Globalization and Productivity
Volume I

# The Globalization of the World Economy

*Series Editor:* Mark Casson
*Professor of Economics*
*University of Reading, UK*

1. Transforming International Organizations
*William G. Egelhoff*
2. Strategic Alliances
*Paul W. Beamish*
3. Structural Change, Industrial Location and Competitiveness
*Joanne E. Oxley and Bernard Yeung*
4. Developing and Newly Industrializing Countries (Volumes I and II)
*Chris Milner*
5. Historical Foundations of Globalization
*James Foreman-Peck*
6. Trade and Investment Policy (Volumes I and II)
*Thomas L. Brewer*
7. The Globalization of Financial Services
*Mervyn K. Lewis*
8. Foreign Direct Investment and Technological Change (Volumes I and II)
*John Cantwell*
9. The Globalization of Business Firms from Emerging Economies (Volumes I and II)
*Henry Wai-chung Yeung*
10. Globalization and Labour Markets (Volumes I and II)
*David Greenaway and Douglas R. Nelson*
11. Financial Market Integration and International Capital Flows
*Gregor Irwin and David Vines*
12. Governing the Global Environment
*Carlo Carraro*
13. SMEs in the Age of Globalization
*David B. Audretsch*
14. Privatization and Globalization: The Changing Role of the State in Business
*Ram Mudambi*
15. Globalization and the Location of Firms
*John Cantwell*
16. Globalization and Economic and Financial Stability
*H. Peter Gray and John R. Dilyard*
17. Critical Perspectives on Globalization
*Marina Della Giusta, Uma S. Kambhampati and Robert Hunter Wade*
18. Global Supply Chain Management (Volumes I and II)
*Masaaki Kotabe and Michael J. Mol*
19. Globalization and Poverty (Volumes I, II and III)
*Paul Collier and Jan Willem Gunning*
20. Globalization and Productivity (Volumes I and II)
*David Greenaway, Holger Görg and Richard Kneller*

Future titles will include:

Multinational Firms and the Local Economy
*Klaus Meyer*

International Business and Innovation
*John Cantwell*

Radical Economic Perspectives on Globalization
*Gerald A. Epstein*

Globalization and the Global Factory
*Peter Buckley*

Wherever possible, the articles in these volumes have been reproduced as originally published using facsimile reproduction, inclusive of footnotes and pagination to facilitate ease of reference.

For a list of all Edward Elgar published titles visit our site on the World Wide Web at www.e-elgar.com

# Globalization and Productivity Volume I

*Edited by*

David Greenaway
*Professor of Economics, Pro-Vice-Chancellor and Director, Leverhulme Centre for Research on Globalisation and Economic Policy*
*University of Nottingham, UK*

Holger Görg
*Professor of International Economics*
*Christian-Albrechts-University, Kiel*
*and Kiel Institute for the World Economy, Germany*

*and*

Richard Kneller
*Associate Professor of Economics*
*Leverhulme Centre for Research on Globalisation and Economic Policy*
*University of Nottingham, UK*

THE GLOBALIZATION OF THE WORLD ECONOMY

**An Elgar Reference Collection**
Cheltenham, UK • Northampton, MA, USA

Published by
Edward Elgar Publishing Limited
The Lypiatts
15 Lansdown Road
Cheltenham
Glos GL50 2JA
UK

Edward Elgar Publishing, Inc.
William Pratt House
9 Dewey Court
Northampton
Massachusetts 01060
USA



A catalogue record for this book is available from the British Library

Library of Congress Control Number: 2008927967

ISBN 978 1 84542 380 3 (2 volume set)

Printed and bound in Great Britain by MPG Books Ltd, Bodmin, Cornwall

# Contents


*Acknowledgements* vii

*Introduction* David Greenaway, Holger Görg and Richard Kneller ix

**PART I GLOBALIZATION AND AGGREGATE PRODUCTIVITY GROWTH**

**A Openness**

1. Ross Levine and David Renelt (1992), 'A Sensitivity Analysis of Cross-Country Growth Regressions', *American Economic Review*, **82** (4), September, 942–63 5
2. Sebastian Edwards (1993), 'Openness, Trade Liberalization, and Growth in Developing Countries', *Journal of Economic Literature*, **XXXI** (3), September, 1358–93 27
3. Jeffrey A. Frankel and David Romer (1999), 'Does Trade Cause Growth?', *American Economic Review*, **89** (3), June, 379–99 63
4. Francisco Rodríguez and Dani Rodrik (2001), 'Trade Policy and Economic Growth: A Skeptic's Guide to the Cross-National Evidence', in Ben S. Bernanke and Kenneth S. Rogoff (eds), *NBER Macroeconomics Annual 2000*, **15**, Cambridge MA and London: MIT Press, 261–325 84

**B International Technology Diffusion**

5. David T. Coe and Elhanan Helpman (1995), 'International R&D Spillovers', *European Economic Review*, **39** (5), May, 859–87 151
6. Wolfgang Keller (1998), 'Are International R&D Spillovers Trade-Related? Analyzing Spillovers Among Randomly Matched Trade Partners', *European Economic Review*, **42** (8), September, 1469–81 180
7. Jonathan Eaton and Samuel Kortum (1999), 'International Technology Diffusion: Theory and Measurement', *International Economic Review*, **40** (3), August, 537–70 193
8. Bruno van Pottelsberghe de la Potterie and Frank Lichtenberg (2001), 'Does Foreign Direct Investment Transfer Technology Across Borders?', *Review of Economics and Statistics*, **83** (3), August, 490–97 227
9. Wolfgang Keller (2004), 'International Technology Diffusion', *Journal of Economic Literature*, **XLII** (3), September, 752–82 235

## PART II TRADE ADJUSTMENT AND PRODUCTIVITY GROWTH

### A Macro


10. Gene M. Grossman and Elhanan Helpman (1990), 'Comparative Advantage and Long-Run Growth', *American Economic Review*, **80** (4), September, 796–815 271
11. Luis A. Rivera-Batiz and Paul M. Romer (1991), 'Economic Integration and Endogenous Growth', *Quarterly Journal of Economics*, **CVI** (2), May, 531–55 291
12. Anne O. Krueger (1997), 'Trade Policy and Economic Development: How We Learn', *American Economic Review*, **87** (1), March, 1–22 316
13. Dani Rodrik (1998), 'Globalisation, Social Conflict and Economic Growth', *World Economy*, **21** (2), March, 143–58 338
14. David Greenaway, Wyn Morgan and Peter Wright (2002), 'Trade Liberalisation and Growth in Developing Countries', *Journal of Development Economics*, **67** (1), February, 229–44 354


### B Micro


15. Ann E. Harrison (1994), 'Productivity, Imperfect Competition and Trade Reform: Theory and Evidence', *Journal of International Economics*, **36** (1/2), February, 53–73 373
16. Nina Pavcnik (2002), 'Trade Liberalization, Exit, and Productivity Improvements: Evidence from Chilean Plants', *Review of Economic Studies*, **69** (1), January, 245–76 394
17. Marc J. Melitz (2003), 'The Impact of Trade on Intra-Industry Reallocations and Aggregate Industry Productivity', *Econometrica*, **71** (6), November, 1695–725 426
18. James R. Tybout (2003), 'Plant- and Firm-Level Evidence on "New" Trade Theories', in E. Kwan Choi and James Harrigan (eds), *Handbook of International Trade*, **13**, Oxford: Blackwell Publishing Ltd, 388–415 457

*Name Index* 485

# Acknowledgements

The editors and publishers wish to thank the authors and the following publishers who have kindly given permission for the use of copyright material.

American Economic Association for articles: Gene M. Grossman and Elhanan Helpman (1990), 'Comparative Advantage and Long-Run Growth', *American Economic Review*, **80** (4), September, 796–815; Ross Levine and David Renelt (1992), 'A Sensitivity Analysis of Cross-Country Growth Regressions', *American Economic Review*, **82** (4), September, 942–63; Sebastian Edwards (1993), 'Openness, Trade Liberalization, and Growth in Developing Countries', *Journal of Economic Literature*, **XXXI** (3), September, 1358–93; Anne O. Krueger (1997), 'Trade Policy and Economic Development: How We Learn', *American Economic Review*, **87** (1), March, 1–22; Jeffrey A. Frankel and David Romer (1999), 'Does Trade Cause Growth?', *American Economic Review*, **89** (3), June, 379–99; Wolfgang Keller (2004), 'International Technology Diffusion', *Journal of Economic Literature*, **XLII** (3), September, 752–82.

Blackwell Publishing Ltd for articles and excerpt: Dani Rodrik (1998), 'Globalisation, Social Conflict and Economic Growth', *World Economy*, **21** (2), March, 143–58; Jonathan Eaton and Samuel Kortum (1999), 'International Technology Diffusion: Theory and Measurement', *International Economic Review*, **40** (3), August, 537–70; Nina Pavcnik (2002), 'Trade Liberalization, Exit, and Productivity Improvements: Evidence from Chilean Plants', *Review of Economic Studies*, **69** (1), January, 245–76; James R. Tybout (2003), 'Plant- and Firm-Level Evidence on "New" Trade Theories', in E. Kwan Choi and James Harrigan (eds), *Handbook of International Trade*, **13**, 388–415.

Econometric Society for article: Marc J. Melitz (2003), 'The Impact of Trade on Intra-Industry Reallocations and Aggregate Industry Productivity', *Econometrica*, **71** (6), November, 1695–725.

Elsevier for articles: Ann E. Harrison (1994), 'Productivity, Imperfect Competition and Trade Reform: Theory and Evidence', *Journal of International Economics*, **36** (1/2), February, 53–73; David T. Coe and Elhanan Helpman (1995), 'International R&D Spillovers', *European Economic Review*, **39** (5), May, 859–87; Wolfgang Keller (1998), 'Are International R&D Spillovers Trade-Related? Analyzing Spillovers Among Randomly Matched Trade Partners', *European Economic Review*, **42** (8), September, 1469–81; David Greenaway, Wyn Morgan and Peter Wright (2002), 'Trade Liberalisation and Growth in Developing Countries', *Journal of Development Economics*, **67** (1), February, 229–44.

MIT Press Books for excerpt: Francisco Rodríguez and Dani Rodrik (2001), 'Trade Policy and Economic Growth: A Skeptic's Guide to the Cross-National Evidence', in Ben S. Bernanke and Kenneth S. Rogoff (eds), *NBER Macroeconomics Annual 2000*, **15**, 261–325.

MIT Press Journals for articles: Luis A. Rivera-Batiz and Paul M. Romer (1991), 'Economic Integration and Endogenous Growth', *Quarterly Journal of Economics*, **CVI** (2), May, 531–55; Bruno van Pottelsberghe de la Potterie and Frank Lichtenberg (2001), 'Does Foreign Direct Investment Transfer Technology Across Borders?', *Review of Economics and Statistics*, **83** (3), August, 490–97.

Finally, the Editors wish to acknowledge financial support provided by the Leverhulme Trust under Programme Grant F/00 114/AM.

Every effort has been made to trace all the copyright holders but if any have been inadvertently overlooked the publishers will be pleased to make the necessary arrangement at the first opportunity.

In addition the publishers wish to thank the Library of Indiana University at Bloomington, USA and the Library of the University of Warwick, UK, for their assistance in obtaining these articles.

# Introduction

*David Greenaway, Holger Görg and Richard Kneller*

Productivity growth is a key driver of economic growth, which in turn underpins wealth creation and poverty reduction. The drivers of productivity growth are therefore high on the agenda of the policymaking community in most (if not all) countries. They are also high on the agenda of the research community and a rich and deep literature has developed.

Part of that literature has focused on productivity growth in open economies and the transmission channels that link more openness to productivity improvement. Until fairly recently this was largely a macro literature. Over the last ten years however, new theoretical developments have underpinned an explosion of empirical work which is micro- rather than macro-based.

These two volumes comprise 42 papers, spanning both the micro and macro literature: Part I of Volume I covers Globalization and Aggregate Productivity Growth; Part II of Volume I Trade Adjustment and Productivity Growth; Part I of Volume II Inward Foreign Direct Investment; Part II of Volume II Outward FDI, International Outsourcing and Exporting; and Part III of Volume II Exporting and Productivity.

## Part I, Volume I: Globalization and Aggregate Productivity Growth

The relationship between openness to international trade and economic growth, which forms the first chapter of the collection, has been an area of fierce academic debate. As Edwards (1993; Chapter 2, Volume I) makes clear, nor is it a new debate. Dating even from the early economic literature at various points in time, the majority view, and therefore the policy position, in particular of developing countries, has swung between inward orientated strategies to outward orientated ones, with the transition between the latter to the former over the 1980s and 1990s perhaps the most marked.

At a simplistic level the academic literature can be split into two periods that date along similar lines. The period of greatest empirical scrutiny coming with the explosion of interest in the determinants of economic growth and development that followed the publication of Romer (1986, 1990) and Lucas (1988) and the birth of the endogenous growth model. These models were influential because they provided a role for openness to international trade to affect growth rates that was denied in the neoclassical growth model of Solow (1956). Their exogenous technical progress was the key driver to long-run growth. Indeed Edward argues these new growth models were *the* important motivation in shifting policy towards a more outward orientated strategy. More so than the cross-country regression analysis conducted up to that point.

The majority of the studies reviewed by Edwards (1993) fall into one of two broad categories: a) case studies and b) cross-country econometric studies. Edwards recognizes and discusses the limitations of each, although of particular interest in the context of the remaining papers in this section are the criticisms of cross-country regressions. Edwards writes:

> Much of the cross-country regression based studies have been plagued by empirical and conceptual shortcomings ... many papers have been characterised by a lack of care in dealing with issues related to endogeneity and measurement errors. All of this has resulted, in many cases, in unconvincing results whose fragility has been exposed by subsequent work.

The second review paper in this section, that by Rodríguez and Rodrik (2001; Chapter 4, Volume I), was written at the other end of the period of intensive research activity. As Rodríguez and Rodrik (2001) themselves write in the introduction, their study begins where that of Edwards (1993) ends. It is noteworthy however, that despite the wealth of new evidence and the increasing sophistication of the methods applied to the data over that period, the conclusions from the two papers are nearly identical. Indeed, read out of context it would be easy to believe that this quote came from either paper.

Despite similarities in the negativity of the conclusions there are a number of differences in motivation and coverage between the two reviews that are worth highlighting. First, their focus is concerned with evidence on trade policy, compared to the literature on outward oriented strategies covered by Edwards. This reflects a change in the focus of the empirical literature which in part resulted from the increased availability data on trade policy. Second, they review evidence from cross-country empirical studies only. Other empirical methodologies do not feature. Rodríguez and Rodrik (2001) argue that the cross-country empirical literature had a policy influence over this period that Edwards did not believe existed earlier.

The papers chosen for review by Rodríguez and Rodrik (2001) are on the basis of citation counts and as representative examples of methodologies commonly used in the literature. The principal message of the paper is that there is a significant gap between the policy conclusions being drawn and the empirical facts established by the empirical literature on this topic. In particular they show that once the shortcomings of the measures of trade policy are addressed, the relationship between trade policy and growth is much weaker. In this sense it focuses on the measurement error highlighted by Edwards (1993).

The remaining papers of this part of Volume I focus on the particular issues of robustness (Levine and Renelt – Chapter 1) and endogeneity. These are themes that arise continuously through the volume as a whole (for example, Frankel and Romer – Chapter 3).

While Levine and Renelt (1992) test the robustness of a wide range of possible determinants of growth, they devote a section of their paper to that of the volume and structure of trade as well as trade policy measures, including import indicators, measures of total trade, measures of trade policy and the degree of distortion between domestic and international prices. They note immediately that substituting a measure of export trade for total trade or imports yields essentially the same results, cautioning the ability of researchers to identify whether import orientated or export orientated strategies, the focus of the early empirical literature, are the more appropriate. They also discuss the robustness of these variables more generally. Using error bounds analysis they rotate these international trade variables against a set of other potential covariates. They conclude that none can be identified as robust. In particular they note the results are sensitive to the inclusion of a measure of investment, suggesting that most of their effect comes through resource accumulation. This is interesting given that the focus in much of the remainder of the volume is uncovering the relationship between openness and productivity.

The issue of endogeneity is perhaps even more problematic to account for. It occurs because countries that are relatively wealthy are likely to trade more for reasons other than trade as the causal factor. Given the reduced form nature of the typical growth regression and, ignoring the issues of robustness identified in Levine and Renelt (1992), the disagreement over the appropriate control variables to include, the effect of trade of growth is likely to be biased because trade itself is endogenous, but potentially also because it is mismeasured (Rodríguez and Rodrik, 2001) or there is some omitted factor. The difficulty is in establishing instruments that are correlated with the endogenous variable, trade, but not with the error term in the growth regression.

The central premise of Frankel and Romer (1999) is that geographic variables are valid instruments. They construct their instruments by estimating a gravity equation for bilateral trade as a function of geographic variables such as their size, distance and so on. Interestingly they find from this approach that conventional regressions underestimate the size of the effect of international trade on income levels. The effect of the endogeneity bias is downwards, not upwards as is often thought.

The results achieved by Frankel and Romer (1999) are questioned by Rodríguez and Rodrik (2001). Their concern centres on the appropriateness of geography as a valid instrument. They state that it is likely that geography has an effect on income through a number of channels of which international trade is one. The assumption that the effects of geography occur only through trade is made explicitly in the introduction of Frankel and Romer. Rodríguez and Rodrik go on to give examples of how trade affected public health, the quality of institutions and the quantity and quality of natural endowments.

Taken together, one outcome from the research in this part of the collection was almost certainly to highlight the empirical and measurement issues that are important in establishing the relationship between openness and growth, and therefore to raise the bar for subsequent empirical work. A second outcome has been a greater call for greater evidence derived from case studies (Srinivasan and Bhagwati, 2001). A final outcome has perhaps been to motivate researchers to use data, for example, industry or micro data, that might help to overcome the limitations of the macro approach, and to be more explicit about the mechanisms under investigation.

In part as a consequence of the failure to establish robust evidence of a correlation between openness and economic growth, a separate strand of the literature began to develop that considered a particular mechanism through which openness might affect income levels. This part of Volume I considers the role of one particular mechanism, known as international technology transfer. The basic premise of the argument here is that technical progress embodied in new materials, intermediate manufactured products, capital equipment and so on, are traded on international markets allowing countries to import the R&D investments made in other countries. This international technology transfer is especially important for productivity growth in countries that undertake little domestic R&D and therefore have fewer domestic sources of new technology.

Perhaps again, the deeper motivation behind this literature was however the development of new theoretical models of endogenous research and development (R&D) in Grossman and Helpman (1991) and Rivera-Batiz and Romer (1991). Important insights here were that technology is non-rival and there are both public and private returns. This allows technology to flow across national borders in a manner that is distinct from the other inputs into the production function such as human or physical capital.

An influential model of international technology diffusion was that of Eaton and Kortum (1999; Chapter 7, Volume I). This model incorporates the production of ideas into a model with innovation, imitation, patent protection and technology gaps. Patent protection influences the rate of return to new invention, but because the rate of diffusion of technologies differs between countries, does not imply that new inventions are patented in all countries. Countries are poor because the rate of adoption of new knowledge is low, reducing the returns to patents in those countries. Other interesting insights derived from the model include that knowledge diffusion is slower between countries than within them, and that even large rich countries derive a significant part of their overall productivity growth from the knowledge developed abroad. Applying the model to the data, the authors estimate that for the US half of productivity growth originates from the technology developed abroad.

Empirically an important article in this literature was that of Coe and Helpman (1995; Chapter 5, Volume I). In their model they regress the level of productivity in 22 high income countries against the stock and domestic and foreign R&D and find support for the view that international trade is an important channel through which countries benefit from the research efforts of others. Crucial within this is the construction of the stock of foreign R&D. Coe and Helpman model it as a weighted average of the stock of knowledge in each foreign country, where the bilateral import shares provide the weights. The more a country imports from a foreign country with a large stock of knowledge the more the domestic country benefits from the knowledge embodied in intermediate goods. To capture differences in the level of imports on the stock of foreign countries between countries the authors then interact this term with the level of imports. When a country has the same structure of imports as another it is the country that trades most intensively relative to its GDP that is expected to benefit most.

Development of this literature centred on two issues: the channels through which this knowledge diffusion occurs and the appropriate construction of measures of the stock of foreign knowledge. The first issue is taken forward by van Pottelsberghe and Lichtenberg (2001; Chapter 8, Volume I), who extend Coe and Helpman (1995) to allow for the effects of FDI. The relationship hypothesized for FDI differs from that of imports in that both inward and outward FDI are seen as potentially important. Countries benefit from the knowledge that foreign multinationals bring with them when they locate production abroad and also from the technologies that their own domestic firms source from overseas when they go multinational. The authors find that as well as imports, outward FDI can be an important channel for international knowledge transfer. In contrast, they can find no evidence that inward FDI is important. A result that is broadly consistent with the results found in Part I of Volume II on inward FDI from the firm perspective.

Doubts over the validity of the foreign R&D stock variable used by Coe and Helpman (1995) were raised by Keller (1998; Chapter 6, Volume I). Keller (1998) repeated Coe and Helpman's (1995) regressions using counterfactual (or constructed) 'import' shares and obtained similarly high coefficients and levels of explained variation. This led him to conclude that the import composition of a country does not have a strong influence on the regression results as Coe and Helpman claimed. Subsequent work by Keller (2000) based on industry level data for industrialized countries has, however, given partial support to the import composition effect of Coe and Helpman (1995). The composition of a country's imports is important only when it receives a disproportionately high share of its imports from one country.

Other criticisms can be found in Xu and Wang (1999), Mayer (2001) and in Lichtenberg and van Pottelsberghe (1998). The first two argue that when the import variable more closely resembles imports of capital goods the model better fits the variation in the data. Lichtenberg and van Pottelsberghe (1998) in comparison focus on the choice of denominator. They demonstrate that the import-share weighting scheme is highly sensitive to a potential merger between countries and contended that what really matters is the real R&D intensity embodied in the import flows of the home country from the foreign country. As such, they propose that the denominator of the weighting variable be foreign country GDP rather than the total imports of the home country. This was shown to significantly reduce the 'aggregation bias' associated with Coe and Helpman's measure and also to empirically outperform it.

These criticisms are outlined more fully in the final paper included in Part I, that of Keller (2004; Chapter 9, Volume I). This paper provides an effective review of the literature on international technology diffusion and covers both the macro evidence and several aspects of the micro literature discussed elsewhere in this volume. Perhaps of interest is the generally positive nature of the conclusions reached when compared to those of Edwards (1993) and Rodríguez and Rodrik (2001)

## Part II, Volume I: Trade Adjustment and Productivity Growth

There is clearly overlap between the literature represented in Part I, especially that on openness and economic growth, and the papers in Part II. Nonetheless, trade adjustment and growth merits consideration in its own right, for two reasons: first, over the last 30 years or so the vast majority of developing countries have undergone trade reforms of one form or another and it is important to know whether in some sense these have been successful; second, because the analysis is grounded in the evaluation of transitions. This part of the collection therefore focuses specifically on these issues and encompasses both macro- and micro-based contributions to the literature of some importance.

The first two macro papers are key contributions to embedding trade in endogenous growth models. Grossman and Helpman (1990; Chapter 10, Volume I) build on Romer (1990) to investigate what difference comparative advantage in R&D makes to long-run growth. In a rich analysis of commercial policy they show that tariff intervention could cause long-run growth rates to decline, while subsidies to R&D could accelerate growth, but only if applied across (both) countries. Rivera-Batiz and Romer (1991; Chapter 11, Volume I) also focus on trade and long-run growth. What is key in their models is the existence of scale economies in the R&D sector. This turns out to be crucial to stimulating growth when integration takes place between two (identical) economies. They stress the importance of such scale effects to growth generation and therefore the risks associated with mitigating them through trade restrictions.

Krueger (1997; Chapter 12, Volume I) reflects on the drivers behind the extensive trade reforms initiated by so many developing countries in the 1980s and 1990s. Her central thesis is that 'ideas and evidence matter'. With regard to the former, she argues that the resurgence of neoclassical ideas (including endogenous growth theory) was instrumental in persuading governments and those that advise them that outward orientated trade policies are more likely to promote growth than inward orientated policies. This, she argues, was reinforced by evidence; in particular the spectacular growth rates of South East Asian economies like Singapore, Korea and Taiwan. Rodrik (1998; Chapter 13, Volume I) challenges this, arguing that trade policy (and trade reform) may be necessary for growth but they are certainly not sufficient. Thus, if one looks more deeply at the experience of the 'Asian Tigers', macroeconomic stability and the avoidance of major distributional conflict was, he claims, more important than reforms to trade policy.

In the final 'macro' papers of this section Greenaway, Morgan and Wright (2002; Chapter 14, Volume I) conduct an analysis of over 70 countries in a panel data set which spans the 1980s and 1990s. They deploy three different measures of liberalization, embedded in an empirical new growth model and report important differences between the short and long run. Specifically, on average, things get worse before they get better. So, although there are long-run links between trade reform and growth, there may be output losses in the short run while adjustment takes place.

In recent years attention has shifted to more micro-based analysis of adjustment in part driven by the growing availability of enterprise level data and in part due to the increasing sophistication of tools available to integrate that data. We include these 'micro' papers: one theoretical, two empirical studies and one review paper.

The theoretical paper is Melitz (2003; Chapter 17, Volume I), which has very quickly established itself as the standard reference paper in this literature. Melitz makes a fundamental contribution by connecting what happens to enterprises when trade costs fall and aggregate productivity. The key ingredients in his model are sunk costs to entering foreign markets and firm heterogeneity. So, when trade costs fall the most productive firms survive and expand and the least productive go out of business. As a result we have two drivers of aggregate industry productivity, a scale effect and a reallocation effect. As we will see in Part III of Volume II there is a significant empirical literature which explores these (and other) insights from Melitz.

Harrison (1994; Chapter 15, Volume I) is one of the earliest attempts to link trade reform and productivity using panel data. Her focus is a set of reforms in Côte d'Ivoire in 1985 and their impact on firm profitability and productivity. Her panel includes almost 250 Ivorian firms, with pre-reform data going back to 1979 and post-reform data to 1987. In general, she found that firms in the most protected sectors had the highest mark-ups and lowest productivity and productivity was up to four times higher in less protected sectors. As a result, trade reforms prompted a significant boost to firm level productivity.

Pavcnik (2002; Chapter 16, Volume I) focuses on one of the most dramatic liberalizations of the last 30 years, that in Chile in the late 1970s and early 1980s. To track the impact of this at the plant level, she estimates productivity at this level in the manufacturing sector. She concentrates primarily on exit and finds robust evidence that, in import competing sectors, exit contributes to aggregate productivity growth largely through a reallocation effect. Thus, although this paper pre-dates Melitz (2003) its findings are wholly consistent with that model's predictions.

Tybout (2003; Chapter 18, Volume I) is an early survey of the literature on plant and firm level evidence on trade and productivity. Although that literature has burgeoned since the paper was published, it is nonetheless an important contribution in part because of its comprehensive nature and in part because of its insightful 'agenda setting' dimension.

## Part I, Volume II: Inward Foreign Direct Investment

Over the last decades foreign direct investment (FDI) worldwide has increased tremendously, amounting to a total stock of US £10 trillion in 2005. This has for a long time given rise to examining what the effects of this increasing importance of multinational companies are for the countries involved. A large literature has developed examining whether domestic firms can benefit from the presence of foreign multinationals in their economy.

On the theoretical side, models with imperfect competition and increasing returns to scale show that the development of domestic industry can be fostered if multinationals create backward linkages with domestic suppliers. With increasing returns in the production of inputs, greater demand for locally produced inputs raises the variety of available inputs and, hence, fosters the development of local suppliers. In turn, the increased variety benefits other (domestic and foreign) final good producers in the industry who are able to produce more efficiently. These ideas are captured in two models by Rodríguez-Clare (1996; Chapter 2, Volume II) and Markusen and Venables (1999; Chapter 4, Volume II).

Another mechanism by which domestic firms may be able to benefit from multinationals in their economy is through workers moving between them. If workers have superior knowledge when working in multinationals (for example, through training received) then a worker moving from a multinational to a domestic firm brings with her some of the knowledge which can then be utilized in the domestic firm and improve its technology. This is thus an externality that will raise the domestic firm's efficiency and productivity. Fosfuri, Motta and Rønde (2001; Chapter 5, Volume II) develop a model which incorporates this phenomenon and which analyses the conditions under which such spillovers are likely to arise.

The empirical literature on the benefits or costs from inward foreign direct investment dates back to Caves (1974) if not earlier. Much of that early literature focused on the implications of inward FDI for developing countries, and in particular on the effects on productivity of domestic firms. The fear was that multinationals through increased competition crowd out domestic enterprise, leading to a dependency of the economy on foreign investors. In a series of papers Magnus Blomström investigated this issue for Mexico. One of his papers, Blomström (1986) is replicated in Chapter 1, Volume II. Using cross-section data at the industry level he shows that inward foreign direct investment is positively correlated with domestic productivity.

One shortcoming with this type of analysis is that cross-section data do not allow the researcher to say much about causality of the effect. Aitken and Harrison (1999; Chapter 3, Volume II) use firm level panel data for Venezuela and exploit the panel nature of their data to be more confident about causality running from inward FDI to domestic productivity. In a complete turnaround to Blomström and others' results they show, however, that the use of panel data indicates that inward FDI in an industry leads to a reduction in productivity in domestic firms. They attribute this adverse effect to increased competition from new multinational enterprises crowding out domestic industry. However, in an early expansion of this literature to developed countries, Girma, Greenaway and Wakelin (2001; Chapter 6, Volume II) use firm level panel data for the United Kingdom and show, using a similar estimation approach to Aitken and Harrison, that inward FDI leads to increases in productivity in domestic firms at least in certain industries.

Hence, a dispute was 'born' in the literature that is still far from resolved – is the overall effect from inward FDI on domestic productivity positive or negative? Does it depend on country characteristics, or other variables that need to be controlled for? Or are we just not measuring the right thing? Many of these questions have been debated in the literature, and a review paper by Görg and Greenaway (2004; Chapter 7, Volume II) provides a comprehensive discussion of these and attempts some answers. A related discussion, also focusing on these points, is provided by Lipsey and Sjöholm (2005).

Perhaps the question of measurement has led to the most fruitful developments in the recent empirical literature. Early studies looked at the impact of a measure of the importance of FDI in an industry on productivity of firms in the same industry – what has been termed horizontal spillovers. These studies, however, treat the channel through which spillovers may work as a 'black box'. In recent advances on this literature, Javorcik (2004; Chapter 8, Volume II) and Görg and Strobl (2005; Chapter 9, Volume II) investigate closely through different mechanisms. The premise in Javorcik (2004) is that domestic suppliers can learn from multinationals if these have backward linkages, that is, source their inputs domestically. She investigates this hypothesis empirically using firm level data for Lithuania, and finds strong support for her assumption. Domestic firms improve their productivity when the presence of multinationals increases in industries to which they supply inputs. Görg and Strobl (2005) concern themselves with worker mobility between multinationals and domestic firms. Using firm and worker level data for Ghana they establish that domestic firms have higher productivity if their owners have worked for multinationals before they joined their current firm. This suggests that domestic firms can indeed benefit from employing workers that have had experience working in multinationals.

## Part II, Volume II: Outward FDI, International Outsourcing and Exporting

Given the dramatic rise of multinational companies, the international trade literature has sought to incorporate this type of foreign market access into trade models with imperfect competition. This literature dates back to Helpman (1984), Markusen (1984) and Ethier (1986). The question here is simple to ask, yet complex to answer: Why do firms choose to become multinationals?

In one of the earlier papers using the heterogeneous firm model à la Melitz (2003), Helpman, Melitz and Yeaple (2004; Chapter 14, Volume II) extend this type of model to allow a firm to have three choices: only serve the domestic market, export to a foreign market, or serve a foreign market by setting up an affiliate abroad. There are different levels of sunk costs associated with the different modes of entering foreign markets. Due to the assumptions made about the level of sunk costs (highest for foreign direct investment) the model shows that firms sort into these three categories depending on their efficiency or productivity levels: only the most productive firms become multinationals, those with intermediate productivity levels become exporters, while others only serve the domestic market (or exit completely). That is, faced with the same proximity-concentration tradeoff in Brainard (1997; Chapter 10, Volume II), firms make different choices about how to serve foreign markets.

The Helpman *et al.* paper only considers FDI as a mode to serve foreign markets – that is, a horizontal motive. While this is arguably still the most important type of FDI there is plenty of evidence that vertical FDI (that is, locating abroad to access inputs) is also important (for example, Hanson *et al.*, 2005). Moreover, most firms that invest abroad engage in what has been termed 'complex integration strategies', that is, combine different degrees of horizontal and vertical motives. Yeaple (2003; Chapter 12, Volume II) is one of the first papers to analyse these complex strategies in a formal theoretical setting. He assumes monopolistically competitive firms in a three country (two Northern and one Southern), two factor and two industry setting. In his model, horizontal and vertical FDI create complementarities by reducing the cost of investing abroad in general.

Another form of internationalization of firms that has gained much importance in recent years is the practice of importing intermediate inputs from unaffiliated suppliers abroad. This is generally referred to as international outsourcing, examples of which can be found in Chapters 11, 13 and 14. Grossman and Helpman (2005, Chapter 17, Volume II) focus on the importance of contractual arrangements for outsourcing. In their North–South model firms choose where to search for an outsourcing partner, and this search is costly. The two countries differ in their extent of contractual completeness in the contract between final good producer and supplier. It follows that a higher level of contractibility increases the possibility of international outsourcing.

While this literature is mainly theory driven, some related empirical work is rapidly emerging. The model that appears to lend itself most easily to some empirical analysis is the one by Helpman *et al.* (2004). Papers by Girma, Görg and Strobl (2004; Chapter 15, Volume II) and Girma, Kneller and Pisu (2005; Chapter 16, Volume II) provide empirical analyses related to the theoretically predicted sorting behaviour. They use data for the Republic of Ireland and the UK respectively and find unambiguous support for the conclusion that firms that invest abroad are more productive than either exporters or purely domestic firms. In the UK, it is also the case that exporters are more productive than non-exporters, as predicted, while there is no statistically significant difference in productivity levels between exporters and domestic firms observable in the Irish data. Head and Ries (2003) provide similar evidence using data for Japan.

## Part III, Volume II: Exporting and Productivity

The exporting and productivity literature is closely related to the 'micro' literature in Part II of Volume I. Indeed Melitz (2003) is a standard reference point for most work in this area. The papers in this part are overwhelmingly empirical and important contributions to a literature which has expanded dramatically in both its scope and coverage. Much of this literature has focused on the impact of exporting on enterprise performance in general and on productivity in particular. More specifically microeconometric work has addressed the complementary questions of whether it is more productive firms which enter export markets or whether firms become more productive by exporting.

Bernard and Jensen (1995; Chapter 19, Volume II) are widely credited with triggering the export-productivity (empirical) literature with their work on US manufacturing firms. Among other things, this established that exporters had markedly different characteristics to non-exporters, they tended to be larger, more capital intensive, paid better and were more productive. With regard to the last characteristic, they found that actually firms were more productive *before* they became exporters, which they attributed to there being sunk costs associated with exporting. In other words, firms had to incur some costs, such as market research, product redesign and so on, which means that to cover these and remain competitive, they have to become more productive prior to entry.

The finding that sunk costs are important has been replicated across a large number of studies and embedded in a range of theoretical models. But, Bernard and Jensen (1995) were not the first to identify this, Baldwin (1988; Chapter 18, Volume II) had done so in an earlier paper. In a parsimonious open economy industrial organization model he incorporated sunk costs and clearly linked them to hysteresis effects in the responsiveness of traded goods sectors to exchange rate changes.

Clerides, Lach and Tybout (1998; Chapter 20, Volume II) develop a partial equilibrium model of export market entry and exit which features sunk costs and these are important not only to entry, but also to (hysteresis in) exit. Thus, their model allows for self-selection into export markets. In addition however, it also allows for the possibility of learning by virtue of being in export markets, with learning effects being driven by access to best practice technology or new management and organizational models. They then test for both on panel data for Colombia, Mexico and Morocco. They find clear evidence of self-selection in Colombia and Morocco and some evidence of learning by exporting in Colombia.

Bernard and Jensen (1999; Chapter 21, Volume II) also address the issue of whether 'good' firms become exporters or exporters become 'good' firms. Their reference point is a large sample of US plants for the period 1984–1992. Their conclusion is clear: good plants become exporters, with productivity increasing several years before exports are shipped.

Delgado, Fariñas and Ruano (2002; Chapter 22, Volume II) and Girma, Greenaway and Kneller (2004; Chapter 23, Volume II) address the same issue for Spain and the UK respectively. Both use different methodologies to Bernard and Jensen (1999): Delgado *et al.* use non-parametric methods, while Girma *et al.* use matching and difference in differences to control for unobserved heterogeneity. For Spain, Delgado *et al.* report strong evidence for self-selection, but only weak evidence, confined to younger firms, for learning by exporting. Girma *et al.* also report strong self-selection effects for the UK, but also some learning effects.

This particular literature has grown rapidly and it is synthesized and evaluated in the final paper in this collection, Greenaway and Kneller (2007; Chapter 24, Volume II). This concludes that there is overwhelming evidence of self-selection, as well as reinforcement of other distinctive characteristics of exporting, which are very robust to country type, time period and methodology. It also reports however, growing evidence of learning by exporting, especially for firms originating in smaller countries. As that paper concludes, there is a rich array of issues to be addressed still, not least identifying with greater precision what sunk costs firms actually face and what the precise channels for learning by exporting might be.

## References

Caves, Richard E. (1974), 'Multinational firms, competition, and productivity in host-country markets', *Economica*, **41**(162), 176–93.

Ethier, W.J. (1986), 'The multinational firm', *Quarterly Journal of Economics*, **101**, 805–33.
Grossman, G. and E. Helpman (1991), *Innovation and Growth and Growth in the Global Economy*, Cambridge, MA: MIT Press.
Hanson, G., R. Mataloni and M. Slaughter (2005), 'Vertical production networks in multinational firms', *Review of Economics and Statistics*, **87**, 664–78.
Head, K.C. and J. Ries (2003), 'Heterogeneity and the FDI versus export decision of Japanese manufacturers', *Journal of the Japanese and International Economies*, **17**, 448–67.
Helpman, E. (1984), 'A simple theory of international trade with multinational corporations', *Journal of Political Economy*, **92**, 451–71.
Keller, W. (2000), 'Do trade patterns and technology flows affect productivity growth?', *World Bank Economic Review*, **14**, 17–47.
Lichtenberg, F.R. and B. van Pottelsberghe de la Potterie (1998), 'International R&D spillovers: A comment', *European Economic Review*, **42**, 1483–91.
Lipsey, R.E. and F. Sjöholm (2005), 'Host country impacts of inward FDI: Why such different answers', in M. Blomström, E. Graham and T. Moran (eds), *The Impact of Foreign Direct Investment on Development*, Washington: Institute for International Economics.
Lucas, R. (1988), 'On the mechanisms of economic development', *Journal of Monetary Economics*, **22**, 13–42.
Markusen, J.R. (1984), 'Multinationals, multi-plant economies and the gains from trade', *Journal of International Economics*, **16**, 205–26.
Mayer, Jörg (2001), 'Technology diffusion, human capital and economic growth in developing countries', UNCTAD Discussion Paper #154, UNCTAD Geneva.
Romer, P. (1986), 'Increasing returns and long run growth', *Journal of Political Economy*, **94**(5), 1002–37.
Romer, P. (1990), 'Endogenous technological change', *Journal of Political Economy*, **98**(5), S71–S101.
Solow, R.M. (1956), 'A contribution to the theory of economic growth', *Quarterly Journal of Economics*, **71**, 165–94.
Srinivasan, T.N. and J. Bhagwati (2001), 'Outward-orientation and development: Are revisionists right?', in D. Lal and R.H. Snape (eds), *Trade, Development and Political Economy: Essays in Honour of Anne O. Krueger*, New York: Palgrave.
Xu, B. and J. Wang (1999), 'Capital goods trade and R&D spillovers in the OECD', *Canadian Journal of Economics*, **32**, 1258–74.

# Part I
# Globalization and Aggregate Productivity Growth

# A
# Openness

# [1]

# A Sensitivity Analysis of Cross-Country Growth Regressions

By Ross Levine and David Renelt*

*A vast literature uses cross-country regressions to search for empirical linkages between long-run growth rates and a variety of economic policy, political, and institutional indicators. This paper examines whether the conclusions from existing studies are robust or fragile to small changes in the conditioning information set. We find that almost all results are fragile. We do, however, identify a positive, robust correlation between growth and the share of investment in GDP and between the investment share and the ratio of international trade to GDP. We clarify the conditions under which there is evidence of per capita output convergence.* (*JEL* O47)

A vast literature uses cross-country regressions to search for empirical linkages between long-run average growth rates and a variety of economic policy, political, and institutional factors suggested by theory. Most investigators consider only a small number of explanatory variables in attempting to establish a statistically significant relationship between growth and a particular variable of interest. For example, many authors who examine the relationship between measures of fiscal policy and growth ignore the potential importance of trade policy, while those authors who study the empirical ties between trade and growth commonly ignore the role of fiscal policy.[1] Given that over 50 variables have been found to be significantly correlated with growth in at least one regression, readers may be uncertain as to the confidence they should place in the findings of any one study.[2] This paper addresses the question: how much confidence should we have in the conclusions of cross-country growth regressions? We find that only a few findings can withstand slight alterations in the list of explanatory variables.

As argued by Thomas F. Cooley and Stephen F. LeRoy (1981 p. 825), economic theory "...ordinarily does not generate a complete specification of which variables are to be held constant when statistical tests are performed on the relation between the dependent variable and the independent variables of primary interest." Thus, many candidate regressions have equal theoretical status, but the estimated coefficients on the variables of interest in these regressions may depend importantly on the conditioning set of information. We use a variant of Edward E. Leamer's (1983) extreme-bounds analysis (EBA) to test the robustness of coefficient estimates to alterations in the conditioning

*The World Bank, Washington, DC 20433 and Harvard University, Cambridge, MA 02138, respectively. We received helpful comments from Robert Barro, John Campbell, Maria Carkovic, David Dollar, Bill Easterly, Stanley Fischer, Dale Jorgenson, Lant Pritchett, Dani Rodrik, Paul Romer, Larry Summers, Sara Zervos, two anonymous referees, and seminar participants at Harvard University, M.I.T., the University of Rochester, the Federal Reserve Board, the World Bank, and the NBER Economic Growth Conference in Stanford, April 1991. The findings, interpretations, and conclusions are only those of the authors and should not be attributed to the World Bank, its Board of Governors, its staff, or member countries. Tragically, we lost David Renelt in the spring of 1991 and the spring of his life. We will greatly miss him and all that he would have taught us.

[1]Studies of fiscal policy that exclude trade indicators include Daniel Landau (1983), Rati Ram (1986), Kevin Grier and Gordon Tullock (1989), and Robert J. Barro (1990, 1991). Gershon Feder (1983) and Sebastian Edwards (1989) study trade policy but ignore fiscal indicators. Roger Kormendi and Philip Meguire (1985) and Paul M. Romer (1990a) include variables for both.

[2]See Levine and Renelt (1991) for a review of the empirical growth literature.

set of information. We study a large number of variables that have been the focus of attention in a broad collection of growth studies, and we study the statistical relationship between growth and a wide array of newly constructed policy indicators. We consider the relationship between growth and a particular variable of interest to be robust if it remains statistically significant and of the theoretically predicted sign when the conditioning set of variables in the regression changes. Even though we try not to include variables in the conditioning set that, on a priori grounds, measure the same phenomenon as the variable of interst, almost all identified relationships are very sensitive to slight alterations in the conditioning set of variables, and many publicized coefficients change sign with small changes in the conditioning set of variables.

Two themes emerge from our investigation. First, there are many econometric specifications in which measures of economic policy are significantly correlated with long-run per capita growth rates. The second theme is that the cross-country statistical relationships between long-run average growth rates and almost every particular policy indicator considered by the profession are fragile: small alterations in the "other" explanatory variables overturn past results. In particular, the broad array of fiscal-expenditure variables, monetary-policy indicators, and political-stability indexes considered by the profession are not robustly correlated with growth; and a huge assortment of new indicators that we have constructed to capture exchange rate, trade, tax, and fiscal-expenditure policies are also not robustly correlated with growth. This implies that there is not a reliable, independent statistical relationship between a wide variety of macroeconomic indicators and growth.

Our analysis also identifies some robust relationships and clarifies some past findings. We find a positive and robust correlation between growth and the share of investment in GDP, and we also find that the ratio of trade to output is robustly, positively correlated with the investment share. Furthermore, this paper helps clarify the conditions under which one finds evidence of convergence of per capita output levels.

Before detailing the methodology and the results, it is important to emphasize this paper's boundaries. We do not estimate a structural model, establish causal links, identify growth determinants, make policy recommendations, improve the measurement of policy indicators, or run the full gamut of sensitivity analyses discussed by Leamer (1985) and Michael McAleer et al. (1985). We simply examine whether partial correlations that have drawn the attention of a large empirical literature are robust or fragile to small changes in the list of right-hand-side variables. We find that they are generally fragile.

## I. Methodology and Data

There does not exist a consensus theoretical framework to guide empirical work on growth, and existing models do not completely specify the variables that should be held constant while conducting statistical inference on the relationship between growth and the variables of primary interest.[3] This has produced a diverse and sometimes unwieldy literature, in which few studies control for the variables analyzed by other researchers. To provide evidence on the sensitivity of past findings to small alterations in the explanatory variables, we use a variant of the EBA discussed in Leamer (1983, 1985) and Leamer and Herman Leonard (1983). We first describe the EBA and then return to study the empirical growth literature.

Based on the influential work of Kormendi and Meguire (1985), a common feature of most cross-country growth regressions is that the explanatory variables are entered independently and linearly. Thus,

[3]For example Feder (1983) and Ram (1986) use an augmented neoclassical production function to organize their empirical studies, while Romer (1989) and Barro (1990) use endogenous-growth models that highlight a few aspects of growth. Kormendi and Meguire (1985) and Grier and Tullock (1989) use a variety of models to motivate an assortment of variables that they use in exploratory empirical studies.

our EBA uses equations of the form

$$(1) \qquad Y = \boldsymbol{\beta}_i \mathbf{I} + \beta_m M + \beta_z \mathbf{Z} + u$$

where $Y$ is either per capita GDP growth or the share of investment in GDP, **I** is a set of variables always included in the regression, $M$ is the variable of interest, and **Z** is a subset of variables chosen from a pool of variables identified by past studies as potentially important explanatory variables of growth. Our EBA involves varying the subset of **Z**-variables included in the regression to find the widest range of coefficient estimates on the variable of interest, $M$, that standard hypothesis tests do not reject. In particular, we first choose a variable that has been the focus of past empirical studies, $M$, and run a "base" regression that includes only the **I**-variables and the variable of interest. Then we compute the regression results for all possible linear combinations of up to three **Z**-variables and identify the highest and lowest values for the coefficient on the variable of interest, $\beta_m$, that cannot be rejected at the 0.05 significance level. Thus, the extreme upper bound is defined by the group of **Z**-variables that produces the maximum value of $\beta_m$ plus two standard deviations. The degree of confidence that one can have in the partial correlation between the $Y$ and $M$ variables can be inferred from the extreme bounds on the coefficient $\beta_m$. If $\beta_m$ remains significant and of the same sign at the extreme bounds, then one can maintain a fair amount of confidence in that partial correlation. In such a case, we refer to the result as "robust." If the coefficient does not remain significant or if the coefficient changes sign, then one might feel less confident in the relationship between the $M$ and $Y$ variables, because alterations in the conditioning information set change the statistical inferences that one draws regarding the $M-Y$ relationship. In this case, we refer to the result as "fragile."

One possible objection to this EBA is that it introduces multicollinearity, inflates the coefficient standard errors, and exaggerates the range on the coefficient of interest. Leamer (1978 pp. 170–81), however, points out that the multicollinearity problem really reflects a weak-data problem. If one is unable to find robust partial correlations in a cross-section regression, this means that there is not enough independent variation in that variable to explain cross-country differences in growth. Only when one identifies a significant correlation *while controlling for other relevant variables*, should one have much confidence in the correlation. However, finding a robust partial correlation certainly does not imply that the variable of interest causes growth. The crucial, though nettlesome, issue of empirically identifying causal channels has not been adequately addressed by the cross-country growth literature.

Although we agree with Leamer that multicollinearity is not a procedural problem but rather represents an inability to identify a statistical relationship that is insensitive to the conditioning set of information, our purpose is to convince as wide an audience as possible that certain partial correlations are robust or fragile in as meaningful and noncontroversial a manner as possible. Consequently, we restrict the EBA in three ways. First, to the list of variables always included in the regressions, the **I**-variables, we only allow the procedure to choose up to three **Z**-variables from the pool of variables identified as potentially important for explaining cross-country growth differentials. Consequently, we restrict the total number of explanatory variables included in any one regression to be eight or fewer.[4] The second way we limit the EBA is that we choose a small pool of variables from which the extreme-bounds procedure selects **Z**-variables; we do not search over the massive data set that we have compiled for any variable that might cause the variable of interest to lose its significance. We only search over seven indicators that we argue represent a reasonable conditioning set. Thus, although we examine the sensitivity of the relationship between growth and more variables than

[4]This total is similar to that used by Kormendi and Meguire (1985) and Barro (1991).

that considered by any other study (well over 50 variables), we restrict the pool of variables from which the procedure chooses **Z**-variables to only seven. Third, for every variable of interest, *M*, we further restrict the pool of variables from which we choose **Z**-variables by excluding variables that, a priori, might measure the same phenomenon. For example, when we examine the relationship between growth and the rate of domestic-credit creation over the 1960–1989 period, we do not allow the inflation rate to be a **Z**-variable. These restrictions make it more difficult to implicate past findings as fragile.

When available, the data cover the period 1960–1989 and the Data Appendix describes them in detail. The data set includes 119 countries, but we exclude the major oil exporters. Since detailed government expenditure and tax information become available for a wide selection of countries only in 1974, we conduct much of the analysis over the 1974–1989 period. We use two data sets: data obtained directly from the World Bank and International Monetary Fund (WB/IMF) and data from Barro (1991), which is composed primarily of the Robert Summers and Alan Heston (1988) data set (SH). We find similar results with the two data sets but report primarily results based on the WB/IMF data set.

## II. Some First Results

We choose the **I**-variables based on past empirical studies and economic theory. When the dependent variable is the average annual growth rate of GDP per capita (GYP), the **I**-variables consist of the investment share of GDP (INV), the initial level of real GDP per capita in 1960 from SH (RGDP60), the initial secondary-school enrollment rate (SEC), and the average annual rate of population growth (GPO). Although few empirical studies include all of these variables, most studies control for some subset. Of the 41 growth studies surveyed in Levine and Renelt (1991), 33 include the investment share, 29 include population growth, 13 include a human-capital measure, and 18 include a measure of initial income. In addition, the **I**-variables are consistent with a variety of "new" growth models that rely on constant returns to reproducible inputs or endogenous technological change (e.g., Barro, 1990; Romer, 1990b). Furthermore, with these **I**-variables, we can confirm the findings of a large assortment of empirical studies; and, in recognition of the issues raised by McAleer et al. (1985), we show that changes in the **I**-variables do not alter this paper's conclusions.[5]

Each of these **I**-variables has statistical and conceptual problems. In keeping with this paper's focus on assessing the statistical sensitivity of past findings, we discuss these problems only briefly. Measurement problems with RGDP60 and SEC may induce biased results.[6] In the case of GPO, census data may be very poor, and the causal links with GYP are ambiguous (see e.g., Gary Becker et al., 1990). Furthermore, in the case of SEC, investment in human capital represents more than formal schooling, and enrollment rates do not control for quality. Nonetheless, other measures (i.e., primary-school enrollment, literacy) yield similar results.[7]

There are also problems with including the ratio of physical-capital investment to GDP as an **I**-variable. The causal relationship between GYP and INV is ambiguous,

[5]Gregory N. Mankiw et al. (1992) show that our I-variables (except, instead of SEC, they use average secondary-school enrollment rates over the sample period) enter with the signs predicted by their human-capital-augmented neoclassical growth model.

[6]For example, if initial income is mismeasured, the estimated coefficient on initial income will be biased toward being negative. Romer (1989) shows that initial income and the literacy rate become insignificant when one uses instrumental variables to control for measurement error. Also, see Robert J. Barro and Xavier Sala-i-Martin (1992).

In correspondence, however, Paul M. Romer (pers. comm.) has noted that when one uses the SH measure of initial income but growth rates computed from WB/IMF sources (as we do in this paper), there is no evidence that measurement error affects the coefficient on initial income.

[7]Secondary-school enrollment may be preferable to primary-school enrollment and literacy rates because many countries have reached the upper bound for these other measures. The various education-attainment measures that we tried yielded similar results.

and the justification for including many variables in growth regressions is that they may explain INV. If we include INV, the only channel through which other explanatory variables can explain growth differentials is the efficiency of resource allocation. To partially clarify this ambiguity, we also investigate the partial correlation between INV and the macroeconomic variables of primary interest.

The pool of variables from which we typically allow the EBA to choose **Z**-variables are the average rate of government consumption expenditures to GDP (GOV), the ratio of exports to GDP ($X$), the average inflation rate (PI), the average growth rate of domestic credit (GDC), the standard deviation of inflation (STDI), the standard deviation of domestic credit growth (STDD), and an index for the number of revolutions and coups (REVC). We choose these variables to form the basis of the conditioning information set because the profession has used these variables (or closely related variables) as fiscal, trade, monetary, uncertainty, and political-instability indicators. This pool is kept small to make the results more tangible and digestible. The results do not depend importantly on choosing these variables.

The regression results with the **I**-variables over the 1960–1989 period are

$$\text{(2)}\quad \text{GYP} = \underset{(0.85)}{-0.83} - \underset{(0.14)}{0.35}\,\text{RGDP60} - \underset{(0.22)}{0.38}\,\text{GPO} + \underset{(1.29)}{3.17}\,\text{SEC} + \underset{(2.68)}{17.5}\,\text{INV}$$

($R^2 = 0.46$, number of observations = 101; the coefficient standard errors are in parentheses). The variables have the signs predicted by a wide class of models, and all but GPO are significant at the 0.05 significance level. The **I**-variables explain about half of the cross-section variance in growth rates.

Table 1 presents the EBA tests for each of the **I**-variables. The investment coefficient is positive and robust. At the lower bound, the coefficient on INV is 15.1 with a $t$ statistic of 4.7. This robust positive relationship between GYP and INV is consistent with a wide assortment of growth studies.

A second important finding presented in Table 1 is the robust negative partial correlation between GYP and initial income over the 1960–1989 period. The coefficient on RGDP60 is often used to test the convergence hypothesis: a poor country, other things equal, tends to grow faster than a rich country. Bradford J. De Long (1988) and Romer (1987), for example, argue that there is little empirical support for unconditional convergence. In accord with Barro (1991) and Mankiw et al. (1992), we find evidence of *conditional* convergence over the 1960–1989 period (i.e., we find a robust negative correlation between GYP and RGDP60 as long as the **I**-variables include SEC).

Table 1 also includes EBA tests of GPO and SEC. As illustrated, one should not feel very comfortable assuming that population growth is negatively associated with per capita growth. For some specifications, GPO enters with a significantly negative coefficient, but it enters with an insignificant coefficient with other plausible **Z**-variables. In fact, the coefficient on GPO is insignificantly correlated with growth in the base regression, which implies that one needs to select a particular conditioning information set to obtain a significant negative coefficient on GPO. The initial secondary-school enrollment rate enters with a significantly positive and robust coefficient, which confirms the finding by Barro (1991).

Table 2 provides the EBA of the **I**-variables using the investment share as the dependent variable. None of the **I**-variables is robustly correlated with INV. In fact, the coefficient on initial income is positive for some conditioning sets. The entry in the final column indicates whether the partial correlation is robust or fragile. When the result is fragile, the column indicates how many **Z**-variables need to be added before the variable is insignificant or of the "wrong" sign. In the case of RGDP60, the result is fragile. The corresponding "zero"

TABLE 1—SENSITIVITY RESULTS FOR BASIC VARIABLES (DEPENDENT VARIABLE: GROWTH RATE OF REAL PER CAPITA GDP, 1960–1989)

| *M*-variable | | $\beta$ | Standard error | $t$ | Countries | $R^2$ | Other variables | Robust/fragile |
|---|---|---|---|---|---|---|---|---|
| INV | high: | 19.07 | 2.87 | 6.66 | 98 | 0.54 | STDI, REVC, GOV | robust |
| | base: | 17.49 | 2.68 | 6.53 | 101 | 0.46 | | |
| | low: | 15.13 | 3.21 | 4.72 | 100 | 0.49 | X, PI, REVC | |
| RGDP60 | high: | −0.34 | 0.13 | 2.53 | 98 | 0.54 | STDI, PI, GOV | robust |
| | base: | −0.35 | 0.14 | 2.52 | 101 | 0.46 | | |
| | low: | −0.46 | 0.13 | 3.38 | 85 | 0.56 | GDC, *X*, REVC | |
| GPO | high: | −0.34 | 0.23 | 1.48 | 100 | 0.48 | *X*, STDI, PI | fragile[a] |
| | base: | −0.39 | 0.22 | 1.73 | 101 | 0.46 | | |
| | low: | −0.49 | 0.20 | 2.42 | 85 | 0.56 | *X*, GDC, REVC | |
| SEC | high: | 3.71 | 1.22 | 3.04 | 84 | 0.55 | *X*, GOV, GDC | robust |
| | base: | 3.17 | 1.29 | 2.46 | 101 | 0.46 | | |
| | low: | 2.50 | 1.15 | 2.17 | 85 | 0.62 | *X*, STDD, GDC | |

*Notes:* The base $\beta$ is the estimated coefficient from the regression with the variable of interest (*M*-variable) and the always-included variables (**I**-variables). The **I**-variables, when the dependent variable is the growth rate of real per capita GDP, are INV (investment share of GDP), RGDP60 (real GDP per capita in 1960), GPO (growth in population), and SEC (secondary-school enrollment rate in 1960). The high $\beta$ is the estimated coefficient from the regression with the extreme high bound ($\beta_m$ + two standard deviations); the low $\beta$ is the coefficient from the regression with the extreme lower bound.

The "other variables" are the **Z**-variables included in the base regression that produce the extreme bounds. The robust/fragile designation indicates whether the variable of interest is robust or fragile. If robust, the text provides information about further robustness tests.

[a]The coefficient is insignificant with only the **I**-variables included.

TABLE 2—SENSITIVITY RESULTS FOR BASIC VARIABLES (DEPENDENT VARIABLE: INVESTMENT SHARE, 1960–1989)

| *M*-variable | | $\beta$ | Standard error | $t$ | Countries | $R^2$ | Other variables | Robust/fragile |
|---|---|---|---|---|---|---|---|---|
| RGDP60 | high: | 0.008 | 0.003 | 2.60 | 86 | 0.12 | GDC, PI, STDI | fragile (0) |
| | base: | 0.006 | 0.003 | 2.13 | 104 | 0.04 | | |
| | low: | −0.002 | 0.003 | 0.52 | 100 | 0.24 | PI, GOV, REVC | |
| GPO | high: | −0.002 | 0.005 | 0.35 | 101 | 0.24 | <u>REVC</u>,[a] GOV, STDI | fragile (1) |
| | base: | −0.013 | 0.005 | 2.47 | 106 | 0.06 | | |
| | low: | −0.012 | 0.006 | 2.97 | 87 | 0.12 | GDC, STDI, STDD | |
| SEC | high: | 0.095 | 0.024 | 3.96 | 86 | 0.19 | GDC, STDD, STDI | fragile (1) |
| | base: | 0.080 | 0.023 | 3.45 | 106 | 0.10 | | |
| | low: | 0.022 | 0.024 | 0.93 | 102 | 0.25 | <u>REVC</u>,[a] GOV, STDI | |

*Notes:* The base $\beta$ is the estimated coefficient from the regression with the variable of interest (*M*-variable). When the dependent variable is the investment share, no **I**-variables are included. The high $\beta$ is the estimated coefficient from the regression with the extreme high bound ($\beta_m$ + two standard deviations); the low $\beta$ is the coefficient from the regression with the extreme lower bound. *M*-variable definitions: RGDP60 = real GDP per capita in 1960; GPO = growth in population; SEC = secondary-school enrollment.

The "other variables" are the **Z**-variables included in the base regression that produce the extreme bounds. The underlined variables are the minimum additional variables that make the coefficient of interest insignificant or change sign. The robust/fragile designation indicates whether the variable of interest is robust or fragile. If fragile, the number in parentheses indicates how many additional variables need to be added before the variable is insignificant or of the wrong sign. A zero indicates that the coefficient is insignificant with only the **I**-variables included; if robust, the text provides information about further robustness tests.

[a]If REVC is excluded from the pool of variables from which **Z**-variables are chosen, many other variables cause SEC and GPO to enter insignificantly.

TABLE 3—CROSS-COUNTRY AVERAGES, 1960–1989

| Variable | Fast-growers | Slow-growers | $t$ |
|---|---|---|---|
| Share of investment in GDP | 0.23 | 0.17 | 5.18 |
| Secondary-school enrollment rate in 1960 | 0.30 | 0.10 | 5.46 |
| Primary-school enrollment rate in 1960 | 0.90 | 0.54 | 6.10 |
| Government consumption/GDP | 0.16 | 0.12 | 3.26 |
| Inflation rate | 12.34 | 31.13 | −1.74 |
| Black-market exchange-rate premium | 13.57 | 57.15 | −3.79 |
| Share of exports to GDP | 0.32 | 0.23 | 2.31 |

*Notes:* Mean growth rate = 1.92. Fast-growers are countries with greater than the mean growth rate; slow-growers are countries with less than the mean growth rate.

indicates that no additional variables need to be added to cause the coefficient to be insignificant. This signifies that the variable of interest enters with an insignificant coefficient (or a coefficient of the wrong sign) in the base regression. Thus, only by selectively adding right-hand-side variables can one find a significant coefficient of the theoretically predicted sign. Interestingly, the finding of a nonrobust relationship between RGDP60 and INV and the finding of a conditional robust negative partial correlation between RGDP60 and GYP suggest that per capita income convergence may not operate primarily through increases in domestic savings or international capital inflows.

### III. Macroeconomic Variables and Growth

#### A. *Illustrative Overview*

This paper's primary aim is to evaluate the degree of confidence one should have in the partial correlations between growth and popular macroeconomic indicators. This subsection uses two comprehensive studies of growth (Kormendi and Meguire [1985] and Barro [1991]) and some simple correlations to illustrate this paper's two major themes: many indicators of policy, taken individually or in groups, are correlated with growth, but the relationship between growth and any particular indicator or group of indicators is typically fragile. The following subsections conduct a systematic EBA of past findings.

Tables 3 and 4 anticipate this paper's findings. Countries that grew faster than average over the 1960–1989 period tended to have a higher share of exports in GDP, a higher share of investment in GDP, larger primary- and secondary-school enrollment rates, a lower black-market exchange-rate premium, and lower inflation rates than slower-growing countries. Similarly, Table 4 shows that the investment share, the export share, the black-market premium, and the index of revolutions/coups are significantly correlated with the average real per capita growth rate. Importantly, however, none of these variables is significantly correlated with the residuals from the regression of growth on the I-variables. Thus, while many policy indicators are significantly related to growth, this relationship depends on which factors are being held constant.

Kormendi and Meguire (1985), and Barro (1991) present intuitively appealing results for a variety of macroeconomic variables to explain growth. Table 5 presents equations based on these studies. Equation (ii) is nearly a replication of Barro's (1991) work: it includes INV, GPO, RGDP60, GOV, measures of initial investment in human capital, a dummy variable for socialist economic systems, indicators for revolutions and coups, dummy variables for countries in Latin America and sub-Saharan Africa, and it is based primarily on SH data. All the variables enter with the anticipated sign, and RGDP60, INV, primary-school enrollment rate, GOV, revolution and coups, and the continent dummies are significant. Equation (iii) is based on Kormendi and Meguire (1985): it includes RGDP60, INV, GPO, the average annual growth rate in the share of government consumption to GDP,

TABLE 4—CROSS-COUNTRY CORRELATIONS

| | Variable | | | | | | | | | | |
|---|---|---|---|---|---|---|---|---|---|---|---|
| Variable | GYP | INV | RES | $X$ | GOV | PI | GDC | STDI | STDD | BMP | REVC |
| GYP | 1.00 | 0.59* | 0.73* | 0.32* | 0.09 | −0.16 | −0.04 | −0.14 | −0.16 | −0.38* | −0.36* |
| INV | | 1.00 | 0.00 | 0.50* | 0.28* | −0.04 | 0.06 | −0.01 | 0.14 | −0.43* | −0.40* |
| RES | | | 1.00 | 0.09 | −0.13 | −0.17 | −0.07 | −0.16 | −0.30* | −0.13 | −0.16 |
| $X$ | | | | 1.00 | 0.15 | −0.15 | −0.07 | −0.10 | 0.05 | −0.22* | −0.34* |
| GOV | | | | | 1.00 | −0.16 | 0.08 | −0.14 | 0.17 | −0.19 | −0.29* |
| PI | | | | | | 1.00 | 0.49* | 0.97* | 0.35* | 0.18 | 0.46* |
| GDC | | | | | | | 1.00 | 0.39* | 0.76* | 0.14 | 0.21 |
| STDI | | | | | | | | 1.00 | 0.32* | 0.14 | 0.45* |
| STDD | | | | | | | | | 1.00 | 0.15 | 0.20 |
| BMP | | | | | | | | | | 1.00 | 0.47* |
| REVC | | | | | | | | | | | 1.00 |

*Note:* The variable RES is the ordinary least-squares residual from the regression of average per capita growth (GYP) on the I-variables: initial income (RGDP60), population growth (GPO), secondary-school enrollment rate (SEC), and the investment share (INV).

*Significantly different from zero at the $P = 0.05$ significance level.

GDC, STDD, the average growth rate in the share of exports to GDP, and a measure of civil liberties. As in Kormendi and Meguire (1985), this equation uses WB/IMF data. The coefficients have the anticipated signs, and RGDP60, INV, GPO, GDC, and STDD are significant at the 0.05 level. Equations (ii) and (iii) explain 68 percent and 61 percent, respectively, of the cross-country variation in growth rates.

Since both equations appear to be reasonable but include different independent variables, readers may be wary of the findings of each study. To highlight this quandary, we combine the two equations using the union of the two sets of explanatory variables. These results are shown in equations (iv) and (v), using WB/IMF and SH data, respectively. Only INV, RGDP60, and the continent dummies remain significant with both data sets. Since the continent dummies simply suggest the importance of omitted variables, the results imply that only the share of investment in GDP and the initial income level (out of the long list of explanatory variables given in Table 5) have an independent, statistically significant correlation with cross-country growth differentials computed from both WB/IMF and SH data. These results suggest that many popular cross-country growth findings are sensitive to the conditioning information set. More fundamentally, they illustrate that it is very difficult to isolate a strong empirical relationship between any particular macroeconomic-policy indicator and long-run growth.

### B. *Fiscal-Policy Indicators*

We first use the EBA to analyze fiscal-policy indicators. One of the most important and frequently studied issues in economics is the role of fiscal policy in economic development. Empirical attempts to link aggregate measures of fiscal policy with average per capita growth rates in cross-country studies have tended to use (i) measures of overall size of the government in the economy; (ii) disaggregated measures of government expenditures; or (iii) measures of the growth rate of government expenditures. In addition to examining these fiscal indicators, we examine the role of government deficits and disaggregated measures of government taxes.

Before presenting our results, it is worth mentioning some problems with these fiscal-policy measures. Governments may provide growth-promoting public goods and design taxes to close the gap between private and social costs. On the other hand, governments may waste funds, funnel resources to endeavors that do not encourage

TABLE 5—CROSS-COUNTRY GROWTH REGRESSIONS (DEPENDENT VARIABLE: GROWTH RATE OF REAL PER CAPITA GDP)

| | Regression period [data set] | | | | |
|---|---|---|---|---|---|
| Independent variable | (i) 1960–1989 [WB/IMF] | (ii) 1960–1985 [SH] | (iii) 1960–1989 [WB/IMF] | (iv) 1960–1985 [WB/IMF] | (v) 1960–1985 [SH] |
| Constant | −0.83 | 2.01 | 0.86 | 0.47 | 2.05 |
| | (0.85) | (0.83) | (0.89) | (1.18) | (1.12) |
| Initial GDP per capita (RGDP60) | −0.35* | −0.69* | −0.30* | −0.40* | −0.57* |
| | (0.14) | (0.12) | (0.11) | (0.13) | (0.12) |
| Investment share (INV) | 17.49* | 9.31* | 16.77* | 13.44* | 10.15* |
| | (2.68) | (2.08) | (2.62) | (3.13) | (2.43) |
| Population growth (GPO) | −0.38 | 0.08 | −0.53 | −0.15 | −0.02 |
| | (0.22) | (0.18) | (0.18) | (0.19) | (0.19) |
| Secondary-school enrollment (SEC) | 3.17* | 1.21 | | 0.63 | 0.99 |
| | (1.29) | (1.17) | | (1.26) | (1.23) |
| Primary-school enrollment (PRI) | | 1.79* | | 0.91 | 1.07 |
| | | (0.58) | | (0.73) | (0.70) |
| Government share (GOV) | | −6.37* | | −0.59 | −6.80* |
| | | (2.03) | | (3.73) | (2.30) |
| Growth of government share (GSG) | | | −0.08 | | |
| | | | (0.06) | | |
| Socialist economy (SOC) | | −0.25 | | −0.21 | −0.17 |
| | | (0.38) | | (0.45) | (0.43) |
| Revolution/coups (REVC) | | −1.76* | | −0.86 | −1.75* |
| | | (0.52) | | (0.62) | (0.59) |
| Africa dummy (AFRICA) | | −1.24* | | −1.36* | −1.78* |
| | | (0.37) | | (0.48) | (0.44) |
| Latin America dummy (LAAM) | | −1.13* | | −1.34* | −1.27* |
| | | (0.33) | | (0.38) | (0.36) |
| Growth of domestic credit (GDC) | | | 0.019* | 0.013 | 0.008 |
| | | | (0.009) | (0.008) | (0.007) |
| Standard deviation of domestic credit (STDD) | | | −0.009* | −0.006* | −0.003 |
| | | | (0.003) | (0.003) | (0.003) |
| Export-share growth (XSG) | | | 0.090 | 0.023 | −0.03 |
| | | | (0.052) | (0.047) | (0.041) |
| Civil liberties (CIVL) | | | −0.22 | 0.01 | 0.15 |
| | | | (0.11) | (0.13) | (0.13) |
| Number of observations: | 101 | 103 | 83 | 84 | 86 |
| $R^2$: | 0.46 | 0.68 | 0.61 | 0.67 | 0.73 |

*Notes:* Regressions (i), (iii), and (iv) use primarily World Bank and IMF data, while regressions (ii) and (v) use Summers and Heston data.

*Statistically significant at the $P = 0.05$ level.

TABLE 6—SENSITIVITY RESULTS FOR FISCAL VARIABLES (DEPENDENT VARIABLE: GROWTH RATE OF REAL PER CAPITA GDP)

| *M*-variable (period) | | $\beta$ | Standard error | $t$ | Countries | $R^2$ | Other variables | Robust/fragile |
|---|---|---|---|---|---|---|---|---|
| GOV (1960–1989) | high: | −0.85 | 3.20 | 0.27 | 85 | 0.61 | REVC, STDD, GDC | fragile (0) |
| | base: | −4.17 | 2.96 | 1.41 | 98 | 0.52 | | |
| | low: | −5.52 | 3.33 | 1.66 | 85 | 0.57 | *X*, PI, GDC | |
| TEX (1974–1989) | high | −1.22 | 2.22 | 0.55 | 75 | 0.45 | <u>*X*</u>, STDD, GDC | fragile (1) |
| | base | −5.03 | 2.05 | 2.46 | 85 | 0.36 | | |
| | low | −5.51 | 2.02 | 2.73 | 86 | 0.41 | REVC, PI, STDI | |
| GOVX (1974–1989) | high | −12.95 | 7.81 | 1.66 | 64 | 0.48 | <u>*X*</u>, <u>STDD</u>, STDI | fragile (2) |
| | base | −21.96 | 5.64 | 3.90 | 74 | 0.43 | | |
| | low | −23.73 | 5.64 | 4.21 | 75 | 0.57 | REVC, PI, STDI | |
| DEF (1974–1989) | high | 14.17 | 5.36 | 2.64 | 82 | 0.41 | REVC, PI, STDI | fragile (1) |
| | base | 15.45 | 4.90 | 3.16 | 82 | 0.40 | | |
| | low | 6.22 | 5.98 | 1.04 | 72 | 0.47 | <u>STDD</u>, REVC, PI | |

*Notes:* The base $\beta$ is the estimated coefficient from the regression with the variable of interest (*M*-variable) and the always-included variables (**I**-variables). The **I**-variables, when the dependent variable is the growth rate of real per capita GDP, are INV (investment share of GDP), RGDPxx (initial real GDP per capita), GPO (growth in population), and SEC or SED (initial secondary-school enrollment rate). The high $\beta$ is the estimated coefficient from the regression with the extreme high bound ($\beta_m$ + two standard deviations); the low $\beta$ is the coefficient from the regression with the extreme lower bound. *M*-variable definitions: GOV = government consumption share; TEX = total government expenditure; GOVX = government consumption share minus defense and educational expenditures; DEF = central government surplus/deficit as share.

The "other variables" are the **Z**-variables included in the base regression that produce the extreme bounds. The underlined variables are the minimum additional variables that make the coefficient of interest insignificant or change sign. The robust/fragile designation indicates whether the variable of interest is robust or fragile. If fragile, the column indicates how many additional varaibles need to be added before the variable is insignificant or of the wrong sign. A zero indicates that the coefficient is insignificant with only the **I**-variables included. If robust, the text provides information about further robustness tests.

growth, and impose taxes and regulations that distort private decisions. Aggregate measures of government size will not capture the potentially important implications of how total government expenditures are allocated. Furthermore, even if government funds are always spent on growth-promoting goods, there may be complex, nonlinear trade-offs between the beneficial effects of government services and the deleterious implications of distortionary taxes. Linear cross-country regressions will not appropriately capture these relationships. In addition, disaggregated measures of government expenditures and tax sources are only available for a limited number of countries since the 1970's and are particularly prone to measurement problems. Moreover, since government resources may be spent effectively or ineffectively, using simple expenditure data without accounting for government efficiency may yield inaccurate measures of the actual delivery of public services. While recognizing these problems, we focus on examining the robustness of past findings.

A common measure of the role of the government in economic activity is the ratio of government consumption expenditures to GDP (GOV) (e.g., Landau, 1983; Romer, 1989). Table 6 reports EBA tests of this variable for the period 1960–1989. Although the estimated coefficient on GOV is always negative, the coefficient is not robust. In fact, the coefficient is insignificant in the base regression, so that only by selecting a very particular conditioning set can one identify a significant partial correlation between GOV and GYP within the linear-regression context. Similarly, the growth rate of GOV has a fragile statistical relationship with GYP.

Although subject to data limitations, the ratio of total government expenditures to GDP (TEX) is a more complete proxy for the size of the government in economic activity than GOV. The partial correlation between GYP and TEX, however, is not robust. The sign of the coefficient remains negative but becomes insignificant with the inclusion of only one additional variable. In Table 6, this additional variable is the ratio of exports to GDP, but the inclusion of other macroeconomic indicators (e.g., STDD) also induces an insignificant coefficient on TEX.

The effect of government expenditures on economic growth, however, may depend on the allocation of those funds. Barro (1990) attempts to capture this difference empirically by removing education and defense expenditures from government consumption (GOVX). In Table 6, we provide EBA results for GOVX over the 1974–1989 period, during which data exist for a broad range of countries. In contrast to Barro (1991), however, we show that the coefficient on GOVX becomes insignificant when we alter the conditioning information set (e.g., by adding STDD and $X$).

Continuing to examine the effects of disaggregated government expenditures, we test the ratios of government capital formation, government education expenditures, and government defense expenditures to GDP. None of these variables is robustly correlated with growth rates.[8]

We use the central-government surplus (SUR) to explore the potential negative effects of deficits. For some specifications, SUR enters with a significantly positive coefficient. The mere addition of the STDD, however, causes SUR to enter insignificantly. Many other specifications (e.g., adding GDC) also demonstrate the fragile nature of the link between GYP and SUR.

Table 7 presents EBA tests of the fiscal indicators with INV. Although many theoretical predictions of a negative relationship between the size of the government and growth are based on a negative impact of government activity on capital accumulation, none of the fiscal-policy measures has a robust relationship with INV. In fact, each of the fiscal indicators is either insignificantly correlated with INV or has the wrong sign in the base regressions.

EBA tests of the ratio of export tax receipts to exports, the ratio of import tax receipts to imports, the ratio of corporate tax receipts to GDP, the ratio of individual income tax receipts to GDP, and the ratio of social-security tax receipts to GDP did not yield any robust correlations with either INV or GYP. The coefficient on each of these variables changes sign with different **Z**-variables.[9]

In this subsection, we could not find a robust cross-country relationship between a diverse collection of fiscal-policy indicators and growth. Specifically, although there are econometric specifications that yield significant coefficient estimates between specific fiscal-policy indicators and growth, the coefficients on these same variables become insignificant when the right-hand-side variables are slightly altered. Interestingly, standard fiscal indicators enter with the predicted sign for many econometric specifications when the regression includes investment, but these same indicators are insignificantly correlated with investment (or they enter with the wrong sign). Thus, fiscal policy to the extent that it has an independent relationship with growth, appears to be more strongly correlated with the "efficiency of resource allocation" as opposed

[8]We also tested the growth rate of GOV because Ram (1986) argues that this measure is positively related to growth. An obvious problem with this analysis is that if government services are a normal good, one would expect growth in government services to parallel income growth. This measure enters with a positive coefficient, but when the average annual growth rate of exports (studied by Feder [1983]) and the change in exports as a share of GDP (studied by Romer [1989]) are included, the coefficient on the growth rate of government consumption expenditures becomes insignificant. The high $R^2$ of this equation (0.98) suggests that one only needs to include the growth rates of enough components of GDP to explain the cross-country variance in growth.

[9]See Levine (1991) for an analysis of the effects of different types of taxes on long-run growth.

TABLE 7—SENSITIVITY RESULTS FOR FISCAL VARIABLES (DEPENDENT VARIABLE: INVESTMENT SHARE)

| *M*-variable (period) | | $\beta$ | Standard error | $t$ | Countries | $R^2$ | Other variables | Robust/fragile |
|---|---|---|---|---|---|---|---|---|
| GOV (1960–1989) | high: | 0.244 | 0.13 | 1.90 | 85 | 0.07 | GDC, STDD, STDI | fragile (0) |
| | base: | 0.310 | 0.11 | 2.92 | 102 | 0.08 | | |
| | low: | 0.097 | 0.11 | 0.87 | 85 | 0.31 | *X*, GDC, GOV | |
| GOVX (1974–1989) | high: | −0.018 | 0.15 | 0.12 | 74 | 0.13 | STDI, *X*, PI | fragile (0) |
| | base: | −0.011 | 0.16 | 0.07 | 76 | 0.01 | | |
| | low: | −0.444 | 0.20 | 2.26 | 65 | 0.13 | GDC, PI, REVC | |
| TEX (1974–1989) | high: | 0.110 | 0.05 | 2.19 | 76 | 0.08 | GDC, STDD, STDI | fragile (0) |
| | base: | 0.120 | 0.05 | 2.65 | 87 | 0.08 | | |
| | low: | 0.060 | 0.05 | 1.17 | 75 | 0.23 | GDC, *X*, REVC | |
| DEF (1974–1989) | high: | −0.004 | 0.19 | 0.02 | 72 | 0.04 | PI, GDC, STDI | fragile (0) |
| | base: | −0.009 | 0.14 | 0.06 | 83 | 0.01 | | |
| | low: | −0.158 | 0.15 | 1.05 | 71 | 0.21 | *X*, STDD, REVC | |

*Notes:* The base $\beta$ is the estimated coefficient from the regression with the variable of interest (*M*-variable). When the dependent variable is the investment share, no **I**-variables are included. The high $\beta$ is the estimated coefficient from the regression with the extreme high bound ($\beta_m$ + two standard deviations); the low $\beta$ is the coefficient from the regression with the extreme lower bound. *M*-variable definitions: GOV = government consumption share; GOVX = government consumption share minus defense and educational expenditures; TEX = total government expenditure share; DEF = central-government surplus/deficit as share.

The "other" variables are the **Z**-variables included in the base regression that produce the extreme bounds. The robust/fragile designation indicates whether the variable of interest is robust or fragile. If fragile, the column indicates how many additional variables need to be added before the variable is insignificant or of the wrong sign. A zero indicates that the coefficient is insignificant with only the **I**-variables included. If robust, the text provides information about further robustness tests.

to the accumulation of physical capital per se. These results suggest that the interactions among fiscal policy, investment, and growth may be more complicated than can be captured in simple linear models using fairly aggregate measures of fiscal activity.

## C. *International Trade and Price Distortions*

Over 200 years ago Adam Smith argued that openness to international markets could enhance productivity by encouraging specialization that would be unprofitable in smaller markets. Recently, this argument and other theoretical ties between trade and growth have been formalized by Louis Rivera-Batiz and Romer (1991), Gene M. Grossman and Elhanan Helpman (1990), and Romer (1986, 1990b). Although theoretical discussions frequently focus on the relationship between international trade and growth, empirical examinations have typically examined the relationship between exports and growth. Consequently, we examine the robustness of export indicators used in past studies. In addition, we examine the relationship between growth and import indicators, total-trade indicators, and more direct estimates of trade policy and the distortion between domestic and international prices.

The EBA analysis yields three important results. First, if one substitutes imports or total trade for exports in cross-country growth or investment regressions one obtains essentially the same coefficient estimate and coefficient standard error.[10] Thus, researchers who identify a significant correlation using an export performance measure should not associate this result with exports per se, because it could be obtained using a corresponding measure of imports or total trade. Second, the share of trade in GDP is robustly positively correlated with the share

[10]Although this result may not be surprising, it seems to be frequently overlooked. Many authors interpret their results as establishing an exclusive relationship between exports and growth.

TABLE 8—SENSITIVITY RESULTS FOR TRADE VARIABLES
(DEPENDENT VARIABLE: GROWTH RATE OF REAL PER CAPITA GDP)

| *M*-variable (period) | | $\beta$ | Standard error | *t* | Countries | $R^2$ | Other variables | Robust/fragile |
|---|---|---|---|---|---|---|---|---|
| *X* (1960–1989) | high: | 0.99 | 0.81 | 1.23 | 98 | 0.55 | GOV, PI, STDI | fragile (0) |
| | base: | 0.88 | 0.84 | 1.05 | 100 | 0.47 | | |
| | low: | 0.14 | 0.91 | 0.16 | 86 | 0.57 | GDC, PI, STDI | |
| IMP (1960–1989) | high: | 1.27 | 0.94 | 1.35 | 97 | 0.52 | GOV, PI, STDI | fragile (0) |
| | base: | 0.56 | 0.89 | 0.63 | 99 | 0.44 | | |
| | low: | −1.11 | 1.02 | 1.09 | 85 | 0.55 | GDC, PI, STDI | |
| LEAM1 (1974–1989) | high: | −0.08 | 1.78 | 0.04 | 50 | 0.45 | GOV, PI, REVC | fragile (0) |
| | base: | 1.11 | 1.79 | 0.62 | 50 | 0.36 | | |
| | low: | −2.03 | 1.84 | 1.10 | 41 | 0.51 | DEF, PI, REVC | |
| LEAM2 (1974–1989) | high: | −0.33 | 2.11 | 0.15 | 50 | 0.46 | REVC, PI, STDI | fragile (0) |
| | base: | −0.63 | 2.16 | 0.29 | 50 | 0.36 | | |
| | low: | −4.61 | 2.33 | 1.98 | 41 | 0.51 | REVC, GOV, DEF | |
| BMP (1960–1989) | high: | −0.002 | 0.003 | 0.76 | 90 | 0.56 | REVC, GOV, PI | fragile (0) |
| | base: | −0.003 | 0.003 | 1.02 | 92 | 0.55 | | |
| | low: | −0.005 | 0.003 | 1.53 | 79 | 0.57 | REVC, GOV, GDC | |
| RERDB (1974–1989) | high: | −0.011 | 0.006 | 1.78 | 59 | 0.57 | PI, GOV, GDC | fragile (3) |
| | base: | −0.019 | 0.006 | 3.08 | 63 | 0.53 | | |
| | low: | −0.019 | 0.006 | 3.11 | 63 | 0.58 | PI, REVC, STDI | |

*Notes:* The base $\beta$ is the estimated coefficient from the regression with the variable of interest (*M*-variable) and the always-included variables (**I**-variables). The **I**-variables, when the dependent variable is the growth rate of real per capita GDP, are INV (investment share of GDP), RGDPxx (initial real GDP per capita), GPO (growth in population), and SEC or SED (initial secondary-school enrollment rate). The high $\beta$ is the estimated coefficient from the regression with the extreme high bound ($\beta_m$ + two standard deviations); the low $\beta$ is the coefficient from the regression with the extreme lower bound. *M*-variable definitions: *X* = exports as percentage of GDP; IMP = imports as percentage of GDP; LEAM1 = Leamer's (1988) openness measure based on factor-adjusted trade; LEAM2 = Leamer's (1988) trade-distortion measure based on Heckscher-Ohlin deviations; BMP = black-market exchange-rate premium; RERDB = Dollar's (1992) real exchange-rate distortion for SH benchmark countries.

The "other variables" are the **Z**-variables included in the base regression that produce the extreme bounds. The underlined variables are the minimum additional variables that make the coefficient of interest insignificant or change sign. The robust/fragile designation indicates whether the variable of interest is robust or fragile. If fragile, the column indicates how many additional variables need to be added before the variable is insignificant or of the wrong sign. A zero indicates that the coefficient is insignificant with only the **I**-variables included. If robust, the text provides information about further robustness tests.

of investment in GDP. Finally, when controlling for the share of investment in GDP, we could not find a robust independent relationship between any trade or international price-distortion indicator and growth. These three results indicate that the relationship between trade and growth may be based on enhanced resource accumulation and not necessarily on the improved allocation of resources.

The major results are in Tables 8 and 9. The ratio of exports to GDP (*X*) is not robustly correlated with growth when investment is included as an **I**-variable. In fact, one needs to search beyond the seven variables considered as potential **Z**-variables by the EBA to find a regression in which *X* enters positively and significantly. However, as in Romer (1990a), we find a positive and robust link between *X* and INV. When we substituted the ratio of total trade to GDP or the ratio of imports to GDP for *X*, the results are almost identical.[11] *X* was also found to be robust in the

[11] When we dropped countries with *X* greater than 0.75, the results did not change.

TABLE 9—SENSITIVITY RESULTS FOR TRADE VARIABLES
(DEPENDENT VARIABLE: INVESTMENT SHARE)

| *M*-variable (period) | | $\beta$ | Standard error | *t* | Countries | $R^2$ | Other variables | Robust/fragile |
|---|---|---|---|---|---|---|---|---|
| *X* (1960–1989) | high: | 0.16 | 0.030 | 5.31 | 87 | 0.26 | GDC, STDI | robust |
| | base: | 0.14 | 0.024 | 5.90 | 106 | 0.25 | | |
| | low: | 0.09 | 0.024 | 3.90 | 101 | 0.35 | GOV, REVC, STDI | |
| LEAM1 (1974–1989) | high: | 0.15 | 0.055 | 2.68 | 40 | 0.20 | DEF, STDD, GDC | robust |
| | base: | 0.15 | 0.043 | 3.40 | 50 | 0.19 | | |
| | low: | 0.10 | 0.050 | 2.08 | 48 | 0.24 | REVC, STDD | |
| LEAM2 (1974–1989) | high: | 0.24 | 0.044 | 5.32 | 48 | 0.39 | GOV, STDD | robust |
| | base: | 0.22 | 0.039 | 5.55 | 50 | 0.39 | | |
| | low: | 0.18 | 0.041 | 4.30 | 52 | 0.46 | REVC, PI, GOV | |
| BMP (1960–1989) | high: | −0.0002 | 0.0001 | 1.58 | 79 | 0.19 | GDC, GOV, REVC | fragile (3) |
| | base: | −0.0004 | 0.0001 | 4.54 | 95 | 0.18 | | |
| | low: | −0.0004 | 0.0001 | 3.78 | 81 | 0.18 | PI, STDD, GDC | |
| RERDB (1974–1989) | high: | −0.0002 | 0.0002 | 0.96 | 52 | 0.07 | DEF, REVC | fragile (0) |
| | base: | −0.0002 | 0.0002 | 1.12 | 63 | 0.02 | | |
| | low: | −0.0003 | 0.0002 | 1.46 | 59 | 0.15 | STDD, GDC | |

*Notes:* The base $\beta$ is the estimated coefficient from the regression with the variable of interest (*M*-variable). When the dependent variable is the investment share, no **I**-variables are included. The high $\beta$ is the estimated coefficient from the regression with the extreme high bound ($\beta_m$ + two standard deviations); the low $\beta$ is the coefficient from the regression with the extreme lower bound. *M*-variable definitions: *X* = exports as percentage of GDP; LEAM1 = Leamer's (1988) openness measure based on factor-adjusted trade; LEAM2 = Leamer's (1988) trade-distortion measure based on Heckscher-Ohlin deviations; BMP = black-market exchange-rate premium; RERDB = Dollar's (1992) real exchange-rate distortion for SH benchmark countries.

The "other variables" are the **Z**-variables included in the base regression that produce the extreme bounds. The underlined variables are the minimum additional variables that make the coefficient of interest insignificant or change sign. The robust/fragile designation indicates whether the variable of interest is robust or fragile. If fragile, the column indicates how many additional variables need to be added before the variable is insignificant or of the wrong sign. A zero indicates that the coefficient is insignificant with only the **I**-variables included. If robust, the text provides information about further robustness tests.

growth equation when we dropped investment from the list of **I**-variables. These results suggest an important two-link chain between trade and growth through investment. Interestingly, however, the theoretical ties between growth and trade typically seem to run through improved resource allocation and not through a higher physical investment share.

We also examine more direct measures of trade policy. Leamer (1988) uses the Heckscher-Ohlin-Vanek trade model to construct measures of "openness" and "intervention." The intervention index represents the deviation between the actual and predicted pattern of trade. The openness index represents the difference between the actual and predicted level of trade (as opposed to the pattern of trade). Leamer constructs the openness index so that a higher value represents more openness. As Table 8 indicates, neither the intervention nor the openness index is robustly correlated with GYP. Both of Leamer's indexes, however, are robustly, positively correlated with INV, as seen in Table 9. On the one hand this is not surprising, because both of Leamer's indexes are highly and significantly correlated with *X* (e.g., $r = 0.70$, $P < 0.01$), which we found to be significantly correlated with INV. On the other hand, these results are difficult to interpret because the intervention and openness indexes are *positively* and significantly correlated with each other (e.g., $r = 0.63$, $P < 0.01$).[12]

[12]After carefully examining the relationship among different measures of trade policy, Lant Pritchett (1991

TABLE 10—SENSITIVITY RESULTS FOR MONETARY AND POLITICAL VARIABLES (DEPENDENT VARIABLE: GROWTH OF REAL PER CAPITA GDP 1960–1989)

| *M*-variable | | $\beta$ | Standard error | $t$ | Countries | $R^2$ | Other variables | Robust/fragile |
|---|---|---|---|---|---|---|---|---|
| PI | high: | −0.0022 | 0.0028 | 0.80 | 101 | 0.49 | REVC, *X* | fragile (0) |
| | base: | −0.0039 | 0.0023 | 1.67 | 102 | 0.48 | | |
| | low: | −0.0041 | 0.0026 | 1.57 | 99 | 0.54 | REVC, GOV | |
| STDI | high: | −0.005 | 0.0007 | 0.79 | 101 | 0.49 | REVC, *X* | fragile (0) |
| | base: | −0.0010 | 0.0006 | 1.63 | 102 | 0.48 | | |
| | low: | −0.0010 | 0.0006 | 1.52 | 99 | 0.54 | REVC, GOV | |
| GDC | high: | 0.026 | 0.009 | 2.79 | 86 | 0.64 | *X*, STDI, STDD | fragile (0) |
| | base: | −0.004 | 0.006 | 0.59 | 86 | 0.56 | | |
| | low: | −0.004 | 0.006 | 0.56 | 86 | 0.56 | *X* | |
| STDD | high: | −0.004 | 0.002 | 1.93 | 87 | 0.59 | REVC, GOV, PI | fragile (3) |
| | base: | −0.005 | 0.002 | 2.90 | 88 | 0.60 | | |
| | low: | −0.010 | 0.003 | 3.92 | 86 | 0.64 | *X*, PI, GDC | |
| REVC | high: | 0.217 | 0.758 | 0.29 | 86 | 0.57 | GDC, STDI, *X* | fragile (0) |
| | base: | −1.178 | 0.647 | 1.82 | 102 | 0.48 | | |
| | low: | −1.096 | 0.659 | 1.66 | 101 | 0.48 | *X* | |

*Notes:* The base $\beta$ is the estimated coefficient from the regression with the variable of interest (*M*-variable) and the always-included variables (**I**-variables). The **I**-variables, when the dependent variable is the growth rate of real per capita GDP, are INV (investment share of GDP), RGDP60 (real GDP per capita in 1960), GPO (growth in population), and SEC (secondary-school enrollment rate in 1960). The high $\beta$ is the estimated coefficient from the regression with the extreme high bound ($\beta_m$ + two standard deviations); the low $\beta$ is the coefficient from the regression with the extreme lower bound. *M*-variable definitions: PI = average rate of inflation; STDI = standard deviation of the rate of inflation; GDC = average growth rate of domestic credit; STDD = standard deviation of domestic credit growth; REVC = revolutions and coups.

The "other variables" are the **Z**-variables included in the base regression that produce the extreme bounds. The underlined variables are the minimum additional variables that make the coefficient of interest insignificant or change sign. The robust/fragile designation indicates whether the variable of interest is robust or fragile. If fragile, the column indicates how many additional variables need to be added before the variable is insignificant or of the wrong sign. A zero indicates that the coefficient is insignificant with only the **I**-variables included. If robust, the text provides information about further robustness tests.

We also examine the average black-market exchange-rate premium (BMP). Since this variable represents the interactions of many policies, we find it difficult to interpret this variable as an indicator of any one policy. BMP is not robustly correlated with GYP or INV.[13]

Finally, we examine David Dollar's (1992) measure of the distortion between domestic and international prices. This "real exchange-rate distortion" index is significantly positively correlated with BMP, but it is negatively correlated with *X*. These correlations plus the analysis by Pritchett (1991) suggest that one may want to interpret Dollar's index as a general measure of international distortions and not as a narrow measure of trade policy. For the benchmark countries that have actual as opposed to interpolated data, Table 8 shows that Dollar's index is negatively though not robustly correlated with growth.[14]

p. 29) concludes that "... alternative objective summary measures of policy outward orientation produce entirely different country rankings." This assessment has obviously dour implications for attempts to quantify the relationship between trade policy and growth.

[13]Similar results were found when we excluded OECD countries.

[14]We also examined measures of import penetration (e.g., MP in the Appendix) and indexes of outward orientation (e.g., SCOUT in the Appendix). Neither

TABLE 11—SENSITIVITY RESULTS FOR MONETARY AND POLITICAL VARIABLES (DEPENDENT VARIABLE: INVESTMENT SHARE 1960–1989)

| *M*-variable | | $\beta$ | Standard error | $t$ | Countries | $R^2$ | Other variables | Robust/fragile |
|---|---|---|---|---|---|---|---|---|
| PI | high: | −0.0001 | 0.0003 | 0.16 | 101 | 0.27 | *X*, GOV, STDI | fragile (0) |
| | base: | −0.0001 | 0.0001 | 0.46 | 106 | 0.01 | | |
| | low: | −0.0005 | 0.0004 | 1.25 | 90 | 0.04 | STDD, STDI | |
| STDI | high: | −0.00001 | 0.00002 | 0.24 | 102 | 0.08 | GOV | fragile (0) |
| | base: | −0.00000 | 0.00002 | 0.15 | 106 | 0.00 | | |
| | low: | −0.00005 | 0.00002 | 2.28 | 102 | 0.24 | REVC, GOV | |
| GDC | high: | 0.0003 | 0.0003 | 1.26 | 85 | 0.16 | REVC, GOV | fragile (0) |
| | base: | 0.0001 | 0.0003 | 0.58 | 85 | 0.01 | | |
| | low: | 0.0001 | 0.0003 | 0.46 | 85 | 0.06 | STDI, GOV | |
| STDD | high: | 0.0002 | 0.00007 | 2.14 | 89 | 0.17 | REVC | fragile (0) |
| | base: | 0.0001 | 0.00008 | 1.29 | 90 | 0.02 | | |
| | low: | 0.0001 | 0.00007 | 0.74 | 88 | 0.27 | *X*, GOV, PI | |
| REVC | high: | −0.045 | 0.022 | 2.03 | 88 | 0.30 | *X*, GOV, STDD | robust |
| | base: | −0.088 | 0.020 | 4.47 | 106 | 0.16 | | |
| | low: | −0.106 | 0.025 | 4.24 | 86 | 0.22 | GDC, PI, STDI | |

*Notes:* The base $\beta$ is the estimated coefficient from the regression with the variable of interest (*M*-variable). When the dependent variable is the investment share, no **I**-variables are included. The high $\beta$ is the estimated coefficient from the regression with the extreme high bound ($\beta_m$ + two standard deviations); the low $\beta$ is the coefficient from the regression with the extreme lower bound. *M*-variable definitions: PI = average rate of inflation; STDI = standard deviation of the rate of inflation; GDC = average growth rate of domestic credit; STDD = standard deviation of domestic credit growth; REVC = revolutions and coups.

The "other variables" are the **Z**-variables included in the base regression that produce the extreme bounds. The robust/fragile designation indicates whether the variable of interest is robust or fragile. If fragile, the column indicates how many additional variables need to be added before the variable is insignificant or of the wrong sign. A zero indicates that the coefficient is insignificant with only the **I**-variables included. If robust, the text provides information about further robustness tests.

### D. *Monetary and Political Indicators*

This section examines the empirical relationship between growth and measures of monetary policy and indicators of the political climate. Based on work by Robert E. Lucas (1973), Barro (1976), Stanley Fischer (1979), and Alan C. Stockman (1981), previous researchers have explored the relationship between measures of monetary policy and growth. Kormendi and Meguire (1975) find that the average growth rate of the money supply, the mean growth in the rate of inflation, and the standard deviation of money-supply shocks are negatively related to growth, while Grier and Tullock (1989), using a pooled cross-section, time-series analysis find that the standard deviation of inflation is negatively related to growth. We examined these and other indicators of monetary policy and report the results of four indicators in Tables 10 and 11: PI, the STDI, the GDC, and the STDD. Each indicator has conceptual and statistical problems. For example, PI probably represents less of a direct indicator of monetary policy and more of a conglomerate index of the result of many policies and shocks, while the endogeneity and identification issues associated with GDC may be particularly

was robustly correlated with GYP when INV was included in the regression. Furthermore, in light of studies by Feder (1983) and Kormendi and Meguire (1985), we studied export growth and export growth times the share of exports in GDP. Neither of these variables is robustly correlated with growth when the regression includes corresponding fiscal indicators (e.g., growth of GOV). Given the national-accounts identity, even if we found a robust relationship, it is not clear what worthwhile inferences could be drawn.

acute. Nonetheless, the wide assortment of indicators that we test produce similar results: none of the indicators is robustly correlated with GYP or INV.

The profession has also used a variety of political indicators in searching for explanations of long-run growth. Kormendi and Meguire (1985) find that greater civil liberties are positively related to growth, while Barro (1991) finds a negative relationship between growth and an index of wars and revolutions. We find that indexes of revolutions and coups (REVC) and civil liberties (CIVL) are not robustly correlated with GYP. REVC, however, is robustly, negatively correlated with INV. Thus, not surprisingly, countries that experience a high number of revolutions and coups tend to be countries that invest less of their resources domestically than countries with stable political environments.

### IV. Sensitivity of the Sensitivity Analysis and Variable Groupings

We selected the **I**-variables based on theoretical grounds, past empirical findings, and the ability to replicate past finding with this set of included variables. Nonetheless, we examined the robustness of our findings to alterations in the **I**-variables. We conducted the entire EBA with two alternative sets of **I**-variables. The first set is the original **I**-variables plus the sub-Saharan African and Latin American dummy variables. We added these dummies because a number of previous researchers have found significant effects for the continent variables (see Romer, 1989, 1990a; Grier and Tullock, 1989; Barro, 1991). The second alternative set of **I**-variables includes only INV. The alternative choices of the **I**-variables did not significantly alter the results.[15]

In addition, we experimented with different variable pools from which the EBA chooses **Z**-variables. As long as we included a diverse set of variables in the conditioning set, the determination of whether variables have robust or fragile partial correlations with GYP or INV did not depend on the particular variables chosen for the conditioning set.

To provide some evidence concerning the reasons underlying our findings, we also examined the importance of maximizing the differences in the $\beta_m$'s rather than the differences in $\beta$-bounds ($\beta_m$'s plus two coefficient standard errors). We found that this alteration in the EBA did not alter the results. This suggests, as does the fact that coefficient standard errors are generally similar between upper and lower bounds, that alterations in the **Z**-variables change the estimated $\beta$'s more than the standard errors.

We gauged the sensitivity of our results to data quality and comparability. Wherever possible, we did the analysis using both the SH and WB/IMF data sets, and the results did not importantly change.[16] Also, the SH data set ranks the quality of each country's data from A to D with A being the best-quality data. To test for the importance of data quality, we did the analysis (i) eliminating all quality-D data and (ii) using weighted least squares with A–D as the weights. Again, these specifications did not alter the results.

The restrictions we impose on the EBA, such as limiting the pool of variables from which we choose **Z**-variables and limiting the number of **Z**-variables to three, make it easier to classify a finding as robust. Thus, we conducted additional sensitivity analyses of the robust correlations. We briefly discuss two findings. First, the partial correlation between GYP and INV remains significantly positive even when we allow the EBA to choose five **Z**-variables, drastically expand the pool of variables from which the EBA chooses **Z**-variables, and examine different subperiods and subgroups of countries. Second, the conditional-convergence result is not robust over the 1974–1989 period or when we exclude OECD countries.

[15]SEC is not robustly correlated with growth when the regression includes a dummy variable for sub-Saharan African countries.

[16]The **Z**-variables chosen by the EBA are sometimes different for the two data sets.

Finally, we made some attempts to measure the notion that policies should be interpreted more broadly than any particular measure of fiscal, trade, or monetary performance can capture. For example, BMP is related to exchange-rate policy, monetary policy, trade policy, and political uncertainty; thus, it may be "unfair" to include other policy indicators while examining the partial correlation between BMP and GYP. Of course, if a significant coefficient is then found when other policy indicators are excluded, the significance should not be interpreted as representing a correlation between GYP and BMP per se, but between growth and a general indicator of "distortions." Consequently, we used factor analysis to construct aggregate policy indicators from groups of individual policy indicators. For example, we tested the robustness of various "international" distortion indexes, "domestic" distortion indexes, and "uncertainty" indexes constructed from up to four individual indicators. None was robustly correlated with growth. This again indicates the difficulty of isolating the independent importance of any single policy.

## V. Conclusion

In many respects, this paper is a natural extension of the types of exploratory cross-country empirical investigations of growth pioneered by Kormendi and Meguire (1985) and recently advanced by Barro (1990, 1991). Representative of the large empirical cross-country growth literature, each of these studies uses an assortment of theoretical papers to motivate a variety of economic variables that are then used in cross-country growth regressions. Although each study presents intuitively appealing results, they use different explanatory variables. In addition to showing for the specific cases of Kormendi and Meguire (1985) and Barro (1991) that a union of the two sets of explanatory variables leaves none of the economic policy indicators significantly correlated with growth, this paper systematically evaluates the robustness of the partial correlation between per capita growth rates and a wider assortment of economic indicators than any previous study. We find that very few economic variables are robustly correlated with cross-country growth rates or the ratio of investment expenditures to GDP. We do, however, identify some correlations that, with some qualifications, are robust to slight alterations in the list of independent variables. We hope that this will provide useful information for future theoretical and empirical work.

We briefly summarize our findings as follows.

(i) We found a positive and robust correlation between average growth rates and the average share of investment in GDP.

(ii) We found a positive and robust correlation between the share of investment in GDP and the average share of trade in GDP.

(iii) We found that all findings using the share of exports in GDP could be obtained almost identically using the total trade or import share. Thus, studies that use export indicators should not be interpreted as studying the relationship between growth and exports per se but rather as studying the relationship between growth and trade defined more broadly.

(iv) We found that a large variety of trade policy measures were not robustly correlated with growth when the equation included the investment share.

(v) We found qualified support for the conditional-convergence hypothesis: we find a robust, negative correlation between the initial level income and growth over the 1960–1989 period when the equation includes a measure of the initial level of investment in human capital; but this result does not hold over the 1974–1989 period.

(vi) We found that none of the broad array of fiscal indicators that we studied is robustly correlated with growth or the investment share.

(vii) We found that a large assortment of other economic and political indicators are not robustly correlated with growth or the investment share.

We have tried to distinguish partial growth correlations that seem robust from those that are fragile. We find that, although there are many econometric specifications in which macroeconomic policy indicators—taken individually or in groups—are significantly correlated with growth, the cross-country statistical relationship between long-run average growth rates and almost every particular macroeconomic indicator is fragile. National policies appear to be a complex package, and future researchers may wish to focus on macroeconomic policy regimes and interactions among policies as opposed to the independent influence of any particular policy.

## Data Appendix

*Variables and Sources*

| Variable | Definition and source |
|---|---|
| AFRICA | Dummy variable for sub-Saharan African countries |
| AREA | Land area (in thousands of square kilometers) (Source: *World Bank Social Indicators*) |
| BMP | Black-market exchange-rate premium (Source: *Picks Currency Yearbook* [World Bank Updates]) |
| BMS | Standard deviation of BMP |
| CGC[a] | Central-government gross capital formation (Source: IMF's *Government Finance Statistics Yearbook*) |
| CIVL | Index of civil liberties (Source: Barro, 1991) |
| CTX[a] | Ratio of central-government corporate-income-tax revenue to GDP (Source: IMF's *Government Finance Statistics Yearbook*) |
| DEE[a] | Ratio of central-government defense expenditure to GDP (Source: IMF's *Government Finance Statistics Yearbook*) |
| DEF[a] | Ratio of central-government deficit to GDP (Source: IMF's *Government Finance Statistics Yearbook*) |
| EDE[a] | Ratio of government educational expenditures to GDP (Source: IMF's *Government Finance Statistics Yearbook*) |
| GDC | Growth rate of domestic credit (Source: IMF's *International Financial Statistics*) |
| GGCFD | Real government capital formation (Source: Barro, 1991) |
| GG | Growth of government consumption expenditures (Source: *World Bank National Accounts*) |
| GM | Growth of imports (Source: *World Bank National Accounts*) |
| GOV | Government consumption share of gross domestic product (Source: *World Bank National Accounts*) |
| GOVX[a] | Government consumption less defense and education share of GDP (Source: GOV − DEE − EDE) |
| GPO | Growth of population (Source: *World Bank Social Indicators*) |
| GR | Growth of real per capita GDP (Source: Summers-Heston data set) |
| GSG | Growth of the share of government consumption (GOV) (Source: *World Bank National Accounts*) |
| GX | Growth of exports (Source: *World Bank National Accounts*) |
| GYP | Growth of real per capita gross domestic product (Source: *World Bank National Accounts*) |
| HSGVX | Share of real government consumption expenditures minus defense and education expenditures (Source: Barro, 1991) |
| IMP | Import share of GDP (Source: *World Bank National Accounts*) |
| INV | Investment share of gross domestic product (Source: *World Bank National Accounts*) |
| ITX[a] | Share of central-government individual income tax revenue to GDP (Source: IMF's *Government Finance Statistics Yearbook*) |
| LAAM | Dummy variable for Latin American countries |
| LEAM1 | Measure of overall trade openness (Source: Leamer, 1988) |
| LEAM2 | Measure of overall trade intervention (Source: Leamer, 1988) |
| LIT | Literacy rate in 1960 (Source: *World Bank Social Indicators*) |
| MIX | Dummy variable for mixed government (Source: Barro, 1991) |
| MSG | Growth of import share (Source: *World Bank National Accounts*) |
| MTX[a] | Ratio of import taxes to imports (Source: IMF's *International Financial Statistics* and *Government Finance Statistics Yearbook*) |
| MP | Measure of openness based on import penetration (Source: residuals of regression of IMP on RGDP60, $RGDP60^2$, AREA, and POP) |
| OECD | Dummy for OECD countries (members of the Organization for Economic Cooperation and Development) |
| OIL | Dummy for OPEC countries (members of the Organization of Petroleum Exporting Countries) |
| PI | Average inflation of GDP deflator (Source: *World Bank National Accounts*) |
| POP70 | Population in 1970 (Source: Summers-Heston data set) |
| PRI | Primary-school enrollment rate in 1960 (Source: Barro, 1991) |
| PRJ | Primary-school enrollment rate in 1970 (Source: Barro, 1991) |
| RERD | Real exchange-rate distortion (Source: Dollar, 1991) |

| | |
|---|---|
| RERDB | RERD for Summers-Heston benchmark countries |
| REVC | Number of revolutions and coups per year (Source: Barro, 1991) |
| RGDPxx | Real GDP per capita in 19xx (Source: Summers-Heston data set) |
| SCOUT | Dummy for outward orientation (Source: Moshe Syrquin and Hollis Chenery, 1988) |
| SEC | Secondary-school enrollment rate in 1960 (Source: Barro, 1991) |
| SED | Secondary-school enrollment rate in 1970 (Source: Barro, 1991) |
| SGOV | Real government consumption share of GDP (Source: Summers-Heston data set) |
| SINV | Real investment share of GDP (Source: Summers-Heston data set) |
| SOC | Dummy for socialist economy (Source: Barro, 1991) |
| SST[a] | Ratio of social-security tax revenue to GDP (Source: IMF's *Government Finance Statistics Yearbook*) |
| STDD | Standard deviation of GDC (growth of domestic credit) (Source: IMF's *International Financial Statistics*) |
| STDI | Standard deviation of PI (inflation) (Source: *World Bank National Accounts*) |
| TAX[a] | Ratio of central-government tax revenue to GDP (Source: IMF's *Government Finance Statistics Yearbook*) |
| TEX[a] | Ratio of total government expenditure to GDP (Source: IMF's *Government Finance Statistics Yearbook*) |
| TRD | Ratio of total trade (exports + imports) to GDP (Source: *World Bank National Accounts*) |
| XSG | Growth of export share of GDP (Source: *World Bank National Accounts*) |
| XTX[a] | Ratio of central-government export-tax revenue to exports (Source: IMF's *Government Finance Statistics Yearbook*) |
| *X* | Export share of GDP (Source: *World Bank National Accounts*) |

[a]Only available for 1974–1989 period.

*Country List, 119-Country Sample*

| | | | |
|---|---|---|---|
| Afghanistan | El Salvador | Lesotho | Senegal |
| Algeria | Ethiopia | Liberia | Sierra Leone |
| Angola | Fiji | Luxembourg | Singapore |
| Argentina | Finland | Madagascar | Somalia |
| Australia | France | Malawi | South Africa |
| Austria | Gabon | Malaysia | Spain |
| Bangladesh | Gambia | Mali | Sri Lanka |
| Barbados | Germany | Malta | Sudan |
| Belgium | Ghana | Mauritania | Suriname |
| Benin | Greece | Mauritius | Swaziland |
| Bolivia | Guatemala | Mexico | Sweden |
| Botswana | Guinea-Bissau | Morocco | Switzerland |
| Brazil | Guyana | Mozambique | Syria |
| Burkina Faso | Haiti | Nepal | Taiwan |
| Burma | Honduras | Netherlands | Tanzania |
| Burundi | Hong Kong | New Zealand | Thailand |
| Cameroon | Iceland | Nicaragua | Togo |
| Canada | India | Niger | Trinidad and Tobago |
| Central African Republic | Indonesia | Nigeria | Tunisia |
| Chad | Iran | Norway | Turkey |
| Chile | Iraq | Oman | Uganda |
| Colombia | Ireland | Pakistan | United Kingdom |
| Congo | Israel | Panama | United States |
| Costa Rica | Italy | Papua New Guinea | Uruguay |
| Côte d'Ivoire | Jamaica | Paraguay | Venezuela |
| Cyprus | Japan | Peru | Yemen |
| Denmark | Jordan | Philippines | Zaire |
| Dominican Republic | Kenya | Portugal | Zambia |
| Ecuador | Korea | Rwanda | Zimbabwe |
| Egypt | Kuwait | Saudi Arabia | |

## REFERENCES

**Barro, Robert J.,** "Rational Expectations and the Role of Monetary Policy," *Journal of Monetary Economics*, January 1976, *2*, 1–32.

______, "Government Spending in a Simple Model of Endogenous Growth," *Journal of Political Economy*, October 1990, part 2, *98*, 103–25.

______, "Economic Growth in a Cross Section of Countries," *Quarterly Journal of Economics*, May 1991, *106*, 407–44.

______ **and Sala-i-Martin, Xavier,** "Convergence," *Journal of Political Economy*, April 1992, *100*, 223–51.

**Becker, Gary, Murphy, Kevin and Tamura, Robert,** "Economic Growth, Human Capital and Population Growth," *Journal of Political Economy*, October 1990, part 2, *98*, 12–37.

**Cooley, Thomas F. and LeRoy, Stephen F.,** "Identification and Estimation of Money Demand," *American Economic Review*, December 1981, *71*, 825–44.

**De Long, J. Bradford,** "Productivity Growth, Convergence, and Welfare: Comment," *American Economic Review*, December 1988, *78*, 1138–54.

**Dollar, David,** "Outward-Oriented Developing Economies Really Do Grow More Rapidly: Evidence from 95 LDCs, 1976–1985," *Economic Development and Cultural Change*, April 1992, *40*, 523–44.

**Edwards, Sebastian,** "Openness, Outward Orientation, Trade Liberalization and Economic Performance in Developing Countries," World Bank Working Paper Series No. 191, 1989.

**Feder, Gershon,** "On Exports and Economic Growth," *Journal of Development Economics*, February/April 1983, *12*, 59–74.

**Fischer, Stanley,** "Anticipations and the Nonneutrality of Money," *Journal of Political Economy*, April 1979, *87*, 225–52.

**Grier, Kevin and Tullock, Gordon,** "An Empirical Analysis of Cross-National Economic Growth, 1951–1980," *Journal of Monetary Economics*, September 1989, *24*, 259–76.

**Grossman, Gene M. and Helpman, Elhanan,** "Trade, Innovation, and Growth," *American Economic Review*, May 1990 (*Papers and Proceedings*), *80*, 86–91.

**Kormendi, Roger and Meguire, Philip,** "Macroeconomic Determinants of Growth: Cross-Country Evidence," *Journal of Monetary Economics*, September 1985, *16*, 141–63.

**Landau, Daniel,** "Government Expenditure and Economic Growth: A Cross-Country Study," *Southern Economic Journal*, January 1983, *49*, 783–92.

**Leamer, Edward E.,** *Specification Searches: Ad Hoc Inference from Non-Experimental Data*, New York: Wiley, 1978.

______, "Let's Take the Con Out of Econometrics," *American Economic Review*, March 1983, *73*, 31–43.

______, "Sensitivity Analyses Would Help," *American Economic Review*, June 1985, *75*, 308–13.

______, "Measures of Openness," in R. Baldwin, ed., *Trade Policy Issues and Empirical Analysis*, National Bureau of Economic Research Conference Report Series, Chicago: University of Chicago Press, 1988, pp. 147–200.

______ **and Leonard, Herman,** "Reporting the Fragility of Regression Estimates," *Review of Economics and Statistics*, May 1983, *65*, 306–17.

**Levine, Ross,** "Stock Markets, Growth, and Tax Policy," *Journal of Finance*, September 1991, *46*, 1445–65.

______ **and Renelt, David,** "Cross Country Studies of Growth and Policy: Some Methodological, Conceptual, and Statistical Problems," World Bank Working Paper Series No. 608, 1991.

**Lucas, Robert E., Jr.,** "Some International Evidence on Output–Inflation Tradeoffs," *American Economic Review*, June 1973, *63*, 326–34.

**Mankiw, N. Gregory, Romer, David and Weil, David,** "A Contribution to the Empirics of Economic Growth," *Quarterly Journal of Economics*, May 1992, *152*, 407–37.

**McAleer, Michael, Pagan, Adrian and Volker, Paul A.,** "What Will Take the Con Out of Econometrics?" *American Economic Review*, June 1985, *75*, 293–307.

**Pritchett, Lant,** "Measuring Outward-Orientation in LDCs: Can It Be Done?" World

Bank Working Paper Series No. 566, 1991.

**Ram, Rati,** "Government Size and Economic Growth: A New Framework and Some Evidence from Cross-Section and Time Series Data," *American Economic Review*, March 1986, *76*, 191–203.

**Rivera-Batiz, Louis and Romer, Paul M.,** "Economic Integration and Endogenous Growth," *Quarterly Journal of Economics*, May 1991, *106*, 531–56.

**Romer, Paul M.,** "Increasing Returns and Long-Run Growth," *Journal of Political Economy*, October 1986, *94*, 1002–37.

______, "Crazy Explanations for the Productivity Slowdown," in Stanley Fischer, ed., *NBER Macroeconomics Annual*, Cambridge, MA: MIT Press, 1987, pp. 163–202.

______, "Human Capital and Growth: Theory and Evidence," National Bureau of Economic Research (Cambridge, MA), Working Paper No. 3173, 1989.

______, (1990a) "Capital, Labor, and Productivity," *Brookings Papers on Economic Activity*, special issue, 1990, 337–420.

______, (1990b), "Endogenous Technological Change," *Journal of Political Economy*, October 1990, part 2, *98*, 71–102.

**Stockman, Alan C.,** "Anticipated Inflation and the Capital Stock in a Cash-in-Advance Economy," *Journal of Monetary Economics*, November 1981, *8*, 387–93.

**Summers, Robert and Heston, Alan,** "A New Set of International Comparisons of Real Product and Price Levels Estimates for 130 Countries, 1950–1985," *Review of Income and Wealth*, March 1988, *34*, 1–25.

**Syrquin, Moshe and Chenery, Hollis,** "Patterns of Development, 1950–1983," World Bank Working Paper Series No. 41, 1989.

***Government Finance Statistics Yearbook,*** Washington, DC: International Monetary Fund, various years.

***International Financial Statistics,*** Washington, DC: International Monetary Fund, various years.

***Pick's Currency Yearbook,*** New York: Pick Publishing Corp., various years.

***World Bank National Accounts,*** Washington, DC: World Bank, various years.

***World Bank Social Indicators,*** Washington, DC: World Bank, various years.

# [2]

*Journal of Economic Literature*
*Vol. XXXI (September 1993), pp. 1358–1393*

# Openness, Trade Liberalization, and Growth in Developing Countries

*By* SEBASTIAN EDWARDS
*University of California, Los Angeles,*
*National Bureau of Economic Research,*
*and*
*Institute for Policy Reform*

*I am indebted to three referees for extremely helpful comments. This paper was revised during my stay at the* Kiel Institute for the World Economy, *in March 1992. I thank colleagues and the library staff at Kiel for support. I am grateful to the participants of a seminar at USAID for stimulating discussions. I especially thank Jim Fox for his comments. Roberto Schatan, Fernando Losada, and Abraham Vela, provided able assistance. I am particularly indebted to Miguel Savastano for extensive assistance and comments on earlier versions of this paper. Financial support from the Institute for Policy reform, the University of California Pacific Rim Program, and the National Science Foundation is gratefully acknowledged.*

## I. *Introduction*

THE IDEA that international trade is the engine of growth is very old, going back at least to Adam Smith. However, during long periods in the 20th century, it has not been a very popular one. Protectionist theories, in fact, became dominant and for decades the majority of the developing countries implemented industrialization policies based on a very limited degree of international openness.

These policies, which came to be known as "import substitution industrialization (ISI)" strategies, had their origins in the thinking of Raúl Prebisch (1950) and Hans Singer (1950) and were based on two fundamental premises: (1) a secular deterioration in the international price of raw materials and commodities would result, in the absence of industrialization in the LDCs, in an ever-growing widening of the gap between rich and poor countries; and (2) in order to industrialize, the smaller countries required (temporary) assistance in the form of protection to the newly emerging manufacturing sector. This reasoning was closely related to the *infant industry* argument for industrialization. Prebisch's ideas were particularly influential in Latin America, where as Secretary General of the United Nations Economic Commission for Latin America, he advised most politicians and policy makers.[1]

During the 1950s, 1960s, and 1970s a large number of development economists embraced the protectionist view, and devoted enormous energy to design planning models that relied heavily on the import substitution ideas. However, even though the protectionist paradigm had become dominant, a small group of academics embarked, independently, on major empirical investigations aimed at assessing the consequences of alternative trade regimes. Using different approaches that ranged from the historical to the statistical, these researchers argued that there was abundant evidence suggesting that more open and outward oriented economies had outperformed those countries pursuing protectionism. The obvious policy implication from this literature was that developing countries should move away from protectionist and restrictive trade practices and open their foreign trade sector. This view, which was generally unpopular in development policy circles in the 1960s and 1970s, slowly gained followers among academics. As new evidence was gathered, increasing numbers of skeptical analysts were persuaded by the freer trade perspective. It was not until the late-1980s, however, that the protectionist influence on economic advisors and politicians began to cave in.

There is little doubt that the debt crisis unleashed in 1982 played an important role in reshaping policy views regarding development strategies, growth policy and long-term growth. Politicians sensed that the inward oriented policies followed by the majority of the developing nations since World War II were no longer sustainable. The poor performance of the Latin American countries, most of which had followed with almost religious zeal the dictates of import substitution, offered a dramatic contrast to the rapidly growing East Asian countries that had aggressively implemented outward oriented strategies (see Table 1). Suddenly, this difference in performance which had been documented by the academic literature on trade orientation, became a fundamental topic in the public policy debate.

In the 1980s economists dealing with poorer nations began to recommend, with increasing insistence, development strategies based on market oriented reforms that included as a fundamental component the reduction of trade barriers and the opening of international trade to foreign competition. Even the staff of the United Nations Economic Commission for Latin America (ECLA), at one time the most ardent supporter of protectionist policies, began to favor outward orientation. Moreover, the World Bank, the International Monetary Fund, and other multilateral institutions routinely required the developing countries to embark on trade liberalization and to open up their external sector as a condition for receiving financial assistance. The collapse of the Communist system in Central and Eastern Europe in the late 1980s and early 1990s added impetus to the analysis of policy reform and structural adjustment. The opening of the external sector and the convertibility of the currency are, in fact, at the center of almost every reform package proposed to former Communist nations.

In spite of the recent move towards trade reform in scores of developing countries around the world, there still remain some controversies regarding some aspects of trade policies. A particu-

[1] An interesting summary of his view can be found in Prebisch (1984). Albert Hirschman (1968) provided an early "soul-searching" assessment of the disappointing results experienced under ISI. A review of import substitution theories appears in Henry Bruton (1989). For a discussion of trade policies in the context of Latin America's historical development, see Albert Fishlow (1987).

TABLE 1
GROWTH AND EXPORTS IN LATIN AMERICA AND EAST ASIA: 1965–1989
(PERCENTAGE DISTRIBUTION)

| | Annual Rate of Growth of Real GDP | | Annual Rate of Growth of Manufacturing | | Annual Rate of Growth of Exports | |
|---|---|---|---|---|---|---|
| | 1965–80 | 1980–89 | 1965–80 | 1980–89 | 1965–80 | 1980–89 |
| A. *Selected Latin American Countries* | | | | | | |
| Argentina | 3.5 | −0.3 | 2.7 | −0.6 | 4.7 | 0.6 |
| Brazil | 8.8 | 3.0 | 9.8 | 2.2 | 9.3 | 5.6 |
| Chile | 1.9 | 2.7 | 0.6 | 2.9 | 7.9 | 4.9 |
| Colombia | 5.8 | 3.5 | 6.4 | 3.1 | 1.4 | 9.8 |
| Mexico | 6.5 | 0.7 | 7.4 | 0.7 | 7.6 | 3.7 |
| Peru | 3.9 | 0.4 | 3.8 | 0.4 | 1.6 | 0.4 |
| Venezuela | 3.7 | 1.0 | 5.8 | 4.9 | −9.5 | 11.3 |
| **Latin America & Caribbean (Average)** | 6.0 | 1.6 | 7.0 | 1.5 | −1.0 | 3.6 |
| B. *Selected East Asian Countries* | | | | | | |
| Hong Kong | 8.6 | 7.1 | n.a. | n.a. | 9.5 | 6.2 |
| Indonesia | 8.0 | 5.3 | 12.0 | 12.7 | 9.6 | 2.4 |
| Korea | 9.6 | 9.7 | 18.7 | 13.1 | 27.2 | 13.8 |
| Malaysia | 7.3 | 4.9 | — | 8.0 | 4.4 | 9.8 |
| Singapore | 10.1 | 6.1 | 13.2 | 5.9 | 4.7 | 8.1 |
| Thailand | 7.2 | 7.0 | 11.2 | 8.1 | 8.5 | 12.8 |
| **East Asia (Average)** | 7.2 | 7.9 | 10.6 | 12.6 | 10.0 | 10.0 |

*Source:* World Bank (1989, 1990).

larly important area of disagreement refers to whether "trade liberalization" packages have played an important role in the performance of the outward oriented economies. Jeffrey Sachs (1987), for example, has questioned the premise that trade liberalization is a necessary component of successful outward oriented strategies. He has argued that the success of the East Asian countries was to a large extent due to an active role of government in promoting exports in an environment where imports had not been fully liberalized, and where macroeconomic (and especially fiscal) equilibrium was fostered (see also Sachs 1989). Lance Taylor (1991, p. 119) has recently offered a stronger view, arguing that "the trade liberalization strategy is intellectually moribund," and that there are "no great benefits (plus some loss) in following open trade and capital market strategies" (p. 141). From here he goes on to say that "development strategies oriented internally may be a wise choice towards the century's end" (p. 141).

In this paper I review the modern literature on trade policy in developing countries, trying to evaluate the extent to which the existing empirical evidence supports the currently popular policy view that more open and outward oriented economies have outperformed countries with restrictive trade regimes. I analyze the methodology used in this literature, I scrutinize the techniques implemented and, although the emphasis is mostly empirical, I evaluate the conceptual and theoretical models developed to investigate the relationship between trade orientation and growth. An important question I address in this paper is whether we can trace the recent shift in views regarding protectionist policies to the contributions made by the academic literature on the subject.[2]

Modern empirical work on trade policy and growth can be classified into two broad and distinct categories: (a) large scale multi-country studies that have investigated in detail the experiences of a group of countries with trade policy reform. These studies have typically been sponsored by multilateral institutions and have resulted in book-length investigations of each country included in the sample. And (b) econometric studies that have investigated, on broad cross-country data, the relationship between the pace of exports expansion and aggregate economic growth. In the core of the paper I selectively review groups of works corresponding to each of these categories. The paper concludes with an overall evaluation of the current state of affairs in this field, and with a brief discussion on the recently emerging analyses based on the new theories of endogenous growth. In the concluding section I also provide some reflections on directions for future research.

## II. *Multi-country Studies of Trade Policy in LDCs*

Much of what we know today about the effects of different trade policies on growth and economic performance has been learned from a small number of comparative cross country studies. The typical strategy of these projects has been to engage a number of researchers to undertake detailed, many times book-length, individual country studies. The project coordinator provides, at the end, a synthesis where both the similarities as well as differences across countries are highlighted, and where some general conclusions are offered.

Although these cross-country investigations have unearthed significant information on trade practices in a score of countries, they have been subject to two limitations. First, invariably the authors have found it extremely difficult to compute satisfactory indices of protection and trade orientation, and second, these studies have not been able to provide a fully convincing theoretical framework that links commercial policy, trade orientation, and growth.[3] In this section I discuss some of the most prominent comparative cross-country studies on trade policy in the LDCs. In doing so I explain how different analytical advances have allowed us to understand the issues at hand better, and I point out some of the weaknesses of this general comparative approach.

### II.1 *Import Substitution Policies and Effective Protection*

The studies coordinated by Ian Little, Tibor Scitovsky, and Maurice Scott (1970) and by Bela Balassa (1971) are the pioneer modern multi-country investigations on trade orientation and economic performance in the developing countries. These influential projects analyzed in detail commercial policies in a score of na-

[2] Ann Harrison (1991), Edward Leamer (1992), and James Tybout (1992) have recently provided surveys on different aspects of trade policy in developing countries. In this survey I concentrate on studies rooted in extensive data analysis. Thus I ignore the increasingly popular literature based on computable general equilibrium models. Kemal Dervis, Jaime de Melo, and Sherman Robinson (1982) provide an early treatment of trade liberalization based on this technique.

[3] This problem has, until recently, affected most studies that have tried to link national economic policies to equilibrium long-run growth within the context of the standard neoclassical growth model. The recent work on endogenous growth has, however, provided firmer theoretical grounds. See the discussion in Section V below.

tions, trying to determine the way in which these policies had affected the overall economic structure of these countries. The Little et al. project dealt with Argentina, Brazil, Mexico, India, Pakistan, the Philippines, and Taiwan. The Balassa project analyzed the cases of Chile, Brazil, Mexico, Malaysia, Pakistan, the Philippines, and Norway.[4]

Perhaps the most important contribution of these studies is that they provided comparative evidence on how the structure of protection to intermediate and final goods affected relative profitability to sectoral value added. This was done by computing *effective rates of protection* (ERPs) for each of the countries in the respective projects.

The concept of effective rate of protection, pioneered by W. Max Corden (1966), Balassa (1965), and Harry Johnson (1965), tries to capture in a single indicator the rate of protection granted to *value added* in a given industry. The rate of effective protection to industry $j$ is defined as $\tau_j = (VA_j - VA_j^*)/VA^*_j$, where $VA$ is domestic value added, and $VA^*$ is "world" value added, and is taken to be a proxy for the most efficient way of producing $j$. Assuming a linear relation between inputs and outputs—where $a_{ij}$ denotes an input-output coefficient—the ERP for industry $j$ can be rewritten as:

$$\tau_j = (t_j - \Sigma_i a_{ij} t_i)/(1 - \Sigma_i a_{ij}), \qquad (1)$$

where $t_i$ is the tariff on input $i$. An important property of ERPs is that, to the extent that tariffs on the final good exceed tariffs on intermediate inputs, activities with low value added (e.g., a high $\Sigma a_{ij}$) will tend to have higher "effective" protection than what the nominal tariff would indicate.[5] More interestingly, in those sectors where intermediate inputs are subject to tariffs, the rate of effective protection can be *negative*. This, of course, would be the case if $t_j < \Sigma a_{ij} t_i$. A number of studies have shown that in many developing countries the agricultural sector has, for many years, been subject to negative ERPs.

Both Little, Scitovsky, and Scott (1970) and Balassa (1971) showed that the degree of protection granted to manufacturing value added was significantly higher than suggested by straightforward data on nominal import tariffs. In fact, as Table 2 shows, in many countries the rate of effective protection in the manufacturing sector was almost twice as high as the nominal rate of protection. From this general finding Little, Scitovsky, and Scott concluded that the policies followed in most of the developing world after World War II had excessively encouraged industrialization at the cost of reducing the incentives for expanding agriculture and exports. They further argued that the most important consequences of this protectionist policy had been a worsening of income distribution, a reduction in savings, an increase in the rate of unemployment and a very low rate of capacity utilization.[6] The funda-

[4] From today's perspective the inclusion of Norway as a developing country seems puzzling. It should be pointed out, however, that this study used Norwegian data for 1954.

[5] Subsequent studies also computed domestic resource costs (DRCs) measures of protection. As opposed to ERPs, domestic resource costs measure value-added using shadow prices. DRC can best be defined as measuring the social domestic cost of earning or saving a unit of foreign exchange. See Michael Bruno (1972). It is interesting to note that it is also possible to face a situation where the denominator in the effective rate of protection equation is negative. This is the case of negative value added. See, for example, the discussion in Augustine Tan (1970).

[6] In these, as in related studies, fairly aggregated data were used to construct the ERPs. This introduces some important problems in interpreting the results. See the discussion by Corden (1971) on the computation of average tariffs. In the last few years the concepts of ERPs and DRCs have been criticized for their lack of general equilibrium properties, and for providing, in some circumstances, misleading

TABLE 2
NOMINAL AND EFFECTIVE RATES OF PROTECTION IN SELECTED DEVELOPING COUNTRIES
(PERCENT)*

| | Consumer Durables | | Manufacturing Sector | |
|---|---|---|---|---|
| | Nominal | ERPs | Nominal | ERPs |
| Brazil (1966) | 154 | 285 | 86 | 127 |
| Chile (1961) | 95 | 123 | 89 | 158 |
| Mexico (1960) | 50 | 85 | 20 | 32 |
| Malaysia (1965) | 1 | −5 | 8 | 11 |
| Pakistan (1962–63) | 247 | 510 | 96 | 188 |
| Philippines (1965) | 51 | 81 | 29 | 53 |

*Source:* Balassa (1971).
* Computed using international input-output coefficients.

mental policy recommendation emerging from these studies was that the developing countries should greatly reduce the degree of protection, opening up to international competition. These conclusions were greeted with skepticism by the development establishment. For example, in his review of Little, Scitovsky, and Scott (1970), Paul Streeten (1971) wrote: "The book's arguments for freer trade are . . . not additive[;] . . . they are mutually inconsistent." And he ended his review saying that the book would take its place in history "among the literature of pamphleteering . . ."

In spite of providing a wealth of information on commercial practices, and of presenting what at the time was a highly innovative perspective on trade policy in the developing world, Little, Scitovsky, and Scott and Balassa faced some serious measurement difficulties. First, no attempt was made in any of the specific country studies to calculate the evolution of ERPs through time. Indeed, the data requirements for calculating this indicator at a given moment were so large that the authors were satisfied with providing one, or at most two, snapshots of protection in their specific countries. As a result, no serious effort was made at analyzing *liberalization* episodes. Second, in some instances these two studies generated important differences in ERP calculations for the same country in the same years. For example, when the same technique was used for computing the ERP to the manufacturing sector in the Philippines in 1965, Little, Scitovsky, and Scott's study came up with a figure of 49 percent, while Balassa calculated an ERP of 61 percent.[7]

Neither Little, Scitovsky, and Scott (1970) nor Balassa (1971) ventured into the analysis of how specific countries evolved from one trade regime to another, nor did they investigate empirically and in detail how alternative policies had affected growth in particular historical settings. They concentrated their investigation on the characteristic of the import substitution regimes, without comparing it with alternative ways of organizing the external sector.

conclusions regarding the way in which changes in commercial policies will affect resource reallocation (see, for example, Avinash Dixit 1985).

[7] They used the so-called Corden (1966) method for computing ERPs.

1364 Journal of Economic Literature, Vol. XXXI (September 1993)

### II.2 *Defining Trade Orientation and Liberalization Policies*

The classic NBER study directed by Anne Krueger (1978) and Jagdish Bhagwati (1978) provides the first systematic attempt at formally classifying trade regimes.[8] Trade orientation was measured by the degree by which the protective (and incentives) structure in a country was *biased* against exports. A formal index of the degree of bias was defined as the ratio of the exchange rate effectively paid by importers ($EER_M$) to the exchange rate effectively faced by exporters ($EER_X$). If this ratio is greater than one it is said that the trade regime is biased against exports. More specifically, the effective exchange rate for exports is calculated as the nominal exchange rate applied to exports ($E_X$) corrected by export subsidies ($s$) and other incentives to exports ($r$), including export encouragement schemes:

$$EER_X = E_X(1 + s + r).$$

The effective exchange rate for imports is defined, on the other hand, as the nominal exchange rate applicable to imports $E_M$, corrected by the average (effective) import tariff ($t$), other import surcharges ($n$) and the premium associated with the existence of quantitative restrictions, such as import licenses ($PR$) (see also, Bhagwati 1988):

$$EER_M = E_M(1 + t + n + PR).$$

Naturally, if there are unified nominal exchange rates for commercial transactions then $E_X = E_m = E$. The degree of bias of the trade regime is given by:

$$B = \frac{EER_M}{EER_x} = \frac{E_M(1 + t + n + PR)}{E_x(1 + s + r)}. \quad (2)$$

[8] The study included nine individual country studies: Turkey, Ghana, Israel, Egypt, the Philippines, India, Korea, Chile, and Colombia. The project also included Brazil and Pakistan, but no volume on these countries was published.

When $B$ is smaller than one, the country might be defined as following an export promotion strategy. A unitary value of $B$, on the other hand, reflects the existence of a *neutral* trade regime, while a value of $B$ exceeding unity captures the fact that the country in question is engaged in import substitution policies.

Two points are worth making regarding this index. First, this definition is based on *average* incentives. We can thus have a country that protects some sectors but that still, on average, does not exhibit an anti-export bias. Second, this definition of bias implicitly allows for a continuum of regimes; $B$ can be high, low, somewhat high or relatively low. Even though for analytical purposes it is possible to define threshold values for $B$—$B$ equal to one being the natural threshold—this approach has the advantage of, in principle, avoiding a dichotomized view of trade regimes.

In the Bhagwati-Krueger project trade liberalization was defined as *any policy that reduces the degree of anti-export bias*. In the empirical country cases, the authors mostly concentrated on reductions in the import licenses premium ($PR$) as the fundamental step in liberalization reforms. A particularly important property of this definition of trade *liberalization* is that it does not require zero, or even very low, import tariffs. In fact, according to this definition it is possible to have a "liberalized" economy with very high tariffs. As Krueger has stated:

> Inspection of the definitions of bias and liberalization shows that there is no necessary reason, at least in theory, for a connection between the two. *A regime could be fully liberalized and yet employ exceedingly high tariffs in order to encourage import substitution*. The regime would then be liberalized and highly biased. (1978, p. 89, emphasis added)

With time, however, the definition of *liberalization* has evolved into a sharper concept, almost becoming synonymous with free trade. For instance, some authors have argued that trade liberalization policies should not aim at reducing the degree of anti-export bias, and generating a neutral trade regime—that is a value of *B* equal to one—but should rather strive to produce a *liberal* trade system where *all* trade distortions, including import tariffs and export subsidies, are completely eliminated. This position, however, has been criticized by some authors that have argued that there is no firm evidence linking *liberal* trade regimes with improved economic performance.[9] For instance, in an analysis of the policy options faced by the developing countries affected by the debt crisis, Sachs (1987, p. 294) has argued that the "current focus on liberalization is distracting attention from the more urgent needs of the debtor countries."

In the late 1980s the policy debate on the merits of alternative trade regimes had become confusing and increasingly ideological. At the center of these controversies was the inability to define clearly what was meant exactly by alternative policies and by *trade liberalization* reforms. (See, for example, Colin Bradford and William Branson 1987; Richard Cooper 1987; and Sebastian Edwards 1989b for discussions on this subject.) Bradford and Branson (1987), for instance, argued that "part of the controversy undoubtedly derives from the use of loosely fashioned phrases which sound like dichotomous . . ." (p. 17). Cooper (1987, p. 518), on the other hand, argued that

> it is necessary to distinguish between different types of liberalization to make clear that liberalization can be viewed as a process rather than as a state and to disassociate liberalization from laissez-faire.

As the rest of this paper will show, the literature on the subject has not always been successful in dealing with precise definitions of trade regimes, nor has it been able to handle successfully the difficult issue of measuring the type of trade orientation followed by a particular country.

### II.3 *Quantitative Restrictions, Protectionism, and Liberalization*

Most multi-country studies have emphasized the fact that in developing countries nontariff barriers—quotas, licenses, and prohibitions—have traditionally constituted the most important form of restricting trade. For example, as Table 3 shows, in 1985 a very large proportion of imports into Latin America were either subject to outright prohibitions or to some sort of import licensing mechanism. This means that analyses that focus exclusively on book values of import tariffs will usually produce a highly misleading picture of the extent of protection.

The NBER study directed by Bhagwati-Krueger tackled this issue at the theoretical level through the construction of a series of models that investigated under what circumstances there was an equivalence between tariffs and quotas. At the empirical level, the premium (*PR*) in the bias equation (2) was supposed to capture the importance of existing quantitative restrictions. This premium was formally defined as the percentage difference between the actual domestic price of a particular tradable good and the domestic price that would prevail in the absence of any quantitative restrictions. It is immediately apparent from this definition that gathering actual data on the premium is remarkably difficult: not only would it be necessary to undertake explicit international price comparisons for large numbers of goods, but the difficult issue of computing average values for the premium would have to be faced. Natu-

[9] Deepak Lal and Sarath Rajapatirana (1987) are possibly the most articulate representatives of this view.

TABLE 3
COVERAGE OF NONTARIFF BARRIERS IN SELECTED LATIN AMERICAN COUNTRIES IN THE 1980s

| Country | Year | Percentage of Import Items Subject to: Licenses | Prohibition |
|---|---|---|---|
| Argentina | 1987 | 19.9 | 0.1 |
| Bolivia | 1985 | 17.8 | 11.1 |
| Brazil | 1986 | 21.0 | 19.1 |
| Chile | 1987 | 0.0 | 0.2 |
| Colombia | 1986 | 75.6 | 0.9 |
| Costa Rica | 1982 | 4.1 | 0.0 |
| Ecuador | 1984 | 17.6 | 8.5 |
| El Salvador | 1986 | 0.0 | 10.7 |
| Mexico | 1986 | 22.6 | 0.1 |
| Nicaragua | 1981 | 26.5 | 0.0 |
| Paraguay | 1987 | 2.8 | 3.9 |
| Peru | 1987 | 44.8 | 10.6 |
| Uruguay | 1986 | 3.9 | 0.2 |
| Venezuela | 1987 | 3.0 | 9.4 |

*Source:* UNCTAD (1987).

rally, these problems did not escape the directors of this project. Krueger writes (1978, p. 52):

> Time series estimates of the premium . . . were not obtained for any of the ten countries; in fact the empirical difficulties of obtaining premium data even at a point in time precluded any estimates for some countries.

And from here she went on to say:

> Systematic quantitative analysis is often impossible and must at least partially be replaced by application of economic theory to qualitative evaluation of the incentives created by the regime.

In order to evaluate the effect of trade policies, Krueger and Bhagwati combined the concepts of *premium* and *bias* with the definition of five phases in the evolution of trade regimes. Phase I is characterized by across-the-board imposition of quantitative controls, usually associated with a balance of payments crisis. During Phase II the control system becomes more complex and discriminatory, increasing the anti-export bias of the regime. Phase III is the beginning of the liberalization process and is characterized by the implementation of a (nominal) devaluation and relaxation of some quantitative restrictions (QRs). During Phase IV further steps towards liberalization, through the replacement of quotas by tariffs are implemented. In Phase V the economy has become fully liberalized: current account transactions are fully convertible and QRs are not used any longer. While the first two phases characterize an illiberal trade system, Phases III through V represent different stages in the movement towards free trade. Bhagwati and Krueger found that by the mid-1960s one half of the countries in their sample—Turkey, Ghana, Israel, Egypt, the Philippines, India, Korea, Chile, and Colombia—had evolved from highly protectionist policies to a liberalized stage. So much so, that four of them could be classified as being in Phase IV, while one had attained the fully liberalized Phase V status. Two countries cycled between Phases II and IV, while the other three had a long-term attachment to Phase II distortions. In Section II.5 below, I discuss Krueger's formal empirical evaluation of the relationship among the different phases, exports growth, and overall economic performance.

In the 1980s, and as a way to provide a solid intellectual basis to its new program lending policies, the World Bank commissioned a monumental 19 country comparative study on trade liberalization led by Michael Michaely.[10] The project

[10] The countries are Argentina, Brazil, Chile, Colombia, Greece, Indonesia, Israel, Korea, New Zealand, Pakistan, Peru, the Philippines, Portugal, Singapore, Spain, Sri Lanka, Turkey, Uruguay, and Yugoslavia. The results are published in seven volumes edited by Demetris Papageorgiou, Michael Michaely, and Armeane M. Choksi (1991).

not only analyzed the characteristics and consequences of different trade regimes, as its predecessor had done, but went further, investigating the most appropriate ways of actually implementing a liberalization policy. Issues related to sequencing, speed, and transitional costs were analyzed and compared across countries.

In the light of the difficulties faced by previous studies in classifying countries in different trade regimes, including the problems with measuring the importance of quantitative restrictions, the directors of the World Bank project decided to tackle this problem by asking the individual country authors to construct an *index* of trade liberalization. This index could take values from 1, in the case of a highly repressed external sector, to 20 when foreign trade was fully liberalized, and had to be calculated for as many years as possible between 1948 and 1985. In only one of the 19 countries the liberalization index attained a value of 20—Chile in the late 1970s. The Chilean experience with alternative trade regimes and liberalization policies is briefly described in Section II.6 below.

The analysis of the evolution of this liberalization index through time, in conjunction with the behavior of other variables, allowed Michaely et al. to identify episodes of significant change in trade policy. They defined trade liberalization as

> any change which leads a country's trade system toward neutrality in the sense of bringing its economy closer to the situation which would prevail if there were no governmental interference . . . (Michaely, Papageorgiou, and Choksi 1991, vol. 7, p. xx)

Using this definition, 36 liberalization attempts were identified for the 19 countries in the study. Of these, 19 were considered to be strong liberalizations and 17 were classified as weak efforts. Only 15 of the 36 cases were sustained, in the sense that the reform had not been reversed after a few years.

In spite of the effort made by Michaely et al. to surmount the difficulties in measuring trade orientation, their liberalization index is largely subjective, reflecting the personal perception of the individual country author and, due to this subjectivity it is not comparable across countries. In fact, the directors of this project were aware of this problem and warned the readers that "the index of liberalization is inherently not comparable *across countries:* its assigned level in any year is meaningful only in the context of changes over time in that country" (Michaely, Papageorgiou, and Choksi 1991, v. 7, p. 28). Consequently, the indices could not be used as indicators of trade orientation in their cross country econometric analysis; instead, they had to rely on dummy variables to classify different episodes.[11]

### II.4 *Devaluations and Trade Liberalization*

A central feature of both the Bhagwati-Krueger and Michaely et al. studies is that devaluations are considered an important component, in their own right, of a liberalization policy.[12] The reason for this is that in the presence of quantitative restrictions a (real) devaluation will reduce the rents accrued to those with import license allocations. In terms of Bhagwati and Krueger's framework, this will result in a lower premium (*PR*), and thus in a reduction in the anti-export bias.

The effects of devalutation under quantitative restrictions are illustrated

[11] See Appendix A2 of the Synthesis volume (Vol. 7) of Michaely, Papageorgiou, and Choksi (1991), for a set of regressions relating economic performance to trade policy.

[12] Krueger (1978, p. 53) says that "the feature that distinguishes Phase III from a straightforward alteration in the exchange rate is the prior existence of quantitative restriction."

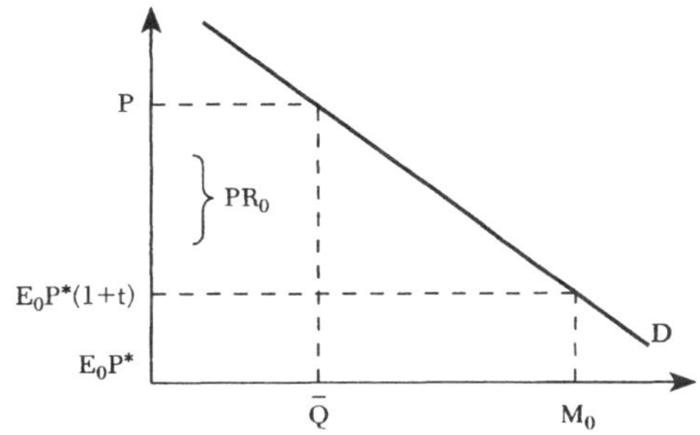


*Figure* 1a. Pre-devaluation situation

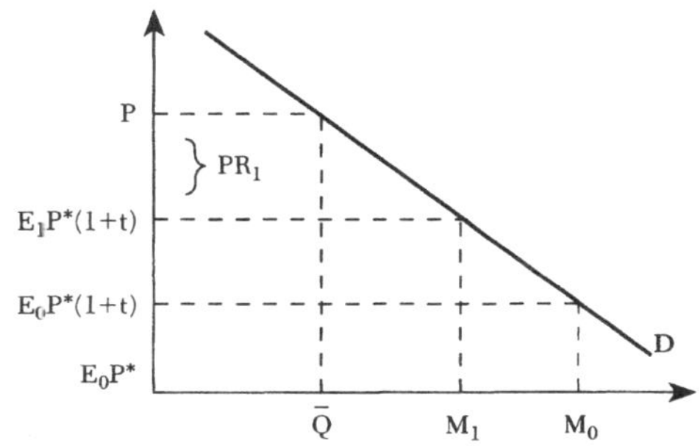


*Figure* 1b. Post-devaluation situation

through the simple (partial equilibrium) analysis in Figure 1. Figure 1a depicts the pre-devaluation situation, where $D$ is the demand schedule for imports, $P^*$ is the international price for imports expressed in foreign currency, $E_o$ is the initial (pre-devaluation) nominal exchange rate, $t$ is the tariff on imports, and $\bar{Q}$ is the maximum amount of this good allowed into the country. Because $\bar{Q}$ is smaller than the quantity demanded in the absence of licenses ($M_0$), there will be rationing and the internal price of this good will exceed its international price inclusive of tariff $E_oP^*(1 + t)$. The domestic price that clears this market is equal to $P$, and the premium associated with the existence of this license is equal to $PR_0$. A devaluation which raises the domestic value of foreign exchange will increase the tariff inclusive world price of imports expressed in domestic currency. That is, $E_1P^*(1 + t) > E_oP^*(1 + t)$, where $E_1$ is the new (higher) nominal exchange rate. As can be seen in Figure 1b, the premium $PR_0$ has now been reduced to $PR_1$ and, as a consequence, there will be a lower anti-exports bias.[13]

Naturally, a devaluation will have no effect on the premium if it is accompanied by an equiproportional increase in the domestic price of nontradables: What is required is a *real exchange rate* (*RER*) depreciation. A key question here—and one that attracted the attention of Krueger (1978) and the Michaely et al. study (1991)—is how to translate a nominal exchange rate adjustment into a real devaluation. If a nominal devaluation is accompanied by expansive fiscal and monetary policies, or if wages and other prices are severely indexed, inflationary pressures will develop and the real exchange rate will rapidly become overvalued. On the other hand, as Edwards (1989a) has found using an extensive cross-country data set, if nominal devaluations are accompanied by a set of consistent macroeconomic policies it is possible to generate significant real exchange rate devaluations and, thus, reductions in the trade system anti-exports bias.[14] In his analysis of 39 major devaluation episodes in the developing countries between 1962 and 1982, Edwards found that in 25 out of 39 cases the nominal exchange rate adjustment succeeded in signifi-

[13] Of course, this simplified partial equilibrium diagram ignores a series of important secondary effects. Still, it neatly captures the core of the argument made by Bhagwati and Krueger.

[14] Edwards (1989a) argues that the role of nominal devaluations is to *facilitate* the elimination of real exchange rate overvaluation. Possibly the first systematic cross-country analysis of devaluations in the developing countries was undertaken by Cooper (1971). Much of the recent work in the area has built on his early contribution.

cantly altering the real exchange rate. Additionally he found that in the vast majority of these cases (20 out of 25), the successful devaluation package had been accompanied by major steps towards dismantling trade, capital, and exchange controls.[15] In every one of these cases exports experienced a rebound and the overall external position of the country experienced a significant improvement relative to its pre-devaluation level.

The Krueger-Bhagwati project detected similar behavior patterns for the anti-export bias in the period following devaluations. Immediately after the nominal exchange rate adjustment, the RER experienced a drastic jump, which was followed by a slow erosion. The magnitude of this subsequent appreciation in the real exchange rate varied across countries: however, two years after the nominal devaluation in 13 of 22 devaluations classified as Phase III cases, the real exchange rate was still depreciated when measured with respect to its pre-Phase III value. What is more important is that in the majority of the cases where data were available, devaluations appeared to have resulted in a reduction of the anti-export bias. Table 4 presents information on the evolution of the trade regime bias—as defined in equation (2)—in selected Phase III episodes: in all but two cases—the two Korean episodes—the bias was lower two years after the devaluation than immediately prior to it.[16]

TABLE 4

ANTI-EXPORT BIAS AND DEVALUATIONS IN SELECTED LIBERALIZATION EPISODES[a]

| Country | Devaluation Episode | Prior to Devaluation | Two Years After Devaluation |
|---|---|---|---|
| Brazil | 1957 | 2.45 | 2.26 |
| | 1961 | 1.78 | 1.41 |
| | 1964 | 1.41 | 1.34 |
| Chile | 1956 | 3.69 | 1.94 |
| | 1959 | 1.94 | 1.99 |
| | 1965 | 1.95 | 1.79 |
| Philippines | 1960–62 | 2.01 | 1.36 |
| | 1970 | 1.37 | 1.16 |
| Korea | 1961 | 0.67 | 0.78 |
| | 1964 | 0.78 | 0.92 |
| Turkey | 1958–59 | 6.31 | 1.80 |

*Source:* Krueger (1978).

[a] The index is defined in detail in equation (2). A lower index reflects a reduction in the extent of anti-export bias.

The analysis of devaluations and trade distortion in the Michaely et al. project not only provided broad support for the findings in earlier studies, but also emphasized the fundamental role of real exchange rate stability in liberalization episodes. In general, countries with a more volatile real exchange rate experienced poorer overall performance than those nations that had managed to maintain a more stable real exchange rate. In a summary of the project, Michaely (1991, p. 119) states that: "The *long term* performance of the real exchange rate clearly differentiates 'liberalizers' from 'non-liberalizers.' "

In most countries in sub-Saharan Africa devaluations and liberalization policies have historically been vehemently opposed by politicians and policy makers. At the center of this hostility towards "trade-enhancing" policies, has been the belief that the successful development of Africa would require a rapid industrialization process. These policies, it was argued, would help the continent achieve "collective self-reliance" and reduce its

[15] See the Appendix to Edwards' (1989a) Chapter 6 for a detailed discussion on the evolution of barriers to international exchange in the period immediately following the 39 devaluation episodes.

[16] One should be cautious, however, in interpreting the data in Table 4, and in attributing the full reduction of the bias to the devaluation itself. In fact, as it was argued above, most devaluation policies are accompanied by relaxations of trade restrictions and controls.

external vulnerability.[17] However, instead of generating growth, self-reliance, and better life conditions, the implementation of inward oriented policies based on planning models during the 1960s and 1970s resulted in severe crises throughout the African continent: market incentives were seriously distorted, food production plummeted, GNP per capita fell by almost one percent per year during the 1970s, corruption became rampant, and shortages were generalized.

In an influential report released in 1981 the World Bank called for major economic reforms in Africa, including the elimination of distortions, the reestablishment of market mechanisms and the encouragement of agricultural exports through large devaluations. There is little doubt that it was this call for massive and generalized *devaluations* throughout the continent that has made this World Bank report particularly controversial. The World Bank critics have argued that nominal devaluations in Africa are fully translated into higher domestic inflation, without reducing the anti-exports bias. More specifically, the skepticism towards the effectiveness of exchange rate adjustments has been largely based on the belief that aggregate agricultural exports in Africa have a very low degree of responsiveness to relative price changes.[18] Recent research, however, has strongly suggested that, contrary to the popular belief, long-run supply elasticities of aggregate exports in Africa are significantly positive. Marian Bond (1983), for example, used country-specific data to estimate supply elasticities for aggregate exports and found point estimates that ranged from 0.07 for Uganda to 0.6 for Senegal. On the other hand, using pooled data for 16 sub-Saharan countries for 1974–82, Balassa (1989) estimated elasticities of aggregate exports ranging from 0.78 to 0.91.

The emergence of massive shortages of manufactured goods in many African countries during the 1980s introduced a new dimension in the debate on effectiveness of devaluation policies. A number of authors argued that, to the extent that producers could not purchase manufactured goods—either consumption goods or intermediate inputs—higher nominal exchange rates would not encourage increases in exports production.[19] This, of course, is a variant of the nominal vs. real devaluation issue. If manufacturing goods shortages are severe enough, their parallel market prices will be so high that for all practical purposes nominal devaluations will have no impact on the real exchange rate and, thus, on producers behavior. Jean-Claude Berthelemy and Christian Morrison (1989) have explicitly incorporated this aspect of African economies in their estimation of aggregate agriculture supply elasticities for the individual country level in Africa. Using data for six countries, they found that these elasticities were higher than those reported by Marian Bond (1983), ranging from 0.1 in Madagascar to 1.0 in Senegal.

As a consequence of the empirical re-

[17] This policy stance was formalized in the "Lagos Plan of Action." See Organization for African Unity (1980). Of course, for those familiar with Latin America's economic history the rhetoric of the Lagos Plan generated a clear sense of déjà vu. However, from a doctrinal perspective the African plan was squarely based on Marxist principles. See, for example, Samir Amin (1973).

[18] For a flavor of the controversy and of the debate that followed the publication of this report, see, for example, David Gordon and Joan Parker (1984). See United Nations Economic Commission for Africa (1990) and Kenneth Shapiro (1984) for a criticism of the World Bank Report. Paul Mosley, Jane Harrigan, and John Toye (1991) provide a critical view of liberalization policies, including devaluations, that were supported by the World Bank during the 1980s. See, also, Taylor (1988).

[19] For a theoretical discussion motivated by the Tanzanian experience see Tessa van der Willingen (1986). See also J. A. Mollett (1984).

sults obtained by studies like the ones reviewed here, there has recently been serious questioning of the validity of the traditional antiliberalization perspective in Africa. In fact, an increasing number of institutions have been slowly embracing the idea that devaluations—and more specifically real exchange rate realignment—provide an effective way for reducing the extent of the anti-export bias in Africa. For example, in a recent study, FAO (1991) has argued the "real devaluation would be necessary to switch production to . . . exportable cash crops . . ." (p. 202). Since the mid-1980s an increasing number of African nations have engaged in reform, including exchange rate adjustment.[20]

### II.5 *Cross-Country Evidence on Trade Orientation and Growth*

What is the effect of trade orientation on economic performance? This is the fundamental issue which multi-country comparative studies ultimately have to address. Given the serious measurement problems involved in tracking the evolution of trade orientation through time this is not an easy question to answer.

In dealing with the relation between trade policy and growth, the most serious analytical difficulty has been the traditional absence of firm theoretical grounds that link national domestic policies to long-run equilibrium growth. Within the framework of the neoclassical growth model, trade and other policies will affect the equilibrium *level* of aggregate output, but not its *rate of growth*. Only recently, with the development of endogenous growth models has this framework been modified to handle policy effects on growth. The traditional trade policy literature has dealt with this analytical problem in two related ways: first, a number of authors argued (either implicitly or explicitly) that movements from one steady state to a new steady state could account for most growth effects of domestic policies; and second, it has been pointed out, in a somewhat loose fashion, that there are some important dynamic advantages of freer trade that affect productivity and growth even in the long run.[21]

Using data from the individual country studies, Krueger (1978) econometrically tested two hypotheses: (1) more liberalized regimes result in higher rates of growth of exports; and (2) a more liberalized trade sector has a positive effect on aggregate growth.[22] In the latter case she conjectured that there are two channels through which openness positively affected growth. First, there are direct effects that operate via "dynamic advantages"—including higher capacity utilization and more efficient investment projects—and second, there are indirect effects that work through exports: more liberalized economies have faster growth of exports and these, in turn, result in more rapidly growing GNP.

In her formal econometric analysis Krueger estimated the following equa-

[20] Ajay Chhibber (1992) has argued that if in Africa nominal devaluations are implemented within the context of restrictive fiscal policies, It is possible to generate significant real exchange rate adjustments. This point has also been forcefully made by Brian Pinto (1991) in a discussion on the unification of parallel and official exchange rates in Africa. Many critics of devaluation have argued that if all African countries engage in these types of policies, terms of trade will worsen, with the net effect of these policies being negative. Balassa (1989), however, argued that if the possibility of diversifying production is taken into account there is no reason for this adverse effect to be severe. For a discussion of recent reforms in Africa see Carol Lancaster (1991).

[21] On "new" endogenous theories of growth see, for example, Paul Romer (1986) and Robert Lucas (1988). Also most of the literature reviewed in Section III implicitly assumes that off-steady state situations capture LDCs experiences even over long periods of time. See, for example, Corden (1986).

[22] A "liberalized" regime was defined as one that had reduced the extent of anti-exports bias.

tion on pooled data for traditional and nontraditional exports:

$$\log X_{it} = a_{0i} + g \log REERX_{it} + rT_t + a_1 d_1 T_t + a_2 d_2 T_t + a_3 d_1 + a_4 d_2 + u_{it},$$

where $X_{it}$ are either nontraditional or traditional exports in country $i$ in period $t$; $REERX$ is the exports effective real exchange rate, defined as the units of domestic currency received by an exporter for each real dollar worth of exports; $T_t$ is a linear time trend; $d_1$ is a dummy that takes the value of one in Phases I and II and zero otherwise; and $d_2$ is a dummy equal to one when the country is in Phases IV or V, and equal to zero in all other phases. She also estimated a real GNP equation on time series for each individual country:[23]

$$\log GNP_t = b_0 + b_1 T_t + b_2 \log X_t + b_3 d_1 T_t + b_4 d_2 T_t + \epsilon_t,$$

where $X_t$ is an index of the dollar value of exports of country $i$ in year $t$, relative to $i$'s average exports over the entire period.

The results strongly confirmed that a more depreciated REERX has a positive impact on nontraditional exports; traditional exports, however, did not appear to be sensitive to real exchange rate changes. For both types of exports the coefficient of $d_2$—the dummy variable for Phases IV and V—was significantly positive, suggesting that the move to a more "liberalized" regime also has a positive effect on exports growth. In terms of their relative contributions to export growth, real exchange rate changes appeared to be substantially more important than movements in the "liberalization" ladder. This prompted Krueger to conclude that "it is bias reduction, to a considerable greater extent than it is liberalization, which brings about export response" (1978, p. 205).

With respect to GNP growth, Krueger argued that her estimates provided strong evidence in favor of an indirect effect of liberalization on growth: higher exports positively affected GNP growth. However, the dummy variables coefficients were not significant in any of the regressions estimated, suggesting that there is no direct effect of liberalization on growth. In Krueger's words:[24]

> [F]actors associated with better export performance explain whatever systematic differences there are in growth rates under different phases of the regime; the fact that the regime itself is liberalized (or restricted) does not seem to have any additional independent influence. (1978, p. 274)

The conclusion that trade regimes per se had no *direct* effect on economic performance troubled some people. Balassa (1982), for example, argued that Krueger's results were seriously affected by an inadequate classification of trade regimes. According to him, by focusing almost exclusively on quantitative restrictions, the NBER study had basically ignored the protective effect of tariffs. He pointed out that, even in the absence of QRs, high tariffs usually introduced a strong bias against exports. In support of this view he cited the Argentinian experience.

As an alternative to the NBER five phases, Balassa (1982) proposed a four-way classification of trade regimes, that ranged from outward orientation—where the export bias stemming both from QRs *and* tariffs had been eliminated—to inward orientation, where the anti-export bias was the highest. Using data on effec-

[23] These equations were estimated for the ten countries in the study for 1954–72, or for subperiods within those years for which data were available.

[24] Notice that although Krueger discussed her results in terms of the effect of trade regimes on *growth*, her regressions considered the real GNP level as the dependent variable.

tive rates of protection, effective export subsidies, and nominal protection, Balassa (1982) classified 11 countries into these four categories.[25] He found that for the period 1960–73 those countries with lower anti-export bias had experienced a faster rate of growth of exports, and he concluded that this was strong evidence favoring the hypothesis that protectionism seriously hampered export expansion.

In trying to test the more controversial proposition that trade regimes affect GDP growth independent of exports, Balassa faced the traditional problem of measuring trade orientation. Instead of using dummy variables, as Krueger (1978) had done in the NBER project, Balassa (1982) decided to use "the growth rate of exports as a proxy for policy orientation" (p. 51). Using Spearman rank coefficients on pooled data for the eleven countries, he found that exports growth and output growth had been positively correlated and concluded that "the expansion of exports and the consequent growth of GNP have been the result of the incentives applied" (1982, p. 59). Although Balassa's comparative analysis was backed by individual country studies, it had some limitations that, in fact, have been present in much of the subsequent literature. Some of these refer to the arbitrary definition of export incentives, the lack of a role for real exchange rates in the explanation of export performance, the use of a highly suspicious proxy (exports growth) for trade orientation, and the inability to deal convincingly with causality issues. In fact, it is not clear whether it is exports growth that causes output expansion, or the other way around.

Michaely et al.'s study returned to the use of dummy variables to classify trade regimes in formally evaluating the effects of trade policy on growth. A number of regressions relating economic performance to different attributes of the trade regime—which, as pointed out, were captured by dummy variables—were estimated. By and large the results supported the view that countries with more intense, sustained liberalizations have outperformed those with failed liberalization attempts. However, in this study as in its predecessors, the problem of measuring trade orientation is not fully resolved. As in previous studies there was a nontrivial degree of arbitrariness in classifying countries as strong or weak liberalizers, and the use of binary dummies precluded the analysis of how different grades of trade liberalization affect growth and other key variables.

### II.6 *Two Examples of Trade Orientation and Liberalization*

Among the countries examined in these projects, Chile and Korea provide two of the most interesting case studies of the evolution of trade policy.

*Chile:* Between 1950 and 1970—the years covered in the Bhagwati-Krueger study—Chile went through three incomplete liberalization attempts: in 1956–57 it reached Phase III, in 1959–61 it moved even further into Phase IV, and in 1965–70 it again reached Phase III (see Table 5). As with most countries in this study, during the period under analysis Chile never reached the stage of full liberalization (Phase V). Moreover, all of its three attempts were short-lived, ending up in frustration and in a reversion to exchange controls, the use of multiple exchange rates, and massive quantitative restrictions. An interesting feature of the three Chilean liberalization attempts is that, although they took place under three different exchange rate systems, they all

[25] The countries considered in this study are: Argentina, Brazil, Chile, Colombia, India, Israel, Korea, Mexico, Singapore, Taiwan, and Yugoslavia.

TABLE 5
PHASES OF EXCHANGE CONTROL REGIMES IN CHILE
1950–1972

| Period | Phase |
|---|---|
| 1950–55 | II |
| 1956–57 | III[a] |
| 1958–59 | II |
| 1959–61 | IV[a] |
| 1962–64 | II |
| 1965–70 | III[a] |
| 1971–72 | II |

*Source:* Jere Behrman (1976).
[a] These are the liberalization episodes identified in the Krueger-Bhagwati study, and defined above.

collapsed, at least in part, due to a highly overvalued real exchange rate.[26]

What makes the Chilean experience particularly interesting is that eventually, in the late 1970s and early 1980s, the country did adopt a very open trade regime with low uniform import tariffs, no exchange or trade controls and minimum restrictions to capital movements. There is no doubt that since 1979 Chile's trade policy corresponds to Phase V in the Bhagwati-Krueger classification: there are no QRs, licenses, or prohibitions. A uniform import tax—that has varied between 10 and 20 percent—has been in effect, and, by and large, real exchange rate overvaluation has been avoided. In fact, Chile is the only country in the Michaely et al. study whose index of liberalization reached the maximum possible level of 20.

In 1973 Chilean import tariffs averaged 105 percent and were highly dispersed, with some goods subject to nominal tariffs of more than 700 percent and others fully exempted from import duties. In addition to tariffs, a battery of quantitative restrictions was applied, including outright import prohibition and prior import deposits of up to 10,000 percent (see de la Cuadra and Hachette 1991). These protective measures were complemented with a highly distortive multiple exchange rate system consisting of 15 different rates. By August of 1975 all quantitative restrictions had been eliminated and the average tariff had been reduced to 44 percent. This tariff reduction process continued until June of 1979 when all tariff items but one (automobiles) were set at 10 percent. In the mid-1980s, in the midst of the debt crisis, temporary tariff hikes were implemented; by 1987, however, a uniform level of 15 percent was firmly established.

The opening of Chile's external sector was accompanied, during most of the period, by a strongly depreciated real exchange rate.[27] The combination of these two policies had a significant impact on Chile's economic structure. The share of manufacture in GNP dropped from 30 percent in 1974 to 22 percent in 1981; productivity in tradable sectors grew substantially and exports became highly diversified. By the early 1990s exports had become the engine of growth and the Chilean experience with trade reform was praised as a big success by the multinational institutions and observers from different ideological persuasions (see World Bank 1989, 1990). Largely thanks to the boom in exports, between 1986 and 1991 Chile experienced the highest rate of growth in Latin America with an

[26] While the 1956–57 liberalization was carried out under floating exchange rates, the 1959–61 was implemented with a fixed nominal exchange rate, and the 1965–70 episode took place under a managed crawling peg system, where the nominal exchange rate was periodically adjusted. See, for example, Sergio de la Cuadra and Dominique Hachette (1991).

[27] During 1980–82, however, the government allowed the real exchange rate to become overvalued. This generated a serious crisis that lasted until 1986–87. Since 1985 Chile has successfully followed a crawling peg nominal exchange rate regime where the official exchange rate is adjusted periodically as a way to avoid devaluation. See Edwards and Alejandra Cox-Edwards (1991) for details.

TABLE 6
PHASES OF EXCHANGE CONTROL REGIMES IN KOREA
1950–1972

| Period | Phase I |
|---|---|
| 1950–53 | I |
| 1954–60 | II |
| 1961–62 | III[a] |
| 1963 | II |
| 1964–65 | III[a] |
| 1966–72 | IV[a] |

*Source:* Krueger (1978).
[a] These are the liberalization episodes identified by the Krueger-Bhagwati study.

TABLE 7
IMPORT TARIFFS AND QUANTITATIVE RESTRICTIONS
IN KOREA 1977–1988

| | Tariff (%) | Percentage of Imports Subject to Licenses & Prohibitions |
|---|---|---|
| 1977 | 29.7 | 50.1 |
| 1979 | 24.8 | 30.9 |
| 1984 | 21.2 | 14.6 |
| 1988 | 9.8 | 4.6 |

*Sources:* Kwang Suk Kim (1991); World Bank (1989).

annual growth of GDP of 4.2 percent.

Perhaps the strongest sign of Chile's success with trade reform is that the new democratic regime of President Patricio Aylwin (elected in December of 1989) decided to continue the opening process, reducing, in June of 1991, import tariffs even further to a uniform 11 percent. What makes this measure particularly remarkable is that President Aylwin's economic team—including the Ministers of Finance and Economics—had been relentless critics of the trade reform process during its implementation in the mid and late 1970s. This remarkable change of opinion is clearly captured by the following quote by Alywin's Minister of finance, at one time one of the most severe critics of the liberalization process:

> Preserving the former government achievements means maintaining an open economy fully integrated into world markets, dynamic growth in exports, with a private sector fully committed to the task of [economic] development. (*Newsweek*, Latin American edition, Mar. 26, 1990)

*Korea:* Between 1963 and 1990 Korea's merchandise exports grew, in real U.S. dollar terms, at an annual rate of 23 percent. This stellar performance has often been mentioned as a premier example of the positive results of outward oriented policies. However, Korea has not always been an open economy. In fact, throughout most of 1950–63 Korea's external sector was highly distorted. During this period most imports were subject to licensing, tariff rates were high (exceeding 50% in 1959–60), and a multiple exchange rate system was in effect. As can be seen from Table 6, with the exception of 1961–62, the Krueger-Bhagwati project classified Korea as a highly repressed economy throughout these years.

A major policy change took place in 1964, when exchange rates were unified, a major devaluation was implemented, and a systematic process of trade liberalization was started. Gradually import tariffs were reduced, the coverage of import licenses was eased, and import prohibitions were eliminated. By the end of the 1980s average import tariffs had been reduced to approximately 10 percent, and import licenses had been virtually eliminated (see Table 7). The transformation of Korea's external sector not only resulted in an accelerated growth of exports, but also affected their composition. While in 1962 manufactured goods amounted to a mere 17 percent of total exports, by 1980 their share had climbed to 75 percent (see Kwang Suk Kim 1991).

Supporting exchange rate and export promotion policies accompanied the Korean trade liberalization experience throughout 1964–90. Since the devaluation of 1964, the Korean authorities have made a concerted effort to maintain a highly depreciated—that is, competitive—*real* exchange rate. Starting in 1980 Korea pegged its nominal exchange rate to a basket of currencies, allowing periodic adjustments that reflect the development of a series of domestic and external factors. This system has allowed Korean exports to remain highly competitive in the world economy, but has generated serious accusations of unfair trade practices by the U.S.[28]

Starting in the 1960s an aggressive export promotion scheme became an important complement of the Korean trade liberalization strategy. Throughout the years exports have been subsidized through a number of channels, including (a) direct cash subsidies (until 1964); (b) direct tax reductions (until 1973); (c) interest rate preferences; (d) indirect tax reductions on intermediate inputs; and (e) tariff exemptions to imported intermediate materials.[29] Kim (1991) has recently calculated that between 1964 and 1980 these subsidies, taken together, amounted to approximately 23 percent. However, as the devolution of indirect taxes and tariff duties paid on imported inputs are not genuine subsidies, he has argued that the relevant figure for evaluating the effect of export subsidies should exclude these items. He estimates that these total net subsidies—comprised of direct cash subsidies, direct tax reductions, and interest rate preference—have been reduced from 23 percent to zero between 1963 and 1983. He has argued, as others have, that in the case of Korea, these export subsidies played a fundamental role during the earlier years of the Korean export boom.

## III. *Trade Orientation, Liberalization, and Unemployment*

One of the most important issues addressed by politicians before embarking on a trade reform program refers to the unemployment consequences of the policies under consideration: Is the liberalization process going to result in short-term unemployment?; What will happen to long-run employment? Many times liberalization attempts have been aborted half-way, as the political authorities fear serious labor market disruptions. This has long been understood by economists. For example, Michaely, Papageorgiou, and Choksi (1991, vol. 7, p. 3) have stated that "[a]voiding high unemployment should . . . be a consideration in any scheme of liberalization." In this section I briefly review the empirical literature on the relationship between trade policy, tariff reforms, and labor market developments in the developing countries.[30]

The most important pioneering studies on structural reform and trade liberalization attempts devoted little effort to analyze the employment consequences of these policies. For example, Little, Scitovsky, and Scott (1970) discuss only briefly the *long-term* employment consequences of industrialization policies, without addressing the short-term consequences on the labor market of their proposed policies of tariff reduction. In fact, their otherwise illuminating discussion on the transition from a repressed to a liberalized trade sector (ch. 10) does not

[28] Rogelio Arellano-Cadena (1990) found that the Korean real exchange rate has had one of the lowest levels of volatility in the developing countries. See Bongsung Oum (1989) for a description of the Korean exchange rate system. See KDI (1989) for an analysis of some of the Korean U.S. fractions.

[29] See Kim (1991) for details on the different export promotion schemes used.

[30] Due to space considerations the discussion is restricted to the empirical literature on the subject. For a theoretical analysis of the main issues involved see, for example, Edwards (1988).

touch explicitly on the employment issue. They do refer, however, to the income distribution effects of trade liberalization policies, arguing that a rapid trade reform would result in drastic changes in income distribution that would, probably, trigger an opposition to the implementation of these policies. In fact, it is this consideration of the potential political opposition to the reforms what prompts them to recommend a *gradual* trade liberalization process. However, no empirical discussion is provided to support the conjecture that more gradual reforms will have a smaller effect on unemployment.

The NBER project directed by Bhagwati (1978) and Krueger (1978) discussed above dealt in a very general way with the question of the employment consequences of trade reforms in the ten countries under study. In her synthesis volume Krueger (1978) devotes little more than two pages to this issue, pointing out that, generally speaking, the evidence from the individual countries indicated that employment grew more rapidly during Phases IV and V—that is, during those phases in which the trade regime was characterized by a more liberalized external sector. Based on data provided by the individual country authors she argues that this effect was particularly strong in the cases of the Philippines and Korea.

The link between trade regimes and employment is the specific subject of another NBER project directed by Krueger (1981). This study focused mainly on the *long-run* relationship between trade orientation and employment creation. Its main purpose was not to inquire how trade reform affected labor markets, but to analyze whether the existence of factor market distortions had resulted in deviations in the observed directions of trade from those suggested by the Heckscher-Ohlin-Samuelson framework. The experiences of ten developing countries were analyzed in detail:[31] Labor coefficients of foreign trade were computed, production functions at the industry level were estimated, and the extent of factor market distortions was assessed. The authors found that, without any exceptions, labor markets were highly distorted in the ten countries under study, with industrial minimum wages being the most prevalent form of distortion. The analysis of the empirical evidence strongly indicated that, in most of the countries, exportable industries (defined as such in a Heckscher-Ohlin sense) tended to be more labor intensive than import competing industries. Moreover, the data showed that the exportable sectors were relatively more intensive in the use of unskilled labor than import competing sectors. Krueger interprets this evidence as suggesting that, in spite of the existence of pervasive distortions in factor markets, the directions of trade in these countries responded to large extent to the Heckscher-Ohlin predictions. The other two general conclusions from this study are that employment tends to grow faster in outward oriented economies—a finding also obtained in the Bhagwati-Krueger study—and that the removal of both factor market distortions and trade restrictions benefits, in the long run, the employment creation process in most of the developing countries.

The World Bank study directed by Balassa (1982) also addressed the long-term employment consequences of different trade regimes. In his synthesis piece on the experiences of eleven countries Balassa points out that, because primary activities and manufacturing for exports are more labor intensive, "reducing tariffs will tend to benefit employment" (p. 65). Nevertheless, neither in the synthesis

[31] Brazil, Chile, Colombia, Indonesia, Ivory Coast, Pakistan, Korea, Thailand, Tunisia, and Uruguay.

paper nor in the individual country studies is the issue of unemployment during the transition addressed in detail.[32]

The most ambitious study on the labor market effects of trade liberalization reforms has been Michaely et al.'s recent World Bank project. In order to deal with the labor market consequences of the reforms, each country author used the methodology he or she found more appropriate and tried to evaluate the extent to which trade reform in that specific episode had affected employment, unemployment and, in some cases, wages.

In analyzing the employment consequences of trade reform Michaely et al. distinguish between gross and net effects. The gross—or in their words "dis-employment"—effect is defined as the unemployment associated with the contraction of some industries after the trade liberalization reform is undertaken. The net effect, on the other hand, is defined as the total change in aggregate unemployment in the economy. Naturally, from an economic perspective the net effect is the most interesting one, because under most circumstances we would expect a reduction in the level of employment in those sectors that lose competitiveness, and an increase in employment in those sectors that, as a consequence of a reform, expand.

In most cases the authors compute variants of the "before" and "after" method in assessing the employment effects of trade reforms. In three of the studies, however (Chile, Spain, and Yugoslavia) a method that attempted to control for the evolution of other economic variables—such as the terms of trade, fluctuations in economic activity and macroeconomic policies—was used. The authors of the Chile and Yugoslavia studies found that, when controlling for other factors, the *net* effect of liberalization on employment was positive: as a consequence of the liberalization program the aggregate rate of unemployment declined in these countries.[33] For Spain the results differed depending on which liberalization episode was considered. While in the first two liberalization attempts (1960–66) and (1970–74) aggregate unemployment increased after the trade reforms, in the third episode (1977–80) there was a *decline* in net unemployment after liberalization.

Regarding the other countries in the study, it was found that unemployment increased *after* the following episodes:[34] Argentina in (1967–70) and (1976–80); Israel in (1952–55) and (1962–68); Indonesia in (1966–72); Korea in (1978–79); the Philippines in (1960–65); and Turkey in (1980–84). In most of these cases, however, the increase in unemployment was rather small, and could be attributed to factors different from the reform itself. These results led the directors of the project to conclude that "by and large, liberalization attempts have *not* incurred significant transition costs by way of unemployment" (Michaely, Papageorgiou, and Choksy, Vol. 7, ch. 6, p. 80, emphasis added).

Undoubtedly, the Michaely et al. project constitutes the most complete and

[32] This study includes Argentina, Brazil, Chile, Colombia, India, Israel, Korea, Mexico, Singapore, Taiwan, and Yugoslavia. The Korean and Taiwan studies, however, analyze in some detail the link between exports growth and employment absorption.

[33] The procedure used compares employment "before" and "after" the trade reform, without controlling for the effect of other variables. However, during the second year (1967) of the Yugoslavian liberalization effort there was an increase in unemployment.

[34] It is interesting to note that, in spite of their "before and after" comparisons, almost every time unemployment does increase after the reform the authors tend to attribute it to causes other than the reform itself. For example, in the Argentinean case they talk about overvaluation, in the Israeli episode they mention restrictive macro policies; in Korea they talk about a recession and so on.

ambitious attempt to deal with the link between structural reforms and the labor market. However, as is usually the case with a collection of multi-authored country studies, the empirical and historical analyses are uneven and, at times, somewhat unfocused. For instance, in some of the country studies, there is no detailed discussion on the role of labor market distortions, minimum wages, or indexation practices.

The link between trade liberalization reforms and labor market adjustment has also been studied for the liberalization experiences of the Southern Cone of Latin America during the 1970s. In particular, in the case of Chile it has been argued that the existence of labor distortions—including minimum wages and wage indexation to past inflation—generated a segmented labor market, with a protected and an unprotected sector. The existence of a protected sector resulted in important wage rigidities that impaired the labor market's ability to adjust to the trade reform and other shocks. For example, Edwards and Cox-Edwards (1991) have calculated that as a result of existing labor market rigidities, the trade liberalization reform generated short-run unemployment in Chile on the order of 3.5 percent.[35]

## IV. *Exports Growth, Trade Orientation, and Aggregate Growth*

The comparative studies reviewed in Section II have provided very detailed information on trade policy practices in LDCs. However, their coverage has been small; in each of them only a handful of countries was actually analyzed. In an effort to broaden the scope of the inquiry a number of authors have used larger cross-country data sets to analyze econometrically the relationship between trade orientation and growth. These studies make no pretense of learning details of trade policy practices of the countries in the sample; their strategy has been to maximize the number of countries included in the analysis. This section reviews and analyzes some of the most important works in this category.

In a highly influential paper that has generated significant additional research effort, Michaely (1977) used simple rank correlations on a 41-country sample for 1950–73 to analyze whether the rate of growth of exports has been associated with GDP growth. In order to avoid spurious results steming from the fact that exports are a component of GDP, Michaely focused on the rate of growth of exports *shares* of GDP, and their relation with output growth. He found that the Spearman rank coefficient was significantly positive (.308) for the sample as a whole. It was larger (0.523), however, for a subsample of 23 middle income countries.[36] Balassa (1978) also used the rank correlation methodology to investigate this issue further. Using pooled data on eleven countries for 1960–73, he again found a positive correlation coefficient between different measures of the rate of growth of exports and output growth.

These results were criticized on three accounts: first, by looking at correlation coefficient, the (possible) role of other factors on growth was ignored. Second, no attempt was made to distinguish between endogenous and exogenous variables; that is, the issue of causality between exports growth and GDP growth was not

[35] Edwards and Cox-Edwards (1991) use a segmented labor market model to quantify the effects of the Chilean trade reform on unemployment. On this issue see, also, Vittorio Corbo, de Melo, and Tybout (1986) and Joseph Ramos (1986).

[36] Countries with GNP per capita exceeding U.S. $300 in 1972 dollars.

satisfactorily addressed. And third, these analyses were not based on firm theoretical grounds.

### IV.1 *Studies Based on Neoclassical Production Functions*

A number of authors have attempted to get around the criticisms of the rank correlation studies by formulating a conceptual framework based on neoclassical production functions. At the center of this approach is the idea that exports contribute to aggregate output in two fundamental ways: first, it is assumed that the exports sector generates positive externalities on nonexports sectors, through more efficient management styles and improved production techniques. Second, it is argued that there is a productivity differential in favor of the exports sector. Thus, an expansion of exports at the cost of other sectors will have a positive net effect on aggregate output.[37]

Feder (1983) captured these ideas in a simple model with an exports sector ($X$) and a nonexports sector ($N$). The two sectoral production functions are:

$$N = F(K^n, L^n, X), \tag{3}$$

$$X = G(K^X, L^X), \tag{4}$$

where $K^i$ and $L^i$ are capital and labor used in the $i$ ($i = N,X$) sector. Denoting partial derivatives by subscripts, the assumption of a productivity differential across sectors is captured by the following equation:

$$\left(\frac{G_K}{F_K}\right) = \left(\frac{G_L}{F_L}\right) = 1 + \delta, \tag{5}$$

where $G_L$, $F_L$ are the marginal productivities of labor, and $G_K$, $F_K$ are the marginal productivities of capital. Then, $\delta$ measures the extent of the productivity differential in favor of exports. If $\delta = 0$, resources are optimally allocated and productivities are equalized across sectors. The assumption of a positive externality of exports is captured by the inclusion of $X$ as an additional productive factor in the production function for the non-exports sector. The magnitude of $F_X$ (the marginal productivity of $X$ in $N$) measures the importance of this externality. If $F_X = 0$ the externality is not present, and exports growth will have no effect on the output of $N$.

Aggregate GDP ($y$) is the sum of $N$ and $X$:

$$y = N + X. \tag{6}$$

After assuming that the marginal productivity of labor is equal to $\beta(y/L)$ (where $\beta$ is a constant), Feder derives the following equation for the rate of growth of GDP:[38]

$$(\dot{y}/y) = \alpha(I/y) + \beta(\dot{L}/L) + [F_x + (\delta/(1 + \delta))](X/y)(\dot{X}/X), \tag{7}$$

where $(I/y)$ is the investment ratio. The presence of the exports growth term on the right hand side of (7) distinguishes this expression from a straightforward growth accounting equation. Notice that in the absence of productivity differentials ($\delta = 0$) and of exports-related externalities ($F_x = 0$), the $(\dot{X}/X)$ term disappears, and equation (7) reverts to a standard neoclassical growth equation. One of the most attractive features of equation (7) is that it can be readily estimated using standard econometric techniques.

Feder used a sample of 31 semi-indus-

[37] Gershon Feder (1983) provides the first formal model on this subject. According to him the productivity differentials across sectors could be due to several factors, including a more competitive environment in which exports operate. He does not explain, however, why these effects are not internalized by economic agents, nor why the productivity differentials tend to persist through time.

[38] This is derived from (3)–(6) and the assumption that $F_L = \beta(y/L)$, where $\beta$ is a constant. $\alpha$ is equal to $F_K$.

trialized countries to estimate (7).[39] All variables were measured as 1964–73 averages, and ordinary least squares were used. The main hypothesis being tested is whether the coefficient of $(\dot{X}/y)(\dot{X}/X)$ was significantly positive as suggested by the theory. The following result was obtained (*t*-statistics in parentheses):

$$(\dot{y}/y) = \underset{(0.180)}{0.002} + \underset{(3.542)}{0.178}\,(I/y) + \underset{(2.862)}{0.747}\,(\dot{L}/L) + \underset{(5.454)}{0.422}\,(X/y)(\dot{X}/X) \qquad \bar{R}^2 = .69.$$

Feder interpreted these findings as providing "strong support to the hypothesis that marginal factor productivities in the export sector are higher than in the non-export sector" (p. 65).

In an effort to disentangle the "exports productivity" (δ) from the "exports externality" ($F_x$) effects, Feder estimated an equation that included $(\dot{X}/X)$ as an additional regressor.[40] He found that both the coefficients of $(X/y)(\dot{X}/X)$ and of $(\dot{X}/X)$ were significantly positive and concluded that although both effects were present, export externalities were relatively more important than productivity differentials. Although these results were highly suggestive and represented an improvement over simple correlations between exports growth and GDP growth, Feder made no attempts to analyze the robustness of his results, nor did he discuss some of the most common econometric problems faced by this type of analysis. As a result of this a number of people remained highly skeptical of the validity of these results.

Following the publication of Feder's paper, a number of authors have tried to expand the analysis in several directions. While some authors have based their analyses strictly on Feder's two sectors formulation, others have resorted to simpler one sector models where exports enter the production function as an additional factor of production: $y = f(K,L,X)$. In this case, the relevant exports-related regressor in the cross-country regressions is $(\dot{X}/X)$ and not, as in Feder, $(X/y)(\dot{X}/X)$. A serious problem with this simpler formulation, however, is that it has not specified the channels through which exports are supposed to affect GDP.

In order to organize the discussion I have classified work on the relationship between exports growth and GDP growth under five general questions:

1) Are poor and middle income countries affected in a similar way by outward orientation? or, is there a required minimum threshold level of development in order to enjoy the benefits of rapid exports growth?
2) How, if at all, do changing world economic conditions affect the benefits derived from outward orientation? Do the results of export promotion in the LDCs depend on whether the world economy is experiencing a boom or a bust?
3) Are there other channels, in addition to productivity differentials and externalities, through which exports expansion affects output growth? In other words, is the equation well

[39] An alternative hypothesis not considered by Feder, or any of the contributors to this literature, is that there is a mutual interdependence between the $N$ and $X$ sectors. In this case equation (7) would also include a term for $\dot{N}/N$. Prior to Feder's effort a number of studies had regressed GDP on exports growth. They were not based, however, on a conceptual framework. See, for example, Robert Emery (1967), Alfred Maizels (1968), Irving Kravis (1970), Constantine Michalopoulos and Keith Jay (1973), Balassa (1978), and William Tyler (1981).

[40] Assuming that the $N$ sector production function is $N = X^{\theta}\,\psi(K^N,L^N)$, we have that $F_x = \theta(N/X)$. Thus, equation (7) can be rewritten as:

$$(\dot{y}/y) = \alpha(I/y) + \beta(\dot{L}/L) + \left(\frac{\delta}{1+\delta} - \theta\right)(X/y)(\dot{X}/X) + \theta(\dot{X}/X).$$

specified? Or, are there omitted variables?

4) Is there an independent role for *trade policy* in these growth equations?
5) Does the causality necessarily go from export growth to GDP growth? Or, alternatively, are these equations subject to simultaneity bias?

### IV.2 *Exports, Growth, and Critical Minimum Effort*

An immediate question that emerged from Feder's results was whether his findings held for all LDCs, or whether it was confined to the middle income nations. After all, in his original piece Michaely (1977) had found that the Spearman rank coefficient was higher for middle income countries than for the whole sample. Additionally, the fact that some of the original work had been restricted to semi-industrialized countries cast some doubt on the general applicability of this growth equation formulation.

From the policy debate perspective this is an important question that has some bearing on the universality of the outward oriented policy recommendation. Gerald Helleiner (1986), for example, has strongly argued that a minimum level of development is required before the benefits of exports promotion can be realized, and that, in consequence, export-promotion policies would have doubtful effects in Africa.

In addressing this issue a number of authors estimated GDP growth equations for both poor and middle income countries for 1960–78. In these analyses the cut-off point has been arbitrarily defined as an income per capita of approximately U.S. $360 (1978 dollars). Other authors have tackled this problem by adding a "poor countries" dummies to the cross country growth equations. Regardless of the technique used and of the period considered, these early studies found that the coefficient of exports growth was significantly larger for the middle income group.[41] Subsequent contributions have tried to combine time series and cross section data, where the sample was divided into middle income and low income countries for two periods (1960–72 and 1973–82). They found that the coefficient of export growth was significantly positive in all but one case—low income countries during 1960–72. However, contrary to the results in previous studies, for 1973–82 the coefficient of exports growth for the poorer nations exceeded that of the middle income countries.

Most authors have addressed the homogeneity question by dividing their samples according to the stage of development. This, however, need not be the most appropriate way to distinguish groups of countries. Inderjit Kohli and Nirvikar Singh (1989) have investigated whether countries can be distinguished by a "minimum critical threshold" related to the trade structure itself, rather than to income per capita. Using data on 41 countries, they divided the sample into "outward oriented" economies—those with a rate of growth of exports exceeding 6 percent per annum, or with a share of exports to GNP larger than 17 percent—and "non-outward oriented" countries. Using Feder's analytical formulation they found that for the period 1960–70 the coefficient of exports growth was significantly positive for both groups of countries. It was significantly larger however, for the "outward oriented" nations.[42] For the more recent period,

[41] Rostam Kavoussi (1984) and Rati Ram (1985) are good representatives of this type of study.

[42] This general result has been recently supported by the findings obtained by Patricia Gray and Singer (1988) using a methodology based on Kravis' (1970) decomposition of the sources of export growth. They decomposed exports growth into three factors: world

however, these coefficients were positive but often insignificant for both groups.

In sum, most studies have found that in GDP growth regressions the importance and significance of the exports growth coefficient varies across groups of countries, casting some doubt on the desirability of pooling all these nations together in the econometric analysis. However, it is unlikely that this issue will be further elucidated until more sophisticated econometric techniques are used on pooled time series-cross section data.

### IV.3 *Export Growth, GDP Growth, and World Market Conditions*

A common criticism of the regression analyses that favor "outward-orientation" is that they are overly simplistic and that, among other things, they tend to ignore the role of world market conditions on the feasibility of a successful trade opening strategy (see, for example, Helleiner 1990).

A number of authors have reacted to this criticism by analyzing whether the earlier results hold under alternative world market environments. The vast majority of these studies have taken a very simple approach, comparing the results of cross country growth equations for two, or more, periods. The favorite breaking point has been the 1973 oil shock. Feder-type regressions have been run for pre- and post-1973 averages across countries, and the estimated coefficients have been casually compared. Each author has tried to distinguish his product by adding some twist to the analysis, such as further dividing the sample between low income and middle income countries. A common feature of most of these studies is that the econometric techniques used are very simple, with no effort made to test for structural breaks, or to deal with problems related to measurement error and simultaneity. Table 8 contains summaries of a number of papers that have dealt with export growth under alternative world market conditions.

The earlier regression-based analyses—Balassa (1985), Ram (1985, 1987)—found that the point estimate on the coefficient on the exports growth variable was higher in the post-oil shock period. This type of result led Balassa to conclude that there are clear "advantages of outward-oriented policies for export performance and for economic growth in the face of external shocks," and that the "reliance on export promotion in response to external shocks under an outward-oriented strategy . . . favorably affected economic growth" (Balassa 1981, p. 189).

A serious limitation of this earlier work, however, is that the regressions for different periods were not always strictly comparable. For instance, Pradumna Rana (1988) pointed out that in his 1985 article Balassa compared results for a pre-1973 regression for 11 countries with results from a 41 country sample for post-1973. When these equations were re-estimated using the same 41 countries sample on pooled data, he found that although the exports growth coefficients were significantly positive for both subsamples, the point estimates for the post-1973 period were smaller than those for the pre-1973 period. (These results have been supported by Kohli and Singh 1989; and Hadi Esfahani 1991.)

Some authors have departed from the regression-based tradition and looked at the effects of world market conditions from a different perspective. A typical approach has been to classify countries between those facing "favorable" and

demand, competitiveness, and diversification. The two latter were identified with "outward orientation" and were used to construct an index of trade policy. Spearman rank coefficients between this index and GDP growth were estimated.

TABLE 8

SELECTED WORK ON EXPORTS GROWTH, GDP GROWTH, AND WORLD MARKET CONDITIONS

| Author | Methodology | Results |
|---|---|---|
| Balassa (1985) | • Uses production function approach with $(\dot{X}/X)$ as regressor.<br>• Compares results for sample of 11 counties in 1960–73 with results for 1973–79 that includes 43 countries adversely affected by the 1973 oil shock. | • Finds that coefficient of $(\dot{X}/X)$ is higher in the 1973–79 period than in the earlier period. |
| Ram (1985) | • Production function framework on 73 countries for 1960–70 and 1970–77.<br>• Breakdown of sample justified by oil shock. | • For both periods coefficient of $(\dot{X}/X)$ significantly positive; higher in 1970–77. |
| Kavoussi (1985) | • Decomposes sources of exports growth using Kravis (1970) technique.<br>• Constructs outward orientation ranking.<br>• Classifies countries between those facing "favorable" and "unfavorable" world market conditions.<br>• Computes Spearman rank coefficients between outward orientation and GDP growth in two periods: 1967–73 and 1973–77. | • Found that countries facing favorable market conditions exhibited a significantly stronger correlation between $(\dot{X}/X)$ and GDP growth than those facing unfavorable conditions. |
| Ram (1987) | • Production function approach on time series and cross sections.<br>• Divides sample in "before oil shock" (1960–72) and "after oil shock" (1973–82).<br>• Sample also divided between low and middle income countries. | • In the vast majority of cases the estimated coefficient of $(\dot{X}/X)$ for the 1973–82 period exceeds that of the earlier period. |
| Rana (1988) | • Comment on Balassa's (1985) paper.<br>• Uses balanced sample of 43 nations for before and after 1973.<br>• Estimates pooled regressions using both OLS and a random effects procedure. | • All estimates of $(\dot{X}/X)$ are significantly positive; those for post-73 period smaller than those for earlier period. |
| Gray & Singer (1988) | • Uses Kavoussi's (1985) exports decomposition technique on 1967–73 and 1973–83.<br>• Divides countries between those facing "above average" world demand and "below average" demand.<br>• Spearman rank coefficient. | • Spearman coefficient significantly positive for countries facing above-average world demand; insignificant for those facing low world demand conditions. |
| Kohli & Singh (1989) | • Feder's model is estimated on 41 countries using samples for 1960–70 and 1970–81.<br>• Sample also divided between "outward oriented" and "non-outward oriented" countries. | • Coefficients of $(\dot{X}/X)$ always significant for earlier period; not always in the later period. |

"unfavorable" world demand. It has been found that, while there is a strong positive correlation between exports growth and GDP growth for countries facing positive world demand conditions, this correlation is very weak, or nonexistent, for countries facing below normal world demand. This finding led Gray and Singer (1988) to conclude that "outward orientation cannot be considered as a universal recommendation for all conditions and for all types of countries" (p. 403).

Although the work on the area has not provided a conclusive answer to the question of how world demand conditions affect the relation between export growth and aggregate GDP, it has provided strong indications that world business cycles play some role in the way the external sector interacts with aggregate GDP. A more precise answer to this general question would require more detailed analysis relying, at least in part, on time series data and on modern and more sophisticated statistical techniques. Additionally, truly persuasive analyses would have to be based on firmer theoretical bases that provide a clear discussion on the specific way in which the different variables in the regressions are supposed to affect economic growth.

### IV.4 *Equation Specification*

The literature analyzed above has been based on the premise that exports generate positive externalities for the rest of the economy. In principle, however, there may be other channels through which export performance (and openness) will affect aggregate economic performance. For example, some authors have argued that, in a two gap setting, export expansion will also affect aggregate growth by helping relax the foreign exchange constraint.[43] This effect works through the following mechanism: By allowing an increase in imports of intermediate inputs, export expansion relaxes a crucial bottleneck and positively affects output growth.

Within the two gap framework, ignoring imported inputs in regression analyses of growth will bias the coefficient of $(X/y)(\dot{X}/X)$ upward, tending to overestimate the magnitude of the effect of exports growth on GDP growth. Using a 31 semi-industrialized country sample, Esfahani (1991) found that once intermediate imports growth is included, the point estimate of $(X/y)(\dot{X}/X)$ drops and, for some subperiods, it becomes insignificant. He also found that in all regressions the coefficient of imports growth was significant, providing some support to his view that export growth tends to help relax the foreign exchange constraint. From these findings Esfahani concludes that

> even though exports do not appear to have had much direct externality effect on GDP . . . , export promotion policies in these countries can be quite valuable in supplying foreign exchange, which relieves import shortages and permits output expansion. (p. 114)

The assumption of a linear relationship between export growth and GDP growth has been questioned by a number of authors. More specifically, it has been argued that the contribution of exports growth to GDP growth is likely to be subject to diminishing returns. When the quadratic term $((X/y)(\dot{X}/X))^2$ is added to Feder-type GDP growth equations, its coefficient is usually significant, providing some evidence of diminishing returns of the effects of export growth on GDP growth. (See, for example, Kohli and Singh 1989; Edmar Bacha 1984; and Jose Ocampo 1986.)

### IV.5 *Trade Policy and GDP Growth in Cross Country Regression Analyses*

Most cross country econometric works on the relationship between trade orientation and growth have (implicitly or explicitly) followed a two-stage methodology: in the first stage it is assumed (rather than tested) that more "liberalized" economies experience faster

[43] See, for example, Esfahani (1991). The two gaps approach is based on the crucial ex post macroeconomic identity $S - I = X - M$ (where $S$ is savings, $I$ investment, $X$ exports, and $M$ imports). Depending on the ex ante values of $X$, $M$, $S$, and $I$ a country can be "foreign exchange constrained" or "savings constrained." A role of economic policy is to relieve the binding gap.

growth of exports.[44] In the second stage it is tested whether countries with faster growth of exports have experienced a more rapid rate of growth of GDP. A positive answer to this second narrower question is then interpreted as providing as evidence supporting the broader proposition that outward orientation and "liberalization" foster growth. The fundamental reason why this rather inelegant two stages approach has become so popular is the difficulty of directly measuring trade policy and trade orientation.

Some authors, however, have made an effort to measure trade orientation and to test specifically the relationship between trade policy and growth. Due to the unavailability of time series on trade policy indicators, most of these studies used proxies for the actual policy variables. Balassa (1985), for example, constructed an index of trade policy as the deviations of actual volume exports from the volume of exports *predicted* by a simple structural model of trade. More specifically, he assumed that exports are a function of income per capita, population, and mineral resources availability. After computing a linear exports equation for a 43 country sample he used the residuals as a measure of trade orientation: positive residuals were interpreted as reflecting "export promotion" policies, while negative residuals were considered a sign of "inward orientation." When this trade orientation variable was included in a GDP growth equation its estimated coefficient was significantly positive. This was interpreted as showing "that trade orientation has significantly influenced the rate of economic growth in the 43 countries studied during the 1973–79 period" (p. 30). Surprisingly, perhaps, in this regression Balassa abandoned the production function framework, and did not include capital accumulation or labor force growth as regressors. Additionally, no effort was made to treat this index of trade orientation as a variable measured with error, or to check for the robustness of the results to alternative specifications of the exports equation.

An alternative approach has been to construct subjective indices of trade orientation. According to this methodology the researcher uses her information to classify countries in different groups. For example, in a very influential study the World Bank (1987) classified trade orientation in 41 developing countries into four groups: strongly outward oriented; moderately outward oriented; moderately inward oriented; and strongly inward oriented (see Table 9). The criteria used for these classifications was largely subjective and not free of controversy. For example, a number of authors have objected to Korea's classification as a strongly outward oriented country, and pointed out that government intervention has played an important part in Korea's success story (Helleiner 1990).

Although it is difficult—if not utterly impossible—to know with confidence how to classify Korea within this type of scheme, there is no doubt that the World Bank subjective classification reported in Table 9 is open to a series of questions. Notice, for instance, that Chile, the only country in the Michaely et al. project to achieve a perfect 20 in the liberalization index during the 1970s, is only classified as moderately outward oriented in the 1973–85 period.[45] More interesting, however, is the fact that the World Bank

[44] Given the discussion in Section II on the definition of "liberalization" it may seem ironic to use this term here. This is deliberate. The literature reviewed in this section has been remarkably vague in defining "liberalization" and "outward orientation."

[45] During the same period both Korea and Singapore, which are classified as strongly outward oriented, achieved a maximum index of 18. Remember, however, that Michaely et al. clearly point out that their liberalization indices are not strictly comparable across countries.

TABLE 9

WORLD BANK CLASSIFICATION OF DEVELOPING COUNTRIES ACCORDING TO TRADE ORIENTATION 1963–1973 AND 1973–1985

| Period | Strongly Outward Oriented | Moderately Outward Oriented | Moderately Inward Oriented | Strongly Inward Oriented |
|---|---|---|---|---|
| 1963–73 | Hong Kong | Brazil | Bolivia | Argentina |
| | Korea | Cameroon | El Salvador | Bangladesh |
| | Singapore | Colombia | Honduras | Burundi |
| | | Costa Rica | Kenya | Chile |
| | | Côte d'Ivoire | Madagascar | Dominican Republic |
| | | Guatemala | Mexico | Ethiopia |
| | | Indonesia | Nicaragua | Ghana |
| | | Israel | Nigeria | India |
| | | Malaysia | Philippines | Pakistan |
| | | Thailand | Senegal | Peru |
| | | | Tunisia | Sri Lanka |
| | | | Yugoslavia | Sudan |
| | | | | Tanzania |
| | | | | Turkey |
| | | | | Uruguay |
| | | | | Zambia |
| 1973–85 | Hong Kong | Brazil | Cameroon | Argentina |
| | Korea | Chile | Colombia | Bangladesh |
| | Singapore | Israel | Costa Rica | Bolivia |
| | | Malaysia | Côte d'Ivoire | Burundi |
| | | Thailand | El Salvador | Dominican Republic |
| | | Tunisia | Guatemala | Ethiopia |
| | | Turkey | Honduras | Ghana |
| | | Uruguay | Indonesia | India |
| | | | Kenya | Madagascar |
| | | | Mexico | Nigeria |
| | | | Nicaragua | Peru |
| | | | Pakistan | Sudan |
| | | | Philippines | Tanzania |
| | | | Senegal | Zambia |
| | | | Sri Lanka | |
| | | | Yugoslavia | |

*Source:* World Bank (1987).

study classifies Korea as strongly outward oriented in both the 1963–73 *and* 1973–85 periods, even though it is well known that during the early years of the 1963–73 period the Korean trade regime was significantly more restrictive than in the later period. In fact, for 1963–73 the Michaely et al. index averaged only 12.4, while for 1973–84 it climbed to 18. This outward orientation index was used to compare overall economic performance across the 41 countries in the sample, and concluded that the evidence "suggests that the economic performance of the outward-oriented economies has been broadly superior to that of inward-oriented economies in all respects" (World Bank 1987, p. 85).

A more direct approach has been taken by Bernard Heitger (1987), who instead of constructing an index of trade orientation has used actually computed effective rates of protection (ERP) as measures of the restrictiveness of trade regimes. Using data on 47 countries for 1960–70 he estimated a GDP growth regression equation including as regressors the average and standard deviation of ERPs across commodities, the investment ratio, initial GDP, and adult literacy. He found for a number of alternative specifications of the regressions that the coefficients of both ERPs variables were significantly negative, providing support to the view that trade distortions negatively affect GDP growth. Even though the data on ERPs used by Heitger are from different years for each country, and that quantitative restrictions are ignored, these results constitute an important step towards a more direct test of the proposition that *trade policy* directly affects economic performance.

### IV.6 *Causality and Simultaneity*

Do countries with rapidly growing exports have a higher rate of aggregate growth, or is it that faster growing countries have a more dynamic export sector? Most studies reviewed above have tended to ignore this issue, assuming that it is exports that drive aggregate GDP (see, however, Ram 1987). There are, however, some nontrivial reasons why more rapid GDP growth could, in principle, result in faster growth of exports. Just dismissing the issue as being irrelevant, as a number of authors have done, does not seem to be fully justified.

Time series techniques have been used to obtain some information on whether there is reverse causality, going from GDP growth to exports growth. Woo Jung and Peyton Marshall (1985), for example, have used annual data on 37 countries to perform Granger "causality" tests. In 22 of the 37 cases it was not possible to establish unequivocally the direction of causality. For only four cases—Indonesia, Egypt, Costa Rica, and Ecuador—was it found that exports growth caused GDP growth. More recently Michael Hutchinson and Singh (1987) have applied Granger "causality" tests to 34 countries, finding that for 18 of them—including Brazil and Korea—it was not possible to establish one-way causality. In ten countries exports growth was found to have "caused" output GDP growth, while in three other cases GDP growth caused exports growth.

Esfahani (1991) has tackled the simultaneity problem in a more direct way by formulating and estimating a three equations model of growth, exports, and imports. He found that when his growth equation was estimated using two stage least squares, the estimated coefficient of $(X/y)(\dot{X}/X)$ became insignificant, casting some doubt on the importance of the exports externalities approach.[46]

## V. *Concluding Remarks*

In this paper I have reviewed the modern empirical literature on the relationship between trade orientation and economic performance. The discussion has focused on two distinct bodies of work: detailed multi-country studies of protectionist practices and liberalization episodes, and cross-country regression analyses on the relationship between exports growth and economic performance.

The country-specific analyses reviewed in Section II have been useful in providing detailed discussions on the way in which different policies have affected economic performance in a number of countries. Moreover in some cases these studies have been highly influential in policy circles. In particular, discussions of successful experiences such as Korea and Chile have greatly influenced the

[46]See also Dominick Salvatore (1983) for a simultaneous equation model on trade and growth.

way in which advisors and politicians think about trade orientation and commercial policy. For example, a recently released document by the United Nations Economic Commission for Latin America (CEPAL 1992) indicates that the contrasting performances between successful and lagging nations played a key role in the Commission's recent switch towards supporting outward orientation. On the other hand, Section IV has shown that much of the cross-country regression based studies have been plagued by empirical and conceptual shortcomings. The theoretical frameworks used have been increasingly simplistic, failing to address important questions such as the exact mechanism through which exports expansion affects GDP growth, and ignoring important potential determinants of growth such as educational attainment. Also, many papers have been characterized by a lack of care in dealing with issues related to endogeneity and measurement errors. All of this has resulted, in many cases, in unconvincing results whose fragility has been exposed by subsequent work. It is difficult to believe, in fact, that cross-country regression analyses of the type reviewed in Section IV of this paper have, on their own, played much of a role in the recent popularity of outward oriented policies.

Recent developments in the theory of endogenous economic growth, largely influenced by Romer (1986) and Lucas (1988), have made important progress towards providing a more convincing and rigorous conceptual framework for the analysis of the relationship between trade policies and growth. In this new vintage of growth models it is possible to establish a *long-run equilibrium* relationship between openness and economic growth. This, of course, is not the case in traditional neoclassical models where in long-run equilibrium the steady-state rate of growth is completely independent of national policies. For example, Feder's (1983) model discussed above relies heavily on the non-steady state assumptions that $\delta > 0$ and $F_x > 0$.

A good example of this new literature is Romer's (1989) model of endogenous growth, where the productive process uses capital, labor, and a large number of specialized inputs. Firms can either engage in production of final goods or in research and development (R&D). More resources devoted to R&D result in a larger availability of intermediate inputs and a higher marginal product of capital. In this model, a more open trade regime allows countries to specialize in the production of a subset of intermediate inputs in which they have comparative advantage. Under freer trade, then, a larger number of inputs is available at a lower cost; as a result there is a higher equilibrium growth. Danny Quah and James Rauch (1990) have also developed a model with intermediate goods where freer trade results in an acceleration in the equilibrium rate of growth. In their model a closed economy has to produce a large array of intermediate goods and, thus, is likely to run into bottlenecks. Freer trade, then, allows the country to relax these bottlenecks and thus to grow faster than under autarky. Gene Grossman and Elhanan Helpman (1991) and Edwards (1992) have taken a different perspective and have emphasized the role of freer trade in generating technological progress. They have built models where a higher degree of openness allows smaller countries to absorb technology developed in the advanced nations at a faster rate and thus to grow, in equilibrium, more rapidly than with a lower degree of openness. What is particularly interesting about this model is that under a plausible constellation of parameters more open economies will grow faster than more restricted ones even in the long run.

In spite of these new theoretical results that allow analysts to relate trade policy to long-run growth, the new models of endogenous growth have made little progress in empirically analyzing these issues. To a large extent the results presented until now have been based on broad cross country regressions on aggregate data, not very different from those in the works reviewed in Section IV.[47] Although some of the regressors used are different, the measures of openness are as unconvincing as those of the more traditional literature. Most recent empirical work on the endogenous growth approach have measured openness as exports share or imports shares (Romer 1989; Quah and Rauch 1990), and have not tried to capture the extent to which commercial *policy* impedes trade. It is, in fact, well known that exports or imports ratios depend heavily on the economy's structure—including the country's size—and that independently of the extent of trade barriers, larger countries will exhibit lower exports ratios than smaller countries. In a word, as the more traditional policy work reviewed in Section IV, these new studies are seriously affected by the difficulty in measuring trade orientation.

An important challenge that lies ahead for research in this area, then, is to obtain more reliable measures of trade policy and to investigate in greater detail the channels through which greater outward orientation affects growth. Researchers, however, should be aware that all encompassing indices of trade policy that are free of measurement error will *not* be found. This means, then, that in order to gain further insights into these issues, it is fundamental to adopt econometric methodologies that deal specifically with errors in variables, that investigate formally the robustness of specific results, and that rely systematically on sensitivity analyses. In fact, from an econometric perspective, one of the most serious shortcomings of the cross-section papers discussed in Section IV—and for that matter of most recent papers inspired on endogenous growth—is the lack of efforts to implement in a systematic way a battery of tests that deal with the degree of robustness (or fragility) of the results.[48]

Applied economists often ask too much of their data sets, and try to extract information that simply is not there. In that sense, cross-country aggregate data sets have little information regarding the relationship between trade policy and growth. Recent theoretical developments in growth theory have suggested that microeconomic analysis could shed some light on the growth process. Issues related to the use of multiple intermediate inputs, the invention of designs and the absorption of technological progress under alternative trade regimes look particularly relevant. However, it is doubtful that these questions will be adequately addressed through the currently common cross country regressions on aggregate data. Episodic historical analyses of the type discussed in Section II are, in fact, more promising. More complete evidence on the precise channels through which trade orientation affects growth, will have to wait, then, for new studies that not only look at history but also dig deeply into the *microeconomics* of innovation, trade, and growth.

REFERENCES

AMIN, SAMIR. "Underdevelopment and Dependence in Black Africa—Their Historical Origins and Contemporary Forms," *Soc. Econ. Stud.*, Mar. 1973, 22(1), pp. 177–96.

[47] Quah and Rauch (1990), however, have stayed away from cross country analyses focusing, instead, on time series data.

[48] Edwards (1992) addresses this measurement problem and uses nine alternative indices of trade orientation to test the proposition that openness positively affects growth. In that paper the sensitivity of results to measurement errors and alternative specifications are discussed in detail.

ARELLANO-CADENA, ROGELIO. "On the Causes and Effects of Real Exchange Rate Variability: A Comparative Analysis of the East Asian and Latin American Experience." Ph.D. Dissertation: U. of California, Los Angeles, 1990.

BACHA, EDMAR. "Growth with Limited Supplies of Foreign Exchange: A Reappraisal of the Two-Gap Model," in *Economic structure and performance: Essays in honor of Hollis B. Chenery*. Eds.: MOSHE SYRQUIN, LANCE TAYLOR, AND LARRY E. WESTPHAL. NY: Academic Press, 1984, pp. 263–80.

BALASSA, BELA. "Tariff Protection in Industrial Countries: An Evaluation," *J. Polit. Econ.*, Dec. 1965, *73*(6), pp. 573–94.

______. *The structure of protection in developing countries*. Baltimore: Johns Hopkins U. Press, 1971.

______. "Exports and Economic Growth: Further Evidence," *J. Devel. Econ.*, June 1978, *5*(2), pp. 181–89.

______. "The Newly-Industrializing Developing Countries after the Oil Crisis," *Weltwirtsch. Arch.*, 1981, *117*(1), pp. 142–94.

______. *Development strategies in semi-industrial economies*. NY and London: Oxford U. Press, 1982.

______. "Exports, Policy Choices, and Economic Growth in Developing Countries after the 1973 Oil Shock," *J. Devel. Econ.*, May/June 1985, *18*(2), pp. 23–35.

______. "Outward Orientation," in *Handbook of development economics*. Vol. 2. Eds.: HOLLIS CHENERY AND T. N. SRINIVASAN. Amsterdam: North-Holland, 1989, pp. 1645–89.

BEHRMAN, JERE. *Foreign trade regimes and economic development*. Vol. 8. *Chile*. NY and London: Columbia U. Press for NBER, 1976.

BERTHELEMY, JEAN-CLAUDE AND MORRISON, CHRISTIAN. *Agricultural development in Africa and the supply of manufactured goods*. Paris: OECD Development Centre, 1989.

BHAGWATI, JAGDISH. *Anatomy and consequences of exchange control regimes*. Cambridge, MA: Ballinger Pub. Co. for NBER, 1978.

______. "Export-Promoting Trade Strategy: Issues and Evidence," *World Bank Res. Observer*, Jan. 1988, *3*(1), pp. 27–57.

BATTACHARYA, A. AND LINN, JOHANNES F. "Trade and Industrial Policies in the Developing Countries of East Asia." World Bank Discussion Paper #27, 1988.

BOND, MARIAN E. "Agricultural Responses to Prices in Sub-Saharan African Countries," *Int. Monet. Fund Staff Pap.*, Dec. 1983, *30*(4), pp. 703–26.

BRADFORD, COLIN I. AND BRANSON, WILLIAM H. *Trade and structural change in Pacific Asia*. Chicago and London: U. of Chicago Press for NBER, 1987.

BRUNO, MICHAEL. "Domestic Resource Costs and Effective Protection: Clarification and Synthesis," *J. Polit. Econ.*, Jan./Feb. 1972, *80*(1), pp. 16–33.

BRUTON, HENRY. "Import Substitution," in *Handbook in development economics*. Vol. 2. Eds.: HOLLIS CHENERY AND T. N. SRINIVASAN. Amsterdam: North-Holland, 1989, pp. 1601–44.

CEPAL. *El desarrollo sustentable: Transformacion productiva, equidad y medio ambiente*. Santiago, Chile: UN-CEPAL, 1991.

CHHIBBER, AJAY. "Exchange Reforms, Supply Response and Inflation in Africa," in *Open economies: Structural adjustment and agriculture*. Eds.: IAN GOLDIN AND L. ALAN WINTERS. Cambridge: Cambridge U. Press, 1992, pp. 125–45.

CLAASSEN, EMIL MARIA AND SALIN, PASCAL. *The impact of stabilization and structural adjustment policies on the rural sector*. Rome: FAO/United Nations, 1991.

COOPER, RICHARD. "Currency Devaluation in Developing Countries," in *Essays in international finance* 86, Princeton, NJ: 1971.

______. "Industrial Policy and Trade Distortion," in *The new protectionist threat to world welfare*. Ed.: DOMINICK SALVATORE. Amsterdam and London: North Holland, 1987, pp. 233–65.

CORBO, VITTORIO; DE MELO, JAIME AND TYBOUT, JAMES. "What Went Wrong with the Recent Reforms in the Southern Core," *Econ. Develop. Cult. Change*, Apr. 1986, *34*(3), pp. 607–40.

CORDEN, WARNER MAX. "The Structure of a Tariff System and the Effective Protection Rate," *J. Polit. Econ.*, May/June 1966, *74*(3), pp. 221–37.

______. "The Substitution Problem in the Theory of Effective Protection," *J. Int. Econ.*, Feb. 1971, *1*(1), pp. 37–57.

______. *Protection, growth, and trade in international economics*. Oxford: Basil Blackwell, 1985.

DE LA CUADRA, SERGIO AND HACHETTE, DOMINIQUE. "Chile," in PAPAGEORGIOU, MICHAELY, AND CHOKSI, Vol. 1, 1991, pp. 169–319.

DERVIS, KEMAL; DE MELO, JAIME AND ROBINSON, SHERMAN. *General equilibrium models for development policy*. NY: Cambridge U. Press, 1982.

DIXIT, AVINASH. "Tax Policy in Open Economies," in *Handbook of public economics*. Eds.: ALAN AUERBACH AND MARTIN FELDSTEIN. NY and Oxford: North-Holland, 1985, pp. 313–74.

EDWARDS, SEBASTIAN. "Terms of Trade, Tariffs, and Labor Market Adjustment in Developing Countries," *World Bank Econ. Rev.*, May 1988, *2*(2), pp. 165–85.

______. *Real exchange rates, devaluation and adjustment: Exchange rate policy in developing countries*. Cambridge, MA: MIT Press, 1989a.

______. "Structural Adjustment Policies in Highly Indebted Countries," in *Developing country debt and economic performance*. Ed.: JEFFREY SACHS. U. of Chicago Press, 1989b, pp. 159–207; 249–62.

______. "Trade Orientation, Distortions, and Growth in Developing Countries," *J. Devel. Econ.*, July 1992, *39*(1), pp. 31–57.

EDWARDS, SEBASTIAN AND COX-EDWARDS, ALEJANDRA. *Monetarism and liberalization: The Chilean experiment*. Rev. ed. Chicago: U. of Chicago Press, 1991.

EMERY, ROBERT. "The Relation of Exports and Economic Growth," *Kyklos*, 1967, *20*(4), pp. 470–84.

ESFAHANI, HADI S. "Exports, Imports, and Economic Growth in Semi-industrialized Countries," *J. Devel. Econ.*, Jan. 1991, *35*(1), pp. 93–116.

FEDER, GERSHON. "On Exports and Economic

Growth," *J. Devel. Econ.*, Feb./Apr. 1983, *12*(1/2), pp. 59–73.

FISHLOW, ALBERT. "The State of Latin American Economics." Stanford-Berkeley Occasional Paper in Latin American Studies, no. 11, 1985.

GORDON, DAVID F. AND PARKER, JOAN C. "The World Bank and Its Critics: The Case of Sub-Saharan Africa," *Rural Africana*, 1984, *19–20*, pp. 3–33.

GRAY, PATRICIA AND SINGER, HANS W. "Trade Policy and Growth of Developing Countries: Some New Data," *World Devel.*, Mar. 1988, *16*(3), pp. 395–403.

GROSSMAN, GENE AND HELPMAN, ELHANAN. *Innovation and growth in the global economy*. Cambridge: MIT Press, 1991.

HARRISON, ANNE. "Openness and Growth: A Time-Series Cross Country Analysis for Developing Countries." World Bank WP#809, Nov. 1991.

HEITGER, BERNHARD. "Import Protection and Export Performance: Their Impact on Economic Growth," *Weltwirtsch. Arch.*, 1987, *123*(2), pp. 249–61.

HELLEINER, GERALD K. "Outward Orientation, Import Instability and African Economic Growth: An Empirical Investigation," in *Theory and reality in development: Essays in honour of Paul Streeten*. Eds.: SANJAYA LALL AND FRANCES STEWART. London: Macmillan, 1986, pp. 139–53.

______. "Trade Strategy in Medium-term Adjustment," *World Devel.*, June 1990, *18*(6), pp. 879–97.

HIRSCHMAN, ALBERT O. "The Political Economy of Import-Substituting Industrialization in Latin America," *Quart. J. Econ.*, Feb. 1968, *82*(1), pp. 1–32.

HUTCHINSON, MICHAEL AND SINGH, NIRVIKAR. "Exports and Growth in Developing Economies: Identifying Externality Effects." Working Paper, U. of California, Santa Cruz, 1987.

JOHNSON, HARRY. "The Theory of Tariff Structure with Special Reference to World Trade and Development," in *Trade and development*. Eds.: HARRY JOHNSON AND PETER KENEN. Geneva: Libraire Droz for the Graduate Institute of International Studies, 1965, pp. 9–29.

JUNG, WOO S. AND MARSHALL, PEYTON J. "Exports, Growth and Causality in Developing Countries," *J. Devel. Econ.*, May/June 1985, *18*(2), pp. 1–12.

KAVOUSSI, ROSTAM M. "Export Expansion and Economic Growth: Further Empirical Evidence," *J. Devel. Econ.*, Jan./Feb. 1984, *14*(1–2), pp. 241–50.

______. "International Trade and Economic Development: The Recent Experience of Developing Countries," *J. Developing Areas*, Apr. 1985, *19*(3), pp. 379–92.

KDI. *Korea's macroeconomic and financial policies*. KDI/11E Proceedings, Conference Series 89–3. Seoul. Korean Development Institute, 1989.

KIM, KWANG SUK. "Korea," in PAPAGEORGIOU, MICHAELY, AND CHOKSI, eds. Vol. 2, 1991.

KOHLI, INDERGIT AND SINGH, NIRVIKAR. "Exports and Growth: Critical Minimum Effort and Diminishing Returns," *J. Devel. Econ.*, Apr. 1989, *30*(2), pp. 391–400.

KRAVIS, IRVING. "Trade as a Handmaiden of Growth," *Econ. J.*, Dec. 1970, *80*(320), pp. 850–72.

KRUEGER, ANNE O. *Foreign trade regimes and economic development: Liberalization attempts and consequences*. Cambridge, MA: Ballinger Pub. Co. for NBER, 1978.

______. *Trade and employment in developing countries*. Chicago: U. of Chicago Press, 1981.

______. "Trade Policies in Developing Countries," in *Handbook of international economics*. Vol. 1. Eds.: RONALD W. JONES AND PETER B. KENEN. Amsterdam: North-Holland; 1985, pp. 519–69.

LAL, DEEPAK AND RAJAPATIRANA, SARATH. "Foreign Trade Regimes and Economic Growth in Developing Countries," *World Bank Res. Observer*, July 1987, *2*(2), pp. 189–217.

LANCASTER, CAROL. *African external reform: The external dimension*. Washington, DC: Institute for International Economics, 1991.

LEAMER, EDWARD E. "Testing Trade Theory." NBER Working Paper #3957, Jan. 1992.

LEWIS, W. ARTHUR. "The Slowing Down of the Engine of Growth," *Amer. Econ. Rev.*, Sept. 1980, *70*(4), pp. 555–64.

LITTLE, IAN; SCITOVSKY, TIBOR AND SCOTT, MAURICE. *Industry and trade in some developing countries*. London & NY: Oxford U. Press for OECD, 1970.

LUCAS, ROBERT E. "On the Mechanics of Economic Development," *J. Monet. Econ.*, July 1988, *22*(1), pp. 3–42.

MAIZELS, ALFRED. *Exports and economic growth in developing countries*. Cambridge U. Press, 1968.

MCKINNON, RONALD I. "Foreign Trade Regimes and Economic Development," *J. Int. Econ.*, Aug. 1979, *9*(3), pp. 429–52.

MICHAELY, MICHAEL. "Exports and Growth: An Empirical Investigation," *J. Devel. Econ.*, Mar. 1977, *4*(1), pp. 49–53.

______. "The Lessons of Experience: An Overview," in *Trade reform: Lessons from eight countries*. Eds.: GEOFFREY SHEPARD AND CARLOS LANGONI. San Francisco: ISC, 1991.

MICHAELY, MICHAEL M.; PAPAGEORGIOU, DEMETRIS AND CHOKSI, ARMEANE. "The Design of Trade Liberalization," *Finance Devel.*, Mar. 1989, *26*(1), pp. 2–5.

______. *Liberalizing foreign trade*. Vol. 7. *Lessons of experience in the developing world*. Oxford and Cambridge, MA: Basil Blackwell, 1991.

MICHALOPOULOS, CONSTANTINE AND JAY, KEITH. "Growth of Exports and Income in the Developing World: A Neoclassical View." AID Working Paper, Washington, DC, 1973.

MOLLETT, J. A. *Planning for agricultural development*. London: Croom Helm, 1984.

MOSLEY, PAUL; HARRIGAN, JANE AND TOYE, JOHN. *Aid and power: The World Bank and policy-based lending in the 1980s*. London and NY: Routledge, 1991.

OCAMPO, JOSE A. "New Developments in Trade Theory and LDCs," *J. Devel. Econ.*, June 1986, *22*(1), pp. 129–70.

ORGANIZATION OF AFRICAN UNITY. "Lagos Plan of Action for the Economic Development of Africa, 1980–2000." Addis Ababa: OAU, 1980.

OUM, BONGSUNG. "Korea's Exchange Rate, Policy in the 1980s: Evaluation and Prospects," in *Korea's macroeconomic and financial policies*. Conference Series 89–3. Seoul: Korean Development Institute, 1989, pp. 57–91.

PAPAGEORGIOU, DEMETRIS; MICHAELY, MICHAEL AND CHOKSI, ARMEANE M., eds. *Liberalizing foreign trade*. Vols. 1–7. Oxford: Blackwell, 1991.

PINTO, BRIAN. "Black Markets for Foreign Exchange, Real Exchange Rates and Inflation," *J. Int. Econ.*, Feb. 1991, *30*(1/2), pp. 121–35.

PREBISCH, RAÚL. *The economic development of Latin America and its principal problems*. NY: United Nations, 1950.

———. "Five Stages in My Thinking on Development," in *Pioneers in development*. Eds.: GERALD MEIER AND DUDLEY SEERS. NY: Oxford U. Press for the World Bank, 1984, pp. 173–96.

QUAH, DANNY AND RAUCH, JAMES E. "Openness and the Rate of Economic Growth." Working Paper, U. of California, San Diego. Oct., 1990.

RAM, RATI. "Exports and Economic Growth: Some Additional Evidence," *Econ. Devel. Cult. Change*, Jan. 1985, *33*(2), pp. 415–25.

———. "Exports and Economic Growth in Developing Countries: Evidence From Time-Series and Cross Section Data," *Econ. Devel. Cult. Change*, Oct. 1987, *36*(1), pp. 51–72.

RAMOS, JOSEPH. *Neoconservative economics in the southern cone of Latin America*. Baltimore and London: John Hopkins U. Press, 1986.

RANA, PRADUMNA B. "Exports, Policy Changes and Economic Growth in Developing Countries after the 1973 Oil Shock: Comments," *J. Devel. Econ.*, Mar. 1988, *28*(2), pp. 261–64.

ROMER, PAUL M. "Increasing Returns and Long-run Growth," *J. Polit. Econ.*, Oct. 1986, *94*(5), pp. 1002–37.

———. "What Determines the Rate of Growth and Technological Change?" World Banking Working Paper #279, 1989.

SACHS, JEFFREY D. "Trade and Exchange Rate Policies in Growth-Oriented Adjustment Programs," in *Growth oriented adjustment programs*. Eds.: VITTORIO CORBO, MORRIS GOLDSTEIN, AND MOHSIN KHAN. Washington, DC: IMF, 1987.

———. "The Debt Overhang of Developing Countries," in *Debt, stabilization and development: Essays in memory of Carlos Diaz-Alejandro*. Eds.: GUILLERMO A. CALVO ET AL. Oxford: Blackwell, 1989, pp. 80–102.

SALVATORE, DOMINICK. "A Simultaneous Equations Model of Trade and Development with Dynamic Policy Simulations," *Kyklos*, 1983, *36*(1), pp. 66–90.

SHAPIRO, KENNETH H. "The Limits of Policy Reform in African Agricultural Development," *Rural Africana*, 1984, *19/20*, pp. 63–68.

SINGER, HANS W. "The Distribution of Gains Between Investing and Borrowing Countries," *Amer. Econ. Rev.*, May 1950, *40*(2), pp. 473–85.

STREETEN, PAUL. "Review of Little, et al.," *Econ. J.*, Mar. 1971, *81*(1), pp. 144–48.

SUMMERS, LARRY H. "The Scientific Illusion of Empirical Macroeconomics," *Scand. J. Econ.*, 1991, *93*(2), pp. 129–48.

TAN, AUGUSTINE H. "Differential Tariffs, Negative Value Added, and the Theory of Effective Protection," *Amer. Econ. Rev.*, Mar. 1970, *60*(1), pp. 107–16.

TAYLOR, LANCE. *Varieties of stabilization experience*. Oxford and NY: Oxford U. Press, Clarendon Press, 1988.

———. "Economic Openness: Problems to the Century's End," in *Economic liberalization: No panacea*. Ed.: TARIQ BANURI. Oxford and NY: Oxford U. Press, Clarendon Press, 1991, pp. 99–147.

TYBOUT, JAMES. "Linking Trade and Productivity: New Research Directions," *World Bank Econ. Rev.*, May 1992, *6*(2), pp. 189–211.

TYLER, WILLIAM. "Growth and Export Expansion in Developing Countries," *J. Devel. Econ.*, Aug. 1981, *9*(1), pp. 121–30.

UNCTAD. *Handbook of trade control measures of developing countries*. 1987.

VAN DER WILLINGEN, TESSA A. "Cash Crop Production and the Balance of Trade in a Less Developed Economy: A Model of Temporary Equilibrium with Rationing," *Oxford Econ. Pap.*, Nov. 1986, *38*(3), pp. 424–42.

WORLD BANK. *Accelerated growth in sub-Saharan Africa*. Washington, DC, 1981.

———. *World development report, 1987*. Oxford U. Press. 1987.

———. *World development report, 1989*. Oxford U. Press, 1989.

———. *World development report*, 1990. Oxford U. Press, 1990.

# [3]

# Does Trade Cause Growth?

*By* JEFFREY A. FRANKEL AND DAVID ROMER*

*Examining the correlation between trade and income cannot identify the direction of causation between the two. Countries' geographic characteristics, however, have important effects on trade, and are plausibly uncorrelated with other determinants of income. This paper therefore constructs measures of the geographic component of countries' trade, and uses those measures to obtain instrumental variables estimates of the effect of trade on income. The results provide no evidence that ordinary least-squares estimates overstate the effects of trade. Further, they suggest that trade has a quantitatively large and robust, though only moderately statistically significant, positive effect on income.* (*JEL* F43, O40)

This paper is an empirical investigation of the impact of international trade on standards of living. From Adam Smith's discussion of specialization and the extent of the market, to the debates about import substitution versus export-led growth, to recent work on increasing returns and endogenous technological progress, economists interested in the determination of standards of living have also been interested in trade. But despite the great effort that has been devoted to studying the issue, there is little persuasive evidence concerning the effect of trade on income.

To see the basic difficulty in trying to estimate trade's impact on income, consider a cross-country regression of income per person on the ratio of exports or imports to GDP (and other variables). Such regressions typically find a moderate positive relationship.[1] But this relationship may not reflect an effect of trade on income. The problem is that the trade share may be endogenous: as Elhanan Helpman (1988), Colin Bradford, Jr. and Naomi Chakwin (1993), Rodrik (1995a), and many others observe, countries whose incomes are high for reasons other than trade may trade more.

Using measures of countries' trade policies in place of (or as an instrument for) the trade share in the regression does not solve the problem.[2] For example, countries that adopt free-market trade policies may also adopt free-market domestic policies and stable fiscal and monetary policies. Since these policies are also likely to affect income, countries' trade policies are likely to be correlated with factors that are omitted from the income equation. Thus they cannot be used to identify the impact of trade (Xavier Sala-i-Martin, 1991).

This paper proposes an alternative instrument for trade. As the literature on the gravity model of trade demonstrates, geography is a powerful determinant of bilateral trade (see, for example, Hans Linneman, 1966, Frankel et al., 1995, and Frankel, 1997). And as we show in this paper, the same is true for countries' overall trade: simply knowing how far a country is from other countries provides considerable information

* Frankel: Kennedy School of Government, Harvard University, Cambridge, MA 02138; Romer: Department of Economics, University of California, Berkeley, CA 94720. We are grateful to Susanto Basu, Michael Dotsey, Steven Durlauf, William Easterly, Robert Hall, Lars Hansen, Charles Jones, N. Gregory Mankiw, Maurice Obstfeld, Glenn Rudebusch, Paul Ruud, James Stock, Shangjin Wei, Richard Zeckhauser, and the referees for helpful comments; to Teresa Cyrus for outstanding research assistance and helpful comments; and to the National Science Foundation for financial support.

[1] See, for example, Michael Michaely (1977), Gershon Feder (1983), Roger C. Kormendi and Philip G. Meguire (1985), Stanley Fischer (1991, 1993), David Dollar (1992), Ross Levine and David Renelt (1992), Sebastian Edwards (1993), Ann Harrison (1996), and the ordinary least-squares regressions in Section II of this paper. Edwards (1995) and Dani Rodrik (1995b) survey the literature.

[2] For examples of this approach, see J. Bradford De Long and Lawrence H. Summers (1991), Fischer (1991, 1993), Dollar (1992), William Easterly (1993), Edwards (1993), Jong-Wha Lee (1993), Jeffrey D. Sachs and Andrew Warner (1995), and Harrison (1996).

about the amount that it trades. For example, the fact that New Zealand is far from most other countries reduces its trade; the fact that Belgium is close to many of the world's most populous countries increases its trade.

Equally important, countries' geographic characteristics are not affected by their incomes, or by government policies and other factors that influence income. More generally, it is difficult to think of reasons that a country's geographic characteristics could have important effects on its income except through their impact on trade. Thus, countries' geographic characteristics can be used to obtain instrumental variables estimates of trade's impact on income. That is the goal of this paper.[3]

The remainder of the paper contains two main sections. The first describes the impact of geographic characteristics on trade in more detail and uses geographic variables to construct an instrument for international trade. As we discuss there, there is one important complication to our basic argument that geographic variables can be used to construct an instrument for international trade in a cross-country income regression. Just as a country's income may be influenced by the amount its residents trade with foreigners, it may also be influenced by the amount its residents trade with one another. And just as geography is an important determinant of international trade, it is also an important determinant of within-country trade. In particular, residents of larger countries tend to engage in more trade with their fellow citizens simply because there are more fellow citizens to trade with. For example, Germans almost surely trade more with Germans than Belgians do with Belgians. This suggests a second geography-based test of the impact of trade on income: we can test whether within-country trade raises income by asking whether larger countries have higher incomes.

The reason that this issue complicates our test of the impact of international trade is that country size and proximity to other countries are negatively correlated. Because Germany is larger than Belgium, the average German is farther from other countries than the average Belgian is. Thus in using proximity to estimate international trade's effect on income, it is necessary to control for country size. Similarly, in using country size to test whether within-country trade raises income, it is necessary to control for international trade.

To construct the instrument for international trade, we first estimate a bilateral trade equation and then aggregate the fitted values of the equation to estimate a geographic component of countries' overall trade. In contrast to conventional gravity equations for bilateral trade, our trade equation includes only geographic characteristics: countries' sizes, their distances from one another, whether they share a border, and whether they are landlocked. This ensures that the instrument depends only on countries' geographic characteristics, not on their incomes or actual trading patterns. We find that these geographic characteristics are important determinants of countries' overall trade.

The second main section of the paper employs the instrument to investigate the impact of trade on income. We estimate cross-country regressions of income per person on international trade and country size by instrumental variables (IV), and compare the results with ordinary least-squares (OLS) estimates of the same equations. There are five main findings.

First, we find no evidence that the positive association between international trade and income arises because countries whose incomes are high for other reasons engage in more trade. On the contrary, in every specification we consider, the IV estimate of the effect of trade is larger than the OLS estimate, often by a considerable margin. Section II, subsection E, investigates possible reasons that the IV estimate exceeds the OLS one.

Second, the point estimates suggest that the impact of trade is substantial. In a typical specification, the estimates imply that increasing the ratio of trade to GDP by one percentage point

[3] Lee (1993) also uses information on countries' distances from one another to construct a measure of their propensity to trade. His approach differs from ours in two major respects. First, his measure is based not only on countries' geographic characteristics, but also on their actual trade patterns; thus it is potentially correlated with other determinants of income. Second, he does not investigate the relationship between income and his measure of the propensity to trade, but only the relationship between income and the interaction of his measure with indicators of distortionary trade policies.

raises income per person by between one-half and two percent.

Third, the estimates also imply that increased size raises income. This supports the hypothesis that greater within-country trade raises income.

Fourth, the large estimated positive effects of trade and size are robust to changes in specification, sample, and construction of the instrument.

Fifth, the impacts of trade and size are not estimated very precisely. The null hypothesis that these variables have no effect is typically only marginally rejected at conventional levels. As a result, the estimates still leave considerable uncertainty about the magnitudes of their effects.

## I. Constructing the Instrument

### A. *Background*

Our basic ideas can be described using a simple three-equation model. First, average income in country $i$ is a function of economic interactions with other countries ("international trade" for short), economic interactions within the country ("within-country trade"), and other factors:

$$\ln Y_i = \alpha + \beta T_i + \gamma W_i + \varepsilon_i. \quad (1)$$

Here $Y_i$ is income per person, $T_i$ is international trade, $W_i$ is within-country trade, and $\varepsilon_i$ reflects other influences on income. As the vast literature on trade describes, there are many channels through which trade can affect income—notably specialization according to comparative advantage, exploitation of increasing returns from larger markets, exchange of ideas through communication and travel, and spread of technology through investment and exposure to new goods. Because proximity promotes all of these types of interactions, our approach cannot identify the specific mechanisms through which trade affects income.

The other two equations concern the determinants of international and within-country trade. International trade is a function of a country's proximity to other countries, $P_i$, and other factors:

$$T_i = \psi + \phi P_i + \delta_i. \quad (2)$$

Similarly, within-country trade is a function of the country's size, $S_i$, and other factors:

$$W_i = \eta + \lambda S_i + \nu_i. \quad (3)$$

The residuals in these three equations, $\varepsilon_i$, $\delta_i$, and $\nu_i$, are likely to be correlated. For example, countries with good transportation systems, or with government policies that promote competition and reliance on markets to allocate resources, are likely to have high international and within-country trade given their geographic characteristics, and high incomes given their trade.

The key identifying assumption of our analysis is that countries' geographic characteristics (their $P_i$'s and $S_i$'s) are uncorrelated with the residuals in equations (1) and (3). Proximity and size are not affected by income or by other factors, such as government policies, that affect income. And as we observe in the introduction, it is difficult to think of important ways that proximity and size might affect income other than through their impact on how much a country's residents interact with foreigners and with one another.

Given the assumption that $P$ and $S$ are uncorrelated with $\varepsilon$, data on $Y$, $T$, $W$, $P$, and $S$ would allow us to estimate equation (1) by instrumental variables: $P$ and $S$ are correlated with $T$ and $W$ [by (2) and (3)], and are uncorrelated with $\varepsilon$ (by our identifying assumption). Unfortunately, however, there are no data on within-country trade. Ideally, we would want data comparable to measures of international trade. That is, we would want a measure of the value of the exchange of all goods and services among individuals within a country, both across and within firms. This measure would probably be many times GDP for most countries. But no such measure exists.

To address this problem, we substitute (3) into (1) to obtain

$$\begin{aligned} \ln Y_i &= \alpha + \beta T_i + \gamma(\eta + \lambda S_i + \nu_i) + \varepsilon_i \\ &= (\alpha + \gamma\eta) + \beta T_i + \gamma\lambda S_i \\ &\quad + (\gamma\nu_i + \varepsilon_i). \end{aligned} \quad (4)$$

Our identifying assumption implies that $P_i$ and $S_i$ are uncorrelated with the composite residual, $\gamma\nu_i + \varepsilon_i$. Thus (4) can be estimated by instrumental variables, with $P_i$ and $S_i$ (and the constant) as the instruments.

Note that estimation of (4) yields an estimate not only of $\beta$, international trade's impact on income, but also of $\gamma\lambda$, country size's impact on income. Since the two components of this coefficient are not identified separately, one cannot obtain an estimate of $\gamma$, the effect of within-country trade on income. But as long as $\lambda$ is positive—that is, as long as larger countries have more within-country trade—the sign of $\gamma$ is the same as the sign of $\gamma\lambda$. Thus, although we cannot estimate the magnitude of the impact of within-country trade on income, we can obtain evidence about its sign.

As we argue in the introduction (and verify below), $P_i$ and $S_i$ are negatively correlated: the larger a country is, the farther its typical resident is from other countries. Thus if we do not control for size in (4), $P_i$ will be negatively correlated with the residual, and thus will not be a valid instrument. Intuitively, smaller countries may engage in more trade with other countries simply because they engage in less within-country trade. This portion of the geographic variation in international trade cannot be used to identify trade's impact on income. Similarly, if we fail to control for $T_i$ in (4), $S_i$ will be negatively correlated with the residual. Thus, our approach requires us to examine the impacts of both international trade and country size.

To estimate (4), we need data on four variables: income ($Y$), international trade ($T$), size ($S$), and proximity ($P$). We measure the first three in the usual ways. Our measure of income is real income per person. Following standard practice, we measure international trade as imports plus exports divided by GDP. This is clearly an imperfect measure of economic interactions with other countries, an issue we return to in Section II, subsection E.[4] Finally, theory provides little guidance about the best measure of size. We therefore use two natural measures, population and area, both in logs. In interpreting the results concerning size, we focus on the sum of the coefficients on log population and log area. Thus we consider the impact of an increase in population and area together, with no change in population density. Such a change clearly increases the scope for within-country trade.[5]

To measure proximity, we need an appropriate weighted average of distance or ease of exchange between a given country and every other country in the world. To choose the weights to put on the different counties, we begin by estimating an equation for bilateral trade as a function of distance, size, and so on. We then use the estimated equation to find fitted values of trade between countries $i$ and $j$ as a share of $i$'s GDP. Finally, we aggregate over $j$ to obtain a geographic component of country $i$'s total trade, $T_i$. It is this geographic component of $T_i$ that we use as our measure of proximity. The remainder of this section describes the specifics of how we do this.

### B. *The Bilateral Trade Equation*

Work on the gravity model of bilateral trade shows that trade between two countries is negatively related to the distance between them and positively related to their sizes, and that a log-linear specification characterizes the data fairly well. Thus, a minimal specification of the bilateral trade equation is

$$(5)\quad \ln(\tau_{ij}/\mathrm{GDP}_i) = a_0 + a_1 \ln D_{ij} + a_2 \ln S_i + a_3 \ln S_j + e_{ij},$$

where $\tau_{ij}$ is bilateral trade between countries $i$ and $j$ (measured as exports plus imports), $D_{ij}$ is the distance between them, and $S_i$ and $S_j$ are measures of their sizes.

This specification omits a considerable amount of geographic information about trade. The equation that we estimate therefore differs from (5) in

[4] Using the log of the trade share instead of the level does not affect our conclusions. Examining import and export shares separately yields, not surprisingly, the result that the geographic components of the two shares are almost identical. Thus our approach cannot separate the effects of imports and exports.

[5] Throughout the paper, we use the labor force as our measure of population in computing income per person and in measuring country size. Using total population instead makes little difference to the results.

three ways. First, as described above, we include two measures of size: log population and log area. Second, whether countries are landlocked and whether they have a common border have important effects on trade; we therefore include dummy variables for these factors. And third, a large part of countries' trade is with their immediate neighbors. Since our goal is to identify geographic influences on overall trade, we therefore include interaction terms of all of the variables with the common-border dummy.

The fact that we are measuring trade relative to country $i$'s GDP means that we are already including a measure of $i$'s size. We therefore do not constrain the coefficients on the population measures for the two countries, or the coefficients on the area measures, to be equal. We do, however, constrain the coefficients on the landlocked dummies, and their interactions with the common-border dummy, to be equal for $i$ and $j$.[6] Thus, the equation we estimate is

$$(6)\ \ln(\tau_{ij}/\mathrm{GDP}_i) = a_0 + a_1 \ln D_{ij} + a_2 \ln N_i + a_3 \ln A_i + a_4 \ln N_j + a_5 \ln A_j + a_6(L_i + L_j) + a_7 B_{ij} + a_8 B_{ij} \ln D_{ij} + a_9 B_{ij} \ln N_i + a_{10} B_{ij} \ln A_i + a_{11} B_{ij} \ln N_j + a_{12} B_{ij} \ln A_j + a_{13} B_{ij}(L_i + L_j) + e_{ij},$$

where $N$ is population, $A$ is area, $L$ is a dummy for landlocked countries, and $B$ is a dummy for a common border between two countries.

### C. *Data and Results*

We use the same bilateral trade data as Frankel et al. (1995) and Frankel (1997); the data are originally from the IFS Direction of Trade statistics. They are for 1985, and cover trade among 63 countries. Following these papers, we drop observations where recorded bilateral trade is zero. Distance is measured as the great-circle distance between countries' principal cities. The information on areas, common borders, and landlocked countries is from Rand McNally (1993). Finally, the data on population are from the Penn World Table.[7]

The results are shown in Table 1. The first column shows the estimated coefficients and standard errors on the variables other than the common-border dummy and its interactions. These estimates are shown in the second column.[8]

The results are generally as expected. Distance has a large and overwhelmingly significant negative impact on bilateral trade; the estimated elasticity of trade with respect to distance is slightly less (in absolute value) than $-1$. Trade between country $i$ and country $j$ is strongly increasing in $j$'s size; the elasticity with respect to $j$'s population is about 0.6. In addition, trade (as a fraction of $i$'s GDP) is decreasing in $i$'s size and in $j$'s area. And if one of the countries is landlocked, trade falls by about a third.

Because only a small fraction of country pairs share a border, the coefficients on the common-border variables are not estimated precisely. Nonetheless, the point estimates imply that sharing a border has a considerable effect on trade. Evaluated at the mean value of the variables conditional on sharing a border, the estimates imply that a common border raises trade by a factor of 2.2. The estimates also imply that the presence of a common border alters the effects of the other variables substantially. For example, the estimated elasticity with respect to country $j$'s population across a shared border is 0.47 rather than 0.61, and the estimated elasticity with respect to distance is $-0.70$ rather than $-0.85$.

Most importantly, the regression confirms

[6] Allowing them to differ changes the results only trivially.

[7] We use Mark 5.6 of the table, which is distributed by the National Bureau of Economic Research. This is an updated version of the data described in Robert Summers and Alan Heston (1991). The capital city is used as the principal city, except for a small number of cases where the capital is far from the center of the country (in terms of population). In these cases, a more centrally located large city is chosen. For the United States, for example, Chicago rather than Washington is used as the principal city.

[8] The coefficient on the common-border variable itself is therefore shown as the coefficient on the interaction of the common-border dummy with the constant.

TABLE 1—THE BILATERAL TRADE EQUATION

| | Variable | Interaction |
|---|---|---|
| Constant | −6.38 | 5.10 |
| | (0.42) | (1.78) |
| Ln distance | −0.85 | 0.15 |
| | (0.04) | (0.30) |
| Ln population (country $i$) | −0.24 | −0.29 |
| | (0.03) | (0.18) |
| Ln area (country $i$) | −0.12 | −0.06 |
| | (0.02) | (0.15) |
| Ln population (country $j$) | 0.61 | −0.14 |
| | (0.03) | (0.18) |
| Ln area (country $j$) | −0.19 | −0.07 |
| | (0.02) | (0.15) |
| Landlocked | −0.36 | 0.33 |
| | (0.08) | (0.33) |
| Sample size | 3220 | |
| $R^2$ | 0.36 | |
| SE of regression | 1.64 | |

*Notes:* The dependent variable is $\ln(\tau_{ij}/\text{GDP}_i)$. The first column reports the coefficient on the variable listed, and the second column reports the coefficient on the variable's interaction with the common-border dummy. Standard errors are in parentheses.

that geographic variables are major determinants of bilateral trade. The $R^2$ of the regression is 0.36. The next step is to aggregate across countries and see if geographic variables are also important to overall trade.[9]

### D. *Implications for Aggregate Trade*

To find the implications of our estimates for the geographic component of countries' overall trade, we aggregate the fitted values from the bilateral trade equation. That is, we first rewrite equation (6) as

$$\ln(\tau_{ij}/\text{GDP}_i) = \mathbf{a}'\mathbf{X}_{ij} + e_{ij}, \tag{7}$$

where $\mathbf{a}$ is the vector of coefficients in (6) ($a_0$, $a_1$, ..., $a_{13}$), and $\mathbf{X}_{ij}$ is the vector of right-hand side variables ($1, \ln D_{ij}, ..., B_{ij}[L_i + L_j]$). Our estimate of the geographic component of country $i$'s overall trade share is then

$$\hat{T}_i = \sum_{j \neq i} e^{\hat{\mathbf{a}}'\mathbf{X}_{ij}}. \tag{8}$$

That is, our estimate of the geographic component of country $i$'s trade is the sum of the estimated geographic components of its bilateral trade with each other country in the world.[10]

All that is needed to perform the calculations in equation (8) are countries' populations and geographic characteristics. We therefore take the sum in (8) not just over the countries covered by the bilateral trade data set, but over all countries in the world.[11] Similarly, we are able to find the constructed trade share, $\hat{T}$, for all countries, not just those for which we have bilateral trade data. Since our income regressions will also require data on trade and income, however, we limit our calculation of $\hat{T}$ to the countries in the Penn World Table. Thus we compute $\hat{T}$ for 150 countries.

### E. *The Quality of the Instrument*

Figure 1 is a scatterplot of the true overall trade share, $T$, against the constructed share, $\hat{T}$. The figure shows that geographic variables account for a major part of the variation in overall trade. The correlation between $T$ and $\hat{T}$ is 0.62. As column (1) of Table 2 shows, a regression of

[9] The standard errors reported in Table 1 are conventional OLS standard errors. It is likely that the residuals of the bilateral trade equation are not completely independent, and thus that the reported standard errors are too low. But as described in Section II, subsection B, uncertainty about the parameters of the bilateral trade equation contributes only a small amount to the standard errors of the cross-country income regressions that we ultimately estimate. For example, doubling the variance-covariance matrix of the estimated parameters of the bilateral trade equation increases the standard error of the coefficient on the trade share in our baseline cross-country regression [column (2) of Table 3] by less than 10 percent.

[10] The expectation of $\tau_{ij}/\text{GDP}_i$ conditional on $\mathbf{X}_{ij}$ is actually equal to $e^{\hat{\mathbf{a}}'\mathbf{X}_{ij}}$ times $E[e^{e_{ij}}]$. Since we are modeling $e_{ij}$ as homoskedastic, however, $E[e^{e_{ij}}]$ is the same for all observations, and thus multiplies $\hat{T}_i$ by a constant. This has no implications for the subsequent analysis, and is therefore omitted for simplicity.

[11] For convenience, we omit a handful of countries with populations less than 100,000: Antigua and Barbuda, Greenland, Kiribati, Liechtenstein, the Marshall Islands, Micronesia, Monaco, Nauru, St. Kitts and Nevis, and San Marino. In addition, for countries that are not in the Penn World Table, we have data on population but not on the labor force. To estimate the labor force for these countries, we multiply their populations by the average ratio of the labor force to population among the countries in the same continent that are in the Penn World Table. We use the Penn World Table's definitions of the continents.

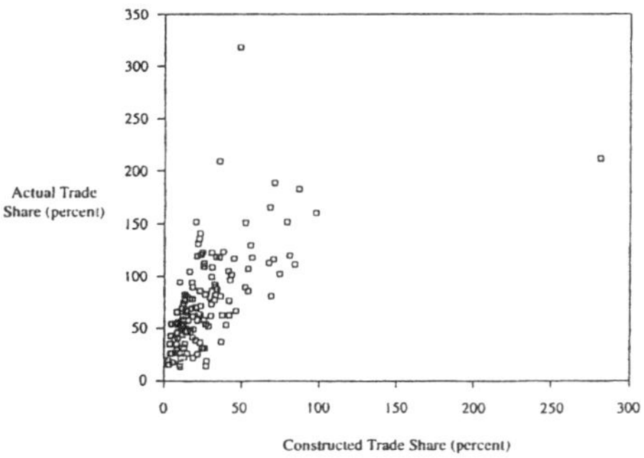


FIGURE 1. ACTUAL VERSUS CONSTRUCTED TRADE SHARE

TABLE 2—THE RELATION BETWEEN ACTUAL AND CONSTRUCTED OVERALL TRADE

| | (1) | (2) | (3) |
|---|---|---|---|
| Constant | 46.41 | 218.58 | 166.97 |
| | (4.10) | (12.89) | (18.88) |
| Constructed trade share | 0.99 | | 0.45 |
| | (0.10) | | (0.12) |
| Ln population | | −6.36 | −4.72 |
| | | (2.09) | (2.06) |
| Ln area | | −8.93 | −6.45 |
| | | (1.70) | (1.77) |
| Sample size | 150 | 150 | 150 |
| $R^2$ | 0.38 | 0.48 | 0.52 |
| SE of regression | 36.33 | 33.49 | 32.19 |

*Notes:* The dependent variable is the actual trade share. Standard errors are in parentheses.

$T$ on a constant and $\hat{T}$ yields a coefficient on $\hat{T}$ of essentially one and a $t$-statistic of 9.5.

As described in subsection A of this section, however, the component of the constructed trade share that is correlated with country size cannot be used to estimate trade's impact on income: smaller countries may engage in more international trade but in less within-country trade. That is, our identification of trade's impact on income will come from the component of the excluded exogenous variable (the constructed trade share) that is uncorrelated with the other exogenous variables (the size measures).

The constructed trade share is in fact highly correlated with country size. For example, the five countries with the smallest constructed shares all have areas over 1,000,000 square miles, and the five with the largest constructed shares all have areas under 10,000 square miles. A regression of the constructed trade share on a constant, log population, and log area yields negative and significant coefficients on both size measures and an $R^2$ of 0.45.

Thus in examining whether geographic variables provide useful information about international trade, we need to ask whether they provide information beyond that contained in country size. Columns (2) and (3) of Table 2 therefore compare a regression of the actual trade share on a constant and the two size measures with a regression that also includes our constructed trade share. As expected, size has a negative effect on trade. Area is highly significant, while population is moderately so. The coefficient on the constructed trade share falls by slightly more than half when the size controls are added.

The important message of columns (2) and (3), however, is that the constructed trade share still contains a considerable amount of information about actual trade. For example, its $t$-statistic in column (3) is 3.6; this corresponds to an $F$-statistic of 13.1. As the results in the next section show, this means that the constructed trade share contains enough information about actual trade for IV estimation to produce only moderate standard errors for the estimated impact of trade. Furthermore, the results of Douglas Staiger and James H. Stock (1997), Charles R. Nelson and Richard Startz (1990), and Alastair R. Hall et al. (1996) imply that these first-stage $F$-statistics are large enough that the finite-sample bias of instrumental variables—which biases the IV estimate toward the OLS estimate—is unlikely to be a serious problem in our IV regressions.

Figure 2, Panel A, shows the partial association between the actual and constructed trade shares controlling for the size measures. The figure shows that although the relationship is not as strong as the simple relationship shown in Figure 1, it is still positive. The figure also shows that there are two large outliers in the relationship: Luxembourg, which has an extremely high fitted trade share given its size, and Singapore, which has an extremely high actual trade share given its size. Figure 2, Panel B, therefore shows the scatterplot with these two observations omitted. Again there is a definite positive relationship.[12]

[12] When these two observations are dropped from the regression in column (3) of Table 2, the coefficient on the constructed trade share rises to 0.69, but the $t$-statistic falls

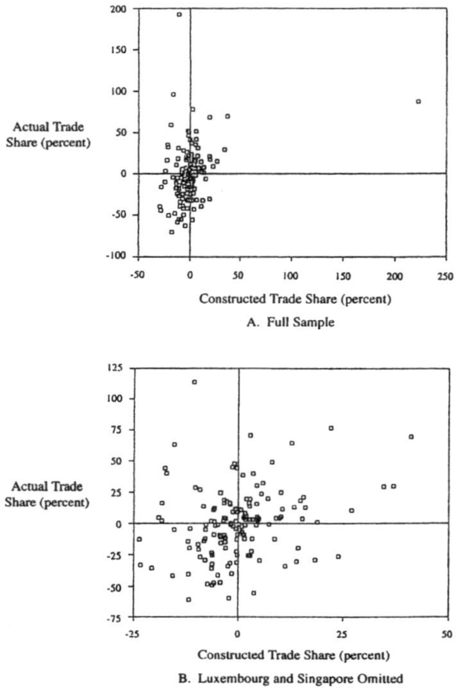


FIGURE 2. PARTIAL ASSOCIATION BETWEEN ACTUAL AND CONSTRUCTED TRADE SHARE

The five countries with the smallest constructed trade shares controlling for size are Western Samoa, Tonga, Fiji, Mauritius, and Vanuatu. All five are geographically isolated islands. Of the five, Western Samoa and Tonga have large negative shares given their size; Fiji and Mauritius have moderate negative shares; and Vanuatu has a moderate positive share. At the other extreme, the five countries with the highest constructed trade shares controlling for size are Luxembourg, Belize, Jordan, Malta, and Djibouti. Of these five, Luxembourg and Jordan have large positive actual trade shares controlling for size, and the other three have moderate positive shares. In sum, countries' geographic characteristics do provide considerable information about their overall trade.

## II. Estimates of Trade's Effect on Income

### A. *Specifications and Samples*

This section uses the instrument constructed in Section I to investigate the relationship between trade and income. The dependent variable in our regressions is log income per person. The data are for 1985 and are from the Penn World Table. Our basic specification is

$$\text{(9)} \quad \ln Y_i = a + bT_i + c_1 \ln N_i + c_2 \ln A_i + u_i,$$

where $Y_i$ is income per person in country $i$, $T_i$ is the trade share, and $N_i$ and $A_i$ are population and area. This specification differs from the one derived from the simple model in Section I, subsection A, only by including two measures of size rather than one [see equation (4)].

We do not include any additional variables in the regression. There are of course many other factors that may affect income. But our argument about the appropriateness of using geographic characteristics to construct an instrument for trade implies that there is no strong reason to expect additional independent determinants of income to be correlated with our instrument; thus they can be included in the error term. In addition, if we included other variables, the estimates of trade's impact on income would leave out any effects operating through its impact on these variables. Suppose, for example, that increased trade raises the rate of return on domestic investment and therefore increases the saving rate. Then by including the saving rate in the regression, we would be omitting trade's impact on income that operates via saving.

As an alternative to including control variables, in subsection D of this section, we decompose countries' incomes in various ways and ask how trade affects each component. In doing so, we can obtain information about the channels through which trade affects income. For example, we ask how trade affects both income at the beginning of the sample and growth

to 3.2 (corresponding to an $F$-statistic of 10.1). This $F$-statistic remains large enough that the finite-sample bias of the IV estimates is still likely to be small.

over the sample period.[13]

Appendix Table A1 reports the basic data used in the tests. It lists, for each country in the sample, its actual trade share in 1985, its constructed trade share, its area and 1985 population, and its income per person in 1985.[14]

We focus on two samples. The first is the full set of 150 countries covered by the Penn World Table. Our instrument is only moderately correlated with trade once we control for size, and much of the variation is among the smallest countries in the sample. Thus it is important to consider a relatively broad sample. And as we describe below, the results for this sample are robust to the exclusion of outliers and of observations where the data are potentially the most subject to error.

Our second sample is the 98-country sample considered by N. Gregory Mankiw et al. (1992). The countries in this sample generally have more reliable data; they are also generally larger, and thus less likely to have their incomes determined by idiosyncratic factors. In addition, data limitations require that we employ a smaller sample when we examine the channels through which trade affects income.

### B. *Basic Results*

Table 3 reports the regressions. Column (1) is an OLS regression of log income per person on a constant, the trade share, and the two size measures. The regression shows a statistically and economically significant relationship between trade and income. The *t*-statistic on the trade share is 3.5; the point estimate implies that an increase in the share of one percentage point is associated with an increase of 0.9 percent in income per person. The regression also suggests that, controlling for international trade, there is a positive (though only marginally significant) relation between country size and income per person; this supports the view that within-country trade is beneficial. The point estimates imply that increasing both population and area by one percent raises income per person by 0.1 percent.

TABLE 3—TRADE AND INCOME

| | (1) | (2) | (3) | (4) |
|---|---|---|---|---|
| Estimation | OLS | IV | OLS | IV |
| Constant | 7.40 | 4.96 | 6.95 | 1.62 |
| | (0.66) | (2.20) | (1.12) | (3.85) |
| Trade share | 0.85 | 1.97 | 0.82 | 2.96 |
| | (0.25) | (0.99) | (0.32) | (1.49) |
| Ln population | 0.12 | 0.19 | 0.21 | 0.35 |
| | (0.06) | (0.09) | (0.10) | (0.15) |
| Ln area | −0.01 | 0.09 | −0.05 | 0.20 |
| | (0.06) | (0.10) | (0.08) | (0.19) |
| Sample size | 150 | 150 | 98 | 98 |
| $R^2$ | 0.09 | 0.09 | 0.11 | 0.09 |
| SE of regression | 1.00 | 1.06 | 1.04 | 1.27 |
| First-stage *F* on excluded instrument | | 13.13 | | 8.45 |

*Notes:* The dependent variable is log income per person in 1985. The 150-country sample includes all countries for which the data are available; the 98-country sample includes only the countries considered by Mankiw et al. (1992). Standard errors are in parentheses.

Column (2) reports the IV estimates of the same equation. The trade share is treated as endogenous, and the constructed trade share is used as an instrument.[15] The coefficient on trade rises sharply. That is, the point estimate suggests that examining the link between trade and income using OLS understates rather than overstates the effect of trade. The estimates now imply that a one-percentage-point increase in the trade share raises income per person by 2.0 percent. In addition, the hypothesis that the IV coefficient is zero is marginally rejected at conventional levels ($t = 2.0$). The coefficient is

[13] Fischer (1993) uses a similar approach to investigate the effects of inflation. Frankel et al. (1996) and the working paper version of this paper (Frankel and Romer, 1996) investigate the effects of controlling for physical and human capital accumulation and population growth, and find that this does not change the character of the results.

[14] The other data used in the analysis are available from the authors on request.

[15] Throughout, the standard errors for the IV regressions account for the fact that the instrument depends on the parameters of the bilateral trade equation. That is, the variance-covariance matrix of the coefficients is estimated as the usual IV formula plus $(\partial\hat{\mathbf{b}}/\partial\hat{\mathbf{a}})\hat{\boldsymbol{\Omega}}(\partial\hat{\mathbf{b}}/\partial\hat{\mathbf{a}})'$, where $\hat{\mathbf{b}}$ is the vector of estimated coefficients from the cross-country income regression, $\hat{\mathbf{a}}$ is the vector of estimated coefficients from the bilateral trade equation, and $\hat{\boldsymbol{\Omega}}$ is the estimated variance-covariance matrix of $\hat{\mathbf{a}}$. In all cases, this additional term makes only a small contribution to the standard errors. In the regression in column (2) of Table 3, for example, this correction increases the standard error on the trade share from 0.91 to 0.99.

much less precisely estimated under IV than under OLS, however. As a result, the hypothesis that the IV and OLS estimates are equal cannot be rejected ($t = 1.2$).[16]

Moving from OLS to IV also increases the estimated impact of country size. The estimated effect of raising both population and area by one percent is now to increase income per person by almost 0.3 percent. This estimate is marginally significantly different from zero ($t = 1.8$).

One interesting aspect of the results concerning size is that the coefficient on area is positive. One might expect increased area, controlling for population, to reduce within-country trade and thus lower income. One possibility is that the positive coefficient is due to sampling error: the $t$-statistic on area is slightly less than one. Another is that greater area has a negative impact via decreased within-country trade, but a larger positive impact via increased natural resources. It is because of this possibility that we focus on the sum of the coefficients on log population and log area in our discussion. As described above, this sum shows the effects of increased size with population density held constant. In addition, as we show below, using population alone to measure size has no major impact on the results.

Columns (3) and (4) consider the 98-country sample. This change has no great effect on the OLS estimates of the coefficients on trade and size, but raises both the IV estimates and their standard errors considerably. The $t$-statistics for the OLS estimates fall moderately, while those for the IV estimates change little.

Frankel et al. (1996) and the working paper version of this paper (Frankel and Romer, 1996) consider a second approach to constructing the instrument for trade. In addition to using information on the proximity of a country's trading partners, these papers use some information about the partners' incomes. Specifically, they include measures of physical and human capital accumulation and population growth. As those papers explain, one can argue that the factor accumulation of a country's trading partners is uncorrelated with determinants of the country's income other than its trade and factor accumulation: once one accounts for the impact of a country's own factor accumulation on its income, the most evident channel through which its partners' factor accumulation may affect its income is by increasing the partners' incomes, and thus increasing the amount the country trades. Thus if one controls for the country's own factor accumulation, its partners' factor accumulation can be used in constructing the instrument.

Not surprisingly, using more information in constructing the instrument increases the precision of the IV estimates of trade's effect on income. But the estimated effect of trade is not systematically different when one moves to the alternative instrument; this supports the argument that it is a valid instrument. The overall results are similar to those we obtain with our basic instrument: the IV estimates of trade's impact on income are much larger than the OLS estimates, and are marginally significantly different from zero.

### C. *Robustness*

A natural question is whether the results are robust. We consider robustness along four dimensions.

First, as described above, Luxembourg and Singapore are major outliers in the relationship between the actual and constructed trade shares. Dropping either or both of these observations, however, does not change the basic pattern of the results. The most noticeable change occurs when Luxembourg is dropped from the baseline regressions in columns (1) and (2) of Table 3. This has effects similar to those of moving to the 98-country sample (which does not include Luxembourg): the OLS estimate of the effect of trade changes little, but the IV estimate and its standard error rise. Similarly, adding Luxembourg to the regressions in columns (3) and (4) of Table 3 moderately reduces the IV estimate of the effect of trade.

[16] That is, we perform a Hausman test (Jerry A. Hausman, 1978) of the hypothesis that actual trade is uncorrelated with the residual, and thus that OLS is unbiased. Under the null, asymptotically the OLS and IV estimates of trade's impact differ only because of sampling error. As a result, the difference between the two estimates divided by the standard error of the difference is distributed asymptotically as a standard normal variable. Furthermore, under the null the variance of the difference between the IV and OLS estimates is just the difference in their variances; that is, the standard error of the difference is the square root of the difference in the squares of their standard errors.

A second concern is the possibility that systematic differences among parts of the world are driving the results. That is, it could be that our IV estimates of the impact of trade arise because the countries in certain regions of the world have systematically higher constructed trade shares given their size and also have systematically higher incomes. In this case, our findings might be the result not of trade, but of other features of those regions.

To address this concern, we reestimate the regressions in Table 3 including a dummy variable for each continent. This modification substantially increases the standard errors of the IV estimates of the impact of trade on income. As a result, the estimates are no longer significantly different from zero. In addition, the IV estimate of the impact of trade for the 150-country sample [column (2) of Table 3] falls to only moderately above the OLS estimate. When Luxembourg is dropped from the sample, however, the IV estimate returns to being much larger than the OLS estimate. For the 98-country sample, in contrast, inclusion of the continent dummies raises the IV estimate slightly and lowers the OLS estimate slightly.

As an alternative way of considering the impact of differences across parts of the world, we follow Robert E. Hall and Charles I. Jones (1999) and include countries' distance from the equator as a control variable. This variable may reflect the impact of climate, or it may be a proxy for omitted country characteristics that are correlated with latitude. With this approach, the IV estimate of trade and size's effects are virtually identical to the OLS estimate for the full sample, and only moderately larger than the OLS estimate for the 98-country sample. Thus there is some evidence that systematic differences among regions are important to our finding that the IV estimates of trade's effects exceed the OLS estimates. Even in this case, however, there is still no evidence that the OLS estimates overstate trade's effects.

Third, our data are highly imperfect in various ways. Potentially most important, for the major oil-producing countries much of measured GDP represents the sale of existing resources rather than genuine value added. Since these countries have among the highest measured incomes in the sample, they have the potential to affect the results substantially. In fact, however, they are not important to our findings: they are already absent from the 98-country sample, and excluding them from the 150-country sample changes the estimates only slightly. As a more general check of the possible importance of data problems, we use the Penn World Table's summary assessments of the quality of countries' data to exclude the countries with the poorest data from the sample. Specifically, we exclude all countries whose data are assigned a grade of "D." This reduces the 150-country sample to 99, and the 98-country sample to 77. These reductions in the sample sizes moderately increase the standard errors of both the OLS and IV estimates of the impact of trade. The point estimates change little, however.

Finally, one can imagine reasons that virtually all the variables used in finding the geographic component of countries' trade might have some endogenous component that is correlated with the error term in the income equation. For example, whether countries have access to an ocean may be endogenous in the truly long run, and may be determined in part by other forces that affect income.[17] Similarly, population is endogenous in the very long run. To check that no single variable that could conceivably be endogenous is driving the results, we redo the construction of the instrument and the regressions in Table 3 in five ways: omitting the landlocked variable from the bilateral trade equation; excluding population from this equation; omitting all interactions with the common-border dummy from this equation; using total population rather than the labor force both in measuring countries' sizes and in computing income per person; and excluding area from both equations.

None of these changes has a major effect on the results. Although the changes sometimes affect the IV estimates noticeably, in every case they remain much larger than the OLS estimates. Moreover, there is no systematic tendency for the changes to reduce the IV

[17] The potential endogeneity of characteristics of borders other than whether countries are landlocked is unlikely to cause serious difficulties, for two reasons. First, the location of borders is largely determined by forces other than government policies and other determinants of current income; that is, the endogenous component of borders appears small. Second, because our estimates control for within-country trade, what is key to our estimates is the overall distribution of population, not the placement of country borders.

estimates; indeed, there are several cases where the changes raise the estimate considerably, or reduce its standard error considerably. Thus, our findings do not hinge on the use of any one of these variables in constructing the fitted trade shares.

### D. *The Channels Through Which Trade Affects Income*

The results thus far provide no information about the mechanisms through which trade raises income. To shed some light on this issue, we decompose income and examine trade's impact on each component.

We consider two decompositions of income. The first follows Hall and Jones (1999). Suppose output in country $i$ is given by

$$Y_i = K_i^{\alpha}[e^{\phi(S_i)}A_iN_i]^{1-\alpha}, \tag{10}$$

where $K$ and $N$ are capital and labor, $S$ is workers' average years of schooling, $\phi(\cdot)$ gives the effects of schooling, and $A$ is a productivity term. Equation (10) could be used to decompose differences in output per worker into the contributions of capital per worker, schooling, and productivity. As Hall and Jones note, however, an increase in $A$ leads to a higher value of $K$ for a given investment rate. Following Peter Klenow and Andrés Rodriguez-Clare (1997), they therefore rewrite (10) as

$$Y_i = (K_i/Y_i)^{\alpha/(1-\alpha)}e^{\phi(S_i)}A_iN_i. \tag{11}$$

Dividing both sides by $N_i$ and taking logs yields

$$\ln(Y_i/N_i) = \frac{\alpha}{1-\alpha}\ln(K_i/Y_i) + \phi(S_i) + \ln A_i. \tag{12}$$

Equation (12) expresses the log of output per worker as the sum of the contributions of capital depth (reflecting such factors as investment and population growth), schooling, and productivity. Hall and Jones set $\alpha = 1/3$ and let $\phi(\cdot)$ be a piecewise linear function with coefficients based on microeconomic evidence. This allows them to measure each component of (12) other than $\ln A_i$ directly from the data, and then find $\ln A_i$ as a residual.

Our second decomposition of income is simpler. We write log output per worker in 1985 as the sum of its value at the beginning of the sample (1960) plus the change during the sample period:

$$\ln(Y_i/N_i)_{1985} = \ln(Y_i/N_i)_{1960} + [\ln(Y_i/N_i)_{1985} - \ln(Y_i/N_i)_{1960}]. \tag{13}$$

For both decompositions, we regress each component of income on a constant, the trade share, and the size measures. Again, we consider both OLS and IV. Since the decompositions cannot be performed for the full sample, we consider only the 98-country sample. The results are reported in Table 4. The first three pairs of columns show the results for the Hall and Jones decomposition, and the remaining two pairs show the results for the decomposition into initial income and subsequent growth.

With both decompositions, the estimates using instrumental variables suggest that trade increases income through each component of income. For the first decomposition, the estimated impacts of trade on physical capital depth and schooling are moderate, and its estimated impact on productivity is large. The estimates imply that a one-percentage-point increase in the trade share raises the contributions of both physical capital depth and schooling to output by about one-half of a percentage point, and the contribution of productivity to output by about two percentage points. For the second decomposition, trade's estimated effects on both initial income and subsequent growth are large. Here the estimates imply that a one-percentage-point increase in the trade share raises both initial income and the change over the sample period by about one and a half percentage points. Further, in every case, the estimates suggest that country size, controlling for international trade, is beneficial. And in every case the IV estimates of the effects of international trade and country size are substantially larger than the OLS estimates.

The standard errors of the IV estimates are

TABLE 4—TRADE AND THE COMPONENTS OF INCOME

| | (1) | (2) | (3) | (4) | (5) | (6) | (7) | (8) | (9) | (10) |
|---|---|---|---|---|---|---|---|---|---|---|
| Dependent variable | $\frac{\alpha}{1-\alpha}\ln(K_i/Y_i)$ | | $\phi(S_i)$ | | $\ln A_i$ | | $\ln(Y/N)_{1960}$ | | $\Delta\ln(Y/N)$ | |
| Estimation | OLS | IV | OLS | IV | OLS | IV | OLS | IV | OLS | IV |
| Constant | −0.72 | −1.29 | 0.10 | −0.37 | 7.47 | 3.05 | 7.45 | 4.27 | −0.50 | −2.65 |
| | (0.34) | (0.93) | (0.30) | (0.81) | (0.74) | (2.84) | (1.03) | (3.07) | (0.39) | (1.66) |
| Trade share | 0.36 | 0.59 | 0.18 | 0.37 | 0.27 | 2.04 | 0.38 | 1.66 | 0.45 | 1.31 |
| | (0.10) | (0.36) | (0.08) | (0.31) | (0.21) | (1.10) | (0.29) | (1.19) | (0.11) | (0.65) |
| Ln population | 0.02 | 0.04 | 0.06 | 0.07 | 0.21 | 0.32 | 0.09 | 0.17 | 0.12 | 0.18 |
| | (0.03) | (0.04) | (0.03) | (0.03) | (0.06) | (0.11) | (0.09) | (0.12) | (0.03) | (0.06) |
| Ln area | 0.04 | 0.07 | −0.01 | 0.01 | −0.13 | 0.08 | −0.02 | 0.13 | −0.03 | 0.07 |
| | (0.02) | (0.05) | (0.02) | (0.04) | (0.05) | (0.14) | (0.07) | (0.15) | (0.03) | (0.08) |
| Sample size | 98 | 98 | 98 | 98 | 98 | 98 | 98 | 98 | 98 | 98 |
| $R^2$ | 0.13 | 0.13 | 0.09 | 0.08 | 0.14 | 0.06 | 0.03 | 0.02 | 0.24 | 0.20 |
| SE of regression | 0.32 | 0.33 | 0.28 | 0.29 | 0.69 | 0.92 | 0.96 | 1.06 | 0.36 | 0.47 |
| First-stage $F$ on excluded instrument | | 8.45 | | 8.45 | | 8.45 | | 8.45 | | 8.45 |

*Note:* Standard errors are in parentheses.

large, however. For productivity and for growth over the sample period, the estimates of trade's effect are marginally significantly different from zero ($t$-statistics of 1.8 and 2.0, respectively). For the other dependent variables, the $t$-statistics are between 1.2 and 1.6. Similarly, the $t$-statistic for the sum of the coefficients on population and area is 1.9 for productivity, 2.0 for growth, and between 1.3 and 1.5 for the other dependent variables. Thus, although the estimates suggest that international and within-country trade raise income through several different channels, they do not allow us to determine their contributions through each channel with great precision.

The results also provide no evidence that OLS is biased. The IV and OLS estimates of trade's impact never differ by a statistically significant amount. Indeed, the $t$-statistic for the null that the estimates are equal exceeds 1.5 only once.[18]

### E. *Why Are the IV Estimates Greater Than the OLS Estimates?*

Both the simple model presented in Section I, subsection A, and prevailing views about the association between trade and income suggest that IV estimates of trade's impact on income will be less than OLS estimates. There are four main reasons. First, countries that adopt free-trade policies are likely to adopt other policies

[18] The result that the IV estimates of the effects of trade and country size on each component of income are positive is extremely robust to the exclusion of outliers, the addition of continent dummies and latitude, the omission of countries with the most questionable data, the use of less information in constructing the instrument, and expanding the sample to include as many countries as possible (132 countries for the Hall and Jones decomposition, 127 countries for the decomposition into initial income and subsequent growth). The one exception is that in the IV regression with $\phi(S_i)$ as the dependent variable, both the coefficient on trade and the sum of the coefficients on population and area are very slightly negative when latitude is included as a control. Likewise, the finding that the IV estimates of the effects of trade and size on productivity, initial income, and growth over the sample are larger than the OLS estimates is extremely robust. Again there is only a single exception: when latitude is included, the IV estimates of the impact of trade and of the combined effect of population and area on initial income are slightly smaller than the OLS estimates. The result that the IV estimates of trade's and size's effects on capital depth and schooling are larger than the OLS estimates, on the other hand, is only moderately robust: for several of our robustness checks, the IV estimates are smaller. The difference is never large, however.

Finally, Hall and Jones's data are for 1988 rather than 1985. This is not important, however: redoing the basic regressions in Table 3 for the 98-country sample using 1988 income per worker changes the results only trivially.

that raise income. Second, countries that are wealthy for reasons other than trade are likely to have better infrastructure and transportation systems. Third, countries that are poor for reasons other than low trade may lack the institutions and resources needed to tax domestic economic activity, and thus may have to rely on tariffs to finance government spending. And fourth, increases in income coming from sources other than trade may increase the variety of goods that households demand and shift the composition of their demand away from basic commodities toward more processed, lighter weight goods. All of these considerations would lead to positive correlation between trade and the error term in an OLS regression, and thus to upward bias in the OLS estimate of trade's effects. And since there is no reason to expect correlation between proximity and these various omitted country characteristics, there is no reason to expect the IV estimate to suffer a similar bias. But we find that the IV estimate is almost always considerably larger than the OLS estimate. Although the difference is not statistically significant, the fact that it is large and positive is surprising.

The OLS estimate is determined by the partial association between income and trade, while the IV estimate is determined by the partial association between income and the component of trade correlated with the instrument. Thus, mechanically, the fact that the OLS estimate is smaller than the IV estimate means that income's partial association with the component of trade that is not correlated with the instrument is weaker than its partial association with the component that is correlated. Figure 3 presents these two partial associations. Since Luxembourg and Singapore are outliers in the relationship between trade and the instrument, they are omitted. Panel A of the figure shows the positive partial association between income and the component of trade correlated with the instrument; it is this association that underlies the positive coefficient on trade in the basic IV regression [column (2) of Table 3]. Panel B of the figure shows that there is also a positive partial association between income and the component of trade not correlated with the instrument. This association, though statistically significant, is smaller than the partial association in Panel A ($\hat{b} = 0.75$, with a standard error of 0.26). It is this smaller relationship that causes the OLS estimate to be less than the IV estimate.

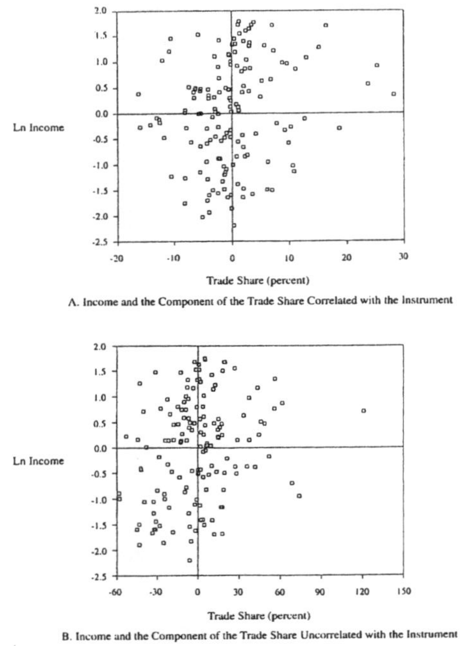


FIGURE 3. PARTIAL ASSOCIATIONS BETWEEN INCOME AND THE TRADE SHARE

The figures show that the difference between the OLS and IV estimates is not due to a handful of observations. (Recall that including Luxembourg and Singapore reduces the IV estimate of trade's effects. Thus the only major outliers are not the source of the gap between the OLS and IV estimates, but in fact reduce it.) In addition, examining which specific countries are important to the estimates suggests that there is no simple omitted country characteristic that is driving the results.

The observations that are responsible for the high estimated IV coefficient are those at the upper right and lower left of Panel A. The most influential observations at the upper right are Qatar, Belgium, the United States, and Israel. The most influential observations at the lower left are Malawi, Lesotho, Burundi, and Haiti. Similarly, the observations that are lowering the OLS estimate relative to the IV estimate are those in the lower right and upper left of Panel B. The most influential observations at the lower right are Qatar, Trinidad and Tobago, Hong Kong, and Syria, while the most influential observations at the upper left are Lesotho, Mauritania, Togo, and Belize.

Thus, in both cases the low-income countries are, not surprisingly, disproportionately from sub-Saharan Africa. But there is no evident characteristic other than proximity that distinguishes the countries with low proximity and low income from those with high proximity and high income. Similarly, there is no clear characteristic other than trade that differentiates the countries with low residual trade and high income from those with high residual trade and low income. Together with our earlier results, this suggests that the finding that the IV estimate exceeds—or at least does not fall short of—the OLS estimate is robust and not the result of omitted country characteristics.

There are two leading explanations of the fact that the IV estimate of trade's impact exceeds the OLS estimate. The first is that it is due to sampling variation. That is, although there no reason to expect systematic correlation between the instrument and the residual, it could be that by chance they are positively correlated. The principal evidence supporting this possibility is that the differences between the IV and OLS estimates, though quantitatively large, are well within the range that can arise from sampling error. In our baseline regressions [columns (1) and (2) of Table 3], the $t$-statistic for the null hypothesis that the OLS and IV estimates are equal is 1.2 ($p$ = 0.25). And in the variations on the baseline regression that we consider, this $t$-statistic never exceeds 2, and it is almost always less than 1.5. Moreover, in a few cases it is essentially zero. Thus, if one believes that theory provides strong grounds for believing that OLS estimates are biased up, our IV estimates do not provide a compelling reason for changing this belief.

The second candidate explanation of the finding that the IV estimates exceed the OLS estimates is that OLS is in fact biased down. The literal shipping of goods between countries does not raise income. Rather, trade is a proxy for the many ways in which interactions between countries raise income—specialization, spread of ideas, and so on. Trade is likely to be highly, but not perfectly, correlated with the extent of such interactions. Thus, trade is an imperfect measure of income-enhancing interactions among countries. And since measurement error leads to downward bias, this would mean that OLS would lead to an understatement of the effect of income-enhancing interactions.[19]

To explore this idea, consider the following simple model. Average income in country $i$ is given by

$$\ln Y_i = a + b_1 I_{1i} + b_2 I_{2i} + \cdots + b_N I_{Ni} + cS_i + e_i, \tag{14}$$

where $I_1, I_2, ..., I_N$ are measures of the various ways in which interactions among countries affect income. This equation has the same form as (4), except that trade has been replaced by $I_1, I_2, ..., I_N$. We want to rewrite this model in a way that expresses the idea that trade is a noisy measure of income-promoting interactions. To do this, we define $T_i^* = (b_1 I_{1i} + b_2 I_{2i} + \cdots + b_N I_{Ni})/b$, where $b = \text{Var}(b_1 I_1 + b_2 I_2 + \cdots + b_N I_N)/\text{Cov}(b_1 I_1 + b_2 I_2 + \cdots + b_N I_N, T)$ and where $T$ is again trade. With this definition, we can rewrite (14) as

$$\ln Y_i = a + bT_i^* + cS_i + e_i. \tag{15}$$

It is straightforward to check that with these definitions, $T - T^*$ is uncorrelated with $T^*$. Thus we can write

$$T_i = T_i^* + u_i, \tag{16}$$

where $u_i$ is uncorrelated with $T_i^*$. Thus, equations (15)–(16) express the idea that actual trade is a noisy measure of income-promoting interactions.

With this formulation, the relationship between income and actual trade is

[19] We are grateful to an anonymous referee and several seminar participants for suggesting this possibility.

$$(17)\quad \ln Y_i = a + bT_i + cS_i + (e_i - bu_i).$$

From (16), $T$ and $u$ are positively correlated. If this correlation is strong enough, it will cause the overall correlation between $T$ and the residual in (17), $e-bu$, to be negative, and thus cause OLS to yield a downward biased estimate of $b$. And again this bias will not carry over to the IV estimates—proximity and other geographic variables are likely to be strongly correlated with income-enhancing interactions, and there is no evident reason for them to be correlated with the idiosyncratic factors that cause trade to move differently from those interactions.

In the univariate case, the expectation of the OLS estimate of $b$ would be given by $E[\hat{b}_{\text{OLS}}] = (V_{T*}/V_T)b$, where $V_{T*}$ and $V_T$ are the variances of $T^*$ and $T$. When size is controlled for, the expression is analogous:

$$(18)\qquad E[\hat{b}_{\text{OLS}}] = \frac{V_{T^*|S}}{V_{T|S}}\, b,$$

where $V_{T*|S}$ and $V_{T|S}$ are the conditional variances of $T^*$ and $T$ given size.

This discussion implies that trade must be a very noisy proxy for income-promoting interactions to account for the gap between the OLS and IV estimates. In our baseline regression for the full sample [columns (1) and (2) of Table 3], the OLS estimate of $b$ is less than half the IV estimate. Thus for the gap between the two estimates to arise from the fact that trade is an imperfect proxy for income-enhancing interactions, the majority of the variation in trade uncorrelated with size would have to be uncorrelated with income-promoting interactions. To put it differently, $u$ in (16) would have to have a standard deviation of 22 percentage points.

We conclude that the most plausible explanation of the bulk of the gap between the IV and OLS estimates is simply sampling error. This implies that our most important finding is not that the IV estimates of trade's effects exceed the OLS estimates, but rather that there is no evidence that the IV estimates are lower. In addition, it implies that our IV estimates may be substantially affected by sampling error, and thus that the OLS estimates are likely to be more accurate estimates of trade's actual impact on income.

## III. Conclusion

This paper investigates the question of how international trade affects standards of living. Although this is an old question, it is a difficult one to answer. The amounts that countries trade are not determined exogenously. As a result, correlations between trade and income cannot identify the effect of trade.

This paper addresses this problem by focusing on the component of trade that is due to geographic factors. Some countries trade more just because they are near well-populated countries, and some trade less because they are isolated. Geographic factors are not a consequence of income or government policy, and there is no likely channel through which they affect income other than through their impact on a country's residents' interactions with residents of other countries and with one another. As a result, the variation in trade that is due to geographic factors can serve as a natural experiment for identifying the effects of trade.

The results of the experiment are consistent across the samples and specifications we consider: trade raises income. The relation between the geographic component of trade and income suggests that a rise of one percentage point in the ratio of trade to GDP increases income per person by at least one-half percent. Trade appears to raise income by spurring the accumulation of physical and human capital and by increasing output for given levels of capital.

The results also suggest that within-country trade raises income. Controlling for international trade, countries that are larger—and that therefore have more opportunities for trade within their borders—have higher incomes. The point estimates suggest that increasing a country's size and area by one percent raises income by one-tenth of a percent or more. And the estimates suggest that within-country trade, like international trade, raises income both .hrough capital accumulation and through income for given levels of capital.

There are two important caveats to these conclusions. First, the effects are not estimated with great precision. The hypotheses that the impacts of trade and size are zero are typically only marginally rejected at standard significance levels. In addition, the hypothesis that the estimates based on the geographic component of trade are the same as the estimates based on overall trade are typically relatively far from rejection. Thus, although the results bolster the case for the benefits of trade, they do not provide decisive evidence for it.

This limitation is probably inherent in the experiment we are considering. Once country size is controlled for, geography appears to account for only a moderate part of the variation in trade. As a result, geographic variables provide only a limited amount of information about the relation between trade and income. Thus, unless additional portions of overall trade that are unaffected by other determinants of income can be identified, it is likely to be difficult to improve greatly on our estimates of the effects of trade.

The second limitation of the results is that they cannot be applied without qualification to the effects of trade policies. There are many ways that trade affects income, and variations in trade that are due to geography and variations that are due to policy may not involve exactly the same mix of the various mechanisms. Thus, differences in trade resulting from policy may not affect income in precisely the same way as differences resulting from geography.

Nonetheless, our estimates of the effects of geography-based differences in trade are at least suggestive about the effects of policy-induced differences. Our point estimates suggest that the impact of geography-based differences in trade are quantitatively large. We also find that the estimated impact is larger than what one obtains by naively using OLS, but is not significantly different from the OLS estimate. These results are not what one would expect if the positive correlation between trade and income reflected an impact of income on trade, or of omitted factors on both variables. In that sense, our results bolster the case for the importance of trade and trade-promoting policies.

## Appendix

Table A1—Basic Data

| Country | Actual trade share | Constructed trade share | Area (thousands of square miles) | Population (millions) | Income per worker |
|---|---|---|---|---|---|
| Algeria | 49.66 | 13.97 | 919.595 | 4.859 | 13434 |
| Angola | 69.10 | 11.51 | 481.354 | 3.512 | 1742 |
| Benin | 76.99 | 42.20 | 43.483 | 1.874 | 2391 |
| Botswana | 121.28 | 24.03 | 231.800 | 0.370 | 6792 |
| Burkina Faso | 52.42 | 14.10 | 105.870 | 4.150 | 940 |
| Burundi | 30.82 | 24.86 | 10.747 | 2.539 | 986 |
| Cameroon | 57.67 | 15.79 | 183.569 | 3.831 | 3869 |
| Cape Verde Islands | 118.02 | 45.11 | 1.557 | 0.120 | 2829 |
| Central African Republic | 65.23 | 15.13 | 241.313 | 1.309 | 1266 |
| Chad | 61.43 | 12.00 | 495.755 | 1.791 | 1146 |
| Comoros | 67.06 | 46.77 | 0.863 | 0.181 | 1400 |
| Congo | 112.81 | 25.77 | 132.046 | 0.760 | 6878 |
| Djibouti | 117.06 | 70.97 | 8.958 | 0.105 | 4647 |
| Egypt | 51.97 | 11.75 | 386.900 | 12.719 | 7142 |
| Ethiopia | 34.13 | 8.44 | 472.432 | 18.385 | 705 |
| Gabon | 100.18 | 30.65 | 103.346 | 0.420 | 9672 |
| Gambia | 89.14 | 52.20 | 4.093 | 0.358 | 1609 |
| Ghana | 21.29 | 18.87 | 92.100 | 4.468 | 2237 |
| Guinea | 71.80 | 23.95 | 94.926 | 2.243 | 1583 |
| Guinea-Bissau | 62.74 | 42.24 | 13.948 | 0.425 | 1354 |
| Ivory Coast | 78.19 | 16.58 | 124.502 | 4.030 | 3740 |
| Kenya | 51.69 | 12.48 | 224.960 | 7.980 | 2014 |
| Lesotho | 152.42 | 20.66 | 11.720 | 0.743 | 2028 |
| Liberia | 79.63 | 29.81 | 43.000 | 0.811 | 2312 |
| Madagascar | 30.99 | 9.90 | 226.660 | 4.498 | 1707 |
| Malawi | 54.09 | 12.67 | 45.747 | 3.180 | 1171 |
| Mali | 73.60 | 12.80 | 482.077 | 2.332 | 1686 |

(continued overleaf)

TABLE A1—*Continued.*

| Country | Actual trade share | Constructed trade share | Area (thousands of square miles) | Population (millions) | Income per worker |
|---|---|---|---|---|---|
| Mauritania | 141.56 | 23.44 | 397.953 | 0.533 | 2674 |
| Mauritius | 109.10 | 31.11 | 0.787 | 0.577 | 7474 |
| Morocco | 58.50 | 12.71 | 172.413 | 6.714 | 6427 |
| Mozambique | 18.38 | 11.11 | 308.642 | 7.290 | 1417 |
| Namibia | 119.81 | 21.31 | 317.818 | 0.380 | 8465 |
| Niger | 51.27 | 12.37 | 489.206 | 3.343 | 1098 |
| Nigeria | 28.53 | 8.68 | 356.700 | 30.743 | 2874 |
| Reunion | 53.14 | 39.92 | 0.969 | 0.216 | 7858 |
| Rwanda | 30.65 | 26.20 | 10.169 | 3.005 | 1539 |
| Senegal | 70.63 | 19.87 | 75.954 | 2.758 | 2688 |
| Seychelles | 111.95 | 84.98 | 0.175 | 0.029 | 7058 |
| Sierra Leone | 19.15 | 27.81 | 27.700 | 1.372 | 2411 |
| Somalia | 25.64 | 14.89 | 246.199 | 2.774 | 1574 |
| South Africa | 55.43 | 8.90 | 471.440 | 11.240 | 9930 |
| Sudan | 21.34 | 10.97 | 967.491 | 7.121 | 2436 |
| Swaziland | 118.71 | 56.87 | 6.704 | 0.277 | 5225 |
| Tanzania | 21.03 | 10.97 | 364.900 | 10.266 | 975 |
| Togo | 105.52 | 41.47 | 21.925 | 1.277 | 1516 |
| Tunisia | 71.33 | 23.83 | 63.379 | 2.280 | 8783 |
| Uganda | 22.54 | 12.97 | 91.343 | 6.236 | 1224 |
| Zaire | 53.15 | 8.97 | 905.365 | 12.321 | 1136 |
| Zambia | 76.96 | 13.81 | 290.586 | 2.274 | 2399 |
| Zimbabwe | 56.40 | 11.27 | 150.699 | 3.135 | 3261 |
| Bahamas | 124.11 | 38.03 | 5.382 | 0.097 | 29815 |
| Barbados | 130.30 | 56.10 | 0.166 | 0.127 | 12212 |
| Belize | 183.27 | 87.48 | 8.866 | 0.049 | 8487 |
| Canada | 54.48 | 4.97 | 3851.809 | 12.595 | 31147 |
| Costa Rica | 63.19 | 23.37 | 19.652 | 0.920 | 9148 |
| Dominica | 103.09 | 75.08 | 0.305 | 0.030 | 6163 |
| Dominican Republic | 64.24 | 22.37 | 18.704 | 1.912 | 7082 |
| El Salvador | 52.21 | 28.91 | 8.260 | 1.564 | 5547 |
| Grenada | 120.63 | 81.25 | 0.133 | 0.039 | 4502 |
| Guatemala | 24.94 | 22.04 | 42.042 | 2.262 | 7358 |
| Haiti | 38.44 | 20.44 | 10.714 | 2.514 | 2125 |
| Honduras | 54.15 | 27.58 | 43.277 | 1.307 | 4652 |
| Jamaica | 131.89 | 22.19 | 4.411 | 1.059 | 4726 |
| Mexico | 25.74 | 4.52 | 761.600 | 24.669 | 17036 |
| Nicaragua | 36.60 | 23.46 | 50.180 | 0.980 | 5900 |
| Panama | 70.96 | 23.56 | 29.761 | 0.760 | 10039 |
| Puerto Rico | 136.74 | 22.75 | 3.515 | 1.101 | 21842 |
| St. Lucia | 165.77 | 68.83 | 0.238 | 0.057 | 5317 |
| St. Vincent & Grenadines | 152.17 | 79.41 | 0.150 | 0.042 | 5796 |
| Trinidad & Tobago | 61.90 | 30.33 | 1.980 | 0.441 | 25529 |
| United States | 18.01 | 2.56 | 3540.939 | 117.362 | 33783 |
| Argentina | 17.10 | 5.60 | 1072.067 | 10.798 | 14955 |
| Bolivia | 30.27 | 8.06 | 424.162 | 1.978 | 5623 |
| Brazil | 19.34 | 3.03 | 3286.470 | 49.609 | 10977 |
| Chile | 53.85 | 7.25 | 292.132 | 4.303 | 9768 |
| Colombia | 26.33 | 7.54 | 439.735 | 9.433 | 9276 |
| Ecuador | 47.63 | 11.42 | 109.484 | 2.820 | 9615 |
| Guyana | 109.95 | 25.92 | 83.000 | 0.280 | 3573 |
| Paraguay | 49.58 | 10.43 | 157.047 | 1.226 | 6241 |
| Peru | 39.42 | 7.03 | 496.222 | 6.107 | 8141 |
| Suriname | 82.99 | 30.96 | 63.251 | 0.124 | 10883 |
| Uruguay | 47.86 | 17.07 | 68.040 | 1.169 | 10216 |
| Venezuela | 40.76 | 8.94 | 352.143 | 5.789 | 18362 |
| Bahrain | 188.70 | 71.82 | 0.240 | 0.178 | 22840 |

TABLE A1—*Continued.*

| Country | Actual trade share | Constructed trade share | Area (thousands of square miles) | Population (millions) | Income per worker |
|---|---|---|---|---|---|
| Bangladesh | 25.78 | 10.31 | 55.598 | 27.684 | 4265 |
| Bhutan | 62.54 | 37.74 | 17.954 | 0.575 | 1504 |
| China | 19.44 | 2.30 | 3689.631 | 612.363 | 2166 |
| Hong Kong | 209.52 | 35.88 | 0.398 | 3.516 | 16447 |
| India | 15.04 | 3.29 | 1229.737 | 295.478 | 2719 |
| Indonesia | 42.66 | 4.47 | 735.268 | 62.136 | 4332 |
| Iran | 15.20 | 10.06 | 636.293 | 13.540 | 13847 |
| Iraq | 49.22 | 19.14 | 169.235 | 4.105 | 15855 |
| Israel | 85.80 | 54.17 | 8.020 | 1.602 | 21953 |
| Japan | 25.54 | 5.47 | 143.574 | 75.526 | 18820 |
| Jordan | 113.50 | 68.18 | 37.297 | 0.601 | 15655 |
| Korea, Republic of | 67.86 | 14.36 | 38.031 | 16.608 | 10361 |
| Kuwait | 96.45 | 42.55 | 6.880 | 0.640 | 35065 |
| Laos | 13.80 | 27.32 | 91.429 | 1.758 | 2739 |
| Malaysia | 104.69 | 16.82 | 128.328 | 6.217 | 10458 |
| Mongolia | 82.72 | 13.52 | 604.829 | 0.894 | 3966 |
| Myanmar | 13.16 | 10.74 | 261.220 | 16.613 | 1332 |
| Nepal | 31.29 | 13.26 | 54.463 | 6.958 | 2244 |
| Oman | 87.06 | 34.19 | 82.030 | 0.368 | 31609 |
| Pakistan | 34.00 | 8.04 | 310.400 | 28.567 | 4249 |
| Philippines | 45.84 | 8.84 | 115.830 | 19.945 | 4229 |
| Qatar | 80.94 | 69.56 | 4.412 | 0.166 | 36646 |
| Saudi Arabia | 79.97 | 14.98 | 865.000 | 3.652 | 28180 |
| Singapore | 318.07 | 48.90 | 0.220 | 1.189 | 17986 |
| Sri Lanka | 62.93 | 13.94 | 25.332 | 5.786 | 5597 |
| Syria | 37.23 | 37.44 | 71.498 | 2.556 | 17166 |
| Taiwan | 94.62 | 17.92 | 13.895 | 8.262 | 12701 |
| Thailand | 51.20 | 9.45 | 198.455 | 26.793 | 4751 |
| United Arab Emirates | 89.66 | 33.42 | 32.000 | 0.694 | 38190 |
| Yemen | 49.34 | 16.83 | 128.560 | 2.369 | 6425 |
| Austria | 81.27 | 36.64 | 32.375 | 3.528 | 23837 |
| Belgium | 151.34 | 52.46 | 11.781 | 4.071 | 27325 |
| Bulgaria | 85.99 | 31.12 | 42.823 | 4.417 | 9662 |
| Cyprus | 107.57 | 54.39 | 3.572 | 0.310 | 13918 |
| Czechoslovakia | 69.45 | 21.07 | 49.383 | 8.137 | 7467 |
| Denmark | 72.99 | 30.89 | 16.631 | 2.780 | 23861 |
| Finland | 57.50 | 21.64 | 130.119 | 2.493 | 23700 |
| France | 47.17 | 15.26 | 211.208 | 24.882 | 27064 |
| Germany, West | 61.52 | 18.47 | 96.010 | 28.085 | 27252 |
| Greece | 53.97 | 27.01 | 50.961 | 3.800 | 16270 |
| Hungary | 82.32 | 26.92 | 35.920 | 5.195 | 10827 |
| Iceland | 81.83 | 33.08 | 39.709 | 0.127 | 23256 |
| Ireland | 118.84 | 33.85 | 26.600 | 1.342 | 19197 |
| Italy | 46.06 | 13.97 | 116.500 | 22.714 | 27189 |
| Luxembourg | 211.94 | 281.29 | 0.999 | 0.157 | 30782 |
| Malta | 160.86 | 98.14 | 0.122 | 0.119 | 15380 |
| Netherlands | 118.76 | 35.84 | 16.041 | 5.855 | 28563 |
| Norway | 86.00 | 23.54 | 125.049 | 2.043 | 28749 |
| Poland | 35.07 | 13.84 | 120.728 | 19.235 | 8079 |
| Portugal | 77.95 | 18.78 | 35.550 | 4.540 | 11343 |
| Romania | 41.62 | 18.80 | 91.699 | 11.275 | 4021 |
| Spain | 43.51 | 12.38 | 194.885 | 13.732 | 21169 |
| Sweden | 69.02 | 18.22 | 173.800 | 4.238 | 26504 |
| Switzerland | 77.69 | 32.57 | 15.941 | 3.222 | 29848 |
| Turkey | 44.40 | 11.26 | 300.947 | 21.829 | 7091 |
| United Kingdom | 56.87 | 13.47 | 94.247 | 27.684 | 22981 |
| Soviet Union | 18.28 | 3.68 | 8600.387 | 142.801 | 13700 |

*(continued overleaf)*

TABLE A1—*Continued.*

| Country | Actual trade share | Constructed trade share | Area (thousands of square miles) | Population (millions) | Income per worker |
|---|---|---|---|---|---|
| Yugoslavia | 57.88 | 25.82 | 39.449 | 10.475 | 11417 |
| Australia | 35.28 | 4.07 | 2966.150 | 7.391 | 28960 |
| Fiji | 89.13 | 18.56 | 7.078 | 0.232 | 9840 |
| New Zealand | 65.25 | 8.19 | 103.884 | 1.438 | 26039 |
| Papua New Guinea | 94.52 | 10.17 | 178.704 | 1.660 | 3374 |
| Solomon Islands | 123.60 | 25.12 | 10.954 | 0.088 | 5109 |
| Tonga | 102.25 | 43.40 | 0.288 | 0.030 | 6022 |
| Vanuatu | 123.33 | 30.86 | 4.707 | 0.042 | 5707 |
| Western Samoa | 92.17 | 32.77 | 1.093 | 0.050 | 5388 |

*Notes:* Actual trade share—Ratio of imports plus exports to GDP, 1985 (Penn World Table, Mark 5.6, Series OPEN).

Constructed trade share—Aggregated fitted values of bilateral trade equation with geographic variables. (See text, Section I, subsections B–D.)

Area—Rand McNally (1993).

Population—Economically active population, 1985 (Penn World Table, Mark 5.6, constructed from real GDP per capita (RGDPCH), real GDP per worker (RGDPW), and total population (POP): RGDPCH*POP/RGDPW).

Income per worker—Real GDP per worker, 1985; 1985 international prices (dollars) (Penn World Table, Mark 5.6, Series RGDPCH).

## REFERENCES


**Bradford, Colin, Jr. and Chakwin, Naomi.** "Alternative Explanations of the Trade-Output Correlation in East Asian Economies." OECD Development Centre Technical Paper No. 87, August 1993.

**De Long, J. Bradford and Summers, Lawrence H.** "Equipment Investment and Economic Growth." *Quarterly Journal of Economics*, May 1991, *106*(2), pp. 445–502.

**Dollar, David.** "Outward-Oriented Developing Economies Really Do Grow More Rapidly: Evidence from 95 LDCs, 1976–1985." *Economic Development and Cultural Change*, April 1992, *40*(3), pp. 523–44.

**Easterly, William.** "How Much Do Distortions Affect Growth?" *Journal of Monetary Economics*, November 1993, *32*(2), pp. 187–212.

**Edwards, Sebastian.** "Openness, Trade Liberalization, and Growth in Developing Countries." *Journal of Economic Literature*, September 1993, *31*(3), pp. 1358–93.

______. "Trade Policy, Exchange Rates, and Growth," in Rudiger Dornbusch and Sebastian Edwards, eds., *Reform, recovery, and growth: Latin America and the Middle East*. Chicago: University of Chicago Press, 1995, pp. 13–49.

**Feder, Gershon.** "On Exports and Economic Growth." *Journal of Development Economics*, February–April 1983, *12*(1–2), pp. 59–73.

**Fischer, Stanley.** "Growth, Macroeconomics, and Development," in Olivier Jean Blanchard and Stanley Fischer, eds., *NBER macroeconomics annual 1991*. Cambridge, MA: MIT Press, 1991, pp. 329–64.

______. "The Role of Macroeconomic Factors in Growth." *Journal of Monetary Economics*, December 1993, *32*(3), pp. 485–512.

**Frankel, Jeffrey A.** *Regional trading blocs in the world trading system*. Washington, DC: Institute of International Economics, 1997.

**Frankel, Jeffrey A. and Romer, David.** "Trade and Growth: An Empirical Investigation." National Bureau of Economic Research (Cambridge, MA) Working Paper No. 5476, March 1996.

**Frankel, Jeffrey A.; Romer, David and Cyrus, Teresa L.** "Trade and Growth in East Asian Countries: Cause and Effect?" National Bureau of Economic Research Working Paper (Cambridge, MA) No. 5732, August 1996.

**Frankel, Jeffrey A.; Stein, Ernesto and Wei, Shang-jin.** "Trading Blocs and the Americas: The Natural, the Unnatural, and the Supernatural." *Journal of Development Economics*, June 1995, *47*(1), pp. 61–95.

**Hall, Alastair R.; Rudebusch, Glenn D. and Wilcox, David W.** "Judging Instrument Relevance in Instrumental Variables Estimation." *International Economic Review*, May 1996, *37*(2), pp. 283–98.

**Hall, Robert E. and Jones, Charles I.** "Why Do Some Countries Produce So Much More Output per Worker than Others?" *Quarterly Journal of Economics*, February 1999, *114*(1), pp. 83–116.

**Harrison, Ann.** "Openness and Growth: A Time-Series, Cross-Country Analysis for Developing Countries." *Journal of Development Economics*, March 1996, *48*(2), pp. 419–47.

**Hausman, Jerry A.** "Specification Tests in Econometrics." *Econometrica*, November 1978, *46*(6), pp. 1251–71.

**Helpman, Elhanan.** "Growth, Technological Progress, and Trade." National Bureau of Economic Research (Cambridge, MA) Reprint No. 1145, 1988.

**Klenow, Peter and Rodriguez-Clare, Andrés.** "The Neoclassical Revival in Growth Economics: Has It Gone Too Far?" in Ben S. Bernanke and Julio J. Rotemberg, eds., *NBER macroeconomics annual 1997*. Cambridge, MA: MIT Press, 1997, pp. 73–103.

**Kormendi, Roger C. and Meguire, Philip G.** "Macroeconomic Determinants of Growth: Cross-Country Evidence." *Journal of Monetary Economics*, September 1985, *16*(2), pp. 141–63.

**Lee, Jong-Wha.** "International Trade, Distortions and Long-Run Economic Growth." *IMF Staff Papers*, June 1993, *40*(2), pp. 299–328.

**Levine, Ross and Renelt, David.** "A Sensitivity Analysis of Cross-Country Growth Regressions." *American Economic Review*, September 1992, *82*(4), pp. 942–63.

**Linneman, Hans.** *An econometric study of international trade flows*. Amsterdam: North-Holland, 1966.

**Mankiw, N. Gregory; Romer, David and Weil, David N.** "A Contribution to the Empirics of Economic Growth." *Quarterly Journal of Economics*, May 1992, *107*(2), pp. 407–37.

**Michaely, Michael.** "Exports and Growth: An Empirical Investigation." *Journal of Development Economics*, March 1977, *4*(1), pp. 49–53.

**Nelson, Charles R. and Startz, Richard.** "Some Further Results on the Exact Small Sample Properties of the Instrumental Variable Estimator." *Econometrica*, July 1990, *58*(4), pp. 967–76.

**Rand McNally.** *Quick reference world atlas*. Chicago: Rand McNally, 1993.

**Rodrik, Dani.** "Getting Interventions Right: How South Korea and Taiwan Grew Rich." *Economic Policy*, April 1995a, (20), pp. 53–97.

______. "Trade and Industrial Policy Reform,"in Jere Behrman and T. N. Srinivasan, eds., *Handbook of development economics*, Vol. 3B. Amsterdam: North-Holland, 1995b, pp. 2925–82.

**Sachs, Jeffrey D. and Warner, Andrew.** "Economic Reform and the Process of Global Integration." *Brookings Papers on Economic Activity*, 1995, (1), pp. 1–95.

**Sala-i-Martin, Xavier.** "Comment," in Olivier Jean Blanchard and Stanley Fischer, eds., *NBER macroeconomics annual 1991*. Cambridge, MA: MIT Press, 1991, pp. 368–78.

**Staiger, Douglas and Stock, James H.** "Instrumental Variables Regression with Weak Instruments." *Econometrica*, May 1997, *65*(3), pp. 557–86.

**Summers, Robert and Heston, Alan.** "The Penn World Table (Mark 5): An Expanded Set of International Comparisons, 1950–1988." *Quarterly Journal of Economics*, May 1991, *106*(2), pp. 327–68.

# [4]

*Francisco Rodríguez and Dani Rodrik*
UNIVERSITY OF MARYLAND AND HARVARD UNIVERSITY

# *Trade Policy and Economic Growth: A Skeptic's Guide to the Cross-National Evidence*

*It isn't what we don't know that kills us. It's what we know that ain't so.*
*—Mark Twain*

## 1. *Introduction*

Do countries with lower barriers to international trade experience faster economic progress? Few questions have been more vigorously debated in the history of economic thought, and none is more central to the vast literature on trade and development.

The prevailing view in policy circles in North America and Europe is that recent economic history provides a conclusive answer in the affirmative. Multilateral institutions such as the World Bank, the IMF, and the OECD regularly promulgate advice predicated on the belief that openness generates predictable and positive consequences for growth. A recent report by the OECD (1998, p. 36) states: "More open and outward-oriented economies consistently outperform countries with restrictive trade and [foreign] investment regimes." According to the IMF (1997, p.

We thank Dan Ben-David, Sebastian Edwards, Jeffrey Frankel, David Romer, Jeffrey Sachs, and Andrew Warner for generously sharing their data with us. We are particularly grateful to Ben-David, Frankel, Romer, Sachs, Warner, and Romain Wacziarg for helpful email exchanges. We have benefited greatly from discussions in seminars at the University of California at Berkeley, University of Maryland, University of Miami, University of Michigan, MIT, the Inter-American Development Bank, Princeton, Yale, IMF, IESA, and the NBER. We also thank Ben Bernanke, Roger Betancourt, Allan Drazen, Gene Grossman, Ann Harrison, Chang-Tai Hsieh, Doug Irwin, Chad Jones, Frank Levy, Douglas Irwin, Rick Mishkin, Arvind Panagariya, Ken Rogoff, James Tybout, and Eduardo Zambrano for helpful comments, Vladimir Kliouev for excellent research assistance, and the Weatherhead Center for International Affairs at Harvard for partial financial support.

84): "Policies toward foreign trade are among the more important factors promoting economic growth and convergence in developing countries."

This view is widespread in the economics profession as well. Krueger (1998, p. 1513), for example, judges that it is straightforward to demonstrate empirically the superior growth performance of countries with "outer-oriented" trade strategies. According to Stiglitz (1998, p. 36), "[m]ost specifications of empirical growth regressions find that some indicator of external openness—whether trade ratios or indices or price distortions or average tariff level—is strongly associated with per-capita income growth." According to Fischer (2000), "[i]ntegration into the world economy is the best way for countries to grow."

Such statements notwithstanding, if there is an inverse relationship between trade barriers and economic growth, it is not one that immediately stands out in the data. See for example Figure 1. The figure displays the (partial) associations over 1975–1994 between the growth rate of per capita GDP and two measures of trade restrictions. The first measure is an average tariff rate, calculated by dividing total import duties by the volume of imports. The second is a coverage ratio for nontariff barriers to trade.[1] The figures show the relationship between these measures and growth after controlling for levels of initial income and secondary education. In both cases, the slope of the relationship is only slightly negative and nowhere near statistical significance. This finding is not atypical. Simple measures of trade barriers tend not to enter significantly in well-specified growth regressions, regardless of time periods, subsamples, or the conditioning variables employed.

Of course, neither of the two measures used above is a perfect indicator of trade restrictions. Simple tariff averages underweight high tariff rates because the corresponding import levels tend to be low. Such averages are also poor proxies for overall trade restrictions when tariff and nontariff barriers are substitutes. As for the nontariff coverage ratios, they do not do a good job of discriminating between barriers that are highly restrictive and barriers with little effect. And conceptual flaws aside, both indicators are clearly measured with some error (due to smuggling, weaknesses in the underlying data, coding problems, etc.).

In part because of concerns related to data quality, the recent literature on openness and growth has resorted to more creative empirical strategies. These strategies include: (1) constructing alternative indicators of openness (Dollar, 1992; Sachs and Warner, 1995); (2) testing robustness by using a wide range of measures of openness, including subjective indica-

1. Data for the first measure come from World Bank (1998). The second is taken from Barro and Lee (1994), and is based on UNCTAD compilations.

Figure 1 PARTIAL ASSOCIATION BETWEEN GROWTH AND DIRECT MEASURES OF TRADE RESTRICTIONS

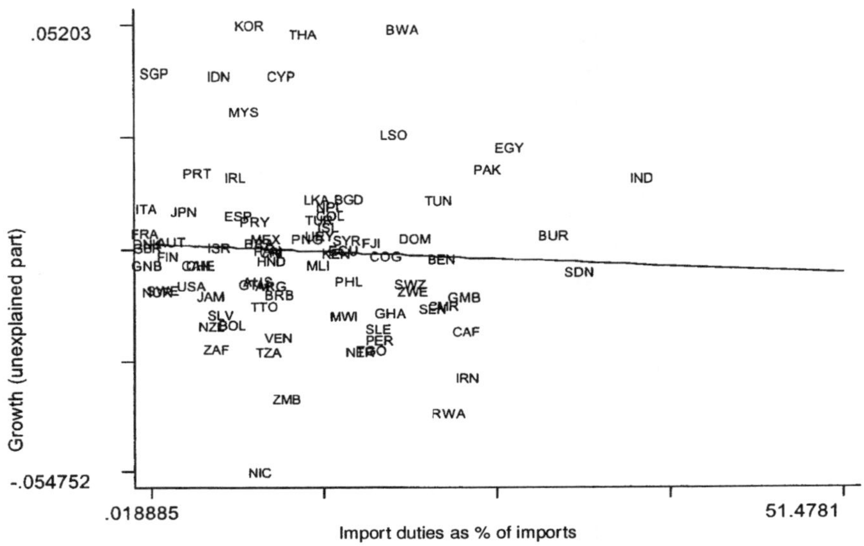


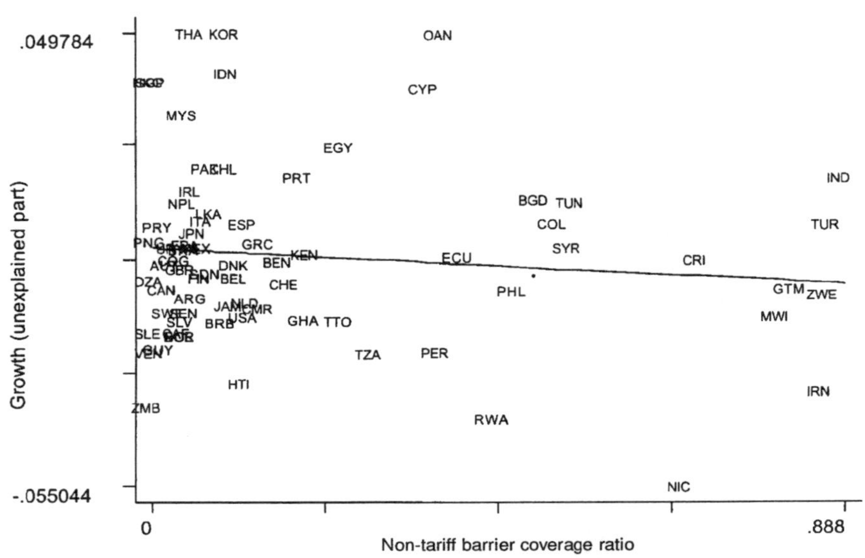

tors (Edwards, 1992, 1998); and (3) comparing convergence experience among groups of liberalizing and nonliberalizing countries (Ben-David, 1993). This recent round of empirical research is generally credited with having yielded stronger and more convincing results on the beneficial consequences of openness than the previous, largely case-based literature. Indeed, the cumulative evidence that has emerged from such studies provides the foundation for the previously noted consensus on the growth-promoting effects of trade openness. The frequency with which these studies are cited in international economics textbooks and in policy discussions is one indicator of the influence that they have exerted.

Our goal in this paper is to scrutinize this new generation of research. We do so by focusing on what the existing literature has to say on the following question: *Do countries with lower policy-induced barriers to international trade grow faster, once other relevant country characteristics are controlled for?* We take this to be the central question of policy relevance in this area. To the extent that the empirical literature demonstrates a positive causal link from openness to growth, the main operational implication is that governments should dismantle their barriers to trade. Therefore, it is critical to ask how well the evidence supports the presumption that doing so would raise growth rates.

Note that this question differs from an alternative one we could have asked: *Does international trade raise growth rates of income?* This is a related, but conceptually distinct question. Trade policies do affect the volume of trade, of course. But there is no strong reason to expect their effect on growth to be quantitatively (or even qualitatively) similar to the consequences of changes in trade volumes that arise from, say, reductions in transport costs or increases in world demand. To the extent that trade restrictions represent policy responses to real or perceived market imperfections or, at the other extreme, are mechanisms for rent extraction, they will work differently from natural or geographical barriers to trade and other exogenous determinants. Frankel and Romer (1999) recognize this point in their recent paper on the relationship between trade volumes and income levels. These authors use the geographical component of trade volumes as an instrument to identify the effects of trade on income levels. They appropriately caution that their results cannot be directly applied to the effects of trade policies.

From an operational standpoint, it is clear that the relevant question is the one having to do with the consequences of trade *policies* rather than trade *volumes*. Hence we focus on the recent empirical literature that attempts to measure the effect of trade policies. Our main finding is that this literature is largely uninformative regarding the question we posed above. There is a significant gap between the message that the consumers of this literature have derived and the facts that the literature has actually demonstrated. The gap emerges from a number of factors. In many cases, the indicators of openness used by researchers are problematic as measures of trade barriers or are highly correlated with other sources of poor economic performance. In other cases, the empirical strategies used to ascertain the link between trade policy and growth have serious shortcomings, the removal of which results in significantly weaker findings.

The literature on openness and growth through the late 1980s was usefully surveyed in a paper by Edwards (1993). This survey covered detailed multicountry analyses (such as Little, Scitovsky, and Scott, 1970, and Balassa, 1971) as well as cross-country econometric studies (such as Feder, 1983, Balassa, 1985, and Esfahani, 1991). Most of the cross-national econometric research that was available up to that point focused on the relationship between exports and growth, and not on trade policy and growth. Edwards's evaluation of this literature was largely negative (1993, p. 1389):

> [M]uch of the cross-country regression-based studies have been plagued by empirical and conceptual shortcomings. The theoretical frameworks used have been increasingly simplistic, failing to address important questions such as the exact mechanism through which export expansion affects GDP growth, and ignoring potential determinants of growth such as educational attainment. Also, many papers have been characterized by a lack of care in dealing with issues related to endogeneity and measurement errors. All of this has resulted, in many cases, in unconvincing results whose fragility has been exposed by subsequent work.

Edwards argued that such weaknesses had reduced the policy impact of the cross-national econometric research covered in his review.

Our paper picks up where Edwards's survey left off. We focus on a number of empirical papers that either were not included in or have appeared since that survey. Judging by the number of citations in publications by governmental and multilateral institutions and in textbooks, this recent round of empirical research has been considerably more influential in policy and academic circles.[2] Our detailed analysis covers the

2. We gave examples of citations from international institutions above. Here are some examples from recent textbooks. Yarbrough and Yarbrough (2000, p. 19) write "[o]n the trade-growth connection, the empirical evidence is clear that countries with open markets experience faster growth," citing Edwards (1998). Caves, Frankel, and Jones (1999, pp. 256–257) warn that "[r]esearch testing this proposition is not unanimous" but then continue to say "productivity growth does seem to increase with openness to the international economy and freedom from price and allocative distortions in the domestic econ-

four papers that are probably the best known in the field: Dollar (1992), Sachs and Warner (1995), Ben-David (1993), and Edwards (1998). We also include an analysis of Frankel and Romer (1999), and shorter discussions of Lee (1993), Harrison (1996), and Wacziarg (1998).

A few words about the selection of papers. The paper by Dollar (1992) was not reviewed in Edwards's survey, perhaps because it had only recently been published. We include it here because it is, by our count, the most heavily cited empirical paper on the link between openness and growth. Sachs and Warner (1995) is a close second, and the index of openness constructed therein has now been widely used in the cross-national research on growth.[3] The other two papers are also well known, but in these cases our decision was based less on citation counts than on the fact that they are representative of different types of methodologies. Ben-David (1993) considers income convergence in countries that have integrated with each other (such as the European Community countries). Edwards (1998) undertakes a robustness analysis using a wide range of trade-policy indicators, including some subjective indicators. Some of the other recent studies on the relationship between trade policy and growth will be discussed in the penultimate section of the paper.

Our bottom line is that the nature of the relationship between trade policy and economic growth remains very much an open question. The issue is far from having been settled on empirical grounds. We are in fact skeptical that there is a general, unambiguous relationship between trade openness and growth waiting to be discovered. We suspect that the relationship is a contingent one, dependent on a host of country and external characteristics. Research aimed at ascertaining the circumstances under which open trade policies are conducive to growth (as well as those under which they may not be) and at scrutinizing the channels through which trade policies influence economic performance is likely to prove more productive.

omy," citing Sachs and Warner (1995) and Dollar (1992). Husted and Melvin (1997) cite Ben-David (1993) in support of the FPE theorem (p. 111), and Sachs and Warner (1995) in support of the statement that "[o]nly a few countries have followed outward-oriented development strategies for extensive periods of time, but those that have done so have been very successful" (p. 287). Krugman and Obstfeld (1997, 260) write that by the late 1980s "[s]tatistical evidence appeared to suggest that developing countries that followed relatively free trade policies had on average grown more rapidly than those that followed protectionist policies (although this statistical evidence has been challenged by some economists)."

3. From its date of publication, Dollar's paper has been cited at least 92 times, according to the *Social Science Citations Index*. Sachs and Warner (1995) is a close second, with 81 citations. Edwards (1992), Ben-David (1993), and Lee (1993) round off the list, with 57, 38, and 17 citations, respectively.

Finally, it is worthwhile reminding the reader that growth and welfare are not the same thing. Trade policies can have positive effects on welfare without affecting the rate of economic growth. Conversely, even if policies that restrict international trade were to reduce economic growth, it does not follow that they would necessarily reduce the level of welfare. Negative coefficients on policy variables in growth regressions are commonly interpreted as indicating that the policies in question are normatively undesirable. Strictly speaking, such inferences are invalid.[4] Our paper centers on the relationship between trade policy and growth because this is the issue that has received the most attention in the existing literature. We caution the reader that the welfare implications of empirical results regarding this link (be they positive or negative) must be treated with caution.

The outline of this paper is as follows. We begin with a conceptual overview of the issues relating to openness and growth. We then turn to an in-depth examination of each of the four papers mentioned previously (Dollar, 1992; Sachs and Warner, 1995; Edwards, 1998; and Ben-David 1993), followed by a section on Frankel and Romer (1999). The penultimate section discusses briefly three other papers (Lee, 1993; Harrison, 1996; and Wacziarg 1998). We offer some final thoughts in the concluding section.

## 2. *Conceptual Issues*

Think of a small economy that takes world prices of tradable goods as given. What is the relationship between trade restrictions and real GDP in such an economy? The modern theory of trade policy as it applies to such a country can be summarized in the following three propositions:

1. In static models with no market imperfections and other pre-existing distortions, the effect of a trade restriction is to reduce the level of real GDP at world prices. In the presence of market failures such as externalities, trade restrictions *may* increase real GDP (although they are hardly ever the first-best means of doing so).
2. In standard models with exogenous technological change and diminishing returns to reproducible factors of production (e.g., the neo-

4. Some of the main problems with economic growth as a measure of welfare are that: (1) the empirically identifiable effect of policies on rates of growth—especially over short intervals—could be different from their effect on levels of income; (2) levels of per capita income may not be good indicators of welfare because they do not capture the distribution of income or the level of access to primary goods and basic capabilities; and (3) high growth rates could be associated with suboptimally low levels of present consumption.

classical model of growth), a trade restriction has no effect on the long-run (steady-state) rate of growth of output.[5] This is true regardless of the existence of market imperfections. However, there may be growth effects during the transition to the steady state. (These transitional effects may be positive or negative, depending on how the long-run level of output is affected by the trade restriction.)

3. In models of endogenous growth generated by nondiminishing returns to reproducible factors of production or by learning-by-doing and other forms of endogenous technological change, the presumption is that lower trade restrictions boost output growth in the world economy as a whole. But a subset of countries may experience diminished growth, depending on their initial factor endowments and levels of technological development.

Taken together, these points imply that there should be no theoretical presumption in favor of finding an unambiguous, negative relationship between trade barriers and growth rates in the types of cross-national data sets typically analyzed.[6] The main complications are twofold. First, in the presence of certain market failures, such as positive production externalities in import-competing sectors, the long-run levels of GDP (measured at world prices) can be higher with trade restrictions than without. In such cases, data sets covering relatively short time spans will reveal a positive (partial) association between trade restrictions and the growth of output along the path of convergence to the new steady state. Second, under conditions of endogenous growth, trade restrictions may also be associated with higher growth rates of output whenever the restrictions promote technologically more dynamic sectors over others. In dynamic models, moreover, an increase in the growth rate of output is neither a necessary nor a sufficient condition for an improvement in *welfare.*

Since endogenous-growth models are often thought to have provided the missing theoretical link between trade openness and long-run growth, it is useful to spend a moment on why such models in fact provide an ambiguous answer. As emphasized by Grossman and Helpman (1991), the general answer to the question "Does trade promote

5. Strictly speaking, this statement is true only when the marginal product of the reproducible factors ("capital") tends to zero in the limit. If this marginal product is bounded below by a sufficiently large positive constant, trade policies can have an effect on long-run growth rates, similar to their effect in the more recent endogenous growth models (point 3 below). See the discussion in Srinivasan (1997).
6. See Buffie (1998) for an extensive theoretical discussion of the issues from the perspective of developing countries.

innovation in a small open economy?" is "It depends."[7] In particular, the answer depends on whether the forces of comparative advantage push the economy's resources in the direction of activities that generate long-run growth (via externalities in research and development, expanding product variety, upgrading product quality, and so on) or divert them from such activities. Grossman and Helpman (1991), Feenstra (1990), Matsuyama (1992), and others have worked out examples where a country that is behind in technological development can be driven by trade to specialize in traditional goods and experience a reduction in its long-run rate of growth. Such models are in fact formalizations of some very old arguments about infant industries and about the need for temporary protection to catch up with more advanced countries.

The issues can be clarified with the help of a simple model of a small open economy with learning-by-doing. The model is a simplified version of that in Matsuyama (1992), except that we analyze the growth implications of varying the import tariff, rather than simply comparing free trade with autarky. The economy is assumed to have two sectors, agriculture ($a$) and manufacturing ($m$), with the latter subject to learning-by-doing that is external to individual firms in the sector but internal to manufacturing as a whole. Let labor be the only mobile factor between the two sectors, and normalize the economy's labor endowment to unity. We can then write the production functions of the manufacturing and agricultural sectors, respectively, as

$$X_t^m = M_t n_t^{\alpha},$$
$$X_t^a = A(1 - n_t)^{\alpha},$$

where $n_t$ stands for the labor force in manufacturing, $\alpha$ is the share of labor in value added in the two sectors (assumed to be identical for simplicity), and $t$ is a time subscript. The productivity coefficient in manufacturing, $M_t$, is a state variable evolving according to

$$\dot{M}_t = \delta X_t^m,$$

where an overdot represents a time derivative and $\delta$ captures the strength of the learning effect.

We assume the economy has an initial comparative disadvantage in manufacturing, and normalize the relative price of manufactures on world markets to unity. If the ad valorem import tariff on manufactures is $\tau$, the domestic relative price of manufactured goods becomes $1 + \tau$.

7. This is a slight paraphrase of Grossman and Helpman (1991, p. 152).

Instantaneous equilibrium in the labor market requires the equality of value marginal products of labor in the two sectors:

$$A(1 - n_t)^{\alpha-1} = (1 + \tau)M_t n_t^{\alpha-1}.$$

It can be checked that an increase in the import tariff has the effect of allocating more of the economy's labor to the manufacturing sector:

$$\frac{dn_t}{d\tau} > 0.$$

Further, for a constant level of $\tau$, $n_t$ evolves according to

$$\hat{n}_t = \frac{\delta}{1 - \alpha}(1 - n_t)n_t^{\alpha},$$

where ^ denotes proportional changes.

Let $Y_t$ denote the value of output in the economy evaluated at world prices:

$$Y_t = M_t n_t^{\alpha} + A(1 - n_t)^{\alpha}.$$

Then the instantaneous rate of growth of output at world prices can be expressed as follows:

$$\hat{Y}_t = \delta\left(\lambda_t + \frac{\alpha}{1 - \alpha}(\lambda_t - n_t)\right)n_t^{\alpha},$$

where $\lambda_t$ is the share of manufacturing output in total output when both are expressed at world prices (i.e., $\lambda_t = X_t^m/Y_t$).

Consider first the case when $\tau = 0$. In this case, it can be checked that $\lambda_t = n_t$ and the expression for the instantaneous growth rate of output simplifies to $\hat{Y}_t = \delta\lambda_t n_t^{\alpha}$, which is strictly positive whenever $n_t > 0$. Growth arises from the dynamic effects of learning, and is faster the larger the manufacturing base $n_t$. A small tariff would have a positive effect on growth on account of this channel because it would enlarge the manufacturing sector (raise $n_t$).

When $\tau > 0$, the manufacturing share of output at world prices is less than the labor share in manufacturing, and $\lambda_t < n_t$. Now the second term in the expression for $\hat{Y}_t$ is negative. The intuition is as follows. The tariff imposes a production-side distortion in the allocation of the economy's resources. For any given gap between $\lambda_t$ and $n_t$, the productive efficiency cost of this distortion rises as manufacturing output (the base of the distortion) gets larger.

Figure 2 GROWTH RATES OF GDP AT WORLD PRICES

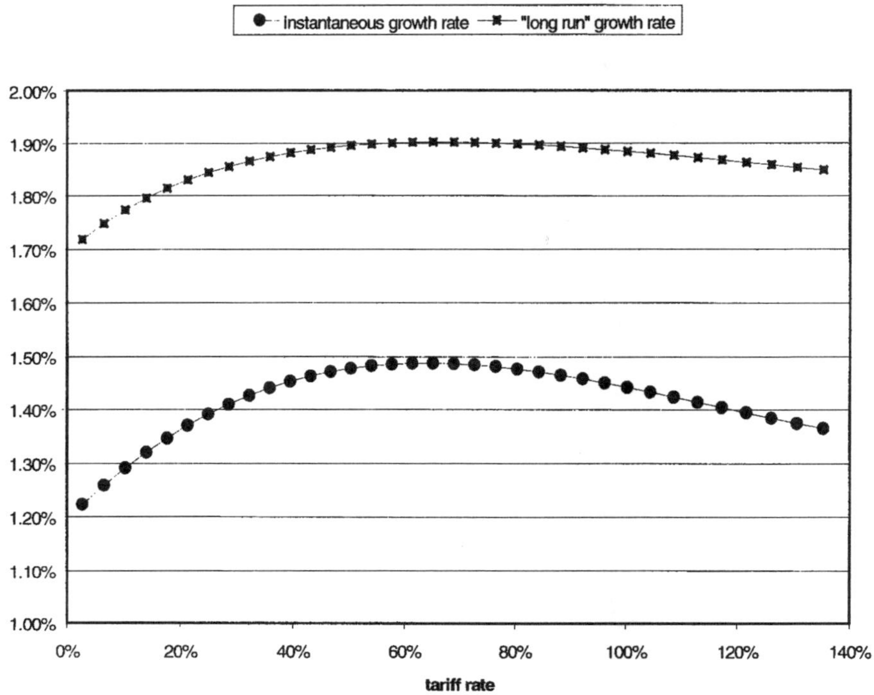


Hence the tariff exerts two contradictory effects on growth. By pulling resources into the manufacturing sector, it enlarges the scope for dynamic scale benefits, thereby increasing growth. But it also imposes a static efficiency loss, the cost of which rises over time as the manufacturing sector becomes larger.[8] Figure 2 shows the relationship between the tariff and the rate of growth of output (at world prices) for a particular parameterization of this model. Two curves are shown, one for the instantaneous rate of growth (based on the expression above), and the other for the average growth rate over a twenty-year horizon [calculated as $\frac{1}{20}(\ln Y_{20} - \ln Y_0)$]. In both cases, growth increases in $\tau$ until a critical level, and then diminishes in $\tau$. This pattern is, however, by no means

8. We emphasize once again that these results on the growth of *output* do not translate directly into welfare consequences. In this particular model, the *level* effect of a tariff distortion also has to be taken into account before a judgment on welfare can be passed. Hence it is possible for welfare to be reduced (raised) even though the growth rate of output is permanently higher (lower).

general, and other types of results can be obtained under different parameterizations.

The model clarifies a number of issues. First, it shows that it is relatively straightforward to write a well-specified model that generates the conclusions that many opponents of trade openness have espoused—namely, that free trade can be detrimental to some countries' economic prospects, especially when these countries are lagging in technological development and have an initial comparative advantage in "nondynamic" sectors. More broadly, the model illustrates that there is no determinate theoretical link between trade protection and growth once real-world phenomena such as learning, technological change, and market imperfections (here captured by a learning-by-doing externality) are taken into account. Third, it highlights the exact sense in which trade restrictions distort market outcomes. A trade barrier has resource-allocation effects because it alters a *domestic* price ratio: it raises the domestic price of import-competing activities relative to the domestic price of exportables, and hence introduces a wedge between the domestic relative-price ratio and the opportunity costs reflected in relative border prices.[9] While this point is obvious, it bears repeating, as some of the empirical work reviewed below interprets openness in a very different manner.

## 3. *David Dollar (1992)*

As mentioned previously, the paper by Dollar (1992) is one of the most heavily cited studies on the relationship between openness and growth. The principal contribution of Dollar's paper lies in the construction of two separate indices, which Dollar demonstrates are each negatively correlated with growth over the 1976–1985 period in a sample of 95 developing countries. The two indices are an "index of real exchange-rate distortion" and an "index of real exchange-rate variability" (henceforth DISTORTION and VARIABILITY). These indices relate to "outward orientation," as understood by Dollar (1992, p. 524), in the following way:

> Outward orientation generally means a combination of two factors: first, the level of protection, especially for inputs into the production process, is

9. Some authors have stressed the effects that the high levels of discretion associated with trade policies can have on rent seeking and thus on economic performance (Krueger, 1974; Bhagwati, 1982). These effects go beyond the direct impact on resource allocation that we discuss. They are however related more directly to the discretionary nature of policies than to their effect on the economy's openness. Discretionary export promotion policies—which will make an economy more open—should in principle be just as conducive to rent seeking as protectionist policies.

relatively low (resulting in a sustainable level of the real exchange rate that is favorable to exporters); and second, there is relatively little variability in the real exchange rate, so that incentives are consistent over time.

We shall argue that DISTORTION has serious conceptual flaws as a measure of trade restrictions, and is in any case not a robust correlate of growth, while VARIABILITY, which appears to be robust, is a measure of instability more than anything else.

In order to implement his approach, Dollar uses data from Summers and Heston (1988, Mark 4.0) on comparative price levels. Their work compares prices of an identical basket of consumption goods across countries. Hence, letting the United States be the benchmark country, these data provide estimates of each country $i$'s price level ($RPL_i$) relative to the United States: $RPL_i = 100 \times P_i/(e_i P_{US})$, where $P_i$ and $P_{US}$ are the respective consumption price indices, and $e_i$ is the nominal exchange rate of country $i$ against the U.S. dollar (in units of home currency per dollar).[10] Since Dollar is interested in the prices of tradable goods only, he attempts to purge the effect of systematic differences arising from the presence of nontradables. To do this, he regresses $RPL_i$ on the level and square of GDP per capita and on regional dummies for Latin America and Africa, as well as year dummies. Let the predicted value from this regression be denoted $\widehat{RPL}_i$. Dollar's index DISTORTION is $RPL_i/\widehat{RPL}_i$, averaged over the ten-year period 1976–1985. VARIABILITY is in turn calculated by taking the coefficient of variation of the annual observations of $RPL_i/\widehat{RPL}_i$ for each country over the same period.

Dollar interprets the variation in the values of DISTORTION across countries as capturing cross-national differences in the restrictiveness of trade policy. He states: "the index derived here measures the extent to which the real exchange rate is distorted away from its free-trade level by the trade regime" and "a country sustaining a high price level over many years would clearly have to be a country with a relatively large amount of protection" (Dollar 1992, p. 524). Since this type of claim is often made in other work as well,[11] we shall spend some time on it before reviewing Dollar's empirical results. We will show that a comparison of price indices for tradables is informative about levels of trade protection only under very restrictive conditions that are unlikely to hold in practice.

10. Our notation differs from Dollar's (1992). In particular, the exchange rate is defined differently.

11. For example, in Bhalla and Lau (1992), whose index is also used in Harrison (1996). We will discuss Harrison's paper in the penultimate section.

### 3.1 TRADE POLICIES AND PRICE LEVELS

We will not discuss further Dollar's method for purging the component of nontradable-goods prices that is systematically related to income and other characteristics.[12] Assuming the method is successful, the DISTORTION measure approximates (up to a random error term) the price of a country's tradables relative to the United States. Letting $P^T$ stand for the price index for tradables and neglecting the error, the DISTORTION index for country $i$ can then be expressed as $P_i^T/(e_i P_{US}^T)$.

Let us, without loss of generality, fix the price level of tradables in the United States, $P_{US}^T$, and assume that free trade prevails there. The question is under what conditions trade restrictions will be associated with higher levels of $P_i^T/(e_i P_{US}^T)$. Obviously, the answer depends on the effect of the restrictions on $P_i^T$ (and possibly on $e_i$).

Note that $P_i^T$ is an aggregate price index derived from the domestic prices of two types of tradables: import-competing goods and exportables. Hence $P_i^T$ can be expressed as a linearly homogenous function of the form

$$P_i^T = \pi(p_i^m, p_i^x),$$

where $p_i^m$ and $p_i^x$ are the domestic prices of import-competing goods and exportables, respectively. Since Summers–Heston price levels are estimated for an identical basket of goods, the price-index function $\pi(\cdot)$ applies equally to the United States:

$$P_{US}^T = \pi(p_{US}^m, p_{US}^x).$$

Next, define $t_i^m$ and $t_i^x$ as the ad valorem equivalent of import restrictions and export restrictions, respectively. Assume that the law of one price holds (we shall relax this below). Then, $p_i^m = e_i p_{US}^m(1 + t_i^m)$ and $p_i^x = e_i p_{US}^x/(1 + t_i^x)$. Consequently, the domestic price of tradables relative to U.S. prices can be expressed as

$$\frac{P_i^T}{e_i P_{US}^T} = \frac{\pi(P_{US}^m(1+t_i^m;), p_{US}^x/1+t_i^x)}{\pi(p_{US}^m, p_{US}^x)} = \frac{(1+t_i^m)\pi\left(p_{US}^m, \dfrac{p_{US}^x}{(1+t_i^x)(1+t_i^m)}\right)}{\pi(p_{US}^m, p_{US}^x)},$$

12. For a good recent discussion of the problems that may arise on this account see Falvey and Gemell (1999).

where we have made use of the linear homogeneity of $\pi(\cdot)$. Note that the nominal exchange rate has dropped out thanks to the assumption of the law of one price.

Consider first the case where there are binding import restrictions, but no export restrictions ($t_i^m > 0$ and $t_i^x = 0$). In this instance, it is apparent that $P_i^T > e_i P_{US}^T$, and trade restrictions do indeed raise the domestic price of tradables (relative to the benchmark country). Judging from the quotations above, this is the case that Dollar seems to have in mind.

On the other hand, consider what happens when the country in question rescinds all import restrictions and imposes instead export restrictions at an ad valorem level that equals that of the import restrictions just lifted ($t_i^m = 0$ and $t_i^x > 0$). From the Lerner (1936) symmetry theorem, it is evident that the switch from import protection to export taxation has no resource-allocation and distributional effects for the economy whatsoever. The relative price between tradables, $p_i^m/p_i^x$, remains unaffected by the switch. Yet, because export restrictions reduce the domestic price of exportables *relative to world prices,* it is now the case that $P_i^T < e_i P_{US}^T$. The country will now appear, by Dollar's measure, to be outward-oriented.

One practical implication is that economies that combine import barriers with export taxes (such as many countries in sub-Saharan Africa) will be judged less protected than those that rely on import restrictions alone. Conversely, countries that dilute the protective effect of import restrictions by using export subsidies ($t_i^x < 0$) will appear more protected than countries that do not do so.

Hence the DISTORTION index is sensitive to the form in which trade restrictions are applied. This follows from the fact that trade policies work by altering relative price *within* an economy; they do not have unambiguous implications for the level of prices in a country relative to another. A necessary condition for Dollar's index to do a good job of ranking trade regimes according to restrictiveness is that export policies (whether they tax or promote exports) play a comparatively minor role. Moreover, as we show in the next section, this is not a sufficient condition.

### 3.2 HOW RELEVANT IS THE LAW OF ONE PRICE IN PRACTICE?

The discussion above was framed in terms that are the most favorable to Dollar's measure, in that we assumed the law of one price (LOP) holds. Under this maintained hypothesis, the prices of tradable goods produced in different countries can diverge from each other, when expressed in a common currency, only when there exist trade restrictions (or transport costs).

However, there is a vast array of evidence suggesting that LOP does not accurately describe the world we live in. In a recent review article,

Rogoff (1996, p. 648) writes of the "startling empirical failure of the law of one price." Rogoff concludes: "commodities where the deviations from the law of one price damp out very quickly are the exception rather than the rule" (Rogoff, 1996, p. 650). Further, the evidence suggests that deviations from LOP are systematically related to movements in nominal exchange rates (see references in Rogoff, 1996). Indeed, it is well known that (nominal) exchange-rate policies in many developing countries are responsible for producing large and sustained swings in *real* exchange rates. Trade barriers or transport costs typically play a much smaller role.

Dollar (1992, p. 525) acknowledges that "there might be short-term fluctuations [unrelated to trade barriers] if purchasing-power parity did not hold continuously," but considers that these fluctuations would average out over time. Rogoff (1996, p. 647) concludes in his survey that the speed of convergence to purchasing-power parity (PPP) is extremely slow, of the order of roughly 15% per year. At this speed of convergence, averages constructed over a time horizon of 10 years (the horizon used in Dollar's paper) would exhibit substantial divergence from PPP in the presence of nominal shocks.

Under this interpretation, a significant portion of the cross-national variation in price levels exhibited in DISTORTION would be due not to trade policies, but to monetary and exchange-rate policies. Unlike trade policies, nominal exchange-rate movements have an unambiguous effect on the domestic price level of traded goods relative to foreign prices when LOP fails: an appreciation raises the price of both import-competing and exportable goods relative to foreign prices, and a depreciation has the reverse effect. Countries where the nominal exchange rate was not allowed to depreciate in line with domestic inflation would exhibit an appreciation of the real exchange rate (a rise in domestic prices relative to foreign levels), and correspondingly would be rated high on the DISTORTION index. Countries with aggressive policies of devaluation (or low inflation relative to the trend depreciation of their nominal exchange rate) would receive low DISTORTION ratings.

Transport costs provide another reason why DISTORTION may be unrelated to trade policies, especially in a large cross-section of countries. Dollar's index would be influenced by geographic variables such as access to sea routes and distance to world markets, even when LOP—appropriately modified to allow for transport costs—holds. Hence in practice DISTORTION is likely to capture the effects of geography as well as of exchange-rate policies. Indeed, when we regress Dollar's DISTORTION index on the black-market premium (a measure of exchange-rate policy), a set of continent dummies, and two trade-related geo-

Table 1 EFFECT OF GEOGRAPHICAL AND EXCHANGE-RATE POLICY VARIABLES ON DOLLAR'S DISTORTION INDEX

| *Variable* | *(1)* | *(2)* |
|---|---|---|
| bmpav | 0.07*** | 0.083** |
| | (1.971) | (2.47) |
| rcoast | −0.045* | −0.053* |
| | (−3.321) | (−3.032) |
| tropics | 0.209*** | 0.145 |
| | (1.829) | (1.004) |
| Latin America | 0.012 | −0.037 |
| | (0.097) | (−0.257) |
| SSA | 0.451* | 0.46** |
| | (3.319) | (2.43) |
| East Asia | −0.12 | −0.145 |
| | (−0.921) | (−0.889) |
| TAR | | −0.017 |
| | | (−0.08) |
| NTB | | −0.276*** |
| | | (−1.851) |
| $R^2$ | 0.52 | 0.58 |
| *N* | 89 | 71 |

Heteroskedasticity-corrected *t*-statistics in parentheses. See appendix for variable definitions. Regressions include a constant term and cover only developing countries. Levels of statistical significance indicated by asterisks: * 99%; ** 95%, *** 90%.

graphic variables (the coastal length over total land area and a dummy for tropical countries), we find that these explain more than 50% of the variation in Dollar's distortion index. Furthermore, two trade-policy variables (tariffs and quotas) enter with the wrong sign (Table 1)!

To summarize, DISTORTION is theoretically appropriate as a measure of trade restrictions when three conditions hold: (1) there are no export taxes or subsidies in use, (2) LOP holds continuously, and (3) there are no systematic differences in national price levels due to transport costs and other geographic factors. Obviously, all of these requirements are counterfactual. Whether one believes that DISTORTION still provides useful empirical information on trade regimes depends on one's priors regarding the practical significance of the three limitations expressed above.[13] Our view is that the second and third of these—the departure from LOP and the effect of geography—are particularly important in practice. We regard it as likely that it is the variation in nominal exchange-rate policies and geography, and not the variation in trade restrictions, that drives the cross-sectional variation of DISTORTION.

### 3.3 WHY VARIABILITY?

As mentioned previously, Dollar (1992) uses his measure of distortion in conjunction with a measure of variability, the latter being the coefficient of variation of DISTORTION measured on an annual basis. He is driven to do this because the country rankings using DISTORTION produce some "anomalies." For example, "Korea and Taiwan have the highest distortion measures of the Asian developing economies" and "the rankings within the developed country groups are not very plausible" (Dollar, 1992, pp. 530–531). The ten least-distorted countries by this measure include not only Hong Kong, Thailand, and Malta, but also Sri Lanka, Bangladesh, Mexico, South Africa, Nepal, Pakistan, and Syria! Burma's rating (90) equals that of the United States. Taiwan (116) is judged more distorted than Argentina (113). Our discussion above indicated that DISTORTION is highly sensitive to the form in which trade policies are applied and to exchange-rate policies as well as omitted geographic characteristics. So such results are not entirely surprising.

Dollar states that the "number of anomalies declines substantially if the real exchange rate distortion measure is combined with real exchange rate variability to produce an outward orientation index" (Dollar, 1992, p. 531). He thus produces a country ranking based on a weighted average of the DISTORTION and VARIABILITY indices. Since these two indices are entered separately in his growth regressions, we shall not discuss this combined index of "outward orientation" further.

However, we do wish to emphasize the obvious point that the VARIABILITY index has little to do with trade restrictions, as commonly understood, or with inward or outward orientation per se. What does VARIABILITY really measure? The ten countries with the highest VARIABILITY scores are Iraq, Uganda, Bolivia, El Salvador, Nicaragua, Guyana, Somalia, Nigeria, Ghana, and Guatemala. For the most part, these are countries that have experienced very high inflation rates and/or se-

13. The sensitivity of Dollar's index to these assumptions highlights a generic difficulty with regression-based indices which use the residual from a regression to proxy for an excluded variable: such indices capture variations in the excluded variable accurately only as long as the model is correctly and fully specified. If some variables are excluded from the estimated equation, they will form part of the index.

vere political disturbances during 1976–1985. It is plausible that VARIABILITY measures economic instability at large. In any case, it is unclear to us why we should think of it as an indicator of trade orientation.

### 3.4 EMPIRICAL RESULTS

The first column of Table 2 shows our replication of the core Dollar (1992) result for 95 developing countries. Dollar's benchmark specification includes on the right-hand side the investment rate (as a share of GDP, averaged over 1976–1985) in addition to DISTORTION and VARIABILITY. As shown in column (1), DISTORTION and VARIABILITY both enter with negative and highly significant coefficients using this specification. [Our results are virtually identical to those in Dollar (1992), with the

Table 2 REPLICATION AND EXTENSION OF DOLLAR'S (1992) RESULTS

| | (1) | (2) | (3) | (4) | (5) |
|---|---|---|---|---|---|
| DISTORTION | −0.018* | −0.008 | −0.003 | −0.004 | −0.008 |
| | (−3.128) | (−1.009) | (−0.406) | (−0.514) | (−0.899) |
| VARIABILITY | −0.080* | −0.080** | −0.103* | −0.107* | −0.099* |
| | (−2.64) | (−2.084) | (−3.3) | (−3.51) | (−3.212) |
| Investment/GDP | 0.137* | 0.100** | | | |
| | (3.515) | (2.278) | | | |
| Latin America | | −0.015** | −0.016* | −0.014** | −0.019* |
| | | (−2.34) | (−2.65) | (−2.362) | (−3.337) |
| East Asia | | 0.007 | 0.010 | 0.011 | 0.004 |
| | | (0.747) | (0.937) | (0.976) | (0.382) |
| SSA | | −0.018** | −0.026* | −0.029* | −0.028* |
| | | (−2.419) | (−3.824) | (−4.129) | (−3.411) |
| Log initial income | | | | −0.004 | −0.011** |
| | | | | (−1.097) | (−2.182) |
| Schooling, 1975 | | | | | 0.005** |
| | | | | | (2.531) |
| $N$ | 95 | 95 | 95 | 95 | 80 |
| $R^2$ | 0.38 | 0.45 | 0.40 | 0.41 | 0.49 |

Dependent variable: growth of real GDP per capita, 1976–1985. Heteroskedasticity-corrected $t$ statistics in parentheses. Regressions include a constant term and cover only developing countries. Levels of statistical significance indicated by asterisks: * 99%; ** 95%; *** 90%.

difference that our *t*-statistics are based on heteroskedasticity-corrected standard errors.]

None of Dollar's runs include standard regressors such as initial income, education, and regional dummies. The other columns of Table 2 show the results as we alter Dollar's specification to make it more compatible with recent cross-national work on growth (e.g., Barro, 1997). First, we add regional dummies for Latin America, East Asia, and sub-Saharan Africa to ensure that the results are not due to omitted factors correlated with geographical location (column 2). Next we drop the investment rate (column 3), and add in succession initial income (column 4) and initial schooling (column 5).[14] The dummies for Latin America and sub-Saharan Africa are negative and statistically significant. Initial income and education also enter significantly, with the expected signs (negative and positive, respectively).

We find that the VARIABILITY index is robust to these changes, but that DISTORTION is not. In fact, as soon as we introduce regional dummies in the regression, the estimated coefficient on DISTORTION comes down sizably and becomes insignificant. Whatever DISTORTION may be measuring, this raises the possibility that the results with this index are spurious, arising from the index's correlation with (omitted) regional effects.

Dollar's original results were based on data from Mark 4.0 of the Summers–Heston database (Summers and Heston, 1988). We have recalculated Dollar's DISTORTION and VARIABILITY indices using the more recent version (Mark 5.6) of the Summers–Heston data, confining ourselves to the same period examined by Dollar (1976–1985). The revised data allow us to generate these indices for 112 developing countries. We have also rerun the regressions for cross sections over different periods, as well as in panel form with fixed effects. We do not report these results here, for reasons of space (see the working-paper version of this paper, Rodríguez and Rodrik, 1999). The bottom line that emerges is similar to the conclusion just stated: the estimated coefficient on VARIABILITY is generally robust to alterations in specifications; the coefficient on DISTORTION is not.

## 4. *Jeffrey Sachs and Andrew Warner (1995)*

We turn next to the paper "Economic reform and the process of global integration" by Jeffrey Sachs and Andrew Warner (1995). This extremely

14. The income variable comes from the Summers–Heston (Mark 4.0) data set used in Dollar (1992). Schooling is from Barro and Lee (1994).

influential paper[15] is an ambitious attempt to solve the measurement-error problem in the literature by constructing an index of openness that combines information about several aspects of trade policy. The Sachs–Warner (SW) openness indicator (OPEN) is a zero–one dummy, which takes the value 0 if the economy was closed according to *any* one of the following criteria:

1. it had average tariff rates higher than 40% (TAR);
2. its nontariff barriers covered on average more than 40% of imports (NTB);
3. it had a socialist economic system (SOC);
4. it had a state monopoly of major exports (MON);
5. its black-market premium exceeded 20% during either the decade of the 1970s or the decade of the 1980s (BMP).[16]

The rationale for combining these indicators into a single dichotomous variable is that they represent different ways in which policymakers can close their economy to international trade. Tariffs set at 50% have exactly the same resource-allocation implications as quotas at a level that raised domestic market prices for importables by 50%. To gauge the effect of openness on growth, it is necessary to use a variable that classifies as closed those countries that were able to effectively restrict their economies' integration into world markets through the use of different combinations of policies that would achieve that result. Furthermore, if these openness indicators are correlated among themselves, introducing them separately in a regression may not yield reliable estimates, due to their possibly high level of collinearity.

The SW dummy has a high and robust coefficient when inserted in growth regressions. The point estimate of its effect on growth (in the original benchmark specification) is 2.44 percentage points[17]: economies that pass all five requirements experience on average economic growth two and a half percentage points higher than those that do not. The $t$-statistic is 5.50 (5.83 if estimated using robust standard errors). This coefficient appears to be highly robust to changes in the list of controls: in a recent paper which subjects 58 potential determinants of growth to

15. A partial listing of papers that have made use of the Sachs–Warner index includes Hall and Jones (1998), Wacziarg (1998), Sala-i-Martin (1997), Burnside and Dollar (1997), and Collins and Bosworth (1996).
16. Sachs and Warner use data from the following sources: Lee (1993) for nontariff barriers, Barro and Lee (1993) for tariffs, World Bank (1994) for state monopoly of exports, Kornai (1992) for the classification of socialist and nonsocial countries, and International Currency Analysis (various years) for black-market premia.
17. In the long run, such an economy would converge to a level of per capita GDP 2.97 times as high as if it had remained closed.

an exhaustive sensitivity analysis, the average *p*-value for the SW index is less than 0.1%.[18]

In this section we ask several questions about Sachs and Warner's results. First, we ask which, if any, of the individual components of the index are responsible for the strength of the SW dummy. We find that the SW dummy's strength derives mainly from the combination of the black-market premium (BMP) and the state-monopoly-of-exports (MON) variables. Very little of the dummy's statistical power would be lost if it were constructed using only these two indicators. In particular, there is little action in the two variables that are the most direct measures of trade policy: tariff and nontariff barriers (TAR and NTB).

We then ask to what extent the black-market premium and state-monopoly variables are measures of trade policy. We suggest that their significance in explaining growth can be traced to their correlation with other determinants of growth: macroeconomic problems in the case of the black-market premium, and location in sub-Saharan Africa in the case of the state-monopoly variable. We conclude that the SW indicator serves as a proxy for a wide range of policy and institutional differences, and that it yields an upward-biased estimate of the effects of trade restrictions proper.

### 4.1 WHICH INDIVIDUAL VARIABLES ACCOUNT FOR THE SIGNIFICANCE OF THE SW DUMMY?

We start by contrasting Sachs and Warner's result with the results of controlling separately for individual components of their index. Column 1 of Table 3 reproduces their baseline regression, and column 2 shows what happens when each of the components of the SW index is inserted separately into the same specification.[19] The variables BMP and MON are highly significant, whereas the rest are not. An *F*-test for the joint significance of the other three components (SOC, TAR, and NTB) yields a *p*-value of 0.25.

18. Sala-i-Martin (1997). The variable used by Sala-i-Martin is the number of years an economy was open according to the SW criteria, whereas here we follow Sachs and Warner's (1995) original article and use a dummy which captures whether or not the economy was open during 1970–1989.

19. We use the same set of controls used by Sachs and Warner. These are log of GDP n 1970, secondary schooling in 1970, primary schooling in 1970, government consumption as a percentage of GDP, number of revolutions and coups per year, number of assassinations per million population, relative price of investment goods, and ratio of investment to GDP. However, our results are highly robust to changes in the list of controls. For example, the simple correlations of TAR, NTB, and SOC with growth are, respectively, −.048, −.083 and −.148. Our result is also not due to multicollinearity: the $R^2$'s from regressions of any one of SOC, NTB, and TAR on the other two are, respectively, 0.02, 0.05, and 0.05.

Table 3 EFFECT OF DIFFERENT OPENNESS INDICATORS ON GROWTH

| | (1) | (2) | (3) | (4) | (5) | (6) | (7) |
|---|---|---|---|---|---|---|---|
| OPEN | 2.44* (5.83) | | | | | | |
| BMP | | −1.701* (−3.65) | | | | | |
| MON | | −2.020* (−2.84) | | | | | |
| SOC | | −1.272 (−1.39) | | | | | |
| NTB | | −0.453 (−0.81) | | | | | |
| TAR | | −0.134 (−0.18) | | | | | |
| BM | | | 2.086* (4.82) | | 2.119* (5.09) | 2.519* (5.94) | 2.063* (4.64) |
| SQT | | | | 0.877*** (1.82) | 0.735 (1.59) | 0.663 (1.30) | |
| SOC | | | | | | | .389 (.56) |
| QT | | | | | | | .657 (1.28) |
| $R^2$ | 0.593 | 0.637 | 0.522 | 0.455 | 0.617 | 0.522 | 0.619 |
| *N* | 79 | 71 | 78 | 75 | 74 | 74 | 74 |

Dependent variable: growth of GDP per capita, 1970–1989. All equations except that for column 6 include the following controls: log of GDP in 1970, investment rate in 1970, government consumption/GDP, assassinations per capita, deviation from world investment prices, secondary-schooling ratio, primary-schooling ratio, revolutions and coups, and a constant term. Column 6 drops the investment rate and deviation from world investment prices. Numbers in parentheses are *t*-statistics based on Huber–White heteroskedasticity-consistent standard errors.

To check whether it is mainly the combination of BMP and MON that drives the Sachs and Warner's result, we ask the following question: suppose that we had built a dummy variable, in the spirit of Sachs and Warner, which classified an economy as closed only if it was closed according to BMP and MON. That is, suppose we ignored the information the other three variables give us as to the economy's openness.

How significant would the coefficient of our variable be in a growth regression? How different would the partition between open and closed economies that it generates be from that generated by the SW dummy? Suppose alternatively that we also constructed an openness dummy based only on the information contained in SOC, NTB, and TAR. How significant would that variable be in a growth regression? And how correlated would it be with the SW index?

Columns (3)–(6) of Table 3 address the question of significance. We denote by BM a variable that takes the value 1 when the economy is open according to criteria 4 and 5 above, whereas SQT equals 1 when the economy passes criteria 1, 2, and 3. We substitute these variables for the SW openness index in the regression Sachs and Warner present in their paper. Entered on its own, BM is highly significant, with an estimated coefficient that is very close to that on OPEN (2.09 vs. 2.44; see column 3). When SQT is substituted for BM, the estimated coefficient on SQT is much smaller (0.88) and significant only at the 90% level (column 4). We next enter BM and SQT simultaneously: the coefficient of SQT now has a $t$-statistic of 1.59, whereas the coefficient on BM retains a $t$-statistic of 5.09 and a point estimate (2.12) close to that on the openness variable in the original equation (column 5). Once the investment rate and investment prices, which are likely to be endogenous, are taken out of the equation, the $t$-statistic on SQT drops to 1.30 and that on BM rises to 5.94 (column 6).

The comparability of the results in Table 3 is hampered by the fact that the sample size changes as we move from one column to the next. This is because not all of the 79 countries in the sample have data for each of the individual SW components. To check whether this introduces any difficulties for our interpretation, we have also run these regressions holding the sample size fixed. We restricted the sample to those countries which have the requisite data for all the components, using both the original specification ($n = 71$) and a specification where we drop two of the SW regressors with $t$-statistics below unity (primary schooling, and revolutions and coups) to gain additional observations ($n = 74$). In both cases, our results were similar to those reported above: Regardless of whether BM and SQT are entered separately or jointly, the coefficient on BM is highly significant (with a point estimate that is statistically indistinguishable from that on OPEN) while the coefficient on SQT is insignificant.[20]

Hence, once BM is included, there is little additional predictive power

20. The largest $t$-statistic we obtained for SQT in these runs is 1.4. These results are not shown, to save space, but are available on request.

coming from regime type (socialist or not), level of tariffs, or coverage of nontariff barriers.[21] The strength of the SW index derives from the low growth performance of countries with either high black-market premia or state export monopolies (as classified by Sachs and Warner).[22]

The reason why BM performs so much better than SQT is that BM generates a partition between closed and open economies that is much closer to that generated by OPEN than the partition generated by SQT. Only six economies are classified differently by BM and by OPEN, while OPEN and SQT disagree in 31 cases. The disagreement between OPEN and SQT is concentrated in 15 African and 12 Latin American economies which SQT fails to qualify as closed but BM (and therefore OPEN) does: the African economies are found to be closed because of their state monopolies of exports, and those of Latin America because of their high black-market premia. The average rate of growth of these economies is 0.24, much lower than the sample average of 1.44.[23]

In view of the overwhelming contribution of the black-market premium and the dummy for state monopoly of exports to the statistical performance of the SW openness index, it is logical to ask what exactly it is that these two variables are capturing. To what extent are they indicators of trade policy? Could they be correlated with other variables that have a detrimental effect on growth, therefore not giving us much useful information on trade openness per se? We turn now to these questions, first with an analysis of the state-monopoly-of-exports variable, and then with a discussion of the black-market premium variable.

21. A different form in which the "horse race" can be run, suggested to us by Jeffrey Sachs, is to introduce OPEN and BM together in the regression, to see if OPEN clearly "wins." When we do this, we find that the point estimate of the coefficient on OPEN is generally larger than that on BM, but that the two coefficients are statistically indistinguishable from each other, because OPEN and BM are highly collinear with each other (as we discuss further below). On the other hand, when OPEN and SQT are entered together, SQT has the wrong (negative) sign and the equality of coefficients can easily be rejected.

22. Harrison and Hanson (1999) have studied the SW dummy and reach a similar conclusion, namely that the effect of trade-policy indicators (tariffs and quotas) on the strength of the SW dummy is small and not significant. The key difference between our work and Harrison and Hanson's is that they introduce the subcomponents of the SW index separately in their regression whereas we construct the subindexes described in the text.

23. Our result is not due to an arbitrary distinction between BM and SQT. SQT performs more poorly than any other openness index constructed on the basis of three of the five indicators used by Sachs and Warner, and BM performs more strongly than any index constructed with two of these five indicators. A similar result applies to partitions along other dimensions: those constructed using four indicators which exclude either BMP or MON do more poorly than any of those which include them; and either BMP or MON individually does better than any of the other indicators. Details of these exercises can be found in the working-paper version of our paper (Rodríguez and Rodrik, 1999).

### 4.2 WHAT DOES THE STATE-MONOPOLY-OF-EXPORTS VARIABLE REPRESENT?

Sachs and Warner's rationale for using an indicator of the existence of a state monopoly on major exports is the well-known equivalence between import and export taxes (Lerner, 1936). The variable MON is meant to capture cases in which governments taxed major exports and therefore reduced the level of trade (exports *and* imports). Sachs and Warner use an index of the degree of distortion caused by export marketing boards, taken from the World Bank study *Adjustment in Africa: Reforms, Results, and the Road Ahead* (World Bank, 1994).[24]

We note that the World bank study covers only 29 African economies that were under structural adjustment programs from 1987 to 1991. This results in a double selection bias. First, non-African economies with restrictive policies towards exports automatically escape scrutiny. Second, African economies with restrictive export policies but not undergoing adjustment programs in the late 1980s are also overlooked. Since Africa was the slowest-growing region during the period covered, and since economies that need to carry out structural adjustment programs are likely to be doing worse than those that do not, the effect is to bias the coefficient on openness upwards on both accounts.

How this selection bias affects the country classification can be illustrated by two examples: Indonesia and Mauritius. Both of these economies are rated as open in Sachs and Warner's sample. Both are excluded from the sample used to construct the state-monopoly-on-exports variable: Indonesia because it is not in Africa, and Mauritius because it was doing well and was not undergoing a World Bank adjustment program during the period covered by the World Bank study. Yet both of these economies would seem to satisfy the conditions necessary to be rated as closed according to the export-monopoly criterion: Indonesian law restricts oil and gas production to the state oil company, Pertamina; and Mauritius sells all of its export sugar production through the Mauritius Sugar Syndicate.[25] Indonesia and Mauritius are also among the ten fastest-growing economies in Sachs and Warner's sample.

24. Sachs and Warner (1995) cite a different source in their paper, but World Bank (1994) appears to be the correct source.

25. See Pertamina (1998) for Indonesia, and Gulhati and Nallari (1990, p. 22) as well as World Bank (1989, p. 6) for Mauritius. Oil represented 61.2% of Indonesian exports and sugar represented between 60–80% of Mauritius exports during the period covered by Sachs and Warner's study (see World Bank, 1983, Table E, and 1998). Although manufactures have recently outstripped sugar as Mauritius's main export, this is a recent development: in 1980 sugar represented 65% of Mauritius's total exports, and agriculture was surpassed by manufacturing as the main source of exports only in 1986 (World Bank, 1998).

One of the problems that this selection bias causes in Sachs and Warner's estimation is that it makes the variable MON virtually indistinguishable from a sub-Saharan Africa dummy.[26] There are 13 African countries (out of 47) in Sachs and Warner's study that are not rated as closed according to MON. (Twelve of these were not included in World Bank study.) But for all but one of these observations MON adds no additional information, either because they are dropped from the sample due to unavailability of other data or because they are rated as closed by other trade-policy indicators used to construct the index. The result is that the only difference between having used an export-marketing-board variable to construct the SW index and having used a sub-Saharan Africa dummy is a single observation. That observation is Mauritius, the fastest-growing African economy in the sample.[27]

We conclude that the export-marketing-board variable, as implemented, is not a good measure of trade policy and creates a serious bias in the estimation. Except for Mauritius, whose classification as open seems to us to be due exclusively to selection bias, the inclusion of MON in the SW dummy is indistinguishable from the use of a sub-Saharan Africa dummy. In that respect, the only information that we can extract from it is that African economies grew more slowly than the rest of the world during the seventies and eighties.

### 4.3 WHAT DOES THE BLACK-MARKET PREMIUM VARIABLE MEASURE?

The second source of strength in the SW openness variable is the black-market premium. Indeed, the simple correlation between the openness dummy and BMP is 0.63. A regression of growth on the black-market premium dummy and all the other controls gives a coefficient of $-1.05$ with a $t$-statistic of nearly 2.5 in absolute value. How good an indicator of openness is the black-market premium?

The black-market premium measures the extent of rationing in the market for foreign currency. The theoretical argument for using the black-market premium in this context is that, under certain conditions, foreign exchange restrictions act as a trade barrier. Using our notation from the previous section (but omitting country subscripts), the domes-

26. This is true despite the fact that the SW dummy's coefficient is still significant after the estimation is carried out controlling for a sub-Saharan Africa dummy. The reason is that the SW dummy still has substantial explanatory power left due to its use of the black-market premium variable.

27. Both Lesotho and Botswana had higher growth rates than Mauritius, but Lesotho was not rated due to insufficient data (Sachs and Warner 1995, p. 85), and Botswana is dropped from their sample because of unavailability of government-consumption data.

tic price of import-competing goods relative to exportables can be expressed as follows:

$$\frac{p^m}{p^x} = \frac{e^m p^{m*} (1 + t^m)(1 + t^x)}{e^x p^{x*}},$$

where an asterisk refers to border prices. We now allow for the possibility that the exchange rates applicable to import and export transactions ($e^m$ and $e^x$, respectively) can differ. Foreign-currency rationing can drive a wedge between these two exchange rates.

Suppose the form that rationing takes is as follows: all imports are financed at the margin by buying foreign currency in the black market, while all export receipts are handed to the central bank at the official exchange rate. In this case, $e^m/e^x = 1 + \text{BMP}$, and the presence of a black-market premium has the same resource-allocation consequences as a trade restriction. On the other hand, if at the margin exporters can sell their foreign-currency receipts on the black market as well, then the wedge between $e^m$ and $e^x$ disappears. In this case, the black-market premium does not work like a trade restriction.[28] Neither does it do so when the premium for foreign currency is generated by restrictions on capital-account (as opposed to current-account) transactions.

But there is a deeper problem with interpreting the black-market premium as an indicator of trade policy. Sachs and Warner rate an economy closed according to BMP if it maintains black-market premia in excess of 20% for a whole decade (the 1970s or the 1980s). Such levels of the black-market premium are indicative of sustained macroeconomic imbalances. Overvaluation of this magnitude is likely to emerge (1) when there is a deep inconsistency between domestic aggregate-demand policies and exchange-rate policy, or (2) when the government tries to maintain a low exchange rate in order to counteract transitory confidence or balance-of-payments crises. Such imbalances may be sparked by political conflicts, external shocks, or sheer mismanagement, and would typically manifest themselves in inflationary pressures, high and growing levels of external debt, and a stop–go pattern of policymaking. In addition, since black-market premia tend to favor government officials who can trade exchange-rate allocations for bribes, we would expect them to be high wherever there are high levels of corruption. Therefore, countries with greater corruption, a less reliable

28. In one respect, Sachs and Warner (1995) treat BMP differently from a trade restriction: the cutoff for tariffs (TAR) is set at 40%, while that for BMP is set at 20%.

bureaucracy, and lower capacity for enforcement of the rule of law are also likely have higher black-market premia.

Hence it is reasonable to suppose that the existence of sizable black-market premia over long periods of time reflects a wide range of policy failures. It is also reasonable to think that these failures will be responsible for low growth. What is more debatable, in our view, is the attribution of the adverse growth consequences exclusively to the trade-restrictive effects of black-market premia.

Many of the relationships just discussed are present in the data. The simple correlations of black-market premia with the level of inflation, the debt/exports ratio, wars, and institutional quality are all sufficiently high to warrant preoccupation. Indeed, of the 48 economies ranked as closed according to the BMP criteria, 40 had one or more of the following characteristics: average inflation over 1975–1990 higher than 10%, debt-to-GNP ratio in 1985 greater than 125%, a terms-of-trade decline of more than 20%, an institutional-quality index less than 5 (on a scale of 1 to 10), or involvement in a war.

We also view the fact that there exist important threshold effects in the black-market premium as indicative that this variable may simply be capturing the effect of widespread macroeconomic and political crises. If we insert the values of the black-market premium in the 1970s and 1980s as continuous variables in the regression, the estimated coefficients are extremely weak, and they fail to pass an *F*-test for joint significance at 10%. The strength of Sachs and Warner's result comes in great part from the dichotomous nature of the variable BMP and from the fact that the 20% threshold allows more weight to be placed on the observations for which the black-market premia—and probably also the underlying macroeconomic imbalances—are sufficiently high.

That the effect of the black-market premium is highly sensitive to the macroeconomic and political variables that one controls for is shown in Table 4, where we present the results of controlling for each of the indicators of macroeconomic and political distress that we have mentioned. In three out of five cases, each of these variables individually is enough to drive the coefficient on BMP below conventional levels of significance. If we insert all our controls together, the estimated coefficient on BMP goes down by more than half and the *t*-statistic drops below 1.

This kind of evidence does not by itself prove that higher black-market premia are unrelated to growth performance. The results in Table 4 might be due to high multicollinearity between the black-market premium and the indicators of macroeconomic and political distress that we have chosen. But what they do show is that there is very little in the data

Table 4 EFFECT OF BLACK-MARKET PREMIUM ON GROWTH BEFORE AND AFTER CONTROLLING FOR MEASURES OF MACROECONOMIC AND POLITICAL DISEQUILIBRIUM;

| | (1) | (2) | (3) | (4) | (5) | (6) | (7) |
|---|---|---|---|---|---|---|---|
| Black-market premium | −1.044** | −0.727 | −0.768 | −1.200* | −0.945** | −0.551 | −0.438 |
| | (−2.47) | (−1.57) | (−1.62) | (−2.84) | (−2.31) | (−1.66) | (−.98) |
| Inflation, 1975–1990 | | −3.201*** | | | | | −1.024 |
| | | (−1.78) | | | | | (−.58) |
| Debt/GDP ratio in 1985 | | | −0.015* | | | | −0.011* |
| | | | (−5.75) | | | | (−3.21) |
| Terms-of-trade shock | | | | 1.038 | | | 3.894 |
| | | | | (0.42) | | | (1.48) |
| War | | | | | −1.378** | | −0.135 |
| | | | | | (−2.32) | | (−0.15) |
| Quality of institutions | | | | | | 0.441* | 0.433*** |
| | | | | | | (2.86) | (2.00) |
| Summary statistics | | | | | | | |
| $R^2$ | 0.476 | 0.382 | 0.589 | 0.496 | 0.507 | 0.567 | 0.703 |
| $N$ | 80 | 76 | 54 | 77 | 80 | 75 | 46 |

Dependent variable: growth of GDP per capita, 1970–1989. All equations include the following controls: log of GDP in 1970, investment rate in 1970, government consumption/GDP, assassinations per capita, deviation from world investment prices, secondary-schooling ratio, primary-schooling ratio, revolutions and coups, and a constant term. Numbers in parentheses are $t$-statistics based on Huber–White heteroskedasticity-consistent standard errors.

to help us distinguish the effect of high black-market premia from those of other plausible right-hand-side variables relating to macroeconomic distress. In other words, they show that the black-market premium is not a good measure of trade policy, because it is also a proxy for many other variables unrelated to trade policy.

### 4.4 SENSITIVITY AND GENERAL IMPLICATIONS

The interpretational problems with the state-monopoly-of-exports and black-market premium variables would not be so important if these two variables were responsible for only part of the effect of the SW index on growth. But the fact that they seem to be its overwhelming determinant makes us worry about the extent to which the results speak meaningfully about the role of trade policies.

The arguments in the previous two sections have shown that the individual coefficients on MON and BMP are not very robust to controlling for variables such as an Africa dummy or indicators of macroeconomic and political distress. However, much of the force of the SW variable comes from its combination of the effects of MON and BMP. The reason is that the SW dummy uses MON to classify as closed all but one of the economies in sub-Saharan Africa and then uses BMP to classify as closed a set of economies with macroeconomic and political difficulties. It thus builds a "supervariable" which is 1 for all non-African economies without macroeconomic or political difficulties. This variable will be statistically stronger than either an African dummy or macroeconomic controls, because it jointly groups information from both.[29]

In the working-paper version of this paper (Rodríguez and Rodrik, 1999) we show that the coefficient on the SW variable, although generally robust to changes in the list of controls, is particularly sensitive to the inclusion of other summary indicators of macroeconomic and political crises. In particular, both the summary indicator of institutional quality developed by Knack and Keefer (1995) and a dummy variable that captures the effect of being in Africa and high macroeconomic disequilibria can easily drive the coefficient of the SW dummy below conventional significance levels. This sensitivity is important not because it shows the existence of a specification in which the SW dummy's significance is not robust, but because this lack of robustness shows up precisely when it is other indicators of political and macroeconomic imbalances that are introduced in the regression. This appears to suggest that

29. If MON and BMP are inserted separately, together with an Africa dummy and a measure of institutional quality, then neither MON nor BMP is individually significant, and the $p$-value for a joint significance test is 0.09 (0.31 after controlling for NTB, TAR, and SOC), but OPEN gets a $t$-statistic of 3.06 and BM one of 2.93 (SQT gets 1.46).

the SW variable may be acting as a proxy for these imbalances rather than as an indicator of trade policy.

We do not pretend to have a good answer to the question of whether it is macroeconomic and political distress that drive trade policy or the other way around.[30] Nor do we give an answer to the question of whether all of these are determined in turn by some other underlying variables such as poor institutions or antimarket ideology. What we believe we have established is that the statistical power of the SW indicator derives not from the direct indicators of trade policy it incorporates, but from two components that we have reasons to believe will yield upward-biased estimates of the effects of trade restrictions. The SW measure is so correlated with plausible groupings of alternative explanatory variables—macroeconomic instability, poor institutions, location in Africa—that it is risky to draw strong inferences about the effect of openness on growth based on its coefficient in a growth regression.

## 5. *Sebastian Edwards (1998)*

The third paper that we discuss is Sebastian Edwards's recent *Economic Journal* paper "Openness, productivity and growth: What do we really know?" (Edwards, 1998). The papers by Dollar and by Sachs and Warner deal with data problems by constructing new openness indicators. Edwards takes the alternative approach of analyzing the robustness of the openness–growth relationship to the use of different existing indicators. Edwards writes: "the difficulties in defining satisfactory summary indexes suggest that researchers should move away from this area, and should instead concentrate on determining whether econometric results are robust to alternative indexes" (1998, p. 386). The presumption is that the imperfections in specific indicators would not seem quite as relevant if the estimated positive coefficient on openness were found to be robust to differences in the way openness is measured.

To carry out this robustness analysis, Edwards runs regressions of total factor productivity growth on nine alternative indicators of openness. (Initial income and a measure of schooling are used as controls.[31])

30. Sachs and Warner's view is that causality goes from restrictive trade policies to macroeconomic instability (personal communication with Sachs). For the purposes of the present paper, we are agnostic about the existence or direction of any causality. An argument that macroeconomic imbalances are largely unrelated to trade policies is not difficult to make, and receives considerable support from cross-national evidence (see Rodrik, 1999, Chap. 4).

31. In an earlier and heavily cited paper, Edwards (1992) carried out a similar analysis for growth rates of real GDP per capita using a somewhat different set of nine alternative indicators of trade-policy distortions. We focus here on Edwards (1998) because it is more recent and the data set used in the earlier paper was not available.

His estimates of total factor productivity growth are the Solow residuals from panel regressions of growth on changes of capital and labor inputs. The nine indicators of openness he uses are: (1) the SW openness index; (2) the World Bank's subjective classification of trade strategies in *World Development Report 1987;* (3) Leamer's (1988) openness index, built on the basis of the average residuals from regressions of trade flows; (4) the average black-market premium; (5) the average import tariffs from UNCTAD via Barro and Lee (1994); (6) the average coverage of nontariff barriers, also from UNCTAD via Barro and Lee (1994); (7) the subjective Heritage Foundation index of distortions in international trade; (8) the ratio of total revenues on trade taxes (exports + imports) to total trade; and (9) Holger Wolf's (1993) regression-based index of import distortions for 1985.

The results Edwards presents are weighted least squares (WLS) regressions of TFP growth on indicators (1)–(9), where the weighting variable is GDP per capita in 1985. They are shown in column 1, rows 1–9, of Table 5: six of the nine indicators are significant, and all but one have the "expected" sign. He repeats the analysis using instrumental weighted least squares (column 2), and finds five of nine indicators significant at 10% (three at 5%) and all having the "correct" sign.[32] He also builds an additional indicator as the first principal component of indicators (1), (4), (5), (6), and (9), which he finds to be significant in WLS estimation (row 10). He concludes that "these results are quite remarkable, suggesting with tremendous consistency that there is a significantly positive relationship between openness and productivity growth."

We will argue that Edwards's evidence does not warrant such strong claims. The robustness of the regression results, we will show, is largely an artifact of weighting and identification assumptions that seem to us to be inappropriate. Of the 19 different specifications reported in Edwards (1998), only three produce results that are statistically significant at conventional levels once we qualify these assumptions. Furthermore, the specifications that pass econometric scrutiny are based on data that suffer from serious anomalies and subjectivity bias.

### 5.1 THE PROBLEM WITH WEIGHTING

The justification for the resort to WLS estimation is not provided in the paper, but it is presumably to correct for possible heteroskedasticity in the residuals. If disturbances are not homoskedastic, ordinary least-squares estimates will be inefficient. If the form of the skedastic function

32. In his paper, Edwards erroneously claims that two additional variables are significant in the IV–2SLS estimation: Leamer's index and tariffs. This mistake was apparently due to two typographical errors in his Table 4, p. 393.

Table 5 ALTERNATIVE WEIGHTING ASSUMPTIONS

| Openness indicator | (1) *Weighted least squares (weight=GDP)* | (2) *Weighted 2SLS (weight=GDP)* | (3) *Weighted least squares (weight=ln GDP)* | (4) *Weighted 2SLS (weight=ln GDP)* | (5) *Robust standard errors* | (6) *2SLS, Robust Standard Errors* |
|---|---|---|---|---|---|---|
| 1. Sachs–Warner | 0.0094** (2.12) | 0.0089*** (1.84) | 0.0101*** (1.81) | 0.0080 (1.28) | 0.0102 (1.54) | 0.0078 (1.06) |
| 2. World Development Report | 0.0075* (3.57) | 0.0131* (3.36) | 0.0070** (2.45) | 0.0126** (2.64) | 0.0068* (3.67) | 0.0126** (2.13) |
| 3. Leamer | 0.0010 (1.03) | 0.0123 (1.40) | 0.0041 (0.82) | −0.0013 (−0.20) | 0.0041 (0.82) | −0.0033 (−0.32) |
| 4. Black-market premium | −0.0217* (−3.59) | −0.0192*** (−1.95) | −0.0108** (−2.57) | −0.0035 (−0.56) | −0.0098*** (−1.79) | −0.0027 (−0.54) |
| 5. Tariffs | −0.0450* (−2.77) | −0.1001 (−1.52) | 0.0065 (0.51) | 0.0013 (0.03) | 0.0114 (0.88) | 0.0079 (0.28) |

*(continued overleaf)*

| | | | | | | |
|---|---|---|---|---|---|---|
| 6. Quotas | −0.0047<br>(−0.45) | −0.0398<br>(−0.42) | 0.0029<br>(0.35) | 0.0461<br>(0.68) | 0.0036<br>(0.43) | 0.0401<br>(0.79) |
| 7. Heritage Foundation | −0.0074*<br>(−4.50) | −0.0133*<br>(−3.75) | −0.0066**<br>(−3.02) | −0.0195*<br>(−3.30) | −0.0064*<br>(−2.87) | −0.0202*<br>(−3.24) |
| 8. Collected-trade-taxes ratio | −0.4849*<br>(3.04) | −1.6668**<br>(−2.15) | −0.2808**<br>(−2.15) | −1.8256<br>(−1.23) | −0.2676**<br>(−2.25) | −1.8368<br>(−1.06) |
| 9. Wolf's index of import distortions | 3.5E-05<br>(0.27) | −2.6E-04<br>(−0.72) | 4.8E-05<br>(0.41) | −3.7E-04<br>(−0.99) | 4.1E-05<br>(0.36) | −3.3E-04<br>(−1.21) |
| 10. Principal-components factor | −0.0070**<br>(−2.38) | | −0.0047<br>(−1.61) | | −0.0043<br>(−1.37) | |

Dependent variable: TFP growth, 1980–1990. These are the estimated coefficients from regressions where each of the trade-policy indicators is entered separately. Each equation also includes log GDP per capita in 1965 and schooling in 1965 as regressors [as in the original Edwards (1998) specification]. *t*-statistics are in parentheses (based on heteroskedasticity-consistent standard errors in column 3).

is known, then it is appropriate to use WLS. This is indeed what Edwards implicitly assumes when he uses GDP per capita as his weighting variable. If it is unknown, White's (1980) covariance-matrix estimator allows for the calculation of heteroskedasticity-robust standard errors that are invariant to the form of the skedastic function.

When there is heteroskedasticity, the standard deviation of the disturbance in the growth equation varies systematically across countries. Edwards's decision to weight his observations by the level of GDP per capita implies an assumption that the standard deviation of the disturbances in the growth equation is inversely proportional to the square root of the level of GDP per capita in 1985. In other words, if the United States is—as it in effect was in 1985 according to the Summers–Heston data—59 times wealthier than Ethiopia, the standard deviation of the growth rate conditional on having the United States's income is 7.7 ($59^{1/2}$) times lower than conditional on having Ethiopia's income. Using the estimates of the residuals' standard deviation from one of Edwards's equations, we can calculate the implied root-mean-square error of the growth rate conditional on having the incomes of the United States and of Ethiopia. The former is 0.8 percentage points, whereas the latter is 6 percentage points. It may be reasonable to suppose that growth data for poor countries are less reliable than those for rich countries, but the errors implied by Edwards's weighting assumption for poor countries' growth data seem to us to be unreasonably high. As a matter of fact, it is hard to think of a reason to be doing regression analysis on a broad cross section of primarily poor countries if we believe that underdeveloped nations' economic data are this uninformative.

Columns 3 and 4 of Table 5 repeat Edwards's regressions using the natural log of 1985 per capita GDP as the weighting variable. In terms of our calculations above, the ratio between the U.S. and Ethiopian standard deviations would now be a more reasonable 1.31. This set of regressions results in six of the eighteen coefficients having the "wrong" sign. Five out of nine coefficients are significant among the least-squares regressions (four at 5%), and two out of nine in the instrumental variables (IV) regressions. The coefficient on the principal-components variable now becomes insignificant.[33]

33. Why does weighting by GDP give such different results? The reason seems to be that there is a relationship between the openness indices used by Edwards and TFP growth at high levels of income. This relationship in itself is apparently driven by the fact that the great majority of economies with restrictive trade practices and high levels of GDP per capita in 1985 were oil exporters. Because of their high incomes, these economies are weighted very heavily in the WLS regressions. It is well known that oil-exporting economies had very low rates of growth during the 1980s (see for example the studies in Gelb, 1988). If one redoes regressions 1–19 using GDP per capita weights but includ-

One way to put aside doubts about the appropriateness of alternative assumptions regarding the nature of the skedastic function is to use White's (1980) heteroskedasticity-consistent standard errors, which are robust to the form of heteroskedasticity. We show these estimates in column 5 and 6 of Table 5. Four out of nine coefficients are now significant among the least-squares regressions (three at 5%), and two out of nine among the IV regressions. Only twelve of the eighteen coefficients have the correct sign. The principal components variable is also insignificant.

5.2 THE PROBLEM WITH IDENTIFICATION

The two significant IV coefficients in Table 5 are moreover quite sensitive to the specification of the instrument lists. In particular, the IV versions of equations 2 and 7 in Table 5 are two of the only three equations in which the Heritage Foundation Index of Property Rights Protection is used as an instrument by Edwards.[34] If this instrument is not excludable from the second-stage regression, Edwards's IV estimation will give biased estimates of the coefficient of openness on growth. Theoretically, it seems to us unreasonable to assert that the protection of property rights can effectively be assumed not to be an important determinant of growth, given the extensive literature concerned precisely with such an effect.[35] In Table 6, columns 1–4, we show that, if property rights are included in the second-stage regression for these two equations, this term gets a significant coefficient in indicator 2 (World Development Report index) and a positive albeit insignificant coefficient in indicator 7 (Heritage Foundation index). Chi-squared tests of the overidentifying restrictions also reject the null hypothesis that these restrictions hold for indicator 2. Furthermore, in both indicators the *t*-statistic on the openness proxy falls to well below 0.5 in absolute value.

If we take seriously the fact that property rights are not excludable from the productivity growth regressions, we are left with the conclusion that, among 17 different specifications in Tables 5 and 6, we find

ing a dummy for oil exporters, one gets very similar results to those in column 3 of Tables 5 and 6. Only the coefficients for the World Development Report index, the Heritage Foundation index, and the least-squares estimate of the collected-taxes ratio remain significant, and the least-squares coefficient on quotas changes sign.

34. His other instruments include TFP growth in the 1970s and the black-market premium, export/GDP, import/GDP and terms-of-trade changes for 1975–1979.

35. Barro (1997) names "the importance of institutions that ensure property rights and free markets" for economic growth as one of the "dominant themes" of his recent research (p. xiv). For examples of the literature emphasizing the importance of property rights for economic growth, see Clague et al. (1996), Acheson and McFetridge (1996), Jodha (1996), Tornell (1997), Park and Ginarte (1997), Grossman and Kim (1996), and Thompson and Rushing (1996).

Table 6 SENSITIVITY TO IDENTIFICATION ASSUMPTIONS AND CHOICE OF TRADE TAX INDICATOR

| | *(1)* | *(2)* | *(3)* | *(4)* | *(5)* | *(6)* | *(7)* | *(8)* |
|---|---|---|---|---|---|---|---|---|
| World Development Report index | 0.0126** | 0.0023 | | | | | | |
| | (2.13) | (0.40) | | | | | | |
| Heritage Foundation index | | | −0.0202* | −0.003 | | | | |
| | | | (−3.24) | (−0.24) | | | | |
| Property rights | | −0.0107* | | −0.010 | | | | |
| | | (−2.91) | | (−1.43) | | | | |
| Collected-taxes ratio (Edwards) | | | | | −0.2676 | | | |
| | | | | | (−2.25)** | | | |
| Average duty (World Bank) | | | | | | 0.0225 | | |
| | | | | | | (1.01) | | |
| Average import duty (World Bank) | | | | | | | 0.0007 | 0.0003 |
| | | | | | | | (2.30)** | (0.884) |
| Average export duty (World Bank) | | | | | | | −0.0003 | |
| | | | | | | | (−1.09) | |
| Test of overidentifying restrictions | 29.3244 | | 5.4072 | | | | | |
| *p*-value | 6.72E-06 | | 0.2480 | | | | | |
| *N* | 30 | 30 | 56 | 56 | 45 | 43 | 43 | 66 |

Dependent variable: TFP Growth, 1980–1990. Each equation also includes log GDP per capita in 1965 and schooling in 1965 as regressors. *t*-statistics based on heteroskedasticity-consistent standard errors in parentheses.

evidence of a negative and statistically significant correlation between trade-restricting policies and productivity growth in only three cases. Those are the ones that use the collected-taxes ratio, the World Development Report index, or the Heritage Foundation index. We take up some problems with these indexes in the next subsection.

### 5.3 DATA ISSUES

Edwards reports that the collected-taxes ratio (which measures trade tax revenue as a proportion of total trade) is calculated from raw data provided by the IMF. We are puzzled by these data, because many of the numbers for developing countries are implausible. India, a country with one of the world's highest tariff rates, is listed as having an average ratio of 2.4% lower than the sample average and barely above the value for Chile (2.3%). The mean value of the collected-taxes ratio in the sample is 2.8%, which strikes us as very low.

We have attempted to replicate Edwards's results using data from the World Bank's World Development Indicators (1998). This source, which was not available at the time Edwards's analysis was first conducted, provides collected trade tax ratios for imports and exports separately, which we have combined to derive an index in the spirit of Edwards's variable.[36] According to this index, India's average trade tax is 37.3% (a more plausible figure than Edwards's 2.4%). We replicate equation 8 of Table 5 with these data, and the results are shown in columns 6–8 of Table 6. The coefficient on average duties is now insignificant and has the "wrong" sign (column 6). If we introduce import and export duties separately (column 7), then import duties in fact get a positive and *significant* coefficient (contrary to the expected negative coefficient), and export duties are insignificant.

One shortcoming of these specifications (including Edwards's) is the small sample size (between 43 and 45). Since export duties are not reported for many countries, one way of increasing the sample size is to introduce *only* the import-duty variable from the World Development Indicators database. This increases the sample size to 66 countries. The estimated coefficient on import duties is once again positive and insignificant (column 8).

These results are in line with others we have reported earlier: there is

36. As our earlier discussion showed, when imports and exports are both taxed, their distortionary effect is multiplicative rather than additive. So instead of summing import and export taxes, we use the formula (1 + mdut)(1 + xdut) − 1, where mdut (xdut) is import (export) duties as a percentage of imports (exports). We take the average of observations for 1980–1985. Our results (on the sign and insignificance of the coefficient on trade taxes) are unchanged, however, when we take the simple sum mdut + xdut.

little evidence that simple averages of trade taxes are significantly and negatively correlated with growth.

The other two variables that are significant are the subjective indexes constructed by the World Bank and the Heritage Foundation. It is striking that two subjective indexes are the only variables that are robust to our econometric analysis, since subjective indexes are well known to suffer from judgment biases. Indeed, a look at the two indexes reveals some striking contrasts. In the Heritage Foundation Index, for example, Chile and Uganda are in the same category (4 on a scale of 1 to 5, where 5 is most protected). Perhaps even more problematic is the fact that the Heritage Foundation index rates policies in 1996, well after the end of Edwards's sample period (1980–1990). Similar problems are present in the World Bank index, where high-growth Korea is rated as more open than moderate-growth Malaysia despite having higher tariff rates and nontariff-barrier coverage as well as a lower export/GDP ratio, and moderate-growth Tunisia—which had average tariffs of 21% and average nontariff coverage of 54%—is classified in the same group as Chile, Malaysia, and Thailand. In fact, in his 1993 literature review, Edwards (1993, pp. 1386–1387) himself drew attention to serious problems with this index. As he noted, Chile, which in other studies is rated as the most open economy in the developing world, was grouped in the second category (moderately outward-oriented); Korea was classified in the group of most open economies for both 1963–1973 and 1973–1985 despite the fact that in the former period the Korean trade regime was considerably more restrictive than in the latter.

In the working-paper version of this paper we report the results of recomputing these subjective indexes using the quantitative information on which they are purportedly based. Given that these underlying data are no different from those used in some of the other empirical work that we have discussed in this and other sections of the paper, it should come as no surprise that these attempts generally yielded insignificant coefficients. The natural conclusion from these results appears to be that either the mismatch in time periods or subjectivity biases or both are the fundamental causes for the significance of the Heritage Foundation and World Bank indexes.

In sum, we do not concur with Edwards's assertion that the cross-country data reveal the existence of a robust relationship between openness and productivity or GDP growth.[37] In our view, there is little evi-

37. Our results are basically unaltered if we use growth of GDP per capita from 1980 to 1990 instead of TFP growth as the dependent variable. In this case the World Bank and Heritage Foundation indexes remain significant, but the collected-trade-taxes ratio is now only significant at a 10% level and the black-market premium is insignificant. Similar results emerge for IV estimation.

dence to support such an assertion. The results reviewed in this section are for the most part highly dependent on questionable weighting and identification assumptions. The trade-policy indicators whose significance is not affected by these assumptions either are subjective indexes apparently highly contaminated by judgement biases or lack robustness to the use of more credible information from alternative data sources.

## 6. *Dan Ben-David (1993)*

Ben-David's (1993) *QJE* paper "Equalizing exchange: Trade liberalization and income convergence" takes an altogether different approach to studying the effect of openness on economic growth. Ben-David analyzes the effect of trade policies on income by asking whether trade liberalization leads to a reduction in the dispersion of income levels among liberalizing countries (i.e., whether it contributes to what has been called $\sigma$-convergence). We pick Ben-David as an example of a strand of the literature which has centered on studying the effect of trade on convergence. Another distinctive aspect of Ben-David's work is that it is nonparametric and not regression-based.

The expectation that trade liberalization might lead to income convergence is grounded in the factor price equalization (FPE) theorem. According to trade theory, free trade in goods leads to the equalization of factor prices under certain conditions (including an equal number of goods and factors, identical technologies, and absence of transport costs). As barriers to trade are relaxed (and assuming in addition that differences in capital–labor ratios and labor-force participation ratios do not countervail), a tendency towards FPE can be set into motion, resulting in convergence in per capita incomes.

There is no necessary relationship between the level of dispersion in incomes and the growth rate. Countries could in principle be converging to lower levels of GDP per capita. But in the case of the European Community, on which Ben-David concentrates, the convergence experienced was indeed to higher incomes. Overall growth from 1945 to 1994 of the EC5 (Belgium, France, the Netherlands, Italy, and Germany) was 3.45% compared to 1.21% percent from 1900 to 1939 and 1.16% from 1870 to 1899. Therefore, if Ben-David's claim is right, convergence in the EEC was achieved by raising the income of poor countries rather than by lowering that of rich countries.

Ben-David's argument goes beyond simply ascertaining that a decrease in dispersion occurred during the postwar era. He tries to show that trade liberalization caused this decrease by discarding other plausible alternatives. Thus he argues (1) that the observed convergence was

Figure 3 EFFECT OF EXCLUDING GERMANY IN DISPERSION CALCULATIONS

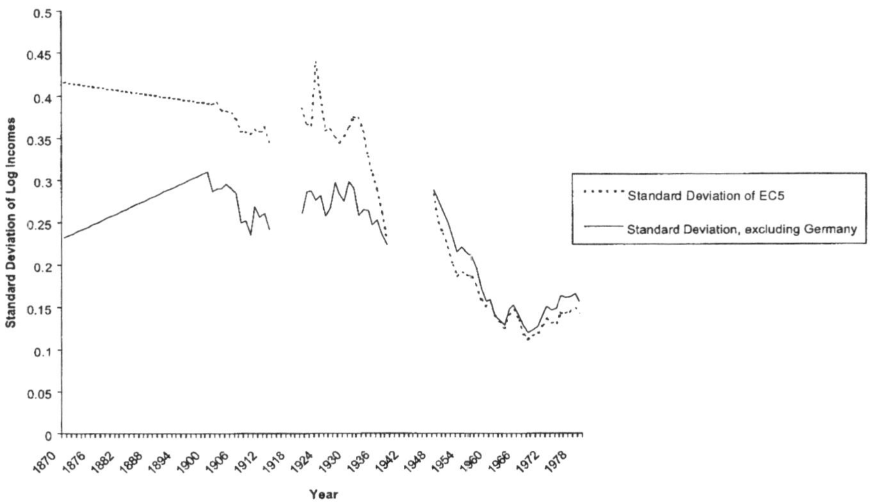


not simply a continuation of a long-term convergence trend unrelated to postwar economic integration; (2) that the European countries that chose not to enter a free-trade agreement did not experience the same extent of convergence as the EEC; and (3) that other subsets of economies in the world that were not economically integrated did not experience convergence. We examine each of his arguments in turn.

### 6.1 WAS EUROPEAN CONVERGENCE A CONTINUATION OF A LONG-TERM TREND?

In support of the argument that the reduction in dispersion was not simply the continuation of a long-run trend, Ben-David argues that the series of per capita income dispersion (solid line in Figure 3) does not show any visible downward tendency before the postwar era. When presenting this series, Ben-David excludes Germany from the calculations,[38] arguing that not doing so would bias the conclusion in favor of convergence:

> Germany was always among the poorest, in per capita terms, of the six countries. Today, it is one of the wealthiest countries in Europe. As a result of its heightened prosperity, it might be claimed that all of the convergence that

38. Luxembourg is also excluded, because Maddison (1982) does not provide data for it.

has been witnessed within the EEC is due to the behavior of Germany. Thus, its exclusion should bias the results away from convergence. (Ben-David, 1993, p. 662)

Note however that the purpose of Figure 3 (Figure VII in Ben-David's paper) is not only to establish the existence of convergence following postwar liberalization, but also to establish the *absence* of a long-term trend in convergence predating it. Thus the exclusion of Germany from the series, which biases the results against convergence, would also bias the results in favor of the hypothesis that there was no prewar convergence trend, had Germany's convergence occurred before the postwar period.

That is indeed what happened. Between 1870 and the eve of World War II, Germany's income went from less than 50% to 75% of the average for the remaining members of the EEC. And by 1958, one year after the EEC was formed, Germany had surpassed Belgium as the leader of the five. The exclusion of Germany therefore has the effect of understating the fall in dispersion before the creation of the EEC. The dashed line in Figure 7, which displays the dispersion of log per capita incomes including Germany, shows this. Once Germany is included in the sample, it appears that dispersion has been on a downward trend since 1870. The hypothesis that postwar convergence was simply a continuation of a long-term trend can no longer be rejected easily, raising doubts about the conclusion that convergence was caused by postwar trade policies.[39]

Figure 4 plots the standard deviation of log incomes for the original members of the EEC, now using Maddison's more recent (1995) estimates and including Germany. We reach the same conclusion as in Figure 3: dispersion has followed a downward trend since the beginning of the twentieth century. From a peak of 0.36 in 1897, dispersion had fallen to 0.25 in 1930, and 0.19 in 1939. By the time the EEC was created, it had fallen to 0.16. It appears therefore that the further reduction in disper-

39. Ben-David (in personal communication) has pointed out to us that much of the prewar convergence is due to the fact that "while the other countries were in the Depression, Germany surged ahead as Hitler built his war machine." Indeed, dispersion appears trendless from 1900 to 1932, and starts falling only as Germany's income rises during the National Socialist period. But we are not sure of what to make of that fact. Germany's income remained high after the war—compared to other European countries—suggesting that not all of the convergence was due to the policies of the Nazi period or to the buildup of the war machine. In any case, Nazi Germany pursued highly protectionist policies, so that its experience sheds doubt on the argument that poor countries that close their economies experience slower growth. Finally, the observation for 1870 in Figure 7 suggests that dispersion was much higher in the late nineteenth century than in 1930. The last point is confirmed when we examine Maddison's (1995) more recent estimates (see Figure 8), which provide a fuller picture of trends in dispersion since 1820. These estimates were not available to Ben-David at the time his paper was written.

Figure 4 DISPERSION OF PER CAPITA INCOMES AND TRADE POLICY EVENTS

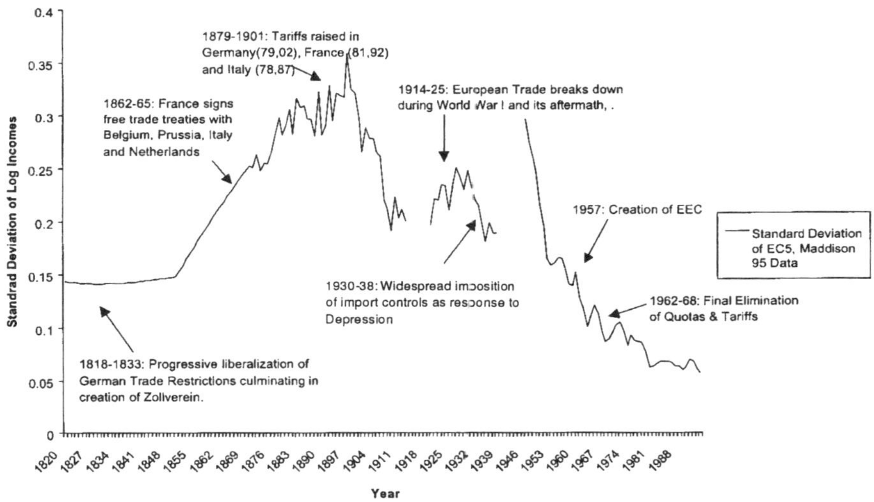


sion that followed the creation of the EEC (to 0.06 by 1994) was a continuation of a long-term trend that predated European integration. Moreover, this conclusion is not sensitive to whether Germany is included in the sample: that is because Maddison's (1995) revised estimates suggest that there was a uniform pattern of convergence during the pre-World War I period, with Italy, France, and Germany *all* catching up with Belgium and the Netherlands.

A closer look at Figure 4 suggests that there is in fact very little association between episodes of economic integration and $\sigma$-convergence over time. The period leading up to 1878 was an era of continuous trade liberalization, at the level of both national markets and international ones. This period witnessed the creation of the German *Zollverein* (1833) and the unification of Italy (1860), as well as the signing of free-trade agreements between Prussia and Belgium (1844), France and Belgium (1842), France and Prussia (1862), France and Italy (1863), and France and the Netherlands (1865).[40] Most of these bilateral agreements had

40. The discussion in this and the following two paragraphs borrows heavily from Chapter V of Pollard (1974). Above we list treaties between countries included in Figure 4, but the extent of trade liberalization from 1820 to 1878 in Europe was impressive. Prussia signed free-trade treaties with Britain (1841 and 1860), Turkey (1839), Greece (1840), Austria (1868), Spain (1868), Switzerland (1869), Mexico (1869), and Japan (1869); France with Britain (1860), Switzerland (1864), Sweden, Norway, the Hanse Towns,

most-favored-nation clauses, extending the benefits of bilateral liberalization to third countries. Yet, despite increasing economic integration, dispersion more than doubled from 1820 to 1880 (from 0.14 to 0.29).[41]

The retreat from free trade started during the 1880s, with Germany's Tariff Act of 1879. Italy raised tariffs in 1878 and 1887, France in 1881 and 1892.[42] This rise in protection followed the depression of the 1870s and was motivated by the desire to protect European farmers from the influx of cheap American grain imports (which began to undersell German grain in 1875) while at the same time compensating industry for the increased wages of workers.[43] Nevertheless, as Figure 4 shows, the period from the 1880s to World War I was, if anything, one of convergence.[44]

The breakdown in world trade that followed World War I and the spread of beggar-thy-neighbor protectionist policies adopted during the Great Depression seem also to have had very little effect on dispersion. Even though fascist governments in Italy and Germany raised agricultural tariffs and other protectionist barriers, and in France the power of agricultural groups was large enough to drive the French price of wheat in 1939 to three times its price in London (Cobban, 1965, p. 156), on the eve of World War II dispersion stood at its lowest level since the 1860s.

In sum, Figure 4 shows no long-run tendency for trade liberalization to be associated with greater convergence in per capita incomes. If anything, it shows increasing dispersion during the nineteenth century and falling dispersion during the twentieth century. While one can interpret this evidence in different ways, we find the most straightforward read-

and Spain (1865), Austria (1866), and Portugal (1867); Belgium with Britain (1862); Italy with Britain (1862) and Turkey and Greece (1839–1940). Aside from the MFN clause, measures were taken to ease international trade such as the inclusion in the Treaties of Berlin of clauses extending commercial freedoms to foreign citizens (1878, 1885). There were even attempts to create customs unions between France and Germany and between France and its neighbors.

41. A caveat applies here: for 1820–1850 we rely on just two observations: one for 1820, and another one for 1850. Since the 1850 observation for Italy was not available, we constructed it as the result of a linear interpolation between the 1820 and the 1870 observation. Even if we disregard the evidence before 1870, the yearly data from 1870–1880 indicate that the increase in dispersion predated the first protectionist measures.

42. Again, tariff adoption was widespread, with only Holland and the United Kingdom resisting the reversion towards protectionism.

43. In effect, high tariffs worked to the detriment of labor in what came to be known in Germany as the "compact of rye and iron." See Gerschenkron (1943) and Rogowski (1989) for detailed discussions of this era. As Rogowski points out, the reversion towards protectionism was more accentuated in capital-poor countries such as Germany, Italy, and France than in capital-rich countries such as Belgium and the Netherlands.

44. O'Rourke's (1997) econometric study of this period (1975–1914), covering a panel of 10 countries, finds that higher tariffs were correlated with *faster* economic growth, and that the estimated effects are quantitatively large.

ing to be that post-World War II convergence was in fact a continuation of a long-run trend that got started around the turn of the twentieth century.

## 6.2 DID NON-EEC EUROPEAN COUNTRIES EXPERIENCE CONVERGENCE?

Ben-David also claims that countries in Europe that did not undertake trade liberalization failed to experience convergence. He supports his argument by showing that (a) there was no convergence among the United Kingdom, Denmark, and Ireland until they began to relax their trade restrictions vis-à-vis Europe, and that (b) EFTA countries experienced significant convergence with the EEC as trade barriers among them were liberalized.

To demonstrate (a), Ben-David plots the standard deviation among the United Kingdom, Denmark, and Ireland, all of which started liberalizing trade with the EEC in the mid-1960s. He shows that their dispersion *among themselves* started falling only after 1965. It is not clear to us why this is the relevant test, since the trade liberalization in question took place between these countries and Europe as well as amongst themselves. In Figure 5, we show that even if there is an indication of convergence among these three countries after 1965, it is not caused by conver-

Figure 5 GDP OF UNITED KINGDOM, DENMARK, AND IRELAND, RELATIVE TO EEC MEAN

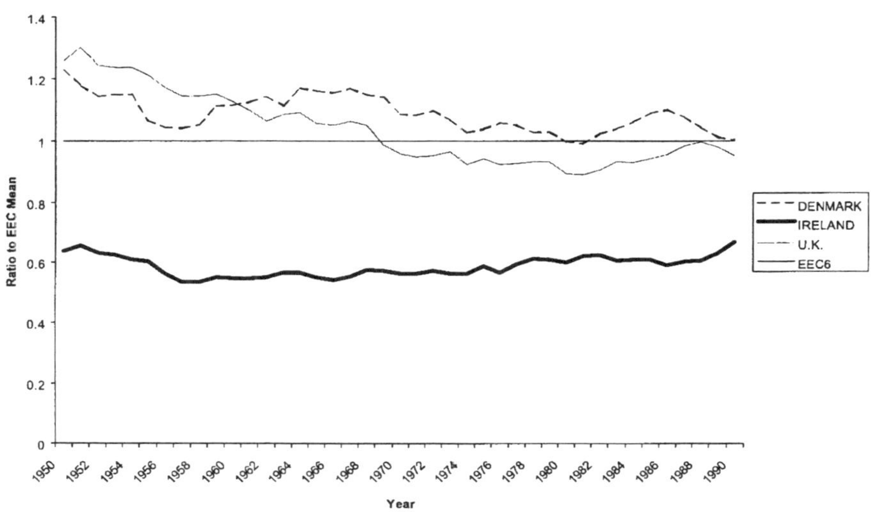

Figure 6 CONTRIBUTION TO VARIANCE AROUND EUROPEAN MEAN

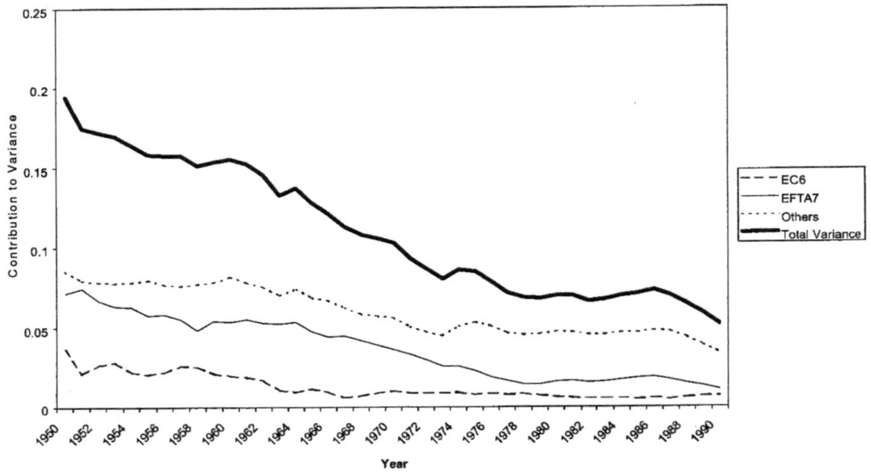


gence to the mean income of EEC members. Ireland has shown very little convergence to the EEC until recent years, and Denmark has oscillated close to the EEC average since the 1950s. The United Kingdom has been converging—downward—to the EEC level steadily (at least) since the 1950s. None of the three countries seem to experience different patterns of convergence after they relaxed trade restrictions with the EEC in 1965.

As regards (b), there has indeed been substantial convergence by EEC and EFTA member countries to the European mean since the 1950s. But we are skeptical whether such convergence can be attributed to trade liberalization. In Figure 6, we plot the contribution to the variance around the European mean[45] of three subsets of European countries: the six members of the European Economic Community, the seven members of the European Free Trade Association,[46] and six remaining European countries which did not join either EFTA or the EEC.[47] It is evident from

45. This is defined as $(1/N_{\text{EUROPE}}) \sum_{i \in J} [(y_i - \bar{y}_{\text{EUROPE}})/\bar{y}_{\text{EUROPE}}]^2$ for $J$ = {EEC6, EFTA6, others}. Normalization by the mean achieves the same purpose as calculating the variance of log incomes (and is more appropriate for large income differences), and putting the expression in terms of the variance (not the standard deviation) ensures that the three components sum to the total.

46. Austria, Switzerland, Sweden, Denmark, Norway, Finland, and the United Kingdom. Even though Portugal was officially a member of EFTA, it was allowed to implement tariffs and to deviate from EFTA policies, so we follow Ben-David in treating it as a non-EFTA country.

47. Cyprus, Greece, Iceland, Ireland, Portugal, and Spain.

Figure 6 that all subgroups have experienced substantial convergence. The non-EFTA and non-EEC countries have seen their contribution to the variance around the European mean fall from 0.085 to 0.034 from 1950 to 1992.[48] European convergence seems to be the result of factors largely unrelated to trade liberalization.

### 6.3 DID OTHER AREAS OF THE WORLD EXPERIENCE CONVERGENCE?

To add plausibility to the story that trade liberalization was behind the European trend towards convergence in the postwar era, Ben-David shows that subsets of countries that have not become integrated have experienced no tendency to converge. He points to the well-known fact that the dispersion of world incomes has not decreased in the postwar era (it has actually increased). He also shows that the dispersion of incomes among the world's 25 richest countries (excluding the EEC6) has not decreased either. He compares these experiences with those of economically integrated Europe and U.S. states to show that convergence seems to occur only when there is substantial trade liberalization.

There is an asymmetry in his selection of diverging and converging areas, however. Whereas the regions he shows to be converging are all close to each other geographically, those which are diverging are not. To have a fair standard of comparison, one must ask whether trade liberalization—or its absence—among geographically adjacent economies would lead towards convergence or divergence.

Did subsets of geographically adjacent economies that liberalized trade tend to observe convergence? There are at least two important cases in which the trends in convergence go counter to what we would expect on the basis of Ben-David's argument. Consider the experiences of East Asia and Latin America, two regions with radically different trade policies and which constitute the canonical examples of open and closed economies. If the liberalizatoin–convergence view is right, the relatively open East Asian economies should have converged, whereas the relatively closed Latin American economies should have diverged. In fact, countries in East Asia have steadily diverged since the 1960s, with the standard deviation of their log incomes going from 0.47 in 1960 to 0.81 in 1989.[49] As for

48. If one includes Turkey as a seventh country in this group, the contribution to dispersion goes from 0.103 in 1950 to 0.053 in 1992. An alternative measure of dispersion around the European mean is the standard deviation of log incomes around the mean log income. The latter measure for the non-EEC, non-EFTA countries falls from 0.15 in 1950 to 0.05 in 1990 (0.20 to 0.10 if Turkey is included).

49. The East Asian countries are Hong Kong, Indonesia, Japan, South Korea, Malaysia, Philippines, Singapore, Taiwan, and Thailand. Data are from Summers and Heston (1994). If the Philippines is excluded, the rise in dispersion is from 0.50 to 0.73.

Latin America, there has been a steady *decrease* in dispersion during the period of import substitution, from 0.55 before the Great Depression to 0.20 in the late 1980s.[50] More striking, dispersion has sharply risen since the late 1980s, just as Latin American countries liberalized their trade. (See Rodríguez and Rodrik, 1999, for more details.)

Another important counterexample comes from the historical experience of the United States. Figure 7 plots the ratio of GDP per capita for the United States to the average GDP per capita for its three main European trading partners (the United Kingdom, France, and Germany) up to 1938.[51] Trade with Europe was approximately two-thirds of total U.S. trade during the nineteenth century,[52] and the bulk of that was with those three countries. It is however evident from Figure 7 that despite declining levels of import duties, the United States and Europe steadily diverged between 1820 and 1938. Again, there seems to be no evident relationship between trade liberalization and income convergence.[53]

We close by drawing attention to Slaughter's (2000) recent examination of the same issue. Slaughter undertakes a systematic analysis by compar-

50. The Latin American countries are Argentina, Brazil, Chile, Colombia, Mexico, and Peru. Data are from Maddison (1995), Summers and Heston (1994), and World Bank (1998). Latin American import substitution policies started rather spontaneously as a response to the collapse of world-wide demand for raw materials in 1929 and the adoption of protectionist measures by the United States and Britain in 1930 and 1931. Most countries abandoned convertibility and imposed trade barriers during this period and did not liberalize until recent years (see Díaz-Alejandro, 1981).

51. The cutoff date of 1938 is chosen because during World War II the Americas overtook Europe as the main destination for U.S. exports. The Americas overtook Europe as the main source of imports much earlier, during World War I. Including observations after 1940 would not change our results: the GDP per capita in 1994 for the United States was still 27% higher than that of its three main European trading partners, despite the fact that after 1944 tariff rates stayed well into the single digits (Bureau of the Census, 1989). Choosing the Americas instead of Europe as a standard of comparison would strengthen our results, as the divergence between U.S. and Latin American incomes during the nineteenth and twentieth centuries has been extremely high (see Haber, 1997), and Canada represents only about half of U.S. trade with the Americas.

52. Before World War II, exports to Europe were 43% of total exports and imports from Europe were 29% of total imports (Bureau of the Census, 1989).

53. Our broader conclusion is not necessarily inconsistent with Ben-David's own reading of the evidence. Ben-David (in personal communication) writes that the main conclusions that can be drawn from his research are that "trade liberalization is associated with income convergence only when (a) the liberalization is comprehensive and (b) the liberalization occurs between countries that trade extensively with each other," and that "there is no evidence that these outcomes hold for poor countries." In fact, Ben-David (1999) has argued that trade flows will be of little use in transferring knowledge to countries with low levels of human capital. This contrasts strongly with much of the discussion in the literature, which has interpreted Ben-David as making the much stronger claim that liberalization leads developing countries to converge with their richer trading partners. A few examples are IMF (1997, p. 84), World Bank (1996, p. 32), Vamvakidis (1996, p. 251), and Richardson *et al.* (1997, p. 100), all of which refer to Ben-David in discussions about developing economies.

Figure 7 RATIO OF U.S. TO EUROPEAN GDP AND IMPORT DUTIES, 1820–1938

ing convergence patterns among liberalizing countries before and after liberalization with the convergence pattern among randomly chosen control countries before and after liberalization. As he emphasizes, this difference-in-differences approach avoids the pitfalls of before-and-after comparisons (nonliberalizing countries too may exhibit the same pattern before and after) or of comparing liberalizing countries with non-liberalizing ones (the liberalizing countries may have been converging prior to the liberalization as well). Hence Slaughter's approach amounts to a more systematic version of the kind of exercise we have carried out above by way of specific illustrations (but using only post-World War II data). Slaughter focuses specifically on four instances of trade liberalization: formation of the EEC, formation of EFTA, liberalization between EEC and EFTA, and Kennedy Round tariff cuts under GATT. His conclusion is that there is no systematic link between trade liberalization and convergence. In fact, he reports that much of the evidence suggests trade liberalization diverges incomes among liberalizers. This parallels our results above.

## 7. *Jeffrey Frankel and David Romer (1999)*

Frankel and Romer's (1999) very recent *AER* paper on trade and incomes has received considerable attention since its publication. This paper analyzes the relationship between trade and income by estimating cross-country regressions of income per capita on the trade–GDP ratio and two measures of country size (population and land area). The authors' aim is to address the problem of the likely endogeneity of trade with respect to income. So the trade share is instrumented by first estimating a gravity equation, where bilateral trade flows are regressed on geographic characteristics (countries' size, their distance from each other, whether they share a common border, and whether they are landlocked). The fitted trade values are then aggregated across partners to create an instrument for the actual trade share. An earlier version of Frankel and Romer's paper included initial income among the regressors in the second-stage equation, so that the results could also be given a growth interpretation. The main finding of the paper is that the IV estimate of the effect of trade on income is if anything greater than the OLS estimate.

As we mentioned in the introduction, this paper is concerned with the relationship between incomes and the *volume* of trade, and does not have immediate implications for trade *policy*. The reason is that the implications of geography-induced differences in trade, on the one hand, and policy-induced variations in trade, on the other, can be in principle quite different. Selective trade policies work as much by altering the structure of trade as they do by reducing its volume. To the extent that policy is targeted on market failures, trade restrictions can augment incomes (or growth rates) even when indiscriminate barriers in the form of geographical constraints would be harmful. Of course, to the extent that selective trade policies are subject to rent seeking, it is also possible that geography-induced variations in trade *under*estimate the real costs of trade restrictions. Ultimately, whether on balance trade policies are used towards benign ends or malign ends is an empirical question, on which Frankel and Romer's paper is silent.

With regard to the role of trade flows proper, we are concerned that Frankel and Romer's geographically constructed trade share may not be a valid instrument. The reason is that geography is likely to be a determinant of income through a multitude of channels, of which trade is (possibly) only one. Geography affects public health (and hence the quality of human capital) through exposure to various diseases. It influences the quality of institutions through the historical experience of colonialism, migrations, and wars. It determines the quantity and quality of natural endowments, including soil fertility, plant variety, and the abundance of minerals. The geographically determined component of trade may be correlated with all these other factors, imparting an upward bias to the IV estimate unless these additional channels are explicitly controlled for in the income equation.

As there is a single instrument used in Frankel and Romer's regressions, conventional exclusion–restriction tests performed conditional on a subset of the instruments being excludable from the second-stage regression cannot be carried out. To check whether Frankel and Romer's result can be attributed to nontrade effects of geography, we simply test whether some summary statistics of the geographical factors influencing trade can be excluded from the second-stage regression. We rerun Frankel and Romer's income regressions, adding three summary indicators of geography: (1) distance from the equator (used in Hall and Jones, 1998); (2) the percentage of a country's land area that is in the tropics (from Radelet, Sachs, and Lee, 1997); and (3) a set of regional dummies.

Table 7 shows the results. Columns 1 and 5 replicate Frankel and Romer's (1999) results in their Table 3, for the OLS and IV versions of the income equation, respectively. The other columns show the consequences of introducing the geography variables. The results are highly

Table 7 FRANKEL–ROMER REGRESSIONS WITH ADDITIONAL GEOGRAPHICAL VARIABLES

| *Variable* | *1* | *2* | *3* | *4* | *5* | *6* | *7* | *8* |
|---|---|---|---|---|---|---|---|---|
| Trade share | 0.85 | 0.57 | 0.46 | 0.61 | 1.97 | 0.34 | 0.21 | 0.25 |
| | (3.47) | (3.00) | (2.36) | (3.88) | (1.99) | (0.41) | (0.26) | (0.41) |
| Disteq | | 3.58 | | | | 3.65 | | |
| | | (9.26) | | | | (7.98) | | |
| Tropics | | | −1.42 | | | | −1.46 | |
| | | | (−9.84) | | | | (−8.03) | |
| East Asia | | | | −1.21 | | | | −1.21 |
| | | | | (−7.71) | | | | (−7.59) |
| Latin America | | | | −0.67 | | | | −0.74 |
| | | | | (−4.48) | | | | (−3.83) |
| Sub-Saharan Africa | | | | −1.94 | | | | −1.99 |
| | | | | (−14.72) | | | | (−12.82) |
| Method | OLS | OLS | OLS | OLS | IV | IV | IV | IV |
| $n$ | 150 | 150 | 145 | 150 | 150 | 150 | 145 | 150 |
| $R^2$ | 0.0949 | 0.4312 | 0.4628 | 0.66 | 0.43 | 0.44 | 0.4563 | 0.65 |

The dependent variable is log of income per person in 1985. IV standard errors include adjustment for generated regressors. All equations include the logs of population and land area. Disteq is distance from equator, as measured by Hall and Jones (1998). Tropics is fraction of country's area in tropics, as measured by Radelet, Sachs, and Lee (1997).

suggestive. The new variables enter with highly significant coefficients, indicating that they belong in the income equation. Moreover, once the additional geography variables are included, (1) the IV coefficient estimates on trade become statistically insignificant (with *t*-statistics around 0.4 or below), and (2) the IV point estimates on trade are reduced below their OLS counterparts. These findings are consistent with the hypothesis that nontrade effects of geography are the main driving force behind the findings of Frankel and Romer.[54]

## 8. Other Recent Work

Before we close, we mention briefly some other recent papers that have examined the connection between openness and economic growth. We focus on three papers in particular: Lee (1993), Harrison (1996), and Wacziarg (1998). These papers are of interest because they contain some methodological innovations.

Lee (1993) reasons, on the basis of an analytical model, that the distortionary effects of trade restrictions should be larger in economies that, in the absence of trade restrictions, would be more exposed to trade. Hence he interacts an indicator of trade policy with a measure of what he calls "free trade openness" (FREEOP).[55] The latter is constructed by regressing observed import shares on land area, distance from major trading partners, import tariffs, and black-market premia, and then calculating the predicted value of imports when the actual values of tariffs black-market premia are replaced by zeros. He finds that this composite measure (FREETAR) enters a growth regression with an estimated coefficient that is negative and statistically significant.

Lee uses two indicators of trade policy: an import-weighted tariff average and the black-market premium. We have discussed above the shortcomings of the latter as a measure of trade policy (when reviewing Sachs and Warner, 1995). The problem with Lee's tariff variable, as Lee (1993, p. 320) acknowledges, is that the underlying tariff data are from "various years in the 1980s"—the tail end of the 1960–1985 period over which his growth regressions are run. This raises the possibility of reverse causation: countries that perform well tend to liberalize their trade regime eventually. To check for this possibility, we have repeated Lee's regression, using the same specification and tariff variable, but over the subse-

54. We have carried out this exercise for various other samples [e.g., the higher-quality 98-country sample used by Frankel and Romer (1999), and samples excluding possible outliers such as Luxembourg and Hong Kong] and reach identical conclusions.

55. Specifically, the composite measure is constructed as FREETAR = FREEOP log(1 + tariff).

quent time period 1980–1994.[56] While the estimated coefficient on FREETAR is negative for this later period, it is nowhere near significant ($t$-statistic −0.80).

Harrison's (1996) main methodological contribution is to examine the relationship between trade policy and growth in a *panel* setting, using fixed effects for countries. This approach has the advantage that it enables the analyst to look for evidence of the effects of trade liberalization *within* countries.[57] But it has the disadvantage that the available time series are necessarily short, requiring the use of annual data or (at most) five-year averages. It may be a lot to ask of such data to reveal much about the relationship between trade policy and growth, because of the likely lags involved and the contamination from business-cycle effects.[58]

Harrison uses seven indicators of trade policy, and finds that three of these "exhibit a robust relationship with GDP growth" (1996, p. 443). These three are the following: (1) the black-market premium, (2) a measure based on the price level of a country's tradables (relative to international prices), and (3) a subjective measure of trade liberalization constructed at the World Bank. We have already discussed at length the problems involved in interpreting measures of each of these types as indicators of trade policy.

Finally, the paper by Wacziarg (1998) is an ambitious attempt to uncover the channels through which openness affects economic growth. Wacziarg's index of trade policy is a linear combination of three indicators: (1) the average import duty rate, (2) the NTB coverage ratio, and (3) the SW indicator.[59] The weights used to construct the combined index come from a regression of trade volumes (as a share of GDP) on these three indicators plus some other determinants. Using a panel made up of five-year averages for 57 countries during 1970–1989, Wacziarg finds that investment is the most important channel through which openness increases growth, accounting for more than 60% of the total effect.

We have two worries about this paper. First, we are not sure that the

56. Since Summers–Heston data are not available for the 1990s, we used World Bank data on GDP per capita (at constant prices).
57. Harrison (1996) cites disappointing results with cross-section regressions as a motivation for going the panel route.
58. Indeed, when Harrison (1996) controls for some business-cycle conditions, about half of her significant coefficients (on openness-related variables) disappear. The empirical evidence on the *short-run* relationship between trade liberalization and economic growth is judiciously reviewed in Greenaway, Morgan, and Wright (1998), who point to both positive and negative findings. These authors attempt to trace out the dynamics of the output response using three different indicators of policy (including the SW index), and report finding a J-curve effect: output first falls and then increases.
59. More specifically, Wacziarg uses the timing of trade liberalization in Sachs and Warner (1995) to assign a value to each country for any given five-year period.

regularities revealed by the data over time horizons of five years or less are particularly informative about the relationship between trade policy and long-run economic performance. It would be interesting to see if the results hold up with averages constructed over a decade or more. Second, as discussed previously, we are skeptical that the SW measure, on which the Wacziarg indicator is partly based, is a meaningful indicator of trade policy. Wacziarg remarks in a footnote (1998, footnote 9) that the "exclusion of [the SW indicator] from the trade policy index reduced the precision of the estimates . . . but did not change the qualitative nature of the results." We would have preferred to see estimates based only on tariff and NTB indicators.

## 9. Concluding Remarks

We have scrutinized in this paper the most prominent recent empirical studies on the relationship between trade barriers and economic growth. While we do not pretend to have undertaken an exhaustive survey, we believe that the weaknesses we have identified are endemic to this literature.

We emphasize that our difficulty with this literature is *not* a variant of the standard robustness criticism often leveled at cross-country growth empirics. Going back at least to Levine and Renelt (1992), a number of authors have pointed to the sensitivity of growth regressions to changes in the list of controls, and to the failure of these coefficients to pass the test of "extreme-bounds analysis." Whatever position one takes on this debate, the general point that we wish to make about the empirical literature on openness and growth is much simpler. For the most part, the strong results in this literature arise either from obvious misspecification or from the use of measures of openness that are proxies for other policy or institutional variables that have an independent detrimental effect on growth. When we do point to the fragility of the coefficients, it is to make the point that the coefficients on the openness indicators are particularly sensitive to controls for these other policy and institutional variables. To the extent that these objections can be conceptualized as variants of the robustness criticism, it is robustness at a much more basic level than that typically discussed in the Bayesian literature.

Still, in view of the voluminous research on the subject, a natural question that arises is whether we shouldn't take comfort from the fact that so many authors, using varying methods, have all arrived at the same conclusion. Don't we learn something from the cumulative evidence, even if individual papers have shortcomings?

We take a different message from this large literature. Had the negative relationship between trade restrictions and economic growth been convincingly demonstrated, we doubt that this issue would continue to generate so much empirical research. We interpret the persistent interest in this area as reflecting the worry that the existing approaches haven't gotten it quite right. One indication of this is that the newer papers are habitually motivated by exegeses on the methodological shortcomings of prior work.

We are especially struck and puzzled by the proliferation of indexes of trade restrictions. It is common to assert in this literature that simple trade-weighted tariff averages or nontariff coverage ratios—which we believe to be the most direct indicators of trade restrictions—are misleading as indicators of the stance of trade policy. Yet we know of no papers that document the existence of serious biases in these direct indicators, much less establish that an alternative indicator performs better (in the relevant sense of calibrating the restrictiveness of trade regimes).[60] An examination of simple averages of taxes on imports and exports and NTB coverage ratios leaves us with the impression that these measures in fact do a decent job of rank-ordering countries according to the restrictiveness of their trade regimes. In the working-paper version of this paper, we provide a simple measure of import duties for a large sample of countries and three different periods, so that the reader can form his/her judgement on this (Rodríguez and Rodrik, 1999, Table VIII.1).[61]

As we mentioned in the introduction, we are skeptical that there is a strong negative relationship in the data between trade barriers and economic growth, at least for levels of trade restrictions observed in practice.[62] We view the search for such a relationship as futile. We think there are two other fruitful avenues for future research.

60. Pritchett (1996) comes closest. The point of his paper, however, is to document the weak correlation between commonly used indicators of trade restrictions, and not to argue for the superiority of one indicator over the others.

61. This is the measure of import tariffs we used in Figure 1 (top panel).

62. In his comment on this paper, Chad Jones acknowledges the fragility of many of the results in the literature, but reports a range of exercises that leads him to conclude, as a best estimate, that trade restrictions are harmful to long-run incomes and that the effects are potentially large. We caution the reader about regressions where the *level* of per capita income is regressed on measures of trade restrictions. It is well known that countries reduce their trade barriers as they get richer, so levels regressions are subject to problems of reverse causality. It is difficult to overcome this problem via instrumentation, since adequate instruments (exogenous variables that are correlated with trade restrictions, but are otherwise uncorrelated with incomes) are particularly difficult to find in this context (as our discussion in Section 7 highlights). When regressions are run in growth form, we find that none of the available continuous measures of trade restrictions (simple tariff averages or nontariff coverage ratios) enter significantly in the vast majority of reasonable specifications. Some dichotomous measures based on the continuous variables do somewhat "better," but only if the break point is set at a sufficiently high level (e.g., a tariff rate or nontariff coverage ratio in excess of 40%).

First, in cross-national work, it might be productive to look for *contingent* relationships between trade policy and growth. Do trade restrictions operate differently in low- vs. high-income countries? In small vs. large countries? In countries with a comparative advantage in primary products vs. those with comparative advantage in manufactured goods? In periods of rapid expansion of world trade vs. periods of stagnant trade? Further, it would help to disaggregate policies and to distinguish the possibly dissimilar effects of different types of trade policies (or of combinations thereof). Are tariff and nontariff barriers to imports of capital goods more harmful to growth than other types of trade restrictions? Does the provision of duty-free access to imported inputs for exporters stimulate growth? Are export-processing zones good for growth? Does the variation in tariff rates (or NTBs) across sectors matter? The cross-national work has yet to provide answers to such questions.

Second, we think there is much to be learned from microeconometric analysis of plant-level datasets. These datasets constitute a rich source for uncovering the ways in which trade policy influences the production, employment, and technological performance of firms (see Roberts and Tybout, 1996). Recent research by Bernard and Jensen (1995, 1998), Aw, Chung, and Roberts (1998), and Clerides, Lach and Tybout (2000) has already shed new light on the relationship between trade and firm performance. For example, these papers (based on the experiences of countries as diverse as the United States, Taiwan, and Mexico) find little evidence that firms derive technological or other benefits from exporting per se; the more common pattern is that efficient producers tend to self-select into export markets. In other words, causality seems to go from productivity to exports, not vice versa. Relating these analyses to trade *policies* is the obvious next step in this line of research.

Let us close by restating our objective in this paper. We do not want to leave the reader with the impression that we think trade protection is good for economic growth. We know of no credible evidence—at least for the post-1945 period—that suggests that trade restrictions are systematically associated with higher growth rates. What we would like the reader to take away from this paper is some caution and humility in interpreting the existing cross-national evidence on the relationship between trade policy and economic growth.

The tendency to greatly overstate the systematic evidence in favor of trade openness has had a substantial influence on policy around the world. Our concern is that the priority afforded to trade policy has generated expectations that are unlikely to be met, and it may have crowded out other institutional reforms with potentially greater payoffs. In the real world, where administrative capacity and political capital are scarce, having a clear sense of policy priorities is of utmost importance. The effects of trade liberalization may be on balance beneficial on standard comparative-advantage grounds; the evidence provides no strong reason to dispute this. What we dispute is the view, increasingly common, that integration into the world economy is such a potent force for economic growth that it can effectively substitute for a development strategy.

## *Data Appendix*

SECTION 1

1. Import duties as a percentage of imports. Source: World Bank (1998).
2. Nontariff barriers. Source: Barro and Lee (1994).

SECTION 3

3. bmpav: average black-market premium. Source: Sachs and Warner (1995).
4. rcoast: coastal length over total land area. Source: Radelet, Sachs, and Lee (1997).
5. tropics: dummy for tropical countries. Source: Radelet, Sachs, and Lee (1997).
6. Latin America: dummy for countries in Latin America and the Caribbean.
7. SSA: dummy for countries in sub-Saharan Africa.
8. East Asia: dummy for countries in East Asia.
9. TAR: own-import-weighted ratio of tariff revenues to trade. Source: Barro and Lee (1994).
10. NTB: own-import-weighted nontariff frequency on capital goods and intermediates. Source: Barro and Lee (1994).
11. DISTORTION: ratio of consumption price level to U.S. price level, measured in identical currencies, divided by the fitted value of a regression on GDP, GDP squared, year dummies, and continent dummies. Source: Dollar (1992).
12. VARIABILITY: Coefficient of variation of DISTORTION. Source: Dollar (1992).
13. Investment/GDP: Source: Summers and Heston (1988) for Table 2.
14. Log initial income: Source: Summers and Heston (1988) for Table 2.
15. Schooling, 1975: Barro and Lee (1994).

SECTION 4

16. BMP: Dummy variable equal to 1 if black-market premium exceeds 20% during either the 1970s or the 1980s. Source: Sachs and Warner (1995).
17. BMP70, BMP80: Black-market premium during (respectively) 1970s and 1980s. Source: Sachs and Warner (1995).
18. MON: Dummy variable equal to 1 if the country had a score of 4 (highest score) on the Export Marketing Index in World Bank (1994). Source: Sachs and Warner (1995).
19. SOC: Dummy variable equal to 1 if the country was classified as socialist in Kornai (1992). Source: Sachs and Warner (1995).
20. TAR: own-import-weighted ratio of tariff revenues to trade. Source: Barro and Lee (1994).
21. NTB: own-import-weighted nontariff frequency on capital goods and intermediates. Source: Barro and Lee (1994).
22. OPEN: Variable equal to 0 if the country had BMP = 1, MON = 1, SOC = 1, TAR > 0.4, or NTB > 0.4. Source: Sachs and Warner (1995).
23. BM, SQT, QT, etc.: Openness indexes constructed using subsets of the Sachs and Warner's information. The label for each index denotes the openness indicators used to construct that index: M = state monopoly of main export, S = socialist economic system, Q = nontariff barriers, T = tariffs, B = black-market premium. For example, SMQT is set to 0 if it is closed according to either of the criteria for S, M, Q, or T, and to 1 otherwise.
24. Inflation, 1975–1990. Source: World Bank (1998).
25. Debt/exports, 1985. Source: World Bank (1998).
26. Change in terms of trade. Source: Barro and Lee (1994).
27. War: dummy for countries that participated in at least one external war over the period 1960–1985. Source: Barro and Lee (1994).
28. Quality of institutions: Institutional quality index from Knack and Keefer (1995).
29. Government budget surplus, 1970–1990. Source: World Bank (1998).
30. Population growth. Source: World Bank (1998).

SECTION 5

31. Sachs–Warner: Same as OPEN in Section 4.
32. World Development Report: World Development Report outward-orientation index, 1973–1985. Source: Edwards (1998).

33. Leamer: Openness index estimated by Leamer (1988) using residuals from disaggregated trade-flow regressions. Source: Edwards (1998).
34. Black-market premium: same as BMP80 in Section 4.
35. Tariffs: Same as TAR in Section 4.
36. Quotas: Same as NTB in Section 4.
37. Heritage Foundation: Subjective index of the extent to which government policies distort trade, from Johnson and Sheehy (1996). Source: Edwards (1998).
38. Collected-trade-taxes ratio: Average for 1980–1985 of ratio of total revenues on international trade taxes to total trade. Source: Edwards (1998).
39. Wolf's index of import distortions: A regression-based index from Wolf (1993). Source: Edwards (1998).
40. Principal-components factor: First principal component of OPEN, black-market premium, tariffs, quotas, and Wolf's index. The equation used to calculate it is
    $COM = -0.469 \times OPEN + 0.320 \times BLACK + 0.494 \times TARIFF + 0.553 \times QR + 0.354 \times WOLF.$
41. Log of GDP per capita, 1985. From Summers and Heston (1994). Source: Edwards (1998).
42. Property rights: Heritage Foundation index of property-rights protection, from Johnson and Sheehy (1996). Source: Edwards (1998).
43. Average import and export duties (World Bank): From World Bank (1998). Average duty is calculated as $(1 + \text{export duty}) \times (1 + \text{import duty}) - 1$.
44. Merged duty index: Simple average of average duty (43) and (38).
45. Trade distortion index based on Lee's data. Analog of Heritage index using data from Lee (1993) in Barro and Lee (1994). Countries are rated on a score of 1 to 5 according to the maximum of tariff rate and nontariff-barrier coverage ratio: higher than 20%: "very high" (a rating of 5); between 15 and 20%: "high" (4); between 10% and 15%: "moderate" (3); between 5% and 10%: "low" (2); and between 0 and 5%: "very low" (1).

SECTION 6

46. Contributions to variance around EC mean, from Summers and Heston (1994).
47. GDP per capita (Figure 3): Maddison (1982). Source: Ben-David (1993).
48. GDP per capita (Figure 4, Table 7): Maddison (1995).

49. GDP per capita (Figures 5–7): Summers and Heston (1994).
50. Ratio of import duties to imports, United States, from Bureau of the Census (1989, Series U211).

REFERENCES

Acheson, A. L. K. and D. McFetridge. (1996). Intellectual property and endogenous growth. In *The Implications of Knowledge-Based Growth for Microeconomic Policies.* P. Howitt (ed.). Calgary: University of Calgary Press.

Aw, B. Y., S. Chung, and M. J. Roberts. (1998). Productivity and turnover in the export market: Micro evidence from Taiwan and South Korea. Pennsylvania State University.

Balassa, B. (1971). *The Structure of Protection in Developing Countries.* Baltimore: Johns Hopkins University Press, 1971.

———. (1985). Exports, policy choices, and economic growth in developing countries after the 1973 oil shock. *Journal of Development Economics* 18(2): 23–35.

Barro, R. J. (1997). *Determinants of Economic Growth: A Cross-Country Empirical Study.* Cambridge, MA: The MIT Press.

———, and J.-W. Lee. (1993). International comparisons of educational attainment. *Journal of Monetary Economics* 32(3):363–394.

———, and ———. (1994). Data set for a panel of 138 countries. Harvard University.

Ben-David, D. (1993). Equalizing exchange: Trade liberalization and income convergence. *Quarterly Journal of Economics* 108(3).

———. (1999). Teach your children well: Planting the seeds of education and harvesting the benefits of trade. Tel Aviv University.

Bernard, A. B., and J. B. Jensen. (1995). Exporters, jobs, and wages in U.S. manufacturing, 1975–1987. In *Brookings Papers on Economic Activity: Microeconomics 1995*, pp. 67–112.

———, and ———. (1998). Exporting and productivity. Presented at 1998 Summer Institute, NBER, Cambridge, MA.

Bhagwati, J. N. (1982). Directly unproductive, rent-seeking (DUP) Activities. *Journal of Political Economy* 90(5):988–1002.

Bhalla, S., and L. J. Lau. (1992). Openness, technological progress, and economic growth in developing countries. World Bank.

Buffie, E. (1998). *Trade Policy in Developing Countries.* Unpublished manuscript.

Bureau of the Census. (1989). *Historical Statistics of the United States, Colonial Times to 1970.* White Plains, NY: Kraus International Publications.

Burnside, C., and D. Dollar. (1997). Aid, policies, and growth. World Bank. Policy Research Working Paper 1777.

Caves, R. E., J. A. Frankel, and R. W. Jones. (1999). *World Trade and Payments: An Introduction.* 8th ed. Reading, MA: Addison-Wesley, 1999.

Clague, C., P. Knack, S. Keefer, and M. Olson. (1996). Property and contract rights in autocracies and democracies. *Journal of Economic Growth* 1(2):243–276.

Clerides, S., S. Lach, and J. Tybout. (2000). Is "Learning-by-exporting" important? Micro-dynamic evidence from Colombia, Mexico, and Morocco. *Quarterly Journal of Economics*, forthcoming.

Cobban, A. (1965). *A History of Modern France.* New York: Braziller.

Collins, S. M. and B. P. Bosworth. (1996). Economic growth in East Asia:

Accumulation versus assimilation. *Brookings Papers on Economic Activity* 1996 (2):135–191.
Díaz-Alejandro, C. (1981). Southern Cone stabilization plans. In *Economic Stabilization in Developing Countries,* W. Cline and S. Weintraub (eds.). Washington: The Brookings Institution.
Dollar, D. (1992). Outward-oriented developing economies really do grow more rapidly: Evidence from 95 LDCs, 1976–85. *Economic Development and Cultural Change* 1992:523–544.
Edwards, S. (1992). Trade orientation, distortions, and growth in developing countries. *Journal of Development Economics* 39(1):31–57.
———. (1993). Openness, trade liberalization, and growth in developing countries. *Journal of Economic Literature* XXXI(3):1358–1393.
———. (1998). Openness, productivity and growth: What do we really know? *Economic Journal* 108(March):383–398.
Esfahani, H. S. (1991). Exports, imports, and growth in semi-industrialized countries. *Journal of Development Economics* 35(1):93–116.
Falvey, R., and N. Gemell. (1999). Factor endowments, nontradables prices and measures of "openness." *Journal of Development Economics* 58(February):101–122.
Feder, G. (1983). On exports and economic growth. *Journal of Development Economics* 12(1/2):59–73.
Feenstra, R. (1990). Trade and uneven growth. Cambridge, MA: National Bureau of Economic Research. NBER Working Paper 3276.
Fischer, S. (2000). Lunch address given at the conference on "Promoting Dialogue: Global Challenges and Global Institutions," Washington: American University.
Frankel, J., and D. Romer. (1999). Does trade cause growth? *American Economic Review* 89(3):379–399.
Gelb, A. H., and Associates. (1988). *Oil Windfalls: Blessing or Curse?* New York: Oxford University Press.
Gerschenkron, A. (1943). *Bread and Democracy in Germany,* Berkeley and Los Angeles: University of California Press.
Greenaway, D., W. Morgan, and P. Wright. (1998). Trade reform, adjustment and growth: What does the evidence tell us? *The Economic Journal* 108 (September):1547–1561.
Grossman, G., and E. Helpman. (1991). *Innovation and Growth in the Global Economy.* Cambridge, MA: The MIT Press.
Grossman, H., and M. Kim. (1996). Predation and accumulation. *Journal of Economic Growth* 1(3):333–350.
Gulhati, R. and R. Nallari. (1990). *Successful Stabilization and Recovery in Mauritius.* Washington: The World Bank.
Haber, S. (1997). *How Latin America Fell Behind: Essays on the Economic Histories of Brazil and Mexico, 1800–1914.* Stanford, CA: Stanford University Press.
Hall, R. E., and C. I. Jones. (1998). Why do some countries produce so much more output per worker than others? Cambridge, MA: National Bureau of Economic Research. NBER Working Paper W6564.
Harrison, A. (1996). Openness and growth: A time-series, cross-country analysis for developing countries. *Journal of Development Economics* 48:419–447.
———, and G. Hanson. (1999). Who gains from trade reform? Some remaining puzzles. *Journal of Development Economics* 50:125–154.

Husted, S., and M. Melvin. (1997). *International Economics,* 4th ed. Reading, MA: Addison-Wesley.

IMF. (1997). *World Economic Outlook,* Washington.

International Currency Analysis. (1995). *World Currency Yearbook.* Brooklyn, NY: International Currency Analysis, Inc.

Jodha, N. (1996). Property rights and development. In *Rights to nature: Ecological, economic, cultural and political principles of institutions for the environment,* S. Hanna (ed.). Washington: Island Press.

Johnson, B. T., and T. P. Sheehy. (1996). *1996 Index of Economic Freedom.* Washington: The Heritage Foundation.

Knack, S., and P. Keefer. (1995). Institutions and economic performance: Cross-country tests using alternative institutional measures. *Economics & Politics,* November, pp. 207–228.

Kornai, J. (1992). *The Socialist System: The Political Economy of Communism.* Princeton, NJ: Princeton University Press.

Krueger, A. O. (1974). The political economy of the rent-seeking society. *American Economic Review* 64(June):291–303.

———. (1998). Why trade liberalisation is good for growth. *The Economic Journal* 108(September):1513–1522.

Krugman, P. R., and M. Obstfeld. (1997). *International Economics: Theory and Policy,* 4th ed. Reading, MA: Addison-Wesley, 1997.

Leamer, E. (1988). Measures of openness. In *Trade Policy and Empirical Analysis,* R. Baldwin (ed.). Chicago: University of Chicago Press.

Lee, J.-W. (1993). International trade, distortions, and long-run economic growth. *International Monetary Fund Staff Papers* 40(2):299–328.

Lerner, A. P. (1936). The symmetry between import and export taxes. *Economica* 11:306–313.

Levine, R., and D. Renelt. (1992). A sensitivity analysis of cross-country growth regressions. *American Economic Review* 82(4):942–963.

Little, I., T. Scitovsky, and M. Scott. (1970). *Industry and Trade in Some Developing Countries.* London and New York: Oxford University Press.

Maddison, A. (1982). *Phases of Capitalist Development.* Oxford and New York: Oxford University Press.

———. (1995). *Monitoring the World Economy: 1820–1992.* Development Centre Studies. Paris and Washington: Organisation for Economic Co-operation and Development, 1995.

Matsuyama, K. (1992). Agricultural productivity, comparative advantage, and economic growth. *Journal of Economic Theory* 58(2):317–334.

OECD. (1998). *Open Markets Matter: The Benefits of Trade and Investment Liberalisation.* Paris: OECD. 1998.

O'Rourke, K. H. (1997). Tariffs and growth in the late nineteenth century. Center for Economic Policy Research. Discussion Paper 1700.

Park, W. and J. C. Ginarte. (1997). Intellectual property rights and economic growth. *Contemporary Economic Policy* 15(3):51–61.

Pertamina. (1998). http://www.pertamina.co.id/ptmhp.htm.

Pollard, S. (1974). *European Economic Integration, 1815–1970.* London: Thames and Hudson.

Pritchett, L. (1996). Measuring outward orientation: Can it be done? *Journal of Development Economics* 49(2).

Radelet, S., J. D. Sachs, and J.-W. Lee. (1997). Economic growth in Asia. Harvard Institute for International Development. Development Discussion Paper.
Richardson, P., et al. (1997). Globalization and linkages: Macro-structural challenges and opportunities. OECD Economic Surveys 28.
Roberts, M. J., and J. R. Tybout, eds. (1996). *Industrial Evolution in Developing Countries.* New York: Oxford University Press for the World Bank.
Rodríguez, F., and D. Rodrik. (1999). Trade policy and economic growth: A skeptic's guide to the cross-national literature. Cambridge, MA: National Bureau of Economic Research. NBER Working Paper 7081.
Rodrik, D. (1999). *The New Global Economy and Developing Countries: Making Openness Work.* Washington: Overseas Development Council.
Rogoff, K. (1996). The purchasing power parity puzzle. *Journal of Economic Literature* XXXIV (June):647–668.
Rogowski, R. (1989). *Commerce and Coalitions: How Trade Affects Domestic Political Alignments.* Princeton: Princeton University Press.
Sachs, J., and A. Warner. (1995). Economic reform and the process of global integration. *Brookings Papers on Economic Activity* 1995(1):1–118.
Sala-i-Martin, X. (1997). I just ran two million regressions. *American Economic Review* 87(2):178–183.
Slaughter, M. J. (2000). Trade liberalization and per capita income convergence: A difference-in-differences analysis. *Journal of International Economics,* forthcoming.
Srinivasan, T. N. (1997). As the century turns: Analytics, empirics, and politics of development. Economic Growth Center, Yale University.
Stiglitz, J. E. (1998). Towards a new paradigm for development: Strategies, policies, and processes. 1998 Prebisch Lecture, UNCTAD, Geneva.
Summers, R., and A. Heston. (1988). A new set of international comparisons of real product and price levels: Estimates for 130 countries, 1950–1985. *Review of Income and Wealth* 34(March):1–25.
———, and ———. (1994). *Penn World Tables Mark 5.6.* http://www.nber.org.
Thompson, M., and F. Rushing. (1996). An empirical analysis of the impact of patent protection on economic growth. *Journal of Economic Development* 21(2): 61–79.
Tornell, A. (1997). Economic growth and decline with endogenous property rights. *Journal of Economic Growth* 2(3):219–250.
Vamvakidis, A. (1996). Regional integration and economic growth. *The World Bank Economic Review* 12(2):251–270.
Wacziarg, R. (1998). Measuring the dynamic gains from trade. *World Bank Working Paper* 2001.
White, H. L. (1980). A heteroskedasticity-consistent covariance matrix estimator and a direct test for heteroskedasticity. *Econometrica* 48:817–838.
Wolf, H. (1993). Trade orientation: Measurement and consequences. *Estudios de Economia* 20(20):52–72.
World Bank. (1983). *Mauritius Economic Memorandum: Recent Developments and Prospects.* Washington: The World Bank.
———. (1989). *Mauritius: Managing Success.* Washington: The World Bank.
———. (1994). *Adjustment in Africa: Reforms, Results, and the Road Ahead.* Washington: The World Bank.
———. (1996). *Global Economic Prospects and the Developing Countries.* Washington: The World Bank.

———. (1998). *World Development Indicators CD-ROM*. Washington: The World Bank.

Yarbrough, B. M., and R. M. Yarbrough. (2000). *The World Economy: Trade and Finance,* 5th ed. Fort Worth, TX: Harcourt College Publishers.

# B
# International Technology Diffusion

# [5]

ELSEVIER European Economic Review 39 (1995) 859–887

EUROPEAN ECONOMIC REVIEW

# International R&D spillovers

David T. Coe [a], Elhanan Helpman [b,c,*]

[a] International Monetary Fund, Washington DC, USA
[b] The Eitan Berglas School of Economics, Tel Aviv University, Tel Aviv 69978, Israel
[c] Canadian Institute for Advanced Research, Toronto, Canada

Received April 1994; final version received November 1994

**Abstract**

A model is presented based on recent theories of economic growth that treat commercially oriented innovation efforts as a major engine of technological progress. We study the extent to which a country's total factor productivity depends not only on domestic R&D capital but also on foreign R&D capital. Our estimates indicate that foreign R&D has beneficial effects on domestic productivity, and that these are stronger the more open an economy is to foreign trade. Moreover, the estimated rates of return on R&D are very high, both in terms of domestic output and international spillovers.

*Keywords:* Productivity; R&D; Spillover

*JEL classification:* O31; O40

## 1. Introduction

Economic growth has many facets. It depends on the utilization of resources, the rate of population growth, the savings rate, the mode of organization of economic activity, technological know how, and more. Whereas the neoclassical theory treated technological progress as an exogenous process and focused instead on capital accumulation as the main endogenous source of output expansion, recent research has provided novel ways of dealing with technical progress. The

* Corresponding author.


*SSDI* 0014-2921(94)00100-6

latter studies view commercially oriented innovation efforts that respond to economic incentives as a major engine of technological progress and productivity growth (see Romer, 1990; Grossman and Helpman, 1991). In this view, innovation feeds on knowledge that results from cumulative R&D experience on the one hand, and it contributes to this stock of knowledge on the other. Consequently an economy's productivity level depends on its cumulative R&D effort and on its effective stock of knowledge, with the two being inter-related. There exists, in fact, convincing empirical evidence that cumulative domestic R&D is an important determinant of productivity (see Griliches, 1988; Coe and Moghadam, 1993).

In a world with international trade in goods and services, foreign direct investment, and an international exchange of information and dissemination of knowledge, a country's productivity depends on its own R&D as well as on the R&D efforts of its trade partners. Own R&D produces traded and nontraded goods and services that bring about more effective use of existing resources and thereby raises a country's productivity level. In addition, own R&D enhances a country's benefits from foreign technical advances, and the better a country takes advantage of technological advances in the rest of the world the more productive it becomes. The benefits from foreign R&D can be both direct and indirect. Direct benefits consist of learning about new technologies and materials, production processes, or organizational methods. Indirect benefits emanate from imports of goods and services that have been developed by trade partners. In either case foreign R&D affects a country's productivity.

We study in this paper the extent to which a country's productivity level depends on domestic and foreign R&D capital stocks. Following much of the theoretical and empirical literature, we use cumulative R&D expenditure as a proxy for a stock of knowledge. For every country in our sample we construct a stock of domestic knowledge that is based on domestic R&D expenditure and a foreign stock of knowledge that is based on R&D spending of its trade partners. For the construction of foreign R&D capital stocks we use import weighted sums of trade partner's cumulative R&D spending. [1] We explain the rationale for this procedure in the theoretical section. For every country we also calculate a measure of total factor productivity defined as the log of output minus a weighted average of the logs of labor and capital inputs, where the weights equal factor shares. Having done these calculations, we estimate the effects of domestic and foreign R&D capital stocks on total factor productivity. Our estimates underline the importance of the interaction between international trade and foreign R&D.

Our sample consists of 21 OECD countries plus Israel during the period 1971–90. We find, using pooled time series cross section data, that both domestic and foreign R&D capital stocks have important effects on total factor productiv-

[1] This is analogous to Terleckyj's (1974) use of input-output weights to model how R&D is imported across industries.

ity. Some of our estimates suggest that foreign R&D capital stocks have stronger effects on domestic productivity the larger the share of domestic imports in GDP. It follows that more open economies extract larger productivity benefits from foreign R&D than less open economies. Moreover, measuring the importance of the R&D capital stock by the elasticity of TFP with respect to the R&D capital stock, our estimates suggest that the foreign R&D capital stock may be at least as important as the domestic R&D capital stock in the smaller countries, while in the larger countries (the G7) the domestic R&D capital stock may be more important.

The next section contains a discussion of the theory that underlies our empirical specification. A brief review of the main features of our data is presented in Section 3, and the sources and construction of the data are described in an appendix. The main empirical findings and their economic interpretations are reported in Section 4. Section 5 concludes.

## 2. Theory

Our empirical equations build on some recent theoretical models of innovation-driven growth. Since the basic models of this theory have been widely discussed, we provide in this section only rudimentary details and focus instead on results that are needed for our purpose. The reader is referred to Helpman (1992) for a review and to Grossman and Helpman (1991) for a detailed description of the models on which we base our discussion.

In the simplest case, an economy manufactures final output $Y$ from an assortment of intermediate inputs. Given the measure of available intermediate inputs $n$, the production function of final output is a linear homogeneous function of the employed inputs. Two stories appear to be common in the formulation of the production function. In one case the inputs are horizontally differentiated. A simple formalization of this view takes the production function to be a symmetric constant elasticity of substitution function, with the elasticity of substitution being larger than one and every input to be manufactured with a unit of labor per unit output. The result is that output is proportional to aggregate employment of intermediates, or to total labor employed in the manufacturing of intermediates. And most importantly, the factor of proportionality is an increasing function of the measure of available inputs $n$.

The measure of available inputs expands as a result of R&D investment. Entrepreneurs who seek monopoly profits invest resources in the development of new intermediate inputs. In this event the measure of available inputs is an increasing function of the country's cumulative R&D effort. It follows that the log of total factor productivity (TFP), as measured by $\log Y - \log L$ (where $L$ stands for the available labor force and no capital is used in production), depends on a measure of cumulative R&D and the share of labor employed in manufacturing. In this model labor is employed either in manufacturing or in R&D. Therefore as long as R&D is a small share of GDP that does not differ greatly across countries and time periods (as it is in our sample where R&D expenditures average about 1.5 percent of GDP with a maximum of about 2 percent), the fraction of labor employed in production is very close to one and remains approximately constant. In this case we expect differences in cumulative R&D to explain most of the variation in TFP.

An alternative model treats intermediate inputs as vertically differentiated; namely, they come in different qualities. Here the effectiveness of an input in manufacturing depends on the number of times it has been improved, and inputs that have been improved more times are more productive. Entrepreneurs invest in research and development to improve inputs. In this model, the average productivity of all inputs depends on cumulative past R&D spending. As a result, this model too implies that total factor productivity is rising with the cumulative R&D effort.

These two examples have disregarded capital and international trade. As for capital, Grossman and Helpman (1991) have shown in Chapter 5 that the presence of capital accumulation does not change the fact that TFP is an increasing function of cumulative R&D, except that with capital as an additional factor of production, $\log TFP$ has to be defined in the usual way as $\log Y - \beta \log K - (1-\beta)\log L$, where $\beta$ is the share of capital in GDP.

Next consider international trade. The previous arguments apply in the absence of international trade in intermediate inputs, regardless of whether final output is traded or not. If this was the relevant case, we would be able to explain variations in a country's total factor productivity with variations in its domestic R&D capital stock. Most international trade takes place in producer goods, however. In this event countries use extensively inputs that are manufactured by trade partners and inputs that were developed by trade partners. How does this change our conclusions?

In order to see as clearly as possible the role of international trade, consider an extreme case in which all intermediate inputs are traded internationally. Under these circumstances our basic relationship between total factor productivity and cumulative R&D remains valid, except that the relevant measure of R&D capital is not the individual country's R&D capital stock, but rather the entire *world's* R&D capital stock. When a country has free access to all inputs available in the world economy, its productivity depends on the world's R&D experience, because independently of where an input has been developed or improved the country can purchase the input and employ it in manufacturing. In this extreme case, domestic R&D has the same productivity effects as foreign R&D.

For empirical implementations of these models neither one of the extreme specifications of tradeability of intermediate inputs seems appropriate; there exist many tradeable inputs; but nontradeable inputs of goods and services are also prevalent. It is therefore most practical to formulate an empirical equation that allows for both traded and nontraded inputs. For these reasons we estimate equations in which variations in TFP are explained by variations in both the domestic and foreign R & D capital stocks. Our simplest equation has the following specification:

$$\log F_i = \alpha_i^0 + \alpha_i^d \log S_i^d + \alpha_i^f \log S_i^f, \tag{1}$$

where $i$ is a country index, $\log F$ is the log of total factor productivity (equal to $\log Y - \beta \log K - (1-\beta)\log L$), $S^d$ represents the domestic R & D capital stock, and $S^f$ represents the foreign R & D capital stock defined as the import-share-weighted average of the domestic R & D capital stocks of trade partners. In this specification we allow the coefficients $\alpha$ to vary across countries. In the implementation, however, we will seek cross-country restrictions on the elasticities $\alpha^d$ and $\alpha^f$. [2] The specification of (1) can be thought of as a multicountry extension of models relating TFP to only the domestic R & D capital stock, which would be a special case with $\alpha^f = 0$.

The specification of (1) may not capture adequately the role of international trade. Although, the foreign stock of knowledge $S^f$ consists of import weighted foreign R & D capital stocks, these weights are fractions that add up to one and therefore do not properly reflect the *level* of imports. It might be expected that whenever two countries have the same composition of imports and face the same composition of R & D capital stocks among trade partners, the country that imports more relative to its GDP may benefit more from foreign R & D. This is in line with the theoretical arguments presented above and can be strengthened with additional arguments that relate productivity gains to trade volumes (see Grossman and Helpman, 1991, Section 6.5). For these reasons a modified specification of (1) that accounts for the interaction between foreign R & D capital stocks and the level of international trade seems preferable. To this end we estimate

$$\log F_i = \alpha_i^0 + \alpha_i^d \log S_i^d + \alpha_i^f m_i \log S_i^f, \tag{2}$$

where $m$ stands for the fraction of imports in GDP. In this equation the elasticity of TFP with respect to the domestic R & D capital stock equals $\alpha^d$ while the elasticity of TFP with respect to the foreign R & D capital stock equals $\alpha^f m$. It follows that whenever $\alpha^f$ is the same for all countries the latter elasticity varies across countries in proportion to their import shares. [3]

---

[2] We always allow the constants $\alpha^0$ to differ across countries for two reasons: first, there may exist country specific effects on productivity that are not captured by the variables used in our equations; and second, variables are transformed into index numbers and TFP is measured in country specific currencies whereas both R&D capital stocks are in U.S. dollars.

[3] An analogy may help to put our use of import shares in context. In microeconomic studies of technological spillovers it is common to seek a metric, such as 'technological closeness' in order to gauge the intensity of spillovers. Scherer (1982) and Jaffe (1986) provide good examples. In our case it is most natural to use import shares as measures of intensity. This is the more so whenever productivity gains are related to imports of intermediate inputs as exemplified by the theoretical model.

Table 1
Summary statistics

| | $F_{1990}/F_{1971}$ | $S^d_{1990}/S^d_{1971}$ | $S^f_{1990}/S^d_{1971}$ | m (in percent) | |
|---|---|---|---|---|---|
| | | | | 1971 | 1990 |
| United States | 1.1 | 2.0 | 3.4 | 5.5 | 11.2 |
| Japan | 1.7 | 4.2 | 1.7 | 9.6 | 9.3 |
| West Germany | 1.2 | 2.6 | 1.6 | 19.1 | 26.1 |
| France | 1.4 | 1.8 | 1.7 | 15.3 | 22.8 |
| Italy | 1.4 | 2.8 | 1.4 | 15.6 | 19.6 |
| United Kingdom | 1.3 | 1.3 | 1.8 | 21.4 | 27.7 |
| Canada | 1.1 | 2.7 | 1.9 | 20.0 | 25.5 |
| Australia | 1.1 | 4.9 | 2.0 | 14.7 | 18.6 |
| Austria | 1.2 | 3.6 | 2.3 | 30.8 | 38.9 |
| Belgium | 1.4 | 2.3 | 1.5 | 43.9 | 88.2 |
| Denmark | 1.2 | 2.3 | 1.9 | 30.9 | 31.1 |
| Finland | 1.4 | 4.5 | 2.2 | 26.8 | 25.4 |
| Greece | 1.2 | 18.7 | 1.7 | 17.0 | 32.0 |
| Ireland | 1.3 | 3.7 | 2.3 | 42.1 | 56.1 |
| Israel | 1.3 | 7.3 | 1.6 | 50.0 | 52.0 |
| Netherlands | 1.2 | 1.5 | 1.9 | 45.1 | 53.9 |
| New Zealand | 0.9 | 2.1 | 2.3 | 25.5 | 22.6 |
| Norway | 1.5 | 4.0 | 2.0 | 45.3 | 37.7 |
| Portugal | 1.3 | 2.0 | 1.4 | 33.6 | 44.9 |
| Spain | 1.2 | 7.0 | 1.2 | 14.7 | 21.4 |
| Sweden | 1.1 | 3.5 | 1.9 | 22.8 | 31.6 |
| Switzerland | 1.1 | 1.3 | 1.9 | 39.1 | 38.3 |

*Source:* Tables A.1, A.3, A.5, and A.6 in Appendix A.

## 3. Data

We provide in the appendix details about data sources and the construction of the variables for estimation purposes. Here we only highlight some features of the data. [4] As shown in Table 1, total factor productivity increased over the 1971–90 period in all countries except New Zealand. But the upward trend was neither uniform across countries nor uniform over time. Japan and Norway experienced the largest increase in productivity of about 70 and 50 percent, respectively; while in New Zealand productivity actually declined. Other countries had intermediate values. Fig. 1 provides plots of TFP for six of these countries; they clearly exhibit substantial fluctuations.

[4] The data used to construct TFP for a number of countries have been revised during the period since our database was established; a preliminary examination of the estimation results based on the updated TFP data indicates that our central conclusions are unchanged.

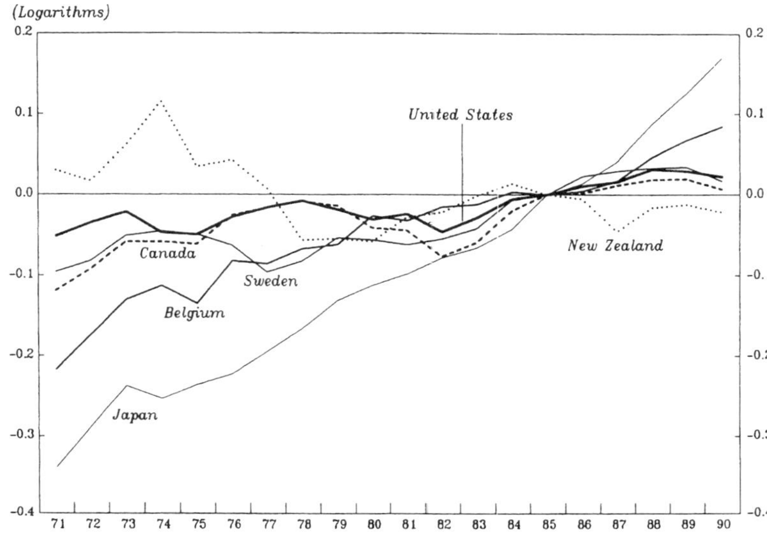


Fig. 1. Total factor productivity.

Between 1971 and 1990 the domestic R&D capital stock increased significantly in most countries. In Greece in particular it increased by a factor of 19, but this is an exception. [5] In Israel and Spain this stock was sevenfold larger by the end of the period than at the beginning, and it had more than quadrupled in Japan, Australia, Finland, and Norway. The United Kingdom and Switzerland experienced the slowest expansion of their domestic R&D capital stock of 20 and 30 percent, respectively. An important point to observe, however, is that the annual changes in this R&D capital stock were not uniform across countries, as can be seen from Fig. 2.

Overall changes in foreign R&D capital stocks were less dramatic than in the domestic R&D capital stocks. Here the United States experienced the fastest expansion: more than threefold. Spain faced the smallest increase of only 20 percent. Other countries enjoyed a doubling of their foreign R&D capital stocks with some variance around this figure. Fluctuations in the foreign R&D capital stocks around their time trends appear to be larger than for the domestic R&D

[5] The level and growth of the R&D capital stocks are sensitive to the assumed depreciation rates and the calculated benchmarks. Table 13 reports estimation results based on a 15 percent rather than a 5 percent depreciation rate.

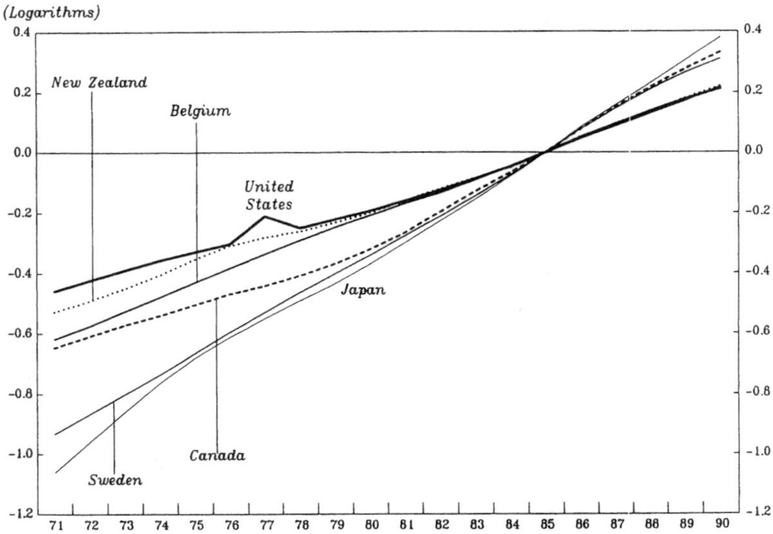


Fig. 2. Domestic research and development capital stocks.

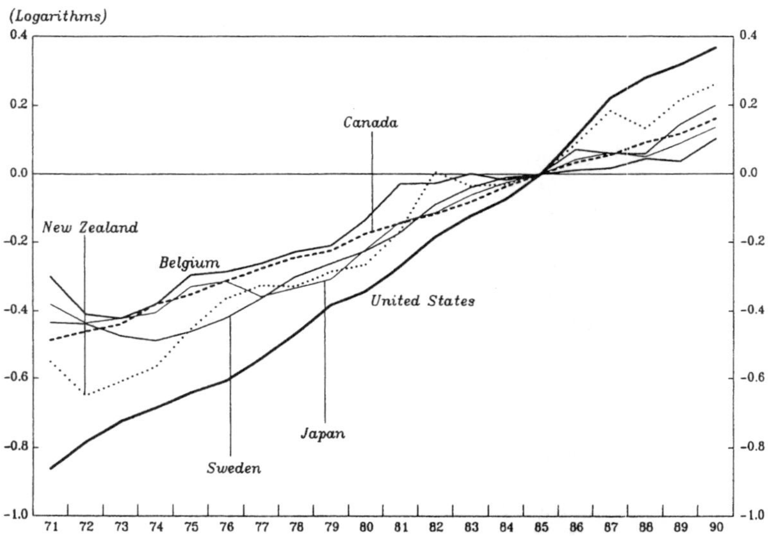


Fig. 3. Trade weighted foreign research and development capital stocks.

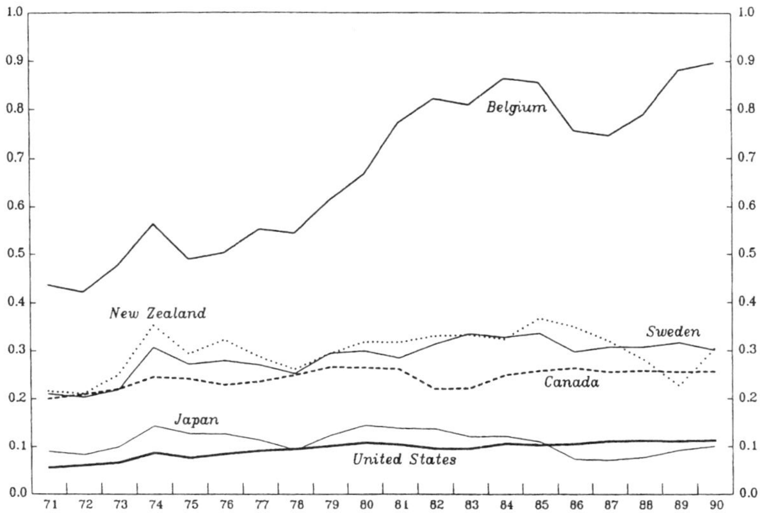


Fig. 4. Import share in GDP.

capital stocks, reflecting the use of bilateral import shares that change from year-to-year, as can be seen by comparing Fig. 3 with Fig. 2.

Finally, Table 1 provides data on import shares. In all countries except for Japan, Finland, New Zealand, Norway, and Switzerland the import share increased between 1971 and 1990. It has more than doubled in the United States and Belgium and only slightly increased in Denmark and Israel. Import shares declined slightly from 1971 to 1990 in Japan, Finland, New Zealand, Norway, and Switzerland. Moreover, there exist substantial differences in import shares across countries. Belgium had by far the largest import share in 1990 (88.2 percent) while Japan had the smallest (9.3 percent). And as shown in Fig. 4, import shares fluctuated over time.

## 4. Empirical findings

Because almost all of our data exhibit a clear trend, and because we want to estimate the long-run relationship between total factor productivity and the foreign and domestic R&D capital stocks, we seek to estimate equations that are cointegrated. [6] The basic idea of cointegration is that if there is a long-run

[6] Cuthbertson et al. (1992) present a useful survey of cointegration; see also Engle and Granger (1987) and Stock (1987).

Table 2
Pooled unit-root tests (annual data 1972–90 for 22 countries, 418 observations) [a]

| | Levin and Lin | |
|---|---|---|
| | (1992) | (1993) |
| log $F$ | −1.85 | 0.54 |
| log $S^d$ | −0.73 | 0 |
| log $S^f$ | −2.00 | 2.58 |
| $m \cdot \log S^f$ | −4.07 | 2.86 |

[a] The critical values at the 10 percent confidence level are −6.78 for Levin and Lin (1992), and −1.64 for Levin and Lin (1993). $F$ = total factor productivity; $S^d$ = domestic R and D capital stock, beginning of year; $S^f$ = foreign R and D capital stock, beginning of year; $m$ = ratio of imports of goods and services to GDP, both in the previous year.

relationship between two or more trended variables, a regression containing all the variables – the cointegrating equation – will have a stationary error term, even if none of the variables taken alone is stationary. If the error term is not stationary, the estimated relationship may be spurious (Granger and Newbold, 1974).

Most studies of the determinants of total factor productivity or output have been based on a change, rather than a levels, specification because differencing was thought necessary to avoid the spurious correlation problem when estimating a relationship between trended variables. The disadvantage of a change specification is that the information embodied in the long-run relationship between the levels of the variables is discarded by differencing. The advantage of the cointegrating approach, in which the relationship is estimated in level terms, is that it exploits rather than discards the relevant information about shared trends that is embodied in the levels data.

Cointegrated equations have attractive econometric properties. The most important is that as the number of observations increases, OLS estimates of the cointegrating equation converge on the true parameter values much faster than in the case where the variables are stationary, i.e., they are 'super consistent' (Stock, 1987). Cointegration techniques have been widely applied to time-series data. It seems natural to test for international R&D spillovers on panel data, however, and the relatively small number of time-series observations that are available for any single country makes the use of a panel data set particularly attractive. We therefore estimate our equations on panel data and interpret the results as pooled cointegrating equations.

Before turning to the estimation results, we need to confirm that our data are nonstationary. When done separately on the time series for each country, the Dickey–Fuller and the augmented Dickey–Fuller tests generally do not reject the presence of a unit root. As is well known, however, the power of these tests is very low, particularly with only twenty annual observations. Levin and Lin (1992, 1993) have recently derived the limiting distributions for unit root tests on panel data, and have shown that the power of these tests increases dramatically as the

Table 3
Total factor productivity estimation results (pooled data 1971–90 for 22 countries, 440 observations) [a]

| | (i) | (ii) | (iii) |
|---|---|---|---|
| $\log S^d$ | 0.097 | 0.089 | 0.078 |
| $G7 \cdot \log S^d$ | | 0.134 | 0.156 |
| $\log S^f$ | 0.092 | 0.060 | |
| $m \cdot \log S^f$ | | | 0.294 |
| Standard error | 0.049 | 0.046 | 0.044 |
| $R^2$ | 0.558 | 0.621 | 0.651 |
| $R^2$ adjusted | 0.534 | 0.600 | 0.630 |
| Cointegration tests: | | | |
| Levin and Lin (1992) | −4.533 | −9.356 | −5.082 |
| Levin and Lin (1993) | 0.570 | 2.201 | 2.266 |
| $t$-statistic on the lagged residual in the EC model | −5.451 | −6.293 | −6.974 |

[a] The dependent variable is log (total factor productivity). All equations include unreported, country-specific constants. The critical value at the 10 percent confidence level is −6.78 for Levin and Lin (1992), and −1.64 for the other two cointegration tests; test statistics that are negative and greater in absolute value than the critical values indicate that the equations are cointegrated. The EC (error correction) model is the first difference of each equation augmented to include the lagged residual from the equations reported above. $S^d$ = domestic R and D capital stock, beginning of year; $S^f$ = foreign R and D capital stock, beginning of year; $G7$ = dummy variable equal to 1.0 for the seven major countries and equal to 0 for the other 15 countries; $m$ = ratio of imports of goods and services to GDP, both in the previous year.

cross-section dimension increases. [7] Unit root tests on the pooled data confirm that the variables are nonstationary, as shown in Table 2.

We report in Table 3 three pooled cointegrating regressions based on Eqs. (1) and (2). [8] All of the equations include unreported country-specific constants. [9] Equation (i) is the basic specification where the estimated coefficients on the domestic and foreign R&D capital stocks are constrained to be the same for all

[7] The test in Levin and Lin (1992) constrains the dynamics of the augmented Dickey-Fuller to be the same across all countries, whereas the test in Levin and Lin (1993) allows the dynamics to differ across countries.

[8] As is standard practice when reporting cointegrating equations, we do not report standard errors for the estimated coefficients because they are, in general, biased and their distribution is not asymptotically normal. In any event, the estimated standard errors are all small relative to the estimated coefficients (one-fourth or less).

[9] Including the country-specific constants generally makes little difference to the estimated parameters. It does, of course, improve the goodness of fit somewhat: the adjusted $R^2$ of equation (iii), for example, increases from 0.532 to 0.630 when the country-specific constants are included. This means that the lion's share of the explained variance is due to our R&D capital stock variables rather than to the country-specific constants.

countries. In equation (ii), the impact of domestic R&D is allowed to differ between the largest seven economies compared with the other 15 economies – this is done by interacting the domestic R&D stock with a dummy variable that takes the value of 1 for the seven largest economies (G7) – while constraining the impact of foreign R&D to be the same for all countries. [10] This latter constraint is dropped in equation (iii) where the foreign R&D capital stock is interacted with the ratio of imports to GDP, thereby allowing for country-specific, time-varying elasticities on foreign R&D that are related to trade shares (as discussed above). If the ratio of imports to GDP is included separately as an additional independent variable, the estimated coefficient is negative. Estimation results based on a variety of alternative specifications and testing for parameter stability are reported in Appendix B.

For the estimated equations to be cointegrated, the residuals must be stationary. Equation (ii) is cointegrated based on Levin and Lin (1992), but none of the equations are cointegrated based on Levin and Lin (1993). Engle and Granger (1987) suggest that a test for cointegration is to include the lagged residuals from the cointegrating equations in the corresponding error-correction model and then test whether the estimated coefficient is negative and significantly different than zero. [11] The relevant *t*-statistics, which are also reported in Table 3, indicate that the error correction terms are significantly different from zero, suggesting that the equations in Table 3 are cointegrated. Given these mixed results, and given that the econometrics of pooled cointegration are not yet fully worked out, we place more emphasis on consistency with the theoretical model and on the a priori plausibility of the estimated parameters than on the tests for cointegration. [12]

The estimated coefficients reported in Table 3 are of the expected sign and the magnitudes of the estimated elasticities are plausible and relatively stable across the different specifications. For the non-G7 countries, the estimated elasticities of TFP with respect to the domestic R&D stock are similar to the 0.06 to 0.1 range typically found in single-country studies (as summarized in Griliches (1988, p.

[10] We tested the hypothesis that the coefficient on the foreign R&D stock also differed between the G7 economies compared with the others by adding the foreign R&D stock interacted with the G7 dummy to equation (ii), but the estimated coefficient was very small. The larger impact of domestic R&D on total factor productivity may reflect the fact that large countries perform R&D across a broader range of possible R&D activities, thereby better exploiting available complementarities. This is more likely the slower or the less perfectly R&D results spillover to foreign countries. Tests of whether the estimated slope coefficients are the same across countries are rejected.

[11] Engle and Granger (1987) propose a two-step approach to cointegration. The first step is to estimate the long-run cointegration equation, which corresponds to the equations reported in Table 3. The second step is to estimate the dynamic error-correction model, which is the first difference of the cointegration equation augmented to include the lagged residuals from the cointegration equation as the error-correction term and other stationary variables that are relevant to the short-run dynamics.

[12] Evidence in favor of cointegration is stronger for some of the equations reported in Table 14 of Appendix B, which are based on an output rather than a total factor productivity specification.

Table 4
Country-specific, time-varying estimates of the impact of R&D capital stocks on total factor productivity [a]

| | Elasticity of total factor productivity with respect to: | | | | |
|---|---|---|---|---|---|
| | World R&D | Foreign R&D | | | Domestic R&D |
| | 1990 | 1971 | 1980 | 1990 | 1971–90 |
| United States | 0.267 | 0.016 | 0.030 | 0.033 | |
| Japan | 0.261 | 0.028 | 0.037 | 0.027 | |
| West Germany | 0.311 | 0.056 | 0.072 | 0.077 | |
| France | 0.301 | 0.045 | 0.061 | 0.067 | 0.234 |
| Italy | 0.292 | 0.046 | 0.067 | 0.058 | |
| United Kingdom | 0.315 | 0.063 | 0.081 | 0.081 | |
| Canada | 0.309 | 0.059 | 0.078 | 0.075 | |
| Australia | 0.132 | 0.043 | 0.049 | 0.055 | |
| Austria | 0.192 | 0.091 | 0.106 | 0.114 | |
| Belgium | 0.337 | 0.129 | 0.181 | 0.260 | |
| Denmark | 0.169 | 0.091 | 0.094 | 0.092 | |
| Finland | 0.152 | 0.079 | 0.088 | 0.075 | |
| Greece | 0.172 | 0.050 | 0.063 | 0.094 | |
| Ireland | 0.243 | 0.124 | 0.180 | 0.165 | 0.078 |
| Israel | 0.231 | 0.147 | 0.154 | 0.153 | |
| Netherlands | 0.236 | 0.133 | 0.146 | 0.158 | |
| New Zealand | 0.144 | 0.075 | 0.086 | 0.066 | |
| Norway | 0.188 | 0.133 | 0.124 | 0.111 | |
| Portugal | 0.210 | 0.099 | 0.117 | 0.132 | |
| Spain | 0.141 | 0.043 | 0.043 | 0.063 | |
| Sweden | 0.171 | 0.067 | 0.087 | 0.093 | |
| Switzerland | 0.190 | 0.115 | 0.106 | 0.113 | |

[a] Based on equation (iii) in Table 3.

15)). For the G7 countries, however, the estimated elasticities of TFP with respect to the domestic R&D stock in equations (ii) and (iii) are considerably larger than those from studies that do not include international R&D spillovers. Our cross-country data and estimation procedure that focuses on the identification of long-run relationships may be better able to estimate the social return to R&D compared with studies for individual countries.

In equation (iii), which corresponds to Eq. (2) in the theory section, the impact of the foreign R&D capital stock varies across countries and over time. Table 4 reports the estimated elasticities of total factor productivity with respect to the foreign R&D capital stocks – which are simply the estimated coefficient from Table 3 multiplied by the import share – for 1971, 1980, and 1990. With the notable exceptions of Norway, Spain, and Switzerland, the estimated impact of foreign R&D rises from 1971 to 1980, usually by a substantial amount. In most of the countries, and especially in Belgium, the estimated impact of foreign R&D rises further during the 1980s. Although the domestic R&D capital stock has a much larger impact on total factor productivity in the large countries compared with the small countries, the smaller countries are more open and hence benefit from foreign R&D more than the larger countries. Indeed, foreign R&D has a larger impact on total factor productivity than does domestic R&D in all of the smaller countries except Australia, Finland, New Zealand, and Spain. Foreign R&D has the strongest impact on Belgium, followed by Ireland, the Netherlands, and Israel.

Estimates of the international R&D spillovers based on equation (iii) are presented in Table 5. Each entry is the estimated elasticity of total factor productivity in the country indicated in the row with respect to the R&D capital stock in the country indicated in the column. [13] Elasticities are largest with respect to the R&D capital stocks of the major countries, because their R&D capital stocks are relatively large and because the major countries account for a relatively high share of other countries' imports, which are used as the weights in the computation of the foreign R&D capital stocks. The estimated R&D spillover elasticities are large. They are largest from the United States and Japan. The estimates imply that a 1 percent increase in the R&D capital stock in these countries increases total factor productivity in their trade partners by an average of 0.04 and 0.01 percent, respectively.

The last row of Table 5 provides average elasticities, taking account of a country's effect on both its own productivity and on the productivity of its trade partners. It shows that a 1 percent increase in the R&D capital stock in the United States raises the average productivity of all 22 countries by about 0.12 percent, while a 1 percent increase in the Japanese R&D capital stock raises the average productivity of the 22 countries by only 0.045 percent. This difference reflects partly the fact that the United States has an R&D capital stock that is about four times as large as Japan's R&D capital stock. Since the elasticity of the United States is less than three times as large as the elasticity of Japan, it follows that the worldwide rate of return on investment in Japanese R&D is larger than the worldwide rate of return on investment in American R&D.

In order to obtain estimates of rates of return on investment in R&D, we need to multiply the elasticities with the appropriate ratios of output to R&D capital stocks. In particular, the rate of return on country $j$'s R&D capital stock in terms of country $i$'s output is

$$\rho_{ij} = \alpha_{ij} \frac{Y_i}{S_j^{\mathrm{d}}}, \tag{3}$$

[13] When the R&D capital stock of country $i$, $S_i^{\mathrm{d}}$, increases by 1 percent, the foreign R&D capital stock of country $j$, $S_j^{\mathrm{f}}$, rises by $m_i^j S_i^{\mathrm{d}} / \Sigma_{k \neq j} m_k^j S_k^{\mathrm{d}}$ percent and country $j$'s output rises by $m^j \alpha^{\mathrm{f}} m_i^j S_i^{\mathrm{d}} / \Sigma_{k \neq j} m_k^i S_k^{\mathrm{d}}$ percent, where $m^j$ is country $j$'s import share and $m_i^j$ is the fraction of $j$'s imports coming from country $i$. The last formula was used to compute the numbers in Table 5.

Table 5
Elasticities of total factor productivity with respect to R&D capital stocks in the G7 countries, 1990

| | U.S. | Japan | Germany | France | Italy | U.K. | Canada |
|---|---|---|---|---|---|---|---|
| United States | ... | 0.0218 | 0.0039 | 0.0014 | 0.0005 | 0.0024 | 0.0024 |
| Japan | 0.0255 | ... | 0.0008 | 0.0003 | 0.0001 | 0.0003 | 0.0001 |
| West Germany | 0.0465 | 0.0098 | ... | 0.0081 | 0.0024 | 0.0060 | 0.0002 |
| France | 0.0369 | 0.0049 | 0.0156 | ... | 0.0025 | 0.0049 | 0.0001 |
| Italy | 0.0254 | 0.0027 | 0.0166 | 0.0076 | ... | 0.0032 | 0.0001 |
| United Kingdom | 0.0530 | 0.0069 | 0.0131 | 0.0047 | 0.0012 | ... | 0.0003 |
| Canada | 0.0717 | 0.0019 | 0.0005 | 0.0002 | 0.0001 | 0.0005 | ... |
| Australia | 0.0409 | 0.0092 | 0.0019 | 0.0005 | 0.0002 | 0.0018 | 0.0001 |
| Austria | 0.0301 | 0.0103 | 0.0611 | 0.0041 | 0.0033 | 0.0030 | 0.0001 |
| Belgium | 0.0930 | 0.0116 | 0.0812 | 0.0339 | 0.0039 | 0.0230 | 0.0004 |
| Denmark | 0.0449 | 0.0063 | 0.0250 | 0.0037 | 0.0012 | 0.0066 | 0.0001 |
| Finland | 0.0357 | 0.0103 | 0.0165 | 0.0027 | 0.0012 | 0.0053 | 0.0001 |
| Greece | 0.0290 | 0.0138 | 0.0287 | 0.0065 | 0.0057 | 0.0071 | 0.0001 |
| Ireland | 0.1032 | 0.0093 | 0.0095 | 0.0029 | 0.0008 | 0.0378 | 0.0001 |
| Israel | 0.1189 | 0.0045 | 0.0121 | 0.0030 | 0.0017 | 0.0083 | 0.0001 |
| Netherlands | 0.0832 | 0.0075 | 0.0430 | 0.0084 | 0.0016 | 0.0112 | 0.0002 |
| New Zealand | 0.0462 | 0.0130 | 0.0020 | 0.0005 | 0.0002 | 0.0036 | 0.0002 |
| Norway | 0.0643 | 0.0084 | 0.0185 | 0.0033 | 0.0012 | 0.0096 | 0.0006 |
| Portugal | 0.0542 | 0.0093 | 0.0294 | 0.0156 | 0.0049 | 0.0128 | 0.0003 |
| Spain | 0.0358 | 0.0047 | 0.0098 | 0.0060 | 0.0018 | 0.0037 | 0.0001 |
| Sweden | 0.0496 | 0.0092 | 0.0204 | 0.0036 | 0.0011 | 0.0070 | 0.0001 |
| Switzerland | 0.0453 | 0.0080 | 0.0400 | 0.0085 | 0.0032 | 0.0057 | 0.0001 |
| Average elasticity of foreign total factor productivity | 0.0422 | 0.0138 | 0.0091 | 0.0032 | 0.0010 | 0.0033 | 0.0011 |
| Elasticity of domestic total factor productivity | 0.2339 | 0.2339 | 0.2339 | 0.2339 | 0.2339 | 0.2339 | 0.2339 |
| Average elasticity of total factor productivity in all 22 countries | 0.1211 | 0.0446 | 0.0266 | 0.0180 | 0.0154 | 0.0179 | 0.0103 |

[a] Estimated elasticity of total factor productivity in the row country with respect to the R&D capital stock in the column country. Based on equation (iii) in Table 3. Averages are calculated using PPP-based GDP weights.

where $\alpha_{ij}$ stands for the elasticity of country $i$'s output with respect to $j$'s domestic R&D capital stock (the entries in Table 5), $Y_i$ stands for country $i$'s output, and $S_j^d$ stands for country $j$'s domestic R&D capital stock. This formula can be used to calculate all cross-country rates of return on R&D investment as well as the rates of return for groups of countries. Rather than report all these rates of return, we report the average rates of return for two groups of countries: the G7 and the remaining 15 smaller countries. These averages should be more accurate than the rates of return for individual countries because the coefficient $\alpha^d$ was estimated to be equal across countries within each group. [14]

Our calculations (based on the data in Tables 5 and A.7) show that in 1990 the average own rate of return from investment in R&D was 123 percent in the G7 countries and 85 percent in the remaining 15 countries. This means that a $100 increase in the R&D capital stock in a G7 country raises its GDP by $123 on average, and that a $100 increase in the R&D capital stock of one of the smaller 15 countries raises its GDP by $85 on average (based on PPP). In addition, in 1990 the average worldwide rate of return from investment in R&D in the G7 countries was 155 percent. These estimated rates of return are very high. For the G7 countries the difference between the worldwide and the own rate of return is about 30 percent, which implies a large international R&D spillover; about one quarter of the total benefits of R&D investment in a G7 country accrue to its trade partners.

Our estimated rates of return are sensitive to the calculated benchmarks for the R&D capital stocks, because they are sensitive to the levels of the R&D capital stocks. A proportional increase in the levels of R&D capital stocks will not affect the estimated coefficients in Table 3 (due to the presence of country dummies), but it will reduce our estimate of own rates of return on investment in R&D. For this reason we place more confidence in the estimated elasticities than in the estimated rates of return. Nevertheless, the estimated rates of return are indicative of the importance of R&D. Of course, our rates of return refer to the social or economy-wide rates of return from R&D, and thus include beneficial externalities that would not be reflected in the private rate of return from R&D investment by a specific enterprise.

Although the calculations of the international spillovers and the rates of return are based on equation (iii) in Table 3, they would be broadly similar if equations (i) and (ii) were used instead. [15] The specification of equation (iii) implies a linear

[14] It follows from (3) that the own rate of return is given by $\rho_{jj} = \alpha_j^d Y_j / S_j^d$ and that the world wide rate of return on country $j$'s R&D is given by $\rho_j = \Sigma_i \rho_{ij} = \alpha_j Y / S_j^d$, where $Y = \Sigma_i Y_i$ is aggregate GDP and $\alpha_j = \Sigma_i \alpha_{ij} Y_i / Y$ is the GDP weighted average elasticity of output with respect to country $j$'s R&D capital stock. Now consider a set $C$ of countries that have the same elasticity $\alpha$. For this group of countries the average own rate of return equals $\rho_{CC} \equiv \Sigma_{j\in C} \rho_j S_j^d / (\Sigma_{i\in C} S_i^d)$.

[15] This is because the elasticities with respect to the domestic R&D capital stocks are of the same order of magnitude, as is the elasticity with respect to the foreign R&D capital stock (after the estimated coefficient in equation (iii) is divided by the average import share).

relationship between the share of imports of goods or services and the benefits from foreign R&D that may not be realistic. For example, Japan has a very low ratio of imports to GDP, but is commonly thought to have benefited greatly from foreign R&D. We consider equation (iii) to be suggestive of the role that the level of trade may play in the international transmission of the benefits of R&D, which is likely to be a fruitful area for further empirical work.

## 5. Closing comments

The emerging new theory of economic growth builds around innovation driven productivity developments. It draws its inspiration from historical studies that have shown the importance of inventive activities for long-run economic growth on the one hand and the role of economic incentives in propagating these activities on the other. This theory also underlines international economic relations, and in particular international trade, as transmission mechanisms that link a country's productivity gains to economic developments in its trade partners (see Grossman and Helpman (1994) for a review).

Although cross-country studies of economic growth have been recently in abundance, they typically focus on explaining output growth, as determined by the accumulation of labor, capital, and some additional economic and political variables. [16] The novelty of the new theory lies, however, in explaining the growth of total factor productivity, which is the component of output growth that is not attributable to the accumulation of inputs. For this reason we have chosen to follow the theory and focus on the central link between productivity and R&D.

Our evidence suggests that there indeed exist close links between productivity and R&D capital stocks. Not only does a country's total factor productivity depend on its own R&D capital stock, but as suggested by the theory, it also depends on the R&D capital stocks of its trade partners. While the beneficial effects on TFP from domestic R&D have been established in the earlier empirical literature, the evidence of the importance of foreign R&D is new. Foreign R&D may have a stronger effect on domestic productivity the more open an economy is to international trade. Some of our estimates of TFP with respect to R&D capital stocks suggest that in the large countries the elasticity is larger with respect to the domestic R&D capital stock than with respect to the foreign R&D capital stock, while in most of the smaller countries the elasticity is larger with respect to the foreign R&D capital stock. And our estimates suggest that the rate of return on

[16] Englander et al. (1988) and Helliwell (1992) also focus on total factor productivity. We report alternative estimates based on an output rather than on a total factor productivity specification in Appendix B.

R & D capital is very high, both in terms of domestic output and in terms of international spillovers.

These results are encouraging; they suggest that our search for international R & D spillovers was not misplaced. Further explorations with disaggregated data and an explicit treatment of R & D capital stock dynamics will undoubtedly provide valuable new insights.

## Acknowledgment

The work on this paper was partly done when Elhanan Helpman was a Visiting Scholar in the Research Department of the International Monetary Fund. He thanks the IMF for its hospitality and the NSF and U.S.–Israel BSF for financial support. Gene Grossman was instrumental in the development of some of the ideas used in this paper and Zvi Eckstein, Zvi Griliches, Leonardo Leiderman, and Manuel Trajtenberg provided enlightening comments on an earlier draft. Andrew Levin, Mark Taylor, and Alexander Hoffmaister provided helpful discussions on the econometric specification and tests. Shoukang Lin helped construct the R & D capital stocks, Aarne Dimanlig did the econometric tests, and Celia Winkler, Nicholas Dopuch, Toh Kuan, and Ehud Yampoler provided research assistance. We are grateful to all of them. The views expressed in this paper are those of the authors and do not represent the views of the International Monetary Fund or any other institution.

## Appendix A: Data sources and definitions

For each country, total factor productivity $F$ is defined as

$$F = Y/[K^{\beta}L^{(1-\beta)}],$$

where $Y$ is value-added in the business sector, $K$ is the stock of business sector capital, and $L$ is employment in the business sector (except for the United States, Japan, and Israel, where $L$ is total hours worked). All variables are constructed as indices with $1985 = 1$. The coefficient $\beta$ is the average share of capital income from 1987–89. $Y$, $K$, and $L$ are from the OECD Analytical Data Base for all countries except Israel, and except for L for the United States, which is from the *Monthly Labor Review* (U.S. Department of Labor), and Japan, which is from the *Monthly Labor Survey* (Japan, Ministry of Labor). For Israel, $Y$ is from the May 1991 Supplement to the *Monthly Bulletin of Statistics* (Israel, Central Bureau of Statistics) and estimates of $K$ and $L$ were provided by Rafi Melnick of the Bank of Israel. The estimates for total factor productivity are reported in Table A.1 and the capital shares are reported in Table A.2.

Table A.1
Total factor productivity (1985 = 1)

| | U.S. | Japan | Germany | France | Italy | U.K. | Canada | Aus'lia | Austria | Belgium | Denmark | Finland | Greece | Ireland | Israel | Nether. | N.Z. | Norway | Portual | Spain | Sweden | Switz. |
|---|---|---|---|---|---|---|---|---|---|---|---|---|---|---|---|---|---|---|---|---|---|---|
| 1971 | 0.950 | 0.712 | 0.873 | 0.807 | 0.771 | 0.823 | 0.888 | 0.885 | 0.891 | 0.805 | 0.846 | 0.784 | 0.867 | 0.825 | 0.858 | 0.836 | 1.030 | 0.691 | 0.889 | 0.899 | 0.909 | 0.973 |
| 1972 | 0.965 | 0.750 | 0.889 | 0.829 | 0.791 | 0.843 | 0.912 | 0.890 | 0.923 | 0.841 | 0.881 | 0.839 | 0.920 | 0.876 | 0.905 | 0.855 | 1.017 | 0.719 | 0.945 | 0.935 | 0.921 | 0.986 |
| 1973 | 0.978 | 0.789 | 0.913 | 0.855 | 0.835 | 0.887 | 0.943 | 0.915 | 0.942 | 0.878 | 0.894 | 0.871 | 0.956 | 0.888 | 0.922 | 0.886 | 1.062 | 0.745 | 1.040 | 0.957 | 0.950 | 1.000 |
| 1974 | 0.954 | 0.776 | 0.904 | 0.863 | 0.858 | 0.862 | 0.943 | 0.900 | 0.956 | 0.894 | 0.869 | 0.864 | 0.896 | 0.905 | 0.943 | 0.909 | 1.122 | 0.777 | 0.976 | 0.963 | 0.955 | 1.003 |
| 1975 | 0.952 | 0.790 | 0.900 | 0.854 | 0.817 | 0.852 | 0.940 | 0.899 | 0.945 | 0.874 | 0.871 | 0.859 | 0.937 | 0.919 | 0.952 | 0.897 | 1.035 | 0.790 | 0.879 | 0.942 | 0.952 | 0.960 |
| 1976 | 0.972 | 0.801 | 0.944 | 0.877 | 0.863 | 0.876 | 0.974 | 0.917 | 0.973 | 0.922 | 0.913 | 0.831 | 0.975 | 0.915 | 0.931 | 0.933 | 1.043 | 0.809 | 0.922 | 0.948 | 0.939 | 0.968 |
| 1977 | 0.984 | 0.823 | 0.956 | 0.892 | 0.879 | 0.891 | 0.983 | 0.904 | 0.991 | 0.918 | 0.911 | 0.834 | 0.987 | 0.958 | 0.920 | 0.946 | 1.007 | 0.818 | 0.960 | 0.955 | 0.909 | 0.983 |
| 1978 | 0.992 | 0.847 | 0.976 | 0.913 | 0.903 | 0.913 | 0.991 | 0.931 | 0.965 | 0.935 | 0.909 | 0.855 | 1.037 | 0.980 | 0.924 | 0.952 | 0.945 | 0.838 | 0.980 | 0.954 | 0.921 | 0.975 |
| 1979 | 0.981 | 0.878 | 0.997 | 0.936 | 0.946 | 0.925 | 0.986 | 0.948 | 0.990 | 0.940 | 0.926 | 0.902 | 1.050 | 0.964 | 0.920 | 0.955 | 0.947 | 0.873 | 1.023 | 0.938 | 0.948 | 0.986 |
| 1980 | 0.969 | 0.894 | 0.980 | 0.941 | 0.969 | 0.905 | 0.959 | 0.940 | 0.999 | 0.974 | 0.916 | 0.925 | 1.040 | 0.967 | 0.948 | 0.947 | 0.943 | 0.904 | 1.044 | 0.949 | 0.945 | 1.006 |
| 1981 | 0.976 | 0.907 | 0.966 | 0.946 | 0.966 | 0.914 | 0.956 | 0.951 | 0.974 | 0.968 | 0.912 | 0.924 | 0.986 | 0.988 | 0.976 | 0.941 | 0.972 | 0.889 | 1.040 | 0.946 | 0.940 | 0.995 |
| 1982 | 0.955 | 0.925 | 0.946 | 0.965 | 0.961 | 0.941 | 0.926 | 0.932 | 0.963 | 0.984 | 0.937 | 0.945 | 0.982 | 0.960 | 0.966 | 0.937 | 0.978 | 0.883 | 1.052 | 0.950 | 0.946 | 0.974 |
| 1983 | 0.972 | 0.936 | 0.964 | 0.967 | 0.963 | 0.977 | 0.943 | 0.935 | 0.981 | 0.988 | 0.956 | 0.963 | 0.967 | 0.947 | 0.963 | 0.960 | 0.998 | 0.926 | 0.994 | 0.961 | 0.959 | 0.979 |
| 1984 | 0.995 | 0.958 | 0.990 | 0.983 | 0.983 | 0.976 | 0.980 | 0.982 | 0.984 | 1.004 | 0.983 | 0.980 | 0.984 | 0.976 | 0.959 | 0.990 | 1.013 | 0.969 | 0.965 | 0.980 | 0.992 | 0.983 |
| 1985 | 1 | 1 | 1 | 1 | 1 | 1 | 1 | 1 | 1 | 1 | 1 | 1 | 1 | 1 | 1 | 1 | 1 | 1 | 1 | 1 | 1 | 1 |
| 1986 | 1.011 | 1.014 | 0.999 | 1.020 | 1.015 | 1.035 | 1.002 | 0.983 | 0.991 | 1.004 | 1.006 | 1.025 | 1.006 | 0.974 | 1.037 | 0.999 | 0.994 | 1.001 | 1.039 | 1.008 | 1.023 | 1.012 |
| 1987 | 1.016 | 1.041 | 0.995 | 1.036 | 1.040 | 1.062 | 1.011 | 1.002 | 0.997 | 1.017 | 0.988 | 1.055 | 0.998 | 1.018 | 1.080 | 0.987 | 0.955 | 0.995 | 1.066 | 1.033 | 1.029 | 1.015 |
| 1988 | 1.032 | 1.091 | 1.017 | 1.070 | 1.067 | 1.072 | 1.019 | 0.999 | 1.027 | 1.048 | 0.984 | 1.108 | 1.024 | 1.035 | 1.095 | 0.997 | 0.984 | 0.992 | 1.084 | 1.051 | 1.033 | 1.028 |
| 1989 | 1.029 | 1.134 | 1.037 | 1.096 | 1.090 | 1.059 | 1.019 | 1.003 | 1.051 | 1.069 | 0.995 | 1.146 | 1.046 | 1.080 | 1.097 | 1.018 | 0.987 | 1.019 | 1.120 | 1.057 | 1.034 | 1.050 |
| 1990 | 1.022 | 1.185 | 1.058 | 1.108 | 1.083 | 1.055 | 1.007 | 0.988 | 1.075 | 1.088 | 1.011 | 1.133 | 1.038 | 1.110 | 1.139 | 1.031 | 0.978 | 1.046 | 1.143 | 1.061 | 1.017 | 1.059 |

Table A.2
Capital shares, R&D capital stock benchmarks, and PPP exchange rates

| | Capital share $\beta$ | R&D expenditure | | R&D stock Benchmark | PPP exchange Rates–1985 |
|---|---|---|---|---|---|
| | | Available | Avg. growth | | |
| United States | 0.335 | 1963–90 | 2.50 | 590,423 | ... |
| Japan | 0.312 | 1965–89 | 8.14 | 33,687 | 243.9 |
| West Germany | 0.401 | 1963–90 | 5.03 | 44,471 | 2.595 |
| France | 0.354 | 1970–90 | 3.46 | 61,555 | 7.489 |
| Italy | 0.376 | 1963–90 | 6.63 | 9,970 | 1343.8 |
| U.K. | 0.311 | 1969–89 | 1.18 | 116,101 | 0.587 |
| Canada | 0.368 | 1967–90 | 5.08 | 9,787 | 1.254 |
| Australia | 0.387 | 1976–88 | 9.66 | 3,632 | 1.151 |
| Austria | 0.358 | 1970–85 | 6.63 | 1,725 | 17.346 |
| Belgium | 0.355 | 1970–88 | 4.32 | 6,497 | 47.087 |
| Denmark | 0.338 | 1970–89 | 4.79 | 2,217 | 10.038 |
| Finland | 0.331 | 1969–89 | 8.05 | 1,012 | 6.080 |
| Greece | 0.290 | 1981–89 | 11.73 | 149 | 81.477 |
| Ireland | 0.281 | 1969–88 | 7.23 | 254 | 0.743 |
| Israel | 0.270 | 1971–89 | 10.65 | 335 | 764.8 |
| Netherlands | 0.390 | 1970–89 | 2.39 | 19,381 | 2.638 |
| New Zealand | 0.370 | 1972–89 | 4.06 | 495 | 1.354 |
| Norway | 0.285 | 1969–89 | 7.19 | 1,282 | 8.924 |
| Portugal | 0.328 | 1971–88 | 4.17 | 345 | 76.573 |
| Spain | 0.391 | 1969–89 | 10.40 | 1,007 | 112.5 |
| Sweden | 0.338 | 1969–89 | 5.96 | 5,491 | 8.373 |
| Switzerland | 0.211 | 1967–89 | 1.57 | 22,810 | 2.447 |

[a] Capital shares are 1987–89 averages. The average annual growth of R&D expenditures relates to the growth over the period for which estimates are available. The R&D capital stock benchmarks are in millions of U.S. dollars (based on PPP exchange rates) in 1985 prices and refer to one year before the first year after which the R&D expenditure estimates are available. PPP exchange rates are U.S. dollars per unit of local currency in 1985.

The estimates of business sector research and development capital stocks are based on R&D expenditure data from the OECD's *Main Science and Technology Indicators* except for Israel which is from the November 1990 Supplement to the *Monthly Bulletin of Statistics*. Real R&D expenditures are nominal expenditures deflated by an R&D price index ($PR$), which is defined as

$$PR = 0.5P + 0.5W,$$

where $P$ is the implicit deflator for business sector output and $W$ is an index of average business sector wages (the same source as for $Y$). This definition of $PR$ implies that half of R&D expenditures are labor costs, which is broadly consistent with available data on the composition of R&D expenditures. For a number of smaller countries, R&D expenditure data are not available over the full 1970–90 period (see Table A.2), in which case an estimated equation relating real R&D

Table A.3
Domestic R & D capital stocks (in U.S. dollars, 1985 = 1)

| | U.S. | Japan | Ger. | France | Italy | U.K. | Canada | Aus'lia | Austria | Belgium | Den. | Finland | Greece | Ireland | Israel | Nether. | N.Z. | Norway | Portugal | Spain | Sweden | Switz. |
|---|---|---|---|---|---|---|---|---|---|---|---|---|---|---|---|---|---|---|---|---|---|---|
| 1971 | 0.632 | 0.346 | 0.486 | 0.656 | 0.493 | 0.864 | 0.523 | 0.358 | 0.360 | 0.539 | 0.582 | 0.336 | 0.094 | 0.405 | 0.264 | 0.794 | 0.590 | 0.377 | 0.667 | 0.234 | 0.394 | 0.876 |
| 1972 | 0.655 | 0.384 | 0.521 | 0.679 | 0.531 | 0.870 | 0.544 | 0.373 | 0.392 | 0.563 | 0.609 | 0.372 | 0.116 | 0.442 | 0.292 | 0.814 | 0.612 | 0.404 | 0.695 | 0.268 | 0.421 | 0.890 |
| 1973 | 0.678 | 0.424 | 0.555 | 0.704 | 0.570 | 0.875 | 0.564 | 0.395 | 0.431 | 0.591 | 0.636 | 0.410 | 0.144 | 0.477 | 0.324 | 0.834 | 0.637 | 0.434 | 0.724 | 0.306 | 0.449 | 0.902 |
| 1974 | 0.700 | 0.466 | 0.584 | 0.726 | 0.602 | 0.884 | 0.583 | 0.434 | 0.469 | 0.620 | 0.661 | 0.448 | 0.175 | 0.507 | 0.355 | 0.848 | 0.667 | 0.465 | 0.747 | 0.354 | 0.479 | 0.913 |
| 1975 | 0.720 | 0.507 | 0.612 | 0.748 | 0.633 | 0.894 | 0.604 | 0.473 | 0.505 | 0.652 | 0.683 | 0.484 | 0.203 | 0.536 | 0.388 | 0.866 | 0.701 | 0.497 | 0.759 | 0.412 | 0.513 | 0.922 |
| 1976 | 0.738 | 0.542 | 0.644 | 0.770 | 0.666 | 0.897 | 0.626 | 0.511 | 0.540 | 0.682 | 0.704 | 0.519 | 0.249 | 0.568 | 0.414 | 0.881 | 0.734 | 0.537 | 0.761 | 0.475 | 0.551 | 0.933 |
| 1977 | 0.811 | 0.577 | 0.673 | 0.792 | 0.694 | 0.905 | 0.644 | 0.559 | 0.581 | 0.714 | 0.728 | 0.553 | 0.303 | 0.599 | 0.453 | 0.897 | 0.755 | 0.577 | 0.758 | 0.538 | 0.589 | 0.941 |
| 1978 | 0.779 | 0.613 | 0.704 | 0.814 | 0.723 | 0.915 | 0.666 | 0.606 | 0.625 | 0.748 | 0.752 | 0.591 | 0.357 | 0.631 | 0.516 | 0.908 | 0.770 | 0.620 | 0.752 | 0.595 | 0.629 | 0.946 |
| 1979 | 0.801 | 0.649 | 0.742 | 0.835 | 0.749 | 0.927 | 0.691 | 0.653 | 0.675 | 0.781 | 0.778 | 0.634 | 0.424 | 0.669 | 0.572 | 0.919 | 0.793 | 0.662 | 0.745 | 0.646 | 0.670 | 0.954 |
| 1980 | 0.826 | 0.691 | 0.786 | 0.858 | 0.781 | 0.940 | 0.725 | 0.704 | 0.727 | 0.813 | 0.805 | 0.680 | 0.485 | 0.708 | 0.622 | 0.930 | 0.819 | 0.709 | 0.765 | 0.696 | 0.711 | 0.962 |
| 1981 | 0.853 | 0.740 | 0.828 | 0.883 | 0.815 | 0.953 | 0.766 | 0.758 | 0.781 | 0.845 | 0.835 | 0.733 | 0.548 | 0.759 | 0.667 | 0.943 | 0.854 | 0.755 | 0.798 | 0.755 | 0.757 | 0.969 |
| 1982 | 0.884 | 0.797 | 0.869 | 0.910 | 0.856 | 0.967 | 0.821 | 0.812 | 0.835 | 0.877 | 0.867 | 0.786 | 0.612 | 0.816 | 0.703 | 0.956 | 0.889 | 0.804 | 0.842 | 0.802 | 0.808 | 0.976 |
| 1983 | 0.918 | 0.857 | 0.911 | 0.939 | 0.900 | 0.979 | 0.880 | 0.863 | 0.889 | 0.914 | 0.905 | 0.849 | 0.720 | 0.873 | 0.755 | 0.968 | 0.919 | 0.860 | 0.890 | 0.867 | 0.866 | 0.981 |
| 1984 | 0.956 | 0.925 | 0.953 | 0.968 | 0.948 | 0.988 | 0.936 | 0.917 | 0.945 | 0.956 | 0.949 | 0.917 | 0.855 | 0.927 | 0.805 | 0.984 | 0.953 | 0.922 | 0.945 | 0.928 | 0.929 | 0.986 |
| 1985 | 1 | 1 | 1 | 1 | 1 | 1 | 1 | 1 | 1 | 1 | 1 | 1 | 1 | 1 | 1 | 1 | 1 | 1 | 1 | 1 | 1 | 1 |
| 1986 | 1.050 | 1.087 | 1.050 | 1.035 | 1.065 | 1.013 | 1.079 | 1.110 | 1.056 | 1.046 | 1.056 | 1.092 | 1.148 | 1.089 | 1.076 | 1.025 | 1.052 | 1.095 | 1.058 | 1.095 | 1.079 | 1.020 |
| 1987 | 1.099 | 1.171 | 1.102 | 1.070 | 1.135 | 1.031 | 1.161 | 1.255 | 1.110 | 1.092 | 1.119 | 1.189 | 1.293 | 1.187 | 1.323 | 1.057 | 1.100 | 1.196 | 1.115 | 1.211 | 1.156 | 1.045 |
| 1988 | 1.146 | 1.259 | 1.155 | 1.108 | 1.208 | 1.050 | 1.241 | 1.404 | 1.166 | 1.139 | 1.187 | 1.291 | 1.448 | 1.290 | 1.550 | 1.092 | 1.146 | 1.297 | 1.176 | 1.332 | 1.232 | 1.068 |
| 1989 | 1.193 | 1.354 | 1.208 | 1.147 | 1.286 | 1.067 | 1.318 | 1.572 | 1.228 | 1.187 | 1.258 | 1.402 | 1.603 | 1.393 | 1.740 | 1.127 | 1.196 | 1.396 | 1.241 | 1.485 | 1.302 | 1.092 |
| 1990 | 1.237 | 1.462 | 1.264 | 1.189 | 1.372 | 1.080 | 1.391 | 1.755 | 1.300 | 1.244 | 1.329 | 1.520 | 1.757 | 1.501 | 1.933 | 1.161 | 1.246 | 1.495 | 1.315 | 1.648 | 1.362 | 1.113 |

Table A.4
Bilateral import shares (percent of total imports from countries listed, 1990)

| | U.S. | Japan | Ger. | France | Italy | U.K. | Canada | Aus'lia | Austria | Belgium | Den. | Finland | Greece | Ireland | Israel | Nether. | N.Z. | Norway | Portugal | Spain | Sweden | Switz. |
|---|---|---|---|---|---|---|---|---|---|---|---|---|---|---|---|---|---|---|---|---|---|---|
| United States | | 45.77 | 9.43 | 9.55 | 7.23 | 13.26 | 75.93 | 29.76 | 4.30 | 5.27 | 8.01 | 8.04 | 4.24 | 17.28 | 21.37 | 10.10 | 20.25 | 9.27 | 5.39 | 11.85 | 9.35 | 7.10 |
| Japan | 32.47 | | 7.94 | 5.12 | 3.06 | 6.90 | 8.21 | 26.74 | 5.87 | 2.64 | 4.50 | 9.32 | 8.10 | 6.28 | 3.23 | 3.64 | 22.94 | 4.85 | 3.73 | 6.27 | 6.96 | 5.05 |
| Germany | 8.58 | 8.49 | | 24.06 | 28.12 | 19.46 | 3.19 | 8.32 | 51.76 | 27.34 | 26.48 | 22.06 | 24.95 | 9.42 | 12.95 | 31.01 | 5.24 | 15.86 | 17.37 | 19.30 | 22.84 | 37.28 |
| France | 4.52 | 5.24 | 14.92 | | 19.51 | 10.54 | 1.74 | 3.24 | 5.23 | 17.36 | 5.89 | 5.39 | 8.52 | 4.41 | 4.85 | 9.20 | 1.87 | 4.26 | 14.04 | 17.90 | 6.08 | 12.08 |
| Italy | 4.26 | 3.59 | 11.15 | 14.29 | | 6.52 | 1.73 | 4.00 | 10.64 | 4.94 | 4.69 | 5.93 | 18.69 | 2.84 | 6.95 | 4.40 | 2.29 | 3.77 | 10.97 | 13.66 | 4.71 | 11.29 |
| UK | 6.31 | 4.21 | 8.56 | 8.88 | 6.43 | | 3.93 | 8.95 | 2.98 | 9.16 | 8.30 | 8.36 | 7.27 | 44.55 | 10.49 | 9.59 | 11.01 | 9.68 | 8.96 | 8.51 | 9.22 | 6.24 |
| Canada | 29.94 | 8.16 | 1.07 | 0.90 | 1.00 | 2.22 | | 3.15 | 0.56 | 0.77 | 0.62 | 1.11 | 0.59 | 0.83 | 0.81 | 0.92 | 2.45 | 2.82 | 1.02 | 0.63 | 0.93 | 0.46 |
| Australia | 1.40 | 10.91 | 0.59 | 0.64 | 0.84 | 0.84 | 0.07 | | 0.08 | 0.48 | 0.35 | 0.46 | 0.13 | 0.14 | 0.43 | 0.39 | 25.91 | 0.43 | 0.38 | 0.45 | 0.50 | 0.14 |
| Austria | 0.40 | 0.49 | 5.17 | 1.05 | 3.06 | 0.91 | 0.32 | 0.48 | | 0.92 | 1.44 | 1.57 | 1.74 | 0.37 | 0.54 | 1.05 | 0.41 | 1.28 | 0.92 | 1.08 | 1.57 | 4.28 |
| Belgium | 1.59 | 1.38 | 8.62 | 11.41 | 6.57 | 5.54 | 0.49 | 1.10 | 3.19 | | 3.84 | 3.55 | 4.81 | 2.34 | 18.22 | 17.08 | 0.86 | 3.33 | 4.76 | 4.14 | 3.58 | 3.84 |
| Denmark | 0.54 | 1.13 | 2.28 | 1.03 | 1.25 | 2.17 | 0.22 | 0.58 | 0.83 | 0.68 | | 3.97 | 1.60 | 1.00 | 0.52 | 1.38 | 0.53 | 8.66 | 1.12 | 0.99 | 7.84 | 1.09 |
| Finland | 0.49 | 0.50 | 1.28 | 0.91 | 0.66 | 1.84 | 0.32 | 0.88 | 0.95 | 0.52 | 3.45 | | 1.16 | 0.90 | 0.72 | 1.22 | 0.41 | 3.92 | 0.76 | 0.87 | 7.69 | 0.73 |
| Greece | 0.18 | 0.17 | 0.84 | 0.51 | 1.53 | 0.38 | 0.06 | 0.22 | 0.51 | 0.22 | 0.34 | 0.36 | | 0.12 | 0.37 | 0.25 | 0.14 | 1.37 | 0.21 | 0.32 | 0.32 | 0.16 |
| Ireland | 0.54 | 0.62 | 1.08 | 1.08 | 0.86 | 4.16 | 0.14 | 0.46 | 0.45 | 0.82 | 0.76 | 0.61 | 0.72 | | 0.32 | 1.12 | 0.30 | 1.24 | 0.41 | 0.90 | 0.73 | 0.63 |
| Israel | 1.11 | 0.72 | 0.34 | 0.35 | 0.38 | 0.47 | 0.13 | 0.39 | 0.18 | 0.76 | 0.16 | 0.20 | 0.53 | 0.21 | | 0.42 | 0.23 | 0.22 | 0.15 | 0.34 | 0.16 | 0.45 |
| Netherland | 1.70 | 1.06 | 12.82 | 6.44 | 7.29 | 9.35 | 0.71 | 1.40 | 3.26 | 20.45 | 6.81 | 4.09 | 9.07 | 4.46 | 4.16 | | 1.43 | 4.32 | 6.59 | 4.29 | 4.79 | 4.51 |
| New Zealand | 0.45 | 1.56 | 0.12 | 0.14 | 0.17 | 0.42 | 0.19 | 5.34 | 0.06 | 0.30 | 0.11 | 0.06 | 0.28 | 0.14 | 0.00 | 0.06 | | 0.05 | 0.08 | 0.16 | 0.06 | 0.05 |
| Norway | 0.71 | 0.53 | 1.80 | 1.76 | 0.52 | 3.53 | 0.68 | 0.56 | 0.46 | 0.95 | 5.20 | 2.96 | 0.51 | 0.41 | 0.26 | 1.62 | 0.33 | | 1.08 | 0.68 | 7.96 | 0.68 |
| Portugal | 0.28 | 0.16 | 0.99 | 1.28 | 0.51 | 1.01 | 0.14 | 0.16 | 0.67 | 0.45 | 1.19 | 1.07 | 0.48 | 0.50 | 0.31 | 0.72 | 0.15 | 1.54 | | 3.05 | 1.36 | 0.41 |
| Spain | 1.20 | 0.65 | 2.62 | 5.48 | 3.22 | 2.81 | 0.49 | 0.59 | 1.01 | 1.65 | 1.24 | 1.36 | 2.36 | 1.35 | 1.28 | 1.58 | 0.42 | 1.43 | 17.67 | | 1.24 | 1.28 |
| Sweden | 1.72 | 1.02 | 3.16 | 2.06 | 2.02 | 3.64 | 0.81 | 2.30 | 2.11 | 2.46 | 14.28 | 17.32 | 2.12 | 1.74 | 1.11 | 2.66 | 1.66 | 19.80 | 1.89 | 2.58 | | 2.22 |
| Switzerland | 1.61 | 3.64 | 5.24 | 3.05 | 5.74 | 4.02 | 0.52 | 1.38 | 4.91 | 1.89 | 2.35 | 2.21 | 2.12 | 0.69 | 11.09 | 1.59 | 1.17 | 1.90 | 2.50 | 2.04 | 2.12 | |
| Total | 100 | 100 | 100 | 100 | 100 | 100 | 100 | 100 | 100 | 100 | 100 | 100 | 100 | 100 | 100 | 100 | 100 | 100 | 100 | 100 | 100 | 100 |

Table A.5
Foreign R & D capital stock (in U.S. dollars, weighted by import shares, 1985 = 1)

| | U.S. | Japan | Ger. | France | Italy | U.K. | Canada | Aus'lia | Austria | Belgium | Den. | Finland | Greece | Ireland | Israel | Nether. | N.Z. | Norway | Portugal | Spain | Sweden | Switz. |
|---|---|---|---|---|---|---|---|---|---|---|---|---|---|---|---|---|---|---|---|---|---|---|
| 1971 | 0.423 | 0.683 | 0.788 | 0.686 | 0.789 | 0.670 | 0.614 | 0.637 | 0.554 | 0.742 | 0.723 | 0.596 | 0.702 | 0.519 | 0.633 | 0.593 | 0.576 | 0.550 | 0.426 | 0.719 | 0.647 | 0.646 |
| 1972 | 0.457 | 0.647 | 0.776 | 0.647 | 0.762 | 0.611 | 0.630 | 0.599 | 0.594 | 0.664 | 0.792 | 0.577 | 0.744 | 0.565 | 0.669 | 0.614 | 0.522 | 0.529 | 0.437 | 0.670 | 0.644 | 0.619 |
| 1973 | 0.485 | 0.656 | 0.699 | 0.654 | 0.747 | 0.608 | 0.644 | 0.606 | 0.594 | 0.656 | 0.743 | 0.573 | 0.769 | 0.551 | 0.597 | 0.584 | 0.544 | 0.544 | 0.507 | 0.686 | 0.622 | 0.633 |
| 1974 | 0.504 | 0.667 | 0.731 | 0.685 | 0.772 | 0.627 | 0.683 | 0.651 | 0.600 | 0.683 | 0.745 | 0.597 | 0.927 | 0.536 | 0.627 | 0.631 | 0.568 | 0.588 | 0.483 | 0.713 | 0.613 | 0.633 |
| 1975 | 0.526 | 0.721 | 0.754 | 0.732 | 0.820 | 0.657 | 0.704 | 0.660 | 0.619 | 0.746 | 0.755 | 0.657 | 1.048 | 0.537 | 0.665 | 0.680 | 0.635 | 0.691 | 0.552 | 0.783 | 0.631 | 0.668 |
| 1976 | 0.545 | 0.732 | 0.759 | 0.728 | 0.889 | 0.667 | 0.733 | 0.670 | 0.643 | 0.753 | 0.765 | 0.706 | 0.939 | 0.575 | 0.828 | 0.744 | 0.695 | 0.657 | 0.679 | 0.831 | 0.656 | 0.735 |
| 1977 | 0.583 | 0.700 | 0.799 | 0.737 | 0.862 | 0.705 | 0.760 | 0.697 | 0.675 | 0.771 | 0.742 | 0.704 | 0.960 | 0.615 | 0.794 | 0.744 | 0.723 | 0.652 | 0.573 | 0.819 | 0.695 | 0.738 |
| 1978 | 0.627 | 0.718 | 0.748 | 0.742 | 0.843 | 0.740 | 0.784 | 0.728 | 0.697 | 0.798 | 0.800 | 0.723 | 0.885 | 0.641 | 0.735 | 0.746 | 0.721 | 0.675 | 0.633 | 0.781 | 0.742 | 0.763 |
| 1979 | 0.682 | 0.737 | 0.783 | 0.768 | 0.848 | 0.739 | 0.799 | 0.785 | 0.732 | 0.812 | 0.815 | 0.766 | 0.933 | 0.640 | 0.714 | 0.761 | 0.752 | 0.701 | 0.684 | 0.845 | 0.770 | 0.825 |
| 1980 | 0.711 | 0.801 | 0.807 | 0.817 | 0.877 | 0.755 | 0.839 | 0.829 | 0.778 | 0.873 | 0.826 | 0.805 | 0.966 | 0.655 | 0.821 | 0.793 | 0.767 | 0.749 | 0.724 | 0.826 | 0.798 | 0.826 |
| 1981 | 0.765 | 0.867 | 0.894 | 0.897 | 0.927 | 0.881 | 0.864 | 0.859 | 0.832 | 0.973 | 0.928 | 0.927 | 1.006 | 0.685 | 0.878 | 0.844 | 0.845 | 0.833 | 0.739 | 0.949 | 0.841 | 0.858 |
| 1982 | 0.832 | 0.892 | 0.945 | 0.954 | 0.976 | 0.888 | 0.888 | 0.930 | 0.922 | 0.974 | 1.126 | 1.096 | 1.049 | 0.774 | 0.945 | 0.918 | 1.007 | 0.925 | 0.810 | 1.045 | 0.913 | 0.917 |
| 1983 | 0.884 | 0.940 | 0.955 | 0.958 | 1.003 | 0.916 | 0.920 | 0.938 | 0.937 | 1.002 | 1.038 | 1.010 | 1.036 | 0.827 | 0.915 | 0.926 | 0.965 | 0.959 | 0.787 | 1.046 | 0.960 | 0.945 |
| 1984 | 0.929 | 0.976 | 0.943 | 0.965 | 0.964 | 0.936 | 0.963 | 0.962 | 0.947 | 0.984 | 0.971 | 1.018 | 1.007 | 0.910 | 0.926 | 0.958 | 0.969 | 0.971 | 0.960 | 0.990 | 0.990 | 1.044 |
| 1985 | 1 | 1 | 1 | 1 | 1 | 1 | 1 | 1 | 1 | 1 | 1 | 1 | 1 | 1 | 1 | 1 | 1 | 1 | 1 | 1 | 1 | 1 |
| 1986 | 1.115 | 1.045 | 1.026 | 1.020 | 1.029 | 1.036 | 1.035 | 1.038 | 1.070 | 1.012 | 1.109 | 1.072 | 1.062 | 1.055 | 0.990 | 1.000 | 1.092 | 0.941 | 0.846 | 0.996 | 1.074 | 1.000 |
| 1987 | 1.247 | 1.065 | 1.018 | 1.033 | 0.998 | 0.995 | 1.058 | 1.071 | 1.080 | 1.018 | 1.125 | 1.027 | 1.052 | 1.056 | 0.912 | 0.981 | 1.200 | 0.958 | 0.667 | 0.859 | 1.063 | 1.022 |
| 1988 | 1.326 | 1.053 | 1.042 | 1.050 | 1.005 | 1.033 | 1.097 | 1.118 | 1.139 | 1.048 | 1.160 | 1.123 | 1.046 | 1.146 | 0.870 | 0.980 | 1.142 | 0.942 | 0.586 | 0.795 | 1.061 | 1.069 |
| 1989 | 1.376 | 1.094 | 1.130 | 1.145 | 1.063 | 1.097 | 1.123 | 1.170 | 1.199 | 1.038 | 1.258 | 1.251 | 1.163 | 1.154 | 0.895 | 1.044 | 1.238 | 1.004 | 0.564 | 0.840 | 1.156 | 1.131 |
| 1990 | 1.444 | 1.146 | 1.268 | 1.187 | 1.094 | 1.220 | 1.175 | 1.270 | 1.268 | 1.108 | 1.384 | 1.292 | 1.178 | 1.195 | 0.991 | 1.140 | 1.299 | 1.125 | 0.585 | 0.874 | 1.220 | 1.230 |

Table A.6
Imports as a share of GDP (ratio)

| | U.S. | Japan | Ger. | France | Italy | U.K. | Canada | Aus'lia | Austria | Belgium | Den. | Finland | Greece | Ireland | Israel | Nether. | N.Z. | Norway | Portugal | Spain | Sweden | Switz. |
|---|---|---|---|---|---|---|---|---|---|---|---|---|---|---|---|---|---|---|---|---|---|---|
| 1970 | 0.0552 | 0.0958 | 0.1914 | 0.1528 | 0.1560 | 0.2145 | 0.2001 | 0.1475 | 0.3081 | 0.4387 | 0.3090 | 0.2678 | 0.1700 | 0.4212 | 0.5002 | 0.4513 | 0.2548 | 0.4535 | 0.3359 | 0.1466 | 0.2282 | 0.3907 |
| 1971 | 0.0568 | 0.0907 | 0.1897 | 0.1534 | 0.1547 | 0.2106 | 0.2008 | 0.1422 | 0.2969 | 0.4362 | 0.2944 | 0.2591 | 0.1675 | 0.4018 | 0.4984 | 0.4469 | 0.2159 | 0.4500 | 0.3283 | 0.1372 | 0.2108 | 0.3597 |
| 1972 | 0.0615 | 0.0835 | 0.1860 | 0.1568 | 0.1628 | 0.2126 | 0.2097 | 0.1217 | 0.2875 | 0.4215 | 0.2650 | 0.2440 | 0.1578 | 0.3776 | 0.4487 | 0.4109 | 0.2112 | 0.4066 | 0.3100 | 0.1477 | 0.2037 | 0.3400 |
| 1973 | 0.0676 | 0.1006 | 0.1891 | 0.1670 | 0.1873 | 0.2552 | 0.2200 | 0.1272 | 0.3071 | 0.4773 | 0.3043 | 0.2576 | 0.1752 | 0.4236 | 0.5781 | 0.4303 | 0.2491 | 0.4521 | 0.3500 | 0.1566 | 0.2184 | 0.3441 |
| 1974 | 0.0874 | 0.1446 | 0.2197 | 0.2170 | 0.2379 | 0.3238 | 0.2456 | 0.1689 | 0.3436 | 0.5638 | 0.3468 | 0.3252 | 0.2167 | 0.5448 | 0.5517 | 0.5005 | 0.3532 | 0.5133 | 0.4212 | 0.1983 | 0.3067 | 0.3829 |
| 1975 | 0.0774 | 0.1286 | 0.2177 | 0.1787 | 0.2010 | 0.2721 | 0.2411 | 0.1430 | 0.3032 | 0.4895 | 0.3102 | 0.2973 | 0.1819 | 0.4345 | 0.5518 | 0.4613 | 0.2932 | 0.5000 | 0.3580 | 0.1775 | 0.2719 | 0.2827 |
| 1976 | 0.0855 | 0.1275 | 0.2342 | 0.2031 | 0.2279 | 0.2924 | 0.2288 | 0.1484 | 0.3413 | 0.5036 | 0.3349 | 0.2633 | 0.1868 | 0.4842 | 0.5268 | 0.4672 | 0.3231 | 0.5216 | 0.3642 | 0.1859 | 0.2790 | 0.3029 |
| 1977 | 0.0924 | 0.1142 | 0.2309 | 0.2036 | 0.2170 | 0.2902 | 0.2352 | 0.1626 | 0.3497 | 0.5534 | 0.3246 | 0.2512 | 0.2030 | 0.5609 | 0.5020 | 0.4528 | 0.2866 | 0.5171 | 0.3825 | 0.1653 | 0.2699 | 0.3408 |
| 1978 | 0.0951 | 0.0938 | 0.2227 | 0.1908 | 0.2069 | 0.2692 | 0.2486 | 0.1632 | 0.3329 | 0.5452 | 0.2995 | 0.2469 | 0.1962 | 0.5282 | 0.5338 | 0.4437 | 0.2612 | 0.4196 | 0.3647 | 0.1439 | 0.2513 | 0.3265 |
| 1979 | 0.1015 | 0.1247 | 0.2441 | 0.2064 | 0.2267 | 0.2742 | 0.2654 | 0.1664 | 0.3610 | 0.6137 | 0.3207 | 0.2979 | 0.2137 | 0.6112 | 0.5251 | 0.4962 | 0.2934 | 0.4229 | 0.3988 | 0.1472 | 0.2943 | 0.3585 |
| 1980 | 0.1085 | 0.1459 | 0.2690 | 0.2275 | 0.2411 | 0.2485 | 0.2644 | 0.1775 | 0.3877 | 0.6679 | 0.3376 | 0.3460 | 0.2328 | 0.5638 | 0.4768 | 0.5305 | 0.3178 | 0.4266 | 0.4123 | 0.1814 | 0.2988 | 0.4028 |
| 1981 | 0.1048 | 0.1393 | 0.2794 | 0.2353 | 0.2483 | 0.2370 | 0.2612 | 0.1787 | 0.3963 | 0.7726 | 0.3581 | 0.3208 | 0.2487 | 0.5646 | 0.5018 | 0.5448 | 0.3169 | 0.3996 | 0.4485 | 0.2018 | 0.2844 | 0.3838 |
| 1982 | 0.0963 | 0.1380 | 0.2747 | 0.2370 | 0.2357 | 0.2430 | 0.2206 | 0.1817 | 0.3639 | 0.8214 | 0.3594 | 0.3002 | 0.2625 | 0.5432 | 0.5177 | 0.5336 | 0.3304 | 0.4097 | 0.4476 | 0.2057 | 0.3135 | 0.3503 |
| 1983 | 0.0964 | 0.1216 | 0.2674 | 0.2265 | 0.2099 | 0.2548 | 0.2214 | 0.1599 | 0.3612 | 0.8089 | 0.3437 | 0.2982 | 0.2614 | 0.5415 | 0.5374 | 0.5386 | 0.3328 | 0.3851 | 0.4290 | 0.2186 | 0.3355 | 0.3524 |
| 1984 | 0.1072 | 0.1227 | 0.2816 | 0.2350 | 0.2253 | 0.2844 | 0.2488 | 0.1720 | 0.3883 | 0.8641 | 0.3545 | 0.2782 | 0.2993 | 0.5865 | 0.5205 | 0.5690 | 0.3241 | 0.3820 | 0.4451 | 0.2136 | 0.3282 | 0.3806 |
| 1985 | 0.1034 | 0.1109 | 0.2901 | 0.2325 | 0.2267 | 0.2767 | 0.2581 | 0.1912 | 0.4055 | 0.8552 | 0.3633 | 0.2833 | 0.3278 | 0.5761 | 0.4985 | 0.5871 | 0.3679 | 0.3890 | 0.4085 | 0.2119 | 0.3363 | 0.3863 |
| 1986 | 0.1058 | 0.0741 | 0.2496 | 0.2016 | 0.1818 | 0.2626 | 0.2637 | 0.1868 | 0.3602 | 0.7563 | 0.3249 | 0.2514 | 0.3089 | 0.5159 | 0.5280 | 0.4970 | 0.3491 | 0.4147 | 0.3551 | 0.1773 | 0.2974 | 0.3550 |
| 1987 | 0.1117 | 0.0723 | 0.2395 | 0.2051 | 0.1825 | 0.2642 | 0.2547 | 0.1762 | 0.3518 | 0.7463 | 0.2961 | 0.2497 | 0.3200 | 0.5121 | 0.5930 | 0.4959 | 0.3200 | 0.3766 | 0.4086 | 0.1922 | 0.3076 | 0.3472 |
| 1988 | 0.1127 | 0.0783 | 0.2434 | 0.2123 | 0.1830 | 0.2648 | 0.2581 | 0.1754 | 0.3694 | 0.7902 | 0.2935 | 0.2488 | 0.3044 | 0.5278 | 0.5654 | 0.5041 | 0.2805 | 0.3740 | 0.4574 | 0.1997 | 0.3074 | 0.3606 |
| 1989 | 0.1119 | 0.0928 | 0.2613 | 0.2278 | 0.1960 | 0.2769 | 0.2548 | 0.1864 | 0.3886 | 0.8819 | 0.3114 | 0.2536 | 0.3202 | 0.5610 | 0.5196 | 0.5385 | 0.2261 | 0.3767 | 0.4487 | 0.2137 | 0.3162 | 0.3826 |
| 1990 | 0.1133 | 0.1010 | 0.2538 | 0.2265 | 0.1950 | 0.2684 | 0.2559 | 0.1759 | 0.3914 | 0.8970 | 0.2996 | 0.2407 | 0.3260 | 0.5331 | 0.5371 | 0.5157 | 0.3035 | 0.3683 | 0.4516 | 0.2047 | 0.3004 | 0.3635 |

Table A.7
GDP and domestic R&D capital stock, 1990 [a]

| | *GDP* | $S^d$ | $GDP/S^d$ | Average ratio |
|---|---|---|---|---|
| United States | 4568.5 | 1041.8 | 4.39 | |
| Japan | 1551.1 | 259.6 | 5.97 | |
| West Germany | 865.9 | 175.3 | 4.94 | |
| France | 712.3 | 115.4 | 6.17 | 5.24 |
| Italy | 688.3 | 46.4 | 14.83 | |
| United Kingdom | 702.1 | 148.2 | 4.74 | |
| Canada | 439.8 | 31.2 | 14.10 | |
| Australia | 228.4 | 9.1 | 25.10 | |
| Austria | 86.6 | 6.6 | 13.12 | |
| Belgium | 116.7 | 15.7 | 7.43 | |
| Denmark | 63.7 | 5.3 | 12.02 | |
| Finland | 64.9 | 5.5 | 11.80 | |
| Greece | 61.2 | 0.5 | 122.40 | |
| Ireland | 24.2 | 1.1 | 22.00 | 10.91 |
| Israel | 45.0 | 2.5 | 18.00 | |
| Netherlands | 174.2 | 29.0 | 6.01 | |
| New Zealand | 34.2 | 1.0 | 34.20 | |
| Norway | 60.4 | 5.9 | 10.24 | |
| Portugal | 55.3 | 0.7 | 79.00 | |
| Spain | 298.7 | 8.7 | 34.33 | |
| Sweden | 113.6 | 21.5 | 5.28 | |
| Switzerland | 145.3 | 31.0 | 4.69 | |

[a] GDP and R&D capital stocks are in 1985 U.S. dollars, based on PPP.

expenditures to real output and investment (all in logarithms) was used to 'predict' the missing R & D expenditure data.

Research and development capital stocks ($S$), which are defined here as beginning of period stocks, were calculated from R & D expenditure ($R$) based on the perpetual inventory model

$$S_t = (1 - \delta) S_{t-1} + R_{t-1},$$

where $\delta$ is the depreciation or obsolescence rate, which was assumed to be 5 percent. [17] The benchmark for $S$ was calculated following the procedure suggested by Griliches (1980), as

$$S_0 = R_0 / (g + \delta),$$

[17] Alternative measures of the R&D capital stocks were also calculated assuming $\delta = 0$, $\delta = 0.1$, and $\delta = 0.15$. Regressions comparable to those reported in Table 3 but using alternative R&D capital stocks assuming $\delta = 0.15$ are reported in Appendix B.

where $g$ is the average annual logarithmic growth of R&D expenditures over the period for which published R&D data were available, $R_0$ is the first year for which the data were available, and $S_0$ is the benchmark for the beginning of the year. The domestic R&D capital stocks were converted into U.S. dollars using 1985 purchasing power parity exchange rates from Gulde and Schulze-Ghattas (1992). The calculated benchmarks and PPP exchange rates are reported in Table A.2, and the estimates of the domestic R&D capital stocks are reported in Table A.3.

For each of the 22 countries, two measures of the foreign R&D capital stock were constructed. The first is simply the sum of the domestic R&D capital stocks of each countries' 21 trading partners. The second estimate of the foreign R&D capital stock is a bilateral import-share weighted average of the domestic R&D capital stocks of each countries' 21 trading partners. The bilateral import shares were calculated for each year from 1970–90 based on data from the IMF's *Direction of Trade*. The bilateral import-share weighting matrix for 1990 is reported in Table A.4, and estimates of the import-share weighted foreign R&D capital stocks are reported in Table A.5. We do not report foreign R&D capital stocks based on simple sums because they are not used in the main text. Experimental estimation using these foreign R&D capital stocks indicated that the import weighted stocks are preferable. Since the latter are also preferable on theoretical grounds we have chosen to concentrate on them.

The ratios of the imports of goods and services to GDP, which are from the IMF's World Economic Outlook database, are reported in Table A.6. The data used to calculate the rates of return to R&D capital are reported in Table A.7.

## Appendix B: Additional estimation results

As noted above, the R&D capital stocks used in the text are based on an assumed depreciation or obsolescence rate of 5 percent. Private rates of depreciation for R&D expenditures are typically estimated to be considerably higher, in part because of the loss of quasi-rents as the knowledge generated by R&D becomes widely known. A number of studies have assumed depreciation rates of 15 percent (Griliches, 1990). Table B.1 reports estimation results comparable to those in Table 3 except that the R&D capital stocks have been constructed assuming a 15 percent depreciation rate. In general, the estimation results are similar to those in Table 3. The main differences are that the elasticity of TFP with respect to the domestic R&D capital stock is increased (although it is reduced somewhat for the G7 countries in equations (ii) and (iii)), while the elasticity with respect to the foreign R&D capital stock is reduced.

Table B.1 also reports estimation results that allow coefficients to change over time based on the specification of equation (iii) in Table 3. Including dummy variables for each year from 1971 to 1989, as is done in equation (iv), reduces the

Table B.1
Estimation results assuming a 15 percent depreciation rate for R&D capital and allowing coefficients to change over time (Pooled data 1971–90 for 22 countries, 440 observations) [a]

| | 15% depreciation rate | | | 5% depreciation rate | | |
|---|---|---|---|---|---|---|
| | (i) | (ii) | (iii) | (iv) | (v) | (vi) |
| $\log S^d$ | 0.140 | 0.123 | 0.109 | 0.032 | 0.041 | 0.060 |
| $G7 \cdot \log S^d$ | | 0.124 | 0.138 | 0.110 | 0.183 | 0.162 |
| $\log S^f$ | 0.048 | 0.033 | | | | |
| $m \cdot \log S^f$ | | | 0.197 | 0.122 | 0.520 | 0.363 |
| $\log S^d \cdot \rightarrow$ | | | | | $T$ 0.005 | $D8$ 0.090 |
| $G7 \cdot \log S^d \cdot \rightarrow$ | | | | | $T$ −0.004 | $D8$ −0.021 |
| $m \cdot \log S^f \cdot \rightarrow$ | | | | | $T$ −0.032 | $D8$ −0.313 |
| Standard error | 0.048 | 0.045 | 0.045 | 0.042 | 0.043 | 0.043 |
| $R^2$ | 0.578 | 0.629 | 0.642 | 0.700 | 0.676 | 0.674 |
| $R^2$ adjusted | 0.555 | 0.608 | 0.621 | 0.668 | 0.654 | 0.652 |
| Cointegration tests: | | | | | | |
| Levin and Lin (1992) | −5.989 | −9.677 | −6.371 | −5.575 | −5.061 | −5.525 |
| Levin and Lin (1993) | 0.266 | 2.036 | 1.756 | 1.578 | 2.536 | 2.666 |
| $t$-statistic on the lagged residual in the EC model | −6.286 | −7.133 | −7.725 | −5.787 | −7.137 | −7.493 |

[a] Equations (i)–(iii) are the same as in Table 3 except that the R&D capital stocks have been constructed using a 15 (rather than 5) percent depreciation rate. Equations (iv)–(vi) are specified the same as equation (iii) in Table 3 except that equation (iv) includes unreported, year-specific dummies for each year from 1971–89; equation (v) allows each of the coefficients to vary over time according to a time trend; and equation (vi) allows each coefficient to shift in 1981–90 compared with 1971–80. The dependent variable is log (total factor productivity). All equations include unreported, country-specific constants. See notes to Table 3. $T$ = time trend equal to 1 in 1971, 2 in 1972, etc.; $D8$ = dummy variable equal to 0 from 1971–80 and equal to 1.0 from 1981–90.

sizes of the estimated coefficients. Some empirical studies have suggested that the beneficial effects of R&D on output or total factor productivity may have changed over time (Griliches, 1988, 1990). To test this, equation (v) includes each of the R&D capital stock variables multiplied by a time trend ($T$). From 1971 ($T = 1$) to 1990 ($T = 20$), the estimated elasticity on the domestic R&D capital stock increases from 0.046 (0.041 + 0.005) to 0.141 for the smaller countries, while it decreases from 0.179 to 0.103 for the G7 countries. The estimated elasticity on foreign R&D falls from 0.488 in 1971 to about 0 in 1986; thereafter it is negative and falls to −0.112 in 1990. This specification implies steady changes in all of the estimated elasticities over the full sample period. Equation (vi) tests for a discrete shift in the estimated coefficients in 1981 by including each of the R&D stock variables multiplied by a dummy variable ($D8$) that is 0 from 1971–80 and 1 from 1981–90. The implications of equations (v) and (vi) are similar: the estimated elasticity of the domestic R&D capital stock increases in the 1980s for the smaller

Table B.2
Production function estimation results (pooled data 1971–90 for 22 countries, 440 observations) [a]

| | (i) | (ii) | (iii) | (iv) |
|---|---|---|---|---|
| $\beta \log K$ | 1.366 | 1.147 | 1.336 | 1.026 |
| $(1-\beta)\log L$ | 0.868 | 0.752 | 0.911 | 0.784 |
| $\log S^d$ | 0.052 | 0.075 | 0.049 | 0.079 |
| $G7 \cdot \log S^d$ | | 0.096 | | 0.128 |
| $\log S^f$ | 0.037 | 0.054 | | |
| $m \cdot \log S^f$ | | | 0.188 | 0.303 |
| Standard error | 0.045 | 0.044 | 0.045 | 0.042 |
| $R^2$ | 0.921 | 0.926 | 0.923 | 0.932 |
| $R^2$ adjusted | 0.916 | 0.922 | 0.919 | 0.927 |
| Cointegration tests: | | | | |
| Levin and Lin (1992) | −5.793 | −5.690 | −6.089 | −6.292 |
| Levin and Lin (1993) | −2.027 | 0.335 | −1.828 | −0.215 |
| *t*-statistic on the lagged residual in the EC model | −6.425 | −7.461 | −6.902 | −8.455 |
| Memoranda: | | | | |
| Average coefficient on | | | | |
| log *K* | 0.458 | 0.384 | 0.448 | 0.344 |
| log *L* | 0.577 | 0.500 | 0.606 | 0.521 |
| Sum | 1.035 | 0.884 | 1.054 | 0.865 |

[a] The dependent variable is log output. All equations include unreported, country-specific constants. See notes to Table 3. $K$ = capital stock; $L$ = employment; $\beta$ = average share of capital in each country over the period 1987–89; the average across all countries is 0.335.

countries and declines somewhat for the G7 countries, while the elasticity of foreign R&D decreases in the 1980s, although it does not become negative.

We report in Table B.2 regressions similar to those in Table 3 except that they are specified as a production function. The coefficients on capital and labor are allowed to vary according to the factor shares in each country; this is done by multiplying capital and labor in each country by its respective factor share ($\beta$). The evidence for cointegration is strongest in equations (i) and (iii), which do not allow the estimated coefficients on the domestic R&D stock to differ between the small and the large economies: both of these equations pass the Levin and Lin (1993) and the t-test for cointegration, and come close to passing the Levin and Lin (1992) test. The sum of the implied coefficients on physical capital and labor are remarkably close to unity, particularly in equations (i) and (iii), indicating constant returns to scale to physical capital and labor (cf. the memoranda to Table B.2). The implied coefficients on capital are somewhat larger than suggested by factor shares, while the opposite is true for the coefficients on labor. The estimated elasticities of output with respect to the R&D capital stocks are somewhat lower than reported in Table 3, but are comparable to results from single-country studies.

## References

Coe, D.T. and R. Moghadam, 1993, Capital and trade as engines of growth in France: An application of Johansen's cointegration methodology, IMF Staff Papers 40, 542–666.
Cuthbertson, K., S.G. Hall and M.P. Taylor, 1992, Applied econometric techniques (University of Michigan Press, Ann Arbor, MI).
Englander, A.S., R. Evenson and M. Hanazaki, 1988, R&D, innovation and the total factor productivity slowdown, OECD Economic Studies 11, 7–42.
Engle, R.F. and C.W.J. Granger, 1987, Cointegration and error correction: Representation, estimation, and testing, Econometrica 55, 251–276.
Granger, C.W.J. and P. Newbold, 1974, Spurious regressions in econometrics, Journal of Econometrics 2, 111–120.
Griliches, Z., 1979, Issues in assessing the contribution of R&D to productivity growth, Bell Journal of Economics 10, 92–116.
Griliches, Z., 1988, Productivity puzzles and R&D: Another nonexplanation, Journal of Economic Perspectives 2, 9–21.
Griliches, Z., 1990, Patent statistics as economic indicators: A survey, Journal of Economic Literature 4, 1661–1707.
Griliches, Z., 1991, The search for R&D spillovers, Working paper no. 3768 (NBER, Cambridge, MA).
Grossman, G.M. and E. Helpman, 1991, Innovation and growth in the global economy (MIT Press, Cambridge, MA).
Grossman, G.M. and E. Helpman, 1994, Endogenous innovation in the theory of growth, Journal of Economic Perspectives 8, 23–44.
Gulde, A.M. and M. Schulze-Ghattas, 1992, Aggregation of economic indicators across countries: Exchange rate versus PPP-based GDP weights, Working paper no. 92/36 (IMF, Washington, DC).
Helliwell, J.F., 1992, Trade and technical progress, Working paper no. 4226 (NBER, Cambridge, MA).
Helpman, E., 1992, Endogenous macroeconomic growth theory, European Economic Review 36, 237–267.
Jaffe, A., 1986, Technological opportunity and spillover of R&D: Evidence from firms' patents, profits, and market value, American Economic Review 76, 984–1001.
Levin, A. and C.F. Lin, 1992, Unit root tests in panel data: Asymptotic and finite-sample properties, Discussion paper no. 92-23 (University of California, San Diego, CA).
Levin, A. and C.F. Lin, 1993, Unit root tests in panel data: New results, Discussion paper no. 93-56 (University of California, San Diego, CA).
Romer, P.M., 1990, Endogenous technical change, Journal of Political Economy 98, S71–S102.
Scherer, F.M., 1982, Interindustry technology flows and productivity growth, Review of Economics and Statistics 64, 627–634.
Stock, J.H., 1987, Asymptotic properties of least squares estimations of co-integrating vectors, Econometrica 55, 1035–1056.
Terleckyj, N.E., 1974, Effects of R&D on the productivity growth of industries, Report no. 140 (National Planning Association, Washington, DC).

# [6]

ELSEVIER European Economic Review 42 (1998) 1469–1481

EUROPEAN ECONOMIC REVIEW

# Are international R&D spillovers trade-related? Analyzing spillovers among randomly matched trade partners

Wolfgang Keller*

*Department of Economics, University of Wisconsin-Madison, 1180 Observatory Drive, Madison, WI 53706, USA*

*National Bureau of Economic Research, Cambridge, MA, USA*

Received 1 April 1996; accepted 7 July 1997

**Abstract**

In this paper, I analyze recent findings by Coe and Helpman (1995) on trade-related international R&D spillovers. A Monte-Carlo-based robustness test is proposed which compares the elasticity of domestic productivity with respect to foreign R&D estimated by Coe and Helpman with an elasticity which is based on counterfactual international trade patterns. It is shown that also these, randomly created trade patterns give rise to positive international R&D spillover estimates, which are often larger, and explain more of the variation in productivity across countries than if 'true' bilateral trade patterns are employed. The finding casts doubt on the claim that patterns of international trade are important in driving R&D spillovers. © 1998 Published by Elsevier Science B.V. All rights reserved.

*JEL classification:* F12; F2; O3; O4; C15

*Keywords:* International R&D spillovers; Trade in differentiated intermediate products; Productivity growth; Counterfactual estimation

* E-mail: wkeller@ssc.wisc.edu.


*PII* S0014-2921(97)00092-5

## 1. Introduction

The recent development of theories of endogenous technological change, in particular by Romer (1990) and Aghion and Howitt (1992), has triggered new work on the relation of trade, growth, and technological change in open economies. Most important in this area is the monograph by Grossman and Helpman (1991). These authors embed the new theories in multi-sector, multi-country general-equilibrium models to analyze the impact of both trade in intermediate as well as final goods on long-run growth. Technology diffuses in this framework through being embodied in intermediate inputs: if R&D expenditures create new intermediate goods which are different (the horizontally differentiated inputs model) or better (the quality ladder model) from those already existing, and if these are exported to other economies, then the importing countries are implicitly utilizing the technology from abroad. If, in addition, the importing country pays less than the intermediate good's full marginal product, then international trade in these intermediate goods triggers productivity increases in the importing country.

Even before the advent of the models of endogenous technological change, a vast literature had developed which related domestic R&D expenditures to total factor productivity (TFP) growth.[1] The particular contribution of the new models of trade and growth therefore lies in the testable hypotheses one can derive with regard to trade and openness. In an influential paper, Coe and Helpman (1995) (henceforth CH) have recently derived and tested two implications of these models. The first regards the composition of imports: ceteris paribus, if one country imports primarily from other countries which have accumulated high levels of technological knowledge, then it should exhibit higher productivity levels than if it would import primarily from countries with comparatively low levels of technological knowledge (import composition effect). The second effect is related to the overall import share of a country: for a given composition of imports, a country should benefit more from foreign R&D creating innovative intermediate goods, the higher is the country's overall import share (overall import share effect).

At the center of the analysis by CH is what the authors call the 'foreign stock of knowledge' of a given country. This variable is constructed as a weighted sum of the cumulative R&D expenditures of the country's trading partners, where the weights are given by the bilateral import shares.[2] According to CH, their analysis

---

[1] See Nadiri (1993) for a survey.

[2] This is analogous to the domestic R&D-TFP literature: as initially proposed by Griliches (1979), authors have frequently tried to capture the degree to which productivity in one industry depends on R&D in others by computing weighted sums of outside R&D, where the weights are, for instance, input–output coefficients.

"underlines the importance of the interaction between international trade and foreign R&D" (p. 860).

They conclude their analysis by stating that

"not only does a country's total factor productivity depend on its own R&D capital stock, but, as suggested by the theory, it also depends on the R&D capital stocks of its trade partners." (p. 875).

Hence, CH argue that their analysis supports the view that international R&D spillovers are trade-related. This is the claim being investigated in the present paper. In doing so, I will focus largely on the import composition effect, as it relates more closely to the recent models of growth and intermediate inputs trade than the overall imports effect, which is likely to be a feature of a larger class of models.[3] The analysis below relies on an approach which I call counterfactual estimation.[4] It consists of Monte-Carlo experiments in which the CH regressions are repeated with foreign knowledge stock variables which are computed on the basis of simulated and counterfactual patterns of international trade. These Monte-Carlo experiments can be viewed as estimating international R&D spillovers among randomly matched trade partners. The inference of whether international R&D spillovers are trade-related or not is then drawn by comparing the estimation results based on 'true' trade patterns with those based on counterfactual trade patterns.

The remainder of the paper is as follows. In Section 2, the empirical implementation as well as the results of CH's estimation are given. Section 3 describes how the counterfactual trade patterns are created in the Monte-Carlo experiments, and presents the international spillover effects estimated from those trade patterns. Section 4 concludes.

## 2. Empirical implementation and results in Coe and Helpman (1995)

The empirical analysis in CH builds on recent work on R&D-driven endogenous technological change and trade in differentiated intermediate inputs. In those models,[5] it is possible to derive an expression for output in country $i$,

[3] While this paper does not address identification issues, they are currently discussed in detail in other work in the international trade literature; see, e.g., Evenett and Keller (1997).

[4] Similar in spirit to the counterfactual estimation approach is Ben-David (1996), who shows that income convergence among countries which trade heavily with each other is faster than among randomly formed groups of countries.

[5] I am referring here specifically to the model of expanding horizontal product varieties. For the so-called quality ladder model, CH show that its implications with respect to the relation of foreign R&D and domestic TFP are essentially the same as those shown below. For more on the derivation of the estimating equation, see CH and Keller (1997); the theory is laid out in detail in Grossman and Helpman (1991).

Table 1
Bilateral import shares in 1980 (%)

| From/to | US | Japan | Germany | France | Italy | UK | Canada | Australia | Austria | Belgium |
|---|---|---|---|---|---|---|---|---|---|---|
| US | 0 | 51.43 | 10.36 | 11.9 | 11.08 | 15.9 | 82.18 | 30.36 | 4.37 | 9.44 |
| Japan | 25.82 | 0 | 4.19 | 3.07 | 2.07 | 4.51 | 4.76 | 23.81 | 3.11 | 2.46 |
| Germany | 9.6 | 5.24 | 0 | 24.21 | 26.47 | 14.93 | 2.46 | 8.42 | 52.69 | 24.25 |
| France | 4.35 | 2.73 | 14.74 | 0 | 22.12 | 10.15 | 1.31 | 2.45 | 5.1 | 17.82 |
| Italy | 3.67 | 1.97 | 10.93 | 14.07 | 0 | 6.07 | 1.04 | 3.51 | 11.73 | 4.43 |
| UK | 8.04 | 4.11 | 9.2 | 8.08 | 7.06 | 0 | 3.36 | 12.98 | 3.55 | 9.96 |
| Canada | 32.89 | 9.95 | 1.46 | 1.16 | 1.63 | 3.72 | 0 | 3.81 | 0.6 | 0.91 |
| Australia | 2.18 | 14.69 | 0.52 | 0.65 | 0.92 | 1.27 | 0.87 | 0 | 0.21 | 0.38 |
| Austria | 0.32 | 0.36 | 3.96 | 0.72 | 3.02 | 0.81 | 0.16 | 0.35 | 0 | 0.47 |
| Belgium | 1.57 | 0.79 | 9.87 | 12.5 | 5.68 | 6.28 | 0.42 | 1.05 | 2.68 | 0 |
| Denmark | 0.6 | 0.67 | 2.31 | 0.96 | 1.4 | 2.91 | 0.2 | 0.5 | 0.88 | 0.57 |
| Finland | 0.38 | 0.25 | 1.19 | 0.79 | 0.6 | 2.09 | 0.11 | 0.9 | 0.6 | 0.37 |
| Greece | 0.25 | 0.08 | 1.11 | 0.51 | 0.78 | 0.35 | 0.04 | 0.13 | 0.27 | 0.19 |
| Ireland | 0.34 | 0.17 | 0.61 | 0.84 | 0.42 | 4.67 | 0.17 | 0.38 | 0.24 | 0.46 |
| Israel | 0.77 | 0.48 | 0.45 | 0.34 | 0.49 | 0.62 | 0.09 | 0.32 | 0.31 | 0.41 |
| Netherlands | 1.6 | 0.8 | 15.77 | 8.1 | 6.67 | 8.97 | 0.45 | 1.55 | 3.48 | 20.16 |
| NZ | 0.62 | 1.75 | 0.11 | 0.19 | 0.19 | 1.09 | 0.25 | 4.74 | 0.07 | 0.19 |
| Norway | 2.14 | 0.39 | 3.12 | 1.4 | 0.45 | 3.8 | 0.14 | 0.32 | 0.44 | 1.03 |
| Portugal | 0.24 | 0.12 | 0.48 | 0.57 | 0.48 | 0.88 | 0.09 | 0.12 | 0.34 | 0.27 |
| Spain | 1.05 | 0.82 | 1.81 | 4.32 | 2.53 | 2.09 | 0.32 | 0.47 | 0.54 | 1.06 |
| Sweden | 1.34 | 0.98 | 2.91 | 2.29 | 1.98 | 3.88 | 0.71 | 2.45 | 2.34 | 1.79 |
| Switzerland | 2.24 | 2.24 | 4.89 | 3.36 | 3.95 | 5 | 0.89 | 1.38 | 6.46 | 3.36 |
| Total | 100 | 100 | 100 | 100 | 100 | 100 | 100 | 100 | 100 | 100 |

denoted $y_i$, as

$$y_i = A_i k_i^{\alpha} n_i^{\alpha} l_i^{1-\alpha}, \quad \forall i, \ 0 < \alpha < 1, \tag{2.1}$$

where $A_i$ is a country-specific constant, $k_i$ are capital services, $l_i$ labor services, and $n_i$ is the range of differentiated intermediate goods employed in country $i$. Note that Eq. (2.1) exhibits constant returns in capital and labor alone, which implies that if an index of TFP is defined as

$$\log F_i = \log y_i - \alpha \log k_i - (1 - \alpha_i) \log l_i, \tag{2.2}$$

it will be positively related to the range of intermediate goods employed:

$$\log F_i = \log A_i + \alpha \log n_i, \quad \forall i. \tag{2.3}$$

With international trade, both domestic as well as foreign intermediate goods can be employed in country $i$. Because the tradability of domestic and foreign

| Denmark | Finland | Greece | Ireland | Israel | Netherlands | NZ | Norway | Portugal | Spain | Sweden | Switzerland |
|---|---|---|---|---|---|---|---|---|---|---|---|
| 7.7 | 9.36 | 7.08 | 9.82 | 28.7 | 11.79 | 19.51 | 9.55 | 16.07 | 25.14 | 9.4 | 7.85 |
| 2.73 | 5.23 | 17.25 | 2.87 | 2.22 | 2.54 | 19.89 | 4.07 | 4.47 | 4.72 | 3.66 | 3.82 |
| 22.17 | 20.37 | 21.63 | 7.7 | 14.66 | 29.81 | 5.12 | 15.81 | 17.09 | 15.77 | 21.56 | 32.04 |
| 5.22 | 4.92 | 9.62 | 5.83 | 5 | 8.98 | 1.47 | 4.13 | 10.61 | 15.9 | 5.56 | 14.27 |
| 3.49 | 3.68 | 13.19 | 2.7 | 5.84 | 4.24 | 1.93 | 2.64 | 7.63 | 9.49 | 3.61 | 11.17 |
| 14.61 | 13.86 | 7.09 | 56.96 | 12.47 | 10.95 | 16.18 | 16.72 | 12.87 | 9.03 | 15.24 | 9.65 |
| 0.6 | 1.18 | 1.15 | 1.51 | 1.48 | 1.01 | 3.35 | 2.74 | 1.33 | 1.52 | 1.19 | 0.65 |
| 0.22 | 0.18 | 0.26 | 0.1 | 0.74 | 0.32 | 25.65 | 0.8 | 0.32 | 0.71 | 0.32 | 0.16 |
| 1.3 | 1.92 | 1.63 | 0.36 | 0.63 | 0.78 | 0.25 | 1.41 | 0.85 | 0.74 | 1.81 | 4.18 |
| 4.14 | 2.7 | 3.05 | 2.23 | 7.5 | 18.05 | 0.58 | 3.86 | 4.55 | 3.06 | 4.22 | 4.78 |
| 0 | 3.86 | 0.93 | 0.79 | 0.52 | 1.17 | 0.51 | 7.03 | 0.84 | 1 | 7.87 | 0.97 |
| 4.58 | 0 | 1.54 | 1.12 | 0.98 | 1.04 | 0.15 | 4.25 | 0.68 | 0.82 | 8.78 | 0.66 |
| 0.24 | 0.18 | 0 | 0.1 | 0.39 | 0.53 | 0.03 | 0.09 | 0.17 | 0.24 | 0.28 | 0.13 |
| 0.37 | 0.32 | 0.56 | 0 | 0.22 | 0.69 | 0.15 | 0.29 | 0.27 | 0.69 | 0.4 | 0.29 |
| 0.19 | 0.41 | 0.57 | 0.31 | 0 | 0.36 | 0.13 | 0.24 | 0.88 | 0.24 | 0.25 | 0.4 |
| 8.51 | 4.1 | 6.01 | 3.16 | 3.52 | 0 | 1.57 | 3.85 | 4.22 | 4.14 | 4.78 | 4.71 |
| 0.12 | 0.11 | 0.72 | 0.18 | 0.02 | 0.06 | 0 | 0.07 | 0.11 | 0.17 | 0.06 | 0.04 |
| 4.96 | 3.4 | 1.38 | 0.47 | 0.37 | 1.87 | 0.2 | 0 | 0.71 | 0.54 | 6.68 | 0.44 |
| 0.55 | 0.77 | 0.25 | 0.34 | 0.3 | 0.37 | 0.1 | 0.67 | 0 | 0.92 | 0.88 | 0.34 |
| 0.89 | 1.43 | 1.4 | 0.95 | 0.74 | 1.2 | 0.58 | 0.85 | 8.1 | 0 | 1.02 | 1.1 |
| 15.39 | 19.46 | 2.69 | 1.8 | 1.37 | 2.48 | 1.7 | 19.08 | 3.35 | 2.25 | 0 | 2.35 |
| 2.04 | 2.55 | 2.01 | 0.69 | 12.32 | 1.75 | 0.94 | 1.86 | 4.89 | 3.01 | 2.41 | 0 |
| 100 | 100 | 100 | 100 | 100 | 100 | 100 | 100 | 100 | 100 | 100 | 100 |

*Source*: IMF (1986).

intermediates differs though, CH separate the domestic from the foreign range of intermediate goods ($n_i^{\mathrm{d}}$ and $n_i^{\mathrm{f}}$, respectively):

$$\log F_i = \log A_i + \beta_1 \log n_i^{\mathrm{d}} + \beta_2 \log n_i^{\mathrm{f}}. \tag{2.4}$$

The expanding product varieties in countries $i$ and $h \neq i$ are the result of R&D investments. With an appropriate choice of units, the range $n_i^{\mathrm{d}}$, $\forall i$, is identical to the cumulative stock of R&D expenditures, $S_i^{\mathrm{d}}$. The unobserved range of foreign intermediates which is employed in $i$, $n_i^{\mathrm{f}}$, is captured by the foreign knowledge stock variable proposed in CH. It is constructed as follows:

$$n_{it}^{\mathrm{f}} = S_{it}^{\mathrm{f}} = \sum_{h \neq i} (m_{hit} S_{ht}^{\mathrm{d}}), \quad \forall i, t. \tag{2.5}$$

Here, $m_{hit}$ is the bilateral import share of country $i$ from country $h$ at time $t$. Hence, the construction of the variable $S_i^{\mathrm{f}}$ weights the cumulative R&D

expenditures of country $i$'s trading partners by their bilateral import share. In this way the specification captures the notion that the domestic economy will reap, ceteris paribus, more international spillovers if it trades relatively more with countries which have invested heavily in R&D, and hence have large domestic knowledge stocks, $S^d$.

With these considerations, CH's first specification is given by

$$\log F_{it} = \beta_{0i} + \beta_1 \log S^d_{it} + \beta_2 \log S^f_{it} + \varepsilon_{it}, \quad \forall i, t, \tag{2.6}$$

where $\varepsilon_i$ is a mean-zero error term, and $\beta_{0i} = \log A_i$ are country-specific intercepts. A second specification allows the effect from domestic R&D to be different in the G-7 group countries relative to the smaller member countries of the OECD:

$$\log F_{it} = \beta_{0i} + \beta_G (G7_i \times \log S^d_{it}) + \beta_1 \log S^d_{it} + \beta_2 \log S^f_{it} + \varepsilon_{it}, \quad \forall i, t, \tag{2.7}$$

where $G7_i$ is equal to one for any G-7 country, otherwise zero.

In order to capture the overall import share effect of trade-related R&D spillovers, CH propose a third specification, with

$$\log F_{it} = \beta_{0i} + \beta_G (G7_i \times \log S^d_{it}) + \beta_1 \log S^d_{it} + \beta_2 (m_{it} \times \log S^f_{it}) + \varepsilon_{it}, \quad \forall i, t. \tag{2.8}$$

Here, $m_{it}$ is country $i$'s overall import share. There are 21 OECD countries plus Israel in the CH sample, for the years 1971–90, making a total of 440 observations. Main data sources are the OECD's *Analytical Data Base* as well as its *Main Science and Technology Indicators*. The bilateral import shares are calculated from the IMF's *Direction of Trade* statistics; its values are shown for the year 1980 in Table 1.[6] For instance, 32.89% of the US imports came from Canada, as opposed to only 1.46% of Germany's. In consequence, the level of the Canadian cumulative R&D expenditures should be much more relevant for US productivity than it should be for Germany's.

The results of the three regression specifications in Eqs. (2.6), (2.7) and (2.8) are given in Table 2, column BIS (for bilateral import shares).[7] The foreign knowledge stock variable enters in all regressions with a positive coefficient which is large relative to the standard error of the parameter estimate.[8] Note, first, that the specification (iii) performs best according to the

[6] For a detailed description of the data employed, see CH.

[7] These results are obtained using the data provided by David Coe. CH report somewhat lower $R^2$ for these regressions, but the point estimates are identical up to two decimals.

[8] In the table, conventional standard errors are given, which would be wrong if the regressions were estimating cointegrating relationships. But see the discussion on super-consistency in CH.

Table 2
TFP estimation results; pooled data with 440 observations

| | (i) | | | (ii) | | | (iii) | | |
|---|---|---|---|---|---|---|---|---|---|
| | BIS | RIS | SS | BIS | RIS | SS | BIS | RIS | SS |
| log $S^d$ | 0.097 | 0.029 | 0.026 | 0.090 | 0.035 | 0.032 | 0.078 | 0.048 | 0.047 |
| | (0.009) | (0.002) | (0.011) | (0.008) | (0.002) | (0.010) | (0.008) | (0.001) | (0.008) |
| G7 × log $S^d$ | | | | 0.135 | 0.097 | 0.095 | 0.157 | 0.159 | 0.159 |
| | | | | (0.016) | (0.002) | (0.016) | (0.015) | (0.001) | (0.014) |
| log $S^f$ | 0.092 | 0.156 | 0.161 | 0.060 | 0.125 | 0.129 | | | |
| | (0.016) | (0.003) | (0.013) | (0.015) | (0.003) | (0.014) | | | |
| $m$ × log $S^f$ | | | | | | | 0.289 | 0.329 | 0.335 |
| | | | | | | | (0.041) | (0.005) | (0.030) |
| $R^2$ | 0.630 | 0.702 | 0.705 | 0.683 | 0.728 | 0.729 | 0.706 | 0.747 | 0.748 |

$R^2$ criterion, which is consistent with the notion that, for a given import composition, international R&D spillovers are higher, the higher is a country's overall import share. Second, with regards to the composition of imports, the question is whether the regressions provide evidence in favor of the hypothesis that international R&D spillovers are related to the trade patterns of differentiated goods.

## 3. Counterfactual estimation: Simulating bilateral import shares

In evaluating the hypothesis that international R&D spillovers are trade-related, the foreign knowledge stock variable $S^f$ constructed by CH is of central interest. A country's R&D benefit from abroad is taken to be a weighted average of these foreign countries' R&D efforts, where the weights are given by the bilateral import shares, $m_{ht}$ (see Eq. (2.5)). In the following, I will compare the estimation results of CH with those obtained from employing foreign knowledge stock variables which are based on random bilateral import shares. That is, rather than constructing the foreign knowledge stock variable $S^f$ using the observed bilateral import shares, alternative foreign knowledge stock variables are computed on the basis of randomly created bilateral import shares (denoted RIS, for random import shares). Then, the CH regressions (i)–(iii) are repeated with the alternative foreign knowledge stocks. Finally, I compare the estimation results obtained by employing observed import patterns with those based on randomly created import patterns. Because each set of random bilateral import shares can be thought of as a counterfactual world of international import relations, I call this approach counterfactual estimation.

The random import shares are constructed as follows: for each Monte-Carlo replication $b$, $b = 1, \ldots, B$, I obtain one matrix $\Gamma(b)$ consisting of 484 ($22 \times 22$) random elements $\gamma_{hi}(b)$ which are drawn from a uniform distribution with support [0, 1] using the (pseudo) random number generator of the GAUSS package.[9] The diagonal elements of $\Gamma(b)$ are then set to zero. In the next step the sum of each column is calculated, $\gamma_{\bullet i}(b) = \sum_{h \neq i} \gamma_{hi}(b)$. Finally, shares $\sigma_{hi}(b)$ are formed by

$$\sigma_{hi}(b) = \frac{\gamma_{hi}(b)}{\gamma_{\bullet i}(b)}, \quad \forall h, i, b, \tag{3.1}$$

with $\sum_h \sigma_{hi}(b) = 1, \forall i, b$. These 484 values $\sigma_{hi}(b)$ form the matrix $\Omega(b)$ of dimension $22 \times 22$. Then, the foreign knowledge stock for this particular replication, $S^{\mathrm{f}}(b)$, is computed from the values of the – observed – cumulative R&D stocks $S^{\mathrm{d}}$ and the matrix $\Omega(b)$ analogous to Eq. (2.5) above:

$$S^{\mathrm{f}}_{it}(b) = \sum_{h \neq i} \sigma_{hi}(b) S^{\mathrm{d}}_{ht}, \quad \forall i, t, b. \tag{3.2}$$

Lastly, I run three regression specifications in analogy to Eqs. (2.6), (2.7) and (2.8) above, the only difference being that the foreign knowledge stock based on actual import patterns is replaced by the foreign knowledge stock variable based on simulated import patterns. For each specification, $B = 1000$ replications are conducted.[10] The column RIS in Table 2 presents the mean and standard deviation (in parentheses) of the parameter estimates from the simulations, denoted $\beta^{\mathrm{m}}_{v}(\bar{b})$, and $\beta^{\mathrm{s}}_{v}(\bar{b})$, respectively, for $v = G, 1, 2$.

The estimates of key interest are the averages of the Monte-Carlo coefficients on the simulated foreign knowledge stocks, $\beta^{\mathrm{m}}_{2}(\bar{b})$, as those reveal how large an international R&D spillover is estimated based on counterfactual import patterns. Note that across all three specifications (i)–(iii), the Monte-Carlo average is larger than the corresponding coefficient based on the 'true' foreign knowledge stock (that is, $\beta^{\mathrm{m}}_{2}(\bar{b}) > \beta_2$). Furthermore, the part of the variation in TFP levels which is accounted for by the simulated foreign knowledge stocks is on average larger than if the 'true' foreign knowledge stock is employed: the $R^2$ in specification (i) is 0.630 for the observed and on average 0.702 for the simulated foreign knowledge stocks. Similar results hold for specifications (ii) and (iii).[11]

---

[9] This function uses a seed value which is updated during the process; the initial seed value is 26 875.

[10] CH use bilateral import shares which are varying from year to year between 1971 and 1991; therefore, also the matrix $\Omega(b)$ varies by year in the Monte-Carlo results presented below. The results are not qualitatively different, however, if a time-invariant import share matrix is employed in the simulations.

[11] Both the result that $\beta^{\mathrm{m}}_{2}(\bar{b}) > \beta_2$ and the fact that the average $R^2$ is larger in the Monte-Carlo replications do not depend on the fact that, in all three specifications (i)–(iii), the coefficient on own-country R&D is estimated to be less (i.e., $\beta^{\mathrm{m}}_{1}(\bar{b}) < \beta_1$) than in the Monte-Carlo simulations.

It is therefore clear that the finding of international R&D spillovers in the context of CH's approach is not limited to employing the observed patterns of international trade: positive and large productivity effects are also estimated if the underlying variable $S^f(b)$ is unrelated to the patterns of international trade. Moreover, the counterfactual international trade patterns generate an even better empirical fit as measured by the $R^2$ criterion. These results imply that it is, on the basis of the CH results, not possible to argue that the import composition of a country matters for productivity in the way predicted by the recent trade and growth theories.

This is seen most clearly by comparing a specific simulated import share matrix $\Omega(b)$ with the actual import share matrix. The former is given in Table 3, while the latter was given for the year 1980 in Table 1. The simulated shares in Table 3 give, in the specification (iii),

$$\log F_{it} = \beta_{0i} + \beta_G(G7_i \times \log S^d_{it}) + \beta_1 \log S^d_{it}$$
$$+ \beta_2(m_{it} \times \log S^f_{it}(b)) + \varepsilon_{it}, \quad \forall i, t,$$

a value of $\beta_2(b)$.of 0.321 (S.E. 0.029), and a $R^2$ of 0.747. This is to be compared to $\beta_2 = 0.289$ (S.E. 0.041), and a $R^2$ of 0.706 in Table 1, BIS.[12] Observe that the simulated pattern of international trade in Table 3 differs considerably from the 'true' pattern given in Table 1. Canada, for instance, has been importing most of its goods from the US; this share was 82.18% in the year 1980. Ireland, however, has been importing primarily from the United Kingdom (56.96% in 1980), whereas only 9.82% of Ireland's imports cam from the US. The theory predicts that Canada benefits more from US technology embodied in intermediate inputs than does Ireland, and, all else equal, that the productivity level in Canada is higher than in Ireland. If the correlation of partner country's cumulative R&D stock and TFP level holds on average in the sample, one expects a positive coefficient $\beta_2$ and a high $R^2$. However, in the simulated world of trade patterns given in Table 3, Canada imports only 2.15% from the US, whereas Ireland imports 6.41% from the US, and one estimates nevertheless a higher coefficient $\beta_2(b)$ (of 0.321 versus 0.289) at the same time where a larger share of variation in TFP levels is accounted for ($R^2(b) = 0.747$ versus 0.706).

Rather than considering alternative international trade patterns in the construction of the foreign knowledge stock, one can also ask what the estimated

[12] For concreteness, the matrix $\Omega(b)$ has been fixed for all years in this simulation, whereas the CH results are derived employing time-varying bilateral import shares. Note, however, that the actual bilateral import shares did not change dramatically over the period of 1971–91 in the countries under consideration.

Table 3
Simulated bilateral import shares: a particular example (%)

| From/to | US | Japan | Germany | France | Italy | UK | Canada | Australia | Austria | Belgium |
|---|---|---|---|---|---|---|---|---|---|---|
| US | 0 | 8.99 | 6.77 | 7.91 | 4.05 | 6.99 | 2.15 | 8.6 | 4.53 | 6.44 |
| Japan | 9.97 | 0 | 3.76 | 3.39 | 0.6 | 4.36 | 7.39 | 0 | 4.78 | 1.29 |
| Germany | 9.91 | 3.55 | 0 | 0.72 | 5.76 | 6.02 | 3.66 | 9.91 | 6.85 | 2.27 |
| France | 0.1 | 2.68 | 3.3 | 0 | 3.28 | 4.66 | 3.35 | 1.01 | 8.22 | 4.71 |
| Italy | 1.7 | 3.99 | 8.14 | 4.57 | 0 | 4.33 | 8.33 | 2.23 | 6.59 | 3.78 |
| UK | 4.28 | 5.36 | 5.17 | 7.51 | 6.2 | 0 | 2.17 | 0.52 | 1.99 | 1.1 |
| Canada | 8.39 | 10.37 | 8.54 | 0.03 | 4.01 | 4.85 | 0 | 8.53 | 7.09 | 4.15 |
| Australia | 5.27 | 0.67 | 8.49 | 2.74 | 9.39 | 2.06 | 9.28 | 0 | 7.59 | 7.95 |
| Austria | 8.3 | 2.78 | 8.64 | 3.12 | 4.4 | 2.27 | 9.04 | 8.22 | 0 | 7.9 |
| Belgium | 10.32 | 9.31 | 5.3 | 4.18 | 1.05 | 1.05 | 3.06 | 3.34 | 6.73 | 0 |
| Denmark | 2.28 | 4.77 | 4.24 | 9.09 | 1.53 | 1.61 | 6.28 | 6.08 | 7.73 | 3.33 |
| Finland | 0.85 | 3.57 | 0.42 | 8.42 | 0.72 | 6.52 | 6.58 | 2.96 | 5.36 | 6.88 |
| Greece | 3.13 | 1.2 | 0.66 | 4.3 | 8.22 | 1.73 | 3.56 | 1.47 | 0.75 | 4.51 |
| Ireland | 2.23 | 10.11 | 5.11 | 6.45 | 8.6 | 6.74 | 5.16 | 0.17 | 6.33 | 5.03 |
| Israel | 8.51 | 2.87 | 1.48 | 7.94 | 3.78 | 7.11 | 0.49 | 4.84 | 0.11 | 2.6 |
| Netherlands | 4.29 | 5 | 0.52 | 3.81 | 6.57 | 7.16 | 7.55 | 4.18 | 4.63 | 6.6 |
| NZ | 4.34 | 2.04 | 9.03 | 2.1 | 4.44 | 5.68 | 2.87 | 8.12 | 3.86 | 2 |
| Norway | 3.78 | 0.96 | 0.57 | 0.17 | 5.74 | 3.99 | 3.79 | 3.02 | 2.44 | 5.45 |
| Portugal | 3.23 | 2.8 | 4.29 | 2.84 | 0.28 | 5.93 | 6.39 | 7.62 | 4.48 | 4.47 |
| Spain | 3.46 | 5.52 | 6.71 | 7.03 | 6.44 | 4.18 | 6.53 | 9.28 | 0.53 | 7.53 |
| Sweden | 0.18 | 9.1 | 2.36 | 9.25 | 9.43 | 5.75 | 1.55 | 6.91 | 3.15 | 6.06 |
| Switzerland | 5.48 | 4.36 | 6.49 | 4.43 | 5.5 | 6.99 | 0.81 | 2.97 | 6.25 | 5.96 |
| Total | 100 | 100 | 100 | 100 | 100 | 100 | 100 | 100 | 100 | 100 |

*(continued overleaf)*

international R&D spillovers are if the foreign knowledge variable is simply computed as the unweighed sum of foreign countries R&D stocks, denoted $\bar{S}^{\mathrm{f}}$,

$$\bar{S}^{\mathrm{f}}_{it} = \sum_{h \neq i} S^{\mathrm{d}}_{ht}, \quad \forall i, t. \tag{3.3}$$

Hence, international trade patterns are completely absent from the construction of the $\bar{S}^{\mathrm{f}}$ variable. The results of substituting the unweighed stock of foreign R&D ($\bar{S}^{\mathrm{f}}$) for the import-share weighted stock of foreign R&D ($S^{\mathrm{f}}$) in the three specifications (i)–(iii) leads to the results shown in Table 2, column SS (for simple sum). For all three specifications, the point estimate on the foreign knowledge stock $\bar{S}^{\mathrm{f}}$ is higher than if import shares are used to construct the $\bar{S}^{\mathrm{f}}$ variable. In addition, the $R^2$ in the SS regressions are higher than those from the BIS (and

| Denmark | Finland | Greece | Ireland | Israel | Netherlands | NZ | Norway | Portugal | Spain | Sweden | Switzerland |
|---|---|---|---|---|---|---|---|---|---|---|---|
| 1.7 | 6.25 | 9.14 | 6.41 | 1.12 | 2.01 | 7.57 | 0.89 | 0.22 | 8.24 | 2.98 | 7.65 |
| 6.65 | 0.91 | 6.86 | 4.29 | 9.92 | 4.99 | 6.55 | 11.5 | 5.21 | 6.07 | 4.78 | 5.86 |
| 6.88 | 3.41 | 1.34 | 4.48 | 9.01 | 9.42 | 7.54 | 3.68 | 8.26 | 5.05 | 1.73 | 8.26 |
| 3.54 | 2.33 | 3.31 | 5.79 | 1.01 | 0.7 | 3.9 | 2.56 | 10.57 | 3.31 | 1.27 | 7.76 |
| 4.58 | 2.66 | 8.07 | 6.25 | 0.77 | 0.81 | 7.7 | 1.39 | 1.09 | 5.95 | 5.37 | 3.62 |
| 2.18 | 4.84 | 2.9 | 3.55 | 1.13 | 4.78 | 0.89 | 2.94 | 0.57 | 6.09 | 8.64 | 5.26 |
| 7.83 | 0.71 | 3.36 | 1.89 | 9.76 | 3.99 | 4.42 | 0.38 | 1.96 | 6 | 3.49 | 0.79 |
| 2.11 | 5.6 | 7 | 1.17 | 3.2 | 8.32 | 1.74 | 4.95 | 2.69 | 0.74 | 7.64 | 2.03 |
| 7.57 | 7.27 | 1.94 | 4.25 | 3.27 | 6.88 | 3.68 | 4.26 | 5.68 | 3.58 | 7.57 | 5.26 |
| 3.06 | 8.34 | 0.01 | 7.09 | 2.48 | 5.81 | 2.75 | 2.41 | 10.03 | 7.12 | 7.28 | 8.01 |
| 0 | 9 | 1.41 | 7.43 | 2.68 | 6.03 | 0.58 | 3 | 1.76 | 4.41 | 1.83 | 2.84 |
| 7.14 | 0 | 2.85 | 7.11 | 10.5 | 8.26 | 2.99 | 5.98 | 3.51 | 0.42 | 7.85 | 6.73 |
| 8.81 | 6.35 | 0 | 6.63 | 6.94 | 3.45 | 7.92 | 10.24 | 3.37 | 5.24 | 5.43 | 2.85 |
| 3.88 | 5.74 | 9.25 | 0 | 6.8 | 0.02 | 6.91 | 0.75 | 3.18 | 5.32 | 2.59 | 5.61 |
| 1.56 | 8.53 | 5.4 | 6.23 | 0 | 8.81 | 4.34 | 5.4 | 0.87 | 4.38 | 3.34 | 1.94 |
| 4.7 | 5.84 | 9.82 | 4.79 | 7.44 | 0 | 6.69 | 10.66 | 2.63 | 5.71 | 8.92 | 3.92 |
| 4.18 | 7.57 | 8.46 | 7.08 | 1.08 | 3.94 | 0 | 5.91 | 10.41 | 4.77 | 1.91 | 7.66 |
| 2.72 | 0.34 | 4.4 | 6.29 | 1.7 | 2.26 | 7.18 | 0 | 6.72 | 5.95 | 8.44 | 8.23 |
| 6.9 | 5.1 | 4.54 | 3.88 | 1.47 | 0.61 | 5.23 | 5.1 | 0 | 0.73 | 3.35 | 1.86 |
| 0.66 | 2.13 | 1.23 | 4.19 | 5.83 | 8.66 | 1.31 | 1.99 | 9.09 | 0 | 0.86 | 2.74 |
| 5.01 | 1.46 | 3.91 | 1.06 | 7.94 | 2.39 | 5.69 | 6.29 | 7.66 | 3.62 | 0 | 1.13 |
| 8.34 | 5.61 | 4.79 | 0.14 | 5.95 | 7.88 | 4.43 | 9.71 | 4.5 | 7.29 | 4.72 | 0 |
| 100 | 100 | 100 | 100 | 100 | 100 | 100 | 100 | 100 | 100 | 100 | 100 |

also the RIS) specifications. Hence, the results employing unweighed sums of foreign R&D in these regressions confirm what the Monte-Carlo results already indicated: the composition of imports of a country plays no particular role in estimating a positive and significant from foreign R&D on domestic productivity levels. Moreover, the variation in the sum of unweighed foreign R&D stocks accounts for more of the variation of TFP levels in this sample than if import-weighted R&D sums are employed.[13]

[13] It is not accidental that the RIS estimates are very similar to the SS ones reported in Table 2: the relation between the average Monte-Carlo estimate and the SS specification is derived in Keller (1997).

## 4. Conclusion

In this paper, I have re-examined the evidence presented in CH on the question of whether international R&D spillovers are related to international trade along the lines of recent models of trade and growth. The results of CH are compared to results from regressions based on counterfactual patterns of international trade. It is shown that, on the basis of CH's results, it is not possible to argue that the actual pattern of international trade is important in their estimation of international R&D spillovers, because counterfactual trade patterns give rise to similarly large (or even larger) estimated international R&D spillovers. We also find positive international spillover effects in specifications which do not incorporate any particular pattern of international trade.

It is important to note, however, that these results do not imply that the pattern of international trade plays no role in the diffusion of embodied technology. Considering the complicated nature of the problem, the quality and degree of aggregation of the data, and the uncertainty with respect to the data generation process underlying the R&D and TFP series, the results in this paper might in fact seem rather unsurprising. However, it is clear from this analysis that the extent to which R&D spillovers are related to the pattern of international trade must be estimated in a model which allows simultaneously for trade-unrelated international technology diffusion.[14]

## Acknowledgements

I would like to thank David Coe and Chiwha Kao for the provision and discussion of the data files. The paper has benefitted from the comments of Elhanan Helpman as one of the editors, an anonymous referee, and seminar participants at the 1996 NBER Summer Institute, the University of Wisconsin, and the World Bank.

## References

Aghion, P., Howitt, P., 1992. A model of growth through creative destruction. Econometrica 60, 323–351.

Ben-David, D., 1996. Trade and convergence among countries. Journal of International Economics 40, 279–298.

Coe, D., Helpman, E., 1995. International R&D spillovers. European Economic Review 39, 859–887.

Evenett, S., Keller, W., 1997. On theories explaining the success of the gravity equation. Mimeo., University of Wisconsin, Madison.

[14] Several of the issues mentioned in the last paragraph have been addressed in Keller (1997).

Griliches, Z., 1979. Issues in assessing the contribution of research and development to productivity growth. Bell Journal of Economics 10, 92–116.

Grossman, G., Helpman, E., 1991. Innovation and Growth in the Global Economy. MIT Press, Cambridge, MA.

International Monetary Fund, 1986. Direction of Trade Statistics. Yearbook 1986, IMF, Washington, DC.

Keller, W., 1997. Trade patterns, technology flows, and productivity growth. Mimeographed, University of Wisconsin, Madison.

Nadiri, M.I., 1993, Innovations and technological spillovers. NBER Working Paper No. 4423, Cambridge, MA.

Romer, P., 1990. Endogenous technological change. Journal of Political Economy 98, S71–S102.

INTERNATIONAL
ECONOMIC
REVIEW

August 1999
Vol. 40, No. 3

# INTERNATIONAL TECHNOLOGY DIFFUSION: THEORY AND MEASUREMENT*

BY JONATHAN EATON AND SAMUEL KORTUM[1]

*Boston University and NBER, U.S.A.*

We model the invention of new technologies and their diffusion across countries. In our model all countries grow at the same steady-state rate, with each country's productivity ranking determined by how rapidly it adopts ideas. Research effort is determined by how much ideas earn at home and abroad. Patents affect the return to ideas. We relate the decision to patent an invention internationally to the cost of patenting in a country and to the expected value of patent protection in that country. We can thus infer the direction and magnitude of the international diffusion of technology from data on international patenting, productivity, and research. We fit the model to data from the five leading research economies. A rough summary of our findings is that the world lies about two-thirds of the way from an extreme of technological autarky to an extreme of free trade in ideas. Research performed abroad is about two-thirds as potent as domestic research. Together the United States and Japan drive at least two-thirds of the growth in each of the countries in our sample.

## 1. INTRODUCTION

What is the geographic scope of technical progress? One camp holds that by its very nature technology is freely available everywhere. A questionable implication is that countries enjoy no relative advantage from being innovative.[2] At the other extreme, the new growth theory typically relates a country's technical advances to only its own innovations. A troubling implication here is that innovative countries leave everyone else behind.[3] In contrast to either polar position, economic historians describe world growth in terms of the gradual diffusion of advances from a small set of innovators.

* Manuscript received September 1997; revised April 1998. An earlier version appeared as "International Patenting and Technology Diffusion," NBER Working Paper No. 4931, 1994.

[1] Akiko Tamura and Deepak Agrawal provided excellent research assistance. We take responsibility for any errors. We gratefully acknowledge the support of the National Science Foundation under Grant No. SBR 9309935-001.

[2] A corollary is that differences in worker productivity across countries must result from differences in capital per worker, where capital may be construed very broadly to include human capital. Mankiw, Romer, and Weil (1992) take this stand.

[3] See, for example, Romer (1990) and Agrion and Howitt (1992).

Innovative countries are the most productive, but their innovations also drive growth elsewhere.[4]

We develop, estimate, and simulate a model of world growth driven by innovation. In the spirit of new growth theory, innovation is endogenous.[5] However, in the spirit of historical accounts, we allow for much richer interdependence among different countries' inventive activity and growth. Our microfoundation of innovation leads naturally to equations for productivity dynamics among countries that are simultaneously inventing and adopting each others' inventions.[6] In steady-state countries all grow at the same rate, with countries that are quicker to adopt innovations taking the lead.[7] Together, the ingredients of our model provide an explanation of why research occurs in different countries, how this research gives rise to innovations, and where these innovations generate increases in productivity.

Reflecting two strands of the new growth literature, we build two versions of the model. In one, the world growth rate is fully endogenous, reacting to research incentives and the extent of diffusion.[8] In the second, the growth rate is only "semiendogenous" and is not influenced by factors affecting research and diffusion.[9]

A fundamental problem in trying to quantify a model with richer and more realistic diffusion patterns is identifying who is getting what from whom. We exploit international patenting to overcome this problem. The international patent system requires inventors to patent in each country where they seek protection from imitators.[10] Our model incorporates an inventor's choice of where to patent an idea, relating the decision to seek patent protection in a particular country in part to the likelihood that it will be used there. This feature of the model allows us to use data on international

[4] Gerschenkron (1962) interprets the comparative experiences of different European countries and Japan during their industrial revolutions in terms of the diffusion of technology. Rosenberg (1982) argues for both the historical importance and practical difficulty of diffusion. "... the transfer of technology has never been easy. Typically high levels of skill and competence are needed in the recipient country" (p. 247). He attributes Britain's decline in relative productivity over the past hundred years to its slowness in "exploiting the new industries that began to emerge in the late nineteenth and earlier twentieth centuries, and that are sometimes referred to collectively as the 'second industrial revolution'" (p. 256). On this same point Lewis (1957) argues that "Britain would have done well enough if she merely imitated German and American innovations. Japan, Belgium, and Swizerland owe more of their success as exporters of manufactures to imitation than they do to innovation."

[5] We build on existing theoretical models of research and economic growth. The last decade saw a spurt of activity on this topic, while Phelps (1966) and Shell (1966) provide earlier contributions.

[6] In particular, we incorporate Kortum's (1997) search model of how research generates innovation.

[7] Several theoretical models of economic growth incorporate diffusion. Nelson and Phelps (1966) provide an early contribution and Parente and Prescott (1994) a recent one. Fagerberg (1994), Grossman and Helpman (1995), and Jovanovic (1996) survey subsequent contributions. These models have been too stylyzed to provide a framework for quantitative analysis in a multicountry setting. In particular, they typically assume a single innovating country. Extending them to a world in which a group of innovators draws on each others' ideas is not straightforward.

[8] Grossman and Helpman (1991a), for example, develop several versions of multicountry growth models in this spirit.

[9] Jones (1995) develops a single-economy version of such a model and finds that it explains the postwar U.S. experience better than a model with fully endogenous growth.

[10] Penrose (1951) provides the classic discussion of the international patenting system. Griliches (1990) surveys the literature on using patents as indicators of inventive activity.

patenting as evidence of who is coming up with ideas and where those ideas are more likely to be used.[11]

Where previous studies provide compelling evidence, we use them to fix key parameters of the model. We estimate the rest by fitting the steady state of our model to research employment, productivity levels, and international patenting among the five leading research economies—the United States, Japan, Germany, the United Kingdom, and France—in the late 1980s.[12] Employment of researchers provides a measure of innovative effort, while productivity reflects countries' use of these innovations. International patenting reflects the link between the sources and uses of innovations.[13]

Inventors patent much more at home than abroad. This propensity could reflect technological immobility, but it also could mean that patents provide much less protection abroad. The patent data themselves cannot sort this out, but these competing explanations have different implications for the distribution of productivity. Since our analysis also takes into account data on productivity and research effort, we can distinguish between the two. We infer that much of the home bias derives from lesser incremental protection provided by foreign patents. Otherwise, the model could not explain the tight distribution of productivity levels relative to the skewness of research effort.

Indeed, our estimates do suggest substantial, but not perfect, sharing of ideas. Relative to the adoption of their own potentially useful ideas, countries generally adopt from one half to three-fourths of those generated abroad. Another way to quantify the extent of diffusion is to decompose each country's growth into the contribution made by its own and others' innovation. We find that the United States and Japan together contribute two-thirds or more to growth in each of the five countries, and only the United States derives most of its growth from its own innovation.

Do inventors' earnings reflect the pervasiveness of diffusion? Not quite. We also decompose earnings from innovation in each country into what emanates from each of the five. We find that inventors in every country earn more from their inventions at home than in any other single country. The U.S. market is the source of about one-fourth of the returns to invention in each of the other four.[14]

[11] Coe and Helpman (1995) confront this issue by equating the direction of technology diffusion to exports. Keller (1998b), however, raises serious doubts about the connection between trade and diffusion. We think that patenting abroad is a much more direct, albeit imperfect, indicator of where ideas are going.

[12] Why do we fit our model only to this one snapshot of the data? By the late 1980s these five countries appear to have converged to roughly similar growth rates. To explain the much faster growth of Japan, Germany, and France in the earlier decades would require us to appeal to the much more unwieldy out-of-steady-state predictions of the model. Eaton and Kortum (1997a) take a first step in that direction.

[13] Others have looked at the determinants of subsets of these variables in partial equilibrium. For example, Coe and Helpman (1995), Park (1995), Keller (1998a), and Eaton and Kortum (1996) attempt to link productivity to research in different countries, taking research as given. These analyses cannot be used to infer the effect of changes in policies or parameters on research effort and productivity, as we do here.

[14] While we find that inventions earn most at home, our analysis implies that only the best and hence most valuable inventions are patented in many countries. This result is consistent with the findings of Harhoff, Scherer, and Vopel (1997) and Putnam (1997).

Putting our general equilibrium approach to work, we simulate the effects of various counterfactuals and policies. While the two versions (fully and semiendogenous growth) of the model produce very similar estimation results, they have quite different implications for simulation.

Using the model and parameter estimates, we can imagine a world in which diffusion patterns are more extreme. We find, for example, that cutting off the United States from the rest of the world would cause its productivity to fall far behind the other four. Going in the opposite direction, removing the impediments to diffusion created by national borders would not only shrink productivity differences, it also would raise productivity overall. With growth fully endogenous, world growth rises by 1 percentage point, whereas, in the case of semiendogenous growth, U.S. productivity rises by 40 percent. The overall level of research effort also rises substantially.

What about the role of patent policy? Our estimates imply that eliminating protection would reduce steady-state growth, when it is fully endogenous, by about 0.1 percentage point and, when it is only semiendogenous, by about 6 percent across the board. In either case there are substantial reductions in research effort in every country. Going to the other extreme, eliminating any imitation of patented ideas would raise growth, when it is fully endogenous, by 0.7 percentage point. With growth semiendogenous, productivity rises by about 40 percent. In both cases research rises by an order of magnitude.

We proceed as follows: In Section 2 we describe our data. Section 3 sets forth our model, while Section 4 characterizes its steady state. In Section 5 we describe the estimation procedure. Section 6 explores the implications of our estimates and their sensitivity to different assumptions. Section 7 simulates several counterfactuals, and Section 8 offers some concluding remarks. The Appendix provides a list of symbols and derivations of results.

## 2. FEATURES OF THE DATA

Our interest is in the generation and sharing of technology among technological leaders. Hence we restrict ourselves to the five leading research nations in the OECD: the United States, Japan, Germany, the United Kingdom, and France. In the late 1980s these countries employed over 80 percent of the OECD's research scientists and engineers (OECD, 1991). Furthermore, each of these five countries obtained between 70 and 80 percent of its foreign patent applications from one of the other four (WIPO, 1990). About 60 percent of the world's gross domestic product (GDP) was produced in these countries (Summers and Heston, 1991). Hence our five countries account for most of the world's inventive activity and a majority of the market for ideas.

Our concern is with the relationships among research and productivity in these countries, and we use patent data as an indicator of the extent to which these countries make use of each others' ideas. Table 1 presents the data. Our task in the model we present below is to capture the basic features of these numbers. We discuss each in turn.

TABLE 1
DATA

| | Germany | France | U.K. | Japan | U.S. |
|---|---|---|---|---|---|
| Adjusted research employment (thousands) | 97 | 41 | 74 | 289 | 477 |
| Workforce (millions) | 29 | 25 | 28 | 61 | 120 |
| Relative output per hour in manufacturing | 0.86 | 0.91 | 0.66 | 0.78 | 1 |
| Patent applications seeking protection in | By inventors from | | | | |
| Germany | 43342 | 5130 | 4739 | 14553 | 18849 |
| France | 13428 | 15365 | 4389 | 10859 | 17627 |
| U.K. | 13029 | 4961 | 24176 | 12984 | 19720 |
| Japan | 7487 | 2685 | 2811 | 65128 | 17505 |
| U.S. | 13159 | 5178 | 6418 | 32829 | 83333 |
| Adjusted GDP ($ billions) | 1751 | 1299 | 921 | 3662 | 5876 |
| Application costs ($) to patent in | Paid by inventors from | | | | |
| Germany | 1066 | 1066 | 1066 | 3066 | 1066 |
| France | 992 | 992 | 992 | 3042 | 992 |
| U.K. | 1200 | 1200 | 1200 | 4020 | 1200 |
| Japan | 4772 | 4772 | 4772 | 9590 | 4772 |
| U.S. | 3390 | 3440 | 1390 | 4210 | 1390 |

SOURCES: R&D RSE's employed in the business sector in 1988, adjusted by the fraction of business sector R&D financed either by the business sector or from abroad, are from OECD (1991). Workforces are from Summers and Heston (1991). Labor productivity levels are manufacturing value added per hour relative to the United States, in 1990 (van Ark, 1996). Patent applications (1988–1990 average) are from WIPO. Domestic applications in Japan are scaled down by a factor of 4.9 (see text). Adjusted GDP is from IMF (1994) with R&D expenditure from OECD (1991) subtracted. Costs of filing a patent application (including translation and agents fees) are from Helfgott (1993). The cost for a Japanese inventor filing an application in Japan is scaled up by a factor of 4.9 (see text).

2.1. *Research.* The first row of Table 1 shows private-sector employment of research and development (R&D) scientists and engineers in 1988 (in thousands).[15] A striking feature is the skewness of the location of research. Nearly half these researchers work in the United States, and Japan employs more than half the remainder. This skewness suggests significant concentration in the generation of ideas in these two countries, but, of course, with technological diffusion, the adoption of these ideas could be much more equal.

Much of the skewness in absolute research activity reflects the scale of the countries in question. Dividing the number of researchers in each country by its workforce, reported in row 2, greatly reduces the range of variation. The two largest countries also have the largest fraction of their workforce engaged in research, but research intensity in the third largest, Germany, is not far behind. Hence, while we do observe skewness in research activity, we do not observe the extreme specialization predicted by some models of international innovation. Finally, in any country, the incentive to

[15] To eliminate researchers working on defense, we multiply these employment numbers by the fraction of business sector R&D financed by either the business sector or from abroad. All data on research are from OECD (1991).

undertake research at the margin seems to die out at a very low level of activity; no more than 0.5 percent of the workforce in any of these countries is engaged as researchers.[16]

2.2. *Productivity.* The third row in Table 1 reports productivity as measured by manufacturing value added per hour in 1990 relative to the United States. We use manufacturing productivity because this represents the major component of what Griliches (1994) terms the "measurable" sector of the economy. In addition, since our interest is in productivity rather than in living standards, we follow Heston and Summer's (1996) recommendation and use van Ark's (1996) data for this purpose.[17]

Regardless of which productivity measure one uses, a striking feature is that differences in productivity levels are nowhere near differences in research effort. Moreover, national growth rates do not appear to be related to research effort. Various measures of productivity growth for our five countries show growth rates bunching together during the postwar period, independent of research effort.[18]

2.3. *Patents.* The next five rows of Table 1 report patent applications, averaged over 1988 through 1990, by country of application and residence of inventor.[19] Note that applications from inventors abroad comprise a large share of the applications in each country. France obtains more applications from the United States than from its own inventors. However, domestic inventors are the single most important source of applications in each of the others.[20]

Foreign patent applications roughly reflect the scale of research activity in the source country (as opposed, for example, to the intensity of research effort there). The United States is the dominant source of foreign patents in the other four countries, followed either by Japan or (in Europe) by Germany.

[16] Of course, research effort involves more than scientists and engineers. Including technical and clerical workers augments these figures by a factor of about 2.3 (based on OECD numbers from all these countries except the United States, for which they are not available).

[17] Summers and Heston's (1991) data on GDP per worker put the United States much further ahead and Japan in the rear.

[18] This tendency appears in van Ark's (1996) data on worker productivity as tabulated in Eaton and Kortum (1997a). It also appears in data on total factor productivity in manufacturing, as shown in Gordon (1996).

[19] Data are from WIPO (1990). We report applications rather than grants because they are much more comparable across countries. Patent applications in Japan by Japanese inventors have been scaled down by a factor of 4.9. The Japanese apply for over 300,000 patents domestically each year, nearly four times the domestic U.S. number. Using data on the number of claims of invention, Okada (1992) finds that Japanese patents granted to foreigners contain on average 4.9 times as many inventive claims as those granted to Japanese inventors. This extremely low level of claims per patent seems particular to Japanese domestic patents. Tong and Frame (1994) show that U.S. patents granted to U.S. inventors, Japanese inventors, and others all have a similar average number of claims per patent.

[20] Putnam (1997) finds that of inventions that are patented in at least one country, 72 percent are patented only there, while 18 percent are patented in three or more countries. Jaffe and Trajtenberg (1998) report that there is also a strong home bias in patent citations; i.e., inventors disproportionately cite other patents originating in the same country. Interestingly, this home bias tends to disappear (or even reverse) when the cited patent has been around for 20 years or more.

Scale, as reflected in GDP (also reported in Table 1), plays a more mixed role in the choice of foreign destinations for patenting.[21] The United States is usually the largest foreign destination for the others. Japan, however, is the least popular destination. Patent costs, reported in the last five rows of Table 1, provide some explanation. Japan is by far the most expensive destination for foreign inventors.[22]

## 3. THE MODEL

Our task now is to construct a model that captures the key features of these data and that will enable us to use them to measure the role of innovation and international technology diffusion in growth. Since we seek to capture the relationships, within and between countries, among technology, research, patenting, and productivity, our model is necessarily intricate. Hence we review its components before describing each in detail. Production of output, described in Section 3.1, combines a continuum of inputs of varying quality, which are themselves produced by labor and capital. An alternative activity for workers is doing research to come up with ideas for better inputs. Section 3.2 describes how ideas are produced and how they disseminate. A key variable describing a country at any moment is the stock of ideas that have reached it up to that point. Our assumptions about production and diffusion imply a relationship between this stock of knowledge and the distribution of input qualities (technologies) in the country. Section 3.3 derives this distribution and its dynamics. In Section 3.4 we show how productivity relates to the stock of ideas through the implied distribution of technologies.

We make assumptions about market structure, with implications for pricing and firm profit, which we discuss in Section 3.5. These assumptions also have implications, which we turn to in Section 3.6, about the value of having an innovation adopted in a country, depending on the imitation rate. We can thus infer the return to patenting in a country and relate the decision to patent an idea to the quality of the idea, the speed of diffusion, the cost of patenting, and market size. This we do in Section 3.7. Putting these things together, we then calculate, in Section 3.8, the expected value of an idea, incorporating the optimal patenting decision in each country.

The value of ideas determines the return to doing research, whereas labor productivity determines the opportunity cost of this activity. In Sections 3.9 and 3.10 we relate the two to solve for the equilibrium amount of research effort and the wage.

[21] These GDP figures are constructed to be consistent with the patent fees discussed below. They are GDP for 1992 in local currencies from the IMF (1994), translated into U.S. dollars at the 1992 fourth quarter exchange rates, also from the IMF (1994). The share of GDP spent on R&D, from OECD (1991), is subtracted.

[22] Patenting costs are based on country-specific filing fees, agents fees, and translation costs taken from Helfgott (1993). We scale up the cost of an application for a Japanese inventor in Japan by the factor of 4.9 so that the costs are compatible with the way that we count Japanese domestic patents. We ignore the more complicated fee structure applying to patents through the European Patent Office and complications introduced by patent renewal fees. Helfgott collected the cost of application data from a survey in 1992 and translated all the figures into U.S. dollars using the exchange rate in effect "near the end of 1992." Since we ignore patent renewal fees and the possible cost of disclosure of information in taking out a patent, our measure of the cost of patenting is a lower bound on the true costs.

Throughout, lengthy derivations are moved to the Appendix. The Appendix also contains a list of symbols.

3.1. *Production.* We consider a world consisting of $n = 1, \ldots, N$ countries. Output in country $n$ at time $t$ ($Y_{nt}$) is produced by combining intermediate inputs subject to a constant-returns-to-scale Cobb-Douglas production function:

$$\ln(Y_{nt}/J) = J^{-1} \int_0^J \ln[Z_{nt}(j)X_{nt}(j)]dj$$

where $X_{nt}(j)$ is the quantity of intermediate input $j$ produced at time $t$ in country $n$ and $Z_{nt}(j)$ is the quality of that input. The range of inputs is fixed over time and the same across countries.[23] Output is homogeneous and tradable across countries, whereas inputs are nontraded.

Each input $j$ is produced by a Cobb-Douglas combination of capital $K(j)$ and labor $L(j)$:

$$X(j) = K(j)^{\phi} L(j)^{1-\phi}$$

where $\phi \in [0, 1]$ is the capital elasticity. We treat this production relationship as the same across inputs, countries, and time. Productivity grows over time as research provides ideas for higher-quality inputs. Imperfect diffusion of these ideas leads to cross-country differences in productivity.

3.2. *Ideas.* An idea, our basic unit of research output, is the result of research effort. While all workers in each country are equally productive making intermediates, they differ in their talent for research. We assume that workers are compensated in proportion to their marginal productivity either as production or as research workers. Hence those who are the most productive at doing research will become researchers.

Consider country $i$ at time $t$ with $L_{it}$ workers. If a fraction $s_{it}$ of these workers are doing research, they create ideas at rate $\alpha_{it} s_{it}^{\beta} L_{it}$. The parameter $\alpha_{it}$ reflects the overall productivity of research effort in country $i$ at time $t$, whereas $\beta$ reflects the rate at which research productivity declines as less talented workers become researchers.[24] We consider alternative specifications of $\alpha_{it}$ in our analysis of the steady state of the model.

There are three dimensions to an idea: its quality, its use, and how long it takes to diffuse. For simplicity, we treat each dimension as independent of the other two.

[23] This production structure slightly generalizes that in Grossman and Helpman (1991b), in which our $J$ is equal to 1. A larger value of $J$ means that the market for a given intermediate is smaller.

[24] This specification arises, for example, if a worker's talent as a researcher is drawn from a Pareto distribution (see Phelps, 1966). Since large countries have more to draw from, this specification naturally introduces "scale effects." Given its research intensity $s$, a larger country invents more. Through the process of diffusion, small countries nevertheless can grow at the same rate as everyone else. In the absence of diffusion, size bias can be eliminated by assuming that inventive output depends only on research intensity. Dinopoulos and Thompson (1996) develop a model along these lines. We find the strong scale effects in patenting compelling evidence for our approach.

An idea's quality $Q$ is a random variable drawn from the cumulative distribution function $F(q)$. The quality of an idea is common to all countries to which it diffuses. We assume a Pareto distribution of qualities, $F(q) = 1 - q^{-\theta}$.[25]

An idea applies to only one out of the continuum of intermediates. The intermediate $j$ to which the idea applies is drawn from the uniform distribution on $[0, J]$.[26]

Ideas do not diffuse immediately. If an idea is discovered at time $t$ in country $i$, then it diffuses to country $n$ at time $t + \tau_{ni}$, for $n = 1, 2, \ldots, N$. We assume that the diffusion lag to country $n$, $\tau_{ni}$, has an exponential distribution with parameter $\epsilon_{ni}$, $\Pr[\tau_{ni} \leq x] = 1 - e^{-\epsilon_{ni} x}$. Thus $\epsilon_{ni}$ is the speed of diffusion from country $i$ to country $n$, and $\epsilon_{ni}^{-1}$ is the mean diffusion lag.[27]

We distinguish between the concepts of diffusion and adoption. An idea has *diffused* to a country when people there know about it and can in principle make use of it. It is *adopted*, however, only if it is actually used. Hence adoption implies diffusion, but not the opposite. While every idea eventually will diffuse to every other country (if the $\epsilon_{ni}$ values are strictly positive), many ideas will never be adopted because they are not as good as ideas already being used.

3.3. *The Technological Frontier.* In equilibrium, only the best available idea for each input in each country is actually used. For each country $n$, $Z_{nt}(j)$ represents the highest-quality idea yet adopted for input $j$ in country $n$ by time $t$, i.e., the state of the art. The state of the art across all inputs forms the technological frontier. Consider an idea of quality $q$ for input $j$ discovered somewhere at time $t$. If the idea diffuses to country $n$ with a lag of $\tau$, then it will be adopted if and only if $q > Z_{nt+\tau}(j)$.

To derive the dynamics of the technological frontier in a given country, we need to know the rate at which ideas were discovered in all countries over all history. Researchers in country $i$ produce a flow of new ideas $\alpha_{it} s_{it}^{\beta} L_{it}$. Let $\dot{\mu}_{nt}$ be the stochastic rate at which ideas diffuse to country $n$ (normalized by the measure of inputs $J$) from all the research that has been done throughout the world. (The corresponding stock is $\mu_{nt} = \int_{-\infty}^{t} \dot{\mu}_{ns} ds$.) An idea may be the result of domestic research or may arrive from

[25] Bental and Peled (1996) and Kortum (1997) also use the Pareto distribution to characterize the pool of undiscovered techniques from which researchers draw. The Pareto distribution has the convenient feature that if we truncate the distribution of $Q$ at some level $z$, then the random variable $Q/z$ ($\geq 1$) inherits the Pareto distribution. Thus, if a new idea is better than current best practice (say $z$), then the distribution of the inventive step ($Q/z$) does not depend on the level of the best practice that is surpassed.

[26] The continuum allows us to abstract from randomness in aggregate outcomes. To simplify further, we ignore the possibility that research could be aimed at improving the quality of a specific input.

[27] Although we can allow any correlations among the diffusion lags to different countries, we do assume that these lags are independent of the quality of the idea that is diffusing. While there is greater incentive to learn about a more important idea, learning about it is likely to prove more difficult. Since our data are unlikely to allow us to identify the direction and magnitude of any correlation between an idea's quality and the time it takes to diffuse, we take the simplest course and treat the two as independent. More disaggregated data might allow the identification of any correlation. In Eaton and Kortum (1996) we relate diffusion parameters to country characteristics, finding that diffusion from country $i$ to country $n$ is related negatively to the distance between the countries, positively to the level of human capital (schooling) in country $n$, and positively to imports of country $n$ from country $i$.

some other country. It may be the outcome of research performed recently or years before. Integrating over the appropriately weighted past research done in country $i$ and summing over source countries, the flow of ideas diffusing to country $n$ is

$$\dot{\mu}_{nt} = J^{-1} \sum_{i=1}^{N} \epsilon_{ni} \int_{-\infty}^{t} e^{-\epsilon_{ni}(t-s)} \alpha_{is} s_{is}^{\beta} L_{is} ds \tag{1}$$

To summarize the technological frontier, we employ the cumulative distribution function $H_n(z;t)$. It represents, for country $n$ at time $t$, the fraction of inputs whose state of the art is below $z$. In the Appendix, we show that

$$H_n(z;t) = e^{-\mu_{nt} z^{-\theta}} \tag{2}$$

Note that the technological frontier depends only on the total stock of ideas $\mu_{nt}$, regardless of when these ideas were adopted for production or where they came from. This feature of the distribution simplifies the analysis drastically.

3.4. *Productivity.* Output is maximized when factors are evenly divided among production of the individual inputs. In this case, total output is

$$A_{nt} K_{nt}^{\phi} [L_{nt}(1 - s_{nt})]^{1-\phi}$$

where total factor productivity, $A_{nt} = \exp\{\int_1^{\infty} \ln(z) dH_n(z;t)\}$, is the geometric mean of the technological frontier. We show in the Appendix that as $\mu_{nt}$ becomes large,

$$A_{nt} = e^{\psi/\theta} \mu_{nt}^{1/\theta} \tag{3}$$

where $\psi \approx 0.5772$ is Euler's constant. Thus productivity growth in a country is proportional to the growth in the stock of ideas that have diffused to that country.

The market structure that we assume does not, in fact, imply an even allocation of production workers among inputs, since the markup of price over cost differs across intermediates. Total factor productivity is proportional to $A_{nt}$, however, as can be seen from equation (11) below. We now discuss the market structure that gives rise to this result.

3.5. *Market Structure.* All producers of intermediates in a country face the same wage $w$ and cost of capital (interest rate plus depreciation) $r'$. Hence they incur the same unit cost of production $c = (r'/\phi)^{\phi}[w/(1-\phi)]^{1-\phi}$. They will not all set the same price, however.

The reason is that the owner of the state-of-the-art idea for an input in a country competes against the previous state of the art for that input, i.e., the state of the art prevailing at the time of invention. Competition is Bertrand, so the owner of the idea charges the highest price at which the previous state of the art is unprofitable.[28] If

[28] Grossman and Helpman (1991b) make similar assumptions. The production technology implies a unit elastic demand for an individual input given the prices of all other inputs. Hence, to maximize profit, the owner of the invention charges the highest price at which it remains the only seller of that input.

the previous state of the art was $z$, an owner of an idea of quality $q > z$ will charge $p = (q/z)c$. Since $q/z$ differs across inputs, so does the price.

At the time of invention, the inventor is the owner of the idea in any country to which it might diffuse. Ownership in any country might be stolen, in which case it passes to a local, monopolistic imitator.[29]

3.6. *The Value of an Idea.* Total purchases of the leading-edge version of intermediate $j$ with price $p(j)$ are $Y/[Jp(j)]$, where we use final output as numeraire. Given the pricing equilibrium, the profit to the owner of the right to use a technology of quality $q$ improving on an existing input of quality $z$ is $\pi = [1 - (z/q)]Y/J$ if $q > z$ and zero otherwise.

The owner can earn a profit only after his or her idea has been adopted and only before it has been surpassed by a more advanced technology. Consider, then, the expected profit in country $n$ at time $s$ from an idea of quality $q$ invented at time $t < s$ in country $i$. The probability of its having diffused there by then is $(1 - e^{-\epsilon_{ni}(s-t)})$. The probability of its not having become obsolete by then is $e^{-(\mu_{ns}-\mu_{nt})q^{-\theta}}$. Finally, we assume that ideas face a hazard $\iota$ of imitation, so the probability of its not having been copied by time $s$ is $e^{-\iota(s-t)}$. The expected discounted value of the right to use an idea from country $i$ of quality $q$ in country $n$, given that the previous state of the art for the relevant input in country $n$ was $z$, is therefore

$$V_{nit}(z, q) = \int_0^\infty \pi_{nt+s}(z, q)e^{-(r+\iota)s}(1 - e^{-\epsilon_{ni}s})e^{-(\mu_{nt+s}-\mu_{nt})q^{-\theta}}ds \tag{4}$$

if $q \geq z$. Otherwise, the value is zero.

We assume that at the time of invention the researcher knows the quality of his or her idea but not the quality of the competing input in any country. The expected value of an idea of quality $q$ from country $i$ in country $n$,

$$V_{nit}(q) = \int_1^q V_{nit}(z, q)dh_n(z; t) \tag{5}$$

is consequently the basis for the patenting decision.

3.7. *The Decision to Patent.* Our modeling of patenting is guided by findings, from surveys of researchers and analyses of patent renewal data, that imitation rates are extremely high and that patenting reduces, but only modestly, the hazard of imitation.[30] Patents need not provide perfect protection from imitation, nor is imitation necessarily immediate if the inventor fails to patent. While we assume that

[29] We assume that imitation does not lead to a lower price. The more natural and appealing assumption, that competition between imitator and inventor drives the markup to zero, substantially complicates the analysis. To keep the analysis as simple as possible, we also assume that the owner of the right to use an idea (whether inventor or imitator) competes with the state of the art at the time of invention. The owner is thus protected from any inferior invention that surpasses the initial state of the art.

[30] For survey evidence, see Mansfield and Romeo (1980), Mansfield et al. (1981), and Levin et al. (1987). Schankerman and Pakes (1986) find that while the total value of patent rights is substantial, it is small relative to total R&D investment. Hence researchers must be appropriating a substantial return to their inventive activity through other means than patents.

patenting does not affect the speed of diffusion, more rapid diffusion increases the incentive to patent because the rewards will be achieved sooner.

Hence we relate the hazard of imitation to whether the inventor has a patent in that country. We denote the hazard of imitation if the idea was patented as $\iota^{pat}$ and if it was not patented as $\iota^{not}$.[31] For a patent to have any value requires, of course, that $\iota^{pat} < \iota^{not}$. If patents provide perfect protection, then $\iota^{pat} = 0$. However, if trade secrets are impossible to keep, then $\iota^{not} = \infty$.

We can distinguish between the expected value of a patented idea $V_{nit}^{pat}(q)$ and an unpatented idea $V_{nit}^{not}(q)$ by evaluating (4) and (5) at imitation rates $\iota^{pat}$ and $\iota^{not}$, respectively. A patent is therefore worth $V_{nit}^{pat}(q) - V_{nit}^{not}(q)$. Although the inventor does not know how long it will take his or her idea to diffuse, all patenting decisions must be made up front.[32]

Denoting by $f_{nit}$ the total fees and other costs to an inventor in country $i$ of patenting in country $n$, the inventor will seek patent protection in that country if $V_{nit}^{pat}(q) - V_{nit}^{not}(q)$ exceeds $f_{nit}$ and not otherwise. The return to patenting rises with the quality of the idea $q$. Hence the condition

$$V_{nit}^{pat}(q) - V_{nit}^{not}(q) = f_{nit} \tag{6}$$

determines a threshold quality level $\bar{q}_{nit}$ such that ideas of higher quality are patented, while those of lower quality are not.[33] We assume that if an idea is potentially useful in a country, then a patent is granted automatically to the inventor seeking protection.

Since researchers in country $i$ produce ideas at rate $\alpha_{it} s_{it}^{\beta} L_{it}$, the rate at which they patent in country $n$, $P_{nit}$, is

$$P_{nit} = \alpha_{it} s_{it}^{\beta} L_{it} (\bar{q}_{nit})^{-\theta} \tag{7}$$

3.8. *The Return to R&D.* The value of an idea of quality $q$ from country $i$ in country $n$ is the maximum of $V_{nit}^{pat}(q) - f_{nit}$ and $V_{nit}^{not}(q)$. The expected value of an idea in that country before its quality is known is therefore the expectation of this amount across all possible values of $q$, which is

$$V_{nit} = \int_{1}^{\bar{q}_{nit}} V_{nit}^{not}(q) dF(q) + \int_{\bar{q}_{nit}}^{\infty} V_{nit}^{pat}(q) dF(q) - f_{nit}(\bar{q}_{nit})^{-\theta} \tag{8}$$

where $F(q)$ is the Pareto distribution. The expected return to an idea of unknown quality in country $i$ at time $t$ is therefore the sum of its expected returns across

[31] We treat the imitation lag, like the diffusion lag, as independent of the quality of the idea in question. While there is greater incentive to try to imitate a bigger idea, imitating it is probably harder, and the inventor has more reason to prevent imitation. Again, our data are unlikely to allow us to identify any correlation between the importance of an idea and its hazard of imitation. Hence, in the absence of any presumption one way or the other, we treat the two as independent.

[32] Specifically, we do not allow the inventor to wait until the idea is adopted in a country to apply for a patent there. This assumption reflects the requirement of most patent systems that patents be taken out in additional countries within 1 year of the first, or priority, application. We assume that inventors do not delay seeking a priority application.

[33] A possibility, of course, is that the cost of patenting would exceed the benefit for any idea regardless of its quality, in which case patenting would be zero and $\bar{q}_{nit}$ infinite. At the other extreme, if $f_{nit} = 0$, then $\bar{q}_{nit} = 1$, so any idea would be patented.

countries, or

$$V_{it} = \sum_{n=1}^{N} V_{nit} \tag{9}$$

This amount is the expected value of an idea.

3.9. *Equilibrium R&D.* The marginal researcher in country $i$ is indifferent between doing research and making intermediates. Equilibrium in the labor market thus implies that the fraction $s_{it}$ of workers doing research in country $i$ will solve

$$\alpha_{it}\beta V_{it}s_{it}^{\beta-1} = w_{it} \tag{10}$$

where $w_{it}$ is what a researcher would earn making intermediates.

3.10. *Technology, Wages, and Income.* Bertrand competition in intermediates implies that the markup over unit cost, $M(j) \equiv p(j)/c$, is low where the currently adopted input is only marginally better than the input it replaced, while $M(j)$ is large where the current input is a substantial improvement over its predecessor. Since expenditure on each input is the same, more factors are allocated to the production of inputs with low markups. Consequently, productivity is lower than it would be if production workers were equally allocated among inputs. As we show in the Appendix, the markup has a time-invariant distribution depending only on the parameter $\theta$.

Even though producers of different inputs in a country set different markups over unit cost, since they face the same wage and interest rate, they employ the same capital-labor ratio $k$. Taking into account the distribution of the markup, aggregate output in country $i$ at time $t$ is

$$Y_{it} = \frac{\kappa_1(\theta)}{\kappa_2(\theta)}A_{it}K_{it}^{\phi}[L_{it}(1-s_{it})]^{1-\phi} = \frac{\kappa_1(\theta)}{\kappa_2(\theta)}A_{it}k_{it}^{\phi}L_{it}(1-s_{it}) \tag{11}$$

where $k_{it} \equiv K_{it}/[L_{it}(1-s_{it})]$ is the ratio of capital to production workers, and the constants $\kappa_1(\theta)$ and $\kappa_2(\theta)$ are derived in the Appendix. The wage is

$$w_{it} = (1-\phi)\kappa_1(\theta)A_{it}k_{it}^{\phi} \tag{12}$$

Since our Cobb-Douglas assumption implies that

$$k_{it} = \frac{\phi}{1-\phi}\frac{w_{it}}{r'}$$

we obtain

$$Y_{it} = \frac{1}{\kappa_2(\theta)}[\kappa_1(\theta)A_{it}(\phi/r')^{\phi}]^{1/(1-\phi)}L_{it}(1-s_{it}) \tag{13}$$

and

$$w_{it} = (1-\phi)[\kappa_1(\theta)A_{it}(\phi/r')^{\phi}]^{1/(1-\phi)} \tag{14}$$

We have now fully specified our model. Given the paths of the workforces $L_{it}$, patenting costs $f_{nit}$, and research productivities $\alpha_{it}$, the state of the world economy at any moment $t$ can be described in terms of the $N$ technology state variables $\mu_{nt}$. Three equations describe the dynamic equilibrium. At each moment individuals decide where to work according to (10) and what ideas to patent according to (6). The labor allocation decisions in turn govern the evolution of the technology state variables according to (1). The economy is in equilibrium when patenting and labor allocation decisions are individually optimal at any moment, given the paths of technology that these decisions will generate. We now turn to the steady state of this three-equation system.

## 4. THE STEADY STATE

The economy is in steady state when the state variables $\mu_{nt}$ grow at a constant common rate that we denote $g$. In order to obtain a steady-state outcome, we make the following assumptions:

1. Workforces in each country grow at a constant rate $g_L \geq 0$.
2. The relative productivity of researchers in a country is proportional to the relative level of technology there. Research productivity in any country also depends on the world stock of ideas. Specifically, we assume that

$$\alpha_{it} = \alpha\left(\frac{\mu_{it}}{\overline{\mu}_t}\right)\overline{\mu}_t^{\gamma}$$

   where $\alpha$ is a constant term, $\overline{\mu}_t = \sum_{i=1}^{N} \mu_{it}$, and $\gamma \leq 1$. To ensure a steady state with growth, we restrict $\gamma = 1$ for $g_L = 0$ and $\gamma < 1$ for $g_L > 0$.
3. Patenting costs are a constant proportion of output, i.e., $f_{nit} = f_{ni} Y_{nt}$.[34]
4. The interest rate $r$ and cost of capital $r'$ are constant across countries and over time.[35]

Features of a steady state are:

1. A constant fraction $s_i$ of workers in each country works as researchers.
2. Patenting is constant.
3. Total factor productivity grows at rate $g/\theta$, the wage grows at rate $g/[\theta(1-\phi)]$, and total output grows at rate $g_Y = g/[\theta(1-\phi)] + g_L$ in all countries.

[34] If patenting costs did not grow with market size, eventually all new ideas, no matter how bad, would be patented. Since we observe a rate of domestic patenting that is not growing over time (with the exception of Japan and a recent jump in the United States), we find it reasonable to assume that patenting costs have not been falling relative to market size.

[35] For most of the analysis we treat $r$ as a parameter even though in general equilibrium the interest rate is determined by intertemporal preferences as they interact with the growth rate. In the standard case of isoelastic marginal utility, in steady state $r = \rho + \sigma g_Y$, where $\rho$ is the discount factor and $\sigma$ the elasticity of marginal utility, with these parameters assumed common across countries. For purposes of estimation (and simulation if $g_Y$ is unaffected), $r$ summarizes all we need to know about the parameteres $\rho$ and $\sigma$.

4. Conditional on an idea eventually being adopted, the mean lag between invention in country $i$ and adoption in $n$ is $1/(\epsilon_{ni} + g)$.[36]
5. Of the ideas generated by country $i$ that would have been useful to $n$ had they diffused immediately after invention in $i$, country $n$ eventually adopts a fraction $\epsilon_{ni}/(\epsilon_{ni} + g)$.[37]

If $g_L = 0$ and $\gamma = 1$, our model exhibits (fully) endogenous growth as in the R&D-based growth models of Romer (1990) and Grossman and Helpman (1991a, 1991b). In these models, the existing stock of knowledge raises research productivity to the extent that constant research effort can generate perpetual growth of knowledge. If $\gamma < 1$, then, as the stock of knowledge increases, innovations become harder to find. Perpetual growth of knowledge requires ever increasing research effort. In steady state population growth thus dictates the rate of productivity growth, as in the single-country semiendogenous growth model of Jones (1995).[38]

We begin by describing the steady-state dynamics of the model given how much research is done. We then turn to steady-state patenting. We finish by solving for how much research will be done.

4.1. *Steady-State Relative Productivities and Growth.* Given a constant research intensity $s_i$ in each country, (1) implies that the stock of ideas in each country $n$ grows at a common rate $g$. These equations can be written in terms of time-invariant variables as

$$g = \frac{\dot{\mu}_n}{\mu_n} = \frac{\alpha}{J} \sum_{i=1}^{N} \frac{\epsilon_{ni}}{\epsilon_{ni} + g} \frac{\mu_i}{\mu_n} s_i^{\beta} \widetilde{L}_i \qquad n = 1, \ldots, N \tag{15}$$

where $\widetilde{L}_i \equiv L_{it}\overline{\mu}_t^{\gamma-1}$ is country $i$'s workforce, scaled by the drag on research productivity imposed by a rising stock of world knowledge in the case of semiendogenous growth ($\gamma < 1$). The $\widetilde{L}_i$ values are constant in either the fully or semiendogenous growth case. With fully endogenous growth, $\gamma = 1$ and $L_i$ is constant, whereas with semiendogenous growth, $g = g_L/(1 - \gamma)$.

Equation (15) decomposes growth in any country into the contribution made by each country, including itself. We can further break down the contribution of any single country into the product of three parts: (1) the generation of ideas in source

[36] This lag differs from the mean diffusion lag $1/\epsilon_{ni}$ because, with growth, ideas that diffuse rapidly are more likely to be adopted, since they are less likely to be obsolete when they arrive.

[37] A larger growth rate relative to the diffusion rate implies that more ideas that might have been useful at the time of invention are obsolete when they finally arrive.

[38] How does the number of existing ideas affect researchers' productivity in developing new ones? On one hand, a larger existing stock of ideas may provide researchers more stimulus for thinking up new ones. On the other, it could mean greater depletion of the stock of possible ideas so that coming up with new ones is harder. In an international context, an additional issue is identifying the relevant country-specific stocks of ideas that researchers have to build on and to compete against. Our specification here implies that for a given world stock of ideas, a country's own stock enhances the productivity of its researchers in proportion. For $\gamma < 1$, however, a larger world pool makes coming up with original ideas harder. While there are other plausible specifications of the effect of knowledge stocks on research productivity, the one we adopt here allows us to nest conveniently the two major approaches appearing in the single-economy literature on R&D and growth.

country $i$, $\alpha\mu_{it}s_i^{\beta}\widetilde{L}_i$, (2) the fraction of those ideas which are potentially useful in country $n$ at the time of invention, $\mu_{nt}^{-1}$ [as shown in (22) of the Appendix], and (3) the fraction of those potentially useful ideas which are eventually adopted, $\epsilon_{ni}/(\epsilon_{ni}+g)$. This last magnitude captures the extent to which research findings are shared between countries and serves as our central measure of diffusion links.

We describe in the Appendix how we solve this system of equations. The solution gives, as a function of the steady-state research intensities $s_i$ across countries, $N-1$ relative levels of total factor productivity:

$$\frac{A_{nt}}{A_{Nt}} = \left(\frac{\mu_{nt}}{\mu_{Nt}}\right)^{1/\theta} \qquad n = 1, \ldots, N-1 \tag{16}$$

In the case of fully endogenous growth, the solution also gives the world rate of total factor productivity growth $\dot{A}/A = g/\theta$. In the case of semiendogenous growth, $\dot{A}/A = g_L/[(1-\gamma)\theta]$ and the solution gives the steady-state level of $\overline{\mu}_t$ relative to any $L_{it}$, which has implications for the world *levels* of productivity rather their rate of growth.

4.2. *Steady-State Patenting.* Of the ideas diffusing to country $n$ from country $i$, equation (6) determines the quality threshold for patenting $\bar{q}_{nit}$. A fraction $\mu_{nt}^{-1}$ is adopted. In steady state, the ratio of patented ideas to adopted ideas is a constant given by[39]

$$\bar{b}_{ni} = \mu_{nt}(\bar{q}_{nit})^{-\theta} \tag{17}$$

Substituting this expression into equation (7), patenting by inventors from country $i$ in country $n$ is

$$P_{ni} = \alpha s_i^{\beta}\widetilde{L}_i\frac{\mu_i}{\mu_n}\bar{b}_{ni} \tag{18}$$

4.3. *Steady-State Labor Market Equilibrium.* Substituting (13) and (14), the condition for steady-state labor market equilibrium in each country, from (10), becomes

$$\alpha\beta s_i^{\beta-1}\sum_{n=1}^{N} v_{ni}\widetilde{L}_n(1-s_n)\left(\frac{\mu_n}{\mu_i}\right)^{\frac{1-\theta+\phi\theta}{\theta(1-\phi)}} = (1-\phi)\kappa_2(\theta) \tag{19}$$

where $v_{ni} \equiv \mu_{nt}V_{nit}/Y_{nt}$ is constant in steady state, as shown by (25) in the Appendix.[40]

To summarize, the $N(N+2)$ equations (15), (17), and (19) determine $N-1$ relative technology levels $\mu$, $N^2$ patenting thresholds $\bar{b}$, and $N$ levels of R&D intensity $s$, and $g$ (with growth fully endogenous) or the level of $\overline{\mu}_t^{\gamma-1}$ relative to each $L_{it}$ (with growth semiendogenous).

[39] Equation 24 in the Appendix allows us to solve directly for each of the constants $\bar{b}_{ni}$ as a function of the parameters of the model.

[40] Since $v_{ni}$ is independent of technology levels, an implication of (19) is that the (partial) elasticity of R&D with respect to the relative level of technology has the sign of $\theta(1-\phi)-1$ (holding research effort elsewhere constant). Researchers in countries with more advanced technologies, as measured by $\mu$, are proportionately more productive as researchers, but their opportunity cost of doing research is also greater in proportion to $\mu^{1/[\theta(1-\phi)]}$. The net effect is more research in advanced countries if $\theta(1-\phi)$ exceeds 1 and less otherwise.

## 5. FITTING THE MODEL

To bring the model to data, we rewrite it as

$$Y = G(\Theta^*, X) \tag{20}$$

where $Y$ is a vector of endogenous variables (productivity growth, relative productivity, research, and patents), $X$ is a vector of exogenous variables (workforces and patenting costs relative to GDP), and $\Theta^*$ is a vector of parameters. The function $G(\cdot)$ represents the simultaneous solution of (15), (17), and (19), as well as the productivity and patenting equations, (16) and (18), respectively.

5.1. *Parameter Restrictions.* In full generality, the parameters of the model, $\theta, \beta, J, \alpha, \iota_{ni}^{pat}, \iota_{ni}^{not}, \epsilon_{ni}, r, g_L, \gamma, \phi$, are too numerous to identify with our equations. To give the model empirical content, we tie things down as follows:

*Imitation rates.* We assume that all patent systems are the same.[41] We allow for the possibility, however, that they treat nationals differently from foreigners. Hence we define $\iota_D^{pat}$ as the imitation rate when an idea is patented domestically and $\iota_F^{pat}$ as the imitation rate when an idea is patented abroad. The corresponding hazards for unpatented ideas are $\iota_D^{not}$ and $\iota_F^{not}$. We set three of these four rates on the basis of survey evidence. The rate at which foreigners imitate nonpatented ideas is set to $\iota_F^{not} = 0.25$ based on Mansfield and Romeo (1980).[42] The imitation rates of domestic patented and unpatented ideas are set to $\iota_D^{pat} = 0.23$ and $\iota_D^{not} = 0.415$, respectively, based on Mansfield, Schwartz, and Wagner (1981).[43]

*Diffusion rates.* We restrict the rate of diffusion from country $i$ to country $n$ to be the product of a parameter governing the speed at which county $n$ adopts new

[41] Rapp and Rozek (1990) classify countries into five categories according to the strength of protection provided by their intellectual property regime. Of our countries, all but Japan are in the highest category (Japan is in the next-to-highest category).

[42] Following the transfer of technology from a U.S. parent company to a foreign subsidiary, Mansfield and Romeo report that it took 4 years, on average, for a non-U.S. competitor to obtain the technology. This average delay implies an imitation rate of 0.25 if the imitation lag is exponentially distributed. Mansfield and Romeo continue: "In fact, the observed distribution is not very different from such an exponential distribution, but the sample is too small to carry out a goodness-of-fit test" (fn. 8, p. 740). We apply this imitation rate to nonpatented ideas, but we could just as well have applied it to patented ideas, since our estimates below imply that patenting ideas abroad has only a small effect on the imitation rate.

[43] "Within 4 years of their introduction, 60 percent of the patented successful innovations in our sample were imitated" (p. 913). Assuming an exponential distribution, these figures imply an imitation rate for domestic patented ideas of 0.23. One interpretation of our model is that there are two types of imitators working independently, one type imitating only unpatented domestic ideas and the other imitating any domestic idea. This specification implies that patenting an idea domestically will do no good with probability $\iota_D^{pat}/\iota_D^{not}$. With probability $[(\iota_D^{not} - \iota_D^{pat})/\iota_D^{not}]e^{-\iota_D^{pat}x}$ patenting an idea will increase the time until imitation by at least $x$ years. Mansfield, Schwartz, and Wagner go on to report that "although patent protection seems to have only a limited effect on entry in about half of the cases, it seems to have a very important effect in a minority of them. For about 15 percent of the innovations, patent protection was estimated to have delayed the time when the first imitator entered the market by 4 years or more." Given $\iota_D^{pat} = 0.23$, the first fact suggests $\iota_D^{not} = 0.46$, while the second suggests $\iota_D^{not} = 0.37$. We average these values and set $\iota_D^{not} = 0.415$.

ideas, a parameter governing the speed at which ideas from country $i$ are ready for adoption, and a parameter governing the percentage increase in adoption speed for domestic ideas. Formally, $\epsilon_{ni} = \epsilon_{n.}\epsilon_{.i}\epsilon_D$, where we normalize $\epsilon_{N.} = 0.1$ and $\epsilon_D = 1$ if $n \neq i$. Thus we require 10 parameters to account for the 25 diffusion rates between and within our 5 countries. Evidence reported by Pakes and Schankerman (1984) suggests that of U.S. inventions that are eventually adopted in the United States, the mean lag to adoption is 1.2 to 2.5 years. Taking the upper end of this range, we restrict $1/(\epsilon_{USUS} + g) = 2.5$. We use this restriction to determine $\epsilon_D$ in terms of the other parameters. The effect of this restriction is to anchor the absolute levels of diffusion to outside evidence.

*Other parameter restrictions.* We set the interest rate to $r = 0.07$, the long-run real return on the U.S. stock market. We fix the capital elasticity $\phi = 0.3$ based on evidence reported in Lysko (1995). We choose $\alpha$ so that, given all the other parameters, the model predicts $g_A = 0.018$, the mean of total factor productivity growth in the U.S., German, and French manufacturing sectors averaged over 1979–1990, from Lysko (1995). For our baseline, we assume the value $g_L = 0$ and $\gamma = 1$ to obtain fully endogenous growth. To explore the semiendogenous growth case, we set $\gamma$ to solve $g_A = 0.018 = g_L/[(1-\gamma)\theta]$ and $g_L = 0.02$, representing a compromise between population growth and growth of research employment.

5.2. *Estimation.* To get at the parameters that have not been measured before, we turn to our data on relative productivity, research, and patenting for our set of five countries. We assume that by the late 1980s their situation can be described by the steady state of our model.

Incorporating our restrictions, and introducing multiplicative measurement error, we rewrite (20) in logarithms as

$$y = g(\Theta, X) + u \tag{21}$$

where $\Theta = (\theta, \beta, J, \iota_F^{pat}, \epsilon_{.1}, \ldots, \epsilon_{.5}, \epsilon_{1.}, \ldots, \epsilon_{4.})'$ and

$$y \equiv \Big[\ln(A_1/A_5), \ldots, \ln(A_4/A_5), \ln R_1, \ldots, \ln R_5, \ln(P_{11}+1), \ldots, \ln(P_{ni}+1), \ldots, \ln(P_{55}+1)\Big]'$$

(which no longer includes productivity growth, since we choose $\alpha$ to match it exactly).[44] The productivity ratios are relative value added per hour in manufacturing, as shown in Table 1, converted to a measure of relative total factor productivity assuming a common interest rate across countries and a capital share of 0.3.[45]

One final adjustment takes into account the employment of clerical and technical workers in research. We assume that employing one research scientist or

[44] Note that in order to allow the model to predict zero patenting, we compare the model's prediction for the number of patents plus one with the actual number of patents plus one. The large amount of patenting that we observe among our five countries makes it reasonable to ignore, for estimation purposes, the count nature of the patent data.

[45] Hence, if $X_i/X_N$ is value added per hour in country $i$ relative to country $N$, then $A_i/A_N = (X_i/X_N)^{0.7}$ is total factor productivity in country $i$ relative to country $N$.

engineer requires the additional employment of 1.3 staff, earning the production wage.[46]

Our estimate $\hat{\Theta}$ of the parameter vector minimizes

$$[y - g(\hat{\Theta}, X)]'\Omega^{-1}[y - g(\hat{\Theta}, X)]$$

where the matrix $\Omega$ reflects our weighting of productivity, research, and patents in the objective function.[47] This procedure would constitute standard nonlinear least squares if the function $g$ had an analytic solution.[48]

## 6. RESULTS

Table 2 reports our parameter estimates for the baseline case, with the first column reporting the case of fully endogenous growth ($g_L = 0$) and the second that of semiendogenous growth ($g_L = 0.02$).[49] First note the remarkable similarity of the parameter estimates in the two cases.

Table 3 reports how well we fit the data for the fully endogenous growth case.[50] The fit with semiendogenous growth (not shown) is nearly identical.

[46] This is the average ratio of R&D clerical and technical workers to R&D scientists and engineers across the countries of our sample for which data were available (all but the United States) (OECD, 1991). Equation 19 becomes

$$\alpha\beta s_i^{\beta-1}\sum_{n=1}^{N} v_{ni}\widetilde{L}_n(1-2.3s_n)\left(\frac{\mu_n}{\mu_i}\right)^{\frac{1-\theta+\phi\theta}{\theta(1-\phi)}} = 2.3(1-\phi)\kappa_2(\theta)$$

[47] Denoting our weights on productivity and patents, relative to research, as $\omega_A$ and $\omega_P$, respectively,

$$\Omega = \begin{bmatrix} \Omega_A & 0 & 0 \\ 0 & I_5 & 0 \\ 0 & 0 & (1/\omega_P)I_{25} \end{bmatrix}$$

where $\Omega_A = (1/\omega_A)[I_4 - \iota_4\iota_4']$, $I_N$ is an $N \times N$ identity matrix, and $\iota_N$ is an $N$-vector of ones. This specification assumes that measurement error is independent across research, patents, and *levels* of productivity. The last induces correlations in relative levels accounted for in $\Omega_A$. The weights reflect the importance that we attach to fitting the different types of data. Given the small number of observations on relative productivity and researchers, we do not attempt to base this weighting on the estimated variances. In our baseline we set $\omega_P = 1/5$ and $\omega_A = 30$, reflecting our desire to take the productivity data more seriously than the patent data. We also examine the implications of alternative weights on productivity.

[48] We have written a GAUSS program to calculate the function $g$. It begins with a parameter vector and data for all the exogenous variables. Next, it finds the set of $b_{ni}$ that solves (17). Then it iterates between (15) and (19) until it finds technology levels and research employments that are consistent with each other. Finally, (3) and (18) are used to infer productivity and patenting. The entire process takes about 1 to 5 minutes (depending on the parameter values) on a Pentium-120 PC. We nest this calculation in a standard minimization routine to find $\hat{\Theta}$.

[49] Table 2 also reports standard errors, although these have limited meaning. They are correct in the very special case in which $\Omega$ reflects the variance matrix of the measurement error (up to a scalar multiple). We use the delta method to calculate standard errors of transformations of the estimated parameters appearing in subsequent tables.

[50] Since we placed so much weight on fitting productivity relative to the other endogenous variables, we explain it nearly perfectly, with a root mean square error (RMSE) of 0.01. The RMSE for research is 0.10, while for patenting it is 0.36. (RMSE is calculated from the differences of the logarithms of the actual and predicted values from Table 3.)

TABLE 2
PARAMETER VALUES

| Definition | Symbol | Parameter Value: Endogenous | Parameter Value: Semiendogenous |
|---|---|---|---|
| Population growth | $g_L$ | 0.00 | 0.02 |
| Parameter of research spillover | $\gamma$ | 1 | 0.40 |
| Parameter of search distribution | $\theta$ | 1.87 (1.06) | 1.85 (1.05) |
| Parameter of talent distribution | $\beta$ | 0.18 (0.02) | 0.16 (0.02) |
| Number of inputs (millions) | $J$ | 1.11 (0.62) | 1.12 (0.62) |
| Imitation rates | | | |
| If not patented at home | $\iota_D^{not}$ | 0.415 | 0.415 |
| If not patented abroad | $\iota_F^{not}$ | 0.250 | 0.250 |
| If patented at home | $\iota_D^{pat}$ | 0.230 | 0.230 |
| If patented abroad | $\iota_F^{pat}$ | 0.244 (0.002) | 0.245 (0.002) |
| Diffusion factor from | | | |
| Germany | $\epsilon_{.1}$ | 0.93 (0.67) | 0.93 (0.67) |
| France | $\epsilon_{.2}$ | 0.28 (0.23) | 0.28 (0.22) |
| U.K. | $\epsilon_{.3}$ | 0.58 (0.56) | 0.56 (0.54) |
| Japan | $\epsilon_{.4}$ | 1.17 (1.10) | 1.20 (1.14) |
| U.S. | $\epsilon_{.5}$ | 0.21 (0.20) | 0.21 (0.20) |
| Diffusion factor to | | | |
| Germany | $\epsilon_{1.}$ | 0.19 (0.13) | 0.20 (0.13) |
| France | $\epsilon_{2.}$ | 0.22 (0.14) | 0.22 (0.14) |
| U.K. | $\epsilon_{3.}$ | 0.07 (0.05) | 0.07 (0.05) |
| Japan | $\epsilon_{4.}$ | 0.11 (0.08) | 0.12 (0.08) |
| U.S. | $\epsilon_{5.}$ | 0.10 | 0.10 |
| Diffusion factor domestic | $\epsilon_D$ | 17.7 | 17.8 |

NOTE: Numbers in parentheses are approximate standard errors. Parameters without standard errors have been calibrated based on outside sources of information (described in the text). We parameterize the diffusion rate to destination $n$ from source $i$ as $\epsilon_{ni} = \epsilon_{n.}\epsilon_{.i}\epsilon_D$, where $\epsilon_D$ takes on the value 1 if $n \neq i$ and the value in the last row of the table if $n = i$. The value of $\epsilon_{5.} = 0.1$ is simply a normalization.

TABLE 3
MODEL FIT

| | Germany | | France | | U.K. | | Japan | | U.S. | |
|---|---|---|---|---|---|---|---|---|---|---|
| Researchers (thousands) | 97 | (110) | 41 | (40) | 74 | (68) | 289 | (329) | 477 | (425) |
| Productivity (relative to U.S.) | 0.90 | (0.91) | 0.94 | (0.94) | 0.75 | (0.75) | 0.84 | (0.85) | 1 | |
| Patents (thousands) for protection in | | | | | By inventors from | | | | | |
| Germany | 43 | (27) | 5 | (6) | 5 | (6) | 15 | (15) | 19 | (36) |
| France | 13 | (10) | 15 | (19) | 4 | (6) | 11 | (13) | 18 | (32) |
| U.K. | 13 | (9) | 5 | (4) | 24 | (20) | 13 | (9) | 20 | (17) |
| Japan | 7 | (8) | 3 | (4) | 3 | (4) | 65 | (45) | 18 | (20) |
| U.S. | 13 | (8) | 5 | (4) | 6 | (6) | 33 | (16) | 83 | (119) |

NOTE: Actual values with predicted values in parentheses. Here and in subsequent tables productivity measures reflect total factor productivity assuming a constant capital-output ratio and a capital share of 0.3.

Since the two cases are so similar, we pursue for now only the fully endogenous growth case. We resurrect semiendogenous growth when we turn to counterfactual experiments.

Our estimate of the research elasticity $\beta$ is precise at a level significantly below the value of one assumed in much theoretical work. We think that this estimate reflects the small but rather even fraction of the workforce engaged in research across our countries. A value closer to 1 implies more international specialization. To explain the near-diagonal dominance of the patenting matrix, our estimates imply that foreign patents provide rather limited protection, reducing the hazard of imitation by about half a percentage point.

Turning to diffusion, we find that ideas from Japan and Germany diffuse most rapidly, while France and Germany are the quickest to exploit ideas. Ideas diffuse much faster within than between countries.

6.1. *Diffusion Lags and Adoption.* The diffusion parameters are not precisely estimated and, on their own, are hard to interpret. Three more meaningful and digestible concepts are (1) the mean lag between the invention of an idea in country $i$ and its arrival in country $n$, regardless of whether or not it is adopted when it arrives $(1/\epsilon_{ni})$, (2) the mean lag between invention and arrival conditional on adoption $[1/(\epsilon_{ni} + g)]$, and (3) the fraction of ideas that are ever adopted of those which were potentially useful when they were invented $[\epsilon_{ni}/(\epsilon_{ni} + g)]$.[51] The second concept corresponds to the adoption lags measured in microeconomic studies (which consider only ideas that are actually adopted). The third concept reflects how much of the research output of one country makes it to another, as one can see in (15). The simple and conditional diffusion lags are estimated about as precisely as the diffusion parameters themselves. However, our central measures of diffusion, the fractions of potentially useful ideas that are adopted, are estimated much more precisely.

As for the unconditional lag, its mean is just over 1 year for domestic ideas and about 21 years for ideas from abroad. The second figure hides considerable variation across individual country pairs. Looking at ideas that eventually will be adopted, the figure for domestic ideas remains about 1 year, while for foreign inventions it decreases to about 11 years. This last figure falls in between the survey results of Mansfield and Romeo (1980) on the mean lags between U.S. adoption and adoption abroad by U.S. subsidiaries (5.8 years for developed countries) and nonsubsidiaries (13.1 years for all countries).[52]

Table 4 presents concept (3), our estimates of ideas that are ever adopted as a fraction of those which would have been adopted if they had diffused instantaneously, along with standard errors (in parentheses). The matrix is highly diagonal-dominant. Over 95 percent of potentially useful domestic ideas are adopted eventually, in contrast with an average of about 60 percent for foreign ideas.

[51] Recall that $g = \theta g_A$, where we set $g_A$ to match average growth in total factor productivity of 0.018 and $\theta$ is estimated.

[52] Jovanovic and Lach (1997) also find evidence of slow international diffusion.

TABLE 4
ADOPTION PERCENTAGES

| Fraction of Potentially Useful Ideas that Are Ever Adopted in | Originating from Research Performed in | | | | |
|---|---|---|---|---|---|
| | Germany | France | U.K. | Japan | U.S. |
| Germany | 0.99 (0.01) | 0.62 (0.14) | 0.77 (0.07) | 0.67 (0.07) | 0.54 (0.16) |
| France | 0.86 (0.07) | 0.97 (0.03) | 0.79 (0.07) | 0.88 (0.06) | 0.57 (0.15) |
| U.K. | 0.65 (0.18) | 0.37 (0.18) | 0.95 (0.05) | 0.70 (0.14) | 0.30 (0.17) |
| Japan | 0.76 (0.13) | 0.49 (0.17) | 0.66 (0.10) | 0.99 (0.02) | 0.41 (0.17) |
| U.S. | 0.73 (0.14) | 0.46 (0.19) | 0.63 (0.17) | 0.78 (0.14) | 0.92 (0.05) |

NOTE: The element in row $n$ and column $i$ is $\epsilon_{ni}/(\epsilon_{ni} + g)$, which in steady state has the interpretation given in the table. Numbers in parentheses are approximate standard errors.

TABLE 5
GROWTH DECOMPOSITION

| Fraction of Productivity Growth in | Due to Research Performed in | | | | |
|---|---|---|---|---|---|
| | Germany | France | U.K. | Japan | U.S. |
| Germany | 0.16 (0.02) | 0.08 (0.01) | 0.07 (0.01) | 0.27 (0.02) | 0.42 (0.04) |
| France | 0.13 (0.01) | 0.11 (0.02) | 0.07 (0.01) | 0.26 (0.02) | 0.42 (0.04) |
| U.K. | 0.15 (0.02) | 0.07 (0.01) | 0.13 (0.02) | 0.32 (0.04) | 0.33 (0.06) |
| Japan | 0.14 (0.02) | 0.07 (0.01) | 0.07 (0.01) | 0.35 (0.05) | 0.36 (0.05) |
| U.S. | 0.10 (0.01) | 0.05 (0.02) | 0.05 (0.01) | 0.20 (0.03) | 0.60 (0.06) |

NOTE: Rows may not sum to 1 due to rounding. Numbers in parentheses are approximate standard errors.

6.2. *The Sources of Growth.* To what extent do countries depend on each other for their growth? Imbedding the figures in Table 4 into (15) provides a means of decomposing growth into its sources by country, taking into account our estimates of the production of potentially useful ideas by each country. Table 5 quantifies this decomposition.

The table portrays a world in which diffusion is pervasive. Differences in the scale of research output swamp the diagonal dominance of the adoption-rate figures in Table 4. The United States, Japan, and Germany, in that order, are the leading contributors to growth in every country. Together, the United States and Japan account for over 65 percent of the growth of each of the five countries.[53]

6.3. *The Rewards to Research.* Do the rewards to inventive activity reflect this breadth of diffusion? While the growth decomposition in Table 5 looks at foreign countries as sources of new technology, Table 6 looks at foreign countries as markets for new technology. We use our estimates to calculate the fraction of the average value of an idea arising from markets in each of the five countries.

[53] In Eaton and Kortum (1996) we perform a similar exercise for a broader sample of countries using a quite different model that does not endogenize research effort. Despite the differences in sample and methodology, the results are remarkably similar. The one difference worth noting is that in this other study Germany and Japan switch places in their rankings as sources of growth for the other European countries.

TABLE 6
INVENTION VALUE DECOMPOSITION

| Fraction of Invention Value from Markets in | For Ideas Originating in | | | | |
|---|---|---|---|---|---|
| | Germany | France | U.K. | Japan | U.S. |
| Germany | 0.33 (0.08) | 0.11 (0.02) | 0.11 (0.02) | 0.10 (0.01) | 0.04 (0.02) |
| France | 0.11 (0.02) | 0.48 (0.13) | 0.11 (0.02) | 0.09 (0.01) | 0.04 (0.02) |
| U.K. | 0.07 (0.01) | 0.05 (0.01) | 0.35 (0.13) | 0.06 (0.01) | 0.02 (0.01) |
| Japan | 0.19 (0.03) | 0.15 (0.02) | 0.17 (0.02) | 0.50 (0.12) | 0.06 (0.02) |
| U.S. | 0.30 (0.10) | 0.22 (0.12) | 0.26 (0.13) | 0.25 (0.11) | 0.84 (0.05) |

NOTE: Columns may not sum to 1 due to rounding. Numbers in parentheses are approximate standard errors.

The return to ideas appears to be much more local than the benefit from ideas. The largest single source of returns is always from the domestic market. Nevertheless, for all but the United States, foreign markets taken as a whole provide at least half the returns. The United States is a valuable market for ideas from all countries and provides over 80 percent of the market for its own ideas.

6.4. *Robustness.* The results that we have presented so far rely on a number of specific assumptions. We now examine the implications of changing a few of the potentially more controversial ones. Specifically, we reestimate the model after either (1) lowering the interest rate from 0.07 to 0.03 (closer to the return on bonds rather than on stocks), (2) doubling the number of research scientists and engineers (to take account of less formal research activity that might escape measurement), (3) increasing the cost of patenting abroad by $10,000 (to proxy for the potential hassle of dealing with foreign legal systems),[54] or (4) reducing the weight placed on productivity in our objective function ($\omega_A$) from 30 to 10.

The one notable effect of the lower interest rate is a lower elasticity of research output with respect to research employment $\beta$ of 0.14. Raising the level of research effort has the opposite impact, raising $\beta$ to 0.35, with no other effect worth mentioning.[55] Higher costs of foreign patenting are, quite logically, manifested entirely in a lower imitation rate of foreign patents, with $\iota_F^{pat} = 0.208$. These changes affect the fit hardly at all, except for the higher fee, which hurts it substantially.

Downweighting productivity in our objective function has broader effects. The major change is that Japan becomes a source of world growth on a par with the United States.[56] However, in trying to fit the patent data better, the model flounders on relative productivity, predicting only tiny differences among countries and putting the

[54] Harvard Business School (1991) documents the frustration vented by U.S. patent seekers in Japan.

[55] Less discounting raises the return to R&D. To explain observed levels of research, our model offsets this effect by reducing the productivity of R&D through a lower $\beta$. By this same logic, when confronted with larger numbers of researchers, our model concludes that research effort is a more productive undertaking.

[56] As shown in Table 3, our baseline, in striving to explain the U.S. productivity edge over Japan, tends to overpredict patenting by U.S. researchers and to underpredict patenting by the Japanese.

United States behind all but the United Kingdom.[57] The reason for this difference is the mixed messages sent by the productivity and patent data about the positions of Japan versus the United States. As shown in Table 1, Japan is 22 percent behind in value added per hour, but given the much smaller scale of its economy, the Japanese patent performance is formidable. While the alternative weighting scheme highlights this intriguing feature of the data, we pay more attention to the message sent by the productivity data, since trying to understand them is our primary objective.

## 7. COUNTERFACTUALS

Exploiting the general equilibrium nature of our model, we finish off by using it to observe hypothetical worlds with different patterns of diffusion and rigor of patent protection. We run two types of experiments, assuming first that growth is fully endogenous and then that it is semiendogenous (using the parameter values in the first and second columns, respectively, of Table 2). In the first case, the counterfactual worlds we explore have different steady-state growth rates, while in the second, levels of productivity differ, but the long-run growth rate is the same.[58]

7.1. *Alternative Patterns of Diffusion.* We can get another perspective on the role of international technology diffusion by simulating the effects of technological autarky. In particular, we calculate what would happen if the single largest economy, the United States, were severed from the others. The results appear in Table 7. (For comparison, we repeat the predictions of the model from Table 3 under the column "baseline.") Our first experiment, "technological isolation," reduces to 0.0001 the rate of diffusion between the United States and the block of four other countries.

When growth is fully endogenous, it falls by about 0.7 of a percentage point. Since the block of four other countries grows faster on its own than does the United States, the U.S. level of productivity must fall relative to the others before the resulting technology gap supports the new steady-state growth rate.[59] Note that research effort falls everywhere. Hence the direct effect of technological isolation—lowering growth by cutting off access to foreign ideas—is exacerbated by a reduction in research effort.

With growth semiendogenous, the U.S. productivity growth path in the new steady state is about two-thirds of what it otherwise would have been. Since the United States has fewer ideas, researchers find it easier to come up with new ones. As a

[57] The RMSE for productivity jumps to 0.19, while for research it falls to 0.08 and for patents to 0.22.

[58] In the simulations reported we fix the interest rate at its baseline value of 0.07. With semiendogenous growth coupled with isoelastic marginal utility, this assumption is innocuous, since the steady-state growth rate is unaffected. In the case of fully endogenous growth coupled with a nonzero elasticity of marginal utility $\sigma$, however, the change in the growth rate would feed back into $r$, with subsequent effects on research activity and growth. We also simulated the fully endogenous growth model endogenizing $r$ and setting $\sigma = 2$ (with the discount rate $\rho$ chosen to match the baseline). The interest rate obviously responded to the change in the growth rate, but the subsequent feedback onto research activity and growth was negligible. Hence the results for this case are very close to those reported in Tables 7 and 8.

[59] Thus in the new steady state the United States is not completely isolated because it obtains many innovations from abroad, albeit years later.

TABLE 7
EXPERIMENTS WITH THE RATE OF DIFFUSION

| | Baseline | | Technological Isolation | | Borderless Diffusion | |
|---|---|---|---|---|---|---|
| | Endog. | Semi | Endog. | Semi | Endog. | Semi |
| Productivity growth: | 0.018 | 0.018 | 0.011 | 0.018 | 0.028 | 0.018 |
| U.S. productivity level: | 1.00 | 1.00 | 1.00 | 0.67 | 1.00 | 1.41 |
| Productivity (per U.S.) | | | | | | |
| Germany | 0.91 | 0.92 | 3.20 | 2.09 | 1.02 | 1.01 |
| France | 0.94 | 0.94 | 3.25 | 2.15 | 1.02 | 1.02 |
| U.K. | 0.75 | 0.75 | 2.94 | 1.87 | 0.98 | 0.99 |
| Japan | 0.85 | 0.85 | 3.13 | 2.05 | 1.01 | 1.00 |
| Research intensity | | | | | | |
| Germany | 0.0037 | 0.0037 | 0.0025 | 0.0040 | 0.0115 | 0.0073 |
| France | 0.0016 | 0.0016 | 0.0012 | 0.0020 | 0.0081 | 0.0053 |
| U.K. | 0.0025 | 0.0025 | 0.0018 | 0.0029 | 0.0101 | 0.0065 |
| Japan | 0.0054 | 0.0054 | 0.0039 | 0.0063 | 0.0119 | 0.0075 |
| U.S. | 0.0035 | 0.0036 | 0.0030 | 0.0049 | 0.0071 | 0.0047 |

NOTE: We do each experiment for both fully endogenous (using the parameters in the first column of Table 2) and semiendogenous growth (using the parameters in the second column of Table 2). In "Baseline" we display the prediction of the model (for fully endogenous growth those predictions are from Table 3). In "Technological Isolation" we set the diffusion rates between the United States and the other four countries equal to 0.0001. Since these diffusion rates are not zero, the United States still grows at the same rate as the other four countries in steady state. In "Borderless Diffusion" we set $\epsilon_D = 17.7$ (in the fully endogenous growth case) or $\epsilon_D = 17.8$ (in the semiendogenous growth case) even for $n \neq i$.

consequence, more research is performed everywhere. For countries other than the United States this effect dominates to the extent that productivity is somewhat higher than in the base case.

Our second experiment, "borderless diffusion," eliminates the effect of country borders on diffusion rates. In particular, we set $\epsilon_D = 17.7$ (or 17.8 in the semiendogenous growth case) even if $n \neq i$. Since ideas now spread more rapidly and evenly across countries, productivity levels become tightly clustered. With growth fully endogenous, the growth rate rises by a percentage point. In the semiendogenous growth case the steady-state level of U.S. productivity rises by 41 percent. In either case technological integration stimulates research, particularly in the smaller countries (Germany, France, and the United Kingdom), which now have a much larger effective market for their ideas.

7.2. *The Strength of Patent Protection.* We conclude with some counterfactual experiments on the strength of patent protection. Table 8 reports the results. In the first experiment we eliminate all forms of patent protection by setting $\iota_D^{pat} = \iota_D^{not} = 0.415$ and $\iota_F^{pat} = \iota_F^{not} = 0.250$ (i.e., making the hazard of imitation of patented ideas as great as for unpatented ones). In the fully endogenous growth case, productivity growth falls by one tenth of a percentage point. In the case of semiendogenous growth, the level of productivity in all countries falls by about 6 percent. In either case, relative productivity levels remain about the same, while research intensity falls.

In the second experiment we make patent protection perfect by setting $\iota_D^{pat} = \iota_F^{pat} = 0$ so that there is no hazard of imitation if an idea is patented. As before, relative

TABLE 8
EXPERIMENTS WITH THE STRENGTH OF PATENT PROTECTION

| | Baseline | | No IPP | | Perfect IPP | |
|---|---|---|---|---|---|---|
| | Endog. | Semi | Endog. | Semi | Endog. | Semi |
| Productivity growth: | 0.0180 | 0.0180 | 0.0168 | 0.0180 | 0.0248 | 0.0180 |
| U.S. productivity level: | 1.00 | 1.00 | 1.00 | 0.94 | 1.00 | 1.41 |
| Productivity (per U.S.) | | | | | | |
| Germany | 0.91 | 0.92 | 0.93 | 0.92 | 0.89 | 0.92 |
| France | 0.94 | 0.94 | 0.95 | 0.95 | 0.92 | 0.94 |
| U.K. | 0.75 | 0.75 | 0.77 | 0.76 | 0.71 | 0.75 |
| Japan | 0.85 | 0.85 | 0.87 | 0.86 | 0.82 | 0.85 |
| Research intensity | | | | | | |
| Germany | 0.0037 | 0.0037 | 0.0030 | 0.0032 | 0.0399 | 0.0443 |
| France | 0.0016 | 0.0016 | 0.0011 | 0.0012 | 0.0207 | 0.0254 |
| U.K. | 0.0025 | 0.0025 | 0.0019 | 0.0021 | 0.0298 | 0.0348 |
| Japan | 0.0054 | 0.0054 | 0.0039 | 0.0042 | 0.0462 | 0.0491 |
| U.S. | 0.0035 | 0.0036 | 0.0017 | 0.0018 | 0.0340 | 0.0373 |

NOTE: We do each experiment for both fully endogenous (using the parameters in the first column of Table 2) and semiendogenous growth (using the parameters in the second column of Table 2). In "Baseline" we display the prediction of the model (for fully endogenous growth those predictions are from Table 3). In "No IPP" we set $\iota_D^{pat} = \iota_D^{not} = 0.415$ and $\iota_F^{pat} = \iota_F^{not} = 0.250$. In "Perfect IPP" we set $\iota_D^{pat} = \iota_F^{pat} = 0$.

productivities do not change much, but productivity growth rises by over a half a percentage point in the fully endogenous growth case while long-run productivity tables rise by almost 40 percent in the semiendogenous growth case. In either case, research effort rises dramatically.

To get a crude sense of the net benefits of patent protection, we compare the steady-state gain in productivity with the cost of diverting labor from production. (In the case of fully endogenous growth, we consider the effect of a permanent percentage increase in productivity with the same present value as the increase in the growth rate.) Moving from no protection to our baseline level raises steady-state output by the equivalent of 2.3 percent (growth fully endogenous) or 6.3 percent (growth semiendogenous), while pulling only about half a percent of the workforce into research away from production. Moving from the baseline to perfect protection generates productivity gains of 15 percent (fully) or 41 percent (semi), at a cost of employing about 8 percent more of the workforce in research.[60]

## 8. CONCLUSION

We have provided a quantitative explanation of research effort, the growth of productivity, and the spread of technology across countries. A rough summary of our findings is that countries lie two-thirds of the way from technological autarky toward free trade in ideas; i.e., research performed abroad is about two-thirds as potent as domestic research. Furthermore, the United States and Japan together drive at least two-thirds of the growth in each of our five countries. Our results jive with a

[60] These calculations, by ignoring the transit to the new steady state, overstate the benefits of patent protection, especially in the semiendogenous growth case.

view of economic history that relates a country's productivity to its ability to adopt ideas.[61]

While these results might suggest that the barriers to the spread of technology are minor, they nevertheless can account for the substantial productivity differences among our five countries. Eliminating international barriers to diffusion would not only bring productivity levels very close together but also would raise productivity substantially everywhere.

Our purpose has been to develop a basic methodology for analyzing the determinants of research and productivity in a multicountry world. While the focus here has been on economic aggregates, the methodology can be extended to accommodate additional dimensions of the data. For example, giving the analysis a sectoral dimension would provide insight into why countries specialize in research as they do and how this specialization shapes comparative advantage in production.[62]

We have taken only a first look at policies toward research (by examining the effects of eliminating or perfecting patent protection). Many more issues of patent protection deserve attention. For example, to what extent is coordination required to obtain an optimal patent system? Moreover, governments pursue a wide range of other policies, including tax incentives, research grants, and government labs, that affect innovation. Our framework is a natural one for evaluating the payoffs from these efforts.[63]

## APPENDIX

A.1. *Symbols Used in the Model.*

| | |
|---|---|
| $Y_{nt}$ | Output in country $n$ at time $t$ |
| $J$ | Range of inputs, $j \in [0, J]$ |
| $X_{nt}(j)$ | Quantity of input $j$ in country $n$ at time $t$ |
| $Z_{nt}(j)$ | Quality of input $j$ in country $n$ at time $t$ |
| $L_{nt}$ | Workforce in country $n$ at time $t$ |
| $K_{nt}$ | Capital stock in country $n$ at time $t$ |
| $s_{it}$ | Fraction of workers doing research in country $i$ at time $t$ |
| $\alpha_{it}$ | Productivity of researchers in country $i$ at time $t$ |
| $\beta$ | Parameter of the distribution of research talent |

[61] Unlike economic historians, however, we have only taken a snapshot of the world at a given moment. In Eaton and Kortum (1997a) we used the model (parameterized with our estimates here) to explain the postwar growth of these five economies as convergence toward the steady state from initial productivity levels. While endogenizing R&D in steady state, as we have done here, requires very intricate numerical integration, outside of steady state the problem is an order of magnitude more difficult. Hence in this out-of-steady-state exercise we conditioned on the actual paths of research. We found that the semiendogenous growth version of the model captures broad movements in productivity quite successfully, while the fully endogenous growth version predicted much more rapid convergence than actually occurred.

[62] In Eaton and Kortum (1999) we introduce international trade into a static version of the model to investigate the extent to which trade, as opposed to the diffusion of knowledge, spreads the benefits of innovation.

[63] Eaton, Gutierrez, and Kortum (1998) use a variant of the framework here to analyze European research policies.

| | |
|---|---|
| $Q$ | Random variable representing the quality of an idea |
| $F(q)$ | Distribution from which the quality of an idea is drawn |
| $\theta$ | Parameter of the quality distribution, $F(q) = 1 - q^{-\theta}$ |
| $\tau$ | Random diffusion lag |
| $\epsilon_{ni}$ | Rate of diffusion from country $i$ to $n$ |
| $\mu_{nt}$ | Stock of ideas that have diffused to country $n$ by time $t$ |
| $H_n(z; t)$ | Cumulative distribution of the technological frontier in country $n$ at time $t$ |
| $A_{nt}$ | Level of productivity in country $n$ at time $t$ |
| $\psi$ | Euler's constant ($\approx$ 0.5772) |
| $c$ | Unit cost of production |
| $r$ | Rate of interest |
| $r'$ | Cost of capital (rate of interest plus depreciation rate) |
| $w_{nt}$ | Wage (in units of output) of production workers in country $n$ at time $t$ |
| $\phi$ | Capital elasticity |
| $p(j)$ | Price (in units of output) of input $j$ |
| $\pi_{nt}(z, q)$ | Profit from marketing input of quality $q$ in country $n$ at time $t$ if the next best input has quality $z$ |
| $V_{nit}(z, q)$ | Expected discounted value as of time $t$ in country $n$ of an idea from country $i$ where the idea has quality $q$ and replaces an input of quality $z$ |
| $V^k_{nit}(q)$ | Expected value of an idea before its use (hence $z$) is known The index $k = pat, not$ specifies if it is patented |
| $\iota_n^{pat}$ | Rate of imitation in country $n$ if the idea is patented |
| $\iota_n^{not}$ | Rate of imitation in country $n$ if the idea is not patented |
| $f_{nit}$ | Cost of seeking protection in country $n$ from country $i$ at time $t$ |
| $\bar{q}_{nit}$ | Cut-off quality to patent in country $n$ from country $i$ on an idea invented at time $t$ |
| $P_{nit}$ | Number of ideas from country $i$ seeking protection in $n$ at time $t$ |
| $b_{nit}$ | Defined as $\mu_{nt}(\bar{q}_{nit})^{-\theta}$ (constant in steady state) |
| $V_{nit}$ | Expected value of an idea from country $i$ in country $n$ at time $t$ (quality unknown but optimal patenting assumed) |
| $V_{it}$ | Expected value of an idea from country $i$ at time $t$ |
| $g$ | Steady-state growth rate of $\mu$, the stock of diffused ideas |
| $g_L$ | Growth rate of the labor force |
| $g_A$ | Growth rate of total factor productivity |
| $v_{ni}$ | Normalized value of an idea from country $i$ in country $n$ defined as $V_{nit}\mu_{nt}/Y_{nt}$ (constant in steady state) |
| $\kappa_1(\theta)$ | Constant relating productivity index to the wage |
| $\kappa_2(\theta)$ | Average value of the inverse of the price markup |

A.2. *Mathematical Appendix.*

A.2.1. *The distribution of the technological frontier.* We derive the distribution of the technological frontier by considering the distribution of the best quality idea at time $t$ for a given input in country $n$. Consider an input that is currently of quality $z$. New ideas will be adopted for this input at a stochastic rate of $\dot{\mu}_{nt} z^{-\theta}$. The probability that no idea is adopted in the time interval $[t, t + dt]$ is thus $e^{-\dot{\mu}_{nt} z^{-\theta} dt}$. Therefore,

$$H_n(z; t + dt) = H_n(z; t) e^{-\dot{\mu}_{nt} z^{-\theta} dt}$$

or

$$\frac{\partial \ln H_n(z; t)}{\partial t} = -\dot{\mu}_{nt} z^{-\theta}$$

Solving this differential equation, with the two initial conditions, (1) $\lim_{s \to -\infty} H_n(z; s) = 1$ for all $z \geq 1$ and (2) $\lim_{s \to -\infty} \mu_{ns} = 0$, yields the cumulative distribution function for the technological frontier, equation 2.

A.2.2. *The productivity equation.* The natural log of the geometric mean of the technological frontier is

$$\ln A_{nt} = \int_1^{\infty} \ln(z) dh_n(z; t)$$

Changing the variable of integration to $x = \mu_{nt} z^{-\theta}$,

$$\ln A_{nt} = \theta^{-1} \int_0^{\mu_{nt}} \ln(\mu_{nt}/x) e^{-x} dx = \theta^{-1} \ln(\mu_{nt})(1 - e^{-\mu_{nt}}) - \theta^{-1} \int_0^{\mu_{nt}} \ln(x) e^{-x} dx$$

For large $\mu_{nt}$ we have an arbitrarily good approximation:

$$\ln A_{nt} = \theta^{-1} \ln(\mu_{nt}) - \theta^{-1} \int_0^{\infty} \ln(x) e^{-x} dx$$

The Laplace transform of $-\psi - \ln t$ is $s^{-1} \ln s$, where $\psi$ is Euler's constant. Evaluating the Laplace transform at $s = 1$ implies

$$\int_0^{\infty} \ln(x) e^{-x} dx = -\psi$$

This gives us the desired result that

$$\ln A_{nt} = \theta^{-1} \ln(\mu_{nt}) + \psi/\theta$$

As we discussed in the introduction, our model implies that an idea is more likely to be adopted in a country with a relatively low level of productivity. The probability that an idea of quality $q$ will prove useful is simply $H_n(q; t)$. Integrating this probability over the Pareto density of $Q$, and noting that $\mu_{nt}$ becomes arbitrarily large over time, we get

$$\int_1^{\infty} H_n(q; t) dF(q) = \int_1^{\infty} \theta q^{-(\theta+1)} e^{-\mu_{nt} q^{-\theta}} dq = \mu_{nt}^{-1} \tag{22}$$

A.2.3. *Wages, productivity, and the distribution of the markup.* From Proposition 3.3 in Kortum (1997), the time invariant distribution of the markup is given by

$$G(m) \equiv 1 - \frac{\theta \ln(m)}{1 - m^{-\theta}} m^{-\theta}$$

This distribution is used to derive our equations for the wage and labor productivity conditional on technology, (12) and (11).

To derive an expression for the wage, start with the result that the quantity purchased of input $j$ is

$$X(j) = \frac{Y}{Jp(j)} = \frac{Y}{JcM(j)}$$

where $M(j)$ is the markup for input $j$. Plugging this into the production function and rearranging,

$$\ln c = \ln(A) - J^{-1} \int_0^J \ln M(j) dj = \ln(A) - \int_1^\infty \ln(m) dG(m)$$

Hence $c_{it} = \kappa_1(\theta) A_{it}$, where $\kappa_1(\theta) \equiv \exp\{-\int_1^\infty \ln(m) dG(m)\}$. The corresponding wage is $w_{it} = (1-\phi)\kappa_1(\theta) A_{it} k_{it}^\phi$ in terms of the capital-labor ratio and $w_{it} = (1-\phi)[\kappa_1(\theta) A_{it} (\phi/r')^\phi]^{1/(1-\phi)}$ in terms of the cost of capital $r'$.

Output is the sum of profit and factor income. Total profit across all inputs is

$$\int_0^J (1 - M(j)^{-1}) \frac{Y_{it}}{J} dj = Y_{it}[1 - \int_1^\infty m^{-1} dG(m)]$$

Output of intermediates is $k^\phi L(1-s)$, while each intermediate costs $c$ in terms of factor payments to produce. Summing factor payments and profits and rearranging, we obtain as an expression for total income

$$Y_{it} = \frac{c_{it}}{\kappa_2(\theta)} k_{it}^\phi L_{it}(1 - s_{it}) = \frac{\kappa_1(\theta)}{\kappa_2(\theta)} A_{it} k_{it}^\phi L_{it}(1 - s_{it})$$

in terms of $k_{it}$ and

$$Y_{it} = \frac{1}{\kappa_2(\theta)} [\kappa_1(\theta) A_{it} (\phi/r')^\phi]^{1/(1-\phi)} L_{it}(1 - s_{it})$$

in terms of the cost of capital $r'$. Here $\kappa_2(\theta) \equiv \int_1^\infty m^{-1} dG(m)$.

A.2.4. *Steady-state relative productivities and growth.* We can write the system of equations (15) in matrix form as

$$\mu g = \Delta(g) \mu \tag{23}$$

where $\mu \equiv (\mu_{1t}/\mu_{Nt}, \ldots, \mu_{N-1t}/\mu_{Nt}, 1)'$ and

$$\Delta(g) = \begin{bmatrix} \delta_{11} & \cdots & \delta_{1N} \\ \vdots & \ddots & \vdots \\ \delta_{N1} & \cdots & \delta_{NN} \end{bmatrix}$$

where

$$\delta_{ni} \equiv \frac{\epsilon_{ni}}{\epsilon_{ni} + g} \frac{\alpha}{J} s_i^{\beta} \widetilde{L}_i$$

In the case of fully endogenous growth, we solve the system iteratively. Based on an initial $g_0$, we set $\Delta_0 = \Delta(g_0)$. The system of equations (23) then constitutes a standard system of linear differential equations. The Frobenius root of this system determines a new growth rate $g_1$. We iterate accordingly until $g_n \approx g_{n-1}$. We then set $g = g_n$. The vector $\mu$ is given by the eigenvector corresponding to the Frobenius root $g$. In the case of semiendogenous growth, $g = g_L/(1-\gamma)$. Thus we iterate on the level of $\overline{\mu}_i^{\gamma-1}$ relative to the $L'_{it}$s rather than on $g$.

A.2.5. *Steady-state patenting thresholds.* In steady state, $Y_{nt}$ grows at a constant rate $g_Y$, while $\mu_{nt}$ grows at a constant rate $g$. In order to obtain an expression for the thresholds in terms of time-invariant variables, we define $b \equiv \mu_{nt} q^{-\theta}$. Imposing these steady-state relationships and integrating equation (4) over the distribution of the technological frontier, we get

$$V_{nit}^{l}(q) = \widetilde{V}_{nit}^{l}(b) = Y_{nt} \frac{\Upsilon(b,\theta)}{J} \int_0^{\infty} e^{-(r+\iota_{ni}^{l}-g_Y)s}(1-e^{-\epsilon_{ni}s})e^{-be^{gs}} ds$$

where $l = pat, not$ depending on whether or not the idea is patented, $\Upsilon(b,\theta) \equiv 1 - e^b b^{1/\theta}\Gamma[(\theta-1)/\theta, b]$, where $\Gamma(a,b) \equiv \int_b^{\infty} e^{-x}x^{a-1}dx$ is the incomplete gamma function. The value of an idea relative to market size therefore does not depend on time:

$$\widetilde{V}_{nit}^{l}(b)/Y_{nt} = v_{ni}^{l}(b) = (Jg)^{-1}\Upsilon(b,\theta)\{\Psi(\widehat{r}_{ni}^{l}/g, b) - \Psi[(\widehat{r}_{ni}^{l} + \epsilon_{ni})/g, b]\}$$

where

$$\widehat{r}_{ni}^{l} \equiv r + \iota_{ni}^{l} - g_Y \quad l = pat, not$$

and $\Psi(a/g, b) \equiv g\int_0^{\infty} e^{-as}e^{-be^{gs}}ds$.[64]

Equation (6) determining the patent threshold then becomes

$$v_{ni}^{pat}(\overline{b}) - v_{ni}^{not}(\overline{b}) = f_{ni} \tag{24}$$

Given $g$, the world growth rate of $\mu$, the only country characteristics that directly affect the patenting threshold are the adoption lag $\epsilon_{ni}$, the strength of patent protection, as reflected by $\iota_{ni}^{pat}$ and $\iota_{ni}^{not}$, and the cost of patenting $f_{ni}$.

[64] In order to compute this integral, we rely on the result that for $b > 0$,

$$\Psi(a/g, b) = b^{a/g}\Gamma(-a/g, b)$$

As a consequence, we also have

$$\Upsilon(b,\theta) = 1 - be^b\Psi\left(\frac{1-\theta}{\theta}, b\right)$$

There is a continued fraction representation for the incomplete gamma function (that admits $d < 0$) leading to a speedy numerical algorithm (from Press et al., 1989, pp. 160–163).

A.2.6. *The steady-state value of an idea.* In the text we define

$$v_{ni} \equiv V_{nit}\mu_{nt}/Y_{nt}$$

Substituting the definitions from the previous section into equation (8), it follows that

$$v_{ni} = \int_0^{\bar{b}_{ni}} v_{ni}^{pat}(b)db + \int_{\bar{b}_{ni}}^{\infty} v_{ni}^{not}(b)db - f_{ni}\bar{b}_{ni} \tag{25}$$

REFERENCES


AGHION, P. AND P. HOWITT, "A Model of Growth Through Creative Destruction," *Econometrica* 60 (1992), 323–351.

VAN ARK, B., "Productivity and Competitiveness in Manufacturing: A Comparison of Europe, Japan and the United States," in K. Wagner and B. van Ark, eds. *International Productivity Differences, Measurement and Explanations: Contributions to Economic Analysis*, Vol. 233 (Amsterdam: North Holland, 1996).

BENTAL, B. AND D. PELED, "Endogenous Technical Progress and Growth: A Search Theoretic Approach." *International Economic Review* 37 (1996), 687–718.

COE, D. AND E. HELPMAN, "International R&D Spillovers," *European Economic Review* 39 (1995), 859–887.

DINOPOULOS, E. AND P. THOMPSON, "A Contribution to the Empirics of Endogenous Growth," *Eastern Economic Journal* 22 (1996), 389–400.

EATON, J., E. GUTIERREZ, AND S. KORTUM, "European Research Policy," *Economic Policy* 27 (1998), 405–438.

———, AND S. KORTUM, "Trade in Ideas: Patenting and Productivity in the OECD," *Journal of International Economics* 40 (1996), 251–278.

——— AND ———, "Engines of Growth: Domestic and Foreign Sources of Innovation," *Japan and the World Economy* 9 (1997a), 235–259.

——— AND ———, "Technology Geography and Trade," mimeo, Boston University, 1999.

FAGERBERG, J., "Technology and International Differences in Growth Rates," *Journal of International Perspectives* 32 (1994), 1147–1175.

GERSCHENKRON, A., *Economic Backwardness in Historical Perspective* (Cambridge. MA: Belknap Press, 1962).

GORDON, R.J. "Problems in the Measurement and Performance of Service-Sector Productivity in the United States," NBER Working Paper No. 5519, 1996.

GRILICHES, Z. "Patent Statistics as Economic Indicators: A Survey," *Journal of Economic Literature* 18 (1990), 1661–1707.

———, "Productivity, R&D, and the Data Constraint," *American Economic Review* 84 (1994), 1–23.

GROSSMAN, G.M. AND E. HELPMAN, *Innovation and Growth in the Global Economy* (Cambridge, MA: MIT Press, 1991a).

——— AND ———, "Quality Ladders in the Theory of Growth," *Review of Economic Studies* 58 (1991b), 43–61.

——— AND ———, "Technology and Trade," in G.M. Grossman and K. Rogoff, eds., *Handbook of International Economics*, Vol. 3 (Amsterdam: North-Holland, 1995).

HARHOFF, D., F.M. SCHERER, AND K. VOPEL, "Exploring the Tail of Patented Invention Value Distributions," mimeo, Harvard University, 1997.

HARVARD BUSINESS SCHOOL, "Fusion Systems Corporation in Japan," Case Study No. 9-390-021, 1991.

HELFGOTT, S., "Patent Filing Costs Around the World." *Journal of the Patent and Trademark Office Society* July (1993), 567–580.

HESTON, A. AND R. SUMMERS, "International Price and Quantity Comparisons: Potentials and Pitfalls," *American Economic Review Papers and Proceedings* 86 (1996), 20–24.

IMF, *International Financial Statistics* (Washington, 1994).

JAFFE, A. AND M. TRAJTENBERG, "International Knowledge Flows; Evidence from Patent Citations," NBER Working Paper No. 6507, 1998.

JONES, C.I., "R&D-Based Models of Economic Growth," *Journal of Political Economy* 103 (1995), 759–784.

JOVANOVIC, B., "Learning and Growth," in D. Kreps and K. Wallis, eds., *Advances in Economics* (Cambridge, England: Cambridge University Press, 1996).

——— AND S. LACH, "Product Innovation and the Business Cycle," *International Economic Review* 38 (1997), 3–22.

KELLER, W., "Trade and Transmission of Technology," mimeo, University of Texas at Austin, 1998a.

———, "Are International R&D Spillovers Trade Related? Analyzing Spillovers Among Randomly Matched Trade Partners," *European Economic Review* 42 (1998b), 1469–1481.

KORTUM, S., "Research, Patenting, and Technological Change," *Econometrica* 65 (1997), 1389–1419.

LEWIS, SIR W.A., "International Competition in Manufactures," *American Economic Review Papers and Proceedings* 47 (1957).

LEVIN, R.C., A.K. KLEVORICK, R.R. NELSON, AND S.G. WINTER, "Appropriating the Returns from Industrial Research and Development," *Brookings Papers on Economic Activity* 3 (1987), 783–820.

LYSKO, W., "Manufacturing Multifactor Productivity in Three Countries," *Monthly Labor Review* (1995), 39–55.

MANKIW, N.G., D. ROMER, AND D.N. WEIL, "A Contribution to the Empirics of Economic Growth," *Quarterly Journal of Economics* 107 (1992), 407–437.

MANSFIELD, E. AND A. ROMEO, "Technology Transfer to Overseas Subsidiaries by U.S.-Based Firms," *Quarterly Journal of Economics* 95 (1980). 737–750.

———, M. SCHWARTZ, AND S. WAGNER, "Imitation Costs and Patents: An Empirical Study," *Economic Journal* 91 (1981), 907–918.

NELSON, R.R. AND E.S. PHELPS, "Investment in Humans, Technological Diffusion, and Economic Growth," *American Economic Review, Papers and Proceedings* 56 (1966), 69–75.

OECD, *Basic Science and Technology Statistics* (Paris, 1991).

OKADA, Y., "Tokkyoseido no Ho to Keizaigaku" ("The Law and Economics of the Patent System"), staff paper, Shinshu University, 1992.

PAKES, A. AND M. SCHANKERMAN, "The Rate of Obsolescence of Patents, Research Gestation Lags, and the Private Rate of Return to Research Resources" in Z. Griliches, ed., *R&D, Patents, and Productivity* (Chicago: University of Chicago Press, 1984).

PARENTE, S.L. AND E.C. PRESCOTT, "Barriers to Technology Adoption and Development," *Journal of Political Economy* 102 (1994), 298–321.

PARK, W., "International R&D Spillovers and OECD Economic Growth," *Economic Enquiry* 33 (1995), 571–591.

PENROSE, E.T., *The Economics of the International Patent System* (Baltimore: Johns Hopkins University Press, 1951).

PHELPS, E.S., "Models of Technical Progress and the Golden Rule of Research," *Review of Economic Studies* 33 (1966), 133–145.

PRESS, W.H., B.P. FLANNERY, S.A. TEUKOLSKY, AND W.T. VETTERLING, *Numerical Recipes* (New York: Cambridge University Press, 1989).

PUTNAM, J., "The Value of International Patent Rights," mimeo, Charles River Associates, Boston, 1997.

RAPP, R. AND R. ROZEK, "Benefits and Costs of Intellectual Property Protection in Developing Countries," *Journal of World Trade* 24 (1990), 75–102.

ROMER, P.M., "Endogenous Technical Change," *Journal of Political Economy* 98 (1990), S71–S102.

ROSENBERG, N., *Inside the Black Box: Technology and Economics* (New York: Cambridge University Press, 1982).

SCHANKERMAN, M. AND A. PAKES, "Estimates of the Value of Patent Rights in European Countries During the Post-1950 Period," *Economic Journal* 96 (1986), 1052–1076.

SHELL, K. "Toward a Theory of Inventive Activity and Capital Accumulation," *American Economic Review* 56 (1966), 62–68.

SUMMERS, R. AND A. HESTON, "The Penn World Table (Mark 5): An Expanded Set of International Comparisons, 1950–1988," *Quarterly Journal of Economics* 106 (1991), 327–368.

TONG, X. AND J.D. FRAME, "Measuring National Technological Performance with Patent Claims Data," *Research Policy* 23 (1994), 133–141.

WIPO, *Industrial Property Statistics* (Geneva: World Intellectual Property Organization, 1990).

# [8]

# DOES FOREIGN DIRECT INVESTMENT TRANSFER TECHNOLOGY ACROSS BORDERS?

Bruno van Pottelsberghe de la Potterie and Frank Lichtenberg*

*Abstract*—Previous studies have found that importing goods from R&D-intensive countries raises a country's productivity. In this paper, we investigate econometrically whether foreign direct investment (FDI) also transfers technology across borders. The data indicates that FDI transfers technology, but only in one direction: a country's productivity is increased if it invests in R&D-intensive foreign countries—particularly in recent years—but not if foreign R&D-intensive countries invest in it. Other findings of the paper are that the ratio of foreign-R&D benefits conveyed by outward FDI to foreign R&D benefits conveyed by imports is higher for large countries than it is for small ones, that failure to account for international R&D spillovers leads to upwardly biased estimates of the output elasticity of the domestic R&D capital stock, and that there are much larger transfers of technology from the United States to Japan than there are from Japan to the United States.

## I. Introduction

Coe and Helpman (1995) presented evidence consistent with the hypothesis that technology spills over across countries through the channel of trade flows, and they provided estimates of the magnitude of these spillovers. In a previous paper (1998), we reexamined two features of their econometric model. First, we argued that the weighting scheme they used to compute foreign R&D capital stocks is subject to an "aggregation bias." We suggested an alternative weighting scheme that is theoretically much less biased and that yielded somewhat better empirical results. Second, we corrected an "indexation" bias and generalized their empirical framework by analyzing how the output elasticity of foreign R&D depends on a country's openness to trade.[1] The empirical results confirmed that the more open to trade a country is, the more likely it is to benefit from foreign R&D.

In this paper, we perform econometric tests of the hypothesis that the extent to which country $i$ benefits (in terms of higher productivity) from the R&D performed by country $j$ depends not only on the volume of country $i$'s imports from country $j$, but also on the extent of foreign direct investment (FDI) between the two countries—both "inward" FDI (investment by country $j$ in country $i$) and "outward" FDI (investment by country $i$ in country $j$). This hypothesis is based on the general notion that the extent to which country $i$ benefits from country $j$'s R&D investment depends on the degree of economic interaction between the countries, or of their exposure to one another.

It may be useful to draw an analogy between learning about foreign technology and learning a foreign language. I might learn a foreign language from foreigners living in my country ("inward FDI"), or I might learn it by living in a foreign country ("outward FDI"). Both are potentially useful and important methods of foreign language (knowledge) acquisition, although the latter perhaps tends to be more effective (it is more likely to involve "total immersion"). Similarly, both inward and outward FDI may facilitate acquisition of foreign technology. Dunning (1994), however, has argued that, although outward FDI is likely to have an unambiguously positive effect on productivity ("where foreign production adds to domestic production, the R&D base of the investing company is strengthened—whatever the nationality of the firm" (p. 81)), inward FDI may decrease indigenous innovative capacity. It may therefor have no effect or even a negative effect on productivity.

In his survey of the empirical literature on international R&D spillovers, Mohnen (1996) tentatively identified the following three "stylized facts": (i) foreign R&D contributes to productivity growth more in small countries than in large countries; (ii) the output elasticity of foreign R&D is higher than the output elasticity of domestic R&D; and (iii) the United States is an important R&D spillover generator but a weak spillover receiver, and spillovers emanating from Japan are weak, if not nonexistent. The methodology that we use allows us to conduct formal econometric tests of each of these hypotheses.

The paper is organized as follows. Section II briefly describes the existing evaluation methodologies of the impact of foreign R&D on domestic productivity growth. Because these studies fail to take into account the role of FDI, an insight is given into their potential effects. It is shown that their net effect may not be predicted, partly because they may be directed towards technology sourcing practices. Section III presents the econometric estimates of the impact on national productivity growth of foreign R&D embodied alternatively into imports, inward FDI, and outward FDI. Section IV concludes.

## II. International R&D Spillovers

Given their inherent complexity, international technological spillovers have no widely accepted measures. The existing quantitative analyses focus on the impact of foreign technology on domestic productivity growth. The spillovers are considered to be either disembodied or embodied in a particular transfer channel. The main channels that have been used so far to measure the impact of international

Received for publication July 1, 1998. Revision accepted for publication June 30, 2000.

Solvay Business School, Brussels University, CEB and DULBEA, and Columbia University, respectively.

The opinions expressed in this paper are those of the authors, and not those of Columbia University or Université Libre de Bruxelles. The authors would like to thank Henri Capron, Michele Cincera, Christophe Dumont, Pierre Mohnen, Peter Pedroni, and two anonymous referees for their useful comments and suggestions.

[1] This indexation bias is relevant only to Coe and Helpman's specification that has the foreign R&D capital stock interacted with the import share.

*The Review of Economics and Statistics*, August 2001, 83(3): 490–497

R&D spillovers on domestic productivity growth are international trade (Coe & Helpman, 1995; Lichtenberg & Van Pottelsberghe, 1998), foreign technology payments (Soete & Patel, 1985), and disembodied R&D spillovers (the so-called vector approach) (Bernstein & Mohnen, 1995).[2] In general, a majority of these studies tend to support the view that international R&D spillovers contribute to the productivity growth of industrialized countries.

Neither inward FDI nor technology sourcing have been examined empirically as a specific means of technology transfer. However, a literature exists on the potential direct effects of inward FDI on the host countries' TFP growth. These studies yield conflicting results. Some of them suggest that inward FDI contributes to the productivity growth of local firms, and others fail to find any positive impacts of FDI.[3] It seems that technological spillovers are not an automatic consequence of inward FDI and that their net effect on the domestic economy is not a priori predictable.

The potential transfers of knowledge associated with inward FDI apparently have two directions. In the case of offshore production, the host country may benefit from technological externalities emanating from foreign companies. However, if foreign companies intend to copy or to source the domestic knowledge base, their home country is more likely to benefit from potential spillovers.

Technology sourcing practices are likely to be targeted towards technological leaders. These countries have accumulated substantial scientific and technological capabilities that are accessible to foreign companies that set up production and research facilities within their boundaries. There is empirical evidence supporting that the sourcing of foreign knowledge is a genuine practice firmly embodied in Multinational Enterprises (MNEs') behavior. The pioneering studies focusing on technology sourcing are those by Kogut and Chang (1991) and Yamawaki (1993), who focus on Japanese FDI in the United States and Europe. Their main finding is that Japanese firms enter the U.S. and European markets by capturing existing local firms when Japanese parents suffer from a technological and/or comparative disadvantage as compared to their U.S. and European competitors. Furthermore, when entry is disaggregated by mode (for example, new plant versus acquisition of equity), the evidence indicates that joint ventures are used for the sourcing and the sharing of U.S. technological capabilities. On the other hand, when Japanese parents possess technological comparative advantages, they choose to establish new plants in the United States or Europe.[4]

Despite this evidence that technology sourcing is a substantial motive for investing abroad, there has been no attempt to evaluate the feedback effects of such practices on the productivity growth of the imitator country. In section III, we evaluate and compare the efficiency of three main channels of technology transfer: trade, inward FDI, and outward FDI. We believe that the latter serves as a measure of the extent of technology sourcing practices.

### III. Empirical Implementation

A generalized version of the methodology employed by Coe and Helpman (1995), as modified by Lichtenberg and van Pottelsberghe (1998), can be used to test whether trade, inward FDI, and outward FDI serve as channels for the international diffusion of technology. Because FDI flows data are scarce over the period 1971–1990, we can investigate the role of FDI for only thirteen out of the 22 industrialized countries originally covered by Coe and Helpman. The focus is on a sample comprising the United States, Japan, and eleven European countries (Luxembourg being associated with Belgium).

Equation (1) is the basic econometric model; it states that the domestic total factor productivity of a country is a function of its domestic R&D capital stock and of different types of foreign R&D capital stocks:

$$\text{Log } F_{it} = \alpha_i + \alpha^d \log SD_{it} + \alpha^f \log SF_{it} + \epsilon_{it} \qquad (1a)$$

where $i = 1, \ldots, 13$ is a country index;

$t = 1, \ldots, 20$ is a time index;
log $F$ is the logarithm of total factor productivity;
$SD$ represents the domestic R&D capital stock;
$SF$ represents the foreign R&D capital stock;
$\alpha_i$ is a country-specific intercept;
$\alpha^d$ is the output elasticity of the domestic R&D capital stock;
$\alpha^f$ is the output elasticity of foreign R&D capital stock; and
$\epsilon$ is the error term.

The data sources and the computation of the total factor productivity index are described in appendix A. In their basic specification, Coe and Helpman allowed the output elasticity of domestic R&D capital stock to differ between G-7 and other countries by interacting the domestic R&D capital stock with a dummy variable that takes the value of

[2] In this case, authors measure the impact of the R&D capital stock of country $j$ on the productivity growth of country $i$. These studies rely on long time series and focus mainly on bilateral R&D spillovers between two or more countries, such as Japan and the United States in Bernstein and Mohnen (1995).

[3] For instance, Nadiri (1991) shows that the effects of an increase in U.S.-owned capital stock on the productivity growth of manufacturing industries in France, Germany, Japan, and the United Kingdom, are positive and significant. An intermediate position is proposed by Cantwell (1989), who highlights that the impact of U.S. FDI on European firms has not been beneficial in all industries. The U.S. investments have contributed to growth only when domestic firms were already technologically strong.

[4] In a similar vein and focusing on European industries, Neven and Siotis (1993, 1996) observe that inward FDI flows from the United States and Japan tend to be higher in those sectors where European technological intensity is higher than that of other industrialized countries.

one for G-7 countries. We implement a similar test, but for all the exogenous variables:

$$\text{Log } F_{it} = \alpha_i + \alpha^d \log SD_{it} + \alpha^{d7} G7 \log SD_{it} + \alpha^f \log SF_{it} + \alpha^{f7} G7 \log SF_{it} + \epsilon_{it} \quad (1b)$$

We adopt Lichtenberg and van Pottelsberghe's procedure for constructing the three different foreign R&D capital stocks. The first one, the import-embodied foreign R&D capital stock, $S^{fm}$, is constructed as follows:

$$S_i^{fm} = \sum_{j \neq i} \frac{m_{ij} S_j^d}{y_j}, \quad (2)$$

where $m_{ij}$ is the flow of imports of goods and services of country $i$ from country $j$, which might be interpreted as embodied with the R&D intensity of country $j$, and $y_{jt}$ is country $j$'s GDP.[5] The second one, the foreign R&D capital stock embodied in inward FDI, $S^{ff}$, is computed as follows:

$$S_i^{ff} = \sum_{j \neq i} \frac{f_{ij}}{k_j} S_j^d, \quad (3)$$

where $f_{ij}$ is (the four-year moving average of) the flow[6] of FDI from country $j$ towards country $i$, and $k_j$ is the gross fixed capital formation of country $j$, both expressed in constant dollars. We would prefer to specify FDI stocks rather than flows, in part because flows are much more volatile, but the construction of FDI stocks is rendered difficult by missing data and by the heterogeneous methodologies adopted in different countries.[7] Use of four-year moving averages both reduces volatility and provides a solution to the missing-data problem.

The hypothesis of technology sourcing is tested with the foreign R&D capital stock embodied in country $i$'s outward FDI:

$$S_i^{ft} = \sum_{j \neq i} \frac{t_{ij}}{k_j} S_j^d, \quad (4)$$

where $t_{ij}$ are the FDI flows of country $i$ towards country $j$. Here, the foreign R&D capital stock of country $i$ corresponds to the sum of all its outward FDI embodied in the R&D capital intensity of the target countries.

Coe and Helpman already noticed that the various variables were clearly trended, as usual in total factor productivity studies. Attempting to estimate a long-term relationship with trended variables requires the error term to be stationary. If the error term is not stationary, the estimated relationship may be spurious. An alternative solution is to estimate the model based on a change specification (growth rate) rather than a level, as a significant number of growth studies do. However, a change specification leads to short-run relationships (deviation from the long-term relationship; see the discussion by Coe and Helpman, pp. 867–870). Two test statistics put forward by Levin and Lin (1992, 1993) were used by the authors to test whether the estimated regression equation is cointegrated (that is, whether the residual is stationary). Mixed results were obtained, the main equation being cointegrated according to Levin and Lin (1992) but not to Levin and Lin (1993).[8] Given that the econometrics of pooled cointegration were not fully worked out, Coe and Helpman placed "more emphasis on consistency with the theoretical model and on the a priori plausibility of the estimated parameters than on the tests for cointegration" (p. 870). Important progress in the econometrics of cointegration for panel data have been made since the early 1990s. Pedroni (1999) puts forward seven tests that are based on previous ones (such as Levin and Lin (1993) or Im, Pesaran, and Shin (1996)). Four of these tests allow for country-specific cointegration dynamics. The seven tests were applied to the basic specification in level and in growth rates (first difference). The econometric estimates of equation (1a) are presented in table 1, along with the various cointegration tests. The first four columns present within estimates and the next four, the first-differenced estimates. Regressions (i) to (iii) show the estimated output elasticities of domestic R&D and of the foreign R&D capital stock incorporated alternatively into one of the three alternative technology transfer channels. In each regression, the estimated elasticity of the domestic R&D capital stock is positive and significant. Regression (i) includes the foreign R&D capital stock embodied in trade flows. Although the focus is limited to thirteen countries, the estimated output elasticity of the foreign R&D variable (0.117) is very close to the estimates evaluated over 22 industrialized countries (0.109) by Lichtenberg and van Pottelsberghe (1998).

Regarding the impact of outside R&D embodied in inward FDI, regression (ii) shows that there are no significant international R&D spillovers. This suggests that inward FDI does not induce substantial technology transfers from the

[5] Cf. Lichtenberg and van Pottelsberghe (1998) for the comparison of alternative weighting schemes for the construction of the foreign R&D capital stock. Equation (2) is much less sensitive to potential aggregation biases than is the weighting scheme proposed by Coe and Helpman (1995). When the two weighting schemes were nested, the data clearly favored equation (2). Coe and Helpman's methodology has been challenged by Keller (1998) who finds that randomly created bilateral trade shares yield similar results. Keller's evidence does not apply to our methodology, because we do not use bilateral trade shares in total imports and our weights are not constrained to sum to one.

[6] Statistical data on FDI flows are more available than on stocks. In addition, the latter are not comparable across countries, due to heterogeneous evaluation methods.

[7] An alternative specification, with the GDP ($y$) instead of the gross fixed capital formation of country $j$, yields similar results.

[8] The test presented by Levin and Lin (1992) constrains the dynamics of the augmented Dickey-Fuller to be the same across all countries, whereas the test in Levin and Lin (1993) allows the dynamics to differ across countries.

TABLE 1.—TOTAL FACTOR PRODUCTIVITY ESTIMATION RESULTS: TRADE, INWARD FDI, AND OUTWARD FDI, 1971–1990, 260 OBSERVATIONS

| | Within | | | | First Difference | | | |
|---|---|---|---|---|---|---|---|---|
| | (i) | (ii) | (iii) | (iv) | (v) | (vi) | (vii) | (viii) |
| Domestic R&D | | | | | | | | |
| log $S^d$ | 0.045* (0.010) | 0.138* (0.009) | 0.054* (0.008) | 0.017* (0.008) | 0.050* (0.020) | 0.081* (0.020) | 0.062* (0.020) | 0.030 (0.019) |
| Foreign R&D | | | | | | | | |
| log $S^{fm}$ (imports) | 0.154* (0.012) | | | 0.100* (0.010) | 0.067* (0.013) | | | 0.069* (0.013) |
| log $S^{ff}$ (inward FDI) | | −0.006 (0.005) | | | | 0.006 (0.004) | | |
| log $S^{ft}$ (outward FDI) | | | 0.072* (0.005) | 0.053* (0.004) | | | 0.039* (0.009) | 0.040* (0.009) |
| $R^2$-adjusted | 0.779 | 0.628 | 0.805 | 0.857 | 0.147 | 0.063 | 0.120 | 0.213 |
| SSR | 0.457 | 0.771 | 0.403 | 0.295 | 0.175 | 0.192 | 0.181 | 0.161 |
| $F$-test | 62.2* | 30.2* | 72.7* | 98.6* | 22.3* | 9.3* | 17.8* | 23.2* |
| Cointegration tests | | | | | | | | |
| Panel v-statistic | 4.37* | 2.63* | 3.50* | 3.21* | 9.02* | 7.14* | 7.08* | 5.57* |
| Panel ρ-statistic | −1.74* | −1.92* | −0.87 | −0.21 | −4.80* | −3.57* | −3.63* | −2.42* |
| Panel $t$-statistic A | −2.93* | −3.79* | −1.97* | −1.97* | −7.86* | −6.01* | −6.09* | −6.45* |
| Panel $t$-statistic B | −2.91* | −3.99* | −1.74* | −2.13* | −8.48* | −6.64* | −6.38* | −7.40* |
| Group ρ-statistic | −0.27 | −0.25 | 0.59 | 1.20 | −3.41* | −2.25* | −2.30* | −1.06 |
| Group $t$-statistic A | −2.62* | −3.08* | −1.42 | −1.62 | −9.52* | −7.30* | −7.27* | −7.55* |
| Group $t$-statistic B | −2.62* | −3.41* | −1.25 | −2.16* | −10.89* | −8.28* | −7.76* | −9.65* |

The dependent variable is log (total factor productivity), indexed as 1985 = 1. Unreported country-specific fixed effects (within estimates). Standard errors between parentheses. $S^d$ = domestic R&D capital stock; $S^{fm}$ = foreign R&D capital stock embodied in imports; $S^{ff}$ = foreign R&D capital stock embodied in inward FDI; $S^{ft}$ = foreign R&D capital stock embodied in outward FDI; $G7$ = dummy variable equal to one for the G-7 countries and to zero otherwise. * indicates the parameters that are significant at the 10% probability level. The cointegration tests reject the null hypothesis of no cointegration above the absolute value of 1.64 (10% probability threshold); 1.96 (5%) or 2.57 (1%). The panel $t$-statistic A is nonparametric, whereas the B, which corresponds to Levin and Lin (1993) is parametric. All the panel cointegration statistics are reported by Pedroni (1999, table 1).

home country to the host country. One possible explanation would be that the MNEs' aim when establishing subsidiaries abroad is certainly not to diffuse their own technological advantages towards the host country's domestic firms, but rather to exploit more fully their own technological innovations, hence the weak potential diffusion of technology in the host economy. This result is consistent with Dunning's paradigm that companies may prefer to invest abroad in order to take advantage of their own technological base instead of diffusing it internationally.

In regression (iii), the output elasticity of the foreign R&D capital stock embodied in outward FDI flows is positive and highly significant. That is, the hypothesis of technology sourcing is confirmed by our estimates. Through their investments abroad, MNEs seem to be able to source foreign technology bases, thereby increasing the productivity of their home country. Regression (iv) includes the foreign R&D capital stocks embodied in trade and in outward FDI, simultaneously. The output elasticities of the foreign R&D variables associated with outward FDI and imports are both significant and their magnitudes are hardly affected, reinforcing the robustness of our results. The output elasticity of the domestic R&D capital stocks are smaller in regression (iv) than in regressions (i) to (iii). We may infer that not properly taking into account the effective channels of international R&D spillovers leads to upwardly biased estimates of the output elasticity of the domestic R&D capital stock.

Most of the cointegration tests suggest that the regression equation is cointegrated. An interesting feature is that the "panel" tests are more significant than the "group" tests. This is not surprising, because the former take into account country-specific dynamism, whereas the latter constrain the cointegration parameter across countries.[9]

The first-differenced estimates (columns v to viii) broadly confirm the level estimates. The main difference is that the estimated parameters associated with the foreign R&D capital stocks are lower. All cointegration tests confirm that the error term is cointegrated.

Table 2 investigates whether the estimated parameters were higher or lower in the 1970s than they were in the 1980s. It also investigates whether the estimated parameters are different for large industrialized countries (G-7) than for smaller ones. Regression (i) is equivalent to regression (iv) in table 1 for the whole period, and regressions (ii) and (iii) present the econometric results for the seventies (1971–1980) and the eighties (1981–1990), respectively. From the seventies to the eighties, the impact of the R&D capital stock on productivity was stable, as opposed to the impact of foreign R&D capital stocks.

International trade allowed economies to benefit from foreign R&D in both decades, but its role was much greater in the 1970s (7% in the eighties against 14% in the seventies). The reverse is true for outward FDI, which yielded an output elasticity of foreign R&D higher and substantially more significant in the eighties than it did in the seventies. (The estimated parameter is 3.3% in regression (ii) and 5% in regression (iii).) The $F$-test confirms that a significant

[9] Unreported results, similar to those presented in regression (iv) of table 1 but including time dummies lead to the same cointegration tests. The main difference being a lower and marginally significant parameter associated with the domestic R&D capital stock. The inclusion of time dummies does not affect the output elasticity of the foreign R&D capital stocks.

TABLE 2.—TIME AND COUNTRY STABILITY OF THE OUTPUT ELASTICITIES OF DOMESTIC AND FOREIGN R&D

| | Time Stability | | | Larger Countries | | | |
|---|---|---|---|---|---|---|---|
| | 1971–1990 | 1971–1980 | 1981–1990 | | | | |
| | (i) | (ii) | (iii) | (iv) | (v) | (vi) | (vii) |
| Domestic R&D | | | | | | | |
| log $S^d$ | 0.017* (0.008) | 0.037* (0.014) | 0.037* (0.022) | 0.020* (0.010) | 0.089* (0.010) | 0.056* (0.009) | 0.008 (0.009) |
| log $S^d * G7$ | | | | 0.176* (0.022) | 0.193* (0.018) | 0.063* (0.023) | 0.079* (0.022) |
| Foreign R&D | | | | | | | |
| log $S^{fm}$ (imports) | 0.100* (0.010) | 0.136* (0.015) | 0.071* (0.016) | 0.152* (0.016) | | | 0.134* (0.014) |
| log $S^{fm} * G7$ | | | | −0.069* (0.022) | | | −0.088* (0.020) |
| log $S^{ft}$ (inward FDI) | | | | | −0.001 (0.007) | | |
| log $S^{ff} * G7$ | | | | | −0.001) (0.009) | | |
| log $S^{ft}$ (outward FDI) | 0.053* (0.004) | 0.033* (0.010) | 0.050* (0.009) | | | 0.046* (0.007) | 0.029* (0.006) |
| log $S^{ft} * G7$ | | | | | | 0.021* (0.010) | 0.032* (0.009) |
| $R^2$-adjusted | 0.857 | 0.951 | 0.715 | 0.828 | 0.747 | 0.829 | 0.878 |
| SSR | 0.295 | 0.080 | 0.080 | 0.353 | 0.520 | 0.352 | 0.249 |
| *F*-test: struct. change | | | 107* | | | | |

The dependent variable is log (total factor productivity); the right-side variables are $S^d$ = the domestic R&D capital stock, $S^{fm}$ = the stock of foreign R&D embodied in imports, $S^{ft}$ = the stock of foreign R&D embodied in outward FDI; all regressions include unreported country dummies. Standard errors between parentheses, and * indicates that the parameter is significantly different from zero at a 10% probability threshold.

structural change took place between the two decades. From these figures, we may infer that the practice of technology sourcing intensified over the last two decades, emerging overall during the eighties.

Columns (iv) to (vii) of table 2 show the results that allow all the output elasticities with respect to technology variables to differ between G-7 and other countries. This is done by interacting the right-side variables with a dummy variable that takes the value of one for G-7 countries. Regarding the output elasticities with respect to the domestic R&D capital stock and the foreign R&D embodied into outward FDI, it clearly appears that their impact is much higher for the G-7 countries than for smaller countries. The reverse is true for the foreign R&D embodied into trade flows.

Average rates of return to R&D may be obtained by dividing the estimated elasticities by the appropriate ratios of R&D capital stocks to GDP. Our calculations (based on the estimated elasticities of regressions (i) and (vii) of table 2) show that the average rates of return to domestic R&D capital stocks over the period 1971–1990 were 68% in the G-7 countries and 15% in the smaller countries. Concerning the rate of return to foreign R&D, the estimates suggest that a $100 increase in the foreign R&D capital stock of a particular country would increase its GDP by $813 through import flows and by $1,656 through outward foreign direct investment. These very high values are due to the way in which the foreign R&D capital stocks are constructed. An increase of $100 of the foreign R&D capital stock would require a much larger increase of the foreign countries' domestic R&D capital stock, because they are weighted by their GDP and embodied in the flows of imports and/or outward FDI.

We may compute two matrices of bilateral elasticities of output with respect to foreign R&D from the estimated parameters of regression (i) of table 2. In the case of import-embodied spillovers, the elasticity of country $i$'s output with respect to country $j$'s domestic R&D capital stock, $\alpha_{ij}^{fm}$, may be expressed as follows:

$$\alpha_{ij}^{fm} = \frac{\partial \log y_i}{\partial \log S_j^d} = \frac{\partial \log y_i}{\partial \log S_i^{fm}} \cdot \frac{\partial \log S_i^{fm}}{\partial \log S_j^d} = \alpha_i^{fm} \cdot \frac{\partial \log S_i^{fm}}{\partial \log S_j^d} = \alpha_i^{fm} \cdot \frac{\partial S_i^{fm}}{\partial S_j^d} \cdot \frac{S_j^d}{S_i^{fm}}, \tag{5}$$

and because the foreign R&D capital stock depends on the domestic R&D capital stock of each other country:

$$S_i^{fm} = \sum_j \frac{m_{ij} S_j^d}{y_j},$$

equation (5) becomes

$$\alpha_{ij}^{fm} = \alpha_i^{fm} \cdot \frac{m_{ij}}{y_j} \cdot \frac{S_j^d}{S_i^{fm}} = \alpha^{fm} \cdot \frac{m_{ij}}{y_j} \cdot \frac{S_j^d}{S_i^{fm}} \tag{6}$$

Therefore, the elasticity of country $i$'s output with respect to country $j$'s domestic R&D capital stock is an increasing function of its imports from country $j$, and of country $j$'s intensity in R&D. The computed bilateral elasticities for the two channels of R&D spillovers—imports and outward FDI—are presented in table 3.

The figures in table 3 indicate, for example, that a 1% increase in the U.S. R&D capital stock raises Japanese output by 0.0272% through trade flows and by 0.0274% through the Japanese outward FDI in the United States. On the other hand, a 1% increase in the Japanese R&D capital stock raises U.S. output by 0.0120% through trade flows and by only 0.0005% through U.S. outward FDI in the Japanese economy. Technology transfers are indubitably more intense from the United States to Japan than the other way round. When the channel of import flows is considered, we do not find weaker diffusion of Japanese technology with any other country. However, when the channel of technology sourcing is considered, Japanese R&D benefits other countries less than Japan benefits from foreign technology bases.

TABLE 3.—INTERNATIONAL OUTPUT ELASTICITIES OF DOMESTIC R&D CAPITAL STOCKS, 1971–1990

| | GER | FRA | ITA | UK | BEL | DK | GRC | IE | NTH | PT | SP | USA | JAP | Average |
|---|---|---|---|---|---|---|---|---|---|---|---|---|---|---|
| Import flows | | | | | | | | | | | | | | |
| GER | | 0.0145 | 0.0049 | 0.0151 | 0.0068 | 0.0008 | 0.0000 | 0.0002 | 0.0159 | 0.0001 | 0.0003 | 0.0142 | 0.0041 | 0.0127 |
| FRA | 0.0200 | | 0.0047 | 0.0124 | 0.0067 | 0.0003 | 0.0000 | 0.0001 | 0.0062 | 0.0001 | 0.0005 | 0.0124 | 0.0022 | 0.0115 |
| ITA | 0.0211 | 0.0147 | | 0.0089 | 0.0032 | 0.0004 | 0.0000 | 0.0001 | 0.0058 | 0.0000 | 0.0003 | 0.0104 | 0.0013 | 0.0103 |
| UK | 0.0211 | 0.0116 | 0.0031 | | 0.0048 | 0.0011 | 0.0000 | 0.0011 | 0.0117 | 0.0002 | 0.0004 | 0.0248 | 0.0048 | 0.0198 |
| BEL | 0.0584 | 0.0380 | 0.0044 | 0.0361 | | 0.0005 | 0.0000 | 0.0003 | 0.0460 | 0.0001 | 0.0004 | 0.0221 | 0.0036 | 0.0258 |
| DK | 0.0326 | 0.0067 | 0.0022 | 0.0256 | 0.0036 | | 0.0000 | 0.0001 | 0.0091 | 0.0001 | 0.0002 | 0.0132 | 0.0037 | 0.0142 |
| GRC | 0.0241 | 0.0087 | 0.0061 | 0.0113 | 0.0028 | 0.0005 | | 0.0001 | 0.0073 | 0.0000 | 0.0003 | 0.0084 | 0.0067 | 0.0098 |
| IE | 0.0110 | 0.0061 | 0.0016 | 0.1105 | 0.0020 | 0.0004 | 0.0000 | | 0.0051 | 0.0001 | 0.0002 | 0.0273 | 0.0035 | 0.0289 |
| NTH | 0.0555 | 0.0153 | 0.0033 | 0.0282 | 0.0204 | 0.0008 | 0.0000 | 0.0003 | | 0.0001 | 0.0004 | 0.0284 | 0.0038 | 0.0264 |
| PT | 0.0273 | 0.0188 | 0.0063 | 0.0304 | 0.0046 | 0.0005 | 0.0000 | 0.0001 | 0.0088 | | 0.0027 | 0.0246 | 0.0045 | 0.0218 |
| SP | 0.0126 | 0.0102 | 0.0029 | 0.0108 | 0.0016 | 0.0002 | 0.0000 | 0.0001 | 0.0028 | 0.0001 | | 0.0161 | 0.0025 | 0.0126 |
| USA | 0.0052 | 0.0023 | 0.0010 | 0.0074 | 0.0007 | 0.0001 | 0.0000 | 0.0001 | 0.0011 | 0.0000 | 0.0001 | | 0.0118 | 0.0064 |
| JAP | 0.0027 | 0.0013 | 0.0004 | 0.0025 | 0.0003 | 0.0001 | 0.0000 | 0.0000 | 0.0004 | 0.0000 | 0.0000 | 0.0272 | | 0.0183 |
| Outward FDI flows | | | | | | | | | | | | | | |
| GER | | 0.0037 | 0.0007 | 0.0053 | 0.0022 | 0.0001 | 0.0000 | 0.0001 | 0.0020 | 0.0000 | 0.0003 | 0.0198 | 0.0001 | 0.0135 |
| FRA | 0.0032 | | 0.0011 | 0.0110 | 0.0023 | 0.0001 | 0.0000 | 0.0000 | 0.0008 | 0.0000 | 0.0003 | 0.0150 | 0.0000 | 0.0108 |
| ITA | 0.0048 | 0.0119 | | 0.0045 | 0.0019 | 0.0000 | 0.0000 | 0.0000 | 0.0001 | 0.0000 | 0.0006 | 0.0091 | 0.0000 | 0.0071 |
| UK | 0.0009 | 0.0016 | 0.0002 | | 0.0004 | 0.0000 | 0.0000 | 0.0000 | 0.0015 | 0.0000 | 0.0001 | 0.0284 | 0.0000 | 0.0185 |
| BEL | 0.0042 | 0.0054 | 0.0008 | 0.0103 | | 0.0000 | 0.0000 | 0.0000 | 0.0041 | 0.0000 | 0.0002 | 0.0103 | 0.0000 | 0.0079 |
| DK | 0.0039 | 0.0027 | 0.0002 | 0.0178 | 0.0006 | | 0.0000 | 0.0000 | 0.0002 | 0.0000 | 0.0001 | 0.0092 | 0.0000 | 0.0077 |
| GRC | 0.0038 | 0.0021 | 0.0009 | 0.0053 | 0.0000 | 0.0000 | | 0.0000 | 0.0002 | 0.0000 | 0.0000 | 0.0219 | 0.0000 | 0.0137 |
| IE | 0.0001 | 0.0006 | 0.0002 | 0.0177 | 0.0006 | 0.0000 | 0.0000 | | 0.0002 | 0.0000 | 0.0001 | 0.0149 | 0.0000 | 0.0105 |
| NTH | 0.0013 | 0.0020 | 0.0003 | 0.0063 | 0.0012 | 0.0000 | 0.0000 | 0.0000 | | 0.0000 | 0.0002 | 0.0228 | 0.0001 | 0.0143 |
| PT | 0.0025 | 0.0130 | 0.0012 | 0.0117 | 0.0027 | 0.0000 | 0.0000 | 0.0000 | 0.0000 | | 0.0023 | 0.0017 | 0.0000 | 0.0033 |
| SP | 0.0038 | 0.0036 | 0.0014 | 0.0099 | 0.0023 | 0.0000 | 0.0000 | 0.0000 | 0.0001 | 0.0004 | | 0.0120 | 0.0000 | 0.0086 |
| USA | 0.0024 | 0.0021 | 0.0005 | 0.0268 | 0.0011 | 0.0001 | 0.0000 | 0.0001 | 0.0023 | 0.0000 | 0.0002 | | 0.0005 | 0.0076 |
| JAP | 0.0010 | 0.0005 | 0.0001 | 0.0036 | 0.0003 | 0.0000 | 0.0000 | 0.0000 | 0.0003 | 0.0000 | 0.0000 | 0.0274 | | 0.0183 |
| Average foreign output elasticity of domestic R&D capital stock | | | | | | | | | | | | | | |
| Imports | 0.0108 | 0.0061 | 0.0020 | 0.0093 | 0.0026 | 0.0003 | 0.0000 | 0.0001 | 0.0047 | 0.0000 | 0.0002 | 0.0198 | 0.0078 | 0.096 |
| Outward FDI | 0.0023 | 0.0027 | 0.0005 | 0.0158 | 0.0012 | 0.0001 | 0.0000 | 0.0001 | 0.0015 | 0.0000 | 0.0002 | 0.0206 | 0.0003 | 0.035 |
| Sum | 0.0131 | 0.0088 | 0.0025 | 0.0251 | 0.0038 | 0.0004 | 0.0000 | 0.0002 | 0.0062 | 0.0001 | 0.0004 | 0.0404 | 0.0081 | 0.128 |

Estimated elasticity of output in the row country with respect to the R&D capital stock in the column country. Based on regression (iv) of table 1 and on equation (6). Averages in the bottom rows are calculated using GDP weights. Averages in the last column are calculated using domestic R&D capital stocks as weights.

The mean "international" impact of each country's R&D capital stock is illustrated in the bottom rows. A 1% increase in the U.S. (Japanese) R&D capital stock induces a 0.020% (0.008%) increase of foreign output through trade flows and an increase of 0.021% (0.000%) through outward FDI in the USA (Japan). For some countries, the impact of other countries' domestic R&D capital stock is greater through technology sourcing than through import flows. The U.S. R&D capital stock benefits Germany, France, the United Kingdom, Greece, and Japan more through their outward investments into the U.S. boundaries than through their imports from the United States. On average, considerable technological feedbacks are observed through outward FDI directed towards the United Kingdom and the United States. Germany, France, Belgium, and The Netherlands are also "techno-sourced" but to a smaller degree than the United States and the United Kingdom.

The last column shows the average domestic output elasticity of foreign R&D for each country. The domestic output elasticity of foreign R&D embodied in trade flows is the highest in Ireland (2.9%), The Netherlands, Portugal, and Belgium. It is the lowest in the United States (0.64%) and Greece. Other countries for which import-embodied foreign R&D is associated with a relatively high elasticity are the United Kingdom (2%) and Japan (1.8%). Considering the alternative channel of international technology transfer, Japan and the United Kingdom benefit the most from outward FDI: their output elasticities are the highest (about 1.8%). In contrast, the potential technology embodied in outward FDI contributes only marginally to the productivity of Portugal, Italy, the United States, and Denmark.

These results may be compared with those obtained in the existing empirical literature, which were summarized by Mohnen (1996). A first observation was that foreign R&D contributes to productivity growth more in small countries than in large countries.

Figure 1 clearly shows that it depends on the channel considered. The output elasticity of foreign R&D embodied in imports is, indeed, generally higher in smaller countries. Some exceptions show up, characterized by the relatively weak elasticities in Greece and Denmark, and the relatively high elasticities in the United Kingdom and Japan. If the focus is put on the technology sourcing channel, there is no evidence that the foreign R&D embodied in outward FDI benefits more or less the small countries. Figure 2 demonstrates that the larger a country is, the greater the relative

FIGURE 1.—DOMESTIC OUTPUT ELASTICITIES OF FOREIGN R&D EMBODIED IN IMPORTS AND IN OUTWARD FDI

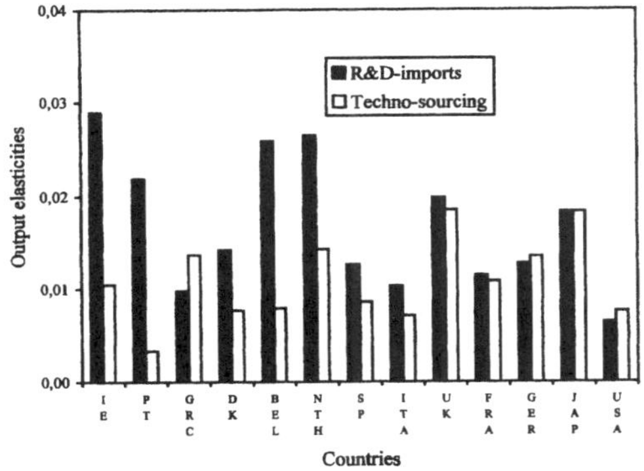


Source: cf. Table 3; last column. The countries are ordered according to their GDP size.

FIGURE 3.—HOW DOMESTIC R&D CONTRIBUTES TO INTERNATIONAL PRODUCTIVITY GROWTH (AVERAGE FOREIGN OUTPUT ELASTICITY OF DOMESTIC R&D, BY COUNTRY)

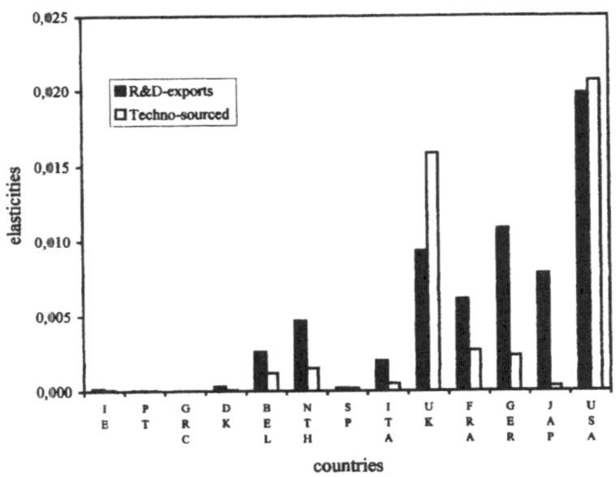


Source: cf. Table 3, bottom rows. The countries are ordered according to their GDP size.

impact of its technology sourcing activities, as compared to the impact of import-embodied foreign R&D.

A second "stylized fact" cited by Mohnen (1996) was that the output elasticity of foreign R&D is higher than the output elasticity of domestic R&D. The last row and the last column of table 3 confirm this statement for the smallest countries: smaller countries all have an aggregate output elasticity of foreign R&D much larger than their output elasticity of domestic R&D. But the reverse is true for large countries, even if the output elasticity of foreign R&D embodied in imports is added to the output elasticity of foreign R&D embodied in outward FDI flows.

The third observation was that the United States is an important R&D spillover generator but a weak spillover receiver, and that the spillovers emanating from Japan are

FIGURE 2.—THE RELATIVE IMPORTANCE OF EACH CHANNEL, BY COUNTRY

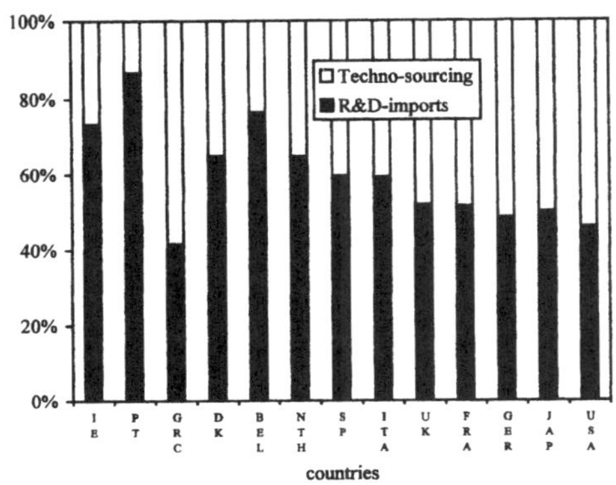


Source: derived from Table 3; last column. The countries are ordered according to their GDP size.

weak, if not nonexistent. Our results for the United States are consistent with the findings of previous studies: the United States appears to benefit less from foreign R&D than other countries benefit from U.S. R&D. (See figure 1 and 3.) One's assessment of Japan's "technology trade balance" depends on the channel of international technology flows considered. Through trade flows, Japan does substantially contribute to foreign productivity, to the same extent that it benefits from outside R&D. However, there is no R&D spillover emanating from outward FDI directed towards Japan, whereas the foreign R&D embodied in Japanese outward FDI contributes to improve its productivity to the same extent that the foreign R&D embodied in its imports does. Concerning outward FDI in the large European countries, Germany and France seem similar to Japan: they benefit more from their own outward FDI abroad than the rest of the world benefits from its outward FDI directed towards them. The United Kingdom is much more similar to the United States in the sense that the benefits it receives from outside R&D are roughly equal to the benefits its R&D confers on the rest of the world, through the channel of technology sourcing.

## IV. Concluding Remarks

We used Coe and Helpman's framework, as modified by Lichtenberg and van Pottelsberghe, to test whether inward and outward FDI are effective in the international diffusion of technology. The empirical results showed that outward FDI flows and import flows are two simultaneous channels through which technology spills over and benefits other industrialized countries. We therefore give credence to the hypothesis of technology sourcing associated with MNEs' activities abroad, and confirm Dunning's (1994) expectation that "where foreign production adds to domestic production, the R&D base of the investing company is strengthened—whatever the nationality of the firm." Contrary to frequent conjectures, inward FDI flows do not seem to contribute to the improvement (or to the reduction) of the technological base of host economies. Our results suggest that inward FDI, on average, take on the characteristics of a Trojan horse; they are intended more to take advantage of the technology base of the host countries than to diffuse the technological advantage originating in the home country. This "technological boomerang" feature emerged mainly during the eighties.

We also found that the ratio of foreign R&D benefits conveyed by outward FDI to foreign R&D benefits conveyed by imports is higher for large countries than it is for small ones, and that failure to account for international R&D spillovers leads to upwardly biased estimates of the output elasticity of the domestic R&D capital stock.

Finally, it is widely believed that the United States is an important R&D spillover generator but a weak spillover receiver, whereas Japan benefits a lot from outside R&D and the R&D spillovers emanating from its boundaries are weak, if not nonexistent. Our results all too amply corroborate the picture for the United States. Concerning Japan, it depends on the channel considered. Japan contributes to international output growth through its exports, but there is no R&D spillovers emanating from outward FDI directed towards Japan.

REFERENCES


Bernstein, J. I., and P. Mohnen, "International R&D Spillovers between U.S. and Japanese R&D Intensive Sectors," NBER working paper no 4682 (1995).

Cantwell, J., "Technological Innovation and Multinational Corporations," (Oxford: Basil Blackwell, 1989).

Coe, D. T., and E. Helpman, "International R&D Spillovers," *European Economic Review* 39(5) (1995), 859–887.

Dunning, J. H., "Multinational Enterprises and the Globalization of Innovatory Capacity," *Research Policy* 23(1) (1994), 67–88.

Im, Pesaran, and Shin, "Testing for Unit Root in Heterogeneous Panels," University of Cambridge discussion paper, University of Cambridge (June 1996).

Kogut, B., and S. J. Chang, "Technological Capabilities and Japanese Foreign Direct Investment in the United States," this REVIEW 73(3) (1991), 401–413.

Keller, W., "Are International R&D Spillovers Trade-Related? Analyzing Spillovers among Randomly Matched Trade Partners," University of Wisconsin-Madison mimeograph (1996).

Levin, A., and C. Lin, "Unit Root Tests in Panel Data: Asymptotic and Finite-Sample Properties," University of California, San Diego discussion paper (December 1992).

———, "Unit Root Tests in Panel Data: New Results," University of California, San Diego discussion paper (May 1993).

Lichtenberg, F., and B. van Pottelsberghe de la Potterie, "International R&D Spillovers: A Comment," *European Economic Review* 42(8) (1998), 1483–1491.

Mohnen, P., "Some Estimates of International R&D Spillovers," Université du Québec à Montréal manuscript (January 1996).

Nadiri, M. I., "U.S. Direct Investment and the Production Structure of the Manufacturing Sector in France, Germany, Japan, and the U.K.," NBER working paper (September 1991).

Neven, D., and G. Siotis, "Foreign Direct Investment in the European Community: Some Policy Issues," *Oxford Review of Economic Policy* 9(2) (1993), 72–93.

———, "Technology Sourcing and FDI in the EC: An Empirical Evaluation," *International Journal of Industrial Organization* 14(5) (1996), 543–560.

Pedroni, P., "Critical Values for Cointegration Tests in Heterogenous Panels with Multiple Regressors," *Oxford Bulletin of Economics and Statistics* 61(1) (1999), 653–670.

Soete, L., and P. Patel, "Recherche-Développement, Importations Technologiques et Croissance "Economique," *Revue Economique* 36(5) (1985), 975–1000.

Yamawaki, H., "International Competitiveness and the Choice of Entry Mode: Japanese Multinationals in US and European Manufacturing Industries," A CEPR Workshop, Oxford. (November 12–13, 1993).


## APPENDIX A

### Data Sources and Definitions

The total factor productivity index $F$ comes from Coe and Helpman (1995, table A.1); it is defined as $F = Y/[K^{\beta}L^{(1-\beta)}]$, where $Y$ is value added in the business sector, $K$ is the stock of business sector capital, and $L$ is employment in the business sector. All variables are constructed as indices with 1985 = 1. The coefficient $\beta$ is the average share of capital income from 1987 to 1989. See Coe and Helpman for a detailed description of the other data sources.

The estimates of domestic business sector R&D capital stocks (lagged one year) are described by Coe and Helpman (p. 878). We have reestimated the value of the domestic R&D capital stocks from the indices provided in table A.3 of Coe and Helpman and the value of the stock in 1990, provided in their table A.7. The domestic R&D capital stocks are in U.S. dollars, based on PPPs and in constant 1985 prices.

The three different foreign R&D capital stocks have been computed from the domestic R&D capital stock of each country. The formulas are presented in the text. The GDP and the Gross Fixed Capital Formation for each country comes from the OECD's *Main Economic Indicators*. For Israel, the GDP data are from the IMF's *Statistical Yearbook*. Bilateral imports flows, in constant 1985 prices, were used for each year, from 1971 to 1990 based on data from the United Nation's *International Trade Statistics Yearbooks*. (Coe and Helpman used data from the IMF's *Direction of Trade*.) The ratios of the imports of goods and services to GDP (both in current price) come from Coe and Helpman's table A.6 and are from the IMF's *Direction of Trade*. National total inward and outward foreign direct investments flows come from three OECD publications: *Recent Trends in International Direct Investment* (1981, 1987) and the *International Direct Investment Statistics Yearbook 1993*. They are deflated in constant 1990 price (GDP deflator). To avoid sharp yearly fluctuations, the series of inward and outward FDI flows have been computed within a four-years moving average framework (the average of the present and the three preceding years). There are no complete time series of bilateral inward FDI flows over the period 1970 to 1990.

We have computed two bilateral inward FDI shares matrices (representing for each country the distribution of inward FDI over the origin countries), one for the 1970s and one for the 1980s from the available data provided by the OECD publications during the two decades. We used these shares to estimate the yearly bilateral inward FDI flows from the total inward FDI flows described here above. From 1970 to 1975, the 1970s weighting matrix has been used. From 1985 to 1990, the 1980s weighting matrix has been used. For each year during the period 1975–1985, we assumed a constant yearly rate of growth of each weighting components of the 1970s matrix to the corresponding components of the 1980s matrix. Because these weighting components have sometimes weak negative values, we have set all negative values to zero, because the stock of foreign R&D may be zero but not negative. The bilateral outward FDI flows are the transposed of the bilateral inward FDI flows, for each country and each year.

*Journal of Economic Literature*
*Vol. XLII (September 2004) pp. 752–782*

# International Technology Diffusion

WOLFGANG KELLER[1]

## 1. *Introduction*

Productivity differences explain a large part of the variation in incomes across countries, and technology plays a key role in determining productivity (William Easterly and Ross Levine 2001; Robert Hall and Charles Jones 1999; Edward Prescott 1998).[2] For most countries, foreign sources of technology account for 90 percent or more of domestic productivity growth. At present, only a handful of rich countries account for most of the world's creation of new technology.[3] The pattern of worldwide technical change is thus determined in large part by international technology diffusion. What determines the extent of technology flows between countries and the means by which technology diffuses? This paper surveys what is known about the extent of international technology diffusion and the channels through which technology is spread.

International technology diffusion is important because it determines the pace at which the world's technology frontier may expand in the future. Do countries' incomes converge over time or not? The answer turns on whether technology diffusion is global or local, as several widely used models show (Gene Grossman and Elhanan Helpman 1991; Peter Howitt 2000; Luis Rivera-Batiz and Paul Romer 1991). [4] A better understanding of technical change therefore provides insights on the likelihood that certain less-developed countries will catch-up to rich countries.

Some of the major channels for technology diffusion across countries may include international trade and foreign direct investment (FDI), both of which are discussed in this survey. There is evidence that imports are a significant channel of technology diffusion. At the same time, the evidence for benefits associated with exporting is weaker. The importance of FDI has long been emphasized in the case-study literature, and recently that

[1] University of Texas, Austin; NBER and CEPR. I have benefited from discussions related to this paper with Bob Baldwin, Elhanan Helpman, Danny Quah, Andres Rodriguez-Claré, Dani Rodrik, Jim Tybout, and Stephen Yeaple. Oded Galor, Peter Howitt, Sam Kortum, Pete Klenow, Pierre Mohnen, Jim Rauch, Carol Shiue, Dan Trefler, and seminar participants at Industry Canada, three anonymous referees and John McMillan provided helpful comments. Support by NSF grant SES 9818902 is gratefully acknowledged.

[2] In addition, institutions and policy have been emphasized as well; see, e.g., Daron Acemoglu, Simon Johnson, and James Robinson (2001); Abhijit Banerjee and Lakshmi Iyer (2003); and Carol Shiue and Wolfgang Keller (2004).

[3] The G-7 countries (the largest seven industrialized countries) accounted for about 84 percent of the world's research and development (R&D) spending in 1995, for example; their share in world GDP was only 64 percent. The world's distribution of production is much less skewed.

[4] The models differ in that some predict global diffusion would lead to convergence in productivity levels while others predict convergence in productivity growth rates; see Philippe Aghion and Peter Howitt (1998) and Charles Jones (1995), as well as the framework in section 2.

evidence has been complemented by some micro-econometric findings.

Despite the global reach of computer programs, there is no indication that a global pool of technology yet exists. This localized character of technology suggests that an important component of it is tacit in nature. Although the relative importance of international technology diffusion appears to be increasing along with higher levels of economic integration, international diffusion of technology is neither inevitable nor automatic. Domestic technology investments are necessary.

Before discussing some of the evidence in more detail (sections 6–8), section 2 presents a conceptual framework that will guide this discussion. The following sections review various measures of technology (section 3) and technology diffusion (section 4) that are available, while section 5 discusses the pros and cons of a number of empirical approaches that have been employed. Section 9 summarizes the overall evidence on international technology diffusion, and section 10 contains a synthesis and some suggestions for future work.

## 2. *International Technology Diffusion: A Framework for Analysis*

Theories of endogenous technical change of the early 1990s (Aghion and Howitt 1992; Grossman and Helpman 1991; Romer 1990; and Paul Segerstrom, T.C.A. Anant, and Elias Dinopoulos 1990) emphasize two aspects of technology:[5, 6]

1. Technology is non-rival in the sense that the marginal costs for an additional agent to use the technology are negligible.[7]
2. The return to technological investments is partly private and partly public.

Point 1 distinguishes technology from rival factor inputs such as human and physical capital; the latter can only be used by one firm at a time, or put differently, the marginal costs of using the same factor somewhere else are infinite. Point 2 highlights that while private returns must be strong enough to keep innovation ongoing, technological investments often create benefits to individuals other than the inventor.[8] These external effects are called technology, or knowledge, spillovers. As an example, the introduction of one product might speed up the invention of a competing product, because the second inventor can learn from the first by carefully studying the product or its product design (the "blueprint").

The focus of this paper is the empirics of international technology diffusion and its effect on productivity.[9] Before discussing the empirical results, I will lay out a model of international technology diffusion, based on Jonathan Eaton and Samuel Kortum (1999) and Kortum (1997), to help clarify the issues.

Consider a model with $n=1,\ldots,N$ countries. Output in $n$ at time $t$, $Y_{nt}$, is produced by combining intermediate inputs subject to a constant-returns-to-scale Cobb-Douglas production function:

$$\ln\left(Y_{nt} / J\right) = J^{-1} \int^{J} \ln\left[Z_{nt}(j) X_{nt}(j)\right] dj, \qquad (1)$$

where $X_{nt}(j)$ is the quantity of intermediate

[5] See Grossman and Helpman (1995) and Aghion and Howitt (1998) for broader overviews. I will also discuss some related work on learning-by-doing and human-capital accumulation that falls into the broad category of models of knowledge accumulation.

[6] Many of these ideas have been discussed in the literature before; important contributors include Paul David, Giovanni Dosi, Robert Evenson, Jan Fagerberg, Richard Nelson, Keith Pavitt, Nathan Rosenberg, Luc Soete, Sidney Winter, Larry Westphal, and others (see Fagerberg 1994, and Robert Evenson and Larry Westphal 1995 for overviews). What distinguishes the recent work is that it includes fully specified general equilibrium models. This means that these technology effects can in principle be estimated in a well-defined framework.

[7] Other authors have coined the terms "perfectly expansible" (David 1992) and "infinitely expansible" (Danny Quah 2001a,b) to positively define this characteristic.

[8] The focus of this work is on technical change driven by private, not public, research. The majority of all research and development (R&D) is privately funded, although public R&D is substantial in many countries.

[9] International technology diffusion in this paper refers to both technology spillovers as well as non-spillovers. As will be discussed below, the two are often difficult to separate.

input $j$ at time $t$ in country $n$ and $Z_{nt}(j)$ is the quality of that input. This quality is increased over time through new ideas, or technologies. The range of inputs is the same across countries and constant over time. Output is homogeneous and tradable, while intermediates are nontraded.

Each input $j$ is produced anywhere by a Cobb-Douglas combination of capital $K(j)$ and labor $L(j)$, $X(j)=K(j)^{\phi}L(j)^{1-\phi}$, with $\phi\in[0,1]$. New technologies are the result of research effort. Consider country $i$ at time $t$ with $L_{it}$ workers. If a fraction $s_{it}$ of them are engaged in research, they create new technologies at rate $\alpha_{it}s_{it}^{\beta}L_{it}$, where $\alpha_{it}$ is the research productivity, and $\beta>0$ characterizes the R&D talent distribution.

Each technology has three dimensions: (i) quality, (ii) use, and (iii) diffusion time lag. First, the quality of a technology is a random variable drawn from the cumulative distribution $F(q)$, $F(q)=1-q^{\theta}$, $\theta>0$. This quality is common to all countries to which the technology diffuses. Second, the technology can be used only in one intermediate sector, which is determined randomly.

Third, technologies become productive only once they have diffused. Diffusion is a stochastic process, with a mean diffusion lag between country $i$ and country $n$ of $\varepsilon_{ni}^{-1}$, or, $\varepsilon_{ni}$ measures the speed of technology diffusion between the countries. The rate at which technologies diffuse to country $n$ at time $t$ is given by

$$\dot{\mu}_{nt} = J^{-1}\sum\nolimits_{i=1}^{N} \underbrace{\varepsilon_{ni}}_{A} \underbrace{\int_{-\infty}^{t} e^{-\varepsilon_{ni}(t-s)}\alpha_{is}s_{is}{}^{\beta}L_{is}\,ds}_{B}, \quad (2)$$

where $A$ in equation (2) is the bilateral speed of diffusion, and $B$ is country $i$'s cumulative output of technologies up to time $t$.[10]

Even though every technology will eventually be in every country (assuming $\varepsilon_{ni}>0$), a given technology may not be employed in production, because by the time it has diffused it is dominated by a higher quality. The stock of technologies in country $n$ at time $t$ is $\mu_{nt}=\int_{-\infty}^{t}\dot{\mu}_{ns}ds$. The fraction of intermediates in country $n$ at time $t$ that are below some quality threshold $\bar{q}$ is decreasing in $u_{nt}$, because the higher is the number of diffused technologies, the greater is the likelihood that the quality in country $n$'s sectors is relatively high.

Let $A_{nt}$ be the geometric mean of qualities across sectors. Final output (1) is maximized when factors are evenly divided across all sectors, and it is given by $A_{nt}K_{nt}^{\phi}[L_{nt}(1-s_{nt})]^{1-\phi}$. This means that $A_{nt}$ is equal to output divided by a factor-share weighted sum of inputs, or total factor productivity (TFP).[11]

To obtain a steady-state equilibrium where $\mu_{nt}$ grows at the same constant rate in all countries in the long run, we assume that the research productivity $\alpha_{it}$ is given by $\alpha_{it}=\alpha(\mu_{it}/\bar{\mu}_t)\,\bar{\mu}_t^{\gamma}$; $\mu_t=\sum_{i=1}^{N}\mu_{it}$, $\gamma\leq 1$, and $\alpha>0$. The higher is $\gamma$, the greater is the strength of the international research spillovers.[12] Finally, steady-state relative TFP levels can be computed as

$$\frac{A_{nt}}{A_{Nt}} = \left(\frac{\mu_{nt}}{\mu_{Nt}}\right)^{1/\theta}, \; n = 1,\dots,N-1, \quad (3)$$

and world TFP growth is proportional to

$$g = \frac{\dot{\mu}_n}{\mu_n} = \frac{\alpha}{J}\sum_{i=1}^{N}\frac{\varepsilon_{ni}}{\varepsilon_{ni}+g}\frac{\mu_i}{\mu_n}s_i{}^{\beta}L_i, \quad n = 1,\dots,N, \quad (4)$$

where $(\mu_i/\mu_n)$ and the share of labor in research, $s_iL_i$, are constant in steady-state. Equation (4) says that world growth is proportional to a weighted sum of research efforts in all countries.

[10] Past R&D is discounted because the technologies might have been superseded by higher-quality, more recent technologies.

[11] Eaton and Kortum (1999) show that due to imperfect competition, TFP is not identical to $A_{nt}$, but it is proportional to it; also see their paper for the exact definition of $A_{nt}$.

[12] For simplicity, we set $\gamma$ to equal one. The parameter $\gamma$ is related to the question of whether the model has "scale effects"; see, e.g., Jones (1995), and Aghion and Howitt (1998) ch. 12, for more details.

The model has a number of implications:

1) Foreign R&D raises domestic TFP: An increase in foreign research leads to a greater inflow of technologies and higher TFP. This holds in both the short and the long-runs (equations 2, 3 respectively).[13]
2) Receiving technology from abroad: A given research effort abroad has a greater effect on domestic TFP, the faster foreign technologies diffuse to the domestic economy ($\varepsilon_{ni}$ in equation 2).
3) Global sources of technology: A country is important in determining the world's rate of growth if it has (i) a relatively high share of the world's research labor and technologies ($s_i L_i$ and $\mu_i$ in equation 4), and/or (ii) a relatively high rate of technology diffusion to other countries (the weight $\varepsilon_{ni}/(\varepsilon_{ni}+g)$ in equation 4 is increasing in $\varepsilon_{ni}$).

International technology diffusion in this framework captures the notion that product quality innovations of country $i$ become available in country $n$ at rate $\varepsilon_{ni}$. Moreover, this is a spillover, because although research is costly in country $i$ (it withdraws labor from final output production), conditional on the technology having diffused, it can be used to produce final output there without incurring additional costs. The diffusion of technology from country $i$ also raises the productivity of research in country $n$ due to the international research spillover (as long as $\gamma>0$). An alternative, partial-spillover interpretation may be that the diffusion lag $\varepsilon_{ni}^{-1}$ is indicative of the strength of costly country-$n$ technology investment to acquire the technology from country $i$.

In either case, it becomes clear that our ability to give the diffusion rates $\varepsilon_{ni}$ a structural interpretation that can be empirically tested is crucial for making further progress. Which are the major channels of international technology diffusion, or, what is behind the rates $\varepsilon_{ni}$? This is the question that is addressed by the major portion of the literature to date, and will be reviewed in sections 6–9. A number of issues are important when thinking about the strength of different diffusion channels. I will briefly turn to them now.

How do technologies move from one country to another? One possibility is through international trade in intermediate goods (Rivera-Batiz and Romer 1991; Grossman and Helpman 1991; and Eaton and Kortum 2002).[14] Employing a foreign intermediate good in final-output production involves the implicit usage of the technology in embodied form. There is a spillover in this process of international technology diffusion to the extent that the intermediate good costs less than its opportunity costs—which include the R&D costs of product development. If trade is an important diffusion channel, one should expect that international technology diffusion is geographically localized, because of the well-documented fact that trade falls with geographic distance (e.g., Edward Leamer and James Levinsohn 1995). In any case, this is a relatively weak form of technology diffusion, because the technology as such is not available domestically—only the manufactured outcome of it is.

Of course, international technology diffusion is not limited to the channel of trade. In principle, just as researchers today "stand on the shoulders" of researchers of the past, one might expect researchers in one country to directly benefit from research conducted in other countries.[15] The model above captures this in that research productivity $\alpha_{it}$ is proportional to the global stock of technologies $\bar{\mu}_t$), which is increasing in world R&D. This is an international R&D spillover (i.e., no domestic opportunity

[13] The same equations indicate that domestic R&D raises TFP as well.

[14] In the model above, this is not explicitly modeled, but it would suggest that $\varepsilon_{ni}$ is related to intermediate inputs trade; see the analysis in Eaton and Kortum (1996).

[15] See Ricardo Caballero and Adam Jaffe (1993) for empirical results in a closed economy.

costs).[16] Moreover, this seems to be a stronger form of diffusion than the intermediate goods trade discussed above: if the foreign technology raises the productivity of domestic researchers, it suggests full mastery of the technology, as opposed to only the ability to use the technology that is embodied in the intermediate good.

Which patterns of technology diffusion should thus be expected? The first type of diffusion above suggests that it should follow the pattern of intermediate goods trade. International R&D spillovers appear to be more difficult to pin down. They are the result of acquiring technology that is not tied to any particular form. In addition to libraries, conferences and other sources, technology may be stored in as little as a couple of bytes, and thus sent over the internet to practically every country in the world at close to zero marginal cost. At the same time, this does not mean that this technology diffusion in fact creates equal levels of technological knowledge in all countries, for the following reasons.

First, irrespective of feasibility, it is not in the interest of the original inventor—who has incurred the R&D cost—to send it to others at no charge. On the contrary, the inventor may decide to spend additional resources to keep the technology secret. Second, even if some domestic technology becomes available abroad, it may be possible to preclude others from using it by patenting the technology. Third, even if the technology is non-rival and can be moved from one country to another at zero marginal costs, operating the technology efficiently often requires making costly investments in terms of complementary skills (see section 8).

Another issue is that technology may in fact not be transferable at essentially zero cost even if all parties involved desire this, such as multinational parents providing technology to their subsidiaries. David Teece (1977) estimates that the costs of such within-firm transfers were on average almost 20 percent of the total project costs in the cases he analyzed.[17] One reason for that is that only the broad outlines of technology are codified—the remainder remains "tacit" (Michael Polanyi 1958).[18] In this view, knowledge is to some extent tacit because the person who is actively engaged in a problem-solving activity cannot necessarily define (and hence prescribe) what exactly she is doing. Technology is only partially codified because it is impossible or at least very costly to fully codify it.

What does this imply for the channels of international technology diffusion? Polanyi (1958, p. 53) argues that tacit knowledge can be passed on only "by example from master to apprentice." A broader view is that non-codified knowledge is often transferred through person-to-person demonstrations and instructions (David 1992). The most effective way of doing this, despite telephone, video, and other remote methods, is face-to-face interaction. This, however, means that technology diffusion implies incurring the costs of moving teacher and student into the same geographic location.

We can summarize the implications of this for the pattern of international technology diffusion as follows.

1) The partial codified nature of technology means that technology diffusion will be incomplete, and technology stocks in different countries will vary. Diffusion will tend to be more geographically localized the higher is the non-codified share in total technology.[19]

[16] Recall that we assume $\gamma$ is equal to 1. More generally, there is an international R&D spillover as long as $\gamma>0$.

[17] For transferring machinery equipment technology, this share was 36 percent (Teece 1977, p. 248); see also Eric von Hippel (1994).

[18] See also Kenneth Arrow (1969), David (1992), and Evenson and Westphal (1995), and references given there.

[19] This follows because the costs of moving people in space are typically increasing in geographic distance; see von Hippel (1994) and Maryann Feldman and Frank Lichtenberg (1997) for empirical support.

2) Because international economic activities (trade, FDI, etc.) lead to additional contacts with foreign persons who may possess advanced technological knowledge (exporter, importer, engineers, researchers), this may stimulate the diffusion of (non-codified) foreign technology.

Trade and interaction with multinationals may thus lead not only to technology diffusion of the limited kind (technology embodied in intermediate goods), but it may also raise the probability of international R&D spillovers.[20]

I now turn to how recent empirical work has studied these issues. The following two sections discuss the data that is available on technology (section 3) and technology diffusion (section 4).

## 3. *Measures of Technology*

Technology is an intangible that is difficult to measure directly. Three widely used indirect approaches are to measure (1) inputs (R&D), (2) outputs (patents), and (3) the effect of technology (higher productivity).

First, internationally comparable data on R&D expenditures have been published by the Organization of Economic Cooperation and Development (OECD) since about 1965. According to the OECD's definition (OECD 2002), only about two dozen relatively rich countries report substantial amounts of R&D, because the definition captures primarily resources spent towards innovation, and not those spent on imitation and technology adoption. Technology investments of middle and poor countries can therefore typically not be analyzed using R&D data.[21]

[20] This process could also in part be sequential: (1) using foreign technology in embodied form, and gradually (2) learning of the technology per se, (3) imitation, and (4) (original) innovation.

[21] However, R&D data becomes more widely available as countries' incomes are rising. There is also increasingly information on poorer countries because surveys encompass the R&D conducted by affiliates of multinational companies located abroad; see e.g. NSF (2004) for R&D expenditures of U.S. firms in China. The main OECD R&D statistics are on a geographic, not ownership, basis.

A drawback of R&D as a measure of technology is that it ignores the stochastic nature of the process of innovation. The current flow of R&D expenditures is thus a noisy measure of technology improvements in that period. Many authors construct R&D stocks from the flows using the perpetual inventory method.[22] Beyond year-to-year noise, the return to R&D expenditures may vary substantially across agents and over time, which limits comparability. One important aspect of this is that the return to publicly funded R&D is lower than the return to privately funded R&D (Frank Lichtenberg 1993), so that many studies focus on business research and development spending.

Second, a patent gives its holder a temporary legal monopoly to use an innovation in a specific market at the price of public disclosure of technical information in the patent description.[23] An innovation must be sufficiently important to be worthy of a patent, which is judged by a trained official (called patent examiner). Relative to R&D, patents have the advantage that patent data has been collected for a longer time (more than 150 years for some countries), and also poorer countries have a substantial number of patents (see WIPO 2003).

There are some issues with using patent data as well. First, a small number of patents accounts for most of the value of all patents. This means that simple patent counts may not measure technology output well. Recent work has addressed this issue in part by using citation-weighted patent data (see Adam Jaffe and Manuel Trajtenberg 2002).[24] Second, the patent decision is an act of choice on the part of the firm, and a large set of innovations is not

[22] This requires an assumption on the rate of R&D depreciation; standard values range between 0 and 10 percent; see Zvi Griliches (1995).

[23] See Griliches (1990) for more discussion.

[24] Typically, a patent contains one or more references to other patents that indicate which earlier knowledge was used to come up with the technology underlying the present patent application; these references are called patent citations.

ever patented.[25] And third, if technology is in part non-codifiable, as argued above, patent statistics will necessarily miss that part.

The third measure of technology discussed here is total factor productivity (TFP). The idea, well-known since the 1950s, is that if one subtracts from output the contribution of inputs such as labor and capital, the remainder is due to the factor "technology."[26] A simple example is the term $A$ in the Cobb-Douglas production function $Y=AK^{\alpha}L^{1-\alpha}$. Other TFP measures are more general and have certain desirable properties that are important for comparability (e.g. the "superlative" index proposed by Richard Caves, Laurits Christensen, and Erwin Diewert 1982).

In contrast to R&D and patents, TFP is a derived measure of technology, as it is computed from data on inputs and output. This introduces measurement error and perhaps biases, because the appropriate data on inputs and outputs is rarely, if ever, available. Hajime Katayama, Shihua Lu, and James Tybout (2003), for example, show that the use of (1) real sales revenues, (2) depreciated capital spending, and (3) real input expenditures; instead of (unavailable) data on the physical quantities (1) of output, (2) of capital, and (3) of intermediate inputs, as is frequently done, will often confound higher productivity with higher mark-ups. [27] Other factors might thus contaminate the use of TFP as a measure of technological efficiency, which ultimately goes back to the concern that TFP is constructed as a residual, and may potentially capture a host of spurious influences (Moses Abramovitz 1956).

Because of these difficulties in computing TFP, researchers have pursued a number of strategies. One is to consider changes in TFP as opposed to TFP levels. This will help in identifying technology (or rather, technical change) if spurious factors do not change over time, or more generally, if they change less than technology. For example, in Katayama, Lu, and Tybout's (2003) case from above, if a firm faces higher adjustment costs to changing its mark-up, this will reduce the mark-up variability in equilibrium. A second strategy has been to employ TFP measures in studies of technical change together with data on R&D (e.g., Griliches 1984). By establishing a relationship between TFP changes and its presumed major cause, R&D spending, the likelihood of measuring changes in technology inappropriately is substantially reduced.

I now turn to measures of technology diffusion and spillovers.[28]

## 4. *Measures of International Technology Diffusion*

The diffusion of technology involves both market transactions and externalities (see above), and obtaining data on the former is fairly straightforward. For instance, firms make royalty payments for their use of patents, licenses, and copyrights, and this data is available for major countries in the international services balance (e.g., OECD 2003). Many economists believe, though, that most international technology diffusion occurs not through market transactions but instead through externalities (spillovers).[29]

[25] The fact that there is variation in the propensity to patent in several dimensions—for instance, it is profitable to patent only in a large-enough market—could also provide important information.

[26] See Charles Hulten (2000) for more details on TFP.

[27] This could have major social welfare implications as consumers benefit from higher productivity but not from higher mark-ups. See also Tor Klette and Griliches (1996), as well as Eric Bartelsman and Mark Doms (2000) for a recent analysis of micro productivity data.

[28] Sometimes firm-level datasets provide information on the fraction of computer-controlled machinery, or whether a firm satisfies certain technological standard; either of these would also provide information about the technological sophistication of the firm.

[29] One reason is that technology is not fully codifiable, so that complete contracts cannot be written. Another reason is market failure in the market for technology due to asymmetric information: the buyer does not know (the productivity of) the technology, while the seller cannot commit to truthful claims about it. This is considered to be a major reason why international technology transfers are often internalized within firms (between multinational parent and subsidiary); see, e.g., William Ethier (1986).

Naturally, data on spillovers does not exist. Measures that are related to it do exist, but typically they capture spillovers only partially, because the measures do not account for costs of acquisition (learning). For instance, if one patent application cites an earlier patent, this generally indicates that the applicant has benefited from the earlier patent.[30] At the same time, it is impossible to know how large these benefits are net of the learning costs that the patent applicant had to incur.

Among the different methods that try to measure international spillovers, the largest set of papers employs international R&D spillover regressions. In one set of papers, if R&D of firm $j$ is positively correlated with TFP in firm $i$, all else equal, this is consistent with international technology spillovers from firm $j$ to firm $i$ (e.g., Keller 2002a).[31] A variant of this approach replaces TFP by the number of patents (e.g. Lee Branstetter 2001b), and Giovanni Peri (2002) presents a hybrid approach by relating patents in region $i$ to patents in other regions, where the latter is instrumented by R&D expenditures.

There are two alternatives to this basic approach, a generalization and a simplification. In the former, a particular channel of technology diffusion is added to the analysis. David Coe and Elhanan Helpman (1995), e.g., analyze the relationship between productivity and foreign R&D conditional on imports from that foreign country. The other alternative to the international R&D spillover regressions is to relate productivity not to foreign R&D, but to other measures of foreign activity; Brian Aitken and Ann Harrison (1999), e.g., study the correlation of inward FDI and domestic firm productivity (so-called FDI spillover regressions).

A common concern in these studies is that, for various reasons, the estimate might give us correlations but not causal effects. These, as well as issues in other approaches, such as estimates of spillovers as the parameter $\varepsilon_{ni}$ in the model of section 2, are discussed in the following section.

## 5. *Empirical Methods*

### 5.1 *Case Studies*

Case studies can offer a rich description of the setting and the major factors that determine international technology diffusion. For instance, the paper by Felipe Larrain, Luis Lopez-Calva, and Andres Rodriguez-Claré (2000) analyzes whether Intel's foreign direct investment into Costa Rica in the 1990s generated any technology spillovers. The authors have spoken to the main actors, including Intel's top management and the government of Costa Rica, about their concerns and motivations. This is informative. The major limitation of case studies is that one does not know how general one particular case is. Nevertheless, there seems to be a role for case study research, especially if the study is—as in the Intel case—backed up by quantitative evidence.[32]

### 5.2 *Econometric Studies*

#### 5.2.1 *Association Studies*

In association studies, authors ask whether a specific foreign activity (FA) leads to a particular domestic technology outcome (DTO):

$$DTO = f(X, FA) + u \qquad (5)$$

In equation (5), $X$ is a vector of control variables, and $u$ is a regression error. For instance, Aitken and Harrison (1999) examine the importance of foreign direct investment (FDI) as a source of international technology spillovers; here, $FA$ is the industry share of employment in foreign-owned firms, and $DTO$ is increases of domestic firm productivity.

[30] It is not a perfect indicator because sometimes citations are added by the patent examiner, not the applicant.

[31] This approach goes back to the closed-economy work by Griliches (1995) and Frederic Scherer (1984).

[32] See section 6.2 for more on this particular case study.

This approach is based on economic theory in the following sense. Often, there are several models that have been proposed to explain, in this case, FDI spillovers, and model-specific evidence often does not yet exist. Association studies try to shed light on the most interesting models by proposing what might be the common reduced-form equation of all these FDI spillover models. In order to accommodate several models, the framework cannot be very specific. This explains why authors of FDI spillover studies employ a simple measure such as the foreign employment share. If FDI has a major effect on domestic firm productivity, it will be picked up by foreign employment no matter what the particular mechanism is.

The generality is attractive, but it also precludes a precise interpretation of the results. Moreover, by using a foreign activity (FA) instead of a foreign technology variable, this approach is prone to estimating technology diffusion only with some error.[33] This matters because calculating a proper causal effect (instead of a correlation) becomes more difficult as the possible causes of spurious correlation multiply. This could be due to business cycle effects or to unobserved heterogeneity. If productivity were exogenous and FDI would vary inversely with trade costs across industries, a positive coefficient of FDI on productivity would suggest spurious FDI spillovers if high-trade cost industries would exhibit on average higher productivity, for example.[34] Endogeneity is another problem; here, it could take the form of foreign investors choosing to move FDI into industries that have high rates of productivity growth (those industries are typically also relatively profitable).

How can these issues be addressed? First, spurious business-cycle effects can be avoided by including time fixed effects, as long as it is the case that the business cycle is common to the entire sample. More difficult is the question whether trend variables are appropriate, given the time-series properties of the data, in particular whether it is stationary. This is an important issue because including trend variables can have a major impact on the results in this area.[35] Panel unit root tests and cointegration analysis can be applied, but that approach is still relatively new, and results vary.[36] This suggests trying out alternative approaches; if results change dramatically depending on the assumption on the data generation process, this warrants at least some discussion.

Second, a standard approach in the presence of unobserved heterogeneity is to use fixed effects.[37] The consequence of course is to reduce the variation in the dependent variable that is left to explain. As such, fixed effects tend to be of little interest, as they rarely capture the economics that is involved. Moreover, the differencing that is implied by the fixed effects can exacerbate measurement error problems (Zvi Griliches and Jerry Hausman 1986). These considerations suggest keeping the number of fixed effects low. At the same time, there is often some uncertainty about the 'true' model, and if a low number of fixed effects means omitted variables bias, the results can be seriously misleading. In general, it will be worth trying alternative specifications.

Fixed effects will of course not work as a control for unobserved heterogeneity if the

[33] Here, using the foreign employment share as the measure of FDI may be justified because multinational enterprises tend to be R&D-intensive and share their technology between parent and subsidiaries.

[34] Lael Brainard (1997) finds that FDI is relatively high in high-trade cost industries.

[35] For instance, Coe and Helpman (1995) report that including a generalized time trend in their regression reduces the international spillover coefficient by about 60 percent, and using conventional standard errors, the parameter might be insignificantly different from zero (table B.1 and table 3, coefficient on m*S$^f$).

[36] For instance, critical values are dependent on the exact specification of the intercept and trend components, as well as how much cross-sectional heterogeneity is allowed for; see G.S. Maddala and In-Moo Kim 1998) for an introduction, and Chris Edmonds (2000) for an application to spillover regressions.

[37] Time-differencing is often used for the same purpose; see e.g. Keller (2000).

heterogeneous effects are actually not time-invariant. Not much is known on the extent to which this has led to biases in the existing studies. At any rate, the dynamic industry framework of Steven Olley and Ariel Pakes (1996) does not rely on this assumption—it allows for time-varying heterogeneity—and it has been employed in a number of micro studies.[38]

The third point, endogeneity, has been recognized in the literature, but it is rarely fully addressed. For instance, Keller (2002a) splits his sample into two, the high- and low-R&D expenditure sectors, based on the fact that four out of his twelve industries account for more than 80 percent of all R&D. For a variety of reasons, endogeneity problems are much more likely to arise in the former than in the latter sectors. Keller's result for the low-R&D sample turns out to be similar to that for the whole sample. In general, association studies conduct often a wide number of robustness analyses. These analyses are hardly definitive in dealing with endogeneity: they are sequential in nature (looking at one suspected problem at a time), they proceed under assumptions that might not hold (e.g., lagging a regressor while assuming that there is no serial correlation), and for other reasons. Nevertheless, such robustness analysis can be very helpful in revealing whether endogeneity might have a first-order effect in a particular context.

Endogeneity issues can in principle be fully addressed by using instrumental variable (IV) techniques. So far these techniques have not been used widely in this literature, although that seems to be changing now. In general, the application of IV techniques has been limited because finding good instruments for technology variables such as R&D stocks is difficult. These are estimated to begin with, and moreover, most variables that are uncorrelated with the error term tend to be not particularly correlated with R&D, especially at the industry- or micro-level.

The lack-of-instruments problem should become smaller because some recent IV techniques use primarily lags of right hand side variables as instruments. The instruments are valid as long as there is not too much persistence—which can be tested for—and the robustness of the approach exceeds earlier techniques because it uses both the variables' levels and their changes (see Richard Blundell and Stephen Bond 1999).

Two papers that have used IV estimation recently are Rachel Griffith, Stephen Redding, and Helen Simpson (2003) and Keller and Yeaple (2003). Both of these papers study the importance of technology spillovers associated with FDI.[39] The Griffith et al. (2003) paper studies the influence of foreign-owned subsidiaries in the United Kingdom. Their instruments, the economic conditions in France and the United States, are quite plausible, because these are the countries from which many of the U.K. subsidiaries come. Using over-identification tests, the authors find that endogeneity is not an issue in their sample. This may be somewhat surprising at first, perhaps suggesting that the instruments are not as good as one might hope for. However, Keller and Yeaple's (2003) IV analysis does not suggest an endogeneity bias either. These authors use industry level transport costs and tariffs as instruments for FDI industry variation in the United States. Keller and Yeaple's IV estimates suggest a higher effect through FDI spillovers than is obtained with OLS. This is the opposite of the suspected endogeneity bias, and could be the result from a FDI variable that does not measure too well the source of technology spillovers.

[38] See, for instance, Sourafel Girma and Katharina Wakelin (2001), Garrick Blalock and Paul Gertler (2002), and Wolfgang Keller and Stephen Yeaple (2003). On Olley and Pakes' (1996) method, see also Zvi Griliches and Jacques Mairesse (1998).

[39] See section 8 for a broader discussion of this.

Despite these results, it is too early to argue that endogeneity does not play a major role in many studies. More research is clearly needed. Other approaches that should be used more broadly are difference-in-difference and other control-group estimations, especially when a clear regime shift ("natural experiment") can be identified.

I now turn to a second class of empirical papers that has been employed in the econometric literature.

5.2.2 *Structure Studies*

These studies incorporate more of the structure of the underlying model than association studies. I distinguish between two types of structure studies. Generally, the first set is given by

$$DTO = f(X,M,FT)+u \qquad (6)$$

where the foreign technology variable, $FT$, replaces the foreign activity variable in equation (5), and the specification adds a specific channel, or mechanism of diffusion (denoted by $M$).

An influential example is the study by Coe and Helpman (1995). These authors test the prediction of the trade and growth models of Grossman and Helpman (1991), and Rivera-Batiz and Romer (1991), in which foreign R&D creates new intermediate inputs and perhaps spillovers that the home country can access through imports. Assume that output is produced according to

$$z = Al^{\alpha}d^{1-\alpha},\ 0<\alpha<1, \qquad (7)$$

where $A$ is a constant, $l$ are labor services, and $d$ is a CES aggregator of differentiated intermediate inputs $x$ of variety $s$

$$d = \left( \int_0^{n^e} x(s)^{1-\alpha}\, ds \right)^{\frac{1}{1-\alpha}}, \qquad (8)$$

where $n^e$ is the range of intermediate goods that are employed in this country.[40] It can be distinct from n, the range of intermediate goods produced in the country. The latter is augmented through R&D (denoted $\chi$); if intermediate goods do not become obsolete, the range of intermediate goods at time $T$ is given by the cumulative resources devoted to R&D, $n_T = S_T \equiv \int_0^T \chi(\tau)d\tau$. The goods $x(s)$ are best thought of as differentiated capital goods, produced with foregone consumption. If the x(s) are symmetric and linearly produced with foregone consumption, one can write the stock of capital as $k = \int_0^n x(s)ds = nx$, which can be used to obtain a reduced-form expression for output as

$$z = A(n^e)^{\alpha}l^{\alpha}k^{1-\alpha}. \qquad (9)$$

Defining TFP as $f \equiv \frac{z}{l^{\alpha}k^{1-\alpha}}$, one obtains

$$\ln f = \ln A + \alpha \ln n^e. \qquad (10)$$

Equation (10) shows that TFP is positively related to the range of intermediate products employed in this country (Ethier 1982).

In a symmetric model with $C$ countries and no trade barriers, in equilibrium all countries will employ all intermediates from all countries. Given that the intermediate designs are produced through national R&D, the range $n^e$ will be the same in all countries, equal to the world's cumulative R&D spending:

$$n_t^{\ e} = \sum_{c=1}^{C} n_{ct} = \sum_{c=1}^{C} S_{ct}. \qquad (11)$$

Coe and Helpman's (1995) test of the model recognizes that there is both country heterogeneity as well as trade barriers by separating domestic and foreign R&D:

$$\ln f_c = \alpha_c + \beta^d \ln S_c + \beta^f \ln S_c^f + \varepsilon_c, \qquad (12)$$

where country $c$'s so-called foreign knowledge stock $S_c^f$ is defined as the bilateral import-share weighted R&D stocks of its trade partners:

$$S_c^{\ f} = \sum_{c' \neq c} m_{cc'} S_{c'}, \qquad (13)$$

This captures the prediction of Grossman and Helpman's (1991) model that if a country

[40] This follows Romer (1990) and Grossman and Helpman (1991); see also Keller (2000); time subscripts are omitted when no ambiguity arises.

imports primarily from high-R&D partner countries, it is likely to receive relatively much technology embodied in intermediate goods, which should be reflected in a higher productivity level; and vice versa.

This approach has been influential because of its plausibility, simplicity, and versatility, and has been widely used to examine alternative channels of international diffusion; for instance, Frank Lichtenberg and Bruno van Pottelsberghe de la Potterie (2000) have examined FDI by substituting bilateral measures of FDI instead of imports.[41] The approach is more specific about the mechanism, which helps in interpreting the results. At the same time, such regressions estimate different models only partially; what determines R&D, for instance, is typically not modeled, which means that endogeneity could be an issue. Given the partial equilibrium nature of the estimation, authors should and generally do consider alternative specifications.

The second set of studies in this section puts relatively less emphasis on a particular model of growth and diffusion, and more emphasis on econometric specification and estimation. A good example is the paper by Sofronis Clerides, Saul Lach, and James Tybout (1998), where the authors provide evidence on learning externalities from exporting using micro data from Columbia, Morocco, and Mexico. Clerides, Lach, and Tybout (1998) extend the sunk cost model of exporting due to Richard Baldwin (1989), Avinash Dixit (1989), and Paul Krugman (1989) to include the possibility that exporting experience lowers the costs of production. Clerides et al. take account of the important point that it is on average the already-productive firms that self-select into the export market. They do this by estimating simultaneously a dynamic discrete choice equation that determines export market participation

$$y_{it} = \begin{cases} 1 \;\; if \;\; 0 \le \beta^{x} X_{it} + \beta^{e} e_{it} + \sum_{j=1}^{J} \beta_j^{c} \ln(AVC_{it-j}) \\ \qquad + \sum_{j=1}^{J} (F^{0} - F^{j}) y_{it-j} + \eta_{it} \\ 0 \;\; otherwise, \end{cases} \tag{14}$$

and an autoregressive cost function,

$$\ln(AVC_{it}) = \gamma_0 + \sum_{j=1}^{J} \gamma_j^{k} \ln(K_{it-j}) + \gamma^{e} \ln(e_t) + \sum_{j=1}^{J} \gamma_j^{c} \ln(AVC_{it-j}) + \sum_{j=1}^{J} \gamma_j^{y} y_{it-j} + \upsilon_{it} \tag{15}$$

where $y_{it}$ is the export indicator of plant $i$ in period t, $X_{it}$ is a vector of exogenous plant characteristics, $e_t$ is the exchange rate, $AVC_{it}$ are average costs, $K_{it}$ is capital, and $F^0$ and $F^j$ are sunk costs terms (of export market participation).

Equation (14) states that one only sees a plant exporting if the profits from doing so are greater than from not exporting (the latent threshold is expressed in terms of observables). Equation (15) estimates whether past exporting experience reduces current cost (captured by the parameters $\gamma_j^{y}$), conditional on past costs and size (proxied by capital). These learning-by-exporting parameters are not constrained in a significant way—recall that $y_{it-j}$ are 0/1 indicator variables—which is probably a good starting point given that it is unknown how learning from exporting works (if indeed it exists). Clerides, Lach, and Tybout (1998) employ alternative estimation methods in their analysis.[42] Moreover, the econometric evidence is combined with descriptive evidence in form of over-time plots of average costs for different types of plants (exporters, non-exporters, etc). The emphasis throughout is to distill the results that emerge consistently from all empirical approaches (they are discussed in section 6.1.2 below). I would

[41] The approach of computing a weighted sum of R&D goes back to Griliches (1979).

[42] This includes full information maximum likelihood and generalized methods of moments, the latter with a generalized cost function.

expect more work along these lines to be very fruitful.

### 5.2.3 *Empirical Analysis with General Equilibrium Models*

Eaton and Kortum (1996, 1997, 1999) have studied international technology diffusion using general equilibrium models. In their models productivity growth is related to increases in the quality of intermediate goods, which is key to Aghion and Howitt's (1992) quality ladder model of growth. Eaton and Kortum add a process that governs technology diffusion between countries (see section 2 above). They then explore the quantitative relationships between R&D, technology diffusion, and domestic productivity.

Eaton and Kortum's work is important because instead of focusing on the reduced-form relationship between a subset of variables, they use their full model for making predictions on all (endogenous) variables: endogeneity as in the single-equation studies above is therefore no longer an issue. Eaton and Kortum study both the long-run equilibrium and the models' predictions for the transitional dynamics (Eaton and Kortum 1999 and 1997, respectively). Eaton and Kortum (1996) shed additional light on the rates of diffusion in their model by using reduced-form techniques. Several of their papers study comparative-static changes in the long-run equilibrium, which is especially useful for economic policy analysis (Eaton, Eva Gutierrez, and Kortum 1998).[43]

There are costs to this approach as well though. First, in order to arrive at a framework that can be analyzed, typically some strong assumptions have to be made. In Eaton and Kortum (1999), for instance, the quality of technology that is discovered in a country is a random variable with a Pareto distribution, while the distribution of the diffusion lag to other countries is exponential. Within the context of a given model, such assumptions are very difficult to test. It means that this empirical work does not so much test or select among several models, as it estimates one particular model. Second, the models are usually too complicated for estimation to identify all model parameters. If, as is common practice, a number of parameters are fixed based on values from earlier studies, this means that the results are partly simulated, and not estimated.[44]

Third, it is often difficult to judge how empirically successful a model is. One measure of success is the difference between actual versus predicted values for the endogenous variables. If a model predicts productivity levels that lie within an error margin of 15 percent of the actual levels, for instance, how much of this is due to "free" model parameters (i.e., those that are set ex-ante)? With those parameters, how much worse would a different, perhaps simpler model fare? And what if the set parameters are adjusted to maximize the fit in the alternative model? Peri (2002), for instance, uses a partial equilibrium approach to estimate technology diffusion in a model similar to Eaton and Kortum (1996) who work in a general equilibrium framework. With $N$ countries, $N \times N$ equations pin down bilateral technology diffusion, and the implied technology stocks determine $(N-1)$ relative productivity levels, as in equation (3) above. According to Peri (2002), the technology stocks do not have a significant effect on productivity. In Eaton and Kortum (1996), that relationship is one element of their model's general equilibrium structure, which means that it could be that the structural assumptions have too strong an influence on the empirical results.

43 See also Eaton and Kortum (2002); Andrew Bernard et al. (2003); and the discussion in 6.2 below.

44 In addition, it can be difficult to find other studies that have estimated a particular model parameter, for instance $\theta$, which governs technology discovery in Eaton and Kortum (1999).

It is important to ask which part of the variation in the data, or which assumptions in the model, are primarily responsible for the results. Despite the sensitivity analysis that may be presented, the informed reader will typically find this question impossible to answer, and this reduces the usefulness of the general equilibrium results.[45]

To summarize, the different empirical approaches each have their advantages and disadvantages. There is a case for adopting a broad estimation framework, as in association studies, if there is model uncertainty, and this case is stronger if endogeneity issues can be addressed. It is useful to impose more structure as more information becomes available, because the structure aides interpretation. General equilibrium models allow us to conduct counterfactuals, which is crucial for policy and welfare analysis, and they will be most influential if the sources of variation that underlie the results are clear.

The following section discusses the importance of different potential channels of international technology diffusion.

## 6. *Channels of International Technology Diffusion*

### 6.1 *Trade*

#### 6.1.1 *Imports and Technology Diffusion*

First, I turn to the evidence on diffusion through intermediate input imports. In Eaton and Kortum (2002, 2001), the authors have combined the structure of technology diffusion in Eaton and Kortum (1999)—see section 2—with the Ricardian model of trade due to Rüdiger Dornbusch, Stanley Fischer, and Paul Samuelson (1977).[46] In Eaton and Kortum's model, trade augments a country's production possibilities for the classic Ricardian reason: trade gives access to foreign goods or, implicitly, technologies. By specializing in their respective comparative advantage goods, countries can gain from trade in the sense that given a country's resources, the efficient level of output with trade is higher than without trade. At the same time, there are no spillovers in this model, in the sense that importers pay the competitive price and importing has no effect on innovation.[47]

Eaton and Kortum assume that unit transport costs are increasing in geographic distance. This implies that the price of intermediate (or equipment) goods in remote countries is relatively high, or, equivalently, that productivity in these countries is relatively low. These effects are shown to be quantitatively important, as differences in the relative price of equipment account for 25 percent of the cross-country productivity differences in a sample of 34 countries (Eaton and Kortum 2001).

However, it is not clear at this point whether this provides strong support for imports as a major channel for technology diffusion. This is because the equipment goods prices predicted by Eaton and Kortum's (2001) model are inversely related to those reported in Robert Summers and Alan Heston's International Comparison Program of Prices data (CIC 2003): while according to Summers and Heston's data, rich countries have higher equipment prices than poorer countries, Eaton and Kortum's model predicts the opposite (Eaton and Kortum 2001, figure 7).

[45] In comparison, it is straightforward to assess partial-equilibrium work. For instance, according to Coe and Helpman (1995), bilateral import patterns are important for explaining variation in productivity; see equation (13). A simple test of that is to drop the import shares in (13), and see whether it leads to a major reduction in explained variation of productivity (Keller 1998; see section 6.1). Empirical work on technology diffusion in general equilibrium has not been subjected to the same level of scrutiny, presumably because the nature of the framework has more to do with simulation, and less with testing to begin with.

[46] See also the extension by Bernard et al. (2003) to plant-level analysis.

[47] As far as I know, the literature to date lacks a model in which imports have a direct effect on technology diffusion, at least for the multi-country case with sectoral differences.

Summers and Heston's price data might be imperfect, but it is unlikely that revisions of this data will reverse how equipment prices correlate with income. At this point, Eaton and Kortum's model, although appealing because it suggests plausibly large productivity effects come from importing foreign technologies, seems to require a major modification in order to be consistent with international equipment goods price data. The latter is not the only core prediction of the model, but it appears to be important enough to put at least a question mark behind the estimated quantitative importance of trade for technology diffusion.

Second, there is evidence on the importance of imports that comes from international R&D spillover regressions. Based on the framework laid out in section 5.2.2 above, Coe and Helpman (1995) relate TFP to domestic and foreign R&D,

$$\ln f_{ct} = \alpha_c + \beta^d \ln S_{ct} + \beta^f \ln S_{ct}^{\ f} + \varepsilon_{ct}, \quad (12')$$

where $S_{ct}^f$ is defined as the bilateral import-share weighted R&D stocks of its trade partners, $S_{ct}^f = \sum_{c' \neq c} m_{cc'} S_{c't}$. A positive effect from the foreign R&D variable $S_{ct}^f$ would imply that a country's productivity is increasing in the extent to which it imports from high- as opposed to low-R&D countries, supporting the hypothesis that imports are a channel of technology diffusion along the lines of the models discussed in Grossman and Helpman (1991). In a sample with 22 OECD countries, Coe and Helpman (1995) estimate a positive and quantitatively large effect from import-weighted foreign R&D. Similar effects are found for technology diffusion from highly industrialized to 77 less developed countries (Coe, Helpman, and Alexander Hoffmaister 1997).

There are some reasons to remain skeptical here as well. First, the analysis of Keller (1998) has shown that the import shares in the construction of the foreign R&D variable $S_{ct}^f$ are not, in fact, essential to obtain Coe and Helpman's (1995) results. Specifically, Keller (1998) uses randomly created shares, denoted by $\mu_{c'c}$, in place of the actual bilateral import shares to create the counterfactual foreign knowledge stock $\tilde{S}_{ct}^f = \sum_{c' \neq c} \mu_{cc'} S_{c't}$. Using this alternative foreign R&D variable yields similarly high coefficients and levels of explained variation as the regressions using $S_{ct}^f$ (that is, imports data).[48] Given that import shares are not essential for Coe and Helpman's (1995) results, their analysis does not allow us to draw strong conclusions regarding the importance of imports as a vehicle for diffusion.[49]

A number of authors have made progress by examining the international R&D spillover regressions further. Bin Xu and Jianmao Wang (1999) emphasize that technology diffusion in recent trade and growth models is associated specifically with differentiated capital goods trade. This is in contrast to the trade data Coe and Helpman (1995) use to construct their import shares (from overall trade). Xu and Wang (1999) show that this distinction matters: the capital goods-foreign R&D variable accounts for about 10 percent more of the variation in productivity than does Coe and Helpman's analysis, and it also performs better than Keller's (1998) counterfactual variable.[50]

It has also been noted that the foreign R&D variable $S_{ct}^f$ captures only current-period bilateral trade; it is clearly possible though that country A benefits from country C's technology without importing from this source, if country C exports to country B, which in turn exports to A. Olivier Lumenga-Neso, Marcelo Olarreaga, and Maurice Schiff (2001) use a specification

[48] Alternatively, Keller (1998) sets all μcc' equal to 1, which produces similar results. This confirms that the import shares are inessential for the results, whether or not they are truly random (see Keller 1997, 2000; and Coe and Hoffmaister 1999).

[49] Keller's (1998) analysis has the same implication for Coe, Helpman, and Hoffmaister's (1997) paper.

[50] Keller (2000) uses specialized machinery imports data at the industry level in a related analysis. His results show that technology diffusion through imports does affect productivity growth for high skewed trade patterns (e.g. for Canada, which imports to about 70 percent from the United States), suggesting that the effect is nonlinear.

that captures such indirect R&D spillovers, and show that it performs better than Coe and Helpman's (1995) and Keller's (1998) models. These results are consistent with the importance of dynamic effects from imports, but more research in an explicitly dynamic framework is needed to learn more about this.

The importance of imports for technology diffusion has also been assessed with patent citation data. Frederic Sjöholm (1996) studies citations in patent applications of Swedish firms to patents owned by foreign inventors. Controlling for a number of other correlates and also conducting an extreme-bounds analysis, Sjöholm finds a positive correlation between Swedish patent citations and bilateral imports. This is consistent with imports contributing to international knowledge spillovers.

Overall, the evidence points to a significant role for important in international technology diffusion. However, the various strands of the literature leave still some questions open, and we do not have yet a firm estimate of the quantitative importance of imports for international technology diffusion.

### 6.1.2 *Exports and Technology Diffusion: Is There Learning-By-Exporting*?

A major question is whether firms learn about foreign technology through exporting experience. There is anecdotal evidence claiming that firms do benefit from interacting with foreign customer, for instance because the latter impose higher product quality standards than domestic customer, while at the same time providing information on how to meet the higher standards. Case studies of the export success of a number of East Asian countries starting in the 1960s are particularly strong in their emphasis on learning-by-exporting effects (Yung-Whee Rhee, Bruce Ross-Larson, and Garry Pursell 1984). The question is whether this evidence can be supported with econometric evidence.

There is abundant evidence that in a given cross-section, exporters are on average more productive than nonexporters (e.g., Bernard and Jensen 1999; Clerides, Lach, and Tybout 1998; Mary Hallward-Driemeier, Giuseppe Iarossi, and Kenneth Sokoloff 2002).[51] That does not settle the issue of causality, however: are exporting firms more productive because of learning effects associated with exporting, or is it rather the case that firms that are more productive to begin with start exporting? The conventional wisdom today is that learning-by-exporting effects are nonexistent. This position is consistent with current evidence, but at the same time there are a number of issues which in my view are worth further research before the question should be considered settled.

An important paper is by Clerides, Lach, and Tybout (1998). These authors study manufacturing plants in Columbia, Morocco, and Mexico during the 1980s to find evidence on learning-by-exporting effects. Their framework is based on a model with sunk costs of (export) market entry, leading to a dynamic discrete choice equation for participation and an autoregressive cost function as a performance measure (see section 5 above).

Clerides, Lach, and Tybout show results for each country separately, and also by major industry. In general, they tend to show no significant effects from past exporting experience on current performance (this is parameter $\gamma_j^y$ in equation 15). Clearly, this does not lend support for the existence of strong positive learning-by-exporting effects. In fact, to the extent that Clerides et al.'s estimates are significant, they go into the wrong direction (exporting raising costs). It would be surprising if indeed there would be negative learning effects, and the authors give a number of

[51] Note that the evidence on learning-by-exporting effects discussed in the following comes from micro studies, while the evidence on diffusion associated with imports discussed above is based on more aggregate studies.

plausible reasons of why this finding may have to be discounted. Another interpretation of the generally insignificant estimates may be that the estimation framework is demanding too much of the data. However, Clerides et al.'s plots of average cost before and after export market entry seem to support their main estimation result of no evidence for learning-by-exporting effects.

While learning-by-exporting has been emphasized to be important primarily for low- and middle-income countries' firms, there is in principle no reason why it is limited to these countries, especially given the firms' heterogeneity in terms of productivity in any given country. Bernard and Jensen (1999) study the learning-by-exporting question using data on U.S. firms. This has the advantage that the sample is relatively large and there is comparatively much experience with data collection and preparation, which may result in lower measurement error.

Unlike Clerides, Lach, and Tybout (1998), Bernard and Jensen (1999) do not model export market participation explicitly. Instead, they study the performance of the different sets of firms separately.[52] Bernard and Jensen estimate that labor productivity growth is about 0.8 percent higher among exporters than nonexporters.[53] This estimate is fairly small, and it becomes even smaller (and insignificant) for longer time horizons.

The estimate of 0.8 percent, however, appears to be a downward-biased estimate of the learning-by-exporting effect because it comes from an analysis conditional on plant survival. In fact, Bernard and Jensen show that conditional on size, exporters are 10 percent more likely to survive than nonexporters.[54] It is plausible that this 10 percent survival probability difference is indicative of higher productivity growth for exporters than nonexporters, because plants tend to fail because their productivity growth is low. This suggests that the overall difference in productivity growth between exporters and nonexporters may be larger than 0.8 percent, although at this point it is not clear how much larger.

Some of these estimates come from a relatively small number of years, and there may be an argument that this time horizon is too short to see major learning-by-exporting effects. Alternatively, Hallward-Driemeier, Iarossi, and Sokoloff (2002) focus on the time before entering the export market. These authors use data from five Southeast Asian countries to show that firms which eventually become exporters make more investments to raise productivity and the quality of their goods than firms that plan to stay out of the export market. This is plausible, but if these investments require—which is likely—real resources, those need to be subtracted from any learning effects the firms receive after they have entered the export market.[55] Moreover, given that the productivity increases predate the firm's entry into the export market, at best these are indirect learning-by-exporting effects.

The analysis has shown that there is no econometric evidence for a strong learning-from-exporting effect. At the same time, there are a number of issues that still need to be addressed. First, it is puzzling that the

[52] Four types of firms can be distinguished: exporters, nonexporters, starters (plants that start exporting), and quitters (plants that stop exporting).

[53] Bernard and Jensen's estimates using TFP instead of labor productivity are lower, but the labor productivity figures are preferred in this case. The TFP measure is a simple regression residual that is fallible to a number of problems (e.g. Griliches and Mairesse 1998).

[54] Size is the main predictor of survival in recent industry-equilibrium models (e.g. Olley and Pakes 1996), because a small firm might have to exit after only one bad shock (or, a small number of successive bad shocks), whereas a large firm has substance enough to weather a longer succession of bad shocks.

[55] This point is related to the fact that none of the estimates I discuss are claimed to be spillover effects; rather, they are "learning" effects, which could be costly to acquire. Clerides, Lach, and Tybout (1998) do estimate spillovers, those that might accrue to *other* plants; this evidence is mixed.

econometric evidence is so strongly at odds with the case-study evidence. Second, there could be heterogeneity across industries masking strong but industry-specific learning effects, especially with respect to high-technology products.[56] Third, the analysis could be improved if we knew more on both the export destination and the exporter, instead of simply an indicator variable (exporting yes/no). For instance, to which firms, in which countries, do the exports go? What are the characteristics of these foreign firms—are they engaged in R&D, for example?

### 6.2 *Foreign Direct Investment*

Foreign direct investment (FDI) has long been considered as an important channel for technology diffusion. It is a plausible channel from a theoretical standpoint, because an influential theory says that firm-specific technology is transferred across international borders by sharing technology among multinational parents and subsidiaries (see, e.g., James Markusen 2002). There are a number of models showing how multinational enterprises (MNEs) might generate technological learning externalities for domestic firms, for instance through labor training and turnover (Andrea Fosfuri, Massimo Motta, and Thomas Rønde 2001) or through the provision of high-quality intermediate inputs (Rodriguez-Claré 1996).[57]

Whether FDI indeed generates substantial technological externalities for domestic firms is also a major policy issue, because governments all over the world spend large amounts of resources to attract subsidiaries of MNEs to their jurisdiction. For instance, in 1994, the U.S. state of Alabama spent $230 million, or $150,000 per newly created job, to attract a new plant of Mercedes-Benz (see Jonathan Haskel, Sonia Pereira, and Matthew Slaughter 2001).

What is the evidence on FDI spillovers? A number of surveys have recently concluded that there is *no* evidence for substantial FDI spillovers (Gordon Hanson 2001; Holger Görg and David Greenaway 2002).[58] However, this view, based primarily on a number of micro-level productivity studies, seems to be overly pessimistic. First of all, some more recent evidence for the micro productivity approach suggests that, on the contrary, FDI spillovers are large and economically important. Second, there are some results outside the micro productivity literature that do provide evidence for FDI spillovers.

A case study of Intel's FDI into Costa Rica, for example, already mentioned in section 5 above, provides interesting information on how widespread the changes can be that FDI by a major high-technology company can trigger in a relatively small country (Larrain, Lopez-Calva, and Rodriguez-Claré 2000).[59]

Other authors have provided econometric evidence on whether multinational enterprises (MNEs) raise the rate of international technology transfer as measured by patent citations (Steven Globermann, Kokko, and Sjohölm 2000; Branstetter 2001a; and Jasjit Singh 2003). Here, the results are less clear. First of all, MNE subsidiaries could either disseminate technology to domestic firms of their host country (inward FDI technology transfer), or MNE subsidiaries might pick up new technologies from the firms in the host country (outward FDI technology sourcing). It turns out that the relative strength of these effects is estimated differently, although the technology sourcing effect appears to be

[56] Industry heterogeneity has recently been emphasized in the literature on FDI (see 6.2); Clerides, Lach, and Tybout (1998), however, do generally not estimate major differences across industries.

[57] See Magnus Blomström and Ari Kokko (1998) and Kamal Saggi (2000) for a more detailed discussion of possible spillover channels associated with FDI.

[58] In the words of another author, "today's policy literature is filled with extravagant claims about positive spillovers from FDI, [but] the hard evidence is sobering" (Dani Rodrik 1999, p. 37).

[59] It is an open question whether, or to what extent these are spillover effects; see also the discussion at the end of this section.

stronger.[60] This result—MNE subsidiaries learn more from the firms in their host country than vice versa—might be indicative of a number of problems, however.

The first is firm heterogeneity: MNE subsidiaries are larger and more technologically intensive than the average firm in the host country, and this might be the reason why they are good at sourcing technology. This interpretation seems to be confirmed by Singh's (2003) finding that patent citations between two MNE subsidiaries are stronger than either from MNE subsidiary to a domestic firm or the reverse. The second issue is endogeneity. It could be that one finds MNE subsidiaries to be sourcing more technology than they provide because the MNE parent set up the subsidiary with the explicit goal of technology sourcing, while the average host-country firm, in contrast, has not made a comparable location decision. This suggests that the estimates are not fully comparable, and future research is needed to settle this issue.

The value of a patent is difficult to estimate (see, e.g., Pakes 1986). An important issue in the patent citation studies is therefore how the economic significance of technology diffusion measured in this way should be assessed. A large literature has thus tried to estimate directly the extent to which FDI leads to productivity increases for domestic firms. Xu (2000), for instance, uses the U.S. Bureau of Economic Analysis' comparable data on U.S. outward FDI into forty countries over almost thirty years (between 1966 and 1994). He finds generally a positive relation between FDI and productivity growth, which is stronger in the richer than in the poorer countries.

Xu's (2000) analysis is at the manufacturing level, which may cause aggregation bias because of heterogeneity across sectors and across firms. For this reason, the literature on FDI spillovers has moved towards using micro (firm or plant) level data (e.g., Aitken and Harrison 1999; Girma and Wakelin 2001; Haskel, Pereira, and Slaughter 2001; Griffith, Redding, and Simpson 2003; Keller and Yeaple 2003).[61] These papers present regressions of productivity on FDI and a number of control variables (they are association studies in the sense of section 5.2 above). If productivity growth of domestic firms is systematically higher in industries with more FDI than in industries with less FDI—and endogeneity and other problems can be ruled out, see section 5.1 above—this provides support for the FDI spillovers hypothesis. Irrespective of the precise spillover mechanism, a greater presence of foreign-owned subsidiaries in a particular industry is plausibly conducive to domestic firms' technological learning if they belong to this industry.

What is the evidence on this? In Aitken and Harrison (1999), the authors estimate a *negative* relationship between FDI and productivity for a sample of Venezuelan plants. The finding of a negative relationship points to a specification error: while FDI spillovers may or may not exist, there is no reason to believe that they would be negative. One possibility, raised by Aitken and Harrison (1999), is that their results capture the increased competition through FDI in addition to spillovers.[62] Haskel, Pereira, and Slaughter (2001), among others, control for such competition effects. These authors, as well as Girma and Wakelin (2001) and Griffith, Redding, and Simpson (2003) study inward FDI for the United Kingdom. While Girma and Wakelin's results are somewhat mixed, Haskel, Pereira, and Slaughter (2001) and Griffith, Redding, and Simpson

[60] Branstetter (2001a) finds evidence for spillovers of both types for Japanese FDI in the U.S., Singh (2003) finds the sourcing effect to be stronger than the transfer effect in a sample of 10 OECD countries, and Globerman, Kokko, and Sjöholm (2000) find only evidence for the outward FDI effect.

[61] Görg and Greenaway (2002) is a recent survey.

[62] Another possibility is endogeneity: FDI into Venezuela targets sectors in which Venezuelan firms are relatively weak. Aitken and Harrison do not treat endogeneity explicitly.

(2003) present evidence in support of a significant positive FDI spillover effect. The implied economic magnitudes are fairly small, however, certainly relative to the subsidies that have been paid to attract FDI.[63]

In contrast, Keller and Yeaple's (2003) study of recent FDI activity in the United States suggests that FDI spillovers are positive and large. They estimate that FDI in the United States accounts for about 11 percent of U.S. manufacturing productivity growth in that period. This estimate is much larger than Haskel, Pereira, and Slaughter's (2001) as well as other estimates, and the question is why. There seem to be two primary reasons.

The first reason is that FDI spillovers appear to be much stronger in relatively high-technology than in relatively low-technology sectors.[64] This explains in part Keller and Yeaple's larger FDI spillover estimate, because in their *Compustat* sample, the share of high-technology firms is higher than in the broader sample of Haskel, Pereira, and Slaughter (2001), for example. The strong difference between sectors, which is implicitly present also in Griffith, Redding, and Simpson (2003), table 5—suggests that FDI might be an important conduit for international technology diffusion, but only some forms of FDI that occur in a limited set of sectors. Other FDI, for instance that primarily seeking lower factor costs, is not likely to generate major spillovers. Moreover, the practice of pooled FDI spillover estimation—across all manufacturing industries—is likely to lead to misleading results.

The second finding of Keller and Yeaple underscores the importance of good measures of foreign economic activity. They use detailed U.S. statistics to allocate the employees of a given MNE subsidiary to potentially *different* industries. In contrast, in most previous studies, all employees are allocated to one, the so-called major industry. To the extent that MNE subsidiaries are diversified and their industry mix changes over time, the major-industry method of measuring FDI is prone to year-to-year volatility that is essentially noise. Keller and Yeaple (2003) show that for their sample, the preferred FDI data yields estimates that are seven times as large as those with the inferior by major-industry FDI data.

We can summarize the literature on FDI spillovers as follows. In contrast to the earlier literature, recent micro productivity studies tend to estimate positive, and in some cases also economically large spillovers associated with FDI. This difference does not appear to be primarily due to endogeneity (or other problems).[65] Moreover, although the current evidence from micro productivity studies comes from the United Kingdom and the United States, there are reasons to believe that the findings might apply in other countries as well. If these micro productivity FDI spillovers hold up in the future, it would also provide support for the FDI learning effects that are found in some of the case studies.

There are other important questions. First, are there effects of FDI outside the industry in which MNE subsidiaries are active? It is plausible to assume that to the extent that MNE subsidiaries buy local intermediate inputs, they have an incentive to provide technological knowledge to their suppliers; a stronger incentive at any rate than to local competitors that produce the same product. Maurice Kugler (2002) as well as Blalock and Gertler (2002) have found some evidence for such vertical FDI spillovers.[66]

Second, could there be more general externalities? Larrain, Lopez-Calva, and

[63] Haskel, Pereira, and Slaughter (2001) present a calculation of costs and benefits.

[64] The two types of sectors are distinguished by R&D intensity; see Keller and Yeaple (2003).

[65] As noted in section 5, instrumental variable estimations are presented in Griffith, Redding, and Simpson (2003) and Keller and Yeaple (2003). In neither case are the least-squares estimated FDI spillovers larger than the corresponding IV-estimates.

[66] See also Beata Smarzynska Javorcik (2004).

Rodriguez-Claré (2000) argue that among the most important consequences of the chipmaker Intel's recent FDI into Costa Rica was that (1) Intel funded schools that taught local workers certain skills (but by no means Intel specific skills), and (2) Intel's FDI served as a signal for other potential foreign investors that it might be time to invest into Costa Rica now. Estimating such signaling effects (if they exist ) is a challenge, because the more diffuse and indirect the alleged externalities are, the more difficult it becomes to identify clean causal effects.

## 7. *Geographic Effects on International Technology Diffusion*

Global technology spillovers favor income convergence, and local spillovers tend to lead to divergence, no matter through which channel technology diffuses. In addition to research on channels of diffusion, another strand of the literature has examined international technology diffusion in its geographic dimension (Jaffe, Trajtenberg, and Rebecca Henderson 1993; Douglas Irwin and Peter Klenow 1994; Eaton and Kortum 1999; Branstetter 2001b; Laura Bottazzi and Peri 2000; and Keller 2002a). An advantage of this is that geography is arguably exogenous in this process.

One question is whether technology diffusion within countries is stronger than across countries. The evidence generally supports this hypothesis, although there are exceptions. In particular, Jaffe, Trajtenberg, and Henderson (1993) compare the geographic location of patent citations with that of the cited patents in the United States. They find that U.S. patents are significantly more often cited by other U.S. patents than they are cited by foreign patents. This is confirmed by Branstetter (2001b), who uses R&D and patenting data on U.S. and Japanese firms to compute weighted R&D spillover stocks analogous to Coe and Helpman's (1995) import share weights (see section 5).[67] He finds that within-country spillovers are much stronger than between-country spillovers. More evidence for stronger diffusion within than across countries comes from Eaton and Kortum's (1999) study: these authors estimate that for the G-5 countries, the rate of domestic technology diffusion is about 200 times the size of the average rate of international technology diffusion between the G-5 countries.[68]

In contrast, Irwin and Klenow (1994) do not find stronger within country spillover compared to across country spillovers. Irwin and Klenow estimate that for eight vintages of semiconductors introduced between 1974 and 1992, the spillovers from one U.S. firm to another U.S. firm are *not* significantly stronger than those between an U.S. firm and a foreign firm. The different results might be obtained because Irwin and Klenow's spillovers, which are identified from the effects of cumulative production on market shares, are different from knowledge spillovers as measured in the other studies.[69] It could also have to do with the particulars of the semiconductor industry at the time. Most of the relatively small number of firms were located in the United States and in Japan, which means that the scope for identifying the within versus between country difference is limited.

[67] Patenting data by technological field allows Branstetter to compute weights that are increasing in the similarity of two firms' patenting activities; this captures the idea that R&D expenditures of another firm are more likely to generate spillovers, the closer the two firms are in technology space.

[68] The average international diffusion rate, $\varepsilon_{ni}$, for $n \neq i$, in Eaton and Kortum (1999) is about 0.088, while the domestic rate of diffusion ($\varepsilon_{ni}$, for n=i) is fixed at 17.7; see their table 2.

[69] Irwin and Klenow (1994) estimate learning-by-doing spillovers, which are more closely related to human-capital models (e.g. Robert Lucas 1988) than to models of technological change. They might be different in that they measure improvements in the efficiency of an already adopted technology, whereas international technology spillovers may capture to a greater extent learning about new and not-yet-adopted technologies. Empirical analysis has not been able to clearly separate one from the other so far.

The analysis has therefore been extended beyond the national versus international distinction by estimating spillovers conditional on geographic distance and the countries' locations relative to each other (Keller 2001, 2002a). Keller (2002a) uses industry-level productivity in nine mostly smaller OECD countries to R&D in the G-5 countries (France, Germany, Japan, the United Kingdom, and the United States) using a simple exponential decay function in distance:

$$\ln TFP_{cit} = \beta \ln\left( S_{cit} + \gamma \sum_{c' \in G5} S_{c'it} \times e^{-\delta D_{c'c}} \right) + \alpha' X + \varepsilon_{cit}. \quad (16)$$

Here, $D_{c'c}$ is the geographic distance between countries $c'$ and $c$, and $X$ is a vector of control variables. If $\delta$ is estimated to be greater than zero, variation in productivity is best accounted for by giving a lower weight to R&D conducted in countries that are located relatively far away, whereas if $\delta=0$, geographic distance and relative location do not matter. Keller (2002a) finds that $\delta$ is positive, and moreover, the decay of technology diffusion implied by the estimate is substantial: with every additional 1,200 kilometers distance there is a 50-percent drop in technology diffusion. Applying this estimate to Australia, for example, with its remote geographic location relative to the G-5 countries, would suggest that Australia benefits extremely little from technology created in the G-5 countries. Along the same lines, Bottazzi and Peri (2003) find a strong geographic decay in their analysis of technology diffusion between European regions using a similar framework. These studies suggest that technology is highly geographically localized in particular regions and countries.

A related question is whether the degree of localization has fallen in recent years. This may be expected as a consequence of transport cost improvements, information and communication technology innovations, increased multinational activity, and other changes. Keller (2002a) examines this by estimating different decay parameters ($\delta$ in equation 16) for the late 1970s and the early 1990s. The estimates indicate that $\delta$ has shrunk substantially over time in absolute value, suggesting that the degree of localization has become smaller. This is consistent with the changes mentioned above leading to a greater international diffusion of technology.

A major concern is that the estimated geography effect may be spurious, perhaps due to unobserved heterogeneity across locations. This issue is addressed in a number of studies, and while the proposed solutions are clearly imperfect, overall the results suggest that geography in fact is an important determinant of technology diffusion.[70] Another concern seems to be more important. This is that we still need to find out exactly what the geography effect means in terms of economic analysis: does this capture trade costs, for instance? We know that trade volumes are strongly declining with distance (Leamer and Levinsohn 1995), so this seems clearly a possibility. Keller (2001) is a first attempt to explain the geographic effects in international technology diffusion in terms of imports, foreign direct investment patterns, and person-to-person communication, but more work is needed that reveals what geography stands for in terms of economic models and behavior.

### 8. *Human Capital and R&D as Determinants of International Technology Diffusion*

As international technology diffusion becomes stronger over time, this favors income convergence, and vice versa, weaker

[70] See Jaffe, Trajtenberg, and Henderson (1993), e.g., who adopt a control group approach: they examine cited and not cited patents that are matched in terms of otherwise similar characteristics. See also Keller's (2002a) discussion of whether his results may be explained by geographic distance being correlated with technological distance (i.e., that geographically proximate countries produce relatively similar products).

diffusion makes divergence more likely. However, this result applies only if the trend towards (or away from) greater diffusion is global, affecting all countries to the same extent. In fact, there seem to be big differences in how effective countries are in adopting foreign technology. Given that the bulk of new technology is created in a handful of the world's richest countries, greater technology diffusion could in fact lead to divergence in the world income distribution: this will happen if today's richer countries are on average better at adopting foreign technology than today's poorer countries. Alternatively, poorer countries could gain more from better technology diffusion than richer countries. After all, poorer countries have more to gain from it, or, in the words of Alexander Gerschenkron (1962), latecomers may benefit from their relative backwardness.

This underlines the importance of identifying the major determinants of successful technology diffusion. Among the many that have been proposed, two stand out: human capital and R&D expenditures. Both are associated with the notion of absorptive capacity, the idea that a firm or country needs to have a certain type of skill in order to be able to successfully adopt foreign technology; see Keller (1996) for a formalization of this idea.[71] These skills can come, first of all, in the form of human capital (Richard Nelson and Edmund Phelps 1966). They can also be in the form of R&D spending, a notion that was first emphasized by Wesley Cohen and Daniel Levinthal (1989). These authors argue that R&D investments are necessary for a firm to acquire outside technology. This is because R&D is critical to enabling the firm to understand and evaluate new technological trends and innovations.

There is evidence that human capital facilitates the adoption of new technology in a closed economy setting (e.g., Ann Bartel and Lichtenberg 1987). Does the same also hold true for international technology adoption? The evidence presented in a number of papers suggests the affirmative. Eaton and Kortum (1996) find that inward technology diffusion is increasing in the level of a country's human capital. In Francesco Caselli and Wilbur Coleman's (2001) study, inward technology diffusion is captured by imports of office, computing, and accounting machinery, on the grounds that many countries do not have a domestic computer industry, so that computer technology comes necessarily from abroad. They find that computer imports are positively correlated with human capital. The results presented by Xu (2000) are consistent with the importance of human capital for technology diffusion as well. He finds that the reason relatively rich countries benefit from hosting U.S. multinational subsidiaries while poorer countries do not as much has to do with a threshold level of human capital in the host country.

Does absorptive capacity in the form of R&D have a similar effect on technology diffusion? To date there exist only a few studies. In one of them, Griffith, Redding, and John Van Reneen (2000) use industry-level data from twelve OECD countries for the years 1974 to 1990 to study the main determinants of productivity dynamics. They show that conditional on a certain productivity gap to the leader country, subsequent productivity growth in an industry is higher, the higher are its R&D expenditures. This is consistent with R&D playing a role similar to that of human capital in providing the necessary skills for technology adoption.

The second question is whether conditional on human capital and R&D speeding up the diffusion of technology, there is more likely to be convergence or divergence. As discussed above, this will depend on the distribution of human capital and R&D across countries, and the evidence on this is mixed

[71] Others distinguish specific and currently embodied from more general skills, and argue that technology diffusion destroys the former skills in the short-run, while in the long-run there is a complementary relationship between technical change and skills (Oded Galor and Daniel Tsiddon 1997).

so far. First, the human-capital threshold identified by Xu (2000) might not have been surpassed by poor countries, which suggests that differences in human capital could lead to divergence. Second, a number of FDI spillover studies have found that it is the less productive firms that benefit most from foreign technology (Haskel, Pereira, and Slaughter 2001; Griffith, Redding and Simpson 2003; and Keller and Yeaple 2003), and that favors convergence.

One difference between Xu (2000) on the one side, and the FDI studies on the other side, is that the latter do not specifically focus on the role that a firm's own R&D (or skills) might have for convergence. A possible explanation for these seemingly contradictory results could be that while the distribution of R&D and skills in favor of the relatively rich is as such a force towards divergence, this is more than outweighed by the stronger benefits that the relatively poor derive from foreign technology that are not conditional on skills and R&D. It is of course also possible that convergence of countries and convergence of firms in a particular country are not comparable in this way. More work in this area is clearly needed.

## 9. *Quantifying Domestic and Foreign Sources of Productivity Growth*

Building on the analysis in section 5, the following equation shows the relation between a country's productivity ($f_c$) and domestic ($S_c$) as well as foreign R&D ($S_c^f$):

$$\ln f_c = \alpha_c + \beta^d \ln S_c + \beta^f \ln S_c^f + \varepsilon_c, \qquad (12")$$

Two hypotheses regarding extreme cases of international technology diffusion can be stated easily. If $\beta^f$ is equal to zero, there is no international technology diffusion at all, whereas if $\beta^d$ is equal to zero, then there is perfect international technology diffusion, or, a global pool of technological knowledge. The discussion so far has indicated that neither of these two cases finds empirical support—$\beta^f$ is clearly greater than zero, but at the same time geographic localization means that $\beta^d$ is not equal to zero either. Going beyond these results, this section asks what we know about the relative magnitude of domestic and foreign technology sources.

Most of the estimates we have come from analyzing samples of relatively rich countries. In poor countries, there is very little comparable data on domestic technology investments. The data on the most important foreign technology sources that is available—R&D in the G-7 countries—by itself is thus not sufficient to assess the *relative* foreign contribution for poorer countries. In order to get some idea nevertheless, I will rely on the differences in relative contribution of foreign technology among OECD countries.

There are several different ways of assessing the relative importance of foreign technology diffusion, roughly corresponding to the different empirical methods described in section 5. One approach is to compare the TFP elasticities of domestic and foreign R&D. Coe and Helpman (1995) estimate a domestic R&D elasticity of about 23 percent for the relatively large G-7 countries, whereas the corresponding foreign R&D elasticity is only about 6 percent (these are approximately equal to $\beta^d$ and $\beta^f$ in equation 12"). Thus, for the G-7 countries the relative contribution from foreign R&D is about 21 percent (0.06 divided by 0.06 plus 0.23). This is almost the same as in Keller's (2002b) analysis of the G-7 countries plus Sweden using data at the industry level, where he arrives at a share of about 20 percent for foreign R&D in the total effect on productivity.

For the smaller OECD countries, Coe and Helpman estimate a domestic R&D elasticity of about 8 percent and a foreign R&D elasticity of about 12 percent. Thus, the ratio of foreign to domestic effect is estimated to be 3:2 for smaller and 1:4 for larger OECD countries. What lies behind the result that foreign R&D is relatively much more important for smaller countries? Here, this follows because smaller countries are more open than larger countries—recall from section 6.1 that the foreign R&D effect is proportional to a country's overall import share in this specification.

This openness effect points to country size as an important determinant of the relative importance of foreign versus domestic technology sources. Is the relative contribution of foreign R&D indeed so much larger for small compared with large countries? A first look at other evidence seems to suggest yes. For instance, Eaton and Kortum (1999) estimate that the part of productivity growth that is due to domestic as opposed to foreign R&D is between 11 percent and 16 percent in Germany, France, and the United Kingdom, around 35 percent for the larger Japan, and about 60 percent for the United States. Keller (2002a) computes the domestic and foreign share from his distance-adjusted estimate of effective R&D (equation 16). For nine countries that are smaller than the United Kingdom, Keller estimates that the domestic source share is about 10 percent, even smaller than Eaton and Kortum's estimate of 11 percent for the United Kingdom.

That size matters in some way is clear, however, because in the limit, as a country's share in the world approaches one, the share due to foreign technology goes to zero. To control for size differences, one possibility is to use GDP data. Doing this gives for the United States a ratio of domestic technology share to GDP share of 60 percent to 48 percent, or 1.24, whereas the corresponding value for the Netherlands is 2.18.[72] This suggests that relative to GDP, productivity growth in the United States relies *less* on domestic sources of technology than in the Netherlands.

[72] These figures are based on results in Eaton and Kortum (1999) and Keller (2002a); GDP data from Heston, Summers, and Bettina Aten (2002). In the year 1990, the United States contributed about 48 percent to the combined size of the G-5 countries plus Sweden, Denmark, and the Netherlands, while the Netherlands accounted for 2.2 percent. Eaton and Kortum estimate that about 60 percent of U.S. productivity growth was due to U.S. R&D, while Keller finds that about 4.7 percent of Dutch productivity growth can be attributed to Dutch R&D.

This may suggest that more generally, the smaller a country, the more intensively it relies on domestic technology sources. If so, it would be interesting to find out whether this is only a country size, or also a distance-to-the-frontier phenomenon. The latter would mean that even though poor countries receive almost all of their technology from abroad—there is a vast pool of technology out there—it is domestic technology efforts that matter most for them. This would be consistent with theories where technology that is invented in frontier countries is less appropriate for poorer countries (e.g., Susanto Basu and David Weil 1998).

## 10. *Concluding Discussion*

What have we learned from this literature so far, and what do we still need to know? I will begin by giving a snapshot summary of the evidence in some major areas. The empirical literature is still quite fragmented, but there are signs of consolidation which I will highlight. I will turn then to an outlook on what research might have a particularly high payoff in the future.

For most countries, foreign sources of technology are of dominant importance (90 percent or more) for productivity growth (section 9). This fact underlines the significance of international technology diffusion and the importance of finding out which activities determine its success, and whether substantial technology spillovers are associated with them. Foreign sources of technology are more important for small (and relatively poor) than for bigger countries, which is what one expects given the size difference in domestic R&D investments.

There is no indication, however, that international learning is inevitable or automatic. Neither does it seem to be easier for countries that are relatively backward, as Gerschenkron (1962) has called it. It could well be that controlling for size, the poorer a country is, the greater is the importance of domestic technology investments. Instead of simply being far from the frontier, the success of countries is in part explained by how their firms engage in international economic activities. What is the evidence on this so far?

Early on, international trade has been suggested as a major channel for technology diffusion. With regard to imports, I think that overall the evidence now supports the notion that importing is associated with technology spillovers. At the same time, there is still an abundance of disparate results that need to be brought together and quantified. Moreover, we do not know yet how strong diffusion is through embodied technology in intermediate goods versus other technology diffusion associated with imports. Learning effects from exporting have been found in the case study literature, whereas authors of econometric studies take a much more skeptical view. While the econometric evidence on learning-by-exporting effects is not as clear cut and negative as it is often stated, right now I do not see evidence in favor of strong important learning-by-exporting effects either.

What about learning effects for domestic firms from FDI? The FDI literature seems to be closer to a consensus than the trade literature is right now. For instance, both micro-econometric studies and case studies point in the same direction. The evidence suggests that there can be FDI spillovers, but they do not occur everywhere to the same degree. The remaining questions include the following: how large are vertical compared to horizontal spillovers, and which firms—stronger or weaker—benefit most from spillovers. In addition, we need to know whether FDI spillovers in richer and poorer countries are equally strong, and last not least whether they are quantitatively large enough to justify the large subsidies that governments provide to attract multinationals.

There is a thin line between recognizing the importance of international technology diffusion and getting carried away in the belief that in today's world technology is global. In fact, technology is not global today, as the studies on the localization of technology diffusion have shown. Yes, we can zap technology in the form of computer programs or designs easily around the globe, but no, this does not mean that there is effectively a global pool of technology. Perhaps it is because technology is in part tacit, requiring the sender at times to actually go there and implement the technology, that there is still a geographic pattern to technology diffusion—although the grip of geography has become weaker recently. We still need to know more about why geography matters—explaining changes in the geographic pattern of technology diffusion will tell us much, I think, about the key mechanisms, especially in analyses that include both rich and poor countries.

In order to decide what kind of research would be most useful at this point, it is worth recalling what the options are. Broadly speaking, those are case studies, econometric analyses, and simulation studies. As long as their respective strengths and weaknesses are recognized, all three can potentially prove to be very useful. Of great importance is whether the data that is employed is closely related to issues of technology and technology diffusion. For instance, FDI spillovers estimated from data on foreign subsidiaries' (and their parents') R&D should tell us much more on technology transfer than a variable like the foreign share of employment. The general principle is: if you know something about actual technological activity, try to use it.

An important question is the appropriate level of data aggregation. This issue was moot for a long time in international economics because there was very little micro data. Recently however, micro data sets have started to become available. It is thus important to know the differences between micro and more aggregate data for studying international technology diffusion, and which of the two, if any, is preferred. Not only can one use micro data today, but moreover it seems to matter a great deal for the results:

generally, the higher is the level of aggregation, the stronger tends to be the evidence for externalities and learning effects. What can explain this difference between micro and more aggregate evidence?

Micro data can capture heterogeneity across firms, something that features prominently even in narrowly defined industries, whereas industry- and aggregate-level studies cannot control for this and may suffer from composition and aggregation biases that tend to lead to inflated spillover estimates. I think that this is indeed sometimes the case. At the same time, firm heterogeneity is less important if one is primarily interested in industry-level outcomes. For example, it may not matter too much for economic policy whether industry productivity rises because all firms benefit from spillovers or because only the more productive firms benefit and become larger while the least productive firms exit.

Simultaneity and endogeneity seem to be more important issues than aggregation, and in this respect there is little difference between micro and more aggregate studies: for instance, interpreting a cross-sectional correlation of foreign ownership and productivity as evidence for FDI spillovers would be just as inappropriate at the firm level as it is at the aggregate level. Instead, the work in question is more or less important depending on how thorough the authors are in trying to identify a truly causal effect.

Most strategies for doing that rely on comparing sets of firms. This comparison, or, taking differences, may allow us to see whether the treatment (say, inward FDI) has an effect. There is no doubt that differencing is crucial for capturing a causal effect. At the same time, the assumptions on the nature of the differences are often quite simple (e.g., firm-specific time-invariant heterogeneity), and it is not clear whether the results would remain the same if firms are actually allowed to react to a major change in their environment.

More generally, I expect the biggest contribution of micro data sets to come from a better estimation of micro behavior, as the data is recorded right at the decision-taking level. And to reach their full potential, empirical micro studies of technology diffusion will probably involve modeling micro structure as well, because it is the structure that shapes behavior. As of now, there is little of that. For instance, currently, empirical studies of technology diffusion are not based on models whose structure explicitly allows for learning and spillover externalities between firms. That is, so far the micro evidence is based on "no-externality" models. This suggests that the micro evidence may become stronger once externalities are included in the models as a matter of theory (some work in this direction is Clerides, Keller, and Tybout 2003).

If the idea of differencing is to control for the averse effects of heterogeneity (across firms or over time), where does one stop? Of course, solving the heterogeneity issue fundamentally means conducting a case study, with a sample of one observation—but it is not necessarily advisable to go that far, at least not as the sole empirical methodology. More generally, can there be a problem of overdifferencing? An important issue is that technology data tends to be not of very high quality, and this limits the amount of differencing that one can do. Once the estimated coefficients look like a collection of random numbers scattered around zero with typically large standard errors, the researcher has probably asked too much of the data. Similarly, is it possible to probe so deeply into the structure of micro behavior that one fails to notice more diffuse, more aggregate, and slower-acting effects? As noted above, one benefit of attracting a major foreign investor, according to Larrain, Lopez-Calva, and Rodriguez-Claré (2000), is that it sends a signal to other potential foreign investors. It is difficult to see how a deeper analysis of micro structure would help to detect these types of effects.

Summarizing, I think that we can expect to obtain additional major results on international technology diffusion in the future, and this will be in part because of the increased usage of micro data and estimation. At the same time, it will be important to keep an open mind and not expect too much from any one empirical methodology.

What are the policy implications of this literature? The evidence is not strong enough yet to provide support for specific policy measures, such as a particular subsidy to a multinational enterprise for locating in a country. This would require more agreement on quantitative effects than there is right now. At this point, the results suggest that the international dimension of technological change is of key importance for most countries. In this situation, a closed-off international economic regime must have detrimental welfare consequences for a country.

There is also evidence that the relative importance of international technology diffusion has been increasing with the level of economic integration in the world. This suggests that the performance advantage of outward-oriented economies over inward-oriented economies will be higher in the future than it is today. What if future research were to establish that international technology diffusion raises productivity more in advanced than in less-developed countries? The implication for less-developed countries would *not* be that a turn towards autarky is beneficial—on the contrary, given the evidence on positive productivity effects from international technology diffusion. Rather, if the benefits from operating in an international economic environment differ across countries, this suggests we should investigate further the major reasons for this—what works, and why?

While there is no consensus yet on the exact magnitude of spillover benefits, it is clear that well-functioning markets and an undistorted trade and foreign-investment regime are conducive to these learning effects. However, the evidence suggests that the latter are quite difficult to pin down. For one, it does not seem to be primarily a matter of simply specializing in the production of high-tech goods. Rather, the goods characteristics are only part of what is important. India, for example, aimed at producing relatively advanced products during its era of import-substitution policy, but their quality was low compared to international standards. In contrast, Southeast Asian countries such as Hong Kong and South Korea were initially specializing in relatively low-tech products, and moved slowly but successfully into the range of higher-tech products.

Instead, technological knowledge spillovers appear to be resulting from a deliberate commitment to learning and matching international performance standards through ongoing interaction with foreigners. Local efforts are clearly necessary for successful technology adoption. At the same time, the ongoing interaction with foreign firms and consumers seems to be a process of knowledge discovery for firms that cannot be had from interacting only with other domestic firms. To model as well as empirically capture these in a convincing way continues to be a challenge.

## References

Abramovitz, Moses. 1956. "Resource and Output Trends in the United States since 1870," *Amer. Econ. Rev.* 46:2, pp. 5–23.

Acemoglu, Daron; Simon Johnson and James Robinson. 2001. "The Colonial Origins of Comparative Development," *Amer. Econ. Rev.* 91:5, pp. 1369–401.

Aghion, Philippe and Peter Howitt. 1992. "A Model of Growth through Creative Destruction," *Econometrica* 60, pp. 323–51.

———. 1998. *Endogenous Growth Theory*. Cambridge, MA: MIT Press.

Aitken, Brian and Ann Harrison. 1999. "Do Domestic Firms Benefit from Foreign Direct Investment? Evidence from Venezuela," *Amer. Econ. Rev.* 89:3, pp. 605–18.

Arrow, Kenneth. 1969. "Classificatory Notes on the Production and Transmission of Technological Knowledge," *Amer. Econ. Rev. Pap. Proceed.* 59:2, pp. 29–35.

Baldwin, Richard. 1989. "Sunk Costs Hysteresis," NBER work. pap. 2911, Cambridge, MA.

Banerjee, Abhijit and Lakshmi Iyer. 2003. "History, Institutions, and Economic Performance: The Legacy of Colonial Land Tenure Systems in India," BREAD work. pap.

Bartel, Ann and Frank Lichtenberg. 1987. "The Comparative Advantage of Educated Workers in

Implementing Technology," *Rev. Econ. Statist.* 69:1, pp. 1–11.

Bartelsman, Eric and Mark Doms. 2000. "Understanding Productivity: Lessons from Longitudinal Microdata," *J. Econ. Lit.* 38:3, pp. 569–94.

Basu, Susanto and David Weil. 1998. "Appropriate Technology and Growth," *Quart. J. Econ.* 113:4, pp. 1025–54.

Bernard, Andrew and Bradford Jensen. 1999. "Exceptional Exporter Performance: Cause, Effect, or Both?" *J. Int. Econ.* 47:1, pp. 1–25.

Bernard, Andrew; Jonathan Eaton, Bradford Jensen and Samuel Kortum. 2003. "Plants and Productivity in International Trade," *Amer. Econ. Rev.* 93:4, pp. 1268–90.

Blalock, Garrick and Paul Gertler. 2002. "Technology Diffusion from Foreign Direct Investment through Supply Chains," work pap., Haas School Bus. UC Berkeley.

Blomström, Magnus and Ari Kokko. 1998. "Multinational Corporations and Spillovers," *J. Econ. Surveys* 12:3, pp. 247–77.

Blundell, Richard, and Stephen Bond. 1999. "GMM Estimation with Persistent Panel Data: An Application to Production Functions," work. pap. 99/4, Inst. Fiscal Studies, London.

Bottazzi, Laura and Giovanni Peri. 2003. "Innovation, Demand, and Knowledge Spillovers: Evidence from European Patent Data," *Europ. Econ. Rev.* 47, pp. 687–710.

Brainard, Lael. 1997. "An Empirical Assessment of the Proximity-Concentration Trade-off between Multinational Sales and Trade," *Amer. Econ. Rev.* 87:4, pp. 520–44.

Branstetter, Lee. 2001a. "Is Foreign Direct Investment a Channel of Knowledge Spillovers? Evidence from Japan's FDI in the United States," NBER work. pap. 8015.

———. 2001b. "Are Knowledge Spillovers International or Intranational in Scope? Microeconometric Evidence from the U.S. and Japan," *J. Int. Econ.* 53, pp. 53–79.

Caballero, Ricardo and Adam Jaffe. 1993. "How High Are the Giant's Shoulders? An Empirical Assessment of Knowledge Spillovers and Creative Destruction in a Model of Growth," NBER *Macroeconomic Annual*, vol. 8. Olivier Blanchard and Stanley Fischer, eds.

Caselli, Francesco and Wilbur Coleman II. 2001. "Cross-Country Technology Diffusion: The Case of Computers," *Amer. Econ. Rev. Pap. Proceed.* 91:2, pp. 328–35.

Caves, Richard; Laurits Christensen and Erwin Diewert. 1982. "Multilateral Comparisons of Output, Input, and Productivity Using Superlative Index Numbers," *Econ. J.* 92:365, pp. 73–86.

CIC. 2003. The International Comparison of Prices Program. Center Int. Comparisons, U. Penn.

Clerides, Sofronis; Wolfgang Keller and James Tybout. 2003. "Foreign Direct Investment, Exports, and Spillovers," in progress, Brown U.

Clerides, Sofronis; Saul Lach and James Tybout. 1998. "Is Learning by Exporting Important? Micro-dynamic Evidence from Colombia, Mexico, and Morocco," *Quart. J. Econ.* 113, pp. 903–48.

Coe, David and Elhanan Helpman. 1995. "International R&D Spillovers," *Europ. Econ. Rev.* 39:5, pp. 859–87.

Coe, David; Elhanan Helpman and Alexander Hoffmaister. 1997. "North-South Spillovers," *Econ. J.* 107, pp. 134–49.

Coe, David and Alexander Hoffmaister. 1999. "Are There International R&D Spillovers among Randomly Matched Trade Partners? A Response to Keller," IMF work. pap. 99/18.

Cohen, Wesley and Daniel Levinthal. 1989. "Innovation and Learning: The Two Faces of R&D," *Econ. J.* 99:397, pp. 569–96.

David, Paul. 1992. "Knowledge, Property, and the Systems Dynamics of Technological Change," in *Proceedings of the World Bank Annual Conference on Development Economics 1992*, Larry Summers and Anwar Shah, eds. pp. 215–48.

Dixit, Avinash. 1989. "Entry and Exit Decisions under Uncertainty," *J. Polit. Econ.* 97:3, pp. 620–38.

Dornbusch, Rüdiger; Stanley Fischer and Paul Samuelson. 1977. "Comparative Advantage, Trade, and Payments in a Ricardian Model with a Continuum of Goods," *Amer. Econ. Rev.* 67:5, pp. 823–39.

Easterly, William and Ross Levine. 2001. "It's Not Factor Accumulation: Stylized Facts and Growth Models," *World Bank Econ. Rev.* 15:2, pp. 177–219.

Eaton, Jonathan; Eva Gutierrez and Samuel Kortum. 1998. "European Technology Policy," *Econ. Pol.* 27, pp. 405–38.

Eaton, Jonathan and Samuel Kortum 1996. "Trade in Ideas: Patenting and Productivity in the OECD," *J. Int. Econ.* 40:3-4, pp. 251–78.

———. 1997. "Engines of Growth: Domestic and Foreign Sources of Innovation," *Japan World Econ.* 9. pp. 235–59.

———. 1999. "International Patenting and Technology Diffusion: Theory and Measurement," *Int. Econ. Rev.* 40, pp. 537–70.

———. 2001. "Trade in Capital Goods," *Europ. Econ. Rev.* 45:7, pp. 1195–235.

———. 2002. "Technology, Geography, and Trade," *Econometrica* 70:5, pp. 1741–79.

Edmonds, Chris. 2001. "Some Panel Cointegration Models of International R&D Spillovers," *J. Macroecon.* 23, pp. 241–60.

Ethier, William. 1986. "The Multinational Firm," *Quart. J. Econ.* 101, pp. 805–33.

———. 1982. "National and International Returns to Scale in the Modern Theory of International Trade," *Amer. Econ. Rev.* 72, pp. 389–405.

Evenson, Robert and Larry Westphal. 1995. "Technology Change and Technology Strategy," in *Handbook of Development Economics*, vol. 3A. Jere Behrman and T.N. Srinivasan, eds. North-Holland.

Fagerberg, Jan. 1994. "Technology and International Differences in Growth Rates," *J. Econ. Lit.* 32:3, pp. 1147–75.

Feldman, Maryann and Frank Lichtenberg. 1997. "The

Impact and Organization of Publicly-Funded Research and Development in the European Community," NBER work. pap. 6040.
Fosfuri, Andrea; Massimo Motta and Thomas Rønde. 2001. "Foreign Direct Investment and Spillovers through Workers' Mobility," *J. Int. Econ.* 53, pp. 205–22.
Galor, Oded and Daniel Tsiddon. 1997. "Technological Progress, Mobility, and Economic Growth," *Amer. Econ. Rev.* 87, pp. 363–82.
Gerschenkron, Alexander. 1962. *Economic Backwardness in Historical Perspective*. Cambridge, MA: Harvard U. Press.
Girma, Sourafel and Katharina Wakelin. 2001. "Regional Underdevelopment: Is FDI the Solution? A Semi-Parametric Analysis," GEP Research Pap. 2001/11, U. Nottingham.
Görg, Holger, and David Greenaway. 2002. "Much Ado About Nothing? Do Domestic Firms Really Benefit from Foreign Direct Investment?" work pap. U. Nottingham.
Globerman, Steven; Ari Kokko and Frederic Sjöholm. 2000. "International Technology Diffusion: Evidence from Swedish Patent Data," *Kyklos* 53, pp. 17–38.
Griffith, Rachel; Stephen Redding and Helen Simpson. 2003. "Productivity Convergence and Foreign Ownership at the Establishment Level," CEPR work. pap. 3765.
Griffith, Rachel; Stephen Redding, and John Van Reenen. 2000. "Mapping Two Faces of R&D: Productivity Growth in a Panel of OECD Industries," forthcoming, *Rev. Econ. Statist.*
Griliches, Zvi. 1979. "Issues in Assessing the Contribution of Research and Development to Productivity Growth," *Bell J. Econ.* 10, pp. 92–116.
———. ed. 1984. *R&D, Patents, and Productivity*. U. Chicago for NBER.
———. 1990. "Patent Statistics as Economic Indicators: A Survey," *J. Econ. Lit.* 28:3, pp. 1661–707.
———. 1995. "R&D and Productivity: Econometric Results and Measurement Issues," in *Handbook of the Economics of Innovation and Technological Change*. Paul Stoneman ed. , Oxford: Blackwell, pp. 52–89.
Griliches, Zvi, and Jerry Hausman. 1986. "Errors in Variables in Panel Data," *J. Econometrics* 31, pp. 93–118.
Griliches, Zvi, and Jacques Mairesse. 1998. "Production Functions: The Search for Identification," in *Econometrics and Economic Theory in the 20th Century: Ragnar Frisch Centennial Symposium*. Steinar Strøm, ed. Cambridge: Cambridge U. Press, pp. 169–203.
Grossman, Gene and Elhanan Helpman. 1991. *Innovation and Growth in the World Economy*, Cambridge, MA: MIT Press.
———. 1995. "Technology and Trade," in *Handbook of International Economics* vol.3. Gene Grossman and Kenneth Rogoff, eds. North-Holland.
Hall, Robert and Charles Jones. 1999. "Why Do Some Countries Produce So Much More Output Per Worker Than Others?" *Quart. J. Econ.* 114:1, pp. 83-116.
Hallward-Driemeier, Mary; Giuseppe Iarossi and Kenneth Sokoloff. 2002. "Exports and Manufacturing Productivity in East Asia: A Comparative Analysis with Firm-Level Data," work. pap., UCLA.
Hanson, Gordon. 2001. "Should Countries Promote Foreign Direct Investment?" G-24, UN Discus. Pap. Series, NY and Geneva.
Haskel, Jonathan; Sonia Pereira and Matthew Slaughter. 2001. "Does Inward Foreign Direct Investment Boost the Productivity of Domestic Firms?" pap. for NBER Summer Institute.
Heston, Alan; Robert Summers and Bettina Aten. 2002. *Penn World Tables Version 6.1*, Center Int. Comparisons, U. Penn.
Howitt, Peter. 2000. "Endogenous Growth and Cross-Country Income Differences," *Amer. Econ Rev.* 90:4, pp. 829–46.
Hulten, Charles. 2000. "Total Factor Productivity: A Short Biography," NBER work. pap. 7471.
Irwin, Douglas and Peter Klenow. 1994. "Learning Spillovers in the Semi-Conductor Industry," *J. Polit. Econ.* 102, pp. 1200–27.
Jaffe, Adam and Manuel Trajtenberg. 2002. *Patents, Citations and Innovations: A Window on the Knowledge Economy*. Cambridge: MIT Press.
Jaffe, Adam; Manuel Trajtenberg and Rebecca Henderson. 1993. "Geographic Localization of Knowledge Spillovers as Evidenced by Patent Citations," *Quart. J. Econ.* 108:3, pp. 577–98.
Jones, Charles. 1995. "R&D-Based Models of Growth," *J. Polit. Econ.* 103:4, pp. 759–84.
Katayama, Hajime; Shihua Lu and James Tybout. 2003. "Why Plant-Level Productivity Studies Are Often Misleading, and an Alternative Approach to Inference," work pap. Penn State U.
Keller, Wolfgang. 1996. "Absorptive Capacity: On the Creation and Acquisition of Technology in Development," *J. Devel. Econ.* 49, pp. 199–227.
———. 1997. "How Trade Patterns and Technology Flows Affect Productivity Growth," World Bank Policy Research work. pap. 1831.
———. 1998. "Are International R&D Spillovers Trade Related? Analyzing Spillovers among Randomly Matched Trade Partners," *Europ. Econ. Rev.* 42, pp. 1469–81.
———. 2000. "Do Trade Patterns and Technology Flows Affect Productivity Growth?" *World Bank Econ. Rev.* 14, pp. 17–47.
———. 2001. "Knowledge Spillovers at the World's Technology Frontier," CEPR work. pap. 2815.
———. 2002a. "Geographic Localization of International Technology Diffusion," *Amer. Econ. Rev.* 92, pp. 120–42.
———. 2002b. "Trade and the Transmission of Technology," *J. Econ. Growth*: 7, pp. 5–24.
Keller, Wolfgang and Stephen Yeaple. 2003. "Multinational Enterprises, International Trade, and Productivity Growth: Firm Level Evidence from the United States," IMF work. pap. 248.
Klette, Tor and Zvi Griliches. 1996. "The Inconsistency of Common Scale Estimators When Output Prices Are Unobserved and Endogenous," *J. Appl. Econometrics* 11, pp. 343–61.

Krugman, Paul. 1989. *Exchange Rate Instability*. Cambridge, MA: MIT Press.

Kugler, Maurice. 2002. "The Diffusion of Externalities from Foreign Direct Investment: Theory Ahead of Measurement," work pap. U. Southhampton.

Larrain, B. Felipe; Luis Lopez-Calva, and Andres Rodriguez-Claré. 2000. "Intel: A Case Study of Foreign Direct Investment in Central America," work. pap. 58, Center Int. Develop., Harvard U.

Leamer, Edward and James Levinsohn. 1995. "International Trade theory: The Evidence," in *Handbook of International Economics*, vol. 3. G. Grossman and K. Rogoff, eds. Elsevier: Amsterdam.

Lichtenberg, Frank. 1993. "R&D Investment and International Productivity Differences," in *Economic Growth in the World Economy*. Symposium 1992. Horst Siebert, ed. Tübingen: Mohr.

Lichtenberg, Frank and Bruno van Pottelsberghe de la Potterie. 2000. "Does Foreign Direct Investment Transfer Technology Across Borders?" forthcoming, *Rev. Econ. Statist.*

Lucas, Robert. 1988. "On the Mechanics of Economic Development," *J. Monet. Econ.* 22, pp. 3–42.

Lumenga-Neso, Olivier; Marcelo Olarreaga and Maurice Schiff. 2001. "On 'Indirect' Trade-Related R&D spillovers," mimeo, World Bank.

Maddala, G.S. and In-Moo Kim. 1998. *Unit Roots, Cointegration, and Structural Change*. Cambridge: Cambridge U. Press.

Markusen, James. 2002. *Multinational Firms and the Theory of International Trade*. Cambridge: MIT Press.

Nelson, Richard and Edmunds Phelps. 1966. "Investment in Humans, Technological Diffusion and Economic Growth," *Amer. Econ. Rev.* 56:2, pp. 69–75.

NSF. 2004. "US–China R&D Linkages: Direct Investment and Industrial Alliances in the 1990s," NSF Info. Brief NSF 04-236.

OECD 2002. *Frascati Manual 2002: Proposed Standard Practice for Surveys on Research and Development*. Paris: OECD.

———. 2003. *Main Science and Technology Indicators*. Paris: OECD.

Olley, Steven and Ariel Pakes. 1996. "The Dynamics of Productivity in the Telecommunications Equipment Industry," *Econometrica* 64:6, pp. 1263–97.

Pakes, Ariel. 1986. "Patents as Options: Some Estimates of the Value of Holding European Patent Stocks," *Econometrica* 54:4, pp. 755–84.

Peri, Giovanni. 2002. "Knowledge Flows and Innovation," work. pap., UC Davis.

Polanyi, Michael. 1958. *Personal Knowledge: Towards a Post-Critical Philosophy*. Chicago: U. Chicago Press.

Prescott, Edward. 1998. "Needed: A Theory of Total Factor Productivity," *Int. Econ. Rev.* 39:3, pp. 525–51.

Quah, Danny. 2001a. "Technology Dissemination and Economic Growth," work. pap., London School Econ.

———. 2001b. "Demand-Driven Knowledge Clusters in a Weightless Economy," work pap., London School Econ.

Rhee, Yong-Whee; Bruce Ross-Larson and Garry Pursell. 1984. *Korea's Competitive Edge: Managing Entry into World Markets*. Baltimore: Johns Hopkins U. Press for World Bank.

Rivera-Batiz, Luis and Paul Romer. 1991. "Economic Integration and Endogenous Growth," *Quart. J. Econ.* 106:2, pp. 531–55.

Rodriguez-Claré, Andres. 1996. "Multinationals, Linkages, and Economic Development," *Amer. Econ. Rev.* 86, pp. 852–73.

Rodrik, Dani. 1999. "The New Global Economy and Developing Countries: Making Openness Work," Policy Essay 24, Overseas Develop. Council, Washington DC.

Romer, Paul. 1990. "Endogenous Technological Change," *J. Polit. Econ.* 98:5, pp. S71–S102.

Saggi, Kamal. 2000. "Trade, Foreign Direct Investment, and International Technology Transfer: A Survey," forthcoming in *World Bank Res. Observer*.

Scherer, Frederic. 1984. "Using Linked Patent and R&D Data to Measure Interindustry Technology Flows," in *R&D, Patents, and Productivity*. Zvi Griliches ed. U. Chicago for NBER, pp. 417–61.

Segerstrom, Paul; T.C.A. Anant and Elias Dinopoulos. 1990. "A Schumpeterian Model of the Product Life Cycle," *Amer. Econ. Rev.* 80:4, pp. 1077–92.

Shiue, Carol H. and Wolfgang Keller. 2004. "Markets in China and Europe on the Eve of the Industrial Revolution," CEPR discus. pap. 4420.

Singh, Jasjit. 2003. "Knowledge Diffusion and Multinational Firms: Evidence using Patent Citation Data," work. pap., Grad. School Bus. Admin. and Econ. Dept., Harvard U.

Sjöholm, Frederic. 1996. "International Transfer of Knowledge: The Role of International Trade and Geographic Proximity," *Weltwirtschaftliches Archiv* 132, pp. 97–115.

Teece, David. 1977. "Technology Transfer by Multinational Firms: The Resource Cost of Transferring Technological Know-How," *Econ. J.* 87, pp. 242–61.

von Hippel, Eric. 1994. "'Sticky Information' and the Locus of Problem Solving: Implications for Innovation," *Manage. Sci.* 40:4, pp. 429–39.

Xu, Bin. 2000. "Multinational Enterprises, Technology Diffusion, and Host Country Productivity Growth," *J. Devel. Econ.*, 62:2, pp. 477–93.

Xu, Bin and Jianmao Wang. 1999. "Capital Goods Trade and R&D Spillovers in the OECD," *Can. J. Econ.* 32:5, pp. 1258–74.

WIPO. 2003. World Intellectual Property Organization, www.wipo.org.

World Bank. 1999. *Knowledge for Development*. World Development Report 1998/99, Washington DC: World Bank.

# Part II
# Trade Adjustment and Productivity Growth

# A
# Macro

# [10]

# Comparative Advantage and Long-Run Growth

By GENE M. GROSSMAN AND ELHANAN HELPMAN*

*We construct a dynamic, two-country model of trade and growth in which endogenous technological progress results from the profit-maximizing behavior of entrepreneurs. We study the role that the external trading environment and that trade and industrial policies play in the determination of long-run growth rates. Cross-country differences in efficiency at R&D versus manufacturing (i.e., comparative advantage) bear importantly on the growth effects of economic structure and commerical policies.* (JEL *411, 111, 621*)

What role do the external trading environment and commercial policy play in the determination of *long-run* economic performance? This central question of international economics has received surprisingly little attention in the theoretical literature over the years.

Previous research on trade and growth has adopted the neoclassical framework to focus on factor accumulation in the open economy. (See the surveys by Ronald Findlay, 1984, and Alasdair Smith, 1984.) This research largely neglects the effects of trade structure on rates of growth, however, addressing instead the reverse causation from growth and accumulation to the pattern of trade.[1] The direction that the research followed almost surely can be ascribed to the well-known property of the standard neoclassical growth model with diminishing returns to capital that (endogenous) growth in per capita income dissipates in the long run. For this reason, the familiar models that incorporate investment only in capital equipment seem ill-suited for analysis of long-run growth.

The available evidence collected since the seminal work of Robert Solow (1957) also leads one to look beyond capital accumulation for an explanation of growth. Exercises in growth accounting for a variety of countries generally find that increases in the capital to labor ratio account for considerably less than half of the last century's growth in per capita incomes.[2] Although econometric efforts to explain the residual have been somewhat disappointing (see, for example, Zvi Griliches, 1979), professional opinion and common sense continue to impute much of this residual to improvements in technology.[3] We share the view, expressed by Paul Romer (1986, 1990), that a full understanding of growth in the long run requires appreciation of the economic determinants of the accumulation of knowledge.

In this paper we draw on the pioneering work by Romer to construct a model that highlights the roles of scale economies and technological progress in the growth process. As in Romer's work, our model im-

*Grossman: Woodrow Wilson School, Princeton University, Princeton, NJ 08544. Helpman: Department of Economics, Tel Aviv University, Ramat Aviv, Israel. We are grateful to Avinash Dixit, Carl Shapiro, and Lars Svensson for their comments on an earlier draft, and to the National Science Foundation and the Alfred P. Sloan Foundation for financial support. Grossman also thanks the World Bank and Helpman thanks the International Monetary Fund for providing support and a stimulating environment during part of our work on this project. These organizations are not responsible for the views expressed herein.

[1]An exception is Max Corden (1971), who studies how the opening up of trade affects the speed of transition to the steady state in a two-factor neoclassical growth model with fixed savings propensities.

[2]See Angus Maddison (1987) for a careful, recent exercise in growth accounting.

[3]The benefits of education and experience undoubtedly contribute part of the explanation for the growth residual. See, for example, Robert Lucas (1988) and Gary Becker and Kevin Murphy (1990) for growth models that highlight the role of human capital accumulation as a source of growth.

plies an endogenous rate of long-run growth in per capita income, and we study its economic determinants. Our primary contribution lies in casting the growth process in a two-country setting. We provide, for the first time, a rigorous analysis linking long-run growth rates to trade policies and other international economic conditions. Moreover, we show that recognition of cross-country differences in economic structure impinge upon conclusions about the long-run effects of domestic shocks and policies.

Our model incorporates the essential insights from Romer (1990), although we introduce some differences in detail. The building blocks are an R&D sector that produces designs or blueprints for new products using primary resources and previously accumulated knowledge, an intermediate-goods sector consisting of oligopolistic producers of differentiated products, and a consumer-goods sector in each country that produces a country-specific final output using labor and intermediate inputs. As in Wilfred Ethier (1982), total factor productivity in final production increases when the number of available varieties of differentiated inputs grows. Thus, resources devoted to R&D contribute over time to productivity in the production of final goods, as well as to the stock of scientific and engineering knowledge.

The new elements in our analysis stem from the assumed presence of cross-country differences in the effectiveness with which primary resources can perform different activities, that is, *comparative advantage*. For simplicity we specify a one-primary-factor model, and allow the productivity of this factor in the three activities to vary internationally. Similar results could be derived from a multifactor model with interindustry differences in factor intensities (see Grossman and Helpman, 1989d, and Grossman, 1989). In any event, we find that many comparative dynamic results hinge on a comparison across countries of parameters reflecting efficiency in R&D relative to efficiency in manufacturing the goods that make use of the knowledge generated by R&D. The effects of policy in a single country, of accumulation of primary resources in a single country, and of a shift in world tastes toward the final output of one of the countries all depend upon the identity of the country in which the change originates in relation to the international pattern of comparative advantage.

We describe the economic setting in Section I below. Then, in Section II, we derive the dynamic equilibrium of the world economy and calculate two reduced-form equations that determine the steady-state growth rate. In Section III, we investigate the structural determinants of long-run growth. There, the implications for growth of variations in consumer preferences, primary-input coefficients in one or both countries, and stocks of available primary resources are considered. Section IV contains policy analysis. We study barriers and inducements to trade in consumer goods and subsidies to research and development. The analysis is extended in Section V to incorporate lags in the dissemination of knowledge and asymmetries in the speed of diffusion within and between countries. We use the extended model to reconsider the effects of trade policies on the steady-state rate of growth. Finally, Section VI provides a brief summary of our findings.

### I. The Model

We study a world economy comprising two countries. Each country engages in three productive activities: the production of a final good, the production of a continuum of varieties of differentiated middle products (i.e., intermediate inputs), and research and development (R&D). A single primary factor is used in production, and is taken to be in fixed and constant supply in each country. Although we refer to this factor as "labor," we have in mind an aggregate of irreproducible resources that for any given level of technical know-how limits aggregate output.

At a point in time, output of final goods in country $i$ is given by

$$Y_i = BA_i L_{Yi}^{1-\beta}\left[\int_0^n x_i(\omega)^\alpha \, d\omega\right]^{\beta/\alpha}, \quad 0<\alpha,\beta<1,$$

where $L_{Yi}$ represents employment in the final-goods sector, $x_i(\omega)$ denotes the input of middle product $\omega$, $A_i$ is a country-specific productivity parameter, and $n$ is (the measure of) the number of varieties of middle products available at that time.[4] This production function exhibits constant returns to scale for given $n$, but an increase in the measure of varieties of middle products raises total factor productivity. This specification, which we borrow from Ethier (1982), captures the notion that an increasing degree of *specialization* generates technical efficiency gains. The economy's potential for augmenting the degree of specialization by developing new middle products implies the existence of dynamic scale economies at the industry level that are external to the individual final-good-producing firms.

Competition in the final-goods sectors ensures marginal-cost pricing. Hence, by appropriate choice of the constant $B$, producer prices satisfy

$$(1)\quad p_{Yi}=\left(\frac{w_i}{A_i}\right)^{1-\beta}\left[\int_0^n p_X(\omega)^{1-\varepsilon}d\omega\right]^{\beta/(1-\varepsilon)},$$

$$\varepsilon=\frac{1}{1-\alpha}>1,$$

where $w_i$ is the wage in country $i$ and $p_X(\omega)$ is the price of variety $\omega$. Final-good producers worldwide pay the same prices for (freely traded) middle products.

At every moment in time, the existing producers of middle products engage in oligopolistic price competition. The producer of a variety $\omega$ in country $i$ chooses $p_X(\omega)$ to maximize profits,

$$\pi_i(\omega)=\left[p_X(\omega)-w_i a_{LXi}\right]\times\frac{p_X(\omega)^{-\varepsilon}}{\int_0^n p_X(\omega)^{1-\varepsilon}d\omega}\beta\Sigma_i p_{Yi}Y_i,$$

where $a_{LXi}$ is the unit labor requirement for production of intermediates in country $i$. This expression for profits comprises the product of profits per unit (in square brackets) and derived demand for variety $\omega$, where the latter incorporates the assumption that neither the prices of competing products nor the value of final production varies with $p_X(\omega)$. The first-order condition for a profit maximum implies the usual fixed-markup pricing rule,

$$(2)\quad \alpha p_X(\omega)=w_i a_{LXi}.$$

It is clear from (2) that varieties originating from the same country bear the same price. Letting $p_{Xi}$ represent the price of a variety produced in country $i$ and $n_i$ be the number of intermediate inputs produced there, equations (1) and (2) imply

$$(3)\quad p_{Yi}=\left(\frac{w_i}{A_i}\right)^{1-\beta}\left(\sum_j n_j p_{Xj}^{1-\varepsilon}\right)^{\beta/(1-\varepsilon)},$$

$$(4)\quad \alpha p_{Xi}=w_i a_{LXi}.$$

With these prices, profits per firm can be expressed as

$$(5)\quad \pi_i=(1-\alpha)p_{Xi}X_i/n_i,$$

where $X_i$ is aggregate output of intermediates in country $i$ ($n_i$ times per-firm output) and is given by

$$(6)\quad X_i=\frac{n_i p_{Xi}^{-\varepsilon}}{\sum_j n_j p_{Xj}^{1-\varepsilon}}\beta\left(\sum_j p_{Yj}Y_j\right).$$

As in our 1989c paper (see also Kenneth Judd, 1985), resources devoted to research generate "blueprints" that expand the measure of differentiated products. Research outlays are made by private, profit-maximizing entrepreneurs, who appropriate some of the benefits from a new technological innovation in the form of a stream of oligopoly profits. We assume that innovators receive indefinite patent protection, but that blueprints are not tradable, so that all profits must be derived from production in

[4] Here, and henceforth, we omit time arguments when no confusion is caused by doing so.

the country in which a middle product has been developed. Then, with free entry by entrepreneurs, if resources are devoted to R&D in country $i$ at time $t$, the present value of future operating profits from producing there—discounted to time $t$—must equal the current cost of R&D. We denote R&D costs by $c_{ni}(t)$ and write the zero-profit condition as

$$\int_t^{\infty} e^{-[R(\tau)-R(t)]}\pi_i(\tau)\,d\tau = c_{ni}(t),$$

where $R(t)$ is the cumulative interest factor from time 0 to time $t$ ($R(0)=1$). Differentiating this condition with respect to $t$, we find

$$\frac{\pi_i + \dot{c}_{ni}}{c_{ni}} = \dot{R}. \tag{7}$$

Equation (7) expresses a standard no-arbitrage condition. Recognizing that $c_{ni}(t)$ represents the value of an input-producing firm in country $i$ at time $t$, (7) equates the instantaneous rate of return on shares in such a firm (the sum of dividends and capital gains) to the rate of interest.

We follow Romer (1990) in assuming that R&D generates a second output, which takes the form of a contribution to the stock of disembodied knowledge. Knowledge here includes all general scientific information, as well as some forms of engineering data with more widespread applicability, generated in the course of developing marketable products. Knowledge contributes to the productivity of further research efforts by reducing the amount of labor needed for an inventor to develop a new product. Due to the more general and non-patentable nature of this product of the R&D effort, appropriation of the resulting returns by the creator seems problematic. We assume to begin with that general knowledge disseminates immediately and costlessly throughout the world. This approximates a situation in which information spreads through technical journals, professional organizations, and interpersonal commercial contacts, and where literature, scientists, and businesspeople move freely across international borders (see Luigi Pasinetti, 1981, ch. 11). We relax this assumption by introducing lags in the dissemination of knowledge in Section V.

With these knowledge spillovers in mind, we specify our R&D technology as follows. If $L_{ni}$ units of labor engage in research in country $i$, they generate a flow of new products $\dot{n}_i$ given by

$$\dot{n}_i = L_{ni}K/a_{Lni}, \tag{8}$$

where $K$ is the current stock of knowledge and $a_{Lni}$ is a country-specific productivity parameter. We take the stock of knowledge to be proportional to cumulative experience in R&D; that is, there are no diminishing returns to research in adding to scientific understanding. By choosing units for $K$ so that the factor of proportionality is unity, we have $K=n$ and

$$\dot{K} = \sum_i L_{ni}K/a_{Lni}. \tag{9}$$

Since knowledge has been assumed to be a free input to each individual entrepreneur, the cost of product development in country $i$ can be written as

$$c_{ni} = w_i a_{Lni}/n. \tag{10}$$

We turn now to the demand side of the model. Consumers worldwide share identical, homothetic preferences. They view the final goods produced in the two countries as imperfect substitutes. We represent preferences by a time-separable intertemporal utility function

$$U_t = \int_t^{\infty} e^{-\rho(\tau-t)} \times \log u[y_1(\tau), y_2(\tau)]\,d\tau, \tag{11}$$

where $\rho$ is the subjective discount rate and $y_i(\tau)$ is consumption of final goods from country $i$ in period $\tau$. The instantaneous sub-utility function $u(\cdot)$ is nondecreasing, strictly quasi-concave, and positively linearly homogeneous.

A typical consumer maximizes (11) subject to an intertemporal budget constraint. With $u(\cdot)$ linearly homogeneous, this optimization problem can be solved in two stages. First, the consumer maximizes static utility for a given level of expenditure at time $\tau$, $E(\tau)$. The solution to this subproblem generates an indirect utility function, $v[p_{Y1}(\tau), p_{Y2}(\tau)]E(\tau)$, where $p_{Yi}$ is the price of $Y_i$. In the absence of barriers to trade in final goods, these prices are common to consumers in the two countries. The second-stage problem involves choosing the time pattern of expenditures to maximize

$$(12)\quad V_t = \int_t^{\infty} e^{-\rho(\tau-t)}\{\log v[p_{Y1}(\tau), p_{Y2}(\tau)] + \log E(\tau)\}\, d\tau$$

subject to

$$(13)\quad \int_t^{\infty} e^{-[R(\tau)-R(t)]}E(\tau) \leq \int_t^{\infty} e^{-[R(\tau)-R(t)]}w(\tau)L\,d\tau + Z(t),$$

where $w(t)$ is the consumer's wage rate at time $t$, $L$ is his labor supply, and $Z(t)$ is the value of his time $t$ asset holdings. The interest factor in (13) is common to all individuals as a result of trade on the integrated world capital market, but the wage rate varies by country.

From the first-order conditions to this problem, we find that the optimal path for expenditure obeys

$$(14)\quad \frac{\dot{E}}{E} = \dot{R} - \rho.$$

Savings are used to accumulate either ownership claims in input-producing firms or riskless bonds issued by these same firms. Arbitrage ensures that the rates of return on these two assets are equal, and in equilibrium consumers are indifferent as to the composition of their portfolios.

## II. Equilibrium Dynamics

During the course of the development of our model in the previous section, we provided some of the equilibrium conditions. For example, we derived pricing equations for goods and a no-arbitrage condition relating equilibrium asset returns. In this section we complete the list of equilibrium requirements by adding conditions that stipulate market clearing in factor and final-goods markets. We then derive and discuss a reduced-form system that describes equilibrium dynamics.

Static equilibrium in the markets for the two final goods implies

$$(15)\quad p_{Yi}Y_i = s_i E,$$

where $s_i(p_{Y1}, p_{Y2})$ is the share of world spending allocated to $Y_i$ and $E$ is world spending on consumer goods. The share function is, of course, homogeneous of degree zero. We establish below that relative commodity prices are constant in the vicinity of a steady state with active R&D sectors in both countries. For this reason, we take $s_i$ to be constant in our subsequent analysis, and omit its functional dependence on relative prices.

The labor-market clearing conditions equate labor supply and labor demand in each country. Using (3) and Shephard's lemma, we see that final-goods producers demand $(1-\beta)p_{Yi}Y_i/w_i$ workers. The demand for labor by middle-products manufacturers is $a_{LXi}X_i$, while (8) and the fact that $K = n$ imply demand for labor by product developers of $(a_{Lni}/n)\dot{n}_i$. Hence,

$$(16)\quad (a_{Lni}/n)\dot{n}_i + a_{LXi}X_i + (1-\beta)p_{Yi}Y_i/w_i = L_i,$$

where $L_i$ is the labor force available in country $i$.

Since we neglect here the monetary determinants of the price level, we may choose freely a time pattern for one nominal variable. It proves convenient to specify the numeraire as follows:

$$p_{X1} = n(a_{LX1}/a_{Ln1})^{1/\varepsilon}. \tag{17a}$$

We show in Appendix A of our 1989a working paper that, with this normalization, a necessary condition for convergence to a steady state with positive R&D in both countries (i.e., nonspecialization) is

$$p_{X2} = n(a_{LX2}/a_{Ln2})^{1/\varepsilon}. \tag{17b}$$

Together, (17a) and (17b) imply that relative prices of middle products are constant along the convergent path, which further implies with (4) the constancy of relative wages, and with (3) the constancy of relative prices of final goods. This last fact justifies our treatment of expenditure shares as fixed.

Let $g(t)$ denote the rate of growth of the number of products and the stock of knowledge; that is, $g \equiv \dot{n}/n = \dot{K}/K$. Then from (17) and (4) we see that prices of intermediates and wages grow at rate $g$, while from (10), product development costs are constant. Equations (5)–(7), (10), (15), and (17) imply

$$X_i = \frac{n_i b_i^{1/\alpha}}{\Sigma_j n_j b_j} \frac{\beta E}{n} \tag{18}$$

and

$$\dot{R} = \frac{1}{\varepsilon - 1} \frac{\beta E}{\Sigma_j n_j b_j}, \tag{19}$$

where $b_i \equiv (a_{Lni}/a_{LXi})^{\alpha}$. The coefficients $b_i$ will serve as our measures of *comparative advantage*. Country 1 enjoys comparative advantage in conducting R&D if and only if $b_1 < b_2$.

Since wages grow at the same rate as $n$, it proves convenient to define $e \equiv E/n$. Letting $\sigma_i \equiv n_i/n$ be the share of products manufactured in country $i$ and noting that $g = \Sigma_i \dot{n}_i/n$, (16), (15), (17), (4), and (18) imply

$$g = H - \frac{\beta e}{\sigma} - \frac{1-\beta}{\alpha} se, \tag{20}$$

where we have defined $H \equiv \Sigma_i L_i/a_{Lni}$, the total *effective* labor force, $\sigma \equiv \Sigma_i \sigma_i b_i$, a weighted average of the comparative advantage parameters with product shares as weights, and $s \equiv \Sigma_i s_i/b_i$. Observe that the parameter $\sigma$, which provides a useful summary of the static intersectoral resource allocation, grows (shrinks) over time if and only if the growth rate of the number of differentiated middle products in the country with comparative *disadvantage* in R&D exceeds (falls short of) that of the other country.

We are now prepared to derive two equations that describe the dynamic evolution of the world economy. From the definition of $e$, we have $\dot{e}/e = \dot{E}/E - g$, or, substituting (14), (19), and (20),

$$\frac{\dot{e}}{e} = \frac{\beta e}{\alpha \sigma} + \frac{1-\beta}{\alpha} se - H - \rho. \tag{21}$$

Hence, the rate of increase of spending per middle product is larger the greater is spending per product and the smaller is the share of the country with comparative disadvantage in R&D in the total number of varieties.

Now, from the definition of the product shares $\sigma_i$, their rates of change are given by $\dot{\sigma}_i/\sigma_i = \dot{n}_i/n_i - \dot{n}/n$. Using (16) together with (17), (4), (18), and (20), we obtain

$$\dot{\sigma}_i = h_i - \frac{s_i}{b_i} \frac{1-\beta}{\alpha} e - \sigma_i \left( H - \frac{1-\beta}{\alpha} se \right), \tag{22}$$

where $h_i \equiv L_i/a_{Lni}$ is effective labor in country $i$, and $\Sigma_i h_i = H$. Since the evolution of the two product shares are related by $\Sigma_i \dot{\sigma}_i = 0$, we can replace (22) by a single differential equation in $\sigma$. Making use of the fact that $\dot{\sigma} = \Sigma_i \dot{\sigma}_i b_i$, we find

$$\dot{\sigma} = h - \frac{1-\beta}{\alpha} e - \sigma \left( H - \frac{1-\beta}{\alpha} se \right), \tag{23}$$

where $h \equiv \Sigma_i h_i b_i$.

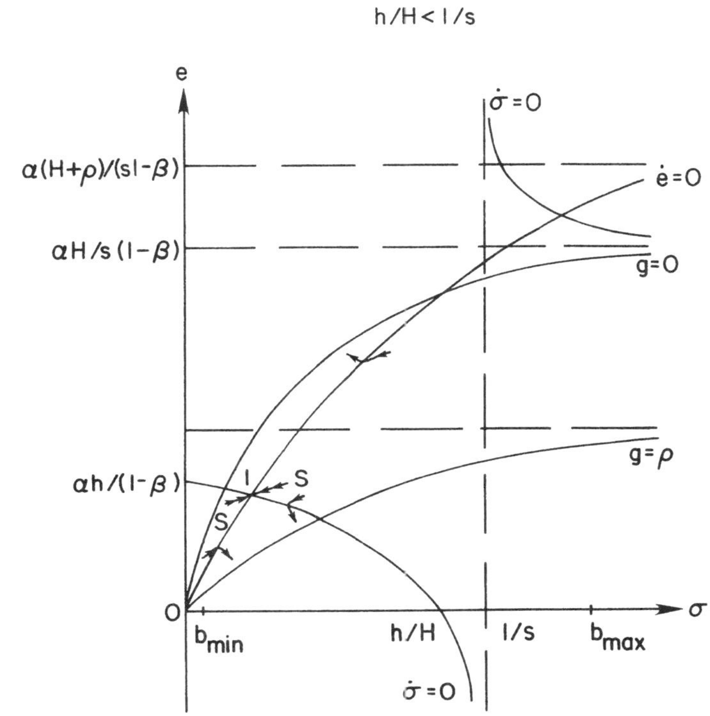


FIGURE 1

Equations (21) and (23) constitute an autonomous system of differential equations in $e$ and $\sigma$. The solution to this system, together with (13), (20), and the definition of $\sigma$, provide a complete description of the evolution of spending and the number of products in each country. From these, the paths for outputs, employments and final-goods prices are easily derived. Thus, we shall use this two-equation system to analyze equilibrium dynamics.[5]

In Figures 1 and 2 we depict the stationary points for $e$. We draw the $\dot{e}=0$ locus as increasing and concave (see (21)). To understand the positive slope of this curve, observe from (19) that the interest rate can be expressed as

$$\dot{R}=\beta e/\sigma(\varepsilon-1). \tag{24}$$

Thus, an increase in spending per product increases the interest rate and (from (20)) reduces the rate of growth of $n$ (the former because the profitability of R&D rises with

[5]A restriction that we have not explicitly taken into account to this point is that product development must be nonnegative in each country. This condition certainly is satisfied in the neighborhood of a steady-state equilibrium with positive growth, but it need not hold all along the convergent path to such an equilibrium. Thus, strictly speaking, the equilibrium dynamics that we describe below apply for sure only in the vicinity of a steady state.

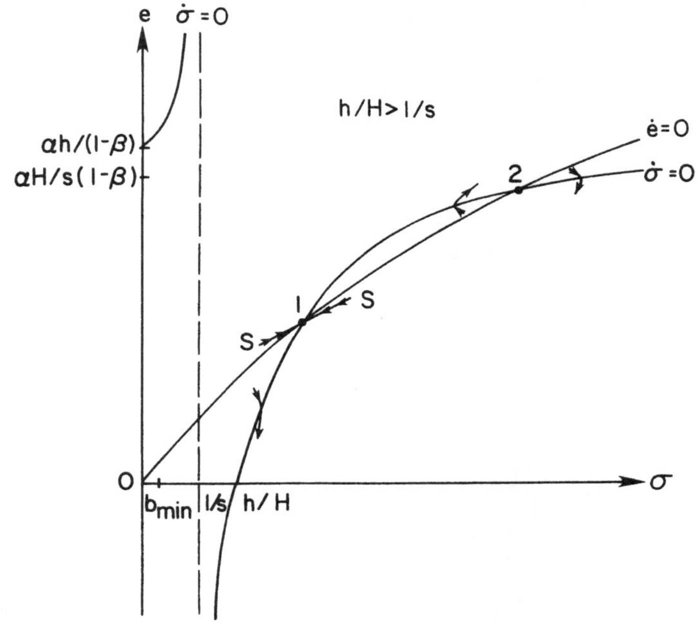


FIGURE 2

derived demand, the latter because more spending means less savings and hence less investment). Since an increase in the interest rate raises the rate of growth of nominal spending, and the rate of growth of $e$ is just the difference between the rates of growth of $E$ and $n$, it follows that an increase in $e$ raises the growth rate of $e$. To compensate for this acceleration in spending per product, if $e$ is to be stationary, $\sigma$ must rise. An increase in $\sigma$ lowers the interest rate and raises the rate of growth of $n$, thereby reducing the rate of growth of $e$.

Next, we distinguish two subcases depending on the relative sizes of $h/H$ and $1/s$.[6] It can be shown that $h/H > 1/s$ if and only if $(b_2 - b_1)(h_2 b_2/s_2 - h_1 b_1/s_1) > 0$. Therefore, the case $h/H > 1/s$, depicted in Figure 2, applies, for example, if the shares of the two countries' final outputs are in proportion to their relative *effective* labor forces; that is, $h_1/s_1 = h_2/s_2$. But a bias in size relative to budget share of final output can reverse the inequality and hence the relationship between $h/H$ and $1/s$. This gives us the case $h/H < 1/s$, shown in Figure 1, with which we begin the discussion.

In general, both $1/s$ and $h/H$ must lie between $b_{\min}$ and $b_{\max}$. The $\dot{\sigma} = 0$ curve in Figure 1 is everywhere downward sloping, crosses the horizontal axis at $h/H$, and is discontinuous at $\sigma = 1/s$. The slope of the curve is understood as follows. For $\dot{\sigma} = 0$, we must have $\dot{\sigma}_1 = 0$, which requires that the resources available for R&D in each country be just sufficient to preserve the country's *share* in the world's number of

[6]A borderline case arises when $b_1 = b_2$; that is, when comparative advantage is absent. Then $h/H = 1/s$, and $\sigma = b$ always. Convergence to the steady-state level of $e$ is immediate in this case; see Grossman and Helpman (1989a).

varieties. Consider country 1 and suppose for concreteness that this country has comparative advantage in R&D. Then an increase in $\sigma$ lowers $\sigma_1$, thereby reducing the resources needed for production of middle products. The fall in $\sigma_1$ also reduces the amount of R&D country 1 must perform to preserve its share in the number of products. *Ceteris paribus*, $\sigma_1$ would tend to rise. An increase in $e$, on the other hand, diverts resources away from R&D to production of middle and final products in country 1. But it also causes the world's rate of product growth to fall, thereby diminishing the amount of R&D country 1 must undertake to maintain its share of middle products. The relative magnitudes of these two effects depend upon country 1's relative size, and on the share of its final product in aggregate spending. In the case under consideration, the second effect dominates, and so the $\dot{\sigma}=0$ curve slopes downward.

In this case, there exists a unique steady state shown as point 1 in the figure. For initial values of $\sigma$ not too different from that at point 1, a unique trajectory (saddle-path) converges to the steady state. This trajectory, labeled $SS$, fulfills all equilibrium requirements and satisfies the intertemporal budget constraint with equality. Along this trajectory (in the vicinity of the steady state), the interest rate and profit rate are declining (see (24)) and nominal expenditure $E$ is rising. If the country with comparative advantage initially has a share of products that is smaller (larger) than its steady-state share, expenditure rises more slowly (rapidly) than the number of products.

The case depicted in Figure 2 arises when $h/H > 1/s$. Then the $\dot{\sigma}=0$ schedule slopes upward. If the curve intersects the $\dot{e}=0$ locus in the positive orthant at all, it must intersect it twice, as at points 1 and 2.[7] The lower point (point 1) represents the steady state with the higher rate of growth (growth rates increase as we move down along the $\dot{e}=0$ schedule, as we demonstrate below) and indeed the growth rate corresponding to point 2 may be negative. More importantly, as we show in Appendix B of our 1989a working paper, the equilibrium at point 1 exhibits saddle-path stability, whereas that at point 2 is locally unstable.[8] To the right of point 1, the saddle-path leading to that point remains trapped in the area bounded by the $\dot{e}=0$ locus and the line segment joining points 1 and 2, and is everywhere upward sloping. Thus, the qualitative properties of the dynamic trajectory that leads to a stable, positive-growth equilibrium in Figure 2 mimic those of the stable saddle-path in Figure 1.

For the remainder of this paper we shall restrict our discussion to stable steady-state equilibria with positive rates of growth. That is, we focus our attention on equilibria such as those at the points labeled 1 in Figures 1 and 2. In the steady state there occurs intraindustry trade in middle products and interindustry trade in consumer goods, with the long-run pattern of trade determined by comparative advantage, productivities in the two final-goods industries, and consumer preferences.

### III. Determinants of Long-Run Growth

Our model generates an endogenous rate of long-run growth. We now are prepared to explore how economic structure and economic policy affect this growth rate. In this section, we derive the implications of sec-

[7]The geometry supports this claim, once we recognize that the $\dot{\sigma}=0$ curve asymptotes to the horizontal line at $\alpha H/s(1-\beta)$, whereas the $\dot{e}=0$ curve asymptotes to the horizontal line at $\alpha(H+\rho)/s(1-\beta)$. The algebra provides confirmation, as simple manipulation reveals that the steady-state growth rate solves a quadratic equation.

[8]We strongly suspect, however, that whenever there exist two positive-growth, steady-state equilibria in the admissible range, there also exists a third (saddle-path stable) steady-state equilibrium with zero growth. We have established the existence of such an equilibrium for some parameter values, but so far have been unable to construct a general existence proof. Since the equilibrium at point 1 in Figure 2 can only be reached if the initial value of $\sigma$ is less than that at point 2, we suspect that initial values of $\sigma$ in excess of that at point 2 (and perhaps only these) imply convergence to a steady state with zero growth.

toral productivity levels, country sizes, and demand composition for the steady-state growth rate. The influence of trade policies and of subsidies to R&D are treated in the next section.

We derive the long-run values of $e$ and $\sigma$ by setting $\dot{e}$ and $\dot{\sigma}$ to zero in (21) and (23). The steady-state magnitudes, $\bar{e}$ and $\bar{\sigma}$, solve

$$\frac{\beta\bar{e}}{\alpha\bar{\sigma}}+\frac{1-\beta}{\alpha}s\bar{e}=H+\rho; \tag{25}$$

$$\frac{1-\beta}{\alpha}\bar{e}(1-\bar{\sigma}s)+\bar{\sigma}H=h. \tag{26}$$

Whenever $1/s>h/H$, these equations provide at most one solution for $(\bar{e},\bar{\sigma})$ consistent with $\bar{g}>0$. When $1/s<h/H$, there may be two such solutions, in which case we select the stable equilibrium, that is, the one with the smaller values for $\bar{e}$ and $\bar{\sigma}$. Stability implies, in this latter case, that the $\dot{\sigma}=0$ curve intersects the $\dot{e}=0$ curve from below (see Appendix B of our 1989a working paper). We make use of this condition, namely,

$$\frac{\beta\bar{e}}{(H+\rho)\bar{\sigma}^2}>\frac{\alpha H-(1-\beta)s\bar{e}}{\bar{\sigma}H-h} \quad \text{for } 1/s<h/H, \tag{27}$$

in signing the comparative-dynamics derivatives that follow.

The growth rate of the number of varieties in the steady-state equilibrium can be derived from the solution to (25) and (26), together with (20). From this, we can easily calculate the growth rate of output. In the steady state, nominal expenditure grows at rate $\bar{g}$, while (3) implies that $p_{Yi}$ grows at rate $[1-\beta/(1-\varepsilon)]\bar{g}$. From these facts and (15), we deduce that final output grows at rate $\beta\bar{g}/(1-\varepsilon)$.

It is worth noting at this point that the steady-state equations (25) and (26), as well as the equation for $\bar{g}$, do not rely on our assumption of perfect capital mobility. In the absence of capital mobility, the steady state would be the same as long as consumers worldwide share identical preferences (and therefore common subjective discount rates).[9]

It is instructive to begin the discussion with the case in which neither country exhibits comparative advantage in conducting R&D; that is, $b_1=b_2=b$. This case has $h=bH$ and $s=1/b$. Then (25) and (26) provide a unique solution for $\bar{e}$ and $\bar{\sigma}$, which upon substitution into (20) yields the long-run growth rate

$$\bar{g}=\frac{\beta(H+\rho)}{\varepsilon}-\rho. \tag{28}$$

This equilibrium growth rate shares much in common with that derived by Romer (1990) for a closed economy. In particular, the growth rate rises with effective labor $H$ and declines with the subjective discount rate. Our measure of effective labor adjusts raw labor for productivity in R&D (recall that $H=\Sigma_i L_i/a_{Lni}$), so greater effectiveness in research in either country, as well as a larger world labor force, necessarily means faster growth. Long-run growth does not, however, depend upon coefficients that determine absolute productivity in the intermediate or final goods sectors (such as $A_i$ or $a_{LXi}$). Nor do properties of the instantaneous utility function $u(\cdot)$, including the product composition of final demand, play any role in the determination of $\bar{g}$. As we shall see presently, all these features (except for the absence of an effect of $A_i$ on $\bar{g}$) are special to a world without any comparative advantage.

Consider next the case with $1/s>h/H$. The curves $\dot{e}=0$ and $\dot{\sigma}=0$ in Figure 3 describe the initial situation, with a unique initial steady state at point 1. Now suppose

[9]The cases of perfect and imperfect capital mobility do differ in their implications for the steady-state share of each country in aggregate spending $E$. However, as should be clear from (25) and (26), the cross-country composition of $E$ does not matter for the issues taken up in the present section.

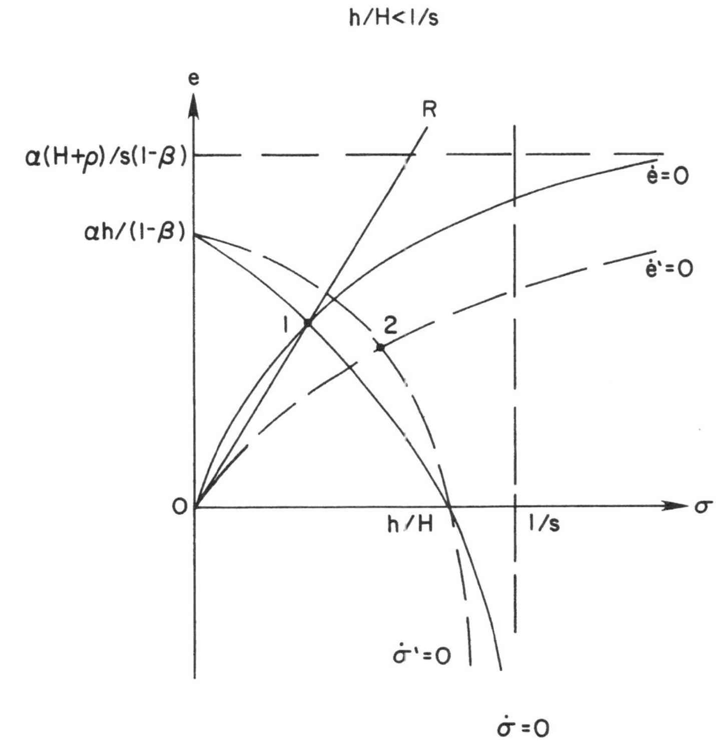


FIGURE 3

that preferences change so that $s$ increases. This corresponds to a shift in tastes in favor of the final good produced by the country with comparative advantage in performing R&D. From (25), we see that the $\dot{e}=0$ curve shifts down, say to $\dot{e}'=0$ in the figure. Equation (26) implies that the $\dot{\sigma}=0$ schedule shifts out (in the positive orthant) to $\dot{\sigma}'=0$. The new steady state occurs at a point such as 2. But observe that all points on $\dot{e}'=0$ to the right of its intersection with ray $OR$ are characterized by slower steady-state growth than at point 1. This claim follows from (20) and (25), whence

$$\bar{g}=\frac{\beta\bar{e}}{(\varepsilon-1)\bar{\sigma}}-\rho. \quad (29)$$

Since the intersection of $\dot{\sigma}'=0$ and $\dot{e}'=0$ necessarily lies to the right of the intersection of the latter curve with $OR$, we have established that an increase in $s$ reduces steady-state growth.

When tastes shift unexpectedly toward the final good of the country with comparative advantage in R&D, resources there must be reallocated to satisfy the relatively higher consumer demand. A process begins whereby labor there shifts out of R&D and the manufacture of middle products. Products accumulate more slowly in this country than in the other, and over time its share of middle products falls (i.e., $\sigma$ rises). Output per middle product changes by the same proportion in both countries (see (18)). So, in the new steady state, the country with comparative disadvantage in R&D is responsible for a relatively larger share of the world's innovation, with adverse consequences for the common steady-state growth rate. Of course, the opposite conclusion applies when $s$ falls. Moreover, the same results obtain at stable equilibrium points when $1/s < h/H$ (see our 1989a working paper). We have thus proven the following:

PROPOSITION 1: *Stronger relative demand for the final good of the country with comparative advantage in R&D lowers the long-run share of that country in the number of middle products and slows long-run growth of the world economy. In the absence of comparative advantage in R&D, the long-run growth rate is independent of the relative demand for final goods.*

Next we consider the dependence of growth on the sizes of the effective labor forces. Effective labor may grow without affecting cross-country comparative advantage either because the stock of irreproducible resources expands, or because the productivity of labor in all uses (or in R&D and intermediate-good production) rises equiproportionately. In the first experiment, suppose that both countries experience equiproportionate, once-and-for-all increases in the sizes of their effective labor forces. We have already seen that this change would augment world growth in the absence of comparative advantage. In our 1989a working paper we prove that the same result carries over to a world with intercountry differences in relative productivities at R&D and manufacturing. We establish the following there:

PROPOSITION 2: *An equiproportionate, once-and-for-all increase in the effective labor forces of both countries accelerates long-run growth.*

Greater resources generate faster growth in our model, as in Romer (1990), essentially because dynamic scale economies characterize long-run production.

We investigate next the effects of an increase in the effective labor force of a single country. Conceptually, it proves convenient to decompose this change into two elements. First, we increase $h$ and $H$ by the same percentage amount. This percentage is chosen to equal the product of the share of the expanding country in the world's effective stock of labor times the percentage increase in effective labor force that the expanding country actually experiences. This accounts for the total percentage change in $H$ when $H_i$ changes. Then we must adjust $h$ with $H$ fixed to arrive at the appropriate change in $h$.

As an intermediate step, let us consider the effects of an increase in $h$ alone. This corresponds to an increase in the effective labor of the country with comparative disadvantage in R&D, and a decrease in the effective labor of the other, so that the sum remains constant. This imaginary reshuffling of the world's resources shifts the $\dot{\sigma} = 0$ schedule upward when $1/s > h/H$, and downward otherwise. In either case, the $\dot{e} = 0$ curve is unaffected and the new steady-state point lies on this curve to the right of the original point. Noting (29), this proves the following:

LEMMA 1: *A reallocation of resources between countries that maintains a constant world stock of effective labor raises the long-run growth rate and increases the long-run product share of the relatively R&D efficient country if and only if the share of this country in effective labor increases.*

When the effective labor force of only country 1 (say) increases, $h$ rises by proportionately more or less than $H$, according to whether country 1 has comparative disadvantage or advantage in R&D. If country 1 has comparative advantage in R&D, then both the uniform increase in $H$ and $h$ and the adjustment (lowering) of $h$, that together comprise the effect of an increase in $H_1$, serve to accelerate world growth. But if country 1 has comparative disadvantage in R&D, the two effects work in opposite directions. The increase in resources, by Proposition 2, speeds growth; but the reallocation of given resources, by Lemma 1, slows growth. The net effect is ambiguous, as the numerical examples that we present in Appendix D of our 1989a working paper serve to demonstrate. We have established the following:

PROPOSITION 3: *The long-run growth rate is higher the larger is the effective labor force of the country with comparative advantage in R&D. A larger effective labor force in the country with comparative disadvantage in R&D may be associated with faster or slower growth, depending upon the extent of productivity differences. In the absence of comparative advantage, long-run growth is faster the larger is the effective labor force of either country.*

These results emphasize the novel features of growth in a world with distinct countries and intercountry differences in relative productivities. They also suggest that findings reported by Paul Krugman (1990) may be somewhat special. A country need not enjoy faster growth by joining the integrated world economy, if the country enjoys substantial comparative advantage in R&D. Moreover, growth in resources or improvements in the productivity of existing resources do not guarantee faster long-run growth in a world equilibrium with free trade. If resources expand or become more efficient in the country with comparative disadvantage in R&D, then the resulting intersectoral reallocation of resources worldwide might slow innovation and growth everywhere.

## IV. Economic Policy

In this section we discuss the effects of tariffs, export subsidies, and R&D subsidies on long-run growth. In order to do so, it is necessary for us to introduce the relevant policy parameters into the equations that describe instantaneous and steady-state equilibrium. To avoid repetition of the detailed arguments presented in Section I, we present here only the necessary modifications of the model and then explain their implications for the steady-state conditions. We restrict attention to small taxes and subsidies; this restriction facilitates exposition, as the channels through which economic policies affect long-run growth can be seen more clearly. We confine our analysis of trade policies to those that impede or encourage trade in final goods.

The introduction of taxes and subsidies to the model necessitates consideration of the government's budget. As usual, we assume that the government collects and redistributes net revenue by lump-sum taxes and subsidies. In a static framework, this specification suffices to determine completely the government's budgetary policy. But in a dynamic framework the budget need not balance period by period, so budgetary policy in general must specify the intertemporal pattern of lump-sum collections and transfers. However, with perfectly foresighted and infinitely lived agents, our model exhibits the Barro-Ricardo neutrality property. Hence, we need not concern ourselves with the intertemporal structure of budget deficits so long as the present value of the government's net cash flow equals zero.

The presence of the aforementioned policies modifies the decision problem for consumers in country 1 in two ways. First, we replace the price of good $i$ in (12) by $T_i p_{Yi}$, where $T_1 = 1$. With this formulation, $p_{Yi}$ remains the producer price of final good $i$, $T_2 > 1$ represents a tariff in country 1 on imports of consumer goods, and $T_2 < 1$ represents a subsidy by country 2 on exports of final output.[10] Second, we add the present value of net taxes to the right-hand side of (13) as a lump-sum addition to consumer wealth. The amount of this collection or redistribution will differ across countries according to their policies.

These modifications do not affect (14), which continues to describe the optimal intertemporal pattern of expenditures for consumers worldwide as a function of the pattern of equilibrium interest rates. In a steady state with $\dot{e} = 0$, (14) reduces to

$$\dot{R} = \bar{g} + \rho. \tag{30}$$

[10] The effects of a country 2 import tariff and a country 1 export subsidy can be derived symmetrically, so we neglect these policies here and leave the maximand for consumers in country 2 as before.

Notice that (30) implies that in any steady state in which countries grow at the same rate, long-run equalization of interest rates obtains. This property of our model holds irrespective of the presence or absence of international capital mobility and the presence or absence of tariffs or export subsidies on final goods and subsidies to research and development.

Turning to the production side, our policies do not alter equations (3)–(8) describing pricing and output relationships in the intermediate and final-goods sectors and the technology for knowledge creation. However, R&D subsidies do change the private cost of R&D. We replace (10) by

$$c_{ni} = w_i a_{Lni} / nS_i, \tag{10'}$$

where $S_i > 1$ represents subsidization of research costs in country $i$. It proves convenient to redefine our numeraire to normalize for the effect of the R&D subsidy on the price of intermediate inputs in country 1. Our new normalization dictates a modified equation for the price of intermediates produced in country 2 as well. Together, these relationships, which replace (17a) and (17b), can be written as

$$p_{Xi} = n(S_i a_{LXi} / a_{Lni})^{1/\varepsilon}. \tag{17'}$$

As for the market-clearing conditions, the factor-markets equation (16) is not affected, but we must replace (15) by

$$p_{Yi}Y_i = \frac{s_{i1}E_1}{T_i} + s_{i2}E_2, \tag{15'}$$

where $E_i$ denotes aggregate spending by consumers in country $i$, and the shares of spending devoted to good $i$ by residents of country 1 and country 2 are $s_{i1} = s_i(p_{Y1}, p_{Y2}T_2)$ and $s_{i2} = s_i(p_{Y1}, p_{Y2})$, respectively. Although import tariffs and export subsidies on final goods do not affect steady-state producer prices of final output in our model,[11] the direct response of spending shares in country 1 to changes in trade policy must now be taken into account. Moreover, R&D subsidies, if introduced at different rates in the two countries, will affect the steady-state value of $p_{Y1}/p_{Y2}$, and may therefore influence the long-run spending shares in both countries.

This completes the necessary modifications of the equilibrium relationships. We can now use the extended model to derive the equations describing steady-state equilibrium in the presence of policy intervention. In a steady state, employment in the R&D sector is given by $a_{Lni}\dot{n}_i / n = a_{Lni}\bar{g}\bar{\sigma}_i$. Making use of (4), (5), (7), (30), (10′), and (17′) (which together imply $\dot{c}_{ni} = 0$ in a steady state), we find employment in the manufacture of middle products equal to $a_{Lni}\bar{\sigma}_i(\bar{g} + \rho)(\varepsilon - 1)/S_i$. Substitution of these terms into (16) yields the steady-state labor market–clearing condition,

$$\bar{g}\bar{\sigma}_i + \frac{(\varepsilon-1)(\bar{g}+\rho)}{S_i}\bar{\sigma}_i + \frac{1-\beta}{\alpha b_i S_i^{1/\varepsilon}}\bar{q}_i = h_i, \tag{31}$$

where $q_i \equiv p_{Yi}Y_i / n$. Next, from (4)–(7), (30), and (17′), we obtain

$$(\varepsilon-1)(\bar{g}+\rho)\left(\sum_i \frac{\bar{\sigma}_i b_i}{S_i^{\alpha}}\right) - \beta\sum_i \bar{q}_i = 0. \tag{32}$$

Naturally, we also require

$$\sum_i \bar{\sigma}_i = 1. \tag{33}$$

Finally, (15′) implies

$$\bar{q}_i = \frac{\bar{s}_{i1}\bar{e}_1}{T_i} + \bar{s}_{i2}\bar{e}_2. \tag{34}$$

It is straightforward, now, to verify that (31)–(34) imply (25) and (26) when $T_i = S_i = 1$ for $i = 1,2$ (with $\bar{e} = \Sigma_i \bar{e}_i$). This provides a

[11] This statement can be verified using equations (3), (4), and (17′).

consistency check on the extended model with policy instruments.

We consider trade policies first. From (34), the ratio $\bar{q}_1/\bar{q}_2$ satisfies

$$\frac{\bar{q}_1}{\bar{q}_2} = \frac{\bar{s}_{11}\bar{e}_1 + \bar{s}_{12}\bar{e}_2}{\bar{s}_{21}\bar{e}_1/T_2 + \bar{s}_{22}\bar{e}_2}. \tag{35}$$

Now, for given expenditure levels $\bar{e}_i$, equations (31)–(33) and (35)—which constitute a system of five equations—provide a solution for $(\bar{g}, \bar{\sigma}_1, \bar{\sigma}_2, \bar{q}_1, \bar{q}_2)$. In this system, the trade policy parameters appear only in (35). Therefore, the long-run effects of trade policy depend only on their effects on $\bar{q}_1/\bar{q}_2$, taking into account the induced adjustment in the spending levels $\bar{e}_1$ and $\bar{e}_2$. Moreover, for small trade policies (i.e, with an initial value of $T_2 = 1$), the spending shares are equal across countries ($\bar{s}_{i1} = \bar{s}_{i2}$), so the effect on $\bar{q}_1/\bar{q}_2$ of changes in the cross-country composition of aggregate spending "washes out."

Further inspection of (35) reveals that an increase in $T_2$ starting from free trade with $T_2 = 1$ (i.e., a small import tariff in country 1) unambiguously raises $\bar{q}_1/\bar{q}_2$.[12] A tariff shifts demand by residents of country 1 toward home consumer products, and since relative producer prices do not change in the long run, steady-state relative quantities must adjust. The effect of this change on the steady state is qualitatively the same as for an exogenous increase in world preference for final good 1, such as we studied in the previous section when we varied $s_1$.

[12]The easiest way to see this is to write the right-hand-side of (35) as

$$(\bar{p}_{Y1}, \bar{p}_{Y2})[\phi_1(\bar{p}_{Y1}, T_2\bar{p}_{Y2})\bar{e}_1 + \phi_1(\bar{p}_{Y1}, \bar{p}_{Y2})\bar{e}_2]/$$
$$[\phi_2(\bar{p}_{Y1}, T_2\bar{p}_{Y2})\bar{e}_1 + \phi_2(\bar{p}_{Y1}, \bar{p}_{Y2})\bar{e}_2],$$

where $\phi_i(\cdot)$ is minus the partial derivative of $v(\cdot)$ from (1) with respect to its $i$th argument divided by $v(\cdot)$. Then an increase in $T_2$ with $\bar{p}_{Y1}/\bar{p}_{Y2}$ constant clearly raises demand for final good 1 in country 1 (the first component of the bracketed term in the numerator increases) and lowers the demand there for final good 2 (the first component of the bracketed term in the denominator falls).

Similarly, a small export subsidy in country 2 (a reduction in $T_2$ to a value slightly below one) biases country 1 demand in favor of foreign final output. So we may apply directly our results from Proposition 1 to state the following:

PROPOSITION 4: *A small import tariff or export subsidy on final goods reduces a country's steady-state share in middle products and R&D. It increases the rate of long-run growth in the world economy if and only if the policy-active country has comparative disadvantage in R&D.*

Commercial policies *do* affect long-run growth rates. They do so by shifting resources in the policy-active country out of the growth-generating activity (R&D) and into production in the favored sector. At the same time, a resource shift of the opposite kind takes place abroad in the dynamic general equilibrium. The net effect on world growth hinges on the identity of the country that favors its consumer-good industry. If import protection or export promotion is undertaken by the country that is relatively less efficient in conducting R&D, then growth accelerates; otherwise, growth decelerates.

Next, we investigate the effects of small subsidies to R&D, introduced from an initial position of *laissez faire*. For these policy experiments, $T_2 = 1$ before and after the policy change, so the expenditure levels $\bar{e}_i$ cancel from (35). Suppose, first, that both countries apply subsidies at equal *ad valorem* rates; that is, $S_1 = S_2 = S$. In this case, relative prices of final output do not change across steady states. Therefore, the spending shares $\bar{s}_{ij}$ do not change. In Appendix C of our 1989a working paper, we totally differentiate (31)–(33) and (35) with respect to $S$ to prove the following:

PROPOSITION 5: *A small R&D subsidy by both countries at a common rate increases the rate of long-run growth in the world economy.*

This proposition is not surprising, and corresponds to a similar result for the closed economy derived by Romer (1990). Since R&D represents the only source of gains in per capita income in our model, stimulation of this activity promotes growth.

What is more interesting, perhaps, is the effect of a small R&D subsidy in a single country. As for bilateral subsidies, a unilateral subsidy promotes growth by bringing more resources into product development in the policy-active country. But now, relative final-good prices change, so the spending shares in (35) must be allowed to vary unless the utility function has a Cobb-Douglas form. Depending on whether the elasticity of substitution between final products exceeds or falls short of one, this induced change in the pattern of spending can be conducive to or detrimental to growth. Moreover, an R&D subsidy in a single country will alter the relative shares of the two countries in product development. If the subsidy is introduced by the country that is relatively less efficient at performing R&D, this effect too can impede growth. In Appendix D of our 1989a working paper we show, by means of a numerical example using a Cobb-Douglas utility function, that an R&D subsidy introduced by the country with comparative disadvantage in R&D might (but need not) reduce the world's growth rate. We also prove in Appendix C that, for the case of constant spending shares, an R&D subsidy must encourage growth if it is undertaken by the country with comparative advantage in R&D. Thus we have the following:

PROPOSITION 6: *The provision of a subsidy to R&D in one country increases long-run growth if spending shares on the two final goods are constant and the policy is undertaken by the country with comparative advantage in R&D. Otherwise, the long-run growth rate may rise or fall.*

Our results here on the long-run growth effects of government policy have no immediate normative implications, both because we perform only steady-state comparisons and because the initial *level* of utility may differ along alternative growth paths. But in our 1989b paper we conduct a complete welfare analysis for a small country with endogenous growth generated by technological progress as here. We find that the market determined rate of growth is suboptimally low due to the presence of the nonappropriable spillovers in the process of knowledge generation. An R&D subsidy that speeds growth improves welfare for the small country until some optimal growth rate is achieved. Further increases in the subsidy rate reduce welfare even as they accelerate growth. We show also that trade policy need not raise welfare, even if it successfully speeds growth. The explanation for this lies in the presence of a second distortion in our economy, one that stems from the pricing of middle products above marginal cost. The mark-up pricing practiced by intermediate producers gives rise to suboptimal use of middle products in the production of final goods. Trade policy that accelerates growth but reduces the output of middle products in the general equilibrium can be detrimental to welfare. Conversely, commercial policy that augments the output of middle products can improve welfare even if the growth implications of such policy are adverse.

These results do not carry over immediately to the current environment, though the considerations we found to be relevant in our 1989b paper are certainly applicable here as well. Normative analysis in the present two-country setting is complicated by the terms-of-trade effects that arise when policy alters the relative price of the final goods, changes the price of intermediates (if sectoral trade in middle products is not balanced), or varies the interest rate. Because of these various terms-of-trade effects we have been unable thus far to find simple conditions under which growth-enhancing policy by one government raises that country's welfare.

## V. Lags in the Diffusion of Knowledge

We have assumed all along that research and development creates as a by-product an addition to the stock of knowledge that facilitates subsequent R&D. Moreover, we supposed that the knowledge so created becomes available immediately to scientists and engineers worldwide. We now relax the latter assumption, in recognition of the fact that privately created knowledge, even if nonappropriable, may enter the public domain via an uneven and time-consuming process. Also, since legal and cultural barriers may inhibit the free movement of people and ideas across national borders, we shall allow here for the possibility that information generated in one country disseminates more rapidly to researchers in the same country than it does to researchers in the trade partner country. After extending the model we will reconsider the effects of trade policies on the steady-state rate of growth.

In place of our earlier assumption that world knowledge accumulates exactly at the rate of product innovation (equation (9)), we suppose now that R&D expenditures contribute to country-specific stocks of knowledge according to

$$(9^{\dagger}) \quad K_i(t) = \lambda_h \int_{-\infty}^{t} e^{\lambda_h(\tau - t)} n_i(\tau) + \lambda_f \int_{-\infty}^{t} e^{\lambda_f(\tau - t)} n_j(\tau)\, d\tau,$$

where $K_i(t)$ is the stock of knowledge capital at time $t$ in country $i$. With this specification, the contribution of a particular R&D project to general knowledge is spread over time. At the moment after completion of the project, none of its findings have percolated through the scientific and professional community. After an infinite amount of time has passed, the R&D project makes, as before, a unit contribution to knowledge. After finite time, the contribution lies between these extremes of zero and one, as given by the exponential lag structure in ($9^{\dagger}$). The parameters $\lambda_h$ and $\lambda_f$ (with $\lambda_h \geq \lambda_f$) distinguish within-country and cross-country rates of diffusion.

The introduction of lags in the diffusion of knowledge alters two of the fundamental equations of the model. First, (8) becomes

$$(8^{\dagger}) \quad \dot{n}_i = L_{ni} K_i / a_{Lni}.$$

Second, we have in place of (10),

$$(10^{\dagger}) \quad c_{ni} = w_i a_{Lni} / K_i.$$

In a steady state with $\dot{n}_1 = \dot{n}_2 = g$, we have $n_i(\tau) = n_i(t) e^{g(\tau - t)}$, so that

$$(36) \quad K_i(t) = \frac{\lambda_h}{\lambda_h + \bar{g}} n_i(t) + \frac{\lambda_f}{\lambda_f + \bar{g}} n_j(t) = \left[ \frac{\lambda_h}{\lambda_h + \bar{g}} \bar{\sigma}_i + \frac{\lambda_f}{\lambda_f + \bar{g}} \bar{\sigma}_j \right] n(t) \equiv \mu_i(\bar{\sigma}_1, \bar{\sigma}_2, \bar{g}) n(t).$$

So in the steady state, knowledge in each country is proportional once again to the total number of middle products. But the factor of proportionality has become country-specific and endogenous. This means that the steady-state labor-input coefficient for R&D in country $i$, $a_{Lni}/\mu_i$, also is endogenous; that is, relative productivity in R&D depends now not only on relative natural abilities in performing this activity, but also on relative cumulative experience in research, as summarized by the $\sigma_i$'s. This consideration leads us to draw a distinction henceforth between *natural* and *acquired* comparative advantage in R&D.

From (36) we see that when $\lambda_h = \lambda_f \to \infty$ (i.e., when diffusion lags are very short), $\mu_1 = \mu_2 \to 1$, and the extended model reverts to the earlier formulation. For $\lambda_h = \lambda_f$ finite, $\mu_1 = \mu_2$, so that the ratio of the natural-plus-acquired productivity parameters for each country is the same as for the natural productivity parameters alone. In this case, the pattern of comparative advantage cannot be reversed by endogenous learning, and all results from before continue to apply. We concentrate here on cases in which the rates of diffusion are *unequal* but the difference between them is small.[13]

[13]A large difference between the within-country and across-country rates of diffusion may imply that, in the steady-state equilibrium, all R&D is carried out by one country. Such specialization, which is common in mod-

We derive the long-run effects of trade policy in the extended model using equations (31)–(33) and (35), but with $S_1 = S_2 = 1$ (no R&D subsidies), with $b_i$ replaced by $b_i / \mu_i^{\alpha}$ (natural plus acquired comparative advantage in place of just natural comparative advantage), and with $h_i$ replaced by $h_i \mu_i$ (natural plus acquired effective labor in place of natural effective labor). For clarity of exposition, we shall also assume for the remainder of this section that the spending shares $s_i$ are constant. This assumption is valid when $u(\cdot)$ takes a Cobb-Douglas form.

The new elements that diffusion lags introduce to the analysis of policy stem from the effects of *relative size* and *demand-side bias*. Before considering these new aspects, let us suppose that labor forces are equal and demand for the two final goods is symmetric. By totally differentiating the system of steady-state equations (see Appendix E of our 1989a working paper), we establish the following:

PROPOSITION 7: *Suppose* $L_1 = L_2$, $s_1 = s_2$, $a_{LX1} = a_{LX2}$, *and* $\lambda_h - \lambda_f > 0$, *but small. Then a tariff on imports of final goods in country i raises the long-run growth rate if and only if* $a_{Lni} > a_{Lnj}$.

In this case, the effects of acquired comparative advantage necessarily *reinforce* those of natural comparative advantage. The country that is relatively more productive in creating new blueprints will attain, in the steady-state equilibrium prior to the introduction of policy, a majority share of the world's middle products. By its greater concentration in R&D, it will gain more experience in research and attain a higher steady-state stock of knowledge. Thus, the effects of learning will augment its initial comparative advantage in R&D. When policy is introduced in one country or the other, the implications of the dynamic resource reallocation for the global efficiency of R&D will be all the more significant.

Now suppose that the two countries differ initially only in (effective) size, as measured by $h_i$. Recall that with equal rates of diffusion, a small tariff in either country does not affect the long-run rate of growth. Now, however, we find the following:

PROPOSITION 8: *Suppose* $b_1 = b_2$, $s_1 = s_2$ *and* $\lambda_h - \lambda_f > 0$, *but small. Then a small tariff on imports of final goods raises the long-run growth rate if and only if the policy is introduced by the country with the relatively smaller effective labor force.*

Here, the larger country will come to acquire comparative advantage in R&D, though it starts with none. The reason is as follows. With differential rates of diffusion, knowledge takes on the characteristics of a *local public good*. The larger country will have more (effective) scientists to benefit from this nonexcludable good as its share in world R&D exceeds one half. So it acquires over time a relatively larger knowledge base and hence a relatively more productive corps of researchers. Trade policy that serves to divert resources away from the R&D sector in the larger country once comparative advantage has been established must be detrimental to growth.

The effects of demand-size bias are similar. The country whose good is in relatively greater demand must devote relatively more of its resources to final-goods production. Thus, its R&D sector initially will be smaller. This country develops over time a comparative disadvantage in R&D, as its learning lags that in its trade partner country. Protection in this country will improve world efficiency of R&D and thereby speed growth.

Once we allow for lags in the diffusion of scientific knowledge and differential speeds of diffusion within versus between countries, we find a richer set of possibilities for the long-run effects of trade policy. Comparative advantage continues to play a critical role in determining whether policy in one country will speed or decelerate growth.

els with a national component to increasing returns to scale, necessarily occurs here if static preferences are Cobb-Douglas and $\lambda_f = 0$ (i.e., all spillovers are internal). Then the equations that we have developed to describe the steady-state equilibrium (which presume non-specialization in each country) would not be valid.

But comparative advantage now must be interpreted with care, because it reflects not only natural ability but also the (endogenous) benefits from cumulative experience.[14] Since steady-state productivity in R&D varies positively with the size of the R&D sector, all determinants of the equilibrium allocation of resources to this sector come to be important in the analysis of policy.

### VI. Conclusions

In this paper, we have analyzed a dynamic, two-country model of trade and growth in which long-run productivity gains stem from the profit-maximizing behavior of entrepreneurs. We have studied the determinants of R&D, where research bears fruit in the form of designs for new intermediate products and in making further research less costly. New intermediate products permit greater specialization in the process of manufacturing consumer goods, thereby enhancing productivity in final production. In order to highlight the role of endogenous technological improvements as a source of growth we have abstracted entirely from factor accumulation. But Romer (1990) has shown that capital accumulation can be introduced into a model such as the one we have studied without affecting the analysis in any significant way.

The interesting features of our analysis arise because of the assumed presence of *cross-country differences* in efficiency at R&D and manufacturing. Considerations of comparative advantage in research versus manufacturing of intermediate goods bear importantly on the implications of economic structure and economic policy for long-run patterns of specialization and long-run rates of growth. We find, for example, that growth in world resources or improvements in R&D efficiency need not speed the rate of steady-state growth, if those changes occur predominantly in the country with comparative disadvantage in R&D.

Concerning policy, we find for the first time a link between trade intervention and long-run growth. Any (small) trade policy that switches spending toward the consumer good produced by the country with comparative advantage in R&D will cause long-run growth rates to decline. Subsidies to R&D will accelerate growth when applied at equal rates in both countries, but need not do so if introduced only in the country with comparative disadvantage in R&D. When knowledge spillovers occur with a time lag and diffusion is faster within the country of origin than across national borders, comparative advantage becomes endogenous. Once we recognize that comparative advantage can be *acquired* as well as natural, we find a role for country size and demand-size bias in determining the long-run effects of policy.

Our emphasis on comparative advantage in research and development highlights only one channel through which trade structure and commercial policy might affect long-run growth. In other contexts, the trade environment might influence the rate of accumulation of human capital or the rate at which a technologically lagging (less developed) country adopts for local use the existing off-the-shelf techniques of production. Investigation of the links between trade regime and these other sources of growth seems to us a worthy topic for future research.

[14]Endogenous comparative advantage also plays a central role in Krugman's (1987) analysis of commodity-specific learning-by-doing. There, as here, productivity increases with cumulative experience. But each good is produced in only one country in Krugman's model, so long-run comparative advantage is fully determined by the initial pattern of specialization.

## REFERENCES

**Becker, Gary S. and Murphy, Kevin M.,** "Economic Growth, Human Capital and Population Growth," *Journal of Political Economy*, forthcoming, 1990.

**Corden, W. Max,** "The Effects of Trade on the Rate of Growth," in J. Bhagwati et al., eds., *Trade, Balance of Payments, and Growth: Papers in Honour of Charles P. Kindleberger*, Amsterdam: North-Holland, 1971.

**Ethier, Wilfred J.,** "National and International Returns to Scale in the Modern Theory of International Trade," *American Economic Review*, June 1982, *72*, 389–405.

**Findlay, Ronald,** "Growth and Development in Trade Models," in R. Jones and P. Kenen, eds., *Handbook of International Economics*, Amsterdam: North-Holland, 1984.

**Griliches, Zvi,** "Issues in Assessing the Contribution of Research and Development in Productivity Growth," *Bell Journal of Economics*, Summer 1979, *10*, 92–116.

**Grossman, Gene M.,** "Explaining Japan's Innovation and Trade: A Model of Quality Competition and Dynamic Comparative Advantage," National Bureau of Economic Research Working Paper No. 3194, December 1989.

______ **and Helpman, Elhanan,** (1989a) "Comparative Advantage and Long-Run Growth," National Bureau of Economic Research Working Paper No. 2809, January 1989.

______ **and** ______, (1989b) "Growth and Welfare in a Small, Open Economy," Woodrow Wilson School Discussion Paper in Economics No. 145, June 1989.

______ **and** ______, (1989c) "Product Development and International Trade," *Journal of Political Economy*, December 1989, *97*, 1261–83.

______ **and** ______, (1989d) "Quality Ladders in the Theory of Growth," National Bureau of Economic Research Working Paper No. 3099, September 1989. (*Review of Economic Studies*, forthcoming.)

______, ______ **and Razin, A.,** eds., *International Trade and Trade Policy*, Cambridge, MA: MIT Press, forthcoming.

**Judd, Kenneth,** "On the Performance of Patents," *Econometrica*, May 1985, *53*, 567–85.

**Krugman, Paul R.,** "The Narrow Moving Band, the Dutch Disease, and the Competitive Consequences of Mrs. Thatcher: Notes on Trade in the Presence of Dynamic Scale Economies," *Journal of Development Economics*, October 1987, *27*, 41–55.

______, "Endogenous Innovation, International Trade and Growth," *Journal of Political Economy*, forthcoming, 1990.

**Lucas, Robert E. Jr.,** "On the Mechanics of Economic Development," *Journal of Monetary Economics*, July 1988, *22*, 3–42.

**Maddison, Angus,** "Growth and Slowdown in Advanced Capitalist Economies: Techniques of Quantitative Assessment," *Journal of Economic Literature*, June 1987, *25*, 649–98.

**Pasinetti, Luigi,** *Structural Change and Economic Growth*, Cambridge: Cambridge University Press, 1981.

**Romer, Paul M.,** "Increasing Returns and Long-Run Growth," *Journal of Political Economy*, October 1986, *94*, 1002–37.

______, "Endogenous Technological Change," *Journal of Political Economy*, forthcoming, 1990.

**Solow, Robert M.,** "Technical Change and the Aggregate Production Function," *Review of Economics and Statistics*, August 1957, *39*, 312–20.

# [11]

# ECONOMIC INTEGRATION AND ENDOGENOUS GROWTH*

Luis A. Rivera-Batiz and Paul M. Romer

In a world with two similar, developed economies, economic integration can cause a permanent increase in the worldwide rate of growth. Starting from a position of isolation, closer integration can be achieved by increasing trade in goods or by increasing flows of ideas. We consider two models with different specifications of the research and development sector that is the source of growth. Either form of integration can increase the long-run rate of growth if it encourages the worldwide exploitation of increasing returns to scale in the research and development sector.

## I. Introduction

Many economists believe that increased economic integration between the developed economies of the world has tended to increase the long-run rate of economic growth. If they were asked to make an intuitive prediction, they would suggest that prospects for growth would be permanently diminished if a barrier were erected that impeded the flow of all goods, ideas, and people between Asia, Europe, and North America. Yet it would be difficult for any of us to offer a rigorous model that has been (or even could be) calibrated to data and that could justify this belief.

We know what some of the basic elements of such a growth model would be. Historical analysis (e.g., Rosenberg [1980]) shows that the creation and transmission of ideas has been extremely important in the development of modern standards of living. Theoretical arguments dating from Adam Smith's analysis of the pin factory have emphasized the potential importance of fixed costs and the extent of the market. There is a long tradition in trade theory of using models with Marshallian external effects to approach questions about increasing returns. More recently, static models with fixed costs and international specialization have been proposed that come closer to Smith's description of the sources of the gains from trade [Dixit and Norman, 1980; Ethier, 1982; Krugman, 1979, 1981; Lancaster, 1980]. There are also dynamic models with fixed costs and differentiated products in which output

*Conversations with Robert Barro, Gene Grossman, Elhanan Helpman, and Danyang Xie about their work on related issues have been very helpful, as were comments by Ray Riezman and Robert Staiger on earlier versions of this paper. The work of the second author was supported by NSF grant #SES88-22052, by a Sloan Foundation Fellowship, and by the Center for Advanced Studies in the Behavioral Sciences, which received support from NSF grant #BNS87-00864.


*The Quarterly Journal of Economics*, May 1991

grows toward a fixed steady state level [Grossman and Helpman, 1989a].

Recent models of endogenous growth have used these ideas to study the effects that trade can have on the long-run rate of growth. (See, for example, the theoretical papers by Dinopoulos, Oehmke, and Segerstrom [1990]; Feenstra [1990]; Grossman and Helpman [1989b, 1989c, 1989d, 1989e, 1990]; Krugman [1990, Ch. 11]; Lucas [1988]; Romer [1990]; Segerstrom, Anant, and Dinopoulos [1990]; and Young [1990]. Backus, Kehoe, and Kehoe [1991] present both theoretical models and cross-country empirical evidence that bears on their models.) These models permit a distinction between a one-shot gain (i.e., a level effect) and a permanent change in the growth rate (i.e., a growth effect) that is extremely important in making an order of magnitude estimate of the benefits of economic integration. Conventional attempts to quantify the effects of integration using the neoclassical growth model often suggest that the gains from integration are small. If these estimates were calculated in the context of an endogenous growth model, integration might be found to be much more important.

The papers written so far have already demonstrated, however, that the growth effects of trade restrictions are very complicated in the most general case. Grossman and Helpman [1989b, 1989c, 1989e, 1990] have been particularly explicit about the fact that no universally applicable conclusions can be drawn. There are some models in which trade restrictions can slow down the worldwide rate of growth. There are others in which they can speed up the worldwide rate of growth.

To provide some intuition for the conjecture described in the first paragraph, that trade between the advanced countries does foster growth, we narrow the focus in this paper. We do not consider the general case of trade between countries with different endowments and technologies. Instead, we focus on the pure scale effects of integration. To set aside the other "comparative advantage" effects that trade induces in multisector trade models, we consider integration only between countries or regions that are similar. Therefore, we do not address the kinds of questions that are relevant for modeling the effects that trade between a poor LDC and a developed country can have on the worldwide rate of growth.

In the early stages of our analysis of integration and growth, it became clear that the theoretical treatment of ideas has a decisive effect on the conclusions one draws. In many of the existing models, flows of ideas cannot be separated from flows of goods. In others, flows of ideas are exogenously limited by national boundaries regardless of the trade regime. In either of these cases, economic integration can refer only to flows of goods along cargo networks. We consider a broader notion of integration, one that assigns an effect to flows of ideas along communication networks.

Flows of ideas deserve attention comparable to that devoted to flows of goods, for public policy can influence international communications and information flows to the same extent that it influences goods flows. Governments often subsidize language training and study abroad. Tax policies directly affect the incentive to station company employees in foreign nations. Immigration and visa policies directly limit the movement of people. Telecommunications networks are either run by government agencies or controlled by regulators. Some governments restrict direct foreign investment, which presumably is important in the international transmission of ideas. Others have made the acquisition of commercial and technical information a high priority task for their intelligence agencies.

Although these are the only ones we consider, it should be clear that flows of goods and flows of ideas are not the only elements in economic integration. Under some assumptions about nominal variables and the operation of financial markets, economic integration will also depend on monetary and institutional arrangements. The growth models we consider are too simple to consider these effects. It should also be clear that economic integration is not synonymous with political integration. Firms in Windsor, Ontario, may be more closely integrated into markets in the United States than they are to markets in the neighboring province of Quebec. Moreover, the notion of full economic integration does not entail the abolition of citizenship distinctions that have taken place in Germany's reunification.

The structure of the paper is as follows. Section II lays out the basic features of the production structure on which all arguments rely. It describes preferences, endowments, and the nature of equilibrium under the two specifications of R&D. Section III describes the equilibrium for both models in the closed economy and complete integration cases, and illustrates the scale effects that are present. Section IV presents the three main thought experiments concerning partial integration. Sections V and VI describe the general lessons that can be learned about the relation between the scale of the market and growth and discuss limitations of the models, extensions, and the relation to other models of endogenous growth.

## II. Specification of the Models

### A. Functional Forms and Decentralization in the Manufacturing Sector

The specification of the production technology for the manufacturing sector is taken from Romer [1990]. Manufacturing output is a function of human capital $H$, labor $L$, and a set $x(i)$ of capital goods indexed by the variable $i$. To avoid complications arising from integer constraints, the index $i$ is modeled as a continuous variable. Technological progress is represented by the invention of new types of capital goods.

There are two types of manufacturing activities: production of consumption goods and production of the physical units of the types of capital goods that have already been invented. A third activity, research and development (R&D), creates designs for new types of capital goods. This activity is discussed in the next section.

Both manufacturing activities use the same production function. Let $x(i)$ denote the stock of capital of type $i$ that is used in production, and let $A$ be the index of the most recently invented good. By the definition of $A$, $x(i) = 0$ for all $i > A$. Output $Y$ is assumed to take the form,

$$Y(H,L,x(\cdot)) = H^{\alpha}L^{\beta}\int_0^A x(i)^{1-\alpha-\beta}di. \tag{1}$$

Since the production function for manufacturing consumption goods is the same as that for manufacturing units of any type of existing capital, the relative prices of consumption goods and all types of existing capital goods are fixed by the technology. For simplicity, we choose units so that all of these relative prices are one. Fixed prices imply that the aggregate capital stock $K = \int_0^A x(i)\, di$ is well defined, as is aggregate output $Y$.

In this specification one unit of any capital good can be produced if one unit of consumption goods is forgone. This does not mean that consumption goods are directly converted into capital goods. Rather, the inputs needed to produce one unit of consumption are shifted from the production of consumption goods into the production of a capital good. Since inputs are used in the same proportions, it is easy to infer the allocation of inputs between the different production activities from the level of output of those activities. Because all the outputs here have the same production function, the consumption sector and all of the sectors producing the different capital goods can be collapsed into a single sector. We can therefore represent total manufacturing output as a function of the total stock of inputs used in the combined manufacturing sectors and can describe the division of inputs between sectors by the constraint $Y = C + K$. For one of the models of R&D described in the next section, we can use this same observation to combine the research sector and the aggregate manufacturing sector into a single sector describing all output in the economy. In the other model the R&D and manufacturing sectors must be kept separate.

There are many equivalent institutional structures that can support a decentralized equilibrium in manufacturing. For instance, the holder of a patent on good $j$ could become a manufacturer, producing and selling good $j$. Alternatively, the patent holder could license the design to other manufacturers for a fee. Formally, it is useful to separate the manufacturing decision from the monopoly pricing decision of the patent holder, so we assume that patent holders contract out manufacturing to separate firms. It is also easier to assume that the patent holder collects rent on its capital goods rather than selling them. For analytical convenience, we therefore describe the institutional arrangements in the following, slightly artificial way. First, there are many firms that rent capital goods $x(i)$ from the patent holders, hire unskilled labor $L$, and employ skilled human capital $H$ to produce manufactured goods. Each of these firms can produce consumption goods for sale to consumers. It can also produce one of the capital goods on contract for the holder of the patent. All of the manufacturing firms have the production function given in equation (1), which is homogeneous of degree one. They are price takers and earn zero profit. Manufacturing output is taken as the numeraire.

The firm that holds the patent on good $j$ bids out the production of the actual capital goods to a specific manufacturer. It purchases physical units of the good for the competitive price, by normalization equal to one. The patent holder then rents out the units to all manufacturing firms at the profit-maximizing monopoly rental rate. It can do this because patent law prohibits any firm from manufacturing a capital good without the consent of the patent holder. The patent is a tradable asset with a price of $P_A$ that is equal to the present discounted value of the stream of monopoly rent minus the cost of the machines. It is easy to verify that this set of institutional arrangements is equivalent to other arrangements. For example, the equivalent licensing fee for each unit of capital sold by a licensee is the present value of the stream of monopoly rent on one machine minus the unit cost of manufacturing it.

### *B. Functional Forms and Decentralization in R&D*

We consider two specifications of the technology of R&D that permit easy analytic solutions. Each specification captures different features of the world, and neither alone gives a complete description of R&D. We use both of them because they help us isolate the exact sense in which economic integration can influence long-run growth. As the example in the next section shows, it would be easy to come to misleading conclusions about integration and growth if one generalized from a single example.

The first specification of the technology for producing designs for new capital goods assumes that human capital and knowledge are the only inputs that influence the output of designs:

$$\dot{A} = \delta HA, \tag{2}$$

where $H$ denotes the stock of human capital used in research. The stock of existing designs $A$ is a measure of general scientific and engineering knowledge as well as practical know-how that accumulated as previous design problems were solved. (See Romer [1990] for additional discussion of this specification.) New designs build on this knowledge, so we refer to this type of R&D process as the knowledge-driven specification of R&D. This specification imposes a sharp factor intensity difference between R&D and manufacturing. Neither unskilled labor nor physical capital has any value in R&D. Because of this difference, the resulting model must be analyzed using a two-sector framework.

A useful polar case is a technology for R&D that uses the same inputs as the manufacturing technology, in the same proportions. If $H$, $L$, and $x_i$ denote inputs used in R&D and $B$ denotes a constant scale factor, output of designs can be written as

$$\dot{A} = BH^{\alpha}L^{\beta}\int_0^A x(i)^{1-\alpha-\beta}di. \tag{3}$$

This specification says that human capital, unskilled labor, and capital goods (such as personal computers or oscilloscopes) are productive in research. But in contrast to the previous specification, knowledge per se has no productive value. Access to the designs for all previous goods, and familiarity with the ideas and know-how that they represent, does not aid the creation of new designs. We refer to this as the lab equipment specification of R&D.

As noted above, the growth model with the knowledge-driven specification for R&D has an unavoidable two-sector structure. The production possibility frontier in the space of designs and manufactured goods takes on the usual curved shape. In the lab equipment model the production functions of the goods and R&D sectors are the same, so the production possibility frontier is a straight line. If the output of goods is reduced by one unit and the inputs released are transferred to the R&D sector, they yield $B$ patents. Thus, the price $P_A$ of a patent in terms of goods is determined on the technology side as $P_A = 1/B$. Since capital goods and consumption goods have the same production technology, we integrated them into a single manufacturing sector in the last section. In the lab equipment model we can go farther and aggregate manufacturing and research into a single sector. Let $H$, $L$, and $x(i)$ denote the entire stock of inputs available in the economy at date $t$. Then we can express the value of total output $C + \dot{K} + \dot{A}/B$ in terms of the total stock of inputs,

$$C + \dot{K} + \frac{\dot{A}}{B} = H^{\alpha}L^{\beta}\int_0^A x(i)^{1-\alpha-\beta}di. \tag{4}$$

The model's symmetry implies that $x(i) = x(j)$ for all $i$ and $j$ less than $A$. We can therefore substitute $K/A = x(i)$ in equation (4) to obtain a reduced-form expression for total output in terms of $H$, $K$, $L$, and $A$:

$$\begin{aligned} C + \dot{K} + \dot{A}/B &= H^{\alpha}L^{\beta}A(K/A)^{1-\alpha-\beta} \\ &= H^{\alpha}L^{\beta}K^{1-\alpha-\beta}A^{\alpha+\beta}. \end{aligned} \tag{5}$$

The knowledge-driven and lab equipment specifications of the R&D sector lead to different assumptions about how equilibrium in the R&D sector is decentralized. In the knowledge-driven model, output of designs is homogeneous of degree two. By Euler's theorem it is not possible for both of the inputs $A$ and $H$ to be paid their marginal product. We make the assumption that $A$ receives no compensation. Holders of patents on previous designs have no technological or legal means of preventing designers of new goods from using the ideas implicit in the existing designs. The stock of $A$ that can be put to use, with no compensation, by any individual researcher is therefore the entire stock of knowledge about previous designs, provided that there exists a communication network that makes this information available. The equilibrium is one with knowledge spillovers or external effects in the R&D sector (but not in the manufacturing sector). In this case, we can describe research as if it were done by independent researchers who use their human capital to produce designs, which they subsequently sell.

In the lab equipment model, output of designs is the same, homogeneous-of-degree-one production function as in the manufacturing sector. As is the case for the manufacturing sector, the equilibrium is one in which patents convey market power but in which there are no other entry restrictions. There are no external effects and no knowledge spillovers. There is free entry into both R&D and manufacturing. The only restriction is that no one can manufacture capital of type $i$ without the consent of the holder of the patent on good $i$. In this case we conceive of R&D as being undertaken by separate firms that hire inputs, produce patentable designs, and sell them for a price $P_A$.

## III. Balanced Growth and Integration

The description of the technology given so far represents output as a function of the inputs $H$, $L$, $K$, and $A$, and specifies the evolution equations for $K$ and $A$. To facilitate the simple balanced growth analysis that we undertake, the stocks of $L$ and $H$ are each taken as given. Increases in either $L$ or $H$ could be accommodated if we undertook the more complicated task of solving a nonlinear system of differential equations with growth rates that vary over time.

The calculation of a balanced growth equilibrium for each of the two specifications of the R&D technology can be summarized in terms of two linear relations between the rate of growth and the interest rate that hold along a balanced growth path. One relation comes from the conditions of equilibrium in production and the other from preferences.

As shown in the Appendix and as illustrated in Figure I, the interest rate implied by equilibrium in the production sector is decreasing in the rate of growth of output for the knowledge-driven model:

$$r_{\text{technology}} = (\delta H - g)/\Lambda. \tag{6}$$

The term in the denominator depends only on the production function parameters, $\Lambda = \alpha(\alpha + \beta)^{-1}(1 - \alpha - \beta)^{-1}$.

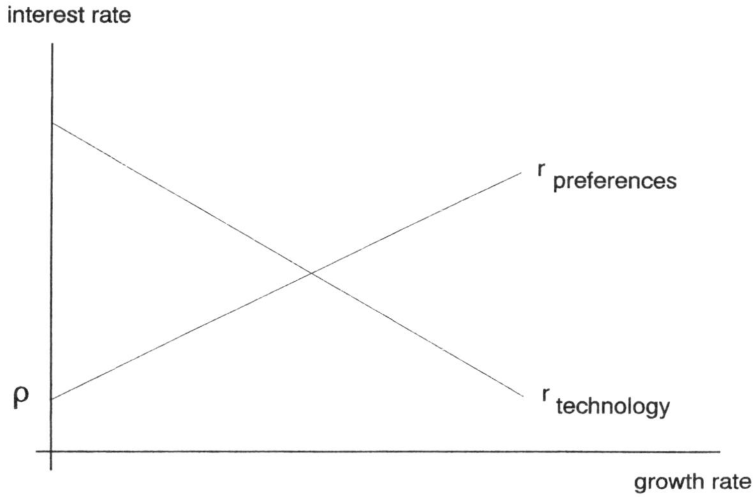


FIGURE I
The Balanced Growth Equilibrium in the Knowledge-Driven Model

The corresponding expression for the interest rate from the lab equipment model is shown in the Appendix to be a function of the production parameters and the stock of $H$ and $L$. It does not, however, depend on the rate of growth:

$$r_{\text{technology}} = \Gamma H^{\alpha} L^{\beta}, \tag{7}$$

where $\Gamma$ is defined by $\Gamma = B^{\alpha+\beta}(\alpha+\beta)^{\alpha+\beta}(1-\alpha-\beta)^{2-\alpha-\beta}$.

In the knowledge-driven specification the negative relation between the interest rate and the growth rate arises because an increase in the interest rate reduces the demand for capital goods. The calculations in the Appendix show that an increase in the interest rate reduces the number of units of each capital good that are rented, and thereby reduces the value of a patent. According to the curved production possibility frontier between designs and manufactured goods, the reduction in the price of the patented design causes a shift in human capital out of the production of new designs and into the production of manufactured goods. This shift slows down the creation of technology and thereby slows growth. In the lab equipment model only a single value of the interest rate is consistent with production of both goods and designs. The relative price of patents and final goods is fixed, so the interest rate is technologically determined.

It remains to specify the preferences that provide the other balanced growth relation between the interest rate and the rate of growth. The simplest formulation to work with is Ramsey preferences with constant elasticity utility,

$$U = \int_0^\infty \frac{C^{1-\sigma}}{1-\sigma} e^{-\rho t}\, dt, \qquad \sigma \in [0,\infty).$$

Under balanced growth the rate of growth of consumption must be equal to the rate of growth of output. Thus, for any fixed rate of growth $g = \dot{C}/C$, we can calculate the implied interest rate from the consumer's first-order conditions for intertemporal optimization:

$$r_{\text{preferences}} = \rho + \sigma g. \tag{8}$$

These preferences yield a positive relation between the interest rate and the growth rate because when consumption is growing more rapidly, current consumption is more valuable compared with future consumption, so the marginal rate of substitution between present and future consumption is higher. Consumers would therefore be willing to borrow at higher interest rates.

There is a parameter restriction that is necessary to ensure that the growth rate is not larger than the interest rate. If it is, present values will not be finite, and the integral that defines utility will diverge. In terms of Figures I and II, the restriction is that the intersection of the two curves must lie above the 45 degree line. This will always be true if $\sigma$ is greater than or equal to one, since in this case, the $r_{\text{preferences}}$ curve always lies above the 45 degree line. If $\sigma$ is less than one, the $r_{\text{technology}}$ curve must not lie too far up and to the right.

Because the rate of growth under each specification is determined by the intersection of two straight lines, it can be calculated directly from the relation between $r$ and $g$ determined on the preference side, equation (8), and the relation between $r$ and $g$ determined by the technology, either equation (6) or (7). The balanced rate of growth for a closed economy under the knowledge-driven model of the research sector is

$$g = (\delta H - \Lambda\rho)/(\Lambda\sigma + 1). \tag{9}$$

The balanced rate of growth for the lab equipment model is

$$g = (\Gamma H^\alpha L^\beta - \rho)/\sigma. \tag{10}$$

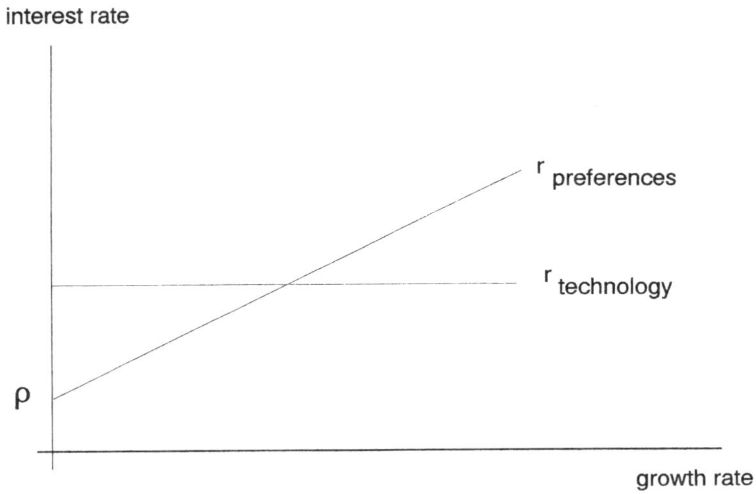


FIGURE II
The Balanced Growth Equilibrium in the Lab Equipment Model

Both of these models have a dependence on scale that is crucial to the analysis of the effects of trade. To see this, consider two economies that have identical endowments of $H$ and $L$. In the long run these economies will have the same stocks of accumulated inputs as well, so that scale effects offer the only lasting source of gains from trade and economic integration.

Suppose that the two economies are physically contiguous, yet are totally isolated from each other by an impenetrable barrier that impedes the flow of goods, people, and ideas. If these economies evolve under isolation, the balanced rate of growth in each is characterized by Figures I and II and calculated in equations (9) and (10). Now suppose that the barrier is removed, so that the economies are completely integrated into a single economy. The change from two economies with endowments $H$ and $L$ to one economy with stocks $2H$ and $2L$ causes an upward shift in the $r_{\text{technology}}$ curve in both figures. Both the rate of growth and the interest rate increase after complete economic integration takes place, regardless of the specification of the technology for R&D. In both models (even the knowledge-driven model with no knowledge spillovers) the rate of growth is too low compared with the rate that would be selected by a social planner.[1] As a result, one would expect integration to be welfare improving. A full welfare analysis, however, would require explicit consideration of the dynamics along the transition path.

With this discussion as background the examples in the next section are designed to address three questions. First, can free trade in goods between countries induce the same increase in the balanced growth rate as complete integration into a single economy? If not, can the free movement of goods, combined with the free movement of ideas, reproduce the rate of growth under full integration? And finally, what is the underlying explanation for the dependence of the growth rate on the extent of the market?

## IV. Trade in Goods and Flows of Ideas

In this section we conduct a series of thought experiments about partial integration. In the first two experiments we focus on the knowledge-driven specification for R&D because it permits a sharp distinction between flows of goods and flows of ideas. In the third we consider the lab equipment specification in which ideas have no direct effect on production.

In the analysis of the knowledge-driven specification, we start with two identical, completely isolated economies that are growing at the balanced growth rate. We first allow for trade in goods, but continue to restrict the flow of ideas. To emphasize the distinction between goods and ideas, we assume that trade in goods does not induce any transmission of ideas. For example, we assume that it is impossible to reverse engineer an imported good to learn the secrets of its design. Under these assumptions we show that trade in goods has no effect on the long-run rate of growth. Then in the second experiment we calculate the additional effect of opening communications networks and permitting flows of ideas. We show that allowing flows of ideas results in a permanently higher growth rate.

In the third experiment we consider the effects of opening trade in goods under the lab equipment specification. In this case trade in goods alone causes the same permanent increase in the

1. For the knowledge-driven model, this is shown in Romer [1990]. For an early version of the lab equipment model, this is shown in Romer [1987]. See Barro and Sala i Martin [1990] for a discussion of the optimality of the no-intervention equilibrium and of tax and subsidy policies that can achieve the socially optimal balanced rate of growth in a variety of endogenous growth models.

rate of growth as complete integration. Since ideas per se have no effect on production, the creation of communications networks has no additional effect.

*A. Flows of Goods with No Flows of Ideas in the Knowledge-Driven Model*

In all of the experiments considered here, the form of trade between the two countries is very simple. By symmetry there are no opportunities for intertemporal trade along a balanced growth path, hence no international lending. Because there is only a single final consumption good, the only trades that take place are exchanges of capital goods produced in one country for capital goods produced in the other.

With the knowledge-driven model of research, it is straightforward to show that opening trade in goods has no permanent effect on the rate of growth. In balanced growth the rate of growth of output is equal to the rate of growth of $A$, $\dot{A}/A = \delta H_A$, which is determined by the split of human capital $H = H_Y + H_A$ between the manufacturing sector and the research sector. Opening trade in goods has two offsetting effects on wages for human capital in these two sectors. Before trade is opened, the number of different types of machines that are used in the manufacturing sector must equal the number that has been designed and produced domestically. Along the new balanced growth path after trade is opened, the number of types of machines used in each country approaches twice the number that has been produced and designed domestically. In their pursuit of monopoly rents, researchers in the two countries will specialize in the production of different types of designs and avoid redundancy, so the worldwide stock of designs will ultimately be twice as large as the stock that has been produced in either country.

With trade in the specialized capital goods, domestic manufacturers can take advantage of foreign designs and vice versa. Ultimately, the level $\bar{x}$ at which each durable is used in each country will return to the level that obtained under isolation. From equation (1) it follows that the increase in $A$ doubles the marginal product of human capital in the manufacturing sector, increasing it from $\partial Y/\partial H = \alpha H_A^{\alpha-1} L^{\beta}\, \bar{x}^{1-\alpha-\beta} A$ to $\partial Y/\partial H = \alpha H_A^{\alpha-1} L^{\beta}\, \bar{x}^{1-\alpha-\beta} (A + A^*)$, where $A^*$ is the set of durables available from abroad.

For the research sector, opening of trade implies that the market for any newly designed good is twice as large as it was in the absence of trade. This doubles the price of the patents and raises the return to investing human capital in research from $P_A \delta A$ to

$2P_A \delta A$. The knowledge represented by $A^*$ is not available for use in research because flows of ideas are not permitted. Since the return to human capital doubles in both of the competing sectors, free trade in goods does not affect the split of human capital between manufacturing and research. Hence, it does not change the balanced rate of economic growth or the interest rate. In terms of Figure I, opening trade in goods does not change the position of either the $r_{\text{preferences}}$ locus or the $r_{\text{technology}}$ locus.

This result does not imply that free trade in goods has no effect on output or welfare. Consider, for example, the extreme case in which two isolated economies start from completely nonintersecting sets of capital goods $A$ and $A^*$ that have the same measure. Before trade in goods, the home country will use capital at the level $\bar{x}$ for $A$ types of capital goods and the foreign country will use capital at the same level $\bar{x}$ for $A^*$ different types of capital goods. If existing capital is freely mobile, each country will immediately exchange half of its capital stock for half of the capital stock of the other country when trade in capital goods is allowed. Each will then be using capital at the level $\bar{x}/2$ on a set of capital goods of measure $A + A^*$. (Over time, the level of usage will climb back to $\bar{x}$ as capital accumulation takes place because the level of $x$ is determined by $r$ and $g$, and on the new balanced growth path these are the same as before.) From the form of production in manufacturing given in equation (1), it follows that immediately after trade is opened output in each country jumps by a factor of $2^{\alpha+\beta}$. This is analogous to the kind of level effect one encounters in the neoclassical model and in static models of trade with differentiated inputs in production (e.g., Ethier [1982]). In the specific model outlined here, free trade in goods can affect the level of output and can therefore affect welfare, but it does not affect long-run growth rates.

If the two different economies start from a position with exactly overlapping sets of goods prior to the opening of trade, the timing of the effect on output is different, but the ultimate effect is the same. The level of output at future dates will differ from what it would have been without trade in goods and will generally be higher. But once the transitory effects have died out, the underlying growth rate will be the same as it was prior to the opening of trade in the capital goods.

### *B. Flows of Information in the Knowledge-Driven Model of Research*

This second example shows that greater flows of ideas can permanently increase the rate of growth in the knowledge-driven model of research. Once we allow for flows of information, we must make some assumption about international protection of intellectual property rights. In each country we have assumed that patents protect any designs produced domestically. Once ideas and designs created abroad become available, the government could try to expropriate the monopoly rents that would accrue to the foreigners by refusing to uphold their patents. To simplify the discussion here, we assume that neither government engages in this practice. A patent in one country is fully respected in the other. (For a discussion of incomplete protection of intellectual property rights, see Rivera-Batiz and Romer [1991].)

Consider the two identical economies with the knowledge-driven specification of the research sector described in the first experiment. Trade in goods has already been allowed, and this creates the incentive for researchers to specialize in different designs. Over time the sets of designs that are in use in the two countries will be almost entirely distinct, so the worldwide stock of knowledge approaches twice the stock of designs in either country. In the absence of communications links, this means that researchers in each country will ultimately be using only one half of the worldwide stock of knowledge. In the domestic country the rate of growth of $A$ is given by $\dot{A} = \delta H_A A$. In the foreign country it is given by $\dot{A}^* = \delta H_A^* A^*$.

Now suppose that flows of ideas between the two countries are permitted. Research in each country now depends on the total worldwide stock of ideas as contained in the union of $A$ and $A^*$. If the ideas in each country are completely nonintersecting, the effective stock of knowledge that could be used in research after communication opens would be twice as large as it was before: $\dot{A} = \dot{A}^* = \delta H_A(A + A^*) = 2\delta H_A A$. Even if the allocation of $H = H_Y + H_A$ between manufacturing and research did not change, the rate of growth of $A$ would double. But the increase in the set of ideas available for use in research increases the productivity of human capital in research and has no effect on its productivity in manufacturing. This change in relative productivity induces a shift of human capital out of manufacturing and into research. For two reasons communication of ideas speeds up growth.

Increasing the flow of ideas has the effect of doubling the productivity of research in each country. Compared with the closed economy model, the formal effect is the same as a doubling of the research productivity parameter $\delta$. This would shift the $r_{\text{technology}}$ curve in Figure I upward and lead to a higher equilibrium growth rate and interest rate. The algebraic solution for the balanced growth rate of $A$ (and therefore also of $Y$, $C$, and $K$) can be determined by replacing $\delta$ with $2\delta$ in equation (9) to obtain $g = (2\delta H - \Lambda\rho)/(\sigma\Lambda + 1)$.

Doubling the value of the productivity parameter $\delta$ has exactly the same effect on the rate of growth of output and designs as a doubling of $H$. And according to the discussion in Section II, doubling $H$ has the same effect on growth as complete integration of the two economies into a single economy. Flows of ideas and goods together have the same effect on the growth rate as does complete integration. Complete integration would permit permanent migration as well, but since ideas and goods are already mobile and because the ratio of $H$ to $L$ was assumed to be the same in the two countries, migration is not necessary to achieve productive efficiency. For symmetric economies, allowing both trade in goods and free flows of ideas is enough to reproduce the resource allocation under complete integration.

So far, we have considered the additional effect that free flows of information would have if free trade in goods were already permitted. It is useful to consider the alternative case in which flows of information are permitted but flows of goods are not. In this case the results hinge on the degree of overlap between the set of ideas that are produced in each country.

In the absence of trade in goods, there would be no incentive for researchers in different countries to specialize in different designs either before or after flows of information are permitted. Moreover, after flows of information are opened, there would be a positive incentive for researchers in one country to copy designs from the other, and little offsetting incentives to enforce property rights. If the firm that owns the patent on good $j$ is not permitted to sell the good in a foreign country, it has no economic stake in the decision by a foreign firm to copy good $j$ and sell it in the foreign market. (The domestic firm would of course have both the incentive and the legal power to stop exports of the copies from the foreign country.) In the extreme case in which identical knowledge is created in each country, opening flows of information has no effect at all on production.

Alternatively, one could imagine that discovery is a random process with a high variance so that truly independent discoveries would take place in the different isolated countries. In this case, permitting the international transmission of ideas would speed up worldwide growth rates to some extent, even in the absence of trade in goods. With free communication each researcher would be working with a larger stock of ideas than would otherwise have been the case. For example, when the first overland routes to China were opened in the Middle Ages, transportation of goods was so expensive that the economic effects of trade in goods was small. But the economic consequences of the ideas that travelers brought back (e.g., the principle behind the magnetic compass and the formula for gunpowder) were large.

### C. Flows of Goods in the Lab Equipment Model of Research

The two previous examples show that there is sometimes a separation between growth effects and level effects. In the first experiment, opening trade in goods had level effects but no growth effects. In the second experiment, opening flows of ideas had both a growth effect and a level effect. (Manufacturing output goes down when $H$ shifts into research, and research output goes up.)

From the first two examples it is tempting to conclude that flows of goods will generally have level effects of the type that are familiar from neoclassical analysis and that it is only flows of ideas that have growth effects. The third example considered shows that this conclusion is wrong. The lab equipment model is constructed so that ideas per se have no effect on production. Hence, permitting international flows of ideas can have no economic effect. Yet we know from the discussion in Section III that complete integration causes a permanent increase in the rate of growth. The experiment considered in this example shows that trade in goods is all that is needed to achieve this result.

Recall that, when trade in goods is permitted in the knowledge-driven model, this increases the profits that the holder of each patent can extract because it increases the market for the good. By itself this increase in the return to producing designs would tend to increase the production of designs, but in the knowledge-driven specification, this effect is exactly offset by the increase in the marginal productivity of human capital in manufacturing.

In the lab equipment specification, opening trade in goods would cause the same kind of increase in the profit earned at each date by the holder of a patent if the interest rate remained constant. But as was noted in subsection II.B, the price of the patent $P_A = 1/B$ is determined by the technology. The only way that the larger market can be reconciled with a fixed price for the patent is if the interest rate increases. A higher interest rate reduces the demand for capital goods, thereby lowering the profit earned by the monopolist at each date. The calculation in the Appendix shows that the required increase in the interest rate is by a factor of $2^{\alpha+\beta}$. When two identical economies are integrated and $2H$ is substituted for $H$ and $2L$ is substituted for $L$ in equation (7), the same increase in $r$ obtains. In each case the higher interest rate leads to higher savings. From Figure II or from equation (10), it follows that this increase in the interest rate leads to the same faster rate of growth as complete integration.

## V. Scale Effects and Growth

In the last example we noted one incorrect conjecture about why tighter economic integration leads to faster growth. From the knowledge-driven model one might conclude that flows of ideas are crucial to the finding that economic integration can speed up growth. But the lab equipment model shows that closer integration can speed up growth even in a model in which flows of ideas have no effect on production. A related conjecture is that knowledge spillovers are fundamental and that increasing the extent of the spillovers is how integrations speeds up growth. The lab equipment model shows that this too is incorrect, for it has no knowledge spillovers.

Finally, one might conclude that it is the increasing returns to scale in the production function for designs, $\dot{A} = \delta H_A A$, that causes integration to have a growth effect in the knowledge-driven model. This conjecture seems to us to come closest to the mark, but it needs to be interpreted carefully. To see why, recall that the production function for designs in the lab equipment model, $\dot{A} = BH_A^{\alpha}L_A^{\beta}\int_0^A x_A(i)^{1-\alpha-\beta}\,di$, exhibits constant returns to scale as a function of $H$, $L$, and the capital goods $x(i)$. There is, nonetheless, a form of increasing returns that is present in this model. It comes from the fixed cost that must be incurred to design a new good. With integration this fixed cost need be incurred only once. Under isolation it must be incurred twice, once in each country.

To bring out the underlying form of increasing returns, recall from equation (5) that we can substitute $x = K_A/A$ into the expression for $\dot{A}$ and write it as a function of $H$, $L$, $K$, and $A$ that is homogeneous of degree $1 + \alpha + \beta$: $\dot{A} = BH_A^{\alpha}L_A^{\beta}K_A^{1-\alpha-\beta}A^{\alpha+\beta}$. Interpreted as a statement about this kind of reduced-form expression, it is correct to say that both models exhibit increasing returns to scale in the production of new designs as a function of the stocks of basic inputs. Consequently, operating two research sectors in isolation is not as efficient as operating a single integrated research sector. To operate an integrated research sector in the knowledge-driven model, two things are required. First, one must avoid redundant effort, that is, devoting resources in one economy to rediscovering a design that already exists in the other. Trade in goods provides the incentive to avoid redundancy. Second, one must make sure that ideas discovered in one country are available for use in research in both countries. Flows of ideas along communications networks serve this function.

In the lab equipment model trade in goods once again provides the incentive to avoid redundant effort. Beyond this, all that is needed to create a single worldwide research sector is to ensure that all types of capital equipment available worldwide are used in all research activities undertaken anywhere in the world. Since ideas do not matter in research, trade in the capital goods is all that is needed.

There is one final point worth emphasizing. Rebelo [1991] offers a general observation about multisector models that is relevant for the experiments considered here. Consider a single-sector model of the form, $C + \dot{K} + \dot{A} = B_0 F_0(K,A)$, where $F_0(\cdot)$ is a homogeneous of degree one function. In this example, $K$ and $A$ can denote any two arbitrary capital goods. If the productivity parameter $B_0$ increases, the balanced growth rate increases. Consider next a two-sector model in which there is an essential fixed factor $L$ that enters as an input in the homogeneous of degree one production function for consumption and capital of type $K$: $C + \dot{K} = B_1 F_1(K_1 A_1 L)$. The capital good $A$, however, is produced by a homogeneous of degree one function $F_2(\cdot)$ of $K$ and $A$ alone: $\dot{A} = B_2 F_2(K_2, A_2)$. In this case a change in the productivity parameter $B_1$ has no effect on the balanced rate of growth. It has only level effects. In contrast, an increase in $B_2$ increases the balanced rate of growth.

The connection between Rebelo's observation and our results is as follows. We do not consider changes in technology parameters like $B_1$ and $B_2$, but we do induce changes in scale for functions that are homogeneous of some degree greater than one. Increases in scale are analogous to increases in the productivity parameters. In the knowledge-driven model trade in goods exploits increasing returns in the sector that produces $C$ and $K$, but not in the sector that produces $A$. It is like an increase in $B_1$ in Rebelo's two-sector model, and induces only level effects. In contrast, flows of ideas increase the productivity in the research sector that produces $A$, and are analogous to an increase in Rebelo's coefficient $B_2$. Finally, trade in goods in the lab equipment model induces a scale effect that is like an increase in $B_0$ in Rebelo's one-sector model.

## VI. Limitations of the Models and Extensions

As noted in the Introduction, the analysis carried out in this paper takes the form of thought experiments for idealized cases. These experiments reveal the following general insight about the connection between economic integration and the rate of economic growth. In a model of endogenous growth, if economic integration lets two economies exploit increasing returns to scale in the equation that represents the engine of growth, integration will raise the long-run rate of growth purely because it increases the extent of the market. Depending on the form of the model, this integration could take the form of trade in goods, flows of ideas, or both.

This conclusion must be tempered by a large number of qualifications. First, there is no consensus yet about whether the equation that is the engine of growth is homogeneous of some degree that is greater than one in the basic inputs (as it is in both of the models considered here) or instead is homogeneous of degree one (as it is, for example, in the papers by Rebelo [1991] and Lucas [1988]).

Second, as noted in the introduction, we have focused on trade between economies with identical endowments and technologies to highlight the scale effects induced by economic integration. In a general two-sector framework, trade between economies that have different endowments or technologies will induce allocation effects that shift resources between the two sectors in each country. For example, Grossman and Helpman [1990] show that trade between countries that have different endowments or technologies will induce shifts between the manufacturing sector and the R&D sector that can either speed up or slow down worldwide growth. If one wants to take the optimistic conclusions reached in this paper literally, they are most likely to apply to integration between similar developed regions of the world, for example, between North America, Europe, and Japan.

There are many details of R&D at the micro level that have been ignored in all of the analysis. We have assumed that giving participants in the economy an incentive to avoid redundancy in research is sufficient to ensure that no redundancy takes place. We have also assumed that patents are infinitely lived and, implicitly, that the institutional structure avoids patent races. We have not considered the role of secrecy in preserving economic value for ideas. All of these restrictions are very strong. Grossman and Helpman [1989d] show how one element of the microeconomic literature on patents, the destruction of monopoly profits by new discoveries, can be included in an aggregate growth model. Other extensions will no doubt follow.

The functional forms used here cannot be literally correct. For example, in both of our models the output of patents at any date increases in proportion to the resources devoted to R&D. This permits the solution for balanced growth paths using linear equations, but it cannot be a good description of actual research opportunities. We would expect that a doubling of research effort would lead to a less than two-fold increase in R&D output, in large part because of the coordination and redundancy problems at the micro level that we have ignored. Addressing these issues would help reconcile a model in which growth rates increase linearly in $H$ in one case, or as a power of $H$ and $L$ in the second, with a historical record showing that growth rates have indeed increased over time, but not nearly as much as the functional forms used here would suggest. More precision in the definition of the input $H$ that is most important for research would also be helpful in this regard. In terms of their effects on research output, one presumably does not literally want to equate two people holding high school degrees with one person holding a Ph.D. degree.

Perhaps the most interesting limitation of the models considered here is one that it shares with many other models: there is no description of how ideas or information affect the production of goods. Once one admits that ideas per se can influence research output, it is apparent that they can influence the output of goods as well. Presumably this is what learning-by-doing models try to capture with the asumption that some production parameter increases with cumulative experience: producing goods yield both goods and ideas, and the ideas raise the productivity of the other inputs. Formal models in the tradition of Arrow [1962] have not yet addressed the importance of communication networks and information flows. When the learning-by-doing models are used in international trade, it is implicitly assumed that there is a communication network that extends throughout one national economy, yet does not cross national boundaries. Little theoretical attention has been given to the analysis of policy choices that can affect the efficiency of international communication networks and to explaining historical episodes (e.g., the emergence of the textile industry in the United States and of the automobile industry in Japan) that reflect large flows of information from developed industries in one country to developing industries in another.

Given these limitations and qualifications, our only claim is to have formalized, and we hope illuminated, an effect that is potentially important. If the discovery of new ideas is central to economic growth, one should expect that increasing returns associated with the opportunity to reuse existing ideas will be present. If the increasing returns extend to the sector of the economy that generates growth, economic integration will induce scale effects that will raise the long-run rate of growth. And because of the remarkable growth of the exponential function, policies that affect long-run rates of growth can have very large cumulative effects on economic welfare. Many other effects may be present as well, but in future theoretical and empirical work, we argue that scale effects on growth that are induced by economic integration are worth watching out for.

## Appendix

### *A. Derivation of Equation (7)*

In the lab equipment model the value of total production in manufacturing and research depends only on the aggregate stocks of inputs, not on their allocation between the two sectors:

$$Y + \frac{\dot{A}}{B} = H^{\alpha} L^{\beta} \int_0^A x(i)^{1-\alpha-\beta} di.$$

Taking its supply of $H$ and $L$ as given, each representative firm in the manufacturing sector chooses levels of $x(i)$ to maximize profits. Consequently, the first-order condition for the problem of maximizing $Y + \dot{A}/B$ minus total input cost $\int p(i)x(i)\, di$ with respect to the use of input $i$ yields the economywide inverse demand curve for good $i$. The rental rate $p$ that results when $x$ units of the capital good are supplied is

$$p = (1 - \alpha - \beta) H^{\alpha} L^{\beta} x^{-(\alpha+\beta)}. \tag{A.1}$$

Input producers choose $x$ to maximize the present value of monopoly rent minus $x$ times the unit cost of each piece of capital, $P_A = \max(px/r) - x$. Using equation (A.1), the first-order condition that determines the number of machines $\bar{x}$ that the holder of the patent on good $i$ rents to manufacturing firms is

$$(1 - \alpha - \beta)^2 H^\alpha L^\beta \bar{x}^{-(\alpha+\beta)} r^{-1} - 1 = 0, \tag{A.2}$$

which implies that $p/r = (1 - \alpha - \beta)^{-1}$. The present discounted value of profit collected by the holder of the patent can then be simplified to

$$P_A = \left(\frac{p\bar{x}}{r}\right) - \bar{x} = \frac{\alpha + \beta}{1 - \alpha - \beta}\bar{x}. \tag{A.3}$$

Since $P_A = 1/B$, this implies that $\bar{x} = (1 - \alpha - \beta)/B(\alpha + \beta)$. Substituting this expression into equation (A.2) yields equation (7) in the text:

$$r_{\text{technology}} = B^{\alpha+\beta}(\alpha + \beta)^{\alpha+\beta}(1 - \alpha - \beta)^{2-\alpha-\beta}H^\alpha L^\beta.$$

*B. Derivation of Equation (6)*

The demand for the capital goods in this model has exactly the same form as in the lab equipment model, with the qualification that since all of the demand comes from the manufacturing sector, $H$ must be replaced by $H_Y$. If we use equation (A.1) with this replacement to substitute for $p$ in the expression for $P_A$, we have

$$P_A = (\alpha + \beta)\frac{p\bar{x}}{r} = \frac{\alpha + \beta}{r}(1 - \alpha - \beta)H_Y^\alpha L^\beta \bar{x}^{1-\alpha+\beta}.$$

Equating the wages of human capital in manufacturing and research yields $P_A \delta A = \alpha H_Y^{\alpha-1} L^\beta A \bar{x}^{1-\alpha-\beta}$. Combining these expressions and solving for $H_Y$ gives $H_Y = (1/\delta), \alpha(\alpha + \beta)^{-1}(1 - \alpha - \beta)^{-1} r = (\Lambda/\delta)r$. Hence, $g = \delta H_A = \delta H - \delta H_Y = \delta H - \Lambda r$.

*C. Trade in Goods in Lab Equipment Model is Equivalent to Complete Integration*

If the interest rate remained constant, the value of a patent $P_A = \pi/r$ would double when trade in goods between two identical markets is introduced in this model. The monopolist that sells in two identical markets and faces constant marginal costs of production will maximize profits in each market independently and earn twice the flow of profits that would accrue from one market alone. Since the value of the patent must remain fixed at $1/B$ by the specification of the technology for producing patents, the interest rate must increase to restore equilibrium.

As shown above, maximization of profit by the monopolist

implies that $p/r$ is constant, so profit is proportional to $\bar{x}$. To offset the doubling of profit that the opening of trade would otherwise induce, $r$ must increase by enough to make the number of units of capital supplied by the monopolist in each country fall by one half. From equation (A.2) this will happen if $r$ increases by a factor of $2^{\alpha+\beta}$. This is the same as the increase in $r$ that results from doubling $H$ and $L$ when the two countries are combined.

UNIVERSITY OF CALIFORNIA, SAN DIEGO
UNIVERSITY OF CALIFORNIA, BERKELEY

## REFERENCES

Arrow, Kenneth J., "The Economic Implications of Learning By Doing," *Review of Economic Studies,* XXIX (June 1962), 155–73.

Backus, David, Patrick Kehoe, and Timothy Kehoe, "In Search of Scale Effects in Trade and Growth," Working Paper No. 451, Federal Reserve Bank of Minneapolis, 1991.

Barro, Robert, and Xavier Sala i Martin, "Public Finance in Models of Economic Growth," National Bureau of Economic Research, Working Paper No. 3362, 1990.

Dinopoulos, Elias, James Oehmke, and Paul Segerstrom, "High Technology Industry Trade and Investment: The Role of Factor Endowments," University of Florida working paper, 1990.

Dixit, Avinash, and V. Norman, *The Theoryof International Trade* (Cambridge, England: Cambridge University Press, 1980).

Ethier, Wilfred J., "National and International Returns to Scale in the Modern Theory of International Trade," *American Economic Review,* LXXII (June 1982), 389–405.

Feenstra, Robert, "Trade and Uneven Growth," National Bureau of Economic Research, Working Paper No. 3276, 1990.

Grossman, Gene, and Elhanan Helpman, "Product Development and International Trade," *Journal of Political Economy,* XCVII (December 1989a), 1261–83.

——, and ——, "Endogenous Product Cycles," National Bureau of Economic Research, Working Paper No. 2113, 1989b.

——, and ——, "Growth and Welfare in a Small Open Economy," National Bureau of Economic Research, Working Paper No. 2809, 1989c.

——, and ——, "Quality Ladders in the Theory of Growth," National Bureau of Economic Research, Working Paper No. 3099, 1989d.

——, and ——, "Comparative Advantage and Long Run Growth," *American Economic Review,* LXXX (September 1990), 796–815.

——, and ——, "Quality Ladders and Product Cycles," *Quarterly Journal of Economics,* CVI (1991), 557–86.

Krugman, Paul, "Increasing Returns, Monopolistic Competition, and International Trade," *Journal of International Economics,* IX (November 1979), 469–79.

——, "Intraindustry Specialization and the Gains from Trade," *Journal of Political Economy,* LXXXIX (October 1981), 959–73.

——, *Rethinking International Trade* (Cambridge MA: MIT Press, 1990).

Lancaster, Kevin, "Intraindustry Trade under Perfect Monopolistic Competition," *Journal of International Economics,* X (1980), 151–75.

Lucas, Robert E., Jr., "On the Mechanics of Economic Development," *Journal of Monetary Economics,* XXII (1988), 3–42.

Rebelo, Sergio, "Long-Run Policy Analysis and Long-Run Growth," *Journal of Political Economy,* forthcoming (1991).

Rivera-Batiz, Luis A., and Paul M. Romer, "International Trade with Endogenous Technological Change," *European Economic Review,* forthcoming (1991).

Romer, Paul M., "Growth Based on Increasing Returns Due to Specialization," *American Economic Review,* LXXVII (May 1987), 56–62.

____, "Endogenous Technological Change," *Journal of Political Economy,* XCVIII (October 1990), S71–S102.

Rosenberg, Nathan, *Inside the Black Box* (Cambridge, England: Cambridge University Press, 1980).

Segerstrom, Paul, T. C. A. Anant, and Elias Dinopoulos, "A Schumpeterian Model of the Product Life Cycle," *American Economic Review,* (1990), 1077–91.

Young, Alwyn, "Learning by Doing and the Dynamic Effects of International Trade," *Quarterly Journal of Economics,* CVI (1991), 369–405.

# [12]

## Trade Policy and Economic Development: How We Learn†

*By* ANNE O. KRUEGER*

The improvement in living standards, life expectancy, and economic growth prospects in developing countries ranks among the most important economic success stories since the Second World War. Growth in some has been dramatic, and while progress has been far from uniform, there are grounds for optimism that future growth prospects can be even better than performance to date.

One factor accounting for that success has been improved understanding and adoption of economic policies much more conducive to satisfactory economic growth than was the case in the 1950's and 1960's. That better understanding, in turn, resulted from a combination and interaction of research and experience with development and development policy.

Ideas with regard to trade policy and economic development are among those that have changed radically. Then and now, it was recognized that trade policy was central to the overall design of policies for economic development. But in the early days, there was a broad consensus that trade policy for development should be based on "import substitution." By this was meant that domestic production of import-competing goods should be started and increased to satisfy the domestic market under incentives provided through whatever level of protection against imports, or even import prohibition, was necessary to achieve it. It was thought that import substitution in manufactures would be synonymous with industrialization, which in turn was seen as the key to development.

The contrast with views today is striking. It is now widely accepted that growth prospects for developing countries are greatly enhanced through an outer-oriented trade regime and fairly uniform incentives (primarily through the exchange rate) for production across exporting and import-competing goods.[1] Some countries have achieved high rates of growth with outer-oriented trade strategies. Policy reform efforts removing protection and shifting to an outer-oriented trade strategy are under way in a number of countries. It is generally believed that import substitution at a minimum outlived its usefulness and that liberalization of trade and payments is crucial for both industrialization and economic development. While other policy changes also are necessary, changing trade policy is among the essential ingredients if there is to be hope for improved economic performance.

And, while there are still some disagreements over particular aspects of trade policy both among academic researchers and policy makers,[2] the current consensus represents a distinct advance over the old one, in terms both of knowledge and of the prospects it offers for rapid economic growth. While it will no doubt be further refined in light of

† Presidential Address delivered at the one-hundred ninth meeting of the American Economic Association, January 5, 1997, New Orleans, LA.

* Herald L. and Carolyn L. Ritch Professor of Humanities and Sciences, Department of Economics, and Senior Fellow, Hoover Institution, Stanford University, Stanford, CA 94305. I am grateful to Ronald McKinnon and Richard Snape for very helpful discussions on an earlier draft of this manuscript. My thanks also go to Chonira Aturupane and Evren Ergin for valuable research assistance. An earlier version of this paper was presented as the Chris Higgins Memorial Lecture at the Economic Society of Australia.

[1] John Williamson (1994 pp. 26–28) summarized the set of policy prescriptions he believed most policy makers and academics concerned with development subscribed to. An outer-oriented trade policy is prominent on his list. He dubbed this set of views "the Washington consensus."

[2] Perhaps the key issue on which there remains disagreement regarding appropriate trade policy is whether there is a role for the state in "picking the winners," or selectivity in incentives confronting different industries. Even those advocating such selectivity, however, would be far less protectionist than were advocates of import substitution in the 1950's, while those advocating uniformity of incentives nonetheless point to key roles for appropriate incentives through macroeconomic policy, provision of infrastructure, enforcement of contract, and other public goods.

experience, a changing world economy, and research, there is no question of ''going back'' to the earlier thinking and understanding of the process.

A number of interesting questions arise about this change in thought and policy. How could it happen that a profession, for which the principle of comparative advantage was one of its key tenets, embraced such protectionist policies? What was the contribution of economic research to the sea change in thinking, policy prescriptions, and politicians' acceptance of the need for policy reform? What sorts of economic research best informed the policy process? In a nutshell, how did we learn? And what was the contribution of economists and their research to the process?

Attempting to answer these questions is the subject of this lecture. Even with a focus limited to trade and development, analysis of the role of research and its usefulness is at least somewhat conjectural. The issue, however, of what types of research inform good policy is an important one. I suspect that the tentative conclusions I draw here may be relevant for other areas of research-informing policy, but leave that to others to demonstrate or refute.[3]

In what follows, I first sketch the initial approach to trade policy in early development research and thought. Next, consideration is given to the evolution of thought, research, and experience with respect to trade and development over the next several decades, and to the ''conventional wisdom'' of the 1990's. Thereafter, I consider the role of research and the sorts of research that proved most fruitful in guiding policy and changing the consensus.

Before proceeding, two caveats are necessary. First, it is very difficult to disentangle views of the proper role for trade policy in development from views about the appropriate role for the state. Partly as a legacy of the Great Depression, partly because of the belief that the Soviet Union had succeeded in its developmental and industrial aspirations through central planning, and partly because of the perceived success of wartime controls, there was widespread agreement—in developed and developing countries alike—that the state should play a major role in economic activity, not only in affecting aggregate demand, but also in regulating private markets and indeed augmenting or supplanting them with state-owned enterprise production of manufactured and other goods. Quite clearly, early views about the necessity for a leading role for the state in guiding resource allocation were incompatible with an open trade policy or outer-oriented trade strategy. Yet to attempt to consider the evolution of both views is well beyond the scope of this paper, and focus here is confined to trade policy.

Second, to focus on research that influenced thinking about economic policy is not to denigrate the importance of research that does not appear to have had immediate policy relevance. First of all, basic research often informs more applied research. Second, in some cases of research that provided little of lasting value, that outcome could not be known at the time. Perhaps some of that research served to demonstrate the infeasibility of certain policy paths,[4] or to demonstrate the futility of further explorations.

Nonetheless, *ex post* it is clear that some lines of research served to hasten the day when policy makers would accept the desirability of removing high walls of protection, while others were irrelevant or served largely to reinforce prejudices and perpetuate the ''old wisdom.'' Perhaps that is inevitable in the ''marketplace of ideas'' as new paradigms are brought forth to replace old ones.

[3] To name just one example from another field, consider the pioneering work of Theodore W. Schultz (1964), challenging the view that irrational peasants were unresponsive to incentives. Once his work was accepted, it was no longer possible to maintain low prices for agricultural commodities and believe that there would be little or no output effects.

[4] An example is the line of research, which continued into the 1970's, improving methodology for planning models. This research certainly contributed greatly to understanding both the functioning of the economy and also to one aspect of what would be necessary in order for the planning approach to succeed. Without those research contributions, it is possible that many would claim that planning failed because it was incorrectly done (rather than, as most would now believe, it was misconceived).

## I. Evolution of Theory, Understanding, and Policy

### A. *The Early Years*

As developing countries gained independence from their former colonial rulers,[5] their leaders had a political mandate to achieve higher living standards and rapid economic growth.[6] It is difficult in the 1990's to recall the extent to which it was then plausible to view the world economy as split into the industrialized countries and the underdeveloped countries, or "first world" and "third world," as they were often called. Underdeveloped countries had markedly lower average educational attainments (including a great deal of illiteracy and a high fraction of the population with no schooling), poor health conditions, and very little infrastructure. They were heavily specialized in the production and export of primary commodities and imported most of their manufactured goods. While differences among the underdeveloped countries were acknowledged, these seemed minor contrasted with the overwhelming realities of their common attributes and widespread poverty.

The new field of development economics was regarded by many as covering underdevelopment because "conventional economics" did not apply (see Albert Hirschman, 1982). Focus on how the developing countries should shape policies for accelerating growth and raising living standards was the central issue.[7]

### B. *Accepted Stylized Facts and Premises*

Early trade and development theories and policy prescriptions were based on some widely accepted stylized facts and premises about the underdeveloped countries. These were a mixture of touristic impressions, half-truths, and misapplied policy inferences. In hindsight, it is surprising how some then-accepted stylized "facts" were so uncritically accepted and held sway for so long. However, it is not possible to understand what thinking about trade and development was except in light of those premises. Indeed, it can be argued that improved understanding of trade and development came about in large part through research which effectively demonstrated the falsity of these premises.

A first premise was based on the fact—then certainly true—that developing economies' production structures were heavily oriented toward primary commodity production. The dependence on foreign trade was believed to be extreme, as there was virtually no production capacity for manufactured goods outside a few light mass-consumed commodities. However, many observers went further and *attributed* the low living standards in developing countries to dependence on primary commodity production and export.

A second "fact," or premise, was that if developing countries adopted policies of free trade, their comparative advantage would forever lie in primary commodity production. It followed that industrialization and, hence, development would not take place if free trade policies were adopted.

A third premise—termed "export pessimism"—was that both the global income and price elasticities of demand for primary commodities were low. Consequently, it was anticipated that export earnings would not grow very rapidly, if at all.[8]

[5] Latin America and a few other countries (including China, Thailand, and Turkey), then deemed "underdeveloped," were not formally colonies prior to the Second World War. However, it was widely believed that they had been "economically dependent." The leaders and elite in most poor countries shared the perception that their economies were "different" from industrialized countries and like other developing countries. The G-77 (77 countries), or nonaligned nations, were all developing countries whose leaders perceived themselves to be in a similar economic situation with similar goals of rapid growth and improved living standards.

[6] As was then conventional, I shall assume here that higher living standards, more rapid growth, and economic development were/are synonymous for purposes of analyzing trade policy.

[7] There was, to be sure, a growing literature on the contribution of technical change and factor accumulation to growth in the industrialized countries. But most development economists saw that research as irrelevant for developing countries.

[8] Another widely held view, closely related to export pessimism, was the proposition that the terms of trade had inexorably deteriorated against primary commodities and would continue to do so. Investigation of this proposition

A fourth premise was that the labor force in developing countries, predominantly engaged in agricultural activities as it was, had a marginal product of labor that was "negligible, zero, or even negative," to quote W. Arthur Lewis (1954 p. 141). The stylized "fact" that there was "surplus" labor, or disguised unemployment in less developed countries (LDCs) was widely accepted.[9] In many analytical formulations, it was explicitly or implicitly assumed that labor was a free good while capital was the scarce factor of production.[10]

Related to the fourth premise was a fifth premise: that capital accumulation was crucial for growth, and in early stages of development it could occur only with the importation of capital goods. Since it was expected that the demand for capital goods imports, and imports of other products used in the production process, would grow rapidly while foreign exchange earnings would not, it appeared that growth could follow only if domestic production of import-competing goods could expand rapidly.

Yet a sixth widely accepted premise was that there was very little response to price incentives in developing countries: peasants were "traditional" in their behavior, and there were "structural" problems within the economy.[11]

Based on these stylized facts and premises, it was a straightforward step to believe that the process of development was that of industrialization, by which was essentially meant the accumulation of capital for investment in manufacturing industry and related infrastructure. Moreover, since most manufactured goods were imported, it seemed to follow logically that, as stated by Chenery (1958 p. 463) among many others: "Industrialization consists primarily in the substitution of domestic production of manufactured goods for imports."

### C. *Initial Policies*

Policy prescriptions were derived from these propositions, or stylized facts. Since it was thought that industrialization was necessary for development and that free trade would leave underdeveloped countries specialized in primary commodity production, it followed that there had to be investment in new manufacturing industries whose output would substitute for imports. Further, it was widely believed that new industries in poor countries could not possibly compete with their established counterparts in the developed world. Therefore, industry would have to be protected during its initial phase. Import-substitution policies therefore became the hallmark of development strategies for manufacturing and the underlying rationale for trade policy.[12]

The case for import substitution was based both on the premises outlined above and also on received doctrine: the infant industry argument. The notion that dynamic considerations and externalities might imply that an industry, although economic, would not be established by private agents had been accepted by economists as a legitimate exception to the case for free trade since Hamilton and List.[13]

tended to demonstrate that at the very least the deterioration had been much less than was believed. John Spraos (1980) provided a classic review of the evidence.

[9] A modern interpretation would be that there are many people in developing countries with very low marginal products of labor. While they are too poor to remain unemployed, the process of development entails equipping people with the capabilities (partly through education) and opportunities to increase their productivity.

[10] To be sure, all analysts recognized the importance of increased provision of education and health services. But for purposes of analyzing trade policy, emphasis was almost exclusively on investment.

[11] This gave rise to a great deal of literature based on "structuralism." According to some, it was the absence of responsiveness to price that made developing countries "different." Structuralism was also used as an argument that inflation was necessary in order to achieve growth. See Hollis B. Chenery (1975) for a fuller description.

[12] There were many important subthemes that are not elaborated here, since they are not essential to the main argument. It should, however, be noted that there were many who believed that the situation of developing countries was "structural" and that marginal changes would not matter. It was then concluded that a "big push" was needed, with many new investments simultaneously generating additional demand and then becoming profitable. Ragnar Nurkse's (1958) "balanced growth" prescription reflected the same viewpoint.

[13] See Robert E. Baldwin's (1969) classic analysis of the argument, which not only sets up the conditions under which there might be an infant industry, but also carefully

It was stipulated that a low-cost producer or producers were already in operation abroad; then, the argument proceeded, a potential entrant in a developing country would be faced with an initial period of high costs, but could in the longer run compete. However, in the presence of dynamic externalities (presumably internal to the industry), it was believed that no individual producer would find it profitable to start production. In these circumstances, the infant industry argument could justify temporary intervention to make entry into the new industry privately profitable provided that, over the longer term, its costs would decline *below* the imported cost by enough to yield an economic return on the intervening loss, which could be viewed as an investment.

Although the infant industry argument was, in a first-best world, an argument for a production subsidy (which would presumably equal the unit value of the externality and might apply as well for production for exports as for the domestic market), it was combined with the appeal for import substitution[14] to yield a justification for protection of newly established manufacturing industries in developing countries.

However, combining the assumptions that industrialization would have to take place through substituting for imports, that there were infant industries requiring initial intervention, and that export earnings were unlikely to increase, the stage was set for trade and industrialization policies.

The premises underlying import-substitution policies were so widely accepted that developing country exceptions were even incorporated into the General Agreement on Tariffs and Trade (GATT) articles. Article XVIII explicitly protected the developing countries from the ''obligations'' of industrialized countries and permitted them to adopt tariffs and quantitative restrictions. They also were entitled to ''special and differential treatment'' in other regards under GATT. That the GATT, the upholder of an open international trading system, would accept an ''exception'' for developing countries shows how deeply entrenched the views supporting import substitution were. It is arguable that the very existence of this exception not only legitimized developing countries' inner-oriented trade policies, but also removed pressures that might otherwise have been brought to bear earlier for them to adopt trade and payments regimes more conducive to economic growth.[15]

### D. *Resulting Evolution of Policies*

In one way or another, provision was made in country after country that, once domestic production became feasible, imports would be restricted. In Brazil, a ''Law of Similars'' provided that firms importing goods that were similar to those available domestically would lose their government privileges, which included not only access to credit and tax treatment, but also eligibility to bid on government contracts and a variety of other valuable rights. In India, imports were licensed, and in the event that there was domestic production, any would-be importer was required to obtain letters from any supplier government officials thought might be capable of producing the good to the effect that the supplier could not meet the specifications. In Turkey, goods were removed from the list of items for which import licenses could be granted once domestic production capacity was available. Similar provisions, or very high tariffs, were used to encourage import substitution in most developing countries.[16]

and critically scrutinizes the various circumstances in which those conditions might hold. Baldwin's article was an important contribution to better understanding of the empirical relevance of the theory, as I shall argue below.

[14] It was also believed that there was a revenue constraint, making the first-best production subsidy infeasible. More recent analyses would also point to the greater potential for corruption inherent in production subsidies as yet another reason why protection might be preferable.

[15] See Kenneth Dam (1970 Ch. 14) for a full discussion.

[16] In Argentina, an effort was made to liberalize the trade regime by lowering tariffs in the late 1970's. To the surprise of officials, there was no apparent effect of the first round of tariff cuts. Subsequent investigation revealed that the tariffs in question had been between 500 and 1,000 percent, and that they had been above the rates at which domestic producers could compete.

In some countries and industries, the trade regime was used as the key policy instrument to provide incentives for import-substituting investment and production by private firms. In other circumstances, state-owned enterprises were established, and investments were made directly by the state sector in new manufacturing activities. In that case, the trade regime provided protection to the state-owned enterprises, although their budget constraints were, in any event, very soft. None of these policies, as adopted, provided means of identifying where dynamic externalities were largest, nor was there any provision for reduction of protection after an initial period. Indeed, protection was virtually automatic for any new import-substitution industry.

A final aspect of early policies also contributed to high and indiscriminate levels of protection. That is, as countries embarked on ambitious development plans, inflation rates rose to levels significantly above those in industrial countries (although far below inflation rates prevailing in many developing countries today). Demand for foreign exchange was rising rapidly in response to the development plans, rising incomes, and domestic inflation. Nonetheless, policy makers in most developing countries chose to maintain their fixed nominal exchange rates. In part, this reflected the perception, noted above, that there was little response to prices and that, indeed, maintaining the nominal exchange rate ''taxed'' agriculture while simultaneously subsidizing capital goods imports. In part, exchange rates were held fixed because it was believed that so doing made imports of capital goods cheaper and thus increased investment. The net result was, of course, real appreciation of the exchange rate, which further intensified *ex ante* payments imbalances, reduced foreign exchange availability, and induced greater restrictiveness in import licensing.

It will be recalled that the 1950's and 1960's were a time of unprecedented economic growth for the industrial countries and for world trade. Buoyed in part by international markets, and in part by the stimuli of increased investment and other aspects of development programs, the rates of growth of per capita incomes rose markedly relative to historical levels in most developing countries, although they remained below those in industrial countries with few exceptions. Even the growth of industry itself was fairly rapid, as the ''easy'' import-substitution opportunities were by and large undertaken first.[17]

However, with real exchange rate appreciation and the pull of resources into newly profitable, import-competing industries, the growth of foreign exchange earnings inevitably slowed. It is not widely appreciated that developing countries, which had a 44 percent share of world exports of agricultural commodities in 1955, lost share to the point where they had only 31 percent by 1970.[18]

With acceleration in the growth of demand for foreign exchange, and deceleration in the growth of supply, foreign exchange difficulties were inevitable. The export pessimism premise had been self-fulfilling, given the policies that were followed. The drop in primary commodity prices in the early 1950's accentuated the phenomenon, but affected the timing more than the actuality of the result. The initial response by most policy makers was to impose rationing of scarce foreign exchange (and require the surrender of foreign exchange from exports) on imports, and the resulting system had little to do with encouraging infant industries.

Although initial rationing of imports was usually on a relatively uniform and across-the-board procedure, controls over foreign trade generally became more restrictive and complex over the next two decades, both in

[17] See Raul Prebisch (1984) for the argument. It can be argued that, with uniform incentives, import substitution would have taken place first in those industries with least comparative disadvantage. In fact, the use of import licensing and prohibitions meant that rates of protection were not uniform even across import-competing activities. In addition, monopoly power in the domestic market was conferred to domestic producers, so that profitability hinged more on the price elasticity of the demand curve than on producers' abilities to reduce costs and compete with imports.

[18] Agricultural protection in Japan, Europe, and the United States may have contributed somewhat to this result. But in most developing countries, the demand for food was growing more rapidly than the supply (as producer prices were suppressed relative to the prices of industrial goods) and, thus, the supply (demand) curve for exports (imports) of agricultural commodities was shifting down (up) (see Krueger, 1990 p. 95).

response to growing "foreign exchange shortage," in reaction to the "unfairness" of the undifferentiated controls, and in response to evasion of the regimes.[19] Periodic balance of payments crises arose in reaction to overvaluation of the real exchange rate, increased indebtedness, and the failure of export earnings to grow.

International Monetary Fund (IMF) "stabilization" programs were undertaken, under which import regimes were simplified and rationalized (as import licensing was, in those years, not abolished). The nominal exchange rate was normally altered (but usually to a new fixed exchange rate in the face of continuing inflation).[20] Even in IMF programs, however, it was seldom intended that the underlying trade policies related to import substitution be changed: the intent, rather, was to rationalize the trade regime and find ways to induce more foreign exchange earnings to finance the capital goods that would be imported to undertake additional import-substitution investments. Growth proceeded in "stop-go" fashion, as periods of foreign exchange crisis were followed by tight(er) monetary and fiscal policies, a consequent reduction in excess demand for imports, and an increase in foreign exchange earnings. When the trade regime was again relaxed, growth resumed and the demand for imports again mushroomed until the next crisis.[21]

### E. *Research Directions and Contributions*

Most research in the 1950's and 1960's was based on the premises outlined above, and supported the basic thrusts of policy. It needs only brief mention here. Some focussed on the possible existence of externalities and the need for "balanced growth," as it was assumed that expansion of any one industry alone would not be feasible because of the limited size of the market.[22] This prescription, of course, was based on the premise that development of manufactured exports was not feasible. Another line of supportive research focussed on planning models, concentrating in large part on interindustry flows and linkages.[23] Empirical research on patterns of development began, focussing on the structure of economies and their growth performance. For more than a decade, the growing disparity between theory and practice was all but ignored.

There was also research providing a rationale for protection of new industries and import substitution. These results demonstrated that domestic distortions could warrant trade intervention[24] in a number of situations. Everett E. Hagen (1958), in perhaps the best known of these, set up a model assuming that urban wages exceeded rural wages exogenously, and demonstrated that a tariff could improve welfare by inducing resources into the (artificially) higher-cost urban industries.

Work also continued on structuralist models, as a number of authors found reasons why developing countries' economic structures were "different" and why, therefore, the usual economic analysis would not apply.[25] Chenery and Michael Bruno (1962), Chenery and Alan Strout (1966), and Chenery and many other coauthors developed the "two-gap" model, using the stylized fact that foreign exchange was "scarce" in developing countries. In this model, export earnings were exogenously given and growing more slowly than the demand for foreign exchange.

[19] For a description, see Jagdish N. Bhagwati (1978).

[20] See William R. Cline and Sydney Weintraub (1981) for analyses of some of these episodes.

[21] See Carlos Díaz-Alejandro (1976) for an analysis of the "stop-go" cycle in Colombia.

[22] For a modern presentation of the "big push" need for balanced growth, see Kevin M. Murphy et al. (1989). The notion of balanced growth and "big push" in the 1940's and 1950's was associated with such analysts as Paul Rosenstein-Rodan (1943) and Nurkse (1958), among others.

[23] See Chenery and Paul Clark (1959) for an exposition. Economists in India probably carried planning models the furthest into practice. The Indian Second Five-Year Plan was explicitly based on the P. C. Mahalanobis (1955) model, and contained estimates of output levels for the subsequent five years which were used as a basis for granting investment licenses. No licenses were issued once the increased capacity already had been allocated. See Bhagwati and Padma Desai (1970) for an account.

[24] There was a huge literature on this subject. See Bhagwati (1971) for a synthesis of many of the papers.

[25] See Christopher Bliss (1989 p. 1194) for a modern statement of the proposition that if demand and supply are sufficiently inelastic, prices do not matter.

Investment was limited by the more binding of two linear constraints: the available savings and the available foreign exchange. There were thus two ''gaps''—between savings and investment, and between demand for, and supply of, foreign exchange. Growth was constrained either by savings or by foreign exchange availability, and the model demonstrated the high potential productivity of foreign aid (in providing foreign exchange), enabling otherwise redundant domestic savings to be used in capital formation. The model, reflecting the views of the day, had little role for the price mechanism.[26]

An example of an analytical effort to clarify circumstances under which one of the stylized facts could be realized was Bhagwati's (1958) and Harry G. Johnson's (1967) demonstration of the possibility of ''immiserizing growth,'' under which a country might increase its output, only to find the price of exports falling so much that the country was worse off. As Bhagwati showed, the conditions under which that might happen were fairly extreme.

An important development was the theory of shadow pricing, which was an offshoot of programming and planning models. It was initially used to demonstrate how reliance on market prices might yield an inappropriate resource allocation. Quickly, however, analysts pointed to the distortions between domestic prices of import-competing and exportable goods because of the trade regime. There is little doubt that cost-benefit techniques improved project selection and enabled improved governmental decision-making with, inter alia, the insistence on use of border prices. The publication of the I. M. D. Little and James A. Mirrlees (1969) volume marked a milestone, after which there was almost no question about the appropriateness of using border prices in project evaluation.

In a related and important development, the theory of effective protection was developed by Johnson (1965a), W. M. Corden (1966), Bela Balassa (1965), and others, providing a framework for analyzing the protection accorded to industries engaged in light processing and much higher value-added activities on a comparable basis. The notion of domestic resource costs (Bruno, 1965; Krueger, 1966), showing the uneven allocation of resources to earning and saving a unit of foreign exchange across activities, was developed to meet the argument that market prices failed to reflect opportunity cost. This research provided a tool with which economists could measure the wide disparities in protection accorded to different import-competing industries.

Recognizing that these estimates were based in part on partial equilibrium analysis,[27] a number of researchers began work on developing techniques for computing general equilibrium results. Based on newly developed solution algorithms, techniques were developed for models which endogenized prices, and thus moved away from the linear models earlier used for analysis.[28]

By the late 1960's and 1970's, there were significant contributions which undermined some of the premises on which import-substitution strategies were based. At an analytical level, one line of research focussed on whether the stylized facts of ''market failure'' in fact warranted the imposition of trade restrictions. Bhagwati and V. K. Ramaswami (1963), Johnson (1965b), Bhagwati (1969), and others demonstrated that a trade instrument (tariff or quota) was usually not a first-best, nor often even second-best, instrument for achieving the objectives in the name of which protection had been granted. The equivalence of tariffs and quotas, an old result in international economics, was revised and refined, as quotas became more frequently used.[29]

Research also began analyzing other aspects of the ways in which protection actually worked. Here, attention focussed on rent-seeking (Krueger, 1974) as a by-product of protection (and, indeed, as a user of resources

[26] See Ronald I. McKinnon (1966), who provided the first demonstration of this important proposition at the time.

[27] They did not, in principle, have to be partial equilibrium estimates if shadow prices were known and used in calculations. In practice, however, that was seldom feasible.

[28] For an exposition of the development of these models into the 1970's, see Kemal Dervis et al. (1982).

[29] See the survey in Bhagwati (1969).

as lobbyists sought protection—see Bhagwati and T. N. Srinivasan, 1980), as resources were used to obtain valuable import licenses, thereby incurring deadweight costs. This, in turn, showed that protection was more costly than earlier, area-under-the-triangle estimates had indicated. It further enabled insights as to the buildup of vested interests that is likely to arise once any policy is undertaken. When policy reforms were attempted, it was clear that those administering earlier policies were in the forefront of those opposing change, alongside the beneficiaries of protection (or other policies).

Related to work on rent-seeking and the tendency for vested interests to spring up around the policies that were adopted, others worked on the theory of overinvoicing and underinvoicing (see Bhagwati, 1974) and smuggling (see Munir A. Sheikh, 1974; Mark Pitt, 1981), again focussing on some of the flaws of the system of protection as practiced in most developing countries.

As trade regimes became more chaotic, empirical work began to document these problems, bolstered by the development of the measurement tools embodied in the concepts of effective rates of protection and domestic resource costs. Researchers focussing on Pakistan discovered that there was actually negative value added in some circumstances, suggesting that it would have been cheaper to pay workers to stay home and import the final product.[30]

The Organization for Economic Cooperation and Development (OECD) sponsored a series of country studies on industrialization led by Little et al. The three synthesized (1970) the results and provided estimates of effective rates of protection in a number of developing countries. These showed how high and indiscriminate protection levels were and demonstrated the extent to which import substitution had failed to achieve many of the objectives set for it. A later series of country studies undertaken under the auspices of the National Bureau of Economic Research, synthesized in works by Bhagwati (1978) and Krueger (1978), provided further systematic empirical evidence of the economic wastefulness and irrationality of the inner-oriented trade regimes.

### F. *East Asian Experience*

At the same time as evidence of the high costs of import-substitution regimes was accumulating, another important development occurred. Starting first in Taiwan, several East Asian economies began growing rapidly under policies diametrically opposite those prevalent under import substitution. Interestingly, the Taiwanese government seems to have listened carefully to the views of S. C. Tsiang,[31] a professor at Cornell University specializing in international economics. Following the precepts of comparative advantage, Tsiang advocated growth through industrialization, but with industrialization taking place through increased capacity for exports, as well as for the domestic market. Taiwan's transformation from a high-inflation, inner-oriented, aid-dependent economy to a major exporting economy is well known.

Korea, whose initial conditions appeared, if anything, even less conducive to growth than those of Taiwan, followed the same pattern. In the late 1950's, Korea's exports had averaged only 3 percent of gross domestic product (GDP) and were growing slowly, if at all, while imports represented 13 percent of GDP. The current account deficit was financed largely by foreign aid, and the domestic savings rate was virtually zero. Major policy reforms took place in Korea in the early 1960's, which greatly increased the return to exporters. There were fairly uniform incentives to all exporters and assurances that the real exchange rate would not appreciate to their detriment. Reforms also reduced the protection to import-competing producers and permitted exporters duty-free importation of needed intermediate goods and raw materials.

The Korean economic performance was transformed, as growth rates entered the double-digit range and living standards

[30] See Corden (1971 p. 51) for a summary of that literature.

[31] For an account of Taiwan's turnaround, see Tsiang (1985).

improved rapidly. Hong Kong and Singapore also became part of the East Asian "miracle" through policies designed to encourage exporting. Growth rates exceeded those previously thought to represent an upper bound on attainable performance.[32]

It was not until the 1980's, however, that the importance of the differences became unarguable. After the second oil price increase of 1979, the worldwide recession of 1980–1982, and the accompanying "debt crisis," the East Asian net importing countries (NICs) rapidly resumed growth, whereas other heavily indebted countries were unable to service their debts and were hard hit by events in the international economy. Research undertaken in attempting to understand the impact of the debt crisis on the developing countries made it abundantly evident that the debt-GDP ratios were not significantly different between the two groups of countries. What was significantly different was the debt-export ratios, as the East Asian countries were able to maintain debt servicing and resume growth because of the greater flexibility of their economies.[33] It also emerged that, even prior to the debt crisis, the rates of growth of inner-oriented developing countries had not increased despite substantial increases in their savings rates.[34]

This is not the place to enter into the debate as to the factors contributing to the success of the East Asian "tigers." For, while there is debate about whether government intervention in "picking the winners" was a key component of the growth strategy,[35] all recognize that the reversal from an import-substitution strategy, the opening up of the economy, and the relative uniformity of incentives across the board were necessary, if not sufficient, for success. Indeed, there is an irony in the fact that the East Asian experience has stimulated some to attempt to identify the "dynamic" factors in exporting that are absent from production for the domestic market. Thus, we have a complete turnaround: in the 1950's and 1960's, the neoclassical argument for an open trade regime was rejected on the grounds that it was "static" and ignored "dynamic considerations"; in the 1990's, there appears to be widespread agreement that the benefits of an open trade regime are largely "dynamic" in nature, and go well beyond the gains from trade under "static" models of an open economy. Just as was the case with the infant industry argument, however, there is a question as to how to identify and measure these "dynamic" gains.

## II. How Did Economists and Researchers Go Wrong?

The "Washington consensus" is very different from the policy consensus that led to the adoption of import-substitution policies in the 1950's and 1960's. While there will no doubt be refinements in that consensus with further experience and research, it is highly unlikely that the ideas of the 1950's and 1960's will be revived.

One can raise three questions about the change in viewpoints. First, how could it be that the economics profession, whose consensus on the principle of comparative advantage was at least as great as that on any other policy issue, endorsed a highly protectionist policy stance?[36] Second, what factors contributed to

[32] Chenery and Strout (1966) actually had a third constraint, "absorption," which restrained growth to 8 percent of GDP or less, on the grounds that more rapid growth would not be feasible.

[33] See Jeffrey Sachs (1985) for an early development of the argument.

[34] The World Bank (1983) documented that this phenomenon of a greatly increased average savings rate with no increase in the growth rate and, therefore, a presumed relatively sharp increase in the incremental capital output ratio, affected most developing countries.

[35] It can be argued that this is a difference between those who see the East Asian trade policies as "free trade" and those who see them as intervention, but of a different type, from that under import substitution. The critical difference is probably between those who would stress uniformity of incentives for earning or saving foreign exchange (and, therefore, would argue that the East Asian NICs were arbitrarily close to a free trade regime), and those who believe the "dynamic externalities" earlier associated with infant industry protection really call for the "right kind" of intervention and argue that the trade strategy was really one of "export substitution."

[36] It can also be asked why it took so long for policy makers in countries such as India to recognize that import substitution (and other policies) as a strategy for development was not delivering the hoped-for results and that a preferable path existed. That is an important question that is well beyond the scope of this paper.

changing the entrenched views of the 1950's and 1960's? Finally, what types of research were most (and least) productive in bringing about better understanding of the role of trade and trade policy in development? I address these questions in turn.

The first is the issue of how the principle of comparative advantage could have been so blithely abandoned. With hindsight, it is almost incredible that such a high fraction of economists could have deviated so far from the basic principles of international trade. What led them to do so? Can any lessons be drawn to avoid (or shorten the duration of) similar mistakes in other applied fields when new policy problems arise?

But, recall the stylized facts that were widely accepted. People were thought not to respond to incentives; exports earnings were thought to be predetermined and slowly growing at best; industrialization was necessary for development; supply response was lacking; and so on. These stylized facts, which were at best simplistic and in most instances simply wrong, permitted economists to conclude that developing economies were "different."

However, it took theory to support these conclusions. Here, one can distinguish several failures. First, there was misapplication of good theory. Second, there was what I shall call the "theory of negative results," which essentially could be used to provide a rationale for virtually any trade intervention. Third, there was good theory harnessed to erroneous stylized facts.

### A. *Misapplication of Good Theory*

Misapplication of good theory was significant.[37] The identification of comparative advantage with the two-factor, two-good model, and the assumption that free trade would imply that developing countries would forever specialize in primary commodities, was an important misapplication. One of the puzzling aspects of the evolution of thinking about policy is the degree to which proponents of open trade regimes failed to refute the allegation that free trade would forever leave developing countries specialized in production of agricultural commodities.[38]

It was not until the 1970's (see Ronald W. Jones, 1971b; Krueger, 1977) that models—motivated in part by the East Asian experience—were developed in which three factors of production (land, labor, and capital) were allocated among sectors, each of which could produce many commodities. As the three-factor models demonstrated, comparative advantage lies within manufacturing and within agriculture, and not between them. Thus, poor unskilled, labor-abundant countries have a comparative advantage in labor-intensive agricultural *and* unskilled labor-intensive manufactured commodities, while countries with a much higher land-labor ratio have a comparative advantage in more land-using agricultural commodities and their comparative advantage in manufacturing lies more in goods with higher capital-unskilled labor ratios. In these models, the overall trade balance in manufactures is a function of the size of the manufacturing sector, itself a function of past capital accumulation and the land-man ratio.

A second serious misapplication of good theory arose because of the nonoperational nature of the theory itself, and the failure to identify circumstances under which policy implementation might be incentive compatible *and* potentially increase welfare. A key culprit in this case was the interpretation of the infant industry argument. As I already discussed, it was widely touted as a basis for import substitution, and generally recognized as a "legitimate" case for a departure from free trade.

One can hardly argue with the proposition that the presence of a positive externality gives rise to a basis for intervention; if the externality is dynamic and temporary, then temporary

[37] Another example of misapplication of good theory was the early defense, such as that of Hagen (1958), of protection because of a domestic distortion. But it took the development of the theory of domestic distortions to correct that, as is discussed below.

[38] Some of Johnson's (1958) research on trade and growth went some way toward refuting this proposition, but still in a $2 \times 2$ framework. Moreover, Johnson's work implied that labor-abundant countries would, while accumulating capital, undergo "ultra anti-trade biassed" growth, which seemed to support import substitution.

intervention, such as infant industry protection, can be called for.

The problem with the argument, as a basis for policy, is that it fails to provide any guidance as to how to distinguish between an infant that will grow up and a would-be producer seeking protection because it is privately profitable. It is not even clear how one could begin, empirically, to identify the domain of the externality. Moreover, even if there were a producer or producers whose increased production would generate dynamic externalities, it does not follow that any level of protection is warranted. And there is nothing in the infant industry argument to provide guidance for quantifying or estimating the likely magnitude of the externality.

Indiscriminate protection in developing countries was defended on infant industry grounds with arguments of capital market failure, labor market failure (as the costs of training, presumably, would be borne by first entrants into industries and then not recouped as others hired workers away), costs of investments in technology, and uncertainty all used. It was not until Baldwin's (1969) seminal article that it was demonstrated that, even when the presumed imperfection existed, it was unlikely that infant industry protection would help correct it. As Baldwin cogently argued, later entrants to an industry might speed up their investments if protection made domestic production more profitable, and the first entrant might even be worse off! It was only after critical examination of these circumstances that the defenders of the infant industry case for import substitution became less vehement.

The infant industry argument also is an excellent example of a theory that is nonoperational because criteria for bureaucrats to identify cases have not been put forward. Quite aside from the unpredictability and immeasurability of the future time path of costs in new factories and the moral hazard associated with asking individual entrepreneurs to indicate how much protection they need, there is nothing to my knowledge in the literature specifying how the policy maker might instruct a bureaucrat to identify (much less measure) a dynamic externality if it were present, how an incentive-compatible mechanism might be devised for improving welfare, how the bureaucrat might measure the height of warranted protection, nor how policy makers might credibly commit to temporary protection. Even *ex post,* it is not entirely clear how one might identify an industry as a successful infant: simply because a firm became profitable and exported does not prove that there was either an externality or a dynamic process at work![39]

### B. *Negative Results*

Much of the theorizing that took place was concerned with what I call ''negative results.'' That is, analysts sought to find reasons why, for example, an exception to free trade should be made. Once the principle of comparative advantage was laid down as a basis for policy, there was little left for theorists to prove supporting an open trading system, so the challenge to theorists was to find conditions under which the free trade precept did not hold. As theory, these findings were significant, but for policy they were unhelpful, and probably served to perpetuate inappropriate policies.

In most real-world circumstances, one strongly suspects that protection exists where theoretical exceptions do not justify it, and that moves to first-best policies would on average lower, and not raise, protection. Judged by that metric, research output relevant for policy would consist more of attempts to measure the costs of these excess levels of protection. In practice, it would be interesting to review the literature and ascertain how many articles, or pages, or other measures of research output were devoted to finding exceptions to the proposition that comparative advantage should form the basis for trade policy, contrasted with those focussing on circumstances where protection was too high! In undergraduate inter-

[39] The same is true of the optimum tariff argument. In the presence of many goods with varying degrees of monopoly power, the formula becomes hopelessly complex. It is certainly true that many tariff structures would lead to lower, rather than higher, welfare in the presence of monopoly power in trade. Yet, in practice, many policy makers have been misled into thinking that they could defend very high tariffs (sometimes even on goods that their countries import in small quantities) on optimum tariff grounds.

national economics courses, sections on trade policy spend considerable time addressing national defense exceptions, the optimum tariff argument, the infant industry argument, second-best arguments, and other arguments for protection. While attention is paid to the reasons why these arguments may not be correct, focus nonetheless centers on the exceptions to the case for free trade, rather than on the reasons for it. While this may be inevitable as a way of reasoning, the temptation to draw inappropriate inferences seems high.

An example will illuminate the argument. Whereas theory suggests criteria for departures from laissez-faire free trade which normally would result in different levels of protection for different industries, a widely used prescription for policy makers is that, if there is to be protection, a uniform tariff is usually preferable to any alternative structure. This proposition rests on several considerations. First, only a uniform tariff can generate a uniform rate of effective protection in the import-competing sectors and, if different goods are subject to different rates of tariff, the resulting differences in effective rates of protection will lead to resource misallocation even within the import-competing industries and have no relation to underlying "dynamic" or market-failure considerations. Second, a uniform tariff simplifies customs administration, making evasion and/or bribery of customs officials more difficult than a varying rate structure. Third, a uniform tariff greatly reduces the opportunities for resource losses in rent-seeking and lobbying. Fourth, given international prices, international value added is more likely to be maximized under a uniform tariff structure than under a variable one.

None of these arguments is sufficient to prove that a uniform tariff is optimal. And, indeed, it is straightforward to develop models in which a uniform tariff is nonoptimal, especially in the presence of income-distribution considerations. In theory, the costs of protection can be minimized by imposing higher tariffs or taxes on goods whose supply and demand is relatively more price inelastic.

Those arguments, as put forward, are all couched in terms of demonstrating the "falsity" of the proposition that a uniform tariff is preferable to variable tariff rates and that there is a departure from uniformity that can potentially improve welfare. But the difficulty with that formulation is that it does not provide a criterion for which departures from uniformity might improve welfare, because a model considering, for example, income-distribution considerations, cannot simultaneously address issues of corruption and administration. And, the fact that income-distribution considerations can warrant a nonuniform tariff structure does not prove that any nonuniform tariff structure is preferable to a uniform one! As such, a negative result gives little or no guide for policy. Nonetheless, it arms lobbyists and others with ammunition to discredit technocrats' efforts to maintain a less irrational structure of protection.

Some good theoretical papers would have done less damage, or at least given less aid and comfort to policy positions that were clearly not those intended in the analyses, if the authors had taken greater pains to note the limitations to their analyses, and the other factors that would have to be taken into account, before their results were applied to policy.

In that regard, it is often overlooked that most policy implementation is carried out by government officials who cannot be expected to have advanced degrees, and sometimes even undergraduate degrees, in economics. In many instances (including formulae for optimal tariff differentiation), the degree of sophistication needed to interpret research results is well beyond that which most bureaucrats will have. As pointed out by Johnson (1970 p. 101):

> ...The fundamental problem is that, as with all second-best arguments, determination of the conditions under which a second-best policy actually leads to an improvement in social welfare requires detailed theoretical and empirical investigation by a first-best economist ... it is therefore very unlikely that a second-best welfare optimum will result based on second-best arguments.

### C. *Good Theory Assuming Counterfactual Situations*

The final abuse of theory was primarily a fault of inappropriate stylized facts. Nonetheless, in many instances, analysts *assumed* signs of variables that were certainly questionable, modelled the situation neatly, and then drew policy conclusions that could hold only if the posited signs were valid. Yet their claims often went beyond the assertion that "if these facts ... then" variety.

As an example to illustrate the point, I have deliberately chosen a good, widely cited paper, because the paper represents good theory, but interprets it, for policy purposes, with dubious "stylized facts." Sudhir Anand and Vijay Joshi (1979) considered a world, such as that envisaged by Hagen (1958), in which workers in the advanced sector receive a higher wage than in the rest of the economy due to unions or other (presumably unalterable) circumstances. They then asked whether maximizing international value added for given employment of domestic resources is an appropriate criterion when income-distribution considerations cannot be separated from productive-efficiency considerations.

In their setup, the clear answer is no, because tradeables are produced by the advanced (presumably unionized) sector, and hence maximizing international value will pull more resources into that sector at the cost of a deteriorating income distribution. Interestingly, they do not address the question of whether the advanced sector is labor or capital intensive. If, as is true for outer-oriented developing countries, the exportables are labor intensive relative to import-competing activity, removing protection to induce a move of more workers to the "advanced" high-wage sector would presumably increase wages of those workers and also those in the rest of the economy: a more equal income distribution would be obtained at the expense of lower real wages for all. Without regard to factor intensity, however, Anand and Joshi (1979 p. 350) conclude that:

> The motivation behind the theory of distortions has been to criticise and to guide trade and industrialisation policies ... Our analysis emphasises the need for caution ... Departures from technical efficiency may be called for as part of the rational response by governments to the limitations they face in carrying out desirable income distribution policies ...[40]

Anand and Joshi (1979) *assumed* that moving toward economic efficiency in tradeables requires paying higher wages because of a distortion. Yet, in fact, the evidence suggests that it has been the highly protected, import-competing industries which have been able to pay above-average wages; removing protection has led to rapid expansion of employment in labor-intensive industries. If the latter stylized fact is correct, and if income-distribution considerations are important, it would suggest that the policy implications of the Anand-Joshi analysis are the opposite of what they suggest—namely, that policy makers should encourage, even beyond the optimum, a shift of resources out of protected industries (presumably by removing protection) and into exportable industries.[41]

## III. What Research Contributed to Improved Policies

Policies that were not consistent with policy makers' growth objectives were cloaked in respectability in the 1950's and 1960's by theory and stylized facts of the type I have already described. I have so far discussed properties of some theories that made them susceptible to misapplication or misuse.

A second question is equally important, however. That is, how did the change in economists' policy prescriptions come about? What led to the reversal to recognition of the importance of an open economy after the conversion to advocacy of import substitution in the 1950's and 1960's? I can address this question more rapidly because much of the answer was implicit in the description of the evolution of developing countries' trade policies.

[40] Another example of the "negative results" research arises from early findings (see Bhagwati and Srinivasan, 1973; Jones, 1971a) that the resource pulls associated with raising an effective rate of protection did not necessarily accord with those associated with increasing a nominal rate of protection. These findings did not significantly affect research efforts in part because the authors made clear the relatively extreme conditions necessary to generate the "perverse" resource pull, and partly because other researchers were able to demonstrate that there seemed to be few, if any, empirical counterparts to the perverse pull cases.

[41] See Pranab Bardhan (1996), tracing how the presumed "efficiency-equity" trade-off has been shown to be false in considerable measure.

Three sets of research efforts can be singled out as having been particularly useful in informing changes in policy, although others, no doubt, also contributed.[42] First, there was research analyzing how import-substitution policies were actually working. Second, and not unrelated to the first, there was the refinement and more appropriate interpretation of theory. Third, there was research demonstrating the feasibility of the alternative.

### A. *Challenging the Stylized Facts and Understanding How Import-Substitution Regimes Worked*

Analyses of the evidence regarding the key stylized facts were in hindsight important steps in undermining the intellectual consensus. Demonstration that there were significant responses to incentives undermined the policy case for ignoring prices. Proof that the terms of trade had deteriorated very little, if at all, began to undermine export pessimism.

Empirical work on the ways in which import-substitution regimes functioned was crucial. Comparative analyses such as those of Little et al. (1970), Bhagwati (1978), Krueger (1978, 1983), and Michael Michaely et al. (1991) clearly contributed significantly to awareness that the effects of import-substitution policies were not idiosyncratic to individual countries. The comparative studies provided a great deal of evidence as to the shortcomings of reliance on import substitution. Evidence that protection was not temporary, that protection levels were high and idiosyncratic, that there was very great discrimination against exports, and that "foreign exchange shortage" was a function of policies and not an exogenously given datum, were all important in challenging the protectionist trade policies still prevailing in most developing countries in the 1980's.

If one considered the evidence regarding the workings of trade policies in any one country taken alone, there were ample grounds for criticism of inner-oriented trade policies, with the monopoly positions they conferred on domestic producers, the high costs of doing business, rent-seeking low quality of products, and so on. It was possible, however, to recognize that and nonetheless conclude that policy makers in that particular country had been inept, or had simply failed to implement policies appropriately. As evidence mounted across countries, the similarity in the evolution of regimes and their consequences was striking. It was increasingly difficult to dismiss the evidence from a particular country as being sui generis or the failing only of the particulars of policy execution in that country.

But, underpinning the analyses of individual country situations, either in the comparative studies or individually, were agreed-upon measurement tools. The empirical studies could not have had their impact without the development and use of measurement tools. As cost-benefit techniques were used, it became increasingly difficult to justify some highly uneconomic projects. And, as measurement of effective rates of protection was undertaken in country after country, the high and erratic nature of protection became evident. Techniques for cost-benefit analysis and measurement of effective rates of protection were important, first of all, in providing analysts with tools with which to demonstrate the chaotic nature of import-substitution policies. In addition, even before the policy consensus changed, there is little doubt that some of the earlier extreme irrationalities of policy were curbed through use of these tools. It became extremely difficult to defend the high average of, and wide variance in, effective rates of protection.

At an empirical level, it seems clear that early demonstrations of the great range of variation in rates of effective protection were useful both in demonstrating some of the problems with trade regimes and also in preventing at least a few of the worst excesses that might otherwise have occurred. More generally, recognition and reintroduction of the proposition that there is a

[42] The ideas and events influencing policy makers in one country may not have been precisely the same as those in the next one. And, of course, no precise measurement of the relative influence of research results and of experience is possible. There is also the question of the role of research, relative to the role of experience itself. However, in fact, the ways in which people in other developing countries learned about the East Asian experience was largely the consequence of research efforts.

response to incentives that cannot be overlooked in policy formulation, combined with the evidence on the erratic and arbitrary nature of incentives provided by trade regimes, forced a reexamination of the premises on which import-substitution policies were based.

Yet another contribution of empirical research was to focus upon the actual workings of policy implementation. In early policy prescriptions, there had been something of a naive tendency to assume that enunciating a desired outcome was itself sufficient to achieve it. This naivete was dispelled, as the theories regarding bureaucratic behavior, rent-seeking, smuggling, and overinvoicing and underinvoicing all enabled observers to examine more critically the ways in which alternative policy prescriptions might have side effects that had earlier been unanticipated.

### B. *Refinement and More Appropriate Interpretation of Theory*

As already seen, some of the intellectual underpinning of import-substitution policies was provided by inappropriate interpretation of theory, or the failure of theory to take into account key institutional or behavioral variables. Analytical developments focussing on conditions under which these interpretations were valid, or examining the ways in which results had to be modified to take into account these institutional and behaviorial aspects, were clearly important in improving understanding.

The entire literature on optimal interventions in the presence of domestic distortions is one important example of a demonstration that earlier interpretations of theory had failed to examine the relevant alternatives. It was invaluable in demonstrating clearly that in most circumstances, the presence of a distortion warranted a first-best policy intervention other than a tariff.[43] For example, in the case of Hagen's (1958) employment-generating case for protection, the optimal intervention literature demonstrated clearly that a first-best intervention would be in the labor market, and that a tariff or quota could not achieve a first-best outcome.

Similarly, developments showing that the comparative advantage results were not the simple ''specialize forever in primary products'' precept proved significant in enabling policy makers to contemplate alteration in trade strategy. Baldwin's (1969) critical examination of the infant industry argument provides yet another example of an analytical contribution that was important in making those concerned with policy consider carefully the effectiveness of the policies they had adopted in achieving their desired goals.

Finally, there was theory that was developed in response to the functioning of import-substitution regimes. Here again, the theory of rent-seeking, as it pointed to the ways in which bureaucrats and others made protection very costly, was important. Further, when it was recognized that bureaucrats, businessmen, and others attempted to capture or thwart policy initiatives not in their self-interest and that they acquired an interest in maintaining the system, once established, and that resources were expended in operating the system, it had to be recognized that changing the system would be politically difficult.

Development of a better understanding of the incentives for underinvoicing and overinvoicing of exports and imports and for smuggling under exchange-control regimes worked in the same direction: not only could these activities prove costly to the exchequer and in terms of resource drains, but the very recognition of their presence served to remind policy makers of the limitations of their instruments.

Finally, good analyses demonstrating how individual import controls actually worked contributed to understanding and made empirical work more effective. The further refinement of theory showing tariff-quota equivalence has already been mentioned. Rent-seeking again comes to mind. But, in addition, individual mechanisms for encouraging import substitution each had their own, often idiosyncratic, incentive effects. A good example is Gene Grossman's (1981) classic analysis of domestic content regulations and their effects.

[43] However, those advocating import substitution seized upon the infeasibility of first-best policy as a defense for following the policies they wished in any event to follow.

### C. *Demonstration of the Viability of Alternative Trade Policies*

Research on the contrast between East Asian and other developing countries and reasons for it obviously turned out to be a major contributing factor in influencing thinking about policy. In a way, research on East Asian experience provided a final blow to the earlier uncritical acceptance of the stylized facts. For, the East Asian experiences demonstrated, as nothing else could have, the feasibility and viability of alternative trade policies: it was no longer possible to associate comparative advantage with reliance on primary commodity exports, and the East Asian experience certainly put an end to the belief that developing countries could not develop rapidly when relying on integration with the international economy.[44]

The experience of the East Asian exporters did several things. Most important, it provided concrete evidence that a developing country could achieve industrialization without relying on domestic markets to absorb almost all additional output. That demonstrated the fallacy of the earlier view that industrialization could take place only through import substitution.[45] Also, the East Asian trade regimes offered significant opportunities for empirical research, and the evidence mounted that properties formerly thought to be those of all developing countries were, in fact, properties resulting from inner-oriented trade and payments regimes.

It cannot be said that either research results or the contrast in economic performance alone led to the change in policies in other developing countries.[46] Both research (especially that which brought the sharply contrasting experiences of the East Asian exporters and the import-substituting countries into focus) and experience contributed.

Whether one should regard the East Asian experience as entirely separate from economic theory, however, is an interesting question. As already mentioned, Tsiang (1985) was himself an international economist, and it was in significant part his efforts that led the Taiwanese authorities to abandon inner-oriented policies and attempt to develop through exports. The theory of comparative advantage was, at least in that instance, a pillar on which policy was built. And, while a variety of factors no doubt contributed to the Korean adoption of outer-oriented trade policies after 1960, the favorable experience of Taiwan undoubtedly facilitated the willingness of decision makers to try the new approach.

The East Asian exporters put to rest the mistaken belief that developing countries relying on the international market would forever be specialized in the production of primary commodities. They also showed that rates of growth well above those realized even in the most rapidly growing import-substitution countries such as Brazil and Turkey could be realized.

## IV. What Lessons Can Be Learned for Research in New Applied Fields?

It is difficult to draw generalizations based on the evolution of analysis, empirical research, and policy in one applied field. Nonetheless, in the hope that insights from other applied areas may reinforce or amend the list, the effort seems worthwhile.

Perhaps the most obvious generalization from the various factors that have been discussed is that empirical research which tests for the presence and order of magnitude of stylized facts which are used in modelling and

[44] To be sure, there are still doubters. Some claim that South Korea and Taiwan were major recipients of foreign aid, which is said to account for much of their rapid growth (although the announcement that foreign aid would diminish was what triggered policy reform in Korea). The status of Hong Kong and Singapore as city-states is alleged by some to render their experience of little relevance. Even today, those resisting policy changes assert that conditions in the 1950's and 1960's were conducive to export expansion in ways in which the world market of the 1990's is not—despite the rapid expansion of exports from China and Southeast Asian countries.

[45] Some have argued that the East Asian outer-oriented trade strategy might not have succeeded without an earlier stage of import substitution. In that view, East Asia moved away from import substitution at the "right time," whereas other countries stayed with the strategy too long. See Gustav Ranis (1984) for one such argument.

[46] For that matter, trade policy reform is still resisted in many countries, notably most of Sub-Saharan Africa.

policy formulation can be invaluable. If the right stylized facts can be used as a basis for theory, and theorists have good indications of the relative quantitative importance of various phenomena, it is clearly far more likely that the theory itself can make a useful contribution.

In the case of trade policy and development, the demonstrations that there were responses to incentives and that developing countries could expand export earnings and did have comparative advantage in other than primary commodities, were clearly crucial to improved understanding of the relationship of trade to development.

For that reason, high marks must go to the analytical research that pointed to measurement techniques such as effective protection and cost benefit, which enabled policy makers and their analysts to obtain empirical quantification, however rough, of the relevant magnitudes.[47]

In like manner, the empirical demonstration of the similarity of policy responses across developing countries, and of the wide and largely irrational variation in incentives for import-competing industries, increased understanding of what was wrong with existing policies.

Overturning, or more accurately interpreting, the accepted stylized facts, therefore, was a first prerequisite for developing a better theory of trade policy for development. But theory was important in many ways, in addition to pointing to appropriate measurement tools. First of all, good policy-relevant theory provided blueprints for those windows of opportunity in which governments genuinely sought to improve economic performance, as was the case in Taiwan and Korea in the early 1960's, and in Chile, Mexico, and India in later decades, to name just a few.[48] Having the "blueprints" on hand from good theory is obviously a major contribution. As already noted, however, that theory is often relatively dull—such as comparative advantage—rather than the more exciting and refined results of complex models.

Second, theory was invaluable when it showed why simple interpretations of received doctrine were in fact wrong. This was the case with the theory of first-best intervention in the case of domestic distortions, and in the case with comparative advantage as interpreted to mean developing countries would specialize in the production of primary commodities, and with the infant industry argument.

These considerations suggest that research results, in order to be most likely to be amenable to policy relevance, should be interpretable into phenomena that are observable, hopefully quantifiable, and recognizable by the policy maker. A negative result, such as that theory does not *always* tell us, can be counterproductive precisely because the policy maker is informed only that a certain generalization (such as comparative advantage and the value of free trade) is not without exception; the generalization can then be ignored.

A more general statement of the problems inherent in theorems which show that major propositions are "not generally true" would encompass all of that theory which is cast in terms of "anything can happen." While it is certainly true that there are conditions under which a wide range of outcomes (Pareto-inferior, a bad equilibrium, Pareto-superior, etc.) are possible from the same policy instrument, it would have challenged the skills of even the most superb theorist to attempt to develop a case for the sorts of chaotic policies prevalent in Turkey in 1957, in Ghana in 1983, and in Argentina in the late 1980's. It is far too easy for analysts to ignore the fact that "an exception" does not rationalize all possible policy alternatives to free trade.

There is a criterion for efficient resource allocation, equating domestic and international marginal rates of transformation. Even if there are "dynamic" factors which contravene part of the static efficiency criterion, they too are measurable. Yet the "anything can happen" theories do not provide guides as to how the

[47] There is another example from a related field. As is well known, multilateral negotiations with regard to agricultural protection were completely stalled until the 1980's. In the 1980's, economists at the OECD proposed the use of a "producer subsidy equivalent" to measure the degree of government intervention in various agricultural commodities across countries. That tool permitted negotiations to begin restricting and dismantling agricultural protection.

[48] See Arnold C. Harberger (1993) for a discussion of the roles played by economists in some key policy reform episodes.

phenomena under examination may be quantified, and thus provide rationalizations (admittedly for those who want them) for policies that cannot by any realistic test pass muster.

Perhaps the lesson is that there is a significant danger that economic theory will be misinterpreted in the policy arena, and researchers could productively take more pains to distance themselves from policy conclusions that are not warranted by their analysis. Theoretical papers which end with "it has been shown that, under conditions $x$ and $y$, policy $z$ may no longer represent an optimum ... Therefore policy should ..." are obviously overstepping their bounds when the empirical relevance of $x$ and $y$ are not yet established, and even more so when conditions other than $x$ and $y$ also may be important (as, for example, with rent-seeking).

But many good theory papers are written where the authors assume that their audience will consist entirely of other theorists. In such instances, good theory may be misused, and it certainly will be in the self-interest of some to harness it to their own ends. It behooves applied economists, as well as the theorists, to be careful to interpret the policy relevance of results in ways which minimize the scope for misinterpretation. This is as true for those seeking to find "dynamic" aspects of exporting, or endogenous aspects of a "big push," as it should have been for those developing the infant industry or optimum tariff arguments. Complex results, such as those noted by Johnson (1970), are particularly suspect in that they can be interpreted in whatever ways suit the decision maker or lobbyist.

Finally, there is theory which provides no guidance as to when or how to observe the phenomenon. In such instances, it is difficult to find policy implications that will not be captured. One possible challenge for theorists might well be to ask for at least one plausible incentive-compatible mechanism under which the inefficiencies they identify might be improved upon by policy makers and bureaucrats. The existence of infant industries, of cases in which there are rents that *might* be captured by appropriate strategic trade policy, and of informational asymmetries and other market imperfections cannot be doubted. But until the magnitude of these phenomena can somehow be measured, or incentive-compatible mechanisms for correcting them can be devised, theorists asserting their presence are simply providing a carte blanche for policy makers and bureaucrats to intervene in whatever ways they like, and this will simultaneously be seized upon by special interests to bolster their causes.

No matter how careful economists are, special interests always will seize their research results in supporting their own objectives. And, no matter how sophisticated and careful research findings are, there always will be politicians formulating, and non-economists administering, policies. Recognition of these propositions could do much to increase the degree to which economists' research results can contribute (positively) to policy formulation.

## REFERENCES

**Anand, Sudhir and Joshi, Vijay.** "Domestic Distortions, Income Distribution and the Theory of Optimum Subsidy." *Economic Journal*, June 1979, *89*(354), pp. 336–52.

**Balassa, Bela.** "Tariff Protection in Industrial Countries: An Evaluation." *Journal of Political Economy*, December 1965, *73*(66), pp. 573–94.

**Baldwin, Robert E.** "The Case Against Infant-Industry Protection." *Journal of Political Economy*, May/June 1969, *77*(3), pp. 295–305.

**Bardhan, Pranab.** "Efficiency, Equity and Poverty Alleviation: Policy Issues in Less Developed Countries." *Economic Journal*, September 1996, *106*(438), pp. 1344–56.

**Bhagwati, Jagdish N.** "International Trade and Economic Expansion." *American Economic Review*, December 1958, *48*(5), pp. 941–53.

______. "On the Equivalence of Tariffs and Quotas," in Jagdish Bhagwati, ed., *Trade, tariffs and growth*. Cambridge, MA: MIT Press, 1969, pp. 248–65.

______. "The Generalized Theory of Distortions and Welfare," in Jagdish Bhagwati, Ronald Jones, Robert Mundell, and Jaroslav Vanek, eds., *Trade, balance of payments and growth*. Amsterdam: North-Holland, 1971, pp. 69–90.

———. "On the Underinvoicing of Imports," in Jagdish Bhagwati, ed., *Illegal transactions in international trade*. Amsterdam: North-Holland, 1974, pp. 138–47.

———. *Foreign trade regimes and economic development: Anatomy and consequences of exchange control regimes*. Cambridge, MA: Ballinger Press, 1978.

**Bhagwati, Jagdish N. and Desai, Padma.** *India: Planning for industrialization and trade policies since 1951*. London: Oxford University Press, 1970.

**Bhagwati, Jagdish N. and Ramaswami, V. K.** "Domestic Distortions, Tariffs, and the Theory of the Optimum Subsidy." *Journal of Political Economy*, February 1963, *71* (1), pp. 44–50.

**Bhagwati, Jagdish N. and Srinivasan, T. N.** "A General Equilibrium Theory of Effective Protection and Resource Allocation." *Journal of International Economics*, August 1973, *3*(3), pp. 259–81.

———. "Revenue Seeking: A Generalization of the Theory of Tariffs." *Journal of Political Economy*, December 1980, *88*(6), pp. 1069–87.

**Bliss, Christopher.** "Trade and Development," in Hollis B. Chenery and T. N. Srinivasan, eds., *Handbook of development economics*, volume 2. Amsterdam: North-Holland, 1989, pp. 1187–1240.

**Bruno, Michael.** "The Optimal Selection of Export-Promoting and Import-Substituting Projects," in *Planning the external sector: Techniques, problems and policies*. New York: United Nations, 1965.

**Chenery, Hollis B.** "The Role of Industrialization in Development Programmes," in A. N. Agarwala and S. P. Singh, eds., *The economics of underdevelopment*. Bombay: Oxford University Press, 1958, pp. 450–71.

———. "The Structuralist Approach to Development Policy." *American Economic Review*, May 1975 (*Papers and Proceedings*), *65*(2), pp. 310–16.

**Chenery, Hollis B. and Bruno, Michael** "Development Alternatives in an Open Economy: The Case of Israel." *Economic Journal*, March 1962, *72*(285), pp. 79–103.

**Chenery, Hollis B. and Clark, Paul.** *Interindustry economics*. New York: Wiley, 1959.

**Chenery, Hollis B. and Strout, Alan.** "Foreign Assistance and Economic Development." *American Economic Review*, September 1966, *56*(4), pp. 679–733.

**Cline, William R. and Weintraub, Sydney,** eds. *Economic stabilization in developing countries*. Washington, DC: Brookings Institution, 1981.

**Corden, W. M.** "The Structure of a Tariff System and the Effective Tariff Rate." *Journal of Political Economy*, June 1966, *74*(3), pp. 221–37.

———. *The theory of protection*. Oxford: Clarendon Press, 1971.

**Dam, Kenneth.** *The GATT: Law and the international economic organization*. Chicago: University of Chicago Press, 1970.

**Dervis, Kemal; de Melo, Jaime and Robinson, Sherman.** *General equilibrium models for development policy*. Cambridge: Cambridge University Press, 1982.

**Díaz-Alejandro, Carlos.** *Foreign trade regimes and economic development: Colombia*. New York: Columbia University Press, 1976.

**Grossman, Gene.** "The Theory of Domestic Content Protection and Preference." *Quarterly Journal of Economics*, November 1981, *96*(4), pp. 583–603.

**Hagen, Everett E.** "An Economic Justification of Protectionism." *Quarterly Journal of Economics*, November 1958, *72*(4), pp. 496–514.

**Harberger, Arnold C.** "Secrets of Success: A Handful of Heroes." *American Economic Review*, May 1993 (*Papers and Proceedings*), *83*(2), pp. 343–50.

**Hirschman, Albert.** "The Rise and Decline of Development Economics," in Mark Gersovitz and W. Arthur Lewis, eds., *The theory and experience of economic development*. London: Allen and Unwin, 1982, pp. 372–90.

**Johnson, Harry G.** *International trade and economic growth*. Cambridge, MA: Harvard University Press, 1958.

———. "The Theory of Tariff Structure, with Special Reference to World Trade and Development," in Harry G. Johnson and Peter B. Kenen, eds., *Trade and development*. Geneva: Librarie Droz, 1965a, pp. 9–29.

———. "Optimal Trade Intervention in the Presence of Domestic Distortions," in Robert E. Baldwin et al., eds., *Trade, growth and the balance of payments—Essays in honor of Gottfried Haberler*. Chicago: Rand McNally, 1965b, pp. 3–34.

———. "The Possibility of Income Losses from Increased Efficiency or Factor Accumulation in the Presence of Tariffs." *Economic Journal*, March 1967, *74*(305), pp. 151–54; reprinted in Harry G. Johnson, ed., *Aspects of the theory of tariffs*. Cambridge, MA: Harvard University Press, 1972, pp. 177–80.

———. "The Efficiency and Welfare Implications of the International Corporation," in I. A. McDougall and R. H. Snape, eds., *Studies in international economics*. Amsterdam: North-Holland, 1970, pp. 83–103.

**Jones, Ronald W.** "Effective Protection and Substitution." *Journal of International Economics*, February 1971a, *1*(1), pp. 59–82.

———. "The Three-Factor Model in Theory, Trade, and History," in Jagdish Bhagwati, Ronald Jones, Robert Mundell, and Jaroslav Vanek, eds., *Trade, balance of payments, and growth*. Amsterdam: North-Holland, 1971b, pp. 3–21.

**Krueger, Anne O.** "Some Economic Costs of Exchange Control: The Turkish Case." *Journal of Political Economy,* October 1966, *74*(5), pp. 466–80.

——— "The Political Economy of the Rent-Seeking Society." *American Economic Review,* June 1974, *64*(3), pp. 291–323.

———. *Growth, factor market distortions, and patterns of trade among many countries*, Princeton Studies in International Finance, No. 40. Princeton, NJ: Princeton University Press, 1977.

———. *Foreign trade regimes and economic development: Liberalization attempts and consequences*. Lexington, MA: Ballinger Press, 1978.

———. *Trade and employment in developing countries*. Chicago: University of Chicago Press, 1983.

———. "Trends in Trade Policies of Developing Countries," in Charles S. Pearson and James Riedel, eds., *The direction of trade policy*. Cambridge, MA: Blackwell, 1990, pp. 87–107.

**Lewis, W. Arthur.** "Economic Development with Unlimited Supplies of Labour." *Manchester School*, May 1954, *22*(2), pp. 139–91.

**Little, I. M. D. and Mirrlees, James A.** *Manual of industrial project analysis in developing countries*. Paris: Organization for Economic Cooperation and Development, 1969.

**Little, I. M. D.; Scitovsky, Tibor and Scott, Maurice.** *Industry and trade in some developing countries*. London: Oxford University Press, 1970.

**Mahalanobis, P. C.** "The Approach of Operational Research to Planning in India." *Sankhya*, December 1955, *16*, pp. 3–62.

**McKinnon, Ronald I.** "Foreign-Exchange Constraints in Economic Development and Efficient Aid Allocation." *Economic Journal*, March 1966, *76*(301), pp. 170–71.

**Michaely, Michael; Papageorgiou, Demetris and Choksi, Armeane.** *Liberalizing foreign trade: Lessons of experience in the developing world*. Cambridge, MA: Blackwell, 1991.

**Murphy, Kevin M.; Shleifer, Andrei and Vishny, Robert W.** "Industrialization and the Big Push." *Journal of Political Economy*, October 1989, *97*(5), pp. 1003–26.

**Nurkse, Ragnar.** *Problems of capital formation in underdeveloped countries*. Oxford: Blackwell, 1958.

**Pitt, Mark.** "Smuggling and Price Disparity." *Journal of International Economics*, November 1981, *11*(4), pp. 447–58.

**Prebisch, Raul.** "Five Stages in My Thinking on Development," in Gerald M. Meier and Dudley Seers, eds., *Pioneers in development*. New York: Oxford University Press, 1984, pp. 175–91.

**Ranis, Gustav.** "Typology in Development Theory: Retrospective and Prospects," in Moshe Syrquin, Lance Taylor, and Larry E. Westphal, eds., *Economic structure and performance*. Orlando, FL: Academic Press, 1984, pp. 23–44.

**Rosenstein-Rodan, Paul.** "Problems of Industrialization in Eastern and South-Eastern Europe." *Economic Journal*, June/September 1943, *53*(210/211), pp. 202–11.

**Sachs, Jeffrey.** "External Debt and Macroeconomic Performance in Latin America and

East Asia.'' *Brookings Papers on Economic Activity*, 1985, (2), pp. 523–64.

**Schultz, Theodore W.** *Transforming traditional agriculture*. New Haven, CT: Yale University Press, 1964.

**Sheikh, Munir A.** ''Smuggling, Protection and Welfare.'' *Journal of International Economics*, November 1974, *4*(4), pp. 355–64.

**Spraos, John.** ''The Statistical Debate on the Net Barter Terms of Trade Between Primary Commodities and Manufactures.'' *Economic Journal*, March 1980, *90*(357), pp. 107–28.

**Tsiang, S. C.** ''Foreign Trade and Investment as Boosters for Take-Off: The Experience of Taiwan,'' in Vittorio Corbo, Anne O. Krueger, and Fernando Ossa, eds., *Export-oriented development strategies*. Boulder, CO: Westview Press, 1985, pp. 27–56.

**Williamson, John.** ''In Search of a Manual for Technopols,'' in John Williamson, ed., *The political economy of policy reform*. Washington, DC: Institute for International Economics, 1994, pp. 9–28.

**World Bank.** *World development report*. New York: Oxford University Press, 1983.

# [13]

# Globalisation, Social Conflict and Economic Growth

*Dani Rodrik*

## 1. Introduction

LET me begin with a confession: until about a month ago, when I began to prepare for this lecture, I had not read any of Raul Prebisch's writings. I was of course familiar with many of Prebisch's ideas – his intellectual leadership at ECLA and UNCTAD, the so-called Prebisch-Singer thesis on the deterioration of the terms of trade for primary products, and his advocacy of import protection as a way of speeding up industrialisation. But like most development economists of my generation, I knew Prebisch second hand and mostly as a label associated with a particular type of development strategy.

It is no secret that this development strategy – import substituting industrialisation (ISI) – has now been out of favour for a while. By the late 1970s, neoclassical economists were pretty unanimous in their condemnation of the ISI strategy. And about a decade later, policy makers all over the developing world had converged on the same verdict. Prebisch's name has become tainted by association with an apparently failed development strategy. Today's conventional wisdom reverses the logic of Prebisch's argument: those developing countries that took Prebisch's advice and withdrew from the world economy, the new consensus goes, eventually floundered, while those that embraced trade prospered beyond expectations.

Anyone who has read Prebisch more closely – and I am now happy to include myself in this company – would object that the usual characterisation of Prebisch as an advocate of protection ignores a lot of subtleties. Prebisch did not favour indiscriminate protection. He anticipated his later critics by recognising that trade protection on its own would not lead to increased productivity in manufactures, and might even result in the opposite.[1]

---

DANI RODRIK is professor of international political economy at the John F. Kennedy School of Government, Harvard University. This is the revised version of the Prebisch Lecture delivered at UNCTAD, Geneva, on 24 October, 1997. The author is grateful to Secretary General Rubens Ricupero for the invitation and for useful comments on the lecture, and to David Greenaway for his suggestions.

[1] He wrote: 'But protection by itself does not increase productivity. On the contrary, if excessive, it tends to weaken the incentive to produce' (Prebisch, 1959, p.259).

But my difficulty with the conventional wisdom, as just stated, goes beyond the details. I believe the development community has internalised the wrong lessons from the experience of countries that adopted the ISI strategy in Latin America and elsewhere. The correct interpretation, I think, goes something like this.

- First, ISI worked rather well for a period of about two decades. It brought unprecedented economic growth to scores of countries in Latin America, the Middle East, and North Africa, and even to some in Sub-Saharan Africa.
- Second, when the economies of these same countries began to fall apart in the second half of the 1970s, the reasons had very little to do with ISI policies per se or the extent of government interventions. Countries that weathered the storm were those in which governments undertook the appropriate *macro*economic adjustments (in the areas of fiscal, monetary and exchange-rate policy) rapidly and decisively.
- Third, and more fundamentally, success in adopting these macroeconomic adjustments was linked to deeper social determinants. It was the ability to manage the domestic social conflicts triggered by the turbulence of the world economy during the 1970s that made the difference between continued growth and economic collapse. Countries with deeper social divisions and weaker institutions of conflict management experienced greater economic deterioration in response to the external shocks of the 1970s.

Each of these points has considerable empirical support, as we shall see. Taken together, they provide an interpretation of recent economic history that is at odds with much current thinking. By emphasising the importance of social conflicts and institutions – at the expense of trade strategy and industrial policies – they also suggest quite a different perspective on development policy.

One of the implications is worth mentioning at the outset. If I am right, the main difference between Latin America, say, and East Asia was not that the former remained closed and isolated while the latter integrated itself with the world economy. The main difference was that the former did a much worse job of dealing with the turbulence emanating from the world economy. It is not openness per se that matters; it is how well you handle it.

## 2. SOME NUMBERS

We have reliable and comparable data on per-capita GDP for most developing countries only since 1960. So I take the period 1960–1975 as the golden era of post-war growth. As Table 1 shows, more than 50 countries experienced growth

TABLE 1
Per-capita GDP Growth Rates

| *Country* | *1960–75* % | *1975–89* % | *Country* | *1960–75* % | *1975–89* % |
|---|---|---|---|---|---|
| Gabon | 7.87 | −3.40 | Ireland | 4.02 | 2.70 |
| **Singapore** | 7.40 | 5.10 | Finland | 3.99 | 2.73 |
| **Japan** | 7.05 | 3.53 | **Thailand** | 3.94 | 4.72 |
| **Korea** | 6.47 | 7.00 | Italy | 3.89 | 2.80 |
| **Botswana** | 6.16 | 6.17 | Turkey | 3.85 | 1.23 |
| Greece | 6.15 | 1.73 | Iceland | 3.80 | 2.54 |
| **Hong Kong** | 6.12 | 6.61 | Belgium | 3.78 | 2.08 |
| Lesotho | 6.00 | 2.15 | Norway | 3.76 | 2.77 |
| **Taiwan** | 5.86 | 6.57 | France | 3.73 | 1.90 |
| Portugal | 5.68 | 2.59 | Austria | 3.71 | 2.29 |
| Spain | 5.66 | 1.64 | Dominican Rep. | 3.56 | 1.14 |
| Syria | 5.61 | 0.30 | Canada | 3.52 | 2.57 |
| **Malta** | 5.46 | 5.39 | Togo | 3.49 | 0.22 |
| Yugoslavia | 5.42 | 1.04 | Netherlands | 3.48 | 1.35 |
| Israel | 4.98 | 1.25 | South Africa | 3.39 | −0.39 |
| Swaziland | 4.76 | −0.86 | Mexico | 3.37 | 0.76 |
| Barbados | 4.60 | 2.57 | Tanzania | 3.37 | n.a. |
| Iran | 4.59 | −3.60 | Cote d'Ivoire | 3.30 | −1.56 |
| Brazil | 4.57 | 1.27 | Jamaica | 3.23 | −1.35 |
| Morocco | 4.27 | 2.20 | Bolivia | 3.19 | −0.77 |
| **Malaysia** | 4.26 | 3.82 | Nicaragua | 3.11 | n.a. |
| Nigeria | 4.15 | −2.41 | Costa Rica | 3.05 | 0.82 |
| Tunisia | 4.14 | 2.25 | Sweden | 3.05 | 1.45 |
| Panama | 4.13 | −0.38 | Egypt | 3.04 | 2.93 |
| Ecuador | 4.04 | 0.48 | Papua New Guinea | 3.02 | −1.27 |

Source: Penn World Tables.

of three per cent or more in GDP per capita during this period. The list includes the East Asian tigers, of course, but also ten countries in Central or South America (Barbados, Brazil, Panama, Ecuador, Dominican Republic, Mexico, Jamaica, Bolivia, Nicaragua and Costa Rica), seven in the Middle East and North Africa (Syria, Israel, Iran, Morocco, Tunisia, Turkey and Egypt), and even nine in Sub-Saharan Africa (Gabon, Botswana, Lesotho, Swaziland, Nigeria, Togo, South Africa, Tanzania and Cote d'Ivoire). The fastest growing country prior to 1975 was not Singapore or Korea, but Gabon! Botswana's growth rate in 1960–75 exceeded that of Hong Kong and Taiwan. Table 1 also shows, however, that very few countries sustained their high growth rates after 1975. Of the 50 countries with growth rates exceeding three per cent in 1960–75, only nine repeated the performance after 1975 – seven countries in East and Southeast Asia, plus Botswana and Malta. Why did growth collapse in so many countries?

The question can be approached from a different angle, by looking at comparative evidence on productivity growth. Table 2, taken from Collins and Bosworth (1996), shows productivity performance in various regions during three

TABLE 2
Economic Performance by Period and Region (Annual Average Growth Rates, in Per Cent)

| | *1960–73* | | *1973–84* | | *1984–94* | |
|---|---|---|---|---|---|---|
| | *GDP per worker* | *TFP* | *GDP per worker* | *TFP* | *GDP per worker* | *TFP* |
| East Asia (excluding China) | 4.2 | 1.3 | 4.0 | 0.5 | 4.4 | 1.6 |
| Latin America | 3.4 | 1.8 | 0.4 | −1.1 | 0.1 | −0.4 |
| Middle East | 4.7 | 2.3 | 0.5 | −2.2 | −1.1 | −1.5 |
| South Asia | 1.8 | 0.1 | 2.5 | 1.2 | 2.7 | 1.5 |
| Africa | 1.9 | 0.3 | −0.6 | −2.0 | −0.6 | −0.4 |
| Non-US industrial countries | 4.8 | 2.2 | 1.8 | 0.2 | 1.7 | 0.7 |
| US | 1.9 | 0.8 | 0.2 | −0.5 | 0.9 | 0.7 |

Source: Collins and Bosworth (1996).

periods: 1960–73, 1973–84, and 1984–94. Productivity is measured by total factor productivity growth (TFPG). Look first at the figures for 1960–73, which contain a striking finding. During this period both Latin America and the Middle East appear to have experienced higher rates of TFPG than East Asia. Annual average growth rates of TFP during 1960–73 are 2.3 per cent and 1.8 per cent in the Middle East and Latin America, respectively, compared to 1.3 per cent in East Asia. East Asian performance starts to look truly superlative only after 1973, when Latin America and the Middle East began to undergo regress in total factor productivity (as did Sub-Saharan Africa).

The moral from these two tables is the following. Had the world come to an end sometime during the mid-1970s, ISI would not have ended up with such a bad reputation, and the East Asian 'miracle' would not occupy the central place in development thinking it occupies today. The puzzle is why so many economies that seemed to be doing well took the express train to hell after 1975.

Now, it is true that most of the countries that had embarked on ISI strategies in the 1960s became casualties of the debt crisis and related macro syndromes. This is what makes the association between ISI strategies and growth collapses (the latter eventually being transformed into 'low growth,' once memories of the high growth period began to fade) superficially plausible and compelling. But there are severe problems with this interpretation. At a conceptual level, I have never seen a good argument about why a set of *microeconomic* policies, which the ISI policies were, should be necessarily and systematically associated with macroeconomic disequilibrium, which is what the debt crisis represented (see the discussion in Rodrik, 1996). In any case, it is clear that there was nothing foreordained about the debt crisis: some of the countries that adhered most rigidly to ISI policies – India being a chief example – were able to avoid protracted debt crises. As Table 2 shows, the only region of the world that experienced a significant rise in TFPG after 1973 was in fact South Asia (i.e., Bangladesh, India, Myanmar, Pakistan and Sri Lanka), which is not exactly the region that comes to mind when one mentions 'outward orientation.'

The point is made somewhat more systematically in Table 3, taken from Rodrik (1996) and based on information from Little et al. (1993) and Easterly (1993). The table evaluates the relevance of three types of potential explanations for whether a country succumbed to the 1982 debt crisis or not: (a) the presence of a significant external shock; (b) the quality of monetary and fiscal policies; and (c) the extent of microeconomic policy distortions. The results point unambiguously to macroeconomic policies as the chief culprit. *All* the countries

TABLE 3
Determinants of the Debt Crisis, 1982

| | *Large External Shock* | *Failure to Adjust Monetary and Fiscal Policy* | *Index of Relative-price Distortion* |
|---|---|---|---|
| | | *Troubled Countries* | |
| Argentina | No | Yes | 0.3054 |
| Brazil | Yes | Yes | 0.2019 |
| Chile | Yes | Yes | 0.4460 |
| Costa Rica | No | Yes | 0.2818 |
| Cote d'Ivoire | Yes | Yes | 0.2438 |
| Mexico | No | Yes | n.a. |
| Morocco | No | Yes | 0.2675 |
| Nigeria | No | Yes | 0.2306 |
| unweighted average | | | 0.2824 |
| | | *Moderately Troubled Countries* | |
| Colombia | No | Yes | 0.2744 |
| Kenya | Yes | Yes | 0.1218 |
| Sri Lanka | Yes | No | 0.8606 |
| unweighted average | | | 0.4189 |
| | | *Untroubled Countries* | |
| Cameroon | Yes | No | 0.2344 |
| India | No | No | 0.2620 |
| Indonesia | No | No | 0.4503 |
| Korea | Yes | No | 0.2128 |
| Pakistan | No | No | 0.3814 |
| Thailand | Yes | No | n.a. |
| Turkey | No | No | n.a. |
| unweighted average | | | 0.3082 |

Source: Little et al. (1993), Table 4.4, except for the relative-price distortion index which is taken from Easterly (1993). The latter index is the variance of the log input prices (relative to US prices) across commodities, measured in 1980. See Easterly (1993) for the method of calculation and the justification for the index.

that Little et al. (1993) classify as having been 'troubled' are also classified as cases of 'failure to adjust monetary and fiscal policy'. *None* of the 'untroubled' countries are similarly classified. With regard to price distortions, these were on average no higher (in fact somewhat lower) in the 'troubled' countries than in the 'untroubled' countries. Likewise, there is no clear-cut pattern where external shocks are concerned.

The bottom line is easily summarised. In those countries that experienced a debt crisis, the crisis was the product of monetary and fiscal policies that were incompatible with sustainable external balances; there was too little expenditure reducing and expenditure switching. Trade and industrial policies had very little to do with bringing the crisis on.

## 3. THE DEEPER DETERMINANTS

We have now pushed the puzzle one level deeper. Why did governments in some countries do the obvious thing of adjusting macroeconomic policies and devaluing their currency in a timely fashion while governments elsewhere did not?

Consider the experiences of three countries, all of which were hit by sizable terms-of-trade shocks during the mid- to late 1970s: South Korea, Turkey, and Brazil. Korea suffered the greatest external shock, since trade constitutes a much larger share of national income and the income loss associated with a rise in the price of imported oil was correspondingly larger in Korea than in Brazil or Turkey. Yet Korea grew even faster after 1975, while Turkey and Brazil both experienced an economic collapse.

At one level, there is no great mystery about these differing experiences. The South Korean government undertook a textbook adjustment in 1980 as soon as signs of a payments imbalance appeared. There was a devaluation, tightening of monetary policy, and a programme aimed at increasing energy efficiency in the economy. The result was a single year with moderate inflation and recession, and growth resumed thereafter (see Aghevli and Marquez-Ruarte, 1985).

The Turkish response was quite different. A populist government reacted to the growing current-account deficit in the mid-1970s by going on an unsustainable external borrowing binge. Once foreign bank loans dried up in 1977–78 as a result of concerns about repayment capacity, fiscal and exchange-rate adjustments were delayed. Between 1978 and 1980, inflation rose and the economy went into a tailspin. Some semblance of macroeconomic balance was restored in 1980, but at the cost of huge distributional consequences brought about by changes in key relative prices (the real exchange rate, real wages, and the rural-urban terms of trade). These relative-price changes had the effect of transferring income from farmers and workers to the public sector (see Celasun and Rodrik, 1989). They were greatly facilitated by military rule during 1980–83. These distributional shifts have in turn created a legacy of macroeconomic cycles in Turkey, with real wages going through periods of recovery followed by bust. Largely due to this legacy of instability, inflation has remained high since the early 1980s, and the Turkish economy has underperfomed relative to its potential.

In Brazil, widespread indexation prevented an adjustment in relative prices of the kind that eventually took place in Turkey. Even without *formal* indexation, strategic interaction among social groups resulting in wage-price rigidities appears to have made orthodox adjustment policies of demand restraint extremely costly in terms of output (Simonsen, 1988). Consequently, fiscal and monetary restraint was tried only half-heartedly. The result was a succession of high-inflation plateaus: inflation jumped from 50 per cent per year to 100 per cent in 1979, 200 per cent in 1983, 400 per cent in 1987, 1,000 per cent in 1988, and more than 2,000 per cent in 1990. Each failed stabilisation resulted in higher inflation rates than previously, until the *real* plan of 1994 finally brought price stability.

These country stories underscore the importance of the manner in which different societies react to external shocks. In Korea, adjustment was swift and somehow non-politicised. In Turkey, adjustment was delayed and when it eventually took place it was undertaken in a manner that imposed disproportionate costs on certain segments of society, undercutting the sustainability of macro balances in the longer run. In Brazil, strategic competition among different social groups gave prices a life of their own and rendered traditional remedies for excess demand costly and ineffective.

In short, social conflicts and their management – whether successful or not – played a key role in transmitting the effects of external shocks on to economic performance. I believe that this is a key insight about economic performance and the manner in which the global economy impinges on it. Societies that benefit the most from integration with the world economy are those that have the complementary institutions at home that manage and contain the conflicts that economic interdependence triggers.

Let me make this idea a bit more precise and empirical by drawing on one of my recent papers (Rodrik, 1997a). There I argue that in societies where there are deep social cleavages and the institutions of conflict management are weak, the economic costs of exogenous shocks – such as deteriorations in the terms of trade – are magnified by the distributional conflicts that are triggered. Such conflicts diminish the productivity with which a society's resources are utilised in a number of ways: by delaying needed adjustments in fiscal policies and key relative prices (such as the real exchange rate or real wages) and by diverting activities from the productive and entrepreneurial spheres to the political sphere. Heuristically, the idea can be summarised by the following formula:

$$\Delta\text{growth} = -\text{external shocks} \times \frac{\text{latent social conflict}}{\text{institutions of conflict management}}$$

The effect of shocks on growth is larger the greater the latent social conflict in an economy and the weaker its institutions of conflict management.

The next step is to quantify this formula. In Rodrik (1997a), I use various proxies for the terms on the right-hand side of the equation. External shocks are measured by the income effects of the volatility of the external terms of trade; 'latent social conflict' is proxied by using measures of inequality, ethnic and linguistic fragmentation, and social (dis)trust; 'institutions of conflict management' are proxied by using measures of democracy, quality of governmental institutions, and public spending on social insurance.

Let me focus here on one combination of proxies, which I call *conflict1*. This synthetic indicator is constructed in the spirit of the equation above, by multiplying three terms: (i) my measure of external shocks; (ii) an index of ethnic and linguistic fragmentation, to capture latent conflicts; and (iii) the inverse of an index of democracy, to capture the role of institutions (sources for all the data and methods of construction are discussed in Rodrik, 1997a). The result is then transformed into a standardised variable, so that a unit change in *conflict1* corresponds to a single standard deviation.

Figure 1 summarises the main finding for a sample of 92 countries. The difference in growth rates between 1975–89 and 1960–75 is shown on the vertical axis, while *conflict1* is on the horizontal axis. (In both cases, the influence of other possible determinants of growth differentials has been partialed out.[2]) As the figure shows, there is quite a tight relationship between how high a country ranks on *conflict1* and the extent of growth collapse after 1975 (the $t$-statistic is $-3.77$). The estimated slope coefficient indicates that a one standard-deviation increase in *conflict1* is associated with a growth reduction of 1.2 percentage points. Hence our measure of (externally-induced) social conflict does a very good job of discriminating between countries that managed to hold together after the mid-1970s and those that fell apart.

The next set of charts explores the same theme with a number of variations, to demonstrate that this result is not a fluke. Figure 2 excludes the richer countries from the sample, with the result that the slope coefficient increases in absolute value from $-1.2$ to $-1.4$ (and remains highly significant). Figure 3 excludes Sub-Saharan African countries to see if a few African countries with extreme values are driving the result: the answer is decidedly no, since the estimated coefficient

[2] The basic regression is one where the growth differential is regressed on a set of regional dummies for Latin America, East Asia and Sub-Saharan Africa as well as growth during 1960–75 (the latter to account for convergence effects). The results are robust to the inclusion of other right-hand side variables. In particular, nothing changes if per-capita GDP in 1975 is substituted for growth during 1960–75 (see Rodrik, 1997a).

FIGURE 1
Social Conflict and Growth Collapse

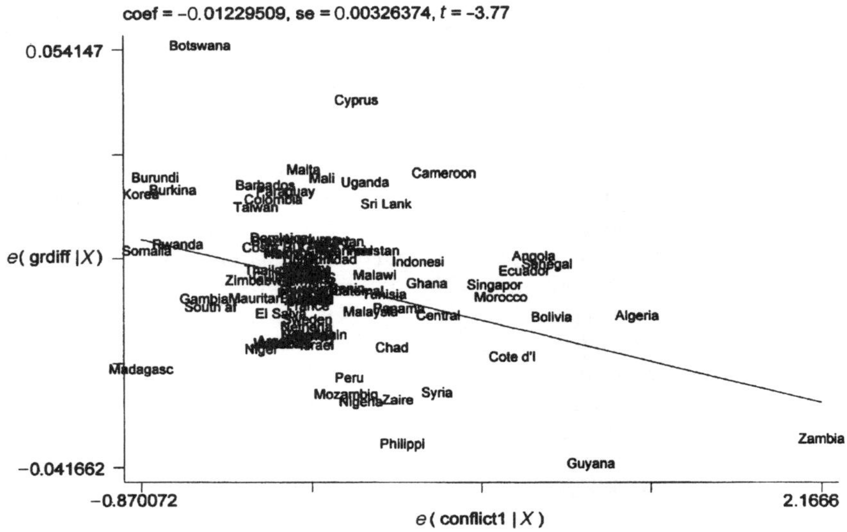


FIGURE 2
Countries with 1975 GDP Per Capita < $5000 (in 1985 Dollars)

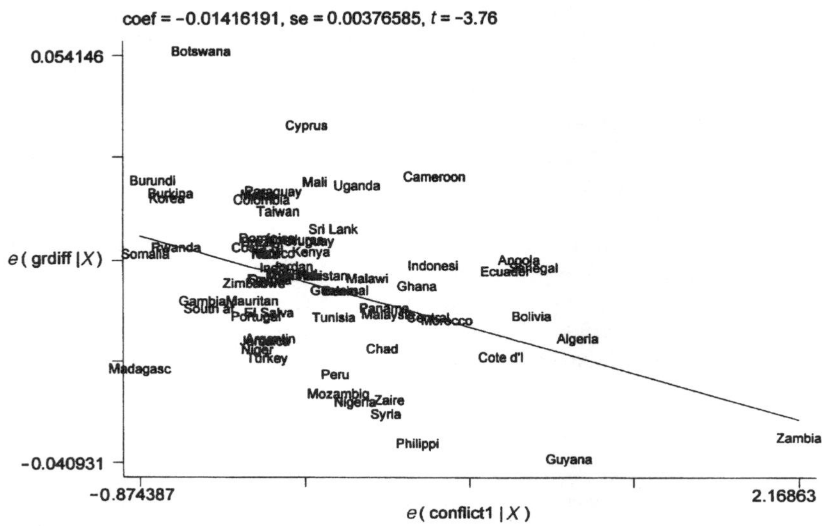

FIGURE 3
Excluding Sub-Saharan Africa

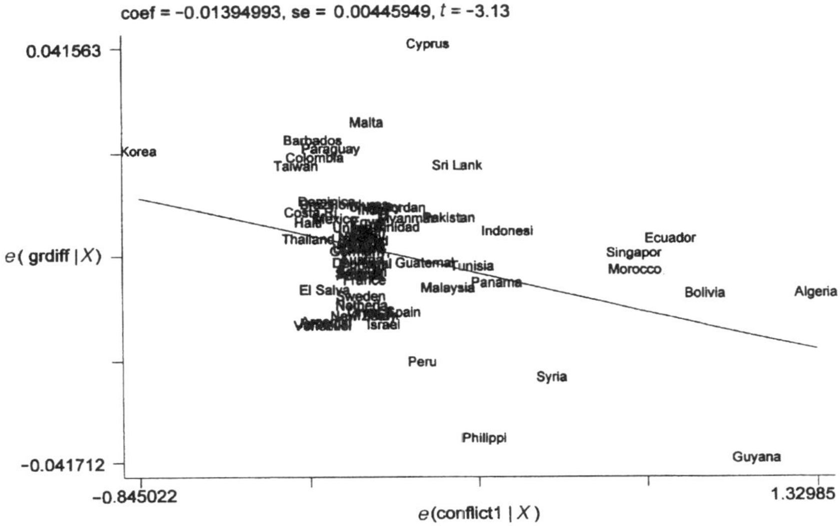


FIGURE 4
Latin America

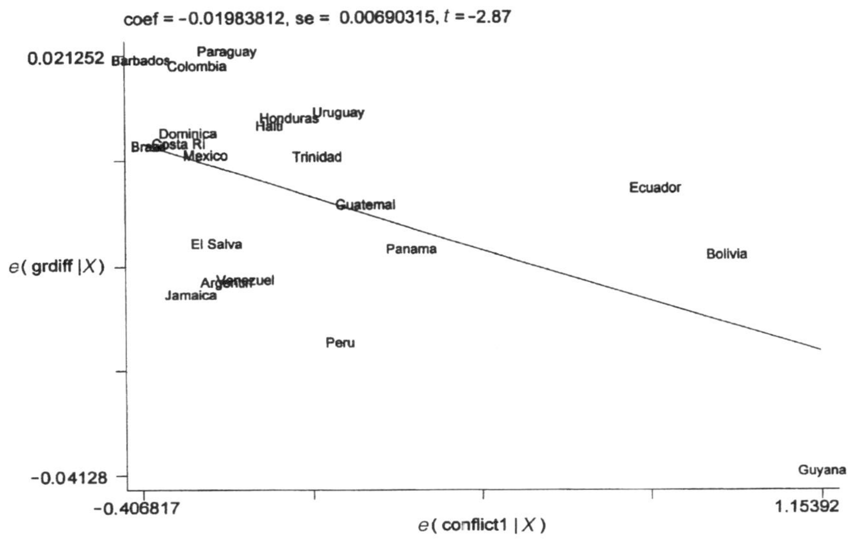

FIGURE 5
Sub-Saharan Africa

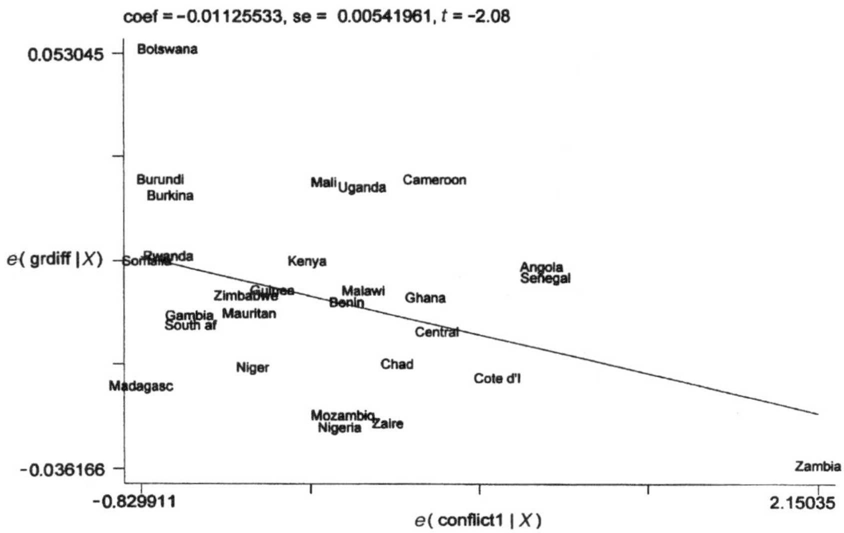


FIGURE 6
Using an Alternative Measure of Social Conflict

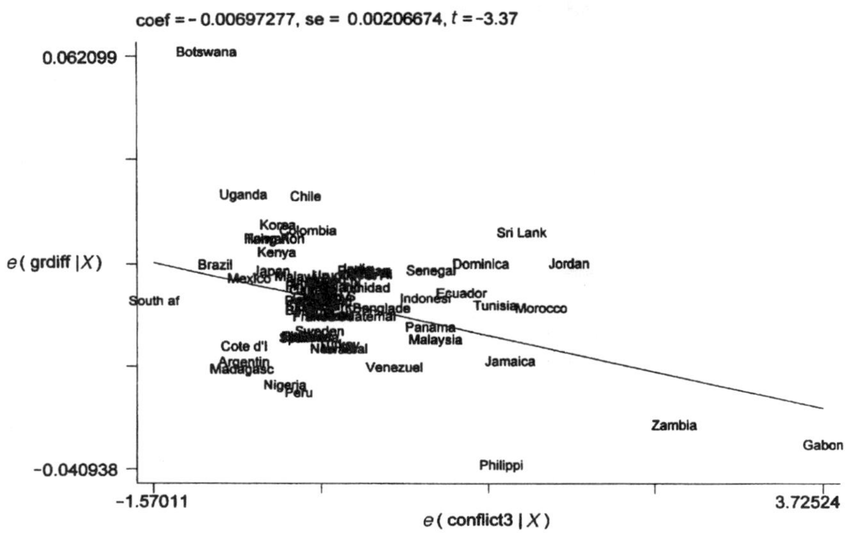

and its level of statistical significance are barely affected. Figures 4 and 5 show that the strong negative relationship holds in samples restricted to Latin American and Sub-Saharan African countries, respectively.

Finally, in Figure 6, I use a different measure of social conflict (*conflict3*), which departs from the previous one in two respects: income inequality during the 1970s is substituted for ethno-linguistic fragmentation and an index of the quality of governmental institutions is substituted for democracy. Once again, we discover a tight relationship between our measure and growth differentials, although the estimated slope coefficient is somewhat smaller at −0.7.

The bottom line is that this broader perspective contributes substantially to an understanding of the growth collapse that was the common fate of so many countries after the 1970s. Countries that experienced the sharpest drops in GDP growth after 1975 were those with divided societies and weak institutions of conflict management. The severity of the external shocks themselves is distinctly secondary as a determinant of cross-country differences in growth across periods.

Furthermore, once latent social conflict and the quality of conflict-management institutions are taken into account, we find that various measures of government policy at the outset of the crisis, such as openness to trade or the size of the public sector, contribute practically nothing to explaining economic performance after 1975 (relative to the earlier period). This is shown in Figures 7–9. Each of these figures depicts the *additional* explanatory power of a specific

FIGURE 7
Government Consumption Levels in 1975 as a Determinant of Growth Collapse

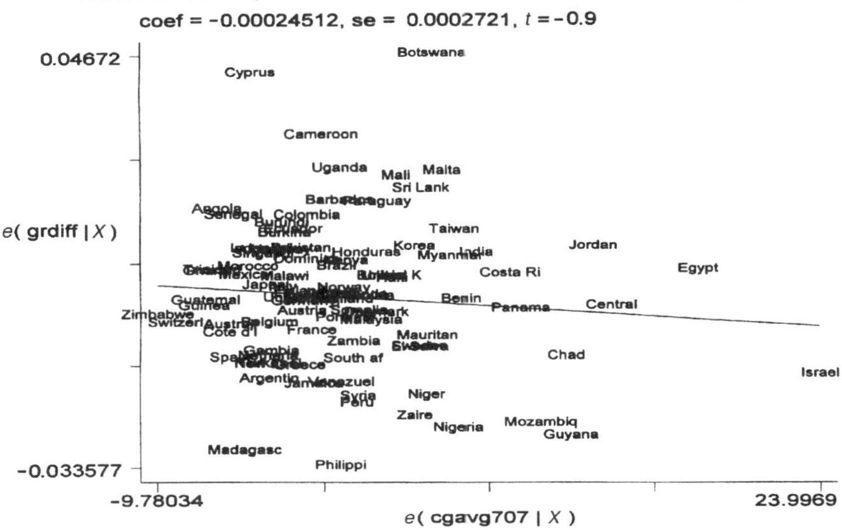

FIGURE 8
Openness to Trade in 1970–74 as a Determinant of Growth Collapse

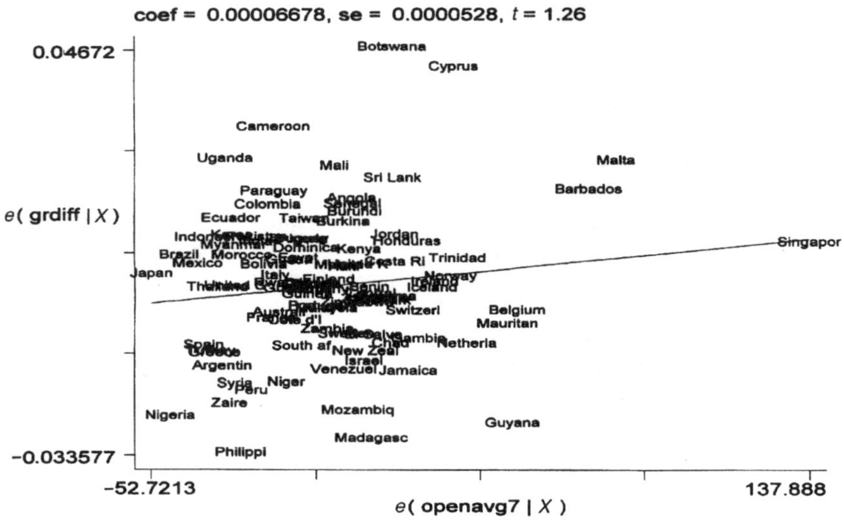


FIGURE 9
Debt-Exports Ratio in 1975 as Determinant of Growth Collapse

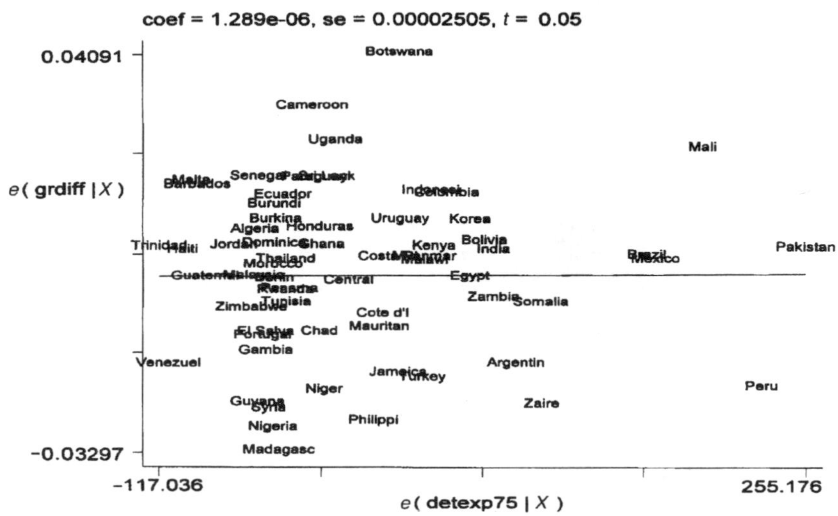

candidate explanation for the growth collapse, after social conflict is controlled (by including *conflict1* in the regression). The three candidates shown are government consumption levels in 1975 (Figure 7), openness to trade (measured by the share of trade in GDP in 1970–74, Figure 8), and the debt-exports ratio in 1975 (Figure 9). In none of these cases is there a statistically significant (partial) association with the growth collapse after 1975. By contrast, the estimated coefficient on *conflict1* is robust to the inclusion of these additional variables on the right-hand side.

## 4. SO WHAT?

Understanding what went wrong in the past is important retrospectively. But it is perhaps even more important prospectively, as we prepare for the future. And this is where we join the debate on globalisation. For the main message that I take from the kind of evidence presented here is that it is not *whether* you globalise that matters, it is *how* you globalise. The world market is a source of disruption and upheaval as much as it is an opportunity for profit and economic growth.[3] Without the complementary institutions at home – in the areas of governance, judiciary, civil and political liberties, social insurance, and of course education – one gets too much of the former and too little of the latter. The weakness of the domestic institutions of conflict management was the Achilles' heel of the development strategy pursued in Latin America, Middle East, and elsewhere, and this is what made these countries so susceptible to the external shocks of the 1970s.

This weakness persists. Reforms in the areas of macroeconomic policy, trade policy, deregulation, and privatisation have not been matched by deeper reforms of political institutions, bureaucracies, judiciaries, and social safety nets. Meanwhile, the world economy has hardly become a safer place – ask the Thais or the Indonesians if you have any doubt. This I believe leaves developing countries highly vulnerable. Without an internal strategy of institutional reform to complement the external strategy of opening up, they risk exposing themselves to the kinds of protracted crises from which many of them have begun to recover only recently. There are at least three components of such a strategy.

(a) *Improving the credibility of the state apparatus*. There has been much progress on the *macroeconomic* policy front in some countries, especially in Latin America. But now this credibility has to be extended beyond the macroeconomic field. There is a great need to improve the quality of the judiciary

[3] There is a large and growing literature on the impact of globalisation on industrialised and developing countries, focusing primarily on the adverse distributional effects. UNCTAD's (1997) recent report is among the most pessimistic. For other perspectives, see Lawrence (1996) and Rodrik (1997b). The same issues were also treated insightfully in Bhagwati's 1996 Prebisch Lecture. See Bhagwati (1997).

and of the public bureaucracy, and to root out corruption. The state cannot play the role of honest broker in mediating social conflict – as it does so often in East Asia – if it is not perceived as honest and competent.

(b) *Improving mechanisms of voice*. There is a need to improve the channels through which non-elites (indigenous peoples, workers, farmers) can make themselves heard, and to bring them (or their representatives) into the decision-making councils. The top-down, technocratic style that is well-suited to macroeconomic stabilisation is not well-suited to the challenges of the second stage of reform. These later reforms will not achieve popular legitimacy unless they are perceived to be the result of a broader deliberation at the national level. So from this perspective, a strong, widely-based trade union movement is a good thing, not a bad thing. Having strong, disciplined political parties is a good thing, not a bad thing. A strong executive is also good, but even better when it uses its autonomy to reach out and strike bargains and alliances with the popular sectors.

(c) *Improving social safety nets and social insurance*. It has now become commonplace to point out that market-oriented reforms require social safety nets to prevent people from falling through the cracks. But I don't think it is sufficiently appreciated what an important role social insurance played in those countries that were the most successful in integrating themselves into the world economy in the postwar period (or reintegrating themselves as in the case of Western Europe).

- In Europe, the idea of providing social protection in order to insulate and cushion broad segments of society from market risks – particularly those having an external origin – was (and to some extend remains) an ingrained habit of mind. We see this in the welfare state that has grown during the postwar era and in the huge growth in income transfers. I think it is only a mild exaggeration to say that the European welfare state was the flip side of the open economy.
- In East Asia, the same function was performed not by social programmes and income transfers, but by a combination of enterprise policies (such as lifetime employment and the provision of social services), extensive product and labour market regulations (which slowed down the pace of change), and a much more gradual, controlled type of external liberalisation.

As we have now come to realise, the approaches in Europe and East Asia both have their problems. What is clear, however, is that the provision of social insurance is an *important component* of market reforms – it cushions the blow on those most severely affected, it helps maintain the legitimacy of these reforms, and it avoids a backlash against the distributional and social consequences of globalisation.

Obviously, there is no 'how-to' manual on accomplishing these things. Much more thought and a fair bit of institutional innovation is needed. What is key, however, is to recognise that globalisation requires strong institutions at home (of the type I just sketched out). In the absence of such institutions, globalisation is likely to foster domestic social conflicts which are damaging not only in their own right, but are also detrimental to economic growth in the long run.

## REFERENCES

Aghevli, B. and J. Marquez-Ruarte (1985), 'A Case of Successful Adjustment: Korea's Experience during 1980–84', IMF Occasional Paper 39 (Washington, DC).

Bhagwati, J. (1997), 'The Golden Age: From a Sceptical South to a Fearful North', *The World Economy*, **20**, 3, 256–89.

Celasun, M., and D. Rodrik (1989), 'Debt, Adjustment, and Growth: Turkey', Book IV of J. Sachs and S. Collins (eds.), *Developing Country Debt and Economic Performance: vol. 3, Country Studies – Indonesia, Korea, Philippines, Turkey* (Chicago and London, University of Chicago Press).

Collins, S. and B. Bosworth (1996), 'Economic Growth in East Asia: Accumulation versus Assimilation', *Brookings Papers on Economic Activity*, **2**, 135–91.

Easterly, W. (1993), 'How Much Do Distortions Affect Growth?' *Journal of Monetary Economics*, **32**, 2, 187–212.

Lawrence, R. (1996), *Single World, Divided Nations? International Trade and OECD Labor Markets* (OECD, Paris).

Little, I.M.D. et al. (1993), *Boom, Crisis, and Adjustment: The Macroeconomic Experience of Developing Countries, New York* (Oxford University Press for the World Bank).

Prebisch, R. (1959), 'Commercial Policy in the Underdeveloped Countries,' *American Economic Review* **49**, 2, 251–73.

Rodrik, D. (1996), 'Understanding Economic Policy Reform', *Journal of Economic Literature*, **XXIV**, 9–41.

Rodrik, D. (1997a), 'Where Did All the Growth Go? External Shocks, Social Conflict, and Growth Collapses', unpublished paper (Harvard University).

Rodrik, D. (1997b), *Has Globalization Gone Too Far?* (Institute for International Economics, Washington, DC).

Simonsen, M. H. (1988), 'Price Stabilisation and Incomes Policy: Theory and the Brazilian Case Study', in Michael Bruno et al. (eds.), *Inflation Stabilisation: The Experience of Israel, Argentina, Brazil, Bolivia, and Mexico* (MIT Press, Cambridge, MA).

UNCTAD (1997), *Trade and Development Report, 1997* (Geneva).

# [14]

ELSEVIER

Journal of Development Economics
Vol. 67 (2002) 229–244

JOURNAL OF
Development
ECONOMICS

www.elsevier.com/locate/econbase

# Trade liberalisation and growth in developing countries

David Greenaway *, Wyn Morgan, Peter Wright

*School of Economics, University of Nottingham, Nottingham NG7 2RD, UK*

Received 1 January 1998; accepted 1 May 2001

**Abstract**

Trade liberalisation in developing countries over the last 20 years has often been implemented with the expectation of growth being stimulated; yet the evidence on its growth enhancing effects is mixed. This paper argues that problems with mis-specification and the diversity of liberalisation indices used are in part responsible for the inconclusiveness. Using a dynamic panel framework and three different indicators of liberalisation, the paper finds that liberalisation does appear to impact upon growth, albeit with a lag. The evidence points to a *J* curve type response and this finding is robust to changes in specification, sample size and data period. © 2002 Elsevier Science B.V. All rights reserved.

*JEL classification:* F14; 040
*Keywords:* Trade liberalisation; Growth

## 1. Introduction

The role of trade policy in economic development has been a key debate in the development literature for most of the second half of the twentieth century. Whereas the prevailing wisdom in the 1950s and 1960s favoured import substitution, that in the 1970s and 1980s favoured export promotion/outward orientation. The evolution of thinking on trade orientation and growth has been charted by

* Corresponding author.
*E-mail address:* david.greenaway@nottingham.ac.uk (D. Greenaway).


PII: S0304-3878(01)00185-7

Krueger (1997). She emphasises the accumulation of evidence of a positive correlation between growth of exports and the growth of GDP, countries with a more open trade orientation appearing to grow faster through time. Edwards (1998) has argued that the positive association between trade and openness is robust to the measure of openness used, though Rodriquez and Rodrik (1999) challenge this conclusion, arguing that although there is little systematic evidence linking inward oriented trade policies and growth, the evidence linking outward orientation and growth overstates the relationship between the two.

A possible link between openness and growth has been an important factor in stimulating an unprecedented wave of unilateral trade reforms, with over 100 countries committing to some kind of trade liberalisation over the last 20 years. Many of these programmes have been voluntary; most however have been tied to the policy conditionality which is central to World Bank Structural Adjustment Loans (SALs).[1] Indeed, trade reforms account for a higher proportion of loan conditions than any other area of policy. The fundamental rationale for this degree of commitment to programmes of trade reform is the obvious belief that liberalisation is a pre-requisite to a transition from a relatively closed to a relatively open economy. If openness is indeed positively related to growth, then it follows that liberalisation is a requirement for growth. In this paper, we investigate whether or not liberalisation appears to have "worked" in the sense of stimulating growth in the short run.

Although not as extensive as that on trade orientation and growth, there is a literature on trade reform/trade liberalisation and (short run) growth. It is fair to say that this literature is fairly inconclusive. Some studies have identified a positive association, others find no association, or even a negative association. Some of the reasons why the literature is inconclusive relate to the fact that different analysts use different proxies for liberalisation and rely on different methodologies. In addition, of course, a given sample will include liberalisations of differing intensities and durations. We add to this literature in three ways. First, we investigate the relationship between liberalisation and growth in a panel framework allowing us to capture both inter-country and inter-temporal variation. Second, we exploit our panel to model the relationship as a dynamic rather than a purely static one. Third, in contrast to previous work which typically relies on a single indicator of liberalisation, we experiment with three different proxies with complementary features. Our results suggest that first, much is to be gained by working in a panel context; second, previous cross-country work which failed to model the dynamics of the liberalisation–growth relationship may be missing an important element; third, the results help explain why the current empirical literature is inconclusive.

[1] A detailed account of the SAL process and its ingredients can be found in Greenaway and Milner (1993).

The remainder of the paper is structured as follows: Section 2 briefly reviews the empirical literature to date. Section 3 sets out our model specification and the empirical methodology. Sections 4 and 5 report the details and discuss the implications of our results and Section 6 concludes.

## 2. Liberalisation and growth: a brief review of the literature

A substantial literature on the effects of trade liberalisation on a range of macroeconomic aggregates and microeconomic adjustment processes has developed, in parallel with the proliferation of trade reform programmes. Several major reviews have been published, including Edwards (1993), Krueger (1997), Rodrik (1997) and Rodriguez and Rodrik (1999). To provide context to our analysis, we focus only on a few key contributions. Prior to doing so, however, we first of all comment on the identification of liberalisation episodes, since this in itself is not straightforward and one of the contributions of this paper is the use of a range of alternative liberalisation measures.

### *2.1. Indicators of liberalisation*

Even at the conceptual level, liberalisation is not unambiguous. In the simple $2 \times 2 \times 2$ trade model, one naturally thinks of it as tariff liberalisation. In a more sophisticated setting with instruments affecting the domestic prices of both importables and exportables, one can conceive of it as a move towards relative price neutrality. Finally, one can think of second best liberalisation, i.e. the substitution of more efficient for less efficient instruments—typically tariffs for quotas.

This ambiguity is reflected in the range of measures used empirically. A widely used indicator is changes in nominal tariffs. For example, Table 1 reports changes in tariffs for 26 countries which liberalised in the 1980s, 22 of which recorded a decrease in average tariffs. This has the virtue of simplicity: it is relatively straightforward to compute and interpret. It also has some important limitations, however. First, there may be instrument substitution taking place: nominal tariffs may well be lowered but at the same time safeguard or anti-dumping measures introduced. Second, depending on the pattern of tariff reductions, average effective protection can increase at the same time as nominal tariffs decline. An alternative strategy therefore is to estimate convergence to relative price neutrality, or changes in the degree of anti-export bias. Krueger's (1978) bias measure and Balassa's (1982) relative exchange rate measure are good examples. The data requirements are extremely demanding, however, which limits their use. A third approach is to combine information on changes in a range of trade policy measures to compute some kind of index of liberalisation. This strategy acknowledges that, in practice, trade reforms are multi-faceted, and it has been adopted by, for example, Papageorgiou et al. (1991) (PMC) and IMF (1998). Because they have a high

Table 1
Elements of recent trade liberalisations

| Country | Average nominal tariff[a] | | | Tax[b] | ER |
|---|---|---|---|---|---|
| | Pre-Reform | Current | Ratio | Dependence | |
| *South Asia* | | | | | |
| Bangladesh (1989, 1992) | 94 | 50 | 0.53 | 0.42 | −5.3 |
| India (1990, 1993) | 128 | 71 | 0.55 | 0.30 | −7.7 |
| Pakistan (1987, 1990) | 69 | 65 | 0.94 | 0.38 | −11.7 |
| Sri Lanka (1985, 1992) | 31 | 25 | 0.81 | 0.22 | −0.5 |
| Average | 80 | 53 | 0.71 | 0.40[c] | |
| *East Asia* | | | | | |
| China (1986, 1992) | 38 | 43 | 1.13 | | −43.9 |
| Philippines (1985, 1992) | 28 | 24 | 0.88 | 0.29 | 1.8 |
| Indonesia (1985, 1990) | 27 | 22 | 0.81 | 0.03 | −23.2 |
| Korea (1984, 1992) | 24 | 10 | 0.42 | 0.17 | 13.1 |
| Thailand (1986, 1990)[d] | 13 | 11 | 0.88 | 0.22 | −0.5 |
| Average | 29 | 25 | 0.82 | −0.65[c] | |
| *SSA* | | | | | |
| Cote d'Ivoire (1985, 1989) | 26 | 33 | 1.27 | 0.31 | CFA |
| Ghana (1983, 1991) | 30 | 17 | 0.57 | 0.18 | −11.1 |
| Kenya (1987, 1992) | 40 | 34 | 0.85 | 0.23 | −5.4 |
| Madagascar (1988, 1990) | 46 | 36 | 0.78 | 0.32 | −11.2 |
| Nigeria (1984, 1990) | 35 | 33 | 0.93 | 0.23 | −71.2 |
| Senegal (1986, 1991) | 98 | 90 | 0.92 | 0.43 | CFA |
| Tanzania (1986, 1992) | 30 | 33 | 1.10 | 0.07 | −145.2 |
| Zaire (1984, 1990) | 24 | 25 | 1.04 | 0.14 | −13.1 |
| Average | 41 | 38 | 0.94 | 0.29[c] | |
| *Latin America* | | | | | |
| Colombia (1984, 1992) | 61 | 12 | 0.20 | 0.13 | −36.1 |
| Peru (1988, 1992) | 57 | 17 | 0.30 | 0.22 | 106.7 |
| Costa Rica (1985, 1992) | 53 | 15 | 0.28 | 0.13 | −15.8 |
| Brazil (1987, 1992) | 51 | 21 | 0.41 | 0.02 | 9.5 |
| Venezuela (1989, 1991) | 37 | 19 | 0.51 | 0.05 | 0.2 |
| Chile (1984, 1991) | 35 | 11 | 0.31 | 0.11 | −14.5 |
| Argentina (1988, 1992) | 29 | 12 | 0.41 | 0.05 | 43.7 |
| Mexico (1985, 1987) | 29 | 10 | 0.34 | 0.03 | 3.7 |
| Average | 44 | 15 | 0.35 | 0.74[c] | |

Years given in parenthesis are pre-reform and current.

[a]Unweighted average nominal tariff (tends to be biased upwards), rounded Ratio is Current Pre-Reform—lower ratio implies greater tariff reductions.

[b]Tax dependence is tariff revenue as proportion of tax revenue in 1984.

[c]Figure is the rank correlation between countries ranked in descending order of tax dependence against descending order of tariff ratio; i.e. a high positive correlation implies that countries most dependent on tariffs are least able to reduce average tariffs.

[d]Import-weighted average nominal tariff.

information content such indexes can be a rich resource. Their key constraint is that, having a degree of subjectivity, they are less valuable when it comes to comparative analysis.[2]

### 2.2. Evidence on the impact of liberalisation

Establishing whether or not liberalisation has impacted on growth is not straightforward, for three reasons. First we need to frame an appropriate counterfactual. Is it sensible to assume a continuation of pre-existing policies and performance? In practical terms this may be all one can do, but it does have an important shortcoming: some liberalisations which are policy conditioned are initiated at a time of crisis and this clearly gives rise to a potential endogeneity problem (which we address below). Second, how does one disentangle the effects of trade reforms from other effects? Third, supply responses will differ from economy to economy: how long should one wait before conducting an assessment of reforms?

Broadly speaking, three methodologies have been widely used; cross-country, time series and computable general equilibrium modelling. We disregard the last, since CGE modelling tends to be used for scenario analysis rather than evaluating outcomes. The cross-country literature falls into two genres, 'with–without' and 'before–after'. 'With–without' has been used by *inter alia* World Bank (1990) and Mosley et al. (1991). It involves taking a sample of countries subject to trade reforms, matching them with non-reform comparators and ascribing any difference to the reform programme. 'Before–after', which is again used by World Bank (1990) and Mosley et al. (1991), introduces a time dimension in that it compares 'with–withouts' for a few years before and a few years after. In some cases, like PMC (1991), it is only the 'withs' that are examined, in that case for 3 years before and after.

Examples of time series analysis include Harrigan and Mosley (1981), PMC (1991), Greenaway and Sapsford (1994), Greenaway et al. (1997). Harrigan and Mosley (1981) focus on SALs as one of a number of possible determinants of growth, export and investment performance in a standard growth model. Greenaway and Sapsford (1994) use a structural break approach in a neo-classical growth model; Greenaway et al. (1997) model growth as a smooth transition process then search for evidence of a coincidence of 'take off' and liberalisation.

The study which reports the most favourable growth enhancing effects for liberalisation is PMC (1991) who evaluate 36 liberalisation episodes in 19 countries. Moreover, they conclude that more rapid growth of real GDP is secured with minimal transitional costs (in unemployment and fiscal constraints). These

[2] For critiques of that methodology, see Collier (1993) and Greenaway (1993).

conclusions were challenged by Greenaway (1993) and Collier (1993) largely on the grounds that the underlying measure of liberalisation is flawed. Moreover, Greenaway et al. (1997) look specifically at the timing of the PMC episodes and find no systematic evidence of a connection between trade reforms and growth acceleration. In some cases, there is a positive correlation, in some a negative correlation, in others no apparent correlation whatsoever. This seems to be the story where the remaining evidence is concerned. There are many cases where a positive link from liberalisation to growth is reported; equally there are many cases where no association is reported. Moreover, as Rodriquez and Rodrik (1999) show, many of the reported results are not very robust to changes in specification and/or sample frame. Given the diversity of components of liberalisation programmes, the range of indicators used and the fact that dynamics are rarely modelled, this is perhaps not surprising.

## 3. Modelling liberalisation in a panel framework

To investigate the impact of such potential shortcomings, we constructed a dataset of up to 73 countries.[3] For this sample, we estimate a 'core' new growth theory model of the type which has now become standard. We then introduce liberalisation. Rather than using a single measure, we take those of Sachs and Warner (1995), Dean et al. (1994) and one based on World Bank (1993). (The characteristics of each are explained below.) For each, we estimate a dynamic panel model to evaluate the short run impact and transitional effects of liberalisation on the growth of real per capita GDP.

### *3.1. The core growth model*

Following the work of Levine and Renelt (1992), which searched for a set of robust variables to model growth and the theoretical contributions to the new growth theory literature following Romer (1990), a degree of convergence on the most appropriate empirical specification for modelling growth has occurred.[4] Most models include as explanatory variables: investment; population growth; initial per capita GDP; and initial human capital. We include these, together with terms of trade variable and our liberalisation proxies. The former is included because our samples include developing countries and the empirical literature demonstrates clearly that terms of trade shocks have a significant impact on growth.[5] Liberalisa-

[3] Details of dataset construction are available from the authors on request.

[4] For a recent review of evidence, see Temple (1999).

[5] See the literature around the Bevan et al. project, for example Bevan et al. (1993).

tion is included for obvious reasons. Thus our base specification is one which is fundamentally a Levine–Renelt 'core variables' specification, with the addition of the terms of trade and liberalisation. The approach is very much in keeping with the work of, *inter alia*, Barro (1991), Easterly and Levine (1997) and Sachs (1997) though as we shall see below in contrast to that work our estimating model is dynamic rather than static. The base specification is[6]

$$\Delta \ln y_{i,t} = \beta_1 \ln y_{i,65} + \beta_2 \mathrm{SCH}_{i,65} + \beta_3 \Delta \ln \mathrm{TTI}_{i,t} + \beta_4 \Delta \ln \mathrm{POP}_{i,t} + \beta_5 \left( \frac{\mathrm{INV}}{\mathrm{GDP}} \right)_{i,t} + \beta_6 \mathrm{LIB}_{i,t} + \Delta \varepsilon_{i,t} \qquad (1)$$

where $y_{i,t}$ = real GDP per head; ln $y_{i,65}$ = real GDP per head as at 1965; $\mathrm{SCH}_{i,65}$ = level of secondary school enrolment as at 1965; $\mathrm{TTI}_{i,t}$ = terms of trade index; $\mathrm{POP}_{i,t}$ = population; $([\mathrm{INV}]/[\mathrm{GDP}])_{i,t}$ = the ratio of gross domestic investment to GDP; $\mathrm{LIB}_{i,t}$ = dummy capturing liberalisation episode.

Specifications of this type have been widely used, not to model movements from one steady state to another but to investigate the transitional effects of liberalisation and other policy switches, by for example Easterley (1993), Fischer (1993) and Boone (1996). Although they have been widely used, Eq. (1) may be dynamically mis-specified. We therefore specify a second estimating equation of the form

$$\Delta \ln y_{i,t} = \alpha \Delta \ln y_{i,t-1} + \beta_1 \ln y_{i,65} + \beta_2 \mathrm{SCH}_{i,65} + \beta_3 \Delta \ln \mathrm{TTI}_{i,t} + \beta_4 \Delta \ln \mathrm{POP}_{i,t} + \beta_5 \left( \frac{\mathrm{INV}}{\mathrm{GDP}} \right)_{i,t} + \beta_6 \mathrm{LIB}_{i,t} + \Delta \varepsilon_{i,t} \qquad (2)$$

where $y_{i,t-1}$ are lags of GDP per head. This has an obvious intuitive appeal in that it models growth in a dynamic context and permits us to track the short run effects of liberalisation. However, including lags induces a correlation between the error term and the lagged dependent variable. To provide consistent estimates, an instrumental variable procedure is adopted, which instruments the lagged dependent variable. Although a number of candidates are possible, the Arellano and Bond (1991) approach is adopted as this will generate the most efficient estimates.[7] (As we report later, we also estimate our model using an alternative procedure to investigate whether our results are robust to changes in estimation methodology.)

[6] All data series are drawn from World Bank data series and the Barro–Lee data series. Full details are available from the authors on request.

[7] Consistency of the GMM estimator requires lack of second order serial correlation in the dynamic formulation, so tests for this are presented with the results. Overall instrumental validity is also examined using a Sargan test of over-identifying restrictions.

### *3.2. Indicators of liberalisation*

As we saw earlier, one of the key difficulties in trying to assess the relationship between liberalisation and growth is gaining an accurate measure of the point at which a country is deemed to have liberalised. Clearly such a process does not happen instantaneously but it is possible to suggest when moves toward greater market freedoms occurred. The simplest option is to use a statement of intent, such as the date when a World Bank SAL is agreed, for example, on the grounds that this signals the beginning of reform. Thus, our first indicator of liberalisation is a dummy variable, which is activated at the time of a country's first SAL (or equivalent World Bank intervention). The advantage of this approach is that it is extensive in its breadth of coverage of developing countries. While accepting that the receipt of a Bank loan does not necessarily imply immediate liberalisation, it is a signal of intent.

Our second indicator uses a range of data, and draws on the work of Dean et al. (1994) who examine post-1985 liberalisation in a sample of 32 developing countries. Timing of liberalisation is assessed by reference to four indicators: tariffs, quotas, export impediments and promoters and exchange rate misalignment. The authors evaluate levels and changes in tariffs, quotas and so on and then identify a year (or years) when liberalisation has taken place. In contrast to the SAL indicator therefore, which proxies intent, the Dean et al. (1994) indicator is based on outcomes of trade reforms. As with the SAL indicator, this again enters our model as a dummy variable.

Our final indicator draws upon Sachs and Warner (1995) who develop a measure of movement from "closed" to "open" trade policy regimes. Using the Summers and Heston (1991) 'international comparisons' dataset, they assess whether an economy is open or closed by reference to five criteria: non-tariff barrier coverage; average tariffs; the black-market exchange rate premium; whether the economy is socialist or not; whether a state monopoly exists over major exports. As Sachs and Warner (1995) concede, there is a degree of arbitrariness in their measure in that the critical average tariff level is deemed to be 39% and the critical level for coverage of NTBs is also deemed to be 39%. Many would regard these levels as too high to be consistent with an economy being 'open'. Nonetheless, it offers a further alternative to our SAL and the Dean et al. (1994) indicators. Again we enter this in our estimating equation as a dummy variable.[8]

## 4. Empirical results

The results of estimating Eqs. (1) and (2) are reported in Tables 2–4. Refer first to Table 2. Here the model is estimated using the Sachs–Warner liberalisation

[8] The Sachs–Warner indicator is in fact one of the most widely used in growth analysis. Recent examples include Sala-i-Martin (1997) and Burnside and Dollar (2000).

Table 2
Growth equations incorporating Sachs and Warner liberalisation index

| Variable | 1 | | 2 | | 3 | |
|---|---|---|---|---|---|---|
| | Coefficient | $t$-ratio | Coefficient | $t$-ratio | Coefficient | $t$-ratio |
| Constant | 0.043 | 2.118** | 0.042 | 1.941* | 0.001 | 0.214 |
| $\Delta \ln y_{t-1}$ | | | | | 0.500 | 9.508** |
| $\Delta \ln y_{t-2}$ | | | | | 0.076 | 1.329 |
| $\Delta \ln y_{t-3}$ | | | | | 0.324 | 8.284** |
| $\ln y_{65}$ | −0.010 | −4.286** | −0.008 | −2.813** | −0.003 | −5.717** |
| $SCH_{65}$ | 0.007 | 2.869** | 0.009 | 3.408** | 0.003 | 3.722** |
| $\Delta$lnTTI | 0.029 | 2.630** | 0.031 | 2.867** | 0.031 | 5.141** |
| $\Delta$lnPOP | −0.681 | −1.840* | −1.171 | −3.221** | −0.411 | −6.133** |
| INV/GDP | 0.114 | 3.258** | 0.125 | 2.925** | 0.005 | 0.554 |
| Sachs1 | 0.027 | 6.457** | | | | |
| Sachs2 | | | −0.008 | −0.963 | 0.010 | 2.001** |
| $\text{Sachs2}_{t-1}$ | | | 0.008 | 0.926 | 0.017 | 4.286** |
| $\text{Sachs2}_{t-2}$ | | | 0.015 | 1.966** | 0.020 | 5.576** |
| 1st Order serial correlation | 3.786** | | 3.756** | | −1.639 | |
| 2nd Order serial correlation | 1.439 | | 2.073** | | −0.986 | |
| Sargan Test | | | | | 0.634 | |
| No. of countries | 69 | | 69 | | 69 | |
| Period | 1975–1993 | | 1975–1993 | | 1975–1993 | |

(a) Heteroskedastic robust asymptotic $t$-ratios are in parentheses.
(b) The Sargan Test for the validity of the set of instruments is defined as $\text{Prob}(J > \chi_p^2)$, where $p$ is the number of over-identifying instruments.
(c) Time dummies are not reported.
* Indicates significance at the 90% level.
** Indicates significance at the 95% level.

proxy. Column 1 refers to the base specification with the Sachs–Warner index included on the basis of a 0 prior to and 1 after reform. In other words, liberalisation is picked up in the form of an intercept shift, which measures average annual per capita growth changes following reform. All of the independent variables have the predicted sign. Thus, a low initial GDP and high initial level of schooling are associated with faster growth in GDP per capita as are a higher investment ratio and favourable terms of trade movement. Faster population growth is associated with slower GDP per capita growth and liberalisation appears to have on average a favourable and substantial (2.7%) impact on growth in the years following liberalisation.[9] All of the coefficient estimates are statistically significant most at the 5% level at least.

[9] For the benchmark Sachs–Warner equation report a growth effect of 2.44% for their dummy.

Table 3
Growth equations incorporating Dean et al. (1994) liberalisation index

| Variable | 1 | | 2 | | 3 | |
|---|---|---|---|---|---|---|
| | Coefficient | $t$-ratio | Coefficient | $t$-ratio | Coefficient | $t$-ratio |
| Constant | 0.020 | 1.026 | 0.023 | 1.146 | 0.034 | 5.491** |
| $\Delta \ln y_{t-1}$ | | | | | 0.624 | 6.454** |
| $\Delta \ln y_{t-2}$ | | | | | −0.139 | −2.173** |
| $\ln y_{65}$ | −0.006 | −3.023** | −0.007 | −3.330** | −0.005 | −4.708** |
| $SCH_{65}$ | 0.008 | 2.664** | 0.008 | 2.711** | 0.004 | 2.454** |
| ΔlnTTI | 0.027 | 1.655* | 0.028 | 1.767* | 0.003 | 0.382 |
| ΔlnPOP | −1.068 | −4.436** | −1.034 | −4.215** | −0.634 | −4.697** |
| INV/GDP | 0.214 | 6.418 | 0.220 | 6.544** | 0.101 | 3.287** |
| dean1 | 0.009 | 1.777* | | | | |
| dean2 | | | −0.001 | −0.132 | −0.005 | −0.924 |
| $dean2_{t-1}$ | | | 0.002 | 0.289 | 0.004 | 0.803 |
| $dean2_{t-2}$ | | | 0.018 | 2.380** | 0.011 | 2.615** |
| 1st Order serial correlation | 3.763** | | 3.814** | | −2.470** | |
| 2nd Order serial correlation | 2.324** | | 2.620** | | 0.048 | |
| Sargan Test | | | | | 0.916 | |
| No of countries | 73 | | 73 | | 73 | |
| Period | 1986–1993 | | 1986–1993 | | 1986–1993 | |

(a) Heteroskedastic robust asymptotic $t$-ratios are in parentheses.
(b) The Sargan Test for the validity of the set of instruments is defined as Prob($J > \chi^2_p$), where $p$ is the number of over-identifying instruments.e
(c) Time dummies are not reported.
* Indicates significance at the 90% level.
** Indicates significance at the 95% level.

To look more closely at the timing of reform on growth, column 2 allows for the same base specification but the liberalisation proxy (Sachs 2) switches on in the year of liberalisation only. This therefore indicates the growth impact of reform in the first year only rather than an average post reform effect. Lags pick up the impact of reform in subsequent years. The magnitude, signs and significance of the independent variables are robust to this change, with population growth increasing in significance. What is most interesting, however, is the arrangement of signs on the liberalisation indicator: negative (but insignificant) in year 1; positive (but insignificant) in year 2 and positive, larger and significant in year 3; suggesting evidence of a $J$ curve type effect of liberalisation on per capita GDP growth.

Equations like those in columns 1 and 2 are routinely used in studies of liberalisation (see for example Easterly and Levine, 1997; Sachs, 1997) yet there are indications of mis-specification. Although first order serial correlation would be expected in differenced equations of this form, as the bottom panel reveals,

Table 4
Growth equations incorporating World Bank Index

| Variable | 1 | | 2 | | 3 | | 4 | |
|---|---|---|---|---|---|---|---|---|
| | Coefficient | $t$-ratio | Coefficient | $t$-ratio | Coefficient | $t$-ratio | Coefficient | $t$-ratio |
| Constant | 0.067 | 3.861** | 0.072 | 4.352** | 0.034 | 5.424** | 0.037 | 5.727** |
| $\Delta \ln y_{t-1}$ | | | | | 0.541 | 7.476** | 0.512 | 7.176** |
| $\Delta \ln y_{t-2}$ | | | | | −0.077 | −2.598** | −0.085 | −2.791** |
| $\ln y_{65}$ | −0.009 | −3.775** | −0.009 | −4.249** | −0.005 | −6.414** | −0.005 | −6.827** |
| $SCH_{65}$ | 0.010 | 3.271** | 0.010 | 3.273** | 0.004 | 3.513** | 0.004 | 3.866** |
| $\Delta \ln TTI$ | 0.001 | 0.028 | 0.005 | 0.280 | 0.002 | 0.299 | 0.003 | 0.504 |
| $\Delta \ln POP$ | −1.510 | −5.219** | −1.479 | −5.028** | −0.966 | −7.580** | −0.996 | −7.633** |
| INV/GDP | 0.155 | 3.099** | 0.153 | 3.276** | 0.089 | 5.164** | 0.094 | 5.393** |
| W.Bank1 | 0.064 | 1.067 | | | | | | |
| W.Bank2 | | | −0.004 | −0.641 | −0.004 | −0.814 | | |
| $W.Bank2_{t-1}$ | | | 0.005 | 0.614 | 0.009 | 1.748* | | |
| $W.Bank2_{t-2}$ | | | 0.000 | 0.013 | −0.002 | −0.680 | | |
| Crisis | | | | | | | 0.001 | 0.324 |
| $Crisis_{t-1}$ | | | | | | | 0.001 | 0.157 |
| $Crisis_{t-2}$ | | | | | | | −0.004 | −1.051 |
| NonCrisis | | | | | | | −0.021 | −1.922* |
| $NonCrisis_{t-1}$ | | | | | | | 0.030 | 2.884** |
| $NonCrisis_{t-2}$ | | | | | | | 0.002 | 0.401 |
| 1st Order serial correlation | | 2.929** | | 3.291** | | −2.713** | | −2.554** |
| 2nd Order serial correlation | | 0.869 | | 0.573 | | −0.531 | | −0.314 |
| Sargan Test | | | | | | 0.722 | | 0.624 |
| No. of countries | 73 | | 73 | | 73 | | 73 | |
| Period | 1979–1991 | | 1979–1991 | | 1979–1991 | | 1979–1991 | |

(a) Heteroskedastic robust asymptotic $t$-ratios are in parentheses.
(b) The Sargan Test for the validity of the set of instruments is defined as $\text{Prob}(J > \chi_p^2)$, where $p$ is the number of over-identifying instruments.
(c) Time dummies are not reported.
* Indicates significance at the 90% level.
** Indicates significance at the 95% level.

there is evidence of second order serial correlation in column 1 which is indicative of dynamic mis-specification. To correct for this an instrumental variables approach in a dynamic setting as per Eq. (2) above was estimated and the results reported in column 3. First of all, note that the Sargan test for the validity of instruments is satisfied and also note that the second order serial correlation problem has been dealt with. From the upper panel, we see that all the independent variables have the predicted sign and all apart from the investment ratio are statistically significant. The liberalisation effect is positive and significant in all 3 years, with a contemporaneous impact effect of just under 1%, with an additional 1.5% in year 2 and 2% in the subsequent year. Again, a lagged reaction to trade reform is suggested though this time without the initial decline in GDP per capita.

Table 3 reports results using the Dean et al. (1994) indicator. Columns 1, 2 and 3 have exactly the same interpretation as in Table 2. Dean 1 and Dean 2 proxies of liberalisation should be interpreted in the same way as Sachs 1 and 2: the first is an average year on year growth impact of reform and the second examines timing issues. As with Table 2, coefficients have the expected sign in columns 1 and 2 and all, apart from the terms of trade variable, are statistically significant. From column 1, we see that liberalisation has a positive impact on growth though this is only significant at the 90% level and somewhat smaller in magnitude than with the Sachs–Warner measure (0.9%). The arrangement of signs in column 2 is negative (and insignificant), positive (and insignificant) and positive (and significant) in year 3, again pointing to a *J* curve reaction. Again, however, there are problems of serial correlation and so we estimate our dynamic equation with instruments on the lagged dependent variables, the results of which are reported in column 3. All the independent variables have the expected sign and are significant (apart, again,

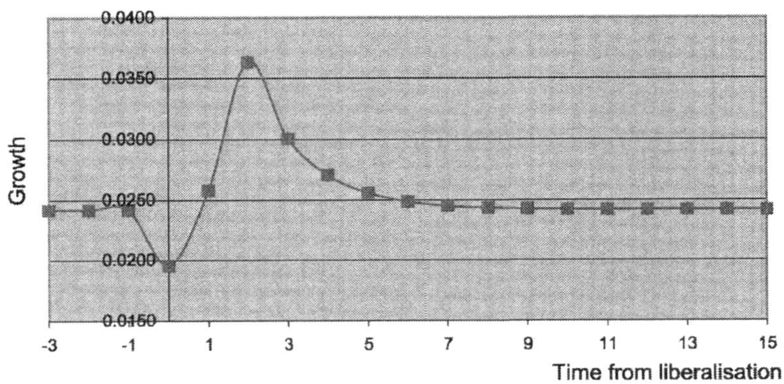


Fig. 1. Impact of liberalisation on growth (Dean et al., 1994).

from the terms of trade), suggesting a robust specification and the diagnostics suggest an appropriately specified equation. The arrangement of signs and significance on the liberalisation variable still points to a *J* curve response, with the strongest effect (1.1%) coming through in the third year (with this coefficient estimate also being statistically significant). Fig. 1 illustrates the path graphically.

In Table 3, we turn to the results when using the World Bank SAL indicator where we take the commencement of a SAL as our marker for liberalisation. The pattern of results is qualitatively similar to those for the other two indicators. In the base equations (columns 1 and 2), all coefficients have the expected sign and, with the exception of the terms of trade proxy, are statistically significant. In column 1, the liberalisation proxy suggests an improvement in GDP per capita growth of 0.6% but this is not statistically significant. In column 2, we report a negative/positive/positive arrangement of signs but again none are significant. Finally, in the dynamic equation (column 3) all coefficient estimates have the expected sign and, with the exception of TTI, all are significant. Here we find a negative/positive/negative arrangement of signs on the liberalisation variable though on this occasion none are statistically significant.

## 5. Discussion, interpretation and robustness

We have reported results for a base 'new growth' model similar to that used by many analysts. Since we feel there are good reasons for believing this to be a mis-specified growth model, we have also estimated a dynamic version. Because the 'measurement' of liberalisation is controversial, rather than confine ourselves to a single measure we have three different indicators. Overall, a number of findings come through. First, the outcomes for our core growth model are as expected: initial GDP, initial schooling, the investment ratio, population growth and (sometimes) terms of trade changes are all influential in determining cross-country patterns of growth. Second, we get similar patterns of results on the liberalisation effect across several measures of markers for liberalisation. This is especially interesting, in part because we have explored the dynamics of liberalisation to good effect and in part because of the consistent story which seems to be revealed. This is that the short run impact of liberalisation on the growth of real GDP per capita is unlikely to be instantaneous: we have clear evidence of a *J* curve effect, evidence which is consistent across samples and measures of liberalisation. Third, orders of magnitude for impact effects (1 year) and medium-run effects (3 years) exhibit some consistency but also some differences. The growth effects are strongest when the Sachs–Warner index is used and weakest with the SAL indicator. This is not surprising since the Sachs–Warner indicator is effectively a measure of ex post openness, i.e. it only includes as 'liberalised' those which have actually opened. By contrast, the SAL indicator is ex ante; in effect it is a statement of intent to liberalise. That being so, it includes trade reformers, which are destined to fail as well as reformers destined for success.

But how robust are our results? We ran an exhaustive series of robustness tests using both Arellano–Bond and generalised instrumental variables regression. The latter suggested a simpler form of dynamic specification than Arellano–Bond. When this specification was estimated, however, the results were little different from those reported above (details are available from the authors on request). As a second check on robustness, we standardised the sample frame by number of countries (69) and time period (1986–1991). With regard to the former, dropping four countries from the Dean and World Bank samples made no material difference to the results. Setting a common sample period had more of an impact, which is not surprising for two reasons: we discard a great deal of useful information and we shorten the time period significantly. Nevertheless, the broad picture remains similar, with the same core variables being significant and a *J* curve pattern of short run growth effects. The only change of note is that the Sachs–Warner results weaken, which is not surprising since, in general, this dates liberalisation earlier than the other two. (Again, detailed results are available from the authors on request.)

As a third check, we investigate whether dropping investment or the terms of trade variables from the estimating equation had an impact. The former is of particular interest since, as well as affecting the level of investment, it could be argued that the coefficient on investment might be affected by liberalisation (or other policy reforms which accompany liberalisation). We experimented both by dropping investment from the regression and instrumenting it. In neither case are the main conclusions relating to the impact of reforms altered, though the magnitude of coefficient estimates are sensitive to the inclusion of investment and the way in which it is instrumented. Conducting similar experiments with the terms of trade variable had no material impact. (Detailed tables of results are available from the authors on request.)

One interesting, and consistent, finding is the lack of significance of the World Bank SAL indicator. Many SALs are introduced contemporaneously with IMF Stabilisation Loans, which in turn are often introduced in crisis conditions. Thus there may be a potential endogeneity problem here. Thus, as a fourth robustness check, we explicitly distinguished between 'crisis' and 'non-crisis' countries in the sample by reference to the timing of their SAL vis-à-vis their stabilisation loan. Specifically, if a stabilisation loan was agreed 12 months before or after a SAL, we treated this as a crisis case; those where the timing was outside this interval were treated as non-crisis. The results of re-estimating our growth equation with this refinement are reported in column 4 of Table 4. As can be seen, the coefficient estimates are smaller in magnitude for the 'crisis' countries and none are significant. Not only are the coefficients larger for the non-crisis countries, they are also statistically significant. This suggests two things. First, there may well be differences between liberalisation outcomes in countries where trade reforms are forced on by a crisis as a consequence of the less favourable initial conditions. Second, it reinforces the point made earlier about care being taken in the choice of liberalisation proxies.

## 6. Conclusions

In this paper, we have tested a dynamic model of growth in the context of several samples and, more importantly, several measures of liberalisation. Our results suggest that liberalisation may impact favourably on growth of real GDP per capita. However, the effect would appear to be lagged and relatively modest. That is not so surprising since liberalisations vary in their depth and intensity and never amount to an immediate shift to free trade. The liberalisations, which are picked up, are often first rather than final steps. Through time of course economies become more open, partly as a consequence of incremental trade reforms but also due to other factors: reductions in transportation and communication costs, technological change and so on. The pay-off to this increased openness may be greater, as manifested in consistently higher coefficients from the Sachs–Warner proxy.

Our results suggest that at least four factors may be at work in explaining why the previous literature on the growth effects of liberalisation is so inconsistent. First there is the obvious point that sample sizes and composition vary as do methodological approaches. Second, different analysts have used different measures; some are ex ante indicators of liberalisation, some are ex post and others are clearly indicators of openness. Third it is clear that many models which have been estimated are mis-specified. Fourth, it is important to model the dynamics in order to distinguish between impact and medium run effects.


## Acknowledgements

The authors acknowledge detailed comments from two anonymous referees and advice from Sebastian Edwards on two earlier drafts of this paper. Helpful comments were also received from participants in a seminar at the Chinese University of Hong Kong and the Annual Congress of the Economic Society of Australia. Finally, financial support from the Leverhulme Trust under Programme Grant F114/BF is gratefully acknowledged.


## References


Arellano, M., Bond, S., 1991. Some test of specification for panel data: Monte Carlo evidence and an application to employment equations. Review of Economic Studies 58, 277–292.

Balassa, B., 1982. Development Strategies in Semi-Industrialised Countries. Johns Hopkins Univ. Press, Baltimore.

Barro, R.J., 1991. Economic growth in a cross-section of countries. Quarterly Journal of Economics 5, 181–189.

Bevan, D., Collier, P., Gunning, J., 1993. Trade stocks in developing countries. European Economic Review 37, 557–565.
Boone, P., 1996. Politics and the effectiveness of foreign aid. European Economic Review 40, 289–328.
Burnside, C., Dollar, D., 2000. Aid, policies and growth. American Economic Review 90, 847–868.
Dean, J., Desai, S., Riedel, J., 1994. Trade Policy Reform in Developing Countries Since 1985: A Review of the Evidence, World Bank Development Policy Group mimeo.
Easterley, W., 1993. How much do distortions affect growth? Journal of Monetary Economics 32, 187–212.
Easterley, W., Levine, R., 1997. Africa's growth tragedy: policies and ethnic divisions. Quarterly Journal of Economics 112, 1203–1250.
Edwards, S., 1993. Openness, trade liberalisation and growth in developing countries. Journal of Economic Literature 31, 1358–1393.
Edwards, S., 1998. Openness, productivity and growth: what do we really know? Economic Journal 108, 383–398.
Fischer, S., 1993. The role of macroeconomics factors in growth. Journal of Monetary Economics 32, 485–512.
Greenaway, D., 1993. Liberalising foreign trade through rose tinted glasses. Economic Journal 103, 208–223.
Greenaway, D., Milner, C.R., 1993. Trade and Industrial Policy in Developing Countries. Macmillan, London.
Greenaway, D., Sapsford, D., 1994. What does liberalisation do for exports and growth? Weltwirtschaftliches Archiv 130, 152–174.
Greenaway, D., Leybourne, S.J., Sapsford, D., 1997. Modelling growth (and liberalisation) using smooth transitions analysis. Economic Inquiry 35, 798–814.
Harrigan, J., Mosley, P., 1981. Evaluating the impact of world bank structural adjustment lending: 1980–87. Journal of Development Studies 27, 63–94.
IMF, 1998. Trade Liberalisation in IMF-Supported Programs (Washington DC, IMF).
Krueger, A.O., 1978. Foreign Trade Regimes and Economic Liberalisation. Ballinger, Lexington, MA.
Krueger, A.O., 1997. Trade policy and economic development: how we learn. American Economic Review 87, 1–22.
Levine, R., Renelt, D., 1992. A sensitivity of cross country growth regressions. American Economic Review 82, 946–963.
Mosley, P., Harrigan, J., Toye, J. (Eds.), Aid and Power: The World Bank and Policy-based Lending, Volume 1: Analysis and Policy Proposals. Routledge, London.
Papageorgiou, D., Michaely, M., Choksi, A. (Eds.), Liberalising Foreign Trade. Blackwell, Oxford.
Rodriguez, F., Rodrik, D., 1999. Trade Policy and Economic Growth: A Skeptic's Guide to the Cross-National Evidence Working Paper 7081, NBER.
Rodrik, D., 1997. Globalisation, social conflict and growth. The World Economy 21, 143–158.
Romer, D., 1990. Endogenous technological change. Journal of Political Economy 98, 71–102.
Sachs, J.D., 1997. Fundamental sources of long run growth. American Economic Review 87, 184–188.
Sachs, J.D., Warner, A., 1995. Economic reform and the process of global integration. Brookings Papers on Economic Activity 1, 1–118.
Sala-i-Martin, X., 1997. I just ran two million regressions. American Economic Review 87, 178–183.
Summers, R., Heston, A., 1991. The Penn World Table (Mark 5): an expanded set of international comparisons 1950–88. Quarterly Journal of Economics 106, 327–368.
Temple, J., 1999. The new growth evidence. Journal of Economic Literature 37, 112–156.
World Bank, 1990. Report on Adjustment Lending II: Policies for the Recovery of Growth, Document R90-99, Washington DC, The World Bank.
World Bank, 1993. Report on Adjustment Lending III, Washington DC, The World Bank.

# B
# Micro

# [15]

Journal of International Economics 36 (1994) 53–73. North-Holland

# Productivity, imperfect competition and trade reform

## Theory and evidence

Ann E. Harrison*

*The World Bank, 1818 H Street, N.W., Washington, DC 20433, USA*

Received November 1990, revised version received February 1993

Research on productivity often examines the relationship between productivity increases and structural changes in an economy, such as trade policy reform. If, however, policy reforms affect the nature of competition, then the productivity changes associated with trade reform may be mismeasured. Using a panel of manufacturing firms in the Cote d'Ivoire, this paper measures changing profit margins and productivity following a 1985 trade reform. The paper also exploits cross-section differences in protection, using data on tariffs and import penetration. Ignoring the impact of liberalization on competition leads to biased estimates of the relationship between trade reform and productivity growth.

## 1. Introduction

The earliest arguments for gains from trade are based on the concept of allocative efficiency. In a static framework, protection is costly because resources are not allocated in areas where a country has a comparative advantage. The recent emphasis on imperfectly competitive markets in international trade creates yet another argument for gains from trade: in a protected market dominated by only a few domestic firms, trade reform increases competition.[1]

Improving the allocation of resources or curbing firms' excess market power only generates a one-time increase in growth. Yet the 'new' endoge-

*Correspondence to*: Ann E. Harrison, The World Bank, 1818 H Street, N.W., Washington, DC 20433, USA.

*This paper is a revised version of an earlier draft circulated as World Bank Staff Working Paper 451 in July 1990. I would like to thank David Card, Avinash Dixit, Gene Grossman, Zvi Griliches, Jim Levinsohn, Ramon Lopez, Jaime de Melo, John Newman, John Page, J. David Richardson, Duncan Thomas and Jim Tybout for helpful comments and suggestions. Extensive comments by an anonymous referee are also very much appreciated. This paper was prepared under funding from the World Bank research project 'Industrial Competition, Productive Efficiency, and Their Relation to Trade Regimes' (RPO-674-46). This research reflects the work of the individual author and does not reflect the views and policies of the World Bank or the countries it represents.

[1]For an overview of this literature, see Helpman and Krugman (1989).


*SSDI* 0022-1996(93)01289-Q

nous growth theories [see Grossman and Helpman (1990) for an overview] suggest that trade policies also affect long-run growth. Moving towards free trade could permanently increase growth rates by accelerating the rate of technological change. An ever-expanding global market may raise the returns to innovaton, while more advanced technology may be embodied in imported inputs. Yet Grossman and Helpman also point out that protection could accelerate growth if it shifts resources towards manufacturing and away from research in countries with no comparative advantage in R & D. In the context of these theories, the impact of trade policies on long-run growth is ultimately an empirical question.

Despite the volume of empirical work which addresses the correlation between trade and growth, efforts to measure gains from trade at the micro level have been inconclusive. In developing countries, where small domestic markets make oligopoly behavior more likely, only a few studies link trade reform with increased competition.[2] Even more striking is the lack of conclusive evidence on the linkages between trade reform and productivity growth. There is now plant-level evidence confirming a positive relationship between trade reform and efficiency for some countries [see, for example, Tybout et al. (1991)]. Yet recent overviews on the links between trade reform and productivity growth [Bhagwati (1988), Nishimizu and Page (1990), and Tybout (1992)] suggest that the debate is still unresolved.

One possible explanation for the lack of definitive results may depend on how productivity is measured. The measurement of productivity pioneered by Solow (1957) has been used extensively to analyze technology change in both developing and developed countries. Solow derived a productivity measure, referred to as total or multi-factor productivity (TFP), which depends on two assumptions: constant returns to scale and perfect competition in product markets. Yet shifts in trade policy are likely to alter the competitive environment, particularly in developing countries where domestic markets are often dominated by several firms.

Although the potential biases from assuming perfect competition have long been recognized, this paper implements a simple approach to correct estimated TFP growth for these biases. Extending a methodology pioneered by Hall (1988) and Domowitz et al. (1988) on aggregate data, this paper uses plant-level data to explore changes in market power and productivity following a 1985 trade reform in Cote d'Ivoire. The results suggest that

[2]See, for example, de Melo and Urata (1986) who compare reported price–cost margins for two census years before and after reforms in Chile. New evidence showing that import penetration lowers price–cost margins in several developing countries will be included in Roberts and Tybout (in process). Research on developed country data includes Domowitz et al. (1986), who use aggregate data to find a negative relationship between import penetration and reported price–cost margins. See also Schmalensee (1989) for an overview of the research on developed countries.

price–cost margins fell in only a few sectors following the reform. We also explore the relationship between mark-ups and trade regime using alternative measures of 'openness', such as import penetration and tariffs. Using these alternative measures does show that increased openness to trade lowers excess profits.

When productivity estimates are modified to account for changes in price–cost margins and returns to scale, there is a stronger positive correlation between trade reform and productivity. Section 2 outlines the theoretical approach and shows how ignoring the effects of liberalization on competition may lead researchers to mismeasure the effect of trade reform on productivity. Section 3 discusses trade policy changes in the Cote d'Ivoire and briefly describes the data. We present estimation results in section 4. Section 5 incorporates the findings on market power and returns to scale to derive modified TFP estimates.

## 2. Correcting biases in productivity measurement

Our framework extends Hall (1988) and Domowitz et al. (1988). We begin with a production function for firm $i$ in industry $j$ at time $t$:

$$Y_{ijt}=A_{jt}f_{it}G(L_{ijt},K_{ijt},M_{ijt}). \tag{1}$$

Output, $Y_{ijt}$, is produced by firm $i$ with inputs labor, $L$, capital, $K$, and materials, $M$. $A_{jt}$ is an industry-specific index of Hicks-neutral technical progress, while $f_{it}$ is a firm-specific parameter which allows for firm-specific differences in technology. Totally differentiating (1), and dividing through by $Y$, we have

$$\begin{aligned}\mathrm{d}Y/Y_{ijt}=&(\partial Y/\partial L)(\mathrm{d}L/Y)_{ijt}+(\partial Y/\partial K)(\mathrm{d}K/Y)_{ijt}\\&+(\partial Y/\partial M)(\mathrm{d}M/Y)_{ijt}+\mathrm{d}A/A_{jt}+\mathrm{d}f_{it}/f_{it}.\end{aligned} \tag{2}$$

The element of imperfect competition enters (2) because firms with market power do not set the value of marginal product, $P(\partial Y/\partial L)$, equal to the factor price. If we assume Cournot behavior by firms, then we can derive the first-order conditions from each firm's profit maximization and write each of the partial derivatives $\partial Y/\partial L$, $\partial Y/\partial K$, and $\partial Y/\partial M$ as follows:

$$\partial Y/\partial L_{ijt}=(w/p)_{jt}\left[\frac{1}{1+(S_{ij}/e_j)}\right](w/p)_{jt}\mu_{ij}, \tag{3a}$$

$$\partial Y/\partial K_{ijt}=(r/p)_{jt}\left[\frac{1}{1+(S_{ij}/e_j)}\right](r/p)_{jt}\mu_{ij}, \tag{3b}$$

$$\partial Y/\partial M_{ijt}=(n/p)_{jt}\left[\frac{1}{1+(S_{ij}/e_j)}\right](n/p)_{jt}\mu_{ij}. \tag{3c}$$

Factor prices are given by $w$ (the wage), $r$ (the rental cost of capital), and $n$ (the price of material inputs). If firm $i$ is not perfectly competitive, then the value of the marginal product exceeds the factor cost by some mark-up, $\mu$. To simplify the estimation, we will assume that the mark-up only varies across sectors. This is equivalent to assuming that market shares do not vary substantially across firms within the same sector.

Substituting (3a)–(3c) into (2) and rearranging terms, we have

$$\frac{\mathrm{d}Y}{Y_{ijt}}=\mu_j\left[\frac{wL}{PY}\frac{\mathrm{d}L}{L}+\frac{rK}{PY}\frac{\mathrm{d}K}{K}+\frac{nM}{PY}\frac{\mathrm{d}M}{M}\right]+(\mathrm{d}A/A)_{jt}+\mathrm{d}f_{it}/f_{it}. \tag{4}$$

The value of $wL/PY$, $rk/PY$, and $nM/PY$ is simply the share of each factor (labor, capital, materials) in total output. We shall denote the share of labor and materials as $\alpha_l$ and $\alpha_m$. Under constant returns to scale, the factor shares would sum to $1/\mu$, but we will retain a general formulation and allow the sum of the factor shares to equal $\beta/\mu$, where $\beta$ may be less than or greater than one.[3] Rewriting (4):

$$\mathrm{d}y_{ijt}=\mu_j[\alpha_l\,\mathrm{d}l+\alpha_m\,\mathrm{d}m]_{ijt}+(\beta-1)_j\mathrm{d}K/K_{ijt}+\mathrm{d}A/A_{jt}+\mathrm{d}f_{it}/f_{it}. \tag{5}$$

Lower case variables $y$, $l$ and $m$ are equal to $\ln(Y/K)$, $\ln(L/K)$, and $\ln(M/K)$. The mark-up, $\mu$, is just the coefficient on the changes in $L/K$ and $M/K$, weighted by their respective shares in output.

To see how estimates of productivity change, $\mathrm{d}A/A$, could be biased due to the presence of imperfect competition, for the moment we will assume constant returns to scale ($\beta=1$), ignore the firm-specific effect, and rewrite (5) as

$$\mathrm{d}y-\alpha_l\mathrm{d}l-\alpha_m\mathrm{d}m=\phi=(\mu-1)(\alpha_l\mathrm{d}l+\alpha_m\mathrm{d}m)+\mathrm{d}A/A. \tag{6}$$

We will refer to $\phi$ as the 'observed' productivity measure, and to $\mathrm{d}A/A$ as the 'true' productivity change. Under perfect competition, $\mu=1$ and $\phi=\mathrm{d}A/A$. The Solow measure of productivity, $\mathrm{d}A/A$, is unbiased.

If $\mu$ is greater than 1, however, there are two possible sources of bias. First, we may get bias in estimating the *rate* of productivity change, $\mathrm{d}A/A$. If $l$ and

[3]Say we have a production function given by $Y=AL^aM^bK^c$, where $a+b+c$ sum to $\beta$, the scale parameter. If we take logs and differentiate, we see that

$$\frac{\mathrm{d}Y}{\mathrm{d}L}\frac{L}{Y}+\frac{\mathrm{d}Y}{\mathrm{d}M}\frac{M}{Y}+\frac{\mathrm{d}Y}{\mathrm{d}K}\frac{K}{Y}=a+b+c=\beta. \tag{a.1}$$

But from our first-order conditions, $(\mathrm{d}Y/\mathrm{d}L)(L/Y)=\mu\alpha_l$, etc. so we have $\mu\alpha_l+\mu\alpha_m+\mu\alpha_k=\beta$.

| | CASE A | CASE B |
|---|---|---|
| | $\alpha_l dl + \alpha_m dm > 0$ | $\alpha_l dl + \alpha_m dm < 0$ |
| Pre-reform $\mu > 1$ | $\phi_1 > dA_1/A_1$ | $\phi_1 < dA_1/A_1$ |
| Post-reform $\mu = 1$ | $\phi_2 = dA_2/A_2$ | $\phi_2 = dA_2/A_2$ |
| Net change | $\phi_2 - \phi_1 < dA_2/A_2 - dA_1/A_1$ | $\phi_2 - \phi_1 > dA_2/A_2 - dA_1/A_1$ |
| Bias | Productivity gains under-estimated | Productivity gains over-estimated |

Fig. 1. Direction of bias in productivity estimates: $dA/A$ = true productivity; $\phi$ = observed productivity.

$m$ are rising (falling), then $dA/A$ is over (under) estimated. Second, *changes* in the trend rate of growth of productivity will be mismeasured. Fig. 1 outlines the possible biases in estimating changes in the trend rate of growth of productivity. As an example, we explore the case where price–cost margins exceed one and firms have market power prior to a trade reform. In this case, the rate of observed productivity growth, $\phi$, will be greater (less) than the true measure if $l$ and $m$ are rising (falling). If the trade reform is accompanied by a fall in market power (possibly due to increases in the perceived elasticity of demand), price–cost margins fall to unity and measured productivity will equal the true productivity measure, $dA/A$. However, if we are interested in comparing productivity before and after the changes in trade policy, we are likely to incorrectly assess the true change in $dA/A$. As illustrated in fig. 1, the direction of the bias cannot be predicted using (6).

To see how observed productivity estimates are affected by assuming constant returns to scale, let us take the perfectly competitive case ($\mu = 1$) and rewrite (5) as (6′):

$$dy - \alpha_l dl - \alpha_m dm = \phi = (\beta - 1) dK/K + dA/A. \tag{6′}$$

If $\beta$ exceeds 1, then the technology is characterized by increasing returns to scale. Observed productivity in this case is the sum of $dA/A$ and productivity gains from exploiting increasing returns to scale (which are positive when $dK/K$ is rising). Under a decreasing returns to scale technology, TFP growth is equal to the exogenous productivity term $dA/A$ *minus* the efficiency losses that occur when a firm expands production. When observed productivity, $\phi$, differs from the exogenous productivity term, $dA/A$, due to scale effects, one could argue that this difference is not necessarily due to 'bias'. In this case, observed productivity growth reflects both changes in Hicks-neutral technical progress and the impact of scale effects on economic efficiency.

## 3. Trade policy in the Cote d'Ivoire

The trade regime in the Cote d'Ivoire became increasingly restrictive in the 1970s. In 1973, a major restructuring of the tariff code increased nominal tariff rates and raised levels of effective protection by implementing an escalated tariff structure. In the second half of the 1970s and in the early 1980s, quantitative restrictions and arbitrary reference prices were introduced on a wide range of imports competing with domestic manufactures. Table 1 indicates the extent of tariff protection across industrial sectors before the reform. Textiles and food-related manufacturing received the highest nominal tariff protection, ranging from 60 to 163 percent. The pattern of effective protection, which is only available for 1980, is very similar: food processing and textiles were the most protected, followed by chemicals. Quota coverage, as measured by the number of import licenses in each sector in 1982, also follows the same pattern: textile imports were the most restricted, followed by food-related products and chemicals.

During the boom years in the second half of the 1970s, the Cote d'Ivoire benefited from the surge in world coffee and cocoa prices. The increases in revenue, most of which were captured by the government, were used to promote investment and expand public spending and infrastructure. The severe macroeconomic imbalances that followed the fall in coffee prices forced the government to adopt an austerity program in 1982. The adjustment program was followed by a major trade reform introduced in mid-1984.

The trade reform was implemented in 1985 and extended in 1986 and early 1987. The reform removed quantitative restrictions and reference prices, rationalized the tariff structure, and introduced temporary tariff surcharges. Although average tariffs did decline by 30 percent (see table 1), the goal of the tariff reform was to equalize effective protection across different sectors by lowering tariffs on final goods and raising tariffs on inputs and intermediate goods. The surcharges declined over a five-year period to allow firms previously protected by non-tariff measures to adjust.

Cote d'Ivoire's nominal exchange rate is fixed in relation to the French franc at a rate which is the same for a number of franc zone African countries. When the French franc appreciated against the U.S. dollar between 1985 and 1988, the Ivorian franc became considerably overvalued in real terms. Consequently, the reform was conducted in conjunction with an environment which lowered the competitiveness of exports on world markets.

Table 1

Sample means for selected variables.

| Sector | 1979–1984 Output growth | 1979–1984 Labor output growth | 1979–1984 TFPG[a] | 1979–1984 Tariff | 1985–1987 Output growth | 1985–1987 Labor output growth | 1985–1987 TFPG[a] | 1985–1987 Tariff |
|---|---|---|---|---|---|---|---|---|
| Grain processing | −0.2 | 5.1 | −1.7 | 0.50 | 3.2 | −10.1 | 1.4 | 0.48 |
| Food processing | 6.1 | 8.8 | 2.4 | 0.60 | −2.7 | −5.7 | 0.9 | 0.59 |
| Other food | 8.5 | 2.9 | −0.5 | 1.63 | 4.0 | 1.5 | 1.3 | 1.33 |
| Textiles | 4.0 | 1.5 | 0.4 | 0.95 | 0.7 | −2.9 | −1.9 | 0.72 |
| Chemicals | 2.0 | −5.6 | 0.3 | 0.58 | 12.7 | 3.2 | 3.7 | 0.58 |
| Transport | 2.2 | −0.8 | −1.7 | 0.73 | 7.2 | −6.5 | 1.7 | 0.69 |
| Machinery | 7.2 | −6.5 | 2.7 | 0.49 | −3.5 | −2.5 | 4.7 | 0.47 |
| Wood products | −7.2 | −0.2 | −0.6 | 0.64 | −0.4 | 0.0 | −3.6 | 0.46 |
| Paper products | −0.2 | 2.2 | −0.8 | 0.57 | 9.6 | −4.6 | 6.2 | 0.56 |
| All sectors | 2.0 | −1.7 | 0.4 | 1.02[b] | 4.8 | −2.5 | 1.4 | 0.72 |

[a]TFP is defined using the Tornquist index number formula, with $TFP=[\ln Y_t-\ln Y_{t-1}]-[\alpha_l\ (\ln L_t-\ln L_{t-1})+\alpha_m\ (\ln M_t-\ln M_{t-1})+(1-\alpha_l-\alpha_m)\ (\ln K_t-\ln K_{t-1})]$. Labor and material shares are defined as follows: $\alpha_l=(1/2)\ (\alpha_{lt}+\alpha_{lt-1})$, $\alpha_m=(1/2)\ (\alpha_{mt}+\alpha_{mt-1})$.

[b]Average tariffs over all sectors computed using a weighted average, using firm output as weights. A value of 0.50 indicates an ad valorem tariff of 50 percent.

Although the government simulated a partial devaluation through an export subsidy scheme for manufactured exports, the first subsidy payments were delayed until mid-1986 and payments were concentrated in several large firms. The government's inability to compensate exporting firms for the real appreciation meant that the export sector was adversely affected. Consequently, we should see a fall in price–cost margins for exporting sectors in the post-trade-reform period.

To account for changes in behavior and productivity during the trade reforms in Cote d'Ivoire, (5) is modified to allow for a change in mark-ups by firms during the post-1985 period. Changes in behavior are captured by adding an interactive slope dummy to $dx$ in (5). If trade reform induced a shift in the overall level of productivity growth, then we should also include an intercept dummy:

$$dy_{ijt} = B_{1j} dx_{ijt} + B_{2j} [D\,dx]_{ijt} + B_{3j} D + B_{4j} dk_{ijt} + dA/A_{jt} + df_{it}/f_{it}, \quad (7)$$

where

$B_{1j} = \mu_j$,
$B_{4j} = (\beta - 1)_j$,
$dx = [\alpha_l\, dl + \alpha_m\, dm]$,
$dk = dK/K$,

$D$ is 1 for 1985–1987 and 0 otherwise. If trade policy changes led to more competitive firm behavior, the coefficient $B_2$ on $[D\,dx]$ should be negative, reflecting the fall in mark-ups when firms are exposed to international competition. If the reform led to overall increases in productivity growth, then $B_3$ should be positive. The coefficient $B_4$ is equal to the scale parameter $\beta$ minus one.

The model presented in section 2 assumes that we correctly observe capital services, $K$. Yet capital services may fluctuate as capacity utilization changes over the business cycle. If we observe recorded capital stock, $K^*$, we can model the true utilization of capital $K$ as equal to $K^*E$, where $E$ reflects changes in utilization of capacity.

Substituting $K^*E$ for $K$, the estimating equation becomes

$$(dy - de)_{ijt} = B_{1j}[dx - (\alpha_l + \alpha_m)\, de]_{ijt} + B_{2j}[D\{dx - (\alpha_l + \alpha_m)\, de\}]_{ijt}$$
$$+ B_{3j} D + B_{4j} dk_{ijt} + dA/A_{jt} + df_{it}/f_{it}. \quad (8)$$

Since we do not have estimates of capacity utilization at the firm level, we employ a measure of total energy use as a proxy. A plant's energy use is the input component most likely to vary as capacity utilization fluctuates.

The productivity term, $dA/A$, can be thought of as the average rate of productivity growth for industry $j$, which will be captured by a constant term $B_{0j}$. We will decompose $\mathrm{d}f_{it}/f_{it}$ into a plant-specific constant, $g_i$, plus a disturbance term, $u_{it}$. The final estimating equation is then given by

$$(\mathrm{d}y - \mathrm{d}e)_{ijt} = B_{0j} + B_{1j}[\mathrm{d}x - (\alpha_l + \alpha_m)\,\mathrm{d}e]_{ijt}$$

$$+ B_{2j}[D\{\mathrm{d}x - (\alpha_l + \alpha_m)\,\mathrm{d}e\}]_{ijt}$$

$$+ B_{3j}D + B_{4j}\,\mathrm{d}k_{ijt} + g_i + u_{it}. \tag{9}$$

*Data*

The firm data are taken from the Banque de Donnees Financieres (BdDF), which is instructed to gather annual information on all industrial firms. The number of firms in individual years ranges from around 250 in the 1970s to nearly 500 in the mid-1980s. Although the coverage of the industrial sector is incomplete (informal enterprises are excluded and small formal firms are under-represented), the BdDF covers almost all large and medium-sized formal manufacturing enterprises. We chose our sample of 246 firms by selecting out those enterprises with a complete time series. Although we include firms which were only present during part of the 1979–1987 period, we exclude firms which had missing values between their entry and exit dates.

We estimate (9) using our panel of 246 Ivorian firms during the period 1979–1987. The approach requires data on real output, capital stock, labor and material inputs, and the shares of labor and materials in total output. Total sales and material inputs were deflated by two-digit sectoral level price deflators to obtain a real output and materials series. We also calculated a material input price deflator based on input–output tables for each of the sectors, but the estimation results were unaffected and are not reported here. Real capital stock was constructed using the perpetual inventory method.[4]

[4]Capital stock was calculated in two steps. First, for those firms that reported across the entire sample period, we used the perpetual inventory method. Real capital stock in period $t$ is defined in eq. (a.1): $K_{it} = (1-d)K_{i,t-1} + I_t$. As a benchmark, we used 1976 capital stock for each firm and then added real investment while accounting for depreciation. Real investment was computed by deflating nominal investment by sector-specific investment price deflators. To construct a base year real capital stock for the remaining sample of firms which entered after 1976, we first constructed a capital stock price deflator ($KPD$) using data on firms that were present in all years:

$$KPD_{jt} = \frac{\sum_{i=1}^{n} K_{ijt}}{\sum_{i=1}^{n} NK_{ijt}}. \tag{a.2}$$

$KPD_{jt}$ is the capital stock deflator for sector $j$ in year $t$. It was constructed using the ratio of the real capital stock computed in (a.1) to the nominal capital stock ($NK$) reported by firms that were present in all years. The real base year capital stock for a firm entering in year $t$ is then given by $K_{ijt} = (KPD_{jt})\ (NK_{it})$, where $t$ is the base year capital stock for firm $i$. For subsequent years, real capital stock is then computed using eq. (a.1).

The total number of employees for each firm was used as a measure of labor input.[5] Since there are only several firms in some of the more disaggregated sectors surveyed by the BdDF, we aggregated our firm sample into nine sectors: grain processing, food processing, other food, textiles, chemicals, transport, machinery, wood, and paper products. Sample means by sector for selected variables are given in table 1. Output growth during the pre-reform period averaged 24 percent, increasing to 4.8 percent during the reform. When trade reforms were introduced in 1985, the economy experienced a period of growth, but 1986 and particularly 1987 were recessionary periods. The burden of the adjustment appears to have fallen disproportionately on the labor force, with the annual average growth of employees falling from $-1.7$ to $-2.5$ percent. One shortcoming of the labor input variable is that it measures the number of permanent employees hired by the firm, but does not include information on temporary workers who may have been hired to replace the permanent labor force. However, the fall in total employment by the formal sector, documented in table 1, has been confirmed by others [see Lorch (1989)].

Table 1 also reports the uncorrected estimate for total factor productivity growth (TFPG), calculated using a Tornquist index number formula. Under trade reform, the adjusted measure shows productivity increased in most sectors but declines in others (food processing, textiles, and wood products). On average, productivity growth accelerated during the trade reform, rising from 0.4 percent to an annual average 1.4 percent growth.

## 4. Estimation

The final estimating equation, eq. (9), contains a firm-specific variable, $g_i$, which allows firms to exhibit different rates of technological change. One way to estimate this equation would be to include dummy variables for each firm. Excluding these firm dummy variables and estimating the equation by ordinary least squares (OLS) would yield biased estimates if any of the explanatory variables are correlated with the firm-specific effect. An alternative procedure is to redefine all the variables as deviations from the mean values for each firm over time, known as the within-group estimator. All the results are estimated using this approach.

### *4.1. Within estimates*

The within estimates are first computed under the assumption of

[5]Unfortunately, the data set does not measure labor input in hours, which would allow us to control for variation in labor intensity across the business cycle.

constant returns to scale. These estimates are presented in table 2.[6] The coefficient $B_1$ should measure the extent of market power across sectors, while $B_2$ indicates the change in price–cost margins under trade reform. The mark-up of price over marginal cost is highest in the food sectors, ranging from 35 percent for the 'other food' category to 20 percent for grain processing. As indicated in table 1, these sectors received the highest levels of protection prior to trade reform. The only sector within the food category without a high mark-up is food processing, a sector which exports about 70 percent of total sales. These results suggest that heavily protected sectors which nevertheless were also highly export oriented were forced to behave competitively due to their participation in global markets.

The coefficient on $B_2$ is statistically significant in three out of the nine sectors. For two of those three sectors, food processing and textiles, the coefficient is negative. In the case of food processing, however, the fall in margins occurred in a sector which generally behaved competitively prior to the reforms. In this sector, the primary impetus behind falling margins was probably the large real appreciation of the exchange rate, which severely affected exporting sectors. In the case of textiles, however, anecdotal evidence suggests that margins also fell due to increased competition from the trade reform. The conversion of quotas to tariffs led to large-scale underinvoicing, which was particularly severe in the textile sector. For the other sectors, which fail to show significant effects of the reform on margins, it is possible that changes in the structure of protection were not dramatic enough to show up in the data. This is corroborated by the data on reported profit margins discussed later in the paper.

The coefficient on $B_3$ indicates the change in productivity growth during the trade policy reforms. The coefficient is positive for five of the nine sectors, but only statistically significant and positive for chemicals and the paper sector. Paper products experienced an unusual increase in growth during the trade reform period. Since productivity is typically procyclical, the statistically significant increase in productivity growth during the reform period may only partly be attributed to changes in the trade regime.

The within estimates are likely to be biased since inputs (including capital stock) and output are simultaneously determined by the firm. Table 2 also presents instrumental variables (IV) estimates. Appropriate instruments should be correlated with material and labor per unit of capital, but independent of any productivity or demand shocks affecting the firm. Natural instruments would include factor prices, such as wages or input prices. As instruments we use the nominal exchange rate, a price index for

[6]If $f_i$ is random and uncorrelated with the explanatory variables, then estimating a fixed effect model using OLS will be unbiased but not as efficient as generalized least squares (GLS) estimation. Since the coefficients and standard errors for the GLS estimates were close to the within estimates, the GLS results are not reported here.

Table 2

Within and instrumental variables (IV) estimates.
Estimating equation: $dy = B_1(\alpha_l dl + \alpha_m dm) + B_2[D(\alpha_l dl + \alpha_m dm)] + B_3 D$.

| Sector | Within estimates $\beta_1$ | $\beta_2$ | $\beta_3$ | $R_2$ | IV[a] $\beta_1$ | $\beta_2$ | $\beta_3$ | Hausman test[b] | Overid test[c] |
|---|---|---|---|---|---|---|---|---|---|
| Grain processing | 1.201 | −0.001 | 0.016 | 0.88 | 1.376 | −0.421 | −0.003 | 0.8 | 7.3 |
| ($N$=83) | (0.089) | (0.113) | (0.113) | | (0.239) | (0.558) | (0.048) | | |
| Food processing | 1.031 | −0.389 | −0.041 | 0.72 | 1.076 | −0.526 | −0.059 | 0.1 | 6.2 |
| ($N$=81) | (0.084) | (0.138) | (0.039) | | (0.227) | (0.407) | (0.062) | | |
| Other food | 1.353 | 0.013 | 0.012 | 0.92 | 1.415 | −0.589 | −0.013 | 1.8 | 4.0 |
| ($N$=121) | (0.049) | (0.090) | (0.023) | | (0.162) | (0.473) | (0.038) | | |
| Textiles | 1.079 | −0.253 | −0.040 | 0.78 | 1.710 | −0.903 | −0.169 | 1.9 | 4.9 |
| ($N$=183) | (0.049) | (0.082) | (0.033) | | (0.463) | (0.563) | (0.107) | | |
| Chemicals | 1.069 | 0.042 | 0.047 | 0.86 | 1.159 | −0.051 | 0.031 | 1.2 | 4.2 |
| ($N$=250) | (0.036) | (0.069) | (0.022) | | (0.091) | (0.377) | (0.027) | | |
| Transport | 1.158 | −0.035 | −0.016 | 0.92 | 1.096 | −0.097 | −0.007 | 1.2 | 0.7 |
| ($N$=113) | (0.049) | (0.069) | (0.027) | | (0.135) | (0.209) | (0.032) | | |
| Machinery | 0.970 | 0.012 | 0.033 | 0.83 | 1.192 | −3.439 | −0.167 | 1.7 | 5.4 |
| ($N$=230) | (0.030) | (0.219) | (0.034) | | (0.165) | (2.178) | (0.134) | | |
| Wood products | 1.137 | 0.080 | −0.036 | 0.87 | 1.268 | −0.172 | 0.052 | 0.2 | 6.1 |
| ($N$=182) | (0.048) | (0.070) | (0.030) | | (0.298) | (0.569) | (0.048) | | |
| Paper products | 1.016 | 0.173 | 0.092 | 0.85 | 0.950 | 0.660 | 0.125 | 1.6 | 5.2 |
| ($N$=115) | (0.059) | (0.089) | (0.031) | | (0.442) | (0.542) | (0.071) | | |
| All sectors | 1.078 | 0.020 | 0.022 | 0.84 | 1.106 | −0.133 | 0.014 | 0.4 | 2.4 |
| ($N$=1358) | (0.016) | (0.028) | (0.010) | | (0.087) | (0.247) | (0.018) | | |

[a]Instruments are $D$; the log of the nominal exchange rate; the log price index for energy; the log of debt; the log of sectoral wages; and $D$ interacted with these four variables.

[b]The critical 5 percent value for the $\chi^2$ (2) = 5.99. A higher value indicates a rejection of the null hypothesis that the OLS and IV estimates are the same.

[c]The over-identification test gives the $\chi^2$ statistic for the hypothesis that the instruments are accepted as valid. The critical 5 percent of the $\chi^2$ (7) = 14.1. A higher value indicates rejection of the test.

energy, the real wage calculated at the sector level, and the firm's reported debt. Exchange rates, wages, and energy prices should be correlated with input decisions but independent of any demand or productivity shocks affecting the firm. We also include the firm's stock of debt under the assumption that the firm's borrowings should be correlated with ability to expand inputs but are predetermined.

Following Bowden and Turkington (1984), we instrument the product $D$ $\mathrm{d}X$ using a non-linear combination of the dummy $D$ and $\mathrm{d}X$. In our case, this is just the set of variables, $D$, instruments for $\mathrm{d}X$, and the product of $D$ and the instruments.[7] The instrumental variable estimates in table 2 were also tested for stability using various alternative sets of instruments. Our experience [which is confirmed by Abbot et al. (1989)] suggests that the standard instruments which are used in these types of regressions, such as GNP, are likely to be correlated with the error term and may lead to biased estimates of price–cost margins. Alternative specifications which employed GNP as an instrument in the first stage of the regression led to rejection of the $\chi^2$ test used to test the model specification. One problem is that instruments which passed the test of exogeneity were sometimes poor explanatory variables for the endogenous variables. In some cases, the first-stage $R^2$ was less than 0.10.

We tested the validity of our instruments using a $\chi^2$ test [see Sargan (1958) for an early exposition or Newey (1985)]. A regression of the residuals from the first stage regression on the instruments yields a $\chi^2$ test of the validity of our instruments. The results, shown in table 2, suggest that in all cases our instruments are valid.

The instrumental variable coefficients in table 3 show a similar pattern to the within estimates. Mark-ups are highest for food-related and textile firms. However, due to the larger standard errors, we only reject the null hypothesis of perfect competition for two food sectors, textiles, and chemicals – the four sectors with the highest tariff and quota protection. Mark-ups generally fell during the trade reform period, as indicated by the negative coefficient on $B_2$. Again, however, none of the estimates, except for textiles, is statistically significant due to the large standard errors. A Hausman test comparing the within and IV estimates confirms the null hypothesis that the two sets of estimates are not statistically different from each other. In the remainder of this paper we present only the within estimates.

### *4.2. Relaxing the assumption of constant returns to scale*

One potential source of misspecification arises from assuming that the

[7] If instead we had regressed $\mathrm{d}x$ on a set of instruments to obtain a predicted value for $\mathrm{d}x$, and then calculated the predicted $\mathrm{d}x$ multiplied by $D1$, this would have yielded a biased coefficient on the product $\mathrm{d}x\ D1$.

Table 3

Within estimates with no restrictions on the scale technology estimating equation: $dy = \beta_1 dx + \beta_2[D\,dx] + \beta_3 D + \beta_4 dk_1$.[a]

| Sector | $\beta_1$ | $\beta_2$ | $\beta_3$ | $\beta_4$ | F-test[b] |
|---|---|---|---|---|---|
| Grain processing | 1.141 | −0.019 | 0.016 | 0.936 | 1.4 |
| | (0.105) | (0.105) | (0.030) | (0.055) | |
| Food processing | 0.725 | −0.172 | −0.054 | 0.688 | 25.1 |
| | (0.078) | (0.103) | (0.036) | (0.062) | |
| Other food | 1.128 | 0.080 | −0.010 | 0.855 | 10.0 |
| | (0.078) | (0.083) | (0.023) | (0.045) | |
| Textiles | 1.036 | −0.182 | −0.039 | 0.951 | 1.3 |
| | (0.062) | (0.080) | (0.031) | (0.044) | |
| Chemicals | 0.772 | 0.046 | 0.070 | 0.740 | 48.0 |
| | (0.052) | (0.057) | (0.020) | (0.038) | |
| Transport | 1.050 | −0.008 | 0.032 | 0.939 | 2.2 |
| | (0.067) | (0.064) | (0.025) | (0.041) | |
| Machinery | 0.862 | −0.007 | 0.030 | 0.900 | 34.2 |
| | (0.037) | (0.179) | (0.033) | (0.026) | |
| Wood products | 1.113 | 0.007 | −0.036 | 0.945 | 1.9 |
| | (0.052) | (0.066) | (0.029) | (0.040) | |
| Paper products | 0.840 | 0.224 | 0.108 | 0.835 | 5.6 |
| | (0.087) | (0.088) | (0.029) | (0.070) | |
| All sectors | 0.947 | 0.040 | 0.024 | 0.881 | 70.8 |
| | (0.020) | (0.026) | (0.009) | (0.014) | |

[a] $dx = \alpha_l dl + \alpha_m dm . dk = d \log K$.
[b] Tests if coefficient on $dk$ is equal to 1.

technology is characterized by constant returns, which permits us to omit $dk$ from eq. (9). If the technology is not characterized by constant returns, then omitting $dk$ leads to biased estimates. The extent of the bias can be computed as the product $R\ (\beta - 1)$, where $\beta - 1$ is the coefficient on $dk$ and $R$ is the coefficient of $dk$ regressed on $dx$.[8] Assuming that $R$ is negative, price–cost margins will be under-estimated with increasing returns to scale ($\beta > 1$). If the technology is characterized by decreasing returns ($\beta < 1$), then margins will be over-estimated.

Table 3 adds $dk$ to both sides of eq. (5) and re-derives the estimating equation, eq. (9). The coefficient on $dk$ is just $\beta$, the scale parameter. A test of constant returns to scale is then a test of whether $\beta = 1$, while increasing (decreasing) returns will be indicated by a value of $\beta$ greater than (less than) unity. As indicated in table 3, the coefficient on $dk$ is generally less than 1, which implies that the technology is characterized by decreasing returns to

[8] See Schmidt (1976).

Table 4

Within estimates: Comparing different measures of openness.

| | Original specification | Import penetration | Tariffs |
|---|---|---|---|
| $\beta_1$ | 0.947 | 1.091 | 0.941 |
| | (0.020) | (0.033) | (0.022) |
| $\beta_2$ | 0.040 | −0.248 | 0.039 |
| | (0.026) | (0.053) | (0.025) |
| $\beta_3$ | 0.024 | −0.186 | 0.016 |
| | (0.009) | (0.093) | (0.021) |
| $\beta_4$ | 0.881 | 0.877 | 0.865 |
| | (0.014) | (0.015) | (0.015) |

scale.[9] As expected, this induced an upward bias in the coefficients reported in table 2. Table 3 shows the same pattern of price–cost margins, but the actual margins are lower. Although a number of previous studies have found increasing, not decreasing returns to scale, scale estimates are typically quite sensitive to functional form and estimation technique. In addition, it is not surprising that manufacturing firms in Cote d'Ivoire exhibit decreasing returns, since larger firms often are publicly owned or receive special treatment from the government.

### *4.3. Alternative measures of trade policy*

One possible objection to our approach could be that the three years of trade reform in the Cote d'Ivoire are too brief a period to allow identification of either its impact on profit margins or productivity growth. A related objection could be raised about the depth of the reform. Since the reform sought to minimize effective rates of protection by raising some (zero) tariff rates and lowering others, the impact of the reform is difficult to measure using a time series of either average tariffs or import penetration. Although average tariffs fell by 30 percent (see table 1), import penetration stayed approximately constant. Nevertheless, combining time-series with cross-sector differences in import penetration or tariffs could be used to exploit differences in trade policy *across* sectors.[10]

We report the results of such estimates in table 4. Instead of interacting d$x$

[9]We also re-estimated the equation in several different ways to test whether our estimation procedure had biased the capital coefficient towards zero. The coefficient on capital remained unchanged when we estimated the equation in levels, suggesting that the within transformation of the data did not exacerbate any downward bias in the coefficient on capital stock.

[10]See also Harrison (1991), who examines the relationship between different measures of trade policy and productivity growth across countries.

with the time dummy to examine the impact of trade reform on margins, we interact d$x$ with either import penetration or tariff rates. Data on import penetration are annual data at the sector level, while tariffs were calculated by sector for two points in time (1984 and 1987). Tariffs were measured using tariff revenues as a fraction of imports. Although this measure does not accurately reflect administrative tariff levels, particularly when there are discretionary and widespread tariff exemptions, it was the only measure available before and after the reform.

The results show a strong and statistically significant negative relationship between price–cost margins and import penetration. The coefficient on the interaction term, $-0.248$, suggests that if imports increased as a share of domestic consumption from 0 to 50 percent, then the excess of price over marginal cost would fall by 12 percent. As expected, price–cost margins rise as tariffs increase, but the relationship is only significant at the 15 percent level.

The coefficient on $B_3$ measures the change in total factor productivity growth when import penetration or tariffs rise. The coefficient is negative and statistically significant for import penetration and positive (but insignificant) for tariffs. This negative relationship between import penetration and productivity growth has been reported in other studies which use aggregate industry data to measure the relationship between productivity growth and import penetration [see, for example, Nishimizu and Page (1990)]. Yet using import penetration as a proxy for trade policy is problematic for several reasons. First, import penetration measures the outcome of changes in trade policy, not the policies themselves. It is quite possible that significant trade reforms could raise productivity without being reflected in import volumes. Second, import penetration does not allow us to distinguish between any positive effect of import competition on productivity growth in the long run and the fact that imports may be drawn to sectors with low productivity growth. Third, the observed relationship could also be explained by the pro-cyclical nature of productivity growth. In the short run, imports may lead to a contraction of output in domestic competing industries, leading to productivity losses. One way to address this problem is to use long-run averages. In section 5 we compute period averages to examine the relationship between corrected productivity growth estimates and import penetration.

### *4.4. Comparison with gross margins*

To examine the impact of trade policy on competition, this paper makes two critical assumptions. First, we assume that trade policy is correctly measured. To test the robustness of our assumption, we have explored different approaches to measuring changes in trade policy – such as changes in policies over time vs. differences in import penetration across sectors.

Table 5

Gross margins and import penetration.

| Sector | Margins pre-reform | Margins post-reform | Average margins over both periods |
|---|---|---|---|
| Grain processing | 12.9 | 13.1 | 13.0 |
| Food processing | 13.1 | 13.9 | 13.4 |
| Other food | 23.4 | 26.6 | 24.5 |
| Textiles | 19.7 | 18.3 | 19.2 |
| Chemicals | 21.3 | 19.2 | 20.4 |
| Transport | 11.9 | 10.9 | 11.5 |
| Machinery | 14.0 | 19.5 | 14.7 |
| Wood products | 13.1 | 7.5 | 11.0 |
| Paper products | 15.2 | 21.0 | 17.7 |

Second, we assume that a fall in $B_2$ can be interpreted as a fall in margins. How valid is this assumption? The empirical literature in industrial organization is still wrestling with how to adequately measure departures from perfect competition.[11] In this subsection we examine one alternative to measuring margins, by examining changes in gross price–cost margins, defined as (revenue – variable costs)/revenue. As noted by Schmalensee (1989) and others, this measure is problematic since more capital-intensive industries or industries with high fixed costs will have higher margins.

Table 5 shows gross margins by sector. Average price–cost margins were estimated for the whole time period, as well as before and after the 1985 trade reform. In some cases the results are consistent with the estimates presented in table 2 and 3, while in other respects the estimates are quite different. Margins are highest in the other food category, textiles and chemicals, and lowest in wood, transport, food, and grain processing. The results are consistent with table 3 for other food (with high margins) and food processing (with the lowest margins). Gross margins did not fall significantly after the 1985 trade reform, which is consistent with our conclusions pointing to small average changes in price–cost margins overall. The sector which experienced the largest change in gross margins is paper products (where margins rose), which is consistent with the estimation results in table 3 showing that paper products are the only sector which exhibited statistically significant increases in margins. Despite these similarities, however, the correlation coefficient between estimates in tables 3 and 5 is almost zero, which suggests that the two sets of estimates may capture different aspects of firm behavior.

[11]See the chapters by Bresnahan and Schmalensee in the *Handbook of Industrial Organization* [Schmalensee and Willig (1989)].

## 5. Modified TFP estimates

Section 2 examined the bias in TFP measurement under imperfect competition and explored the impact on TFP measurement when the technology is characterized by increasing or decreasing returns to scale. Section 4 indicated that the manufacturing sector in Cote d'Ivoire is characterized by market power in some sectors and decreasing returns to scale. This section incorporates those findings to analyze the relationship between openness and modified estimates of productivity growth.

Although productivity may be estimated in a number of different ways, one standard approach is to use the Tornquist index number formula, which is a discrete approximation to the formula derived in eq. (6):

$$\mathrm{TFP} = [\ln Y_t - \ln Y_{t-1}] - [\alpha_l(\ln L_t - \ln L_{t-1}) + \alpha_m(\ln M_t - \ln M_{t-1}) + (1-\alpha_l-\alpha_m)(\ln K_t - \ln K_{t-1})], \tag{10}$$

where $\alpha_l = (1/2)(\alpha_{lt} + \alpha_{lt-1})$ and $\alpha_m = (1/2)(\alpha_{mt} + \alpha_{mt-1})$. If the mark-up factor, $\mu$, and the returns to scale parameter, $B$, are incorporated in the definition, eq. (10) can be written as

$$\mathrm{TFP} = [\ln Y_t - \ln Y_{t-1}] - \mu[\alpha_l(\ln L_t - \ln L_{t-1}) + \alpha_m(\ln M_t - \ln M_{t-1}) + (B/\mu - \alpha_l - \alpha_m)(\ln K_t - \ln K_{t-1})]. \tag{11}$$

Estimates of $\mu$ were taken from table 4 to calculate revised TFP estimates before and after trade reform. The sample was also split into less 'open' and more 'open' using tariffs and import penetration. Estimates of productivity using both the original and revised definitions of TFPG were then recomputed for each of the six categories: time series (before and after reform); import penetration (low and high); tariffs (high and low). The results are presented in table 6. The last column of table 6 also reports (in parentheses) productivity estimates corrected for changes in capacity utilization. The estimates in parentheses are the discrete version of the estimating equation, eq. (9), derived earlier in the paper.

Under the assumption of perfect competition, we find that productivity growth increased from an annual average of 0.4 percent to 1.4 percent following the trade reform. If we relax the assumption of perfect competition and constant returns to scale, the gain in exogenous productivity is 20 percent higher. On average, the adjusted productivity growth now rises from 0.6 percent to 1.8 percent. The alternative estimates, which correct for capacity utilization, show an even greater increase in productivity growth of 2.2 percent, which is consistent with the coefficient $B_3$ in table 4.

Using tariffs as our measure of trade policy also yields the same result:

Table 6

Sensitivity of TFP growth estimates to assumption of perfect competition ($\mu = 1$) and constant returns to scale ($\beta = 1$).

| Time series | $\mu = 1, \beta = 1$ | $\mu \neq 1, \beta = 1$ | $\mu \neq 1, \beta \neq 1$[a] |
|---|---|---|---|
| Pre-reform | 0.4 | 0.5 | 0.6 (−1.0) |
| Post-reform | 1.4 | 1.4 | 1.8 (1.2) |
| Difference | 1.0 | 0.9 | 1.2 (2.2) |
| **Tariffs** | | | |
| High | 0.2 | 0.2 | 0.4 (−0.4) |
| Low | 1.2 | 1.2 | 1.6 (0.8) |
| Difference | 1.0 | 1.0 | 1.2 (1.2) |
| **Import penetration** | | | |
| Low | 0.5 | 0.5 | 0.7 (0.0) |
| High | 1.0 | 1.1 | 1.4 (0.0) |
| Difference | 0.5 | 0.6 | 0.7 (0.0) |

[a]Numbers in parentheses indicate TFP growth adjusted for capacity utilization.

assuming perfect competition and constant returns to scale leads to underestimating the increase in productivity growth from a more open trade regime. Productivity growth is four times higher in sectors with lower tariff levels. Finally, using import penetration as a measure of trade policy yields mixed results. If we define productivity growth as in eq. (11), table 6 shows that productivity growth doubled in sectors with higher import penetration. However, if we correct for capacity utilization, the results show no relationship between import penetration and productivity growth.[12]

## 6. Conclusion

Research on productivity has often focused on the relationship between productivity increases and structural changes in an economy, such as trade policy reform. If, however, those structural changes affect the nature of competition or have scale effects, changes in total factor productivity growth may be mismeasured. In this paper we use a panel of firms from the Cote d'Ivoire to measure the relationship between productivity, market power, and trade reform.

[12]These results differ from reported estimates in table 4, which suggested that increased import penetration lowers productivity growth. Although both the estimates reported in table 4 and the estimates reported in parentheses in table 6 do correct for capacity utilization, import penetration is averaged over time and aggregated across sectors in table 6. Consequently, the short-run negative impact of import penetration on productivity disappears in the aggregated data.

The results suggest that firms in the most protected sectors – primarily food products oriented towards the domestic market – had the highest mark-ups of price over marginal cost. We also find weak evidence that price–cost margins fell between 1985 and 1987. In textiles, the fall in mark-ups suggests that increased competition from imports reduced the market power of existing firms. In the food processing sectors, however, the only significant declines were in exporting sectors, which were adversely affected by the real exchange rate appreciation. We also exploit the cross-section differences in import penetration and tariff rates across manufacturing sectors. Market power, as measured by price–cost margins, is significantly higher in sectors with lower import penetration and higher tariffs.

We then show that assuming perfect competition and constant returns to scale leads to under-estimating the gains in productivity growth following the trade reform. Two of the approaches to measuring the impact of trade policies show a positive association between more open trade policies and higher productivity growth. The time-series approach which compares behavior before and after 1985, shows that productivity growth tripled after the reform. Using tariffs as a trade policy measure shows that productivity growth was four times higher in the less protected sectors. If import penetration is used to capture changes in trade policy, however, the relationship between trade policy and productivity gains is more ambiguous.

Assessing the productivity effects of a trade reform, in contrast to relying on cross-section comparisons, is particularly useful if protection tends to be applied to inefficient sectors. Under those circumstances, time-series data are probably the best hope for disentangling the causal impact of a country's trade policies.

## References

Abbott, T.A., Z. Griliches and J.A. Hausman, 1989, Short run movements in productivity: Market power versus capacity utilization, Mimeo.

Bhagwati, J., 1988, Export-promoting trade strategy: Issues and evidence, The World Bank Research Observer 3, 27–57.

Bowden, R. and D. Turkington, 1984, Instrumental variables (Cambridge University Press, Cambridge).

Domowitz, I., R.G. Hubbard and B.C. Petersen, 1988, Market structure and cyclical fluctuations in U.S. manufacturing, The Review of Economics and Statistics 70, no. 1, 55–66.

Grossman, G. and E. Helpman, 1990, Trade, innovation, and growth, American Economic Review, Papers and Proceedings 80, no. 2, 86–91.

Hall, R.E., 1988, The relation between price and marginal cost in U.S. industry, Journal of Political Economy 96, no. 5, 921–947.

Harrison, A.E., 1991, Openness and growth: A time series, cross-country analysis for developing countries, PRE Working Paper no. 809, The World Bank.

Helpman, E. and P. Krugman, 1989, Trade policy and market structure (MIT Press, Cambridge, MA).

Lorch, K., 1989, Cote d'Ivoire: Industrial competitiveness during economic crisis and adjustment, Mimeo. The World Bank.

Melo, J. de and S. Urata, The influence of increased foreign competition on industrial concentration and profitability, International Journal of Industrial Organization 4, no. 3, 287–304.

Newey, W., 1985, Generalized method of moments specification testing, Journal of Econometrics 29, no. 3, 229–256.

Nishimizu, M. and J.M. Page, Jr., 1990, Trade policy, market orientation, and productivity change in industry, in: J. de Melo and A. Sapir, eds., Trade theory and economic reform: North, south, and east (Basil Blackwell, Oxford) 246–264.

Roberts, M. and J. Tybout, in progress, Industrial competition, productive efficiency, and their relation to trade regimes, Book manuscript.

Sargan, J.D., 1958, The estimation of economic relationships using instrumental variables, Econometrica 26, 393–415.

Schmalensee, R., 1989, Inter-industry studies of structure and performance, in: R. Schmalensee and R. Willig, eds., Handbook of industrial organization (North-Holland, Amsterdam).

Schmalensee, R. and R. Willig, 1989, Handbook of industrial organization (North-Holland, Amsterdam).

Schmidt, P., 1976, Econometrics (Marcel Dekker, New York).

Solow, R.M., 1957, Technical change and the aggregate production function, Review of Economics and Statistics 39, 312–320.

Tybout, J.R., J. de Melo and V. Corbo, 1991, The effects of trade reforms on scale and technical efficiency: New evidence from Chile, Journal of International Economics 31, 231–250.

Tybout, J.R., 1992, Linking trade and productivity: New research directions, The World Bank Economic Review 6, no. 2, 189–211.

# [16]

Review of Economic Studies (2002) **69**, 245–276 0034-6527/02/00100245$02.00


# Trade Liberalization, Exit, and Productivity Improvements: Evidence from Chilean Plants

NINA PAVCNIK
*Dartmouth College and NBER*

*First version received December* 1998; *final version accepted June* 2001 (*Eds.*)

This paper empirically investigates the effects of liberalized trade on plant productivity in the case of Chile. Chile presents an interesting setting to study this relationship since it underwent a massive trade liberalization that significantly exposed its plants to competition from abroad during the late 1970s and early 1980s. Methodologically, I approach this question in two steps. In the first step, I estimate a production function to obtain a measure of plant productivity. I estimate the production function semiparametrically to correct for the presence of selection and simultaneity biases in the estimates of the input coefficients required to construct a productivity measure. I explicitly incorporate plant exit in the estimation to correct for the selection problem induced by liquidated plants. These methodological aspects are important in obtaining a reliable plant-level productivity measure based on *consistent* estimates of the input coefficients. In the second step, I identify the impact of trade on plants' productivity in a regression framework allowing variation in productivity over time and across traded- and nontraded-goods sectors. Using plant-level panel data on Chilean manufacturers, I find evidence of *within* plant productivity improvements that can be attributed to a liberalized trade for the plants in the import-competing sector. In many cases, aggregate productivity improvements stem from the reshuffling of resources and output from less to more efficient producers.

## 1. INTRODUCTION

During the 1980s, many developing countries abandoned their inward-looking development strategies for drastic trade liberalization programmes. The supporters of these reforms claimed that the exposure of home producers to additional import competition and easier access of plants to foreign technology would enhance productivity in domestic industries. Despite the high profile of this topic, surprisingly little is known about the actual effects of trade policy changes on plant's productivity.

The theoretical trade literature offers conflicting predictions about the evolution of plant-level productivity following a trade liberalization episode, especially in cases where imperfect competition is present. Rodrik (1988, 1991) provides an excellent survey of the main issues. On one hand, trade liberalization exposes domestic producers to foreign competition, reduces their market power, and might force them to expand output and move down the average cost curve; this might result in the exploitation of the economies of scale. Gains from scale economies are not very likely in developing countries, where the increasing returns to scale are usually associated with the import-competing industries, whose output is likely to contract as a result of intensified foreign competition. In models such as Rodrik (1988), where plants invest in superior technology to reduce their cost, their incentive to cut costs might increase with their market share. If trade liberalization reduces the domestic market shares of unshielded domestic producers without expanding their international sales, their incentives to invest in improved technology will decrease as protection ceases. This effect reduces the benefits of tariff reductions that lower the relative prices of imported capital goods and ease access to foreign technology for domestic plants.

Although trade liberalization facilitates procurement of foreign technology, it is questionable whether domestic plants actually adopt better technology. A recent series of papers by Eaton and Kortum (1996, 1997) models how the benefits of innovation are spread from one country to another either through diffusion of technology or through the exchange of goods. They find that the impact of diffusion of knowledge on productivity depends crucially on the proximity of a country to the technology source and the flexibility of the domestic labour force. In light of many models predicting that trade diffuses innovation and knowledge, it is also puzzling that studies of convergence of productivity across countries such as Bernard and Jones (1996) find convergence in service rather than manufacturing sector, which is extensively affected by international trade.

While trade theory has considered intraindustry gains from trade liberalization through expansion of economies of scale, it has so far not explored the implications of plant heterogeneity within an industry as most of the traditional trade models rely strongly on a representative plant assumption. Recent work explaining plant-level data by Olley and Pakes (1996), Roberts and Tybout (1996), and Aw, Chen and Roberts (1997), introduces evidence of a significant degree of plant-level heterogeneity within an industry. The presence of plant-level heterogeneity suggests that trade liberalization may yield productivity improvements by reshuffling the resources among plants within the same industry and that plant dynamics such as exit may contribute significantly to this process. In particular, high levels of protection may accommodate the coexistence of producers with different levels of productivity. By reducing protection, trade liberalization lowers domestic prices, potentially forcing high cost producers to exit the market. This would lead to a reallocation of output from less efficient to more efficient producers. These productivity gains emerge only if the irreversibility of investment in capital equipment does not impede the exit of the less productive plants.

Even if trade liberalization enhances plant productivity, such improvements do not occur without costs associated with the exit of plants and large reallocations and displacements of labour and capital. Fear of the initial costs of labour displacement and plant bankruptcies often deters governments from exposing their domestic markets to foreign competition. From a policy perspective, it is therefore important to evaluate the incidence of productivity gains. The goal of this paper is to provide such an evaluation. I approach this topic in two steps. In the first step I estimate a production function to obtain a measure of plant productivity. I estimate the production function semiparametrically to correct for the presence of selection and simultaneity biases in the estimates of input coefficients required to construct a productivity measure. I explicitly incorporate plant exit in the estimation to correct for the selection problem induced by liquidated plants. In the second step I relate productivity changes to liberalized trade exploiting the variation in productivity over time and across traded- and nontraded-goods sectors.

I quantify the incidence of productivity gains using a panel of Chilean manufacturing establishments. Chile presents an interesting setting to study the dynamics of plants' adjustment process to trade liberalization. During the 1974 to 1979 period, Chile implemented a large trade liberalization programme. The country eliminated most of its non-tariff barriers and reduced the tariff rates, often surpassing 100% in 1974, to a uniform across industries 10% *ad valorem* tariff in 1979 (Dornbusch and Edwards (1994)). Its commitment to free trade persisted during the 1980s, except for a transitory period of increased tariff protection starting in 1983 in response to the 1982–1983 recession. These temporary measures peaked in 1984, when tariffs increased uniformly to 35%. Yet Chile remained strongly committed to free trade: it introduced no non-tariff barriers and the tariffs declined to a 20% *ad-valorem* level in mid-1985 (UNCTAD (1992)). Overall, the variation in protection during the early 1980s appears very small relative to the extensive trade liberalization experiment in the late 1970s. These trade developments coincide with massive plant exit, which seems to suggest that plant liquidation played a significant role in the adjustment process. My data covers 1979–1986, a period of significant adjustment, and includes all Chilean manufacturing plants with ten or more employees. The comprehensive nature of the data enables me to analyse the dynamics of the smaller plants that are often unobserved due to data limitations.

Many empirical papers reviewed in the next section of the paper have tackled the relationship between liberalized trade and productivity, but the questions remain far from settled.[1] This paper contributes to the literature in three ways: the identification of trade effects, the measurement of plant-specific productivity, and the incorporation of plant exit in the estimation procedure. One of the main problems in the empirical literature on trade and productivity has been the identification of the effects of liberalized trade. The identification in studies such as Tybout, de Melo and Corbo (1991) and Harrison (1994) relies on the comparison of plant behaviour before and after a trade policy change. As the authors recognize, this approach might attribute productivity variation originating from some other shocks occurring concurrently with trade policy changes, to trade policy reform. To identify the effects of liberalized trade this paper relies not only on productivity variation over time, but also on variation across sectors. I distinguish between sectors that are affected directly by liberalized trade (import-competing and export-oriented sectors) and the nontraded-goods sector to separate productivity effects stemming from liberalized trade from productivity variation stemming from other sources. Since it is very difficult to measure the exposure to trade with a single variable, I check the robustness of my findings to other measures of exposure to trade such as import to output ratios, tariffs, and exchange rates.

In order to obtain a measure of plant-level productivity I estimate a production function in which plant efficiency is modelled as an unobserved plant specific effect. As discussed in detail in Section 2 of the paper, a plant's private knowledge of its productivity affects its behaviour and thus biases the estimates of the coefficients on inputs such as labour and capital in the production function. Since the measure of productivity depends on these estimates, their consistency is crucial for the analysis. Most of the previous studies correct for the biases by relying on simplifying assumptions about the unobserved plant heterogeneity such as time-invariance. I employ semiparametric estimation as in Olley and Pakes (1996) to account for unobserved plant heterogeneity. This approach yields a plant-specific, time-varying productivity measure based on consistent estimates of the production function coefficients; it requires no specific functional form, and is tractable enough to incorporate in the estimation process. A further improvement to previous work is that I explicitly incorporate dynamics like plant exit in the analysis. In particular, I adjust my estimation for the selection bias that is introduced by exiting plants. In the second stage I then investigate whether plant exit contributes to aggregate productivity improvements and whether the effects of exit differ across the plants producing export-oriented, import-competing, and nontraded goods.

My research yields several important findings. First, my results show that selection bias induced by plant closings and simultaneity bias induced by plant dynamics significantly affect the magnitude of the capital coefficient in the production function. This

1. Roberts and Tybout (1996) offer an excellent compilation of studies on this topic.

suggests that Olley and Pakes (1996) semiparametric methodology provides a useful alternative to techniques used in previous studies. Second, I find support for productivity improvements related to liberalized trade. I show that after trade liberalization, the productivity of plants in the import-competing sectors grew 3 to 10% more than in the nontraded-goods sectors. This finding is robust to several econometric specifications and various measures of foreign competition. It suggests that exposure to foreign competition forced plants in sectors that used to be shielded from the international competition to trim their fat. Third, I find that exiting plants are on average about 8% less productive than the plants that continue to produce. Although it is hard to pinpoint the exact mechanism of productivity improvements, this result implies that plant exit also contributes to the reshuffling of resources within the economy. Evidence from the industry-level aggregate productivity indices additionally suggests that the reallocation of market shares and resources from less to more efficient producers is an important channel of productivity improvements. These results have important policy implications that I discuss in the conclusion of the paper.

The next section of the paper provides an overview of the empirical issues, and reviews previous work in this area. Section 3 introduces the model and empirical implementation. Section 4 looks at data and descriptive statistics. Section 5 discusses the estimation results. Section 6 contains my conclusions.

## 2. EMPIRICAL ISSUES AND PREVIOUS LITERATURE

Most of the literature on trade liberalization and productivity obtains a plant-level productivity measure by estimating a production function. Let us describe plant $i$'s technology at time $t$ by a Cobb–Douglas production function:

$$\begin{aligned} y_{it} &= \beta_0 + \beta x_{it} + \beta_k k_{it} + e_{it}, \\ e_{it} &= \omega_{it} + \mu_{it}, \end{aligned} \tag{1}$$

where $y_{it}$ is gross output, $x_{it}$ is a vector of variable intermediate inputs such as labour and materials, and $k_{it}$ is capital used by plant $i$ at time $t$. I express all variables in logarithms so that the input coefficients represent input elasticities. Plant specific term $e_{it}$ is composed of a plant-specific efficiency $\omega_{it}$ that is known by the plant but not by the econometrician and an unexpected productivity shock $\mu_{it}$ that is not known either to the plant or the econometrician. I am interested in the former term. In this framework, any plant-level productivity measure relies on the difference between a plant's actual output and predicted output. It is, then, crucial to obtain consistent estimates of the coefficients in the production function. A plant's private knowledge of its productivity $\omega_{it}$ affects its decision about exiting or staying in the market and its choice of hiring labour, purchasing materials, and investing into new capital. Yet $\omega_{it}$ is unobserved by the econometrician. This information asymmetry introduces two biases in my estimation: simultaneity and selection biases. Although the trade liberalization literature has addressed the first one, it has so far disregarded selection bias stemming from plants' exit.

Let us first focus on the simultaneity bias that arises because a plant's private knowledge of its productivity affects its choice of inputs. If more productive plants are more likely to hire more workers and invest in capital due to higher current and anticipated future profitability, ordinary least squares estimation (OLS) of a production function may lead to estimates of the input coefficients that are higher than their true values. Previous studies have adjusted for this bias in various manner. Comparing pre- and post-trade reform cross-sectional data on the Chilean manufacturing sector, Tybout, de Melo and Corbo (1991) impose normal distribution on the unobserved heterogeneity, assume that the plant-specific efficiency is uncorrelated with the plant's choice of inputs, and use maximum likelihood estimation. Studies such as Harrison (1994) that employ plant-level panel data have corrected for simultaneity bias by assuming that the unobserved plant-specific efficiency is time-invariant. I can then rewrite the production function specified in (1) as

$$y_{it} = \beta_0 + \beta x_{it} + \beta_k k_{it} + \omega_i + \mu_{it},$$

where $\omega_i$ is the plant-specific, time-invariant productivity and estimate it using a fixed effects model. Although the fixed effects model partially solves the simultaneity problem, it only removes the effects of the time-invariant plant's productivity component. During times of large structural adjustments such as trade liberalization, the assumption of unchanging productivity seems worrisome, and the fixed effects methodology may lead to biased estimates of the input coefficients. More importantly, I am ultimately interested in how plant efficiency evolves over time in response to a change in a trade policy regime. The assumption that a plant's productivity is constant over time prevents me from tackling this question.

To correct for this shortcoming, Cornwell, Schmidt and Sickles (1990) propose a plant-specific and time-varying efficiency that can be described as a quadratic function of time. This methodology is also used in Liu (1993) and Liu and Tybout (1996) for Chile. Using the notation in (1) their specification of a production function yields:

$$y_{it} = \beta_0 + \beta x_{it} + \beta_k k_{it} + \omega_{it} + \mu_{it},$$

$$\omega_{it} = \alpha_{1i} + \alpha_{2i} t + \alpha_{3i} t^2.$$

They first estimate the production function by fixed effects to obtain the input coefficient vector $\beta$. They then calculate the residuals by subtracting the actual from the predicted values of output, and for each plant $i$ regress this residual measure on a constant, time, and time squared $(1, t, t^2)$. They construct a productivity measure using the estimates of the coefficients from the last regression $(\alpha_{1i}, \alpha_{2i}, \alpha_{3i})$. Although their approach improves on the fixed effects methodology, it requires a parametric specification of productivity and many degrees of freedom are lost in the estimation process. Moreover, in the presence of simultaneity bias this procedure still uses fixed effects estimation in the first step that provides the residual for the construction of the productivity measure. So although the measure is time varying, it is still likely to be based on biased coefficients.

Alternatively, one could estimate the production function using the GMM estimator proposed in Blundell and Bond (1998). Blundell and Bond (1998) extend the standard first difference GMM estimation as in Arellano and Bond (1991) and use additional moment conditions based on the lagged difference of the explanatory variable as an instrument for the variable in question in the production function expressed in levels. Although their approach is very appealing when time-invariant heterogeneity across plants is correlated with the explanatory variables, their methodology does not account for selection bias stemming from plant exit. It might therefore be more applicable in cases, where plant exit does not play an important role.

The trade liberalization literature has so far abstracted from the effects of self-selection induced by plant closings. Unlike previous studies, I explicitly address the selection issue. In my sample, I only observe those plants that continue to produce. A plant decides to stay in business if its expected future profits exceed its liquidation value. A more productive plant is more profitable today, it anticipates higher profits in the future, and is therefore less likely to close down. If a plant's profits are also positively related to the size of its capital stock, given the level of productivity, plants that are endowed with more capital are more likely to continue their operations than are plants with a lower capital stock. The expectation of productivity $\omega_{it}$ conditional on the surviving plants is then no longer zero, but a decreasing function of capital, yielding a downward bias on the coefficient on capital. Liu (1993) and Liu and Tybout (1996) are the only studies that examine plant exit; they compare the aggregate productivity indices for exiting and surviving plants in the case of Chile. Yet, the comparison is based on the coefficients that are not adjusted for the selection bias induced by plant exit.

The literature on the links between trade liberalization and productivity presents conflicting evidence. Tybout, de Melo and Corbo (1991) find scant support for productivity improvements in the Chilean manufacturing sector after the trade liberalization. Bernard and Jones (1996) study productivity convergence across countries on a sectoral level. They find that productivity growth does not converge in manufacturing sectors, despite the belief that international trade flows expedite this process. Using plant-level panel data from the Ivory Coast, Harrison (1994) finds a positive correlation between trade reform and productivity growth. Tybout and Westbrook (1995) report productivity improvements related to trade liberalization in Mexico. Furthermore, some of these studies are based on the data sets that oversample large and medium-sized manufacturing plants. Chilean data also includes small establishments, which are anecdotally more likely to quickly respond to the changes in the environment, therefore presenting an opportunity to study an important part of plant dynamics. It is this conflicting evidence in addition to the above mentioned econometric issues that motivates the present study.

## 3. EMPIRICAL MODEL

### 3.1. *Theoretical background*

I base my econometric analysis upon the theoretical and empirical work on plant profit-maximizing behaviour in a dynamic framework presented in Ericson and Pakes (1995) and Olley and Pakes (1996). Although Olley and Pakes (1996) address the uncertainty regarding returns to investment in research and development stemming from the regulatory changes in the U.S. telecommunication industry, they provide a good framework to analyse plant dynamics resulting from trade liberalization. Plants belonging to an industry face the same input prices and market structure, but differ in their levels of efficiency and are subject to plant specific uncertainty about future market conditions and investment. A plant's goal is to maximize the expected value of its current and future profits (net cash flow). In each period, a plant first decides whether to close down or continue to produce. A plant continues to produce if its expected future net cash flow exceeds its liquidation value. Conditional on staying in the market, the plant then chooses its inputs. This renders the plant's optimal decision regarding exit and input choices as a function of its observable characteristics such as capital and investment. The plant specific uncertainty about the future market conditions affects these plant choices and leads plants to follow different efficiency paths. This set up is consistent with imperfect competition. In each period, firms consider the market structure and the actions of other firms when making their choice about exit and investment. To capture these interactions among firms, a firm's profits (and ultimately the equilibrium exit and investment rule) are indexed by time.

To elaborate, in a given industry $j$, the profits $\Pi_{ijt}$ of a plant $i$ at time $t$ are a function of its capital $k_{ijt}$ and unobserved productivity $\omega_{ijt}$ ($k_{ijt}$ and $\omega_{ijt}$ are plant state variables):[2]

$$\Pi_{ijt} = f(k_{ijt}, \omega_{ijt}).$$

I assume that each plant can easily adjust its labour force and the use of intermediate materials and treat labour and materials as variable inputs, whereas it takes time to adjust the capital stock. This is not a bad assumption for Chile since it significantly liberated its labour laws and practices in the late 1970s. Overall, the plant's problem can be described by the value function for the dynamic programme:

$$V_t(\omega_t, k_t) = \max \left\{L_t, \sup \Pi_t(\omega_t, k_t) - c(i_t) + dE[V_{t+1}(\omega_{t+1}, k_{t+1})|\Omega_{it}]\right\}$$

and capital accumulation equation:

$$k_{t+1} = (1 - \delta)k_t + i_t, \tag{2}$$

where $L$ is the value of the plant if it liquidates, $c(\ )$ represents the cost associated with investment, $d$ is the discount factor, $\Omega_t$ is the information at time $t$, and $\delta$ is the capital depreciation rate. In order for the model to be econometrically tractable, productivity evolves as a first-order Markov Process which assures that the plant's state variables in the current period depend on the value of the state variables in the previous period. The market conditions that affect plant's profits, but are the same for all plants in a given time period $t$ and industry are captured by the index $t$.

As shown in Ericson and Pakes (1995) the solution to this dynamic programme gives rise to a Markov Perfect Equilibrium strategy for plant's choice of exit and investment. The plant continues to produce if its unobserved productivity exceeds some threshold value $\underline{\omega}_t$ that is a function of the plant's capital:

$$X_t = \begin{cases} 1, & \text{if } \omega_t \geqq \underline{\omega}_t(k_t) \\ 0, & \text{otherwise,} \end{cases} \tag{3}$$

where $X_t = 1$ denotes that a plant stays in the market in period $t$ and $X_t = 0$ denotes a plant's exit. A plant chooses its investment based on its beliefs about future productivity and profitability. Its decision to invest $i_t$, then depends on its capital stock and productivity:

$$i_t = i_t(\omega_t, k_t). \tag{4}$$

The investment and exit rule can be used in the estimation of a production function to yield a measure of productivity. This framework captures the market structure in which the firms compete with each other. The competitive conditions that plants face in a given industry are depicted by a time index in the profit function, the investment function, and the cut-off productivity in the exit rule. In the estimation, I allow the investment and exit function to vary over time.

2. Each industry is characterized by its own profit function. I omit the industry and plant subscripts in my notation in the rest of the paper.

Differences in the exposure of plants to international competition might lead to divergence in plant behaviour and different evolution of plant productivity paths. For example, trade liberalization might force the plants to use their resources more productively and trim their fat. In this framework the industry level productivity improvements induced by trade liberalization could stem from several sources: the exit of less efficient plants, the reshuffling of the resources and output from less to more productive plants, or within plant improvements in productivity—*i.e.* plants becoming leaner by reducing their $X$-inefficiencies or eliminating some other agency problem, or by acquiring better inputs from abroad.

### 3.2. *Empirical implementation*

I incorporate exit and investment rules into the estimation of a production function to identify the coefficients on capital and variable inputs such as skilled and unskilled labour and materials. The semiparametric procedure that yields consistent estimates of the labour and capital coefficients involves three steps. In this section, I first summarize the estimation procedure and then discuss its implementation in this paper.

Let us first focus on the coefficients on variable inputs, labour and materials. Within each period a plant can adjust its variable inputs to innovation in its private knowledge about its unobserved productivity $\omega_t$. By inverting the investment rule specified in equation (4), unobserved productivity can be expressed as a function of observable investment and capital:

$$\omega_t = i_t^{-1}(i_t, k_t) = \theta_t(i_t, k_t). \tag{5}$$

Substituting (5) into (1) yields

$$y_t = \beta x_t + \lambda_t(k_t, i_t) + \mu_t \tag{6}$$

where

$$\lambda_t(k_t, i_t) = \beta_0 + \beta_k k_t + \theta_t(k_t, i_t), \tag{7}$$

I can then obtain consistent estimates of the vector of coefficients on variable inputs $\beta$ by estimating the production function in equation (1) using the partially linear regression model in (6), where the function $\lambda_t$ is modelled as a polynomial series expansion in capital and investment. Since $\lambda_t$ controls for unobserved productivity $\omega_t$, the error term in the production function is no longer correlated with a plant's choice of labour hiring and materials, and the coefficient vector $\beta$ is consistent.[3] This specification of productivity is plant-specific and time varying, and it does not require productivity to be a function with a specific parametric form as in Cornwell, Schmidt and Sickles (1990).

After identifying the vector of variable input coefficients $\beta$, I still need to separate the effect of capital on output from its effect on plant's decision to invest. If productivity is serially correlated, current productivity contains information that a plant might incorporate in forming its expectations about its future profitability. If the plant is not myopic, it bases its investment decision at time $t$ on its expectation of its future profitability and hence its productivity at time $t$. Since capital at $t+1$ includes investment from the pre-

3. Andrews (1991) shows that partially linear regression model with the series estimator of the nonlinear part yields consistent and asymptotically normal estimates of coefficients on the linear part of the model, in my case, $\beta$.

vious period $i_t$ by (2), capital and productivity are then correlated at time $t+1$. In particular, capital at $t+1$ is correlated with the expectation of productivity, $E(\omega_{it+1}|\omega_{it}, k_{it+1}) = \omega_{it+1} - \xi_{it+1}$ (productivity is here decomposed into expected and unanticipated parts). Expectation of the next period's productivity is a function of productivity in this period. Let us denote this function as $g(\omega_t)$. I can substitute the expression for $\omega_t$ from (5) into $g(\,)$ and then the expression for $\theta_t$ from (7) to yield:[4]

$$E[\omega_{t+1}|\omega_t, k_{t+1}] = g(\omega_t) - \beta_0 = g(\theta_t(i_t, k_t)) - \beta_0 = g(\lambda_t - \beta_k k_t) - \beta_0. \tag{8}$$

Substituting (8) into (1) at $t+1$ yields

$$\begin{aligned} y_{t+1} - \beta x_{t+1} &= \beta_0 + \beta_k k_{t+1} + E[\omega_{t+1}|\omega_t, k_{t+1}] + \xi_{t+1} + \mu_{t+1} \\ &= \beta_k k_{t+1} + g(\lambda_t - \beta_k k_t) + \xi_{t+1} + \mu_{t+1}. \end{aligned}$$

Thus, I control for the expectation of productivity in (8) with observable variables. If no plant exits the sample, controlling for the expectation of productivity at $t+1$ conditional on the information available at time $t$ yields consistent estimates of the coefficient on capital in the estimation of the above production function.

Yet, I still need to consider that in my sample, I only observe those plants that select to stay in the market. A plant continues to produce only if its expectation of future profitability exceeds its liquidation value. Otherwise, the plant exits. Using the terminology of the exit rule in (3) a plant stays in the market at time $t+1$ only if its productivity at $t+1$ exceeds some threshold value $\underline{\omega}_{t+1}$. This threshold depends on the plant's capital stock. As explained in Section 2, this truncation leads to a nonzero expectation of productivity that is correlated with capital, thus biasing the coefficient on capital in the estimation of a production function. Conditional on a plant staying in the market, the expression for its expected productivity at $t+1$ becomes

$$E[\omega_{t+1}|\omega_t, k_{t+1}, X_{t+1} = 1] = E[\omega_{t+1}|\omega_t, \omega_{t+1} > \underline{\omega}_{t+1}(k_{t+1})] = \Phi(\omega_t, \underline{\omega}_{t+1}) - \beta_0, \tag{9}$$

where

$$\Phi(\omega_t, \underline{\omega}_{t+1}) \equiv E[\omega_{t+1}|\omega_t, \omega_{t+1} > \underline{\omega}_{t+1}(k_{t+1})] + \beta_0.$$

The expectation of future productivity is thus a function of productivity in the previous period, $\omega_t$, and the cut-off productivity, $\underline{\omega}_{t+1}$. The effect of the latter attenuates the coefficient on capital in the production function. In view of the substantial plant closings in Chile, the self-selection of plants probably plays a significant role in the adjustment process. I already know how to control for $\omega_t$. Next, I find a way to control for $\underline{\omega}_{t+1}$ in estimating the production function.

I can extract information about the cut-off productivity $\underline{\omega}_{t+1}$ by evaluating the probability that a plant continues to produce at time $t+1$. The probability of a plant

4. A constant $\beta_0$ cannot be identified separately from the polynomial expansion in investment and capital.

staying in the market at time $t+1$ can be modelled as a function of its capital and investment:

$$\begin{aligned}\Pr(X_{t+1}=1) &= \Pr\{\omega_{t+1} > \underline{\omega}_{t+1}(k_{t+1}) \mid \underline{\omega}_{t+1}(k_{t+1}), \omega_t\} \\ &= p_t(\underline{\omega}_{t+1}(k_{t+1}), \omega_t) \\ &= p_t(\underline{\omega}_{t+1}(k_t, i_t), \omega_t) \\ &= p_t(k_t, i_t) \equiv P_t, \end{aligned} \tag{10}$$

where the first line follows from the exit rule (3), the third line follows from the capital accumulation equation (2), and the fourth line from the investment rule (4). The intuition is simple. A plant makes its exit decision based on whether its expected future profits exceed its liquidation value. Since a plant's productivity depends on its investment and capital, its probability of staying in the market is then also a function of its investment and capital. Any selection correction is more credible if it does not rely solely on distributional or functional form assumptions, but also on exclusion restrictions: variables that affect the probability that a plant exits the market, but do not affect a plant's output. Investment can be viewed as such a variable because it does not affect current output (assuming it takes time for investment to become productive), but it does reflect the future profitability of a plant.

Assuming that function $p_t$ is invertible, the threshold productivity value, $\underline{\omega}_{t+1}$, can be expressed as a function of a plant's survival probability, $P_t$, and its productivity, $\omega_t$. $\Phi(\omega_t, \underline{\omega}_{t+1})$ from (9) can thus be rewritten as a function of productivity in the previous period, $\omega_t$, and the probability a plant stays in the market, $P_t$:

$$\Phi(\omega_t, \underline{\omega}_{t+1}) = \Phi\{\omega_t, p_t^{-1}(P_t, \omega_t)\} = \Phi(\omega_t, P_t).$$

Moreover, as discussed at the beginning of this section, I can express productivity $\omega_t$ using (5) and (7), so that $\Phi(\omega_t, P_t)$ becomes $\Phi(\omega_t, P_t) = \Phi(\lambda_t - \beta_k k_t, P_t)$. After these substitutions, we can rewrite the production function in (1) at $t+1$ as

$$y_{t+1} - \beta x_{t+1} = \beta_k k_{t+1} + \Phi(\lambda_t - \beta_k k_t, P_t) + \xi_{t+1} + \mu_{t+1}. \tag{11}$$

This is the equation I estimate in the final stage of estimation to obtain a consistent coefficient on capital.

Several estimation issues should be pointed out. First, when I estimate the partially linear regression model in (6), I use a fourth order polynomial expansion in capital and investment to approximate $\lambda_t$. I allow the polynomial to vary over time since the investment rule is indexed by time.[5] This time index accounts for changes in the market structure that firms might adjust to over time. This estimation yields an estimate of the coefficient vector $\beta$ on variable inputs, $\hat{\beta}$, and an estimate of $\lambda_t$, $\hat{\lambda}_t$, that are subsequently used to estimate (11). Estimation of (11) also requires an estimate of a plant's probability of staying in the market, $P_t$. Expression (10) shows that the probability of staying in the market, $P_t$, is a function of investment and capital. I estimate this probability using a probit with regressors that are terms in the fourth order polynomial expansion of capital

5. The coefficients on the variables of interest and the sum of squares did not vary substantively when the reported polynomial or a higher order polynomial was used to estimate (6). I distinguish between 1979–1981, 1982–1983, and 1984–1986 by including time indicators corresponding to these periods. I also interact time indicators with investment and capital.

and investment. As in the estimation of (6), I allow the polynomial to vary over time since the exit rule is indexed by time to account for changes in the market structure across periods. Finally, the estimates of the polynomial expansion lambda $\lambda_t$, $\hat{\lambda}_t$, the coefficients on variable inputs $\beta$, $\hat{\beta}$ and the estimate of the survival probability $P_t$, $\hat{P}_t$, can be used to eliminate the selection and simultaneity bias and obtain a consistent estimate of the coefficient on capital $\beta_k$ in (11). Since the equation is nonlinear in the coefficient on capital $\beta_k$, I utilize the nonlinear least squares technique, using a third order polynomial series expansion in $\hat{P}_t$ and $\hat{\omega}_t = (\hat{\lambda}_t - \beta_k k_t)$ to control for $\Phi(\,)$:

$$\Phi(\omega_t, P_t) = \sum_{j=0}^{3-m} \sum_{m=0}^{3} \beta_{mj} \hat{\omega}_t^m \hat{P}_t^j$$

$$= \sum_{j=0}^{3-m} \sum_{m=0}^{3} \beta_{mj} (\hat{\lambda}_t - \beta_k k_t)^m \hat{P}_t^j.$$

Second, unlike Olley and Pakes (1996), this paper uses series approximation in all the stages of estimation. While the use of a series approximation for $\lambda_t$ in (6) yields estimators with known limiting properties (Andrews (1991)), the use of the series approximation to control for $\Phi(\,)$ in (11) yields an estimator that does not have a well-defined limiting distribution. Pakes and Olley (1995) prove asymptotic results for the case when kernel estimator is used for $\Phi(\,)$. No asymptotic results are proven in the case that uses the series estimator for $\Phi(\,)$. Nevertheless, the use of the series estimator has several advantages. First, it is easier and faster than the kernel approximation. Second, Pakes and Olley (1995) show that for their particular application, the results based on the series estimator in (11) do not differ much from the results obtained using the kernel estimator, so they argue that the convergence of the series estimator in the last stage of estimation is a technicality that still needs to be proven. I therefore use the series estimator. However, since the limiting distribution has not been worked out, I compute and report bootstrap estimates of the standard errors.

Third, the Olley and Pakes (1996) procedure relies on the observations whose investment is nonzero. In order to be able to express unobserved productivity as a function of investment and capital using the optimal investment rule (4), investment needs to be a strictly monotonic function of unobserved productivity. Pakes (1994) shows that this is achieved as long as the marginal productivity of capital is an increasing function of a firm's unobserved productivity, and investment is strictly positive. In my data, many observations have zero investment. In order to check whether the use of these observations significantly affects my findings, I also estimate production functions using only the observations with positive investment and compare the estimates to those obtained when all observations are used. As discussed in Section 5.1 of the paper, the estimates are in most cases relatively close, so the use of zero investment observations does not seem as problematic in practice. More importantly, my findings on the relationship between trade and productivity discussed in Section 5.3, which is the main goal of this paper, do not change if I use the measure of productivity constructed from production function estimates based solely on the observations with strictly positive investment.

Finally, as is common in the literature, the estimation of a production function uses the real value of output rather than physical units of output produced by a given plant as a measure of output. The value of output is deflated using a four-digit industry price index. A measure of productivity based on the real value of output might not reflect the ranking of firms in their productivity if plants charge different markups. Differentiating between the true productivity and the plant specific markups across plants within an industry is a big challenge in the productivity literature. Harrison (1994) is one of the few studies that explicitly models plant markups. She assumes that plants are Cournot competitors and allows the markups to vary over time and across industries, but not across plants within an industry. In her setup, this is the same as assuming that all firms within an industry have the same market share.

In order to empirically distinguish the true efficiency from the plant specific markups within an industry, one would need plant level price data. Otherwise, one needs to impose some assumptions on the joint distribution of productivity and markups. Bernard, Eaton, Jensen and Kortum (2000) provide an example. They set up a model in which they show that, on average, a more efficient plant charges a higher markup. Measured productivity based on the real value of output is then on average higher for plants with higher efficiency. Without detailed price data, one cannot identify if such a relationship holds. This caveat should be considered when interpreting the results in Section 5 of the paper. In my estimation of the relationship between measured productivity and trade, I control for plant specific markups with plant fixed effects. If plants change markups over time and a positive relationship between efficiency and markups does not hold, the interpretation of the results in Section 5 is more convoluted.

## 4. DATA AND PRELIMINARY RESULTS

This paper draws on a census of Chilean manufacturing plants employing ten or more workers provided by Chile's National Institute of Statistics. The panel data set extends from 1979 to 1986. A unit of observation is a plant, not a firm, however, over 90% of the plants are single-plant establishments. The dataset information, variable definitions, and descriptive statistics are provided in Appendix. I characterize each plant in terms of its trade orientation, as being in the export-oriented, the import-competing, or the nontraded goods sector. The trade orientation of an industry is determined at a four-digit ISIC level, on the basis of Chilean trade balance in that particular industry. Plants that belong to a four-digit ISIC industry that exports more than 15% of its total output are characterized as export-oriented. Plants that belong to a four-digit ISIC industry whose ratio of imports to total domestic output exceeds 15% are characterized as import-competing. The rest of the plants belong to the nontraded-goods sector.[6] See Appendix for the sources of trade data and descriptive statistics. This definition of trade orientation could be problematic because of the potential presence of intraindustry trade and because of the potential endogeneity of the definition. In Appendix, I provide some evidence that justifies the use of this trade orientation measure. Nonetheless, given how difficult it is to measure a plant's exposure to trade, I also check the robustness of my analysis to various measures of protection or exposure to trade such as tariffs and import to output ratios. All approaches yield the same conclusions.

The Chilean manufacturing sector experienced significant changes following the trade liberalization period, and plant exit played an important role in the adjustment process.[7] As Table 1 indicates, 35% of the plants that were active in 1979 ceased their production by 1986. The liquidated plants accounted for 25% of the 1979 total manufacturing labour

6. I have experimented with different cut-off points. The results are robust to definitions based on cut-off points between 10 to 25%.

7. Plant entry is also an interesting topic. This paper does not focus on entry because the magnitude of entry was much smaller than the magnitude of exit. It is also unclear how to correct for selection bias from entry because we do not know the population of possible entrants. However, selection bias due to entry might not be that important in this particular application. The average capital level of entering plants is not statistically different from the average capital level of the incumbents.

TABLE 1

*Plants active in 1979 but not in 1986*

| Trade orientation | Share of plants | Share of labour | Share of capital | Share of investment | Share of value added | Share of output |
|---|---|---|---|---|---|---|
| Exiting plants of a given trade orientation as a share of all plants active in 1979 | | | | | | |
| All trade orientations | 0·352 | 0·252 | 0·078 | 0·135 | 0·155 | 0·156 |
| Export-oriented | 0·045 | 0·049 | 0·009 | 0·039 | 0·023 | 0·023 |
| Import-competing | 0·141 | 0·108 | 0·029 | 0·047 | 0·068 | 0·065 |
| Nontraded | 0·165 | 0·095 | 0·040 | 0·049 | 0·064 | 0·067 |
| Exiting plants of a given trade orientation as a share of all exiting plants | | | | | | |
| Export-oriented | 0·129 | 0·194 | 0·117 | 0·289 | 0·149 | 0·148 |
| Import-competing | 0·401 | 0·429 | 0·369 | 0·350 | 0·436 | 0·419 |
| Nontraded | 0·470 | 0·377 | 0·513 | 0·361 | 0·415 | 0·432 |
| Exiting plants of a given trade orientation as a share of all plants active in 1979 in the corresponding trade sector | | | | | | |
| Export-oriented | 0·416 | 0·298 | 0·030 | 0·172 | 0·121 | 0·128 |
| Import-competing | 0·383 | 0·263 | 0·093 | 0·149 | 0·183 | 0·211 |
| Nontraded | 0·316 | 0·224 | 0·104 | 0·107 | 0·147 | 0·132 |

*Note*: This figure also includes plants that exited after the end of 1979, but before the end of 1980 and were excluded in the estimation because of missing capital variable.

force, 13% of the 1979 investment, and 16% of the 1979 manufacturing output.[8] Evidence presented in the top and middle section of Table 1 indicates that the incidence of exit varied across plants in the export-oriented, import-competing, and nontraded goods sectors. Out of the 35% of the plants that exited the market, 13% belonged to the export-oriented sectors, 40% belonged to the import-competing sector, and 47% to the non-traded-goods sector. Similarly, of the 25% of the workers that were employed in 1979 but lost their job thereafter, 19% are displaced from the export-oriented sector, 43% from the import-competing sectors, and 38% from the nontraded goods sector. Finally, out of 16% of the 1979 output attributable to the exiting plants, 15% belonged to the plants exiting from the export-oriented sectors, 42% to the plants from the import-competing sectors, and 43% to the plants from the nontraded-goods sectors.

The above figures suggest that plants in the import-competing sectors experienced the largest displacements in terms of employment, whereas plant closings did not play as significant a role for the plants in the export-oriented industries. Yet, these results might be misleading due to the small size of the export-oriented sector. The bottom part of Table 1 depicts the plants of a given trade orientation that are active in 1979 but not in 1986 as a share of the corresponding trade sector in 1979. 42% of the plants in the export-oriented sector that were active in 1979 are no longer active in 1986. These plants accounted for 30% of employment, 17% of investment and 13% of output in the export-oriented sector in 1979. Similarly, 38% of plants in the import competing sector, and 32% of plants in the non-traded sector, accounting for 26% and 22% of the 1979 employment in the corresponding sectors respectively, are active in 1979 but no longer produce in 1986.

Overall, these descriptive statistics suggest that exit seems to play an important role in the adjustment process after the Chilean trade liberalization. Part of these exit patterns

8. Plants could either exit the data because they go bankrupt or their number of workers falls below 10. Table 1 does not count as exit plants that disappear from the data due to low number of employees and then appear again later in the data. I also do not count as exit a plant switching its ISIC industry sector. Most of these switches occur on a four digit ISIC level, so they do not affect the estimates of production function.

potentially stems from the large recession in 1982 and 1983. Regardless of the causes of the exit, I expect a large attenuation of the capital coefficient in the estimation procedures that ignore self-selection induced by plant closings. This would translate into skewed productivity measures.

## 5. ESTIMATION RESULTS

### 5.1. *Estimates of the production function coefficients*

Table 2 presents estimates of the input coefficients from the production function specified in equation (1). I estimate the production function on a two or three digit ISIC industry level for all individual manufacturing industries: food manufacturing (ISIC 311/312), textiles and apparel (ISIC 32), manufacture of wood and wood products (ISIC 33), manufacture of paper and paper products (ISIC 34), chemical industry (ISIC 35), glass (ISIC 36), basic metals (ISIC 37), and manufacture of machinery and equipment (ISIC 38). This implies that plants producing various four digit ISIC goods within a three or two digit ISIC classification use the same factor proportions, but are imperfect substitutes in consumption, which can lead to different trade orientation within an industry. This assumption is in line with the models of intra-industry trade where goods require the same factor input coefficients in their productions, but play a different role in a country's trade (some are exported, some are import-competing and some are nontraded). Difference in their exposure to international competition might lead to difference in their behaviour and differences in the response of their productivity to international shocks. I include skilled and unskilled labour, materials, and capital as factors of production.

Table 2 reports the estimates of the coefficients based on the OLS, fixed effects, and semiparametric estimation, first using only plants that never exited the sample (balanced panel) and then the full sample (unbalanced panel). According to the theory the coefficients on variable inputs such as skilled and unskilled labour and materials should be biased upwards in the OLS estimation, whereas the direction of the bias on the capital coefficient is ambiguous. My results confirm this. The estimates of the coefficient on labour, materials, and capital based on semiparametric estimation reported in column 5 significantly differ from the OLS and fixed effects estimates. They move in a direction that points at successful elimination of simultaneity and selection bias.

Let us illustrate this point on the input coefficients obtained for the food processing industry. The skilled labour coefficient from semiparametric estimation (0·098) in column 5 is lower than the OLS estimate in column 3 (0·131) based on unbalanced panel. The above finding holds for all industries in my sample but paper, as well as for unskilled labour and materials.[9] Moreover, my estimates of the coefficient on capital exhibit the biggest movement in the direction that points at the successful elimination of the selection and simultaneity bias. Semiparametric estimation yields estimates that are from 45% to over 300% higher than those obtained in the OLS estimations in industries where the coefficient increases. For example, my estimate of the coefficient on capital in column 5 in food processing industry is 0·079 compared to the OLS estimate 0·052 (column 3) and the fixed effects estimate 0·014 (column 4). The coefficient on capital increases in 5 out of 8 industries. In textiles, paper, and machinery the coefficient on capital actually declines, which might indicate that the selection bias is less important than the simultaneity bias.

9. The unskilled labour coefficient obtained by OLS is actually lower than the coefficient obtained by semiparametric method in glass and basic metals.

TABLE 2

*Estimates of production functions*

| | | Balanced panel | | | | Full sample | | | | | |
|---|---|---|---|---|---|---|---|---|---|---|---|
| | | OLS | | Fixed effects | | OLS | | Fixed effects | | Series | |
| | | (1) | | (2) | | (3) | | (4) | | (5) | |
| | | Coef. | S.E. | Coef. | S.E. | Coef. | S.E. | Coef. | S.E. | Coef. | S.E. |
| Food processing | Unskilled labour | 0·152 | 0·007 | 0·185 | 0·012 | 0·178 | 0·006 | 0·210 | 0·010 | 0·153 | 0·007 |
| | Skilled labour | 0·127 | 0·006 | 0·027 | 0·008 | 0·131 | 0·006 | 0·029 | 0·007 | 0·098 | 0·009 |
| | Materials | 0·790 | 0·004 | 0·668 | 0·008 | 0·763 | 0·004 | 0·646 | 0·007 | 0·735 | 0·008 |
| | Capital | 0·046 | 0·003 | 0·011 | 0·007 | 0·052 | 0·003 | 0·014 | 0·006 | 0·079 | 0·034 |
| | *N* | 6432 | | | | 8464 | | | | 7085 | |
| Textiles | Unskilled labour | 0·187 | 0·011 | 0·240 | 0·017 | 0·229 | 0·009 | 0·245 | 0·015 | 0·215 | 0·012 |
| | Skilled labour | 0·184 | 0·010 | 0·088 | 0·014 | 0·183 | 0·009 | 0·088 | 0·012 | 0·177 | 0·011 |
| | Materials | 0·667 | 0·007 | 0·564 | 0·011 | 0·638 | 0·006 | 0·558 | 0·009 | 0·637 | 0·097 |
| | Capital | 0·056 | 0·005 | 0·015 | 0·012 | 0·059 | 0·004 | 0·019 | 0·011 | 0·052 | 0·034 |
| | *N* | 3689 | | | | 5191 | | | | 4265 | |
| Wood | Unskilled labour | 0·233 | 0·016 | 0·268 | 0·026 | 0·247 | 0·013 | 0·273 | 0·022 | 0·195 | 0·015 |
| | Skilled labour | 0·121 | 0·015 | 0·040 | 0·021 | 0·146 | 0·012 | 0·047 | 0·018 | 0·130 | 0·014 |
| | Materials | 0·685 | 0·010 | 0·522 | 0·014 | 0·689 | 0·008 | 0·554 | 0·011 | 0·679 | 0·010 |
| | Capital | 0·055 | 0·007 | 0·023 | 0·018 | 0·050 | 0·006 | −0·002 | 0·016 | 0·101 | 0·051 |
| | *N* | 1649 | | | | 2705 | | | | 2154 | |
| Paper | Unskilled labour | 0·218 | 0·024 | 0·258 | 0·033 | 0·246 | 0·021 | 0·262 | 0·029 | 0·193 | 0·024 |
| | Skilled labour | 0·190 | 0·018 | 0·022 | 0·027 | 0·180 | 0·016 | 0·050 | 0·023 | 0·203 | 0·018 |
| | Materials | 0·624 | 0·013 | 0·515 | 0·025 | 0·597 | 0·011 | 0·514 | 0·021 | 0·601 | 0·014 |
| | Capital | 0·074 | 0·010 | 0·031 | 0·025 | 0·085 | 0·009 | 0·031 | 0·023 | 0·068 | 0·018 |
| | *N* | 1039 | | | | 1398 | | | | 1145 | |
| Chemicals | Unskilled labour | 0·033 | 0·014 | 0·239 | 0·022 | 0·067 | 0·013 | 0·246 | 0·020 | 0·031 | 0·014 |
| | Skilled labour | 0·211 | 0·013 | 0·079 | 0·018 | 0·213 | 0·012 | 0·090 | 0·017 | 0·194 | 0·016 |
| | Materials | 0·691 | 0·009 | 0·483 | 0·013 | 0·698 | 0·008 | 0·473 | 0·013 | 0·673 | 0·012 |
| | Capital | 0·108 | 0·008 | 0·032 | 0·014 | 0·089 | 0·007 | 0·036 | 0·013 | 0·129 | 0·052 |
| | *N* | 2145 | | | | 2540 | | | | 2087 | |
| Glass | Unskilled labour | 0·353 | 0·032 | 0·405 | 0·045 | 0·406 | 0·030 | 0·435 | 0·043 | 0·426 | 0·035 |
| | Skilled labour | 0·285 | 0·035 | 0·068 | 0·042 | 0·226 | 0·031 | 0·056 | 0·038 | 0·183 | 0·036 |
| | Materials | 0·523 | 0·022 | 0·360 | 0·026 | 0·544 | 0·019 | 0·403 | 0·024 | 0·522 | 0·024 |
| | Capital | 0·092 | 0·041 | −0·015 | 0·036 | 0·093 | 0·011 | −0·013 | 0·030 | 0·142 | 0·053 |
| | *N* | 623 | | | | 816 | | | | 666 | |
| Basic metals | Unskilled labour | 0·080 | 0·037 | 0·137 | 0·070 | 0·105 | 0·037 | 0·174 | 0·072 | 0·121 | 0·041 |
| | Skilled labour | 0·158 | 0·034 | 0·008 | 0·070 | 0·156 | 0·034 | 0·006 | 0·072 | 0·117 | 0·043 |
| | Materials | 0·789 | 0·017 | 0·572 | 0·040 | 0·771 | 0·016 | 0·567 | 0·039 | 0·727 | 0·032 |
| | Capital | 0·030 | 0·014 | 0·033 | 0·030 | 0·025 | 0·013 | 0·034 | 0·032 | 0·110 | 0·051 |
| | *N* | 306 | | | | 362 | | | | 255 | |
| Machinery | Unskilled labour | 0·186 | 0·013 | 0·225 | 0·018 | 0·199 | 0·012 | 0·238 | 0·016 | 0·178 | 0·015 |
| | Skilled labour | 0·238 | 0·011 | 0·130 | 0·016 | 0·222 | 0·010 | 0·112 | 0·014 | 0·202 | 0·012 |
| | Materials | 0·611 | 0·008 | 0·530 | 0·012 | 0·619 | 0·007 | 0·548 | 0·010 | 0·617 | 0·009 |
| | Capital | 0·078 | 0·006 | 0·057 | 0·013 | 0·078 | 0·005 | 0·047 | 0·013 | 0·051 | 0·013 |
| | *N* | 3025 | | | | 4015 | | | | 3268 | |

*Note*: Under full sample, the number of observations is lower in the series than in the OLS column because the series estimation requires lagged variables. I have also estimated OLS and fixed effects regressions excluding these observations. The coefficients do not change much. All standard errors in column 5 are bootstrapped using 1000 replications.

The input coefficients also suggest the existence of increasing returns to scale in all sectors, with only slight presence in food processing and the highest in wood and glass industry.

Previous literature has often used fixed effects estimation that relies on the temporal variation in plant behaviour to pinpoint the input coefficients. The fixed effects coefficients are reported in columns 2 and 4, and they are often much lower than those in the OLS or the semiparametric procedure, especially for capital. This is not surprising since the fixed effect estimation relies on the intertemporal variation within a plant, thus overemphasizing any measurement error. Semiparametric estimation therefore provides a useful alternative for estimation of a production function to methods used in previous studies.

As discussed in Section 3.2, semiparametric estimation from Olley and Pakes (1996) technically requires observations with strictly positive investment. Table 2(a) compares the semiparametric estimates of the production function based on all observations (column 1) and based only on observations with strictly positive investment (column 2). In most cases, the coefficients do not vary significantly.[10] The exceptions are the coefficient on the unskilled labour and the coefficient on capital in paper and machinery. However, these are also the two coefficients with the highest standard errors. More importantly, because the estimates of the production function do not vary significantly, the productivity measures and thus my estimates of the relationship between trade and productivity, discussed in Section 5.3 do not change much.

### 5.2. *Productivity measure and aggregate industry productivity indices*

I use the input coefficients based on semiparametric estimation from column 5 in Table 2 to construct a measure of plant productivity. In every industry, the productivity index is obtained by subtracting plant *i*'s predicted output from its actual output at time *t* and then comparing it relative to a reference plant *r*. This methodology has been employed in several studies using panel or cross sectional data such as Aw, Chen, and Roberts (1997), Caves, Christensen and Tretheway (1981) and Klette (1996). It insures that the productivity index has the desired properties such as transitivity and insensitivity to the units of measurement.[11] I obtain such an index by simply subtracting a productivity of a reference plant in a base year (plant with mean output and mean input level in 1979) from an individual plant's productivity measure:

$$pr_{it} = y_{it} - \hat{\beta}_{ls} l^{s}_{it} - \hat{\beta}_{lu} l^{u}_{it} - \hat{\beta}_{m} m_{it} - \hat{\beta}_{k} k_{it} - (y_r - \hat{y}_r),$$

where

$$y_r = \bar{y}_{it}$$

and

$$\hat{y}_r = \hat{\beta}_{ls} \bar{l}^{s}_{it} + \hat{\beta}_{lu} \bar{l}^{u}_{it} + \hat{\beta}_{m} \bar{m}_{it} + \hat{\beta}_{k} \bar{k}_{it}$$

10. The estimates based only on observations with positive investment could be biased due to sample selection. If there is selection bias and the selection affects the production function coefficients the same way as the inclusion of zero investment observations, the similarity of the production function coefficients might not be very informative. The selection bias is likely to occur if observations with zero investment are very different in their use of inputs in the production process from the observations with positive investment. Although the comparison of the means of observable characteristics suggests that there are some differences across the two groups (those with zero investment tend to be smaller in absolute terms), these differences do not seem to be large when one compares the means of the ratio of various inputs to output across the two groups.

11. For a review of this literature see Good, Nadiri and Sickles (1996).

TABLE 2(a)

*Comparison of the semiparametric estimates of production functions*

| | | (1) | | (2) | |
|---|---|---|---|---|---|
| | | Coef. | S.E. | Coef. | S.E. |
| Food processing | Unskilled labour | 0·153 | 0·007 | 0·081 | 0·012 |
| | Skilled labour | 0·098 | 0·009 | 0·119 | 0·011 |
| | Materials | 0·735 | 0·008 | 0·723 | 0·011 |
| | Capital | 0·079 | 0·034 | 0·070 | 0·030 |
| | *N* | 7085 | | 2806 | |
| Textiles | Unskilled labour | 0·215 | 0·012 | 0·183 | 0·020 |
| | Skilled labour | 0·177 | 0·011 | 0·166 | 0·015 |
| | Materials | 0·637 | 0·097 | 0·626 | 0·014 |
| | Capital | 0·052 | 0·034 | 0·056 | 0·032 |
| | *N* | 4265 | | 1591 | |
| Wood | Unskilled labour | 0·195 | 0·015 | 0·149 | 0·023 |
| | Skilled labour | 0·130 | 0·014 | 0·134 | 0·023 |
| | Materials | 0·679 | 0·010 | 0·654 | 0·019 |
| | Capital | 0·101 | 0·051 | 0·107 | 0·020 |
| | *N* | 2154 | | 692 | |
| Paper | Unskilled labour | 0·193 | 0·024 | 0·120 | 0·032 |
| | Skilled labour | 0·203 | 0·018 | 0·224 | 0·025 |
| | Materials | 0·601 | 0·014 | 0·594 | 0·023 |
| | Capital | 0·068 | 0·018 | 0·138 | 0·046 |
| | *N* | 1145 | | 494 | |
| Chemicals | Unskilled labour | 0·031 | 0·014 | 0·018 | 0·017 |
| | Skilled labour | 0·194 | 0·016 | 0·188 | 0·019 |
| | Materials | 0·673 | 0·012 | 0·666 | 0·018 |
| | Capital | 0·129 | 0·052 | 0·138 | 0·021 |
| | *N* | 2087 | | 1247 | |
| Glass | Unskilled labour | 0·426 | 0·035 | 0·400 | 0·049 |
| | Skilled labour | 0·183 | 0·036 | 0·132 | 0·059 |
| | Materials | 0·522 | 0·024 | 0·489 | 0·038 |
| | Capital | 0·142 | 0·053 | 0·113 | 0·040 |
| | *N* | 666 | | 294 | |
| Basic metals | Unskilled labour | 0·121 | 0·041 | 0·117 | 0·063 |
| | Skilled labour | 0·117 | 0·043 | 0·116 | 0·074 |
| | Materials | 0·727 | 0·032 | 0·753 | 0·037 |
| | Capital | 0·110 | 0·051 | 0·079 | 0·029 |
| | *N* | 255 | | 158 | |
| Machinery | Unskilled labour | 0·178 | 0·015 | 0·089 | 0·021 |
| | Skilled labour | 0·202 | 0·012 | 0·231 | 0·016 |
| | Materials | 0·617 | 0·009 | 0·626 | 0·013 |
| | Capital | 0·051 | 0·013 | 0·119 | 0·057 |
| | *N* | 3268 | | 1520 | |

*Note*: All standard errors are bootstrapped using 1000 replications.

and the bar over a variable indicates a mean over all plants in a base year. So, $y_r$ is the mean log output of plants in my base year, 1979, and $\hat{y}_r$ is the predicted mean log output in 1979. This productivity measure presents a logarithmic deviation of a plant from the mean industry practice in a base year.

To check the importance of productivity gains stemming from the reshuffling of resources from the less to more efficient plants I compute aggregate industry productivity measures for each year. In a given year the aggregate industry productivity measure $W_t$ is a weighted average of the plants' individual unweighted productivities $pr_{it}$ with an individual plant's weight $s_{it}$ corresponding to its output's share in total industry output in a particular year. Further, as in Olley and Pakes (1996) I decompose the weighted aggregate productivity measure $W_t$ into two parts: the unweighted aggregate productivity measure and the total covariance between a plant's share of the industry output and its productivity:

$$W_t = \sum_i s_{it} pr_{it}$$
$$= \overline{pr}_t + \sum_i (s_{it} - \bar{s}_t)(pr_{it} - \overline{pr}_t),$$

where the bar over a variable denotes a mean over all plants in a given year. The covariance component represents the contribution to the aggregate weighted productivity resulting from the reallocation of market share and resources across plants of different productivity levels. If the covariance is positive, it indicates that more output is produced by the more efficient plants. So, if trade liberalization induces reallocation of resources within industries from less to more productive plants, the latter measure should be positive, and increasing over time in my sample.

The results of the above decomposition for the industries in my sample are reported in Table 3 in terms of growth relative to 1979. Aggregate productivity, unweighted productivity and covariance growth are reported in columns 1, 2 and 3, respectively. For each industry, the growth figures are normalized, so that they can be interpreted as growth relative to 1979. Note that the figures in columns 2 and 3 add to the figures in column 1 as required by the above decomposition. First, the aggregate productivity column 1 indicates that the aggregate weighted productivity increased from 1979 to 1986 in 6 out of 8 sectors: food processing, textiles, chemicals, glass, basic metals and machinery and equipment; and declined in the wood and paper industry. The aggregate productivity gains over the span of seven years range between 7·6% in the manufacturing of machinery and equipment to around 18% in food, textiles and basic metals, to 33% in glass and 43% in chemicals. Second, as column 2 shows, the growth in aggregate productivity was driven by a substantial growth in unweighted productivity only in food manufacturing and textiles. This suggests that most of the improvements in aggregate productivity resulted from the reallocation of the resources and market share from the less to more productive plants over time. Column 3 reports the growth stemming from this process. The figures suggest that, over time, the more productive plants are producing an increasing share of output in seven out of eight industries. In industries such as paper where the covariance grew by 19·5%, basic metals (25·9%), glass (34%) and chemicals (48·8%), this component of aggregate productivity actually counteracts the declining trend or unchanging unweighted mean productivity.

The above evidence indicates that the productivity of plants in Chile has changed after trade liberalization. The bottom section of Table 3 reports the productivity growth for the manufacturing as a whole and for the sectors of various trade orientations. Aggregate productivity has increased by 19% over seven years: 6·6% due to increased productivity within plants, and 12·7% due to the reallocation of resources from the less to more efficient producers. The table furthermore suggests that aggregate productivity, unweighted productivity and covariance between output and productivity grew the most in the import-competing sectors, and the least in the nontraded goods sectors. To further investigate and identify the effects of trade liberalization on plant level productivity, I now proceed with the analysis of productivity evolution in a regression framework.

TABLE 3

*Decomposition of aggregate productivity growth*

| Industry | Year | Aggregate Productivity | Unweighted Productivity | Covariance | Industry | Year | Aggregate Productivity | Unweighted Productivity | Covariance |
|---|---|---|---|---|---|---|---|---|---|
| Food | 79 | 0·000 | 0·000 | 0·000 | Chemicals | 79 | 0·000 | 0·000 | 0·000 |
| | 80 | 0·005 | 0·008 | −0·003 | | 80 | 0·014 | 0·046 | −0·032 |
| | 81 | 0·008 | 0·058 | −0·049 | | 81 | 0·126 | 0·076 | 0·050 |
| | 82 | 0·209 | 0·099 | 0·110 | | 82 | 0·312 | 0·039 | 0·274 |
| | 83 | 0·144 | 0·049 | 0·095 | | 83 | 0·238 | −0·050 | 0·288 |
| | 84 | 0·116 | 0·044 | 0·072 | | 84 | 0·156 | −0·040 | 0·196 |
| | 85 | 0·092 | 0·014 | 0·078 | | 85 | 0·229 | −0·033 | 0·262 |
| | 86 | 0·179 | 0·129 | 0·050 | | 86 | 0·432 | −0·056 | 0·488 |
| Textiles | 79 | 0·000 | 0·000 | 0·000 | Glass | 79 | 0·000 | 0·000 | 0·000 |
| | 80 | 0·064 | 0·063 | 0·001 | | 80 | 0·137 | −0·036 | 0·174 |
| | 81 | 0·148 | 0·119 | 0·029 | | 81 | 0·109 | −0·073 | 0·182 |
| | 82 | 0·147 | 0·090 | 0·057 | | 82 | 0·155 | −0·044 | 0·200 |
| | 83 | 0·075 | 0·063 | 0·012 | | 83 | 0·231 | −0·052 | 0·283 |
| | 84 | 0·130 | 0·082 | 0·048 | | 84 | 0·257 | −0·071 | 0·328 |
| | 85 | 0·136 | 0·095 | 0·041 | | 85 | 0·193 | −0·095 | 0·287 |
| | 86 | 0·184 | 0·171 | 0·013 | | 86 | 0·329 | −0·011 | 0·340 |
| Wood | 79 | 0·000 | 0·000 | 0·000 | Basic metals | 79 | 0·000 | 0·000 | 0·000 |
| | 80 | −0·052 | −0·030 | −0·022 | | 80 | −0·136 | −0·022 | −0·114 |
| | 81 | −0·125 | −0·071 | −0·054 | | 81 | −0·002 | 0·050 | −0·052 |
| | 82 | 0·070 | −0·076 | 0·145 | | 82 | 0·711 | 0·215 | 0·496 |
| | 83 | 0·148 | −0·051 | 0·198 | | 83 | 0·343 | 0·030 | 0·312 |
| | 84 | 0·169 | 0·038 | 0·131 | | 84 | 0·153 | −0·037 | 0·190 |
| | 85 | 0·019 | −0·038 | 0·058 | | 85 | 0·228 | −0·153 | 0·380 |
| | 86 | −0·035 | 0·045 | −0·081 | | 86 | 0·183 | −0·076 | 0·259 |
| Paper | 79 | 0·000 | 0·000 | 0·000 | Machinery | 79 | 0·000 | 0·000 | 0·000 |
| | 80 | −0·111 | −0·035 | −0·076 | | 80 | 0·031 | −0·025 | 0·005 |
| | 81 | −0·127 | 0·038 | −0·165 | | 81 | 0·125 | 0·070 | 0·055 |
| | 82 | −0·127 | −0·079 | −0·048 | | 82 | 0·131 | 0·027 | 0·105 |
| | 83 | −0·084 | −0·221 | 0·137 | | 83 | 0·077 | 0·025 | 0·053 |
| | 84 | −0·073 | −0·266 | 0·192 | | 84 | 0·137 | 0·072 | 0·064 |
| | 85 | −0·252 | −0·362 | 0·110 | | 85 | 0·083 | 0·032 | 0·051 |
| | 86 | −0·131 | −0·326 | 0·195 | | 86 | 0·076 | 0·040 | 0·036 |
| All | 79 | 0·000 | 0·000 | 0·000 | Import competing | 79 | 0·000 | 0·000 | 0·000 |
| | 80 | −0·010 | 0·018 | −0·027 | | 80 | −0·063 | 0·027 | −0·090 |
| | 81 | 0·051 | 0·054 | −0·003 | | 81 | 0·032 | 0·092 | −0·061 |
| | 82 | 0·329 | 0·048 | 0·281 | | 82 | 0·088 | 0·066 | 0·022 |
| | 83 | 0·174 | 0·010 | 0·164 | | 83 | 0·077 | 0·034 | 0·043 |
| | 84 | 0·117 | 0·025 | 0·092 | | 84 | 0·089 | 0·059 | 0·030 |
| | 85 | 0·120 | −0·003 | 0·123 | | 85 | 0·095 | 0·061 | 0·034 |
| | 86 | 0·193 | 0·066 | 0·127 | | 86 | 0·319 | 0·107 | 0·213 |
| Export oriented | 79 | 0·000 | 0·000 | 0·000 | Nontraded | 79 | 0·000 | 0·000 | 0·000 |
| | 80 | −0·059 | −0·038 | −0·021 | | 80 | 0·044 | 0·021 | 0·024 |
| | 81 | −0·048 | −0·054 | 0·006 | | 81 | 0·101 | 0·047 | 0·054 |
| | 82 | 0·591 | 0·040 | 0·551 | | 82 | 0·228 | 0·038 | 0·190 |
| | 83 | 0·326 | 0·015 | 0·311 | | 83 | 0·127 | −0·004 | 0·131 |
| | 84 | 0·178 | 0·049 | 0·129 | | 84 | 0·114 | 0·000 | 0·114 |
| | 85 | 0·203 | −0·011 | 0·214 | | 85 | 0·101 | −0·040 | 0·142 |
| | 86 | 0·254 | 0·087 | 0·166 | | 86 | 0·062 | 0·038 | 0·024 |

*Note*: The reported growth figures are relative to 1979.

### 5.3. *Estimation of variation in plant-level productivity*

Although the above evidence suggests that plants belonging to sectors with different trade orientations react differently after a trade liberalization episode, I have not formally identified the influence of trade on the evolution of a plant's productivity. Since it is difficult to measure the effects of liberalized trade with a single variable, I approach the relationship in several different ways. First, I utilize the following regression framework:

$$pr_{it} = \alpha_0 + \alpha_1(Time)_{it} + \alpha_2(Trade)_{it} + \alpha_3(Trade * Time)_{it} + \alpha_4 Z_{it} + \nu_{it}, \qquad (12)$$

where $pr_{it}$ is the unweighted productivity measure for plant $i$ at time $t$ defined in Section 5.2, *Time* is a vector of year indicators, *Trade* is a vector of dummy variables indicating trade orientation of a plant (export-oriented, import-competing), *Trade* $*$ *Time* is a vector of interactions of a trade orientation of a plant and a time (for example, import-competing $*$ year84), and $Z_{it}$ is a vector of plant characteristics such as industry affiliation and whether a plant ceases to produce in a given year. The year indicators capture the omitted macroeconomic variables. The nontraded-goods sector, surviving plants, and the year 1979 are the excluded categories.

Previous studies have identified the effects of liberalized trade on productivity by comparing plant's behaviour over time. That approach attributes any variation in productivity originating from other concurrent shocks to trade. My difference in difference framework in equation (12) separates the variation in productivity due to changes in Chilean trade regime from the variation emanating from other sources by exploiting not only the productivity variation over time, but also across plants with different trade orientations. The lack of panel plant level data prior to 1979 unfortunately prevents me from extending my analysis to the period preceding trade policy reform. However, plants might not instantaneously react to the implementation of a change in trade policy. Since I do not observe plants' expectations about the nature and sustainability of a change in trade policy, plants might have responded to the changes in trade regime only after they were convinced of the government's lasting commitment to a liberalized trade regime. Hence, the effects of liberalized trade might persist during the early 1980s, the period that is included in my data. Moreover, if liberalized trade is interpreted in the broader sense of a plant's exposure to foreign markets and competition, the extension of my analysis past the initial policy changes is valid. I later check the robustness of my results based on equation (12) to other measures of exposure to trade.

Liberalized trade directly affects plants in the import-competing and export-oriented sectors, but not the plants in the nontraded-goods sector. On the other hand, other environment changes, for example, the 1982–1983 recession, that occurred while plants were adjusting to the shifts in trade policy, likely impact all sectors. Here I need to assume that the recession does not interact with domestic sectors differently. My difference in difference estimates of the effects of trade are represented by the coefficient vector $\alpha_3$ in (12), whose components are the interactions of the indicator of a plant's trade orientation (export-oriented, import-competing) and year indicators. These coefficients indicate the productivity differential for traded goods compared to the nontraded-goods sector attributable to liberalized trade.

I am trying to test whether liberalized trade makes plants more productive. If trade improves plant productivity in the traded-goods sector, the coefficients in $\alpha_3$ should be positive. Let us first focus on the implications of liberalized trade for plants in the import-competing sectors. If trade lowers the domestic prices of import-competing goods, the domestic plants need to improve their efficiency and trim their fat in order to survive. These are the within plant productivity improvements that I can identify with $\alpha_3$. Unfortunately, it is harder to pinpoint the impact of trade liberalization on the productivity of plants stemming from better access to foreign technology and intermediate inputs. Since all plants might acquire better technology after trade liberalization, this channel might bias my results against finding any effect. In addition, production inefficiency can be eliminated though the liquidation of less efficient plants. I can directly test the incidence of industry rationalization by including an indicator for exiting plants. If plants that cease to produce are less efficient, the coefficient on the exit indicator should be negative.

Trade theory does not offer many guidelines on how exporting plants react to trade liberalization. Potentially, only the best plants could export in the past because of the anti-export bias in the import substituting regimes. Once that bias is eliminated, exporters need to be less productive to compete in the world market, which might imply a reduction in the productivity of the export-oriented sectors. Alternatively, the plants in the export-oriented sector might not change their behaviour much over time. Several recent studies (Aw, Chen and Roberts (1997), Bernard and Jensen (1995)) have found that exporting plants are in general more productive than plants catering solely to the domestic market because only more productive plants enter the export market. None of these studies investigates whether trade liberalization makes exporters more productive relative to other plants.[12]

The regression results are presented in Table 4. In estimating equation (12), I pool plant productivity indices across industries. The inclusion of the 3-digit ISIC industry indicators controls for the variation of productivity between industries, so that the other regressors capture the effects of within industry variation.[13] I report Huber–White standard errors. I also estimate (12) using plant fixed effects and present the results in columns 4–6. I also repeat the analysis in Table 4 using the measure of productivity computed from production function coefficients based on the observations with positive investment (reported in Table 2(a), column 2) with the entire sample and only with observations with strictly positive investment. These results are presented in Tables S.2 and S.3 in the supplement to the paper on the Review's web page. They do not differ much from those in Table 4. Moreover, the results in Table 4 are robust across various specifications, so I focus my discussion on columns 1–3.

First, the coefficient on the exit indicator in column 1 of Table 4 suggests that exiting plants are on average 8·1% less productive than surviving plants. My finding supports the idea that the high levels of trade protection in Chile enabled the coexistence of producers with different levels of productivity, while some of those failed to survive in a more competitive setting of the early 1980s. As protection ceased, the less efficient producers exited. Given the increased exposure to foreign competition, this behaviour might be most pronounced in the import-competing sectors. Yet, the coefficients on the interaction of the exit indicator and importables (−0·007) and the interaction of the exit indicator and exportables (−0·021) in column 2 are insignificant. So, although the exit of less efficient plants contributes to productivity improvements, the exit effects do not vary across plants with different trade orientations. Note that the coefficient on the exit indicator in the plant fixed effect regression in column 4 suggests that the exiting plants are on average only 1·9% less productive than surviving plants. This coefficient is based on variation in exit within a plant, so it excludes plants that never cease to produce. These never exiting plants are on average more productive, so the lower estimate is not surprising.

Second, the positive coefficients on the interaction of a plant's import-competing status and the year indicator in column 3 in Table 4 suggests that plants in the import-

12. These studies observe whether a particular plant exports. Chilean data does not provide such detailed information.

13. Note that the subtraction of the reference plant discussed in Section 5.2 is not necessary for my regression analysis with industry indicators. If I include industry indicators, the reference plant gets absorbed in the means for individual industries. This only changes the coefficients on the constant and industry indicators in the reported regression, but does not affect the coefficients on the year and trade orientation interactions.

TABLE 4

*Estimates of equation 12*

| | (1) Coef. | (1) S.E. | (2) Coef. | (2) S.E. | (3) Coef. | (3) S.E. | (4) Coef. | (4) S.E. | (5) Coef. | (5) S.E. | (6) Coef. | (6) S.E. |
|---|---|---|---|---|---|---|---|---|---|---|---|---|
| Export-oriented | 0·106 | 0·030** | 0·106 | 0·030** | 0·112 | 0·031** | 0·098 | 0·048** | 0·095 | 0·048** | 0·100 | 0·046** |
| Import-competing | 0·105 | 0·021** | 0·105 | 0·021** | 0·103 | 0·021** | −0·024 | 0·040 | −0·025 | 0·040 | −0·007 | 0·039 |
| ex_80 | −0·054 | 0·025** | −0·053 | 0·025** | −0·055 | 0·025** | −0·071 | 0·026** | −0·068 | 0·026** | −0·071 | 0·026** |
| ex_81 | −0·099 | 0·028** | −0·097 | 0·028** | −0·100 | 0·028** | −0·117 | 0·027** | −0·110 | 0·027** | −0·119 | 0·027** |
| ex_82 | 0·005 | 0·032 | 0·007 | 0·032 | 0·003 | 0·032 | −0·054 | 0·028* | −0·042 | 0·028 | −0·055 | 0·028* |
| ex_83 | 0·021 | 0·032 | 0·023 | 0·032 | 0·021 | 0·032 | −0·036 | 0·029 | −0·025 | 0·030 | −0·038 | 0·029 |
| ex_84 | 0·050 | 0·031 | 0·051 | 0·031 | 0·050 | 0·031 | 0·007 | 0·028 | 0·017 | 0·028 | 0·007 | 0·028 |
| ex_85 | 0·030 | 0·030 | 0·032 | 0·031 | 0·028 | 0·030 | −0·001 | 0·029 | 0·013 | 0·030 | −0·003 | 0·029 |
| ex_86 | | | | | 0·043 | 0·036 | | | | | −0·008 | 0·034 |
| im_80 | 0·011 | 0·014 | 0·011 | 0·014 | 0·010 | 0·014 | 0·013 | 0·014 | 0·013 | 0·014 | 0·013 | 0·014 |
| im_81 | 0·047 | 0·015** | 0·047 | 0·015** | 0·046 | 0·015** | 0·044 | 0·014** | 0·044 | 0·014** | 0·044 | 0·014** |
| im_82 | 0·033 | 0·016** | 0·034 | 0·017** | 0·030 | 0·016* | 0·024 | 0·015* | 0·024 | 0·015* | 0·025 | 0·015* |
| im_83 | 0·042 | 0·017** | 0·043 | 0·017** | 0·043 | 0·017** | 0·040 | 0·015** | 0·041 | 0·015** | 0·042 | 0·015** |
| im_84 | 0·062 | 0·017** | 0·062 | 0·017** | 0·063 | 0·017** | 0·059 | 0·015** | 0·059 | 0·015** | 0·061 | 0·015** |
| im_85 | 0·103 | 0·017** | 0·104 | 0·017** | 0·104 | 0·017** | 0·101 | 0·015** | 0·102 | 0·016** | 0·101 | 0·015** |
| im_86 | | | | | 0·071 | 0·019** | | | | | 0·073 | 0·017** |
| Exit indicator | −0·081 | 0·011** | −0·076 | 0·014** | | | −0·019 | 0·010** | −0·010 | 0·013 | | |
| Exit_export indicator | | | −0·021 | 0·036 | | | | | −0·069 | 0·035* | | |
| Exit_import indicator | | | −0·007 | 0·023 | | | | | −0·005 | 0·021 | | |
| Industry indicators | yes | | yes | | yes | | yes | | yes | | yes | |
| Plant indicators | no | | no | | no | | yes | | yes | | yes | |
| Year indicators | yes | | yes | | yes | | yes | | yes | | yes | |
| $R^2$ (adjusted) | 0·057 | | 0·058 | | 0·062 | | 0·498 | | 0·498 | | 0·488 | |
| *N* | 22983 | | 22983 | | 25491 | | 22983 | | 22983 | | 25491 | |

*Note*: ** and * indicate significance at a 5% and 10% level, respectively. Standard errors are corrected for heteroscedasticity. Standard errors in columns 1–3 are also adjusted for repeated observations on the same plant. Columns 1, 2, 4, and 5 do not include observations in 1986 because one cannot define exit for the last year of a panel.

competing sector are on average becoming more productive from 1981 through 1986 relative to the plants in the nontraded goods sector in corresponding years. This difference in productivity increases with time, and the productivity gains for plants in the import-competing sector attributable to liberalized trade range from 3% to 10·4%. These estimates are robust to all of the specifications of equation (12) reported in Table 4.[14] These productivity improvements do not stem simply from the liquidation of inefficient plants, which could increase average productivity in the import competing sectors without any within plant improvements. A comparison of the coefficients in columns 1 and 3 reveals that the inclusion of the exit indicator in the regression hardly changes the coefficients on the interaction of a plant's import-competing status and year indicators. This suggests that continuing plants improve their productivity as they adjust to a more liberalized trading environment. Possible mechanisms are the elimination of the *X*-inefficiencies or some other agency problem, or the adoption of better technology from abroad.

Third, the producers of exportable products do not experience productivity improvements attributable to liberalized trade. Column 3 of Table 4 shows that although plants in export-oriented sectors are in general 11% more productive than the producers of the nontraded goods, this productivity difference diminishes in 1980 and 1981. The coefficient on the interaction of year and export orientation is insignificant from 1982 onwards. The lack of significant improvements in the productivity of exporters could mean that exporters already had to be very productive to compete successfully in foreign markets, so that trade liberalization was not as significant of a shock to them as to plants in the import-competing sector. Aw *et al.* (1997), for example, find that exporting plants in Taiwan are more productive than nonexporters, because exporters need to face extra transportation costs and tougher market conditions to survive, but the exporters do not appear to become more productive through their exporting activity. Additionally, the productivity decline in export-oriented plants in 1980 and 1981 could be attributed to the real exchange rate appreciation as I discuss in more detail below.

The identification of the impact of liberalized trade on the productivity of plants in the export-oriented and import-competing sectors could be affected by real exchange rate fluctuations. If the real exchange rate impacts traded- and nontraded-goods sectors differentially, its effects are not only captured by the year indicators, but also affect the estimates of $\alpha_3$ in equation (12). The real exchange rate might impact measured productivity through changes in the composition of demand for nontradables and tradables. In particular, a real exchange rate appreciation might increase demand for nontradables and decrease demand for domestically produced traded goods. If plants do not adjust their inputs instantaneously and have some spare capacity, the demand fluctuations induced by an exchange rate appreciation (depreciation) could lead to an increase (decrease) in measured productivity for plants in the nontraded goods sector and a decrease (increase) in measured productivity for plants in the export-oriented and import-competing sectors. The Chilean real exchange rate appreciated until 1981 and then depreciated in 1982 due to a nominal exchange rate depreciation, so the spare capacity story is consistent with the observed productivity decline in the export oriented sector in 1980 and 1981. However, this explanation might be less consistent with persistent productivity improvements of

14. A potential alternative interpretation of my results is that import-competing sector always has higher productivity growth. Given the lack of panel plant level data prior to 1979, I cannot directly address this concern. However, my plant fixed effects estimates of $\alpha_3$ for plants in import-competing sectors are partially identified by plants that switch their trade orientation. Also, some anecdotal evidence and evidence based on very aggregate data before my sample period presented in Edwards and Edwards (1987) suggest that this is unlikely to be the case.

plants in the import-competing sector. I thus explore the relationship between the exchange rate and productivity further.

First, the above exchange rate mechanism suggests that productivity growth (decline) stems from expansions (contractions) in output without changes in inputs due to spare capacity. Then, plant productivity growth should be strongly positively correlated with output growth. Simple correlation coefficients reported in Table 5 suggest that the correlation between plant output growth and productivity growth is very small (ranging from 0·089 to 0·226 in various industries). The lack of a strong correlation suggests that the observed productivity improvements could not be explained solely by real exchange shocks. Second, if measured productivity changes occur through plants eliminating (increasing) excess capacity due to demand booms (slowdowns), plant inventories are likely to fluctuate correspondingly. Table 6 reports average inventories of plants with

TABLE 5

*Correlation between productivity growth and output growth*

| Industry | Correlation |
|---|---|
| Food processing | 0·154 |
| Textiles | 0·226 |
| Wood | 0·089 |
| Paper | 0·156 |
| Chemicals | 0·150 |
| Glass | 0·106 |
| Basic metals | 0·109 |
| Machinery | 0·119 |

TABLE 6

*Average plant inventories*

| | Inventories in levels | | | Inventories as a share of output | | |
|---|---|---|---|---|---|---|
| Year | Export-oriented plants | Import-competing plants | Nontraded goods plants | Export-oriented plants | Import-competing plants | Nontraded goods plants |
| 79 | 18,749 | 7,847 | 5,878 | 0·103 | 0·089 | 0·051 |
| | (140,638) | (32,790) | (56,941) | (0·160) | (0·122) | (0·095) |
| 80 | 21,210 | 6,252 | 5,266 | 0·093 | 0·085 | 0·052 |
| | (143,646) | (19,889) | (50,525) | (0·151) | (0·133) | (0·108) |
| 81 | 24,536 | 8,379 | 5,453 | 0·104 | 0·098 | 0·055 |
| | (171,304) | (34,008) | (50,860) | (0·183) | (0·217) | (0·117) |
| 82 | 39,259 | 7,716 | 6,053 | 0·109 | 0·117 | 0·053 |
| | (253,373) | (23,937) | (57,764) | (0·228) | (0·196) | (0·123) |
| 83 | 37,803 | 8,222 | 7,160 | 0·081 | 0·115 | 0·048 |
| | (265,596) | (24,260) | (78,149) | (0·149) | (0·226) | (0·114) |
| 84 | 44,123 | 10,536 | 7,931 | 0·079 | 0·114 | 0·145 |
| | (228,173) | (34,205) | (81,188) | (0·141) | (0·252) | (0·101) |
| 85 | 27,690 | 11,331 | 8,882 | 0·079 | 0·103 | 0·046 |
| | (84,335) | (37,299) | (94,107) | (0·185) | (0·201) | (0·098) |
| 86 | 24,530 | 11,612 | 7,626 | 0·062 | 0·077 | 0·038 |
| | (77,253) | (37,453) | (61,588) | (0·120) | (0·110) | (0·080) |
| Overall | 29,531 | 8,763 | 6,655 | 0·091 | 0·099 | 0·049 |
| | (186,633) | (30,697) | (66,903) | (0·170) | (0·188) | (0·106) |

*Note:* Inventories are measured as the end of the year plant-level inventories in thousands of 1980 Pesos. Reported figures are means and standard deviations.

various trade orientations over time. The level of inventories (and the share of inventories in total output) does not fluctuate much over time, and the fluctuations do not seem to correspond to the timing of the real exchange rate fluctuations.

Finally, if measured productivity reflects exchange rate induced demand changes, the correlation between measured productivity and the real exchange rate should be positive for plants in the nontraded-goods sector and negative for plants in the export-oriented and import-competing sector.[15] To check this hypothesis I regress productivity on the real exchange rate, plant trade orientation indicators, a time trend, and the interaction of the time trend with trade orientation indicators. Plants in the nontraded-goods sectors are the excluded category, so that the effect of the exchange rate on their productivity is given by the coefficient on the exchange rate. The coefficient on the interaction of the exchange rate with the export (import) indicator captures any *additional* effect the exchange rate has on the productivity of plants in the export sector (import-competing sector) *relative* to plants in the nontraded goods sector. Results are reported in Table 7. The real exchange rate is positively correlated with the productivity of plants in the nontraded-goods sector. The negative coefficient on the interaction of the exchange rate with the export-oriented indicator suggests that *relative* to plants in the nontraded goods sector, the real exchange rate appreciation has a negative impact on export-oriented plants. However, the insignificant coefficient on the interaction of the real exchange rate and the import-competing sector indicator means that we cannot reject the hypothesis that the real exchange rate does not impact the productivity of plants in the import-competing sector differently from plants in the nontraded goods sector. In summary, although some of the evidence indicates that the exchange rate story provides a possible alternative explanation for the productivity decline in the export-oriented sectors in 1980 and 1981, there is little evidence that the exchange rate affected plants in the import-competing sectors differently than plants in the nontraded goods sectors. The exclusion of the real exchange rate from my

TABLE 7

*Relationship between productivity and the real exchange rate*

| | |
|---|---|
| Real exchange rate | 0·0006** |
| | (0·0001) |
| Real exchange rate * export indicator | −0·0011** |
| | (0·0003) |
| Real exchange rate * import indicator | 0·0001 |
| | (0·0001) |
| Plant indicators | Yes |
| $R^2$ (adjusted) | 0·48 |

*Note*: ** and * indicate significance at a 5% and 10% level, respectively. Standard errors are corrected for heteroskedasticity. The regression also includes a time trend, export and import indicators, and the interactions of the time trend with export and import indicators as regressors. *N* is 25,491.

15. The real exchange rate is measured by the real effective exchange rate reported in the IMF's International Financial Statistics Yearbook. An increase in the exchange rate means appreciation by the IMF's definition.

initial analysis is thus unlikely to affect the robustness of my results for the import-competing sector.

An additional concern with the interpretation of my results in Table 4 regards the timing of my sample and the impact of a temporary increase in tariffs in 1983 and 1984. Since Chile had uniform tariffs across manufacturing sectors and I use the Census of Manufacturers', the impact of tariffs is captured by year indicators in equation (12), so I do not include a tariff measure in my initial regressions. When I regress plant productivity on tariff levels (columns 1, 2 of Table 8), plant productivity is negatively correlated with tariffs.[16] As a final robustness check of the analysis in Table 4, I relate plant productivity to exposure to foreign competition measured with imports as a share of domestic output at a four-digit ISIC level. Blundell, Griffith and Van Reenen (1999) also follow this approach when examining the relationship between innovation and competition for British firms. The regression results suggest that plants in industries with greater import competition are more productive: the coefficient on the import to output ratio is positive (columns 3, 4 of Table 8). This additional analysis is consistent with my initial finding that liberalized trade enhances the productivity of plants in the import-competing sector. Tables S.4, S.5 and S.6 in the supplement to the paper on the Review's web page repeat the analysis from Tables 5, 7 and 8 using the productivity measure constructed from the estimates of the production function coefficient based only on observations with positive investment. They yield similar conclusions.

## 6. CONCLUSION

This paper studies the effects of liberalized trade on the evolution of plant productivity. In my analysis I pay particular attention to the methodological hurdles that have haunted the previous empirical studies: construction of a productivity measure that is based on *consistent* estimates of the production function coefficients, the identification of the trade effects, and the role of plant exit and the resource reallocations from less to more efficient producers within industries.

TABLE 8

*Relationship between productivity and tariffs, real exchange rate, and import competition*

| | (1) | (2) | (3) | (4) |
|---|---|---|---|---|
| Real exchange rate | | 0·0005** | | 0·0005** |
| | | (0·0001) | | (0·0001) |
| Tariff | −0·2790** | −0·2377** | | −0·2376** |
| | (0·0280) | (0·0286) | | (0·0285) |
| Imports/output | | | 0·0023** | 0·0023** |
| | | | (0·0006) | (0·0006) |
| Plant indicators | yes | yes | yes | yes |
| $R^2$ (adjusted) | 0·48 | 0·48 | 0·48 | 0·48 |

*Note*: ** and * indicate significance at a 5% and 10% level, respectively. Standard errors are corrected for heteroskedasticity. All regressions also include a time trend. $N$ is 25,491.

16. I cannot control for year indicators and tariff levels at the same time because tariffs only vary by year, and they do not vary at all before 1983. Tariff data is reported by the Chilean Central Bank.

These methodological aspects turn out to be important. After I adjust for self selection and simultaneity, the estimate of the capital coefficient on average more than doubles relative to the OLS estimate for 5 out of 8 industries, and decreases on average by 22% relative to the OLS estimates elsewhere. These results reconfirm Olley and Pakes's (1996) finding that one cannot ignore selection and simultaneity issues in the estimation of a production function, and that semiparametric estimation of a production function provides a useful alternative to the methods used in previous studies.

I then analyse the effects of liberalized trade on plant productivity in a regression framework. I identify the impact of trade on productivity by using both the variation of productivity over time and the variation across traded and nontraded goods sectors. This framework allows me to separate productivity variation resulting from liberalized trade from productivity variation stemming from other sources. My results suggest that liberalized trade enhances plant productivity. In particular, using unweighted productivity I show that the productivity of the producers of the import-competing goods improved on average 3 to 10% more than the productivity of plants in the nontraded-goods sectors due to liberalized trade. This finding suggests that the plants responded to intensified foreign competition by trimming their fat. The positive relationship between liberalized trade and productivity is robust to other measures of exposure to trade such as import to output ratios, tariffs, and exchange rate. The evidence for plants in the export-oriented sectors of the economy is less conclusive and could also be consistent with plant responses to real exchange rate fluctuations.

My finding of within-plant productivity improvements for plants in the import-competing sector are consistent with the study by Blundell, Griffith and Van Reenen (1999), who examine the relationship between innovation, market share, and competition using a panel of British firms. Blundell *et al.* (1999) find that firms innovate more in industries facing more import competition and lower domestic concentration ratios. They also find that within each industry, conditional on the level of competition, the firms with a bigger market share innovate more. These incumbents have a stronger incentive to innovate, because the innovation preempts additional entry or the expansion of smaller incumbents and thus shields their profits.

Third, exit in general contributes to productivity gains: exiting plants are on average about 8% less productive than surviving plants. Aggregate industry-level productivity indices in addition suggest that the reshuffling of resources from less to more productive producers contributes to aggregate productivity gains, especially for the plants in the export-oriented and import-competing sectors. The aggregate productivity grew by 25·4% and 31·9% in the export-oriented and import-competing sectors over seven years, respectively, whereas the gains in the nontraded goods sectors amounted to 6%. Overall, the Chilean manufacturing sector grew at an average annual rate of 2·8% after trade liberalization, mostly due to the reshuffling of the resources within the economy (about 2%).

Given the importance of plant heterogeneity within an industry, my findings imply that the barriers to plant turnover are important determinants of the success of trade liberalization. As such, the study complements the recent empirical work by Aw, Chen and Roberts (1997) analysing the importance of plant turnover in Taiwan, where sunk costs do not present a large barrier. My results also substantiate concerns raised in the popular press regarding recent economic turmoil in East Asia. Hurdles such as institutional arrangements that discourage the bankruptcy of less efficient plants have been blamed to restrict economic growth in recent discussions of East Asian economic crisis in the popular press. When the reallocation of resources within industries play an important role in the economic growth, the institutional arrangements that obstruct plant liquidation as in

Japan, or the confinement of such process to smaller businesses as in South Korea can prove very harmful.

Finally, my empirical evidence indicates that channels other than economies of scale yield intraindustry productivity improvements from trade. The incorporation of within industry plant heterogeneity should be a fruitful area for the future theoretical work on welfare gains from trade.

## APPENDIX

This Appendix provides the details of data construction. The original plant-level data set and the variable definitions and construction are described in detail in Liu (1993) and Tybout (1996). I use the information on 4379 plants after eliminating those with incomplete information. The capital variable was initially constructed using a perpetual inventory method by Liu (1993) and is described in detail in Tybout (1996). I have reconstructed the variable so that the capital stock at time $t$ does not contain the investment at time $t$. Since the balance sheet information was only available for the plants in 1980 and 1981, capital measures are based on the book value of capital in those two periods. In my capital variable, I use figures based on the 1981 book value of capital if both 1980 and 1981 are available. Otherwise, capital measure based on the 1980 book value of capital was used. I experimented with several options and all capital measures are highly correlated. Skilled and unskilled labour is measured by the total number of employees in each skill group working in a plant. The data set does not provide the information on hours worked. It also does not provide the information on when a plant was established. Capital, investment, intermediate materials, value added, and output are expressed in constant 1980 pesos. Descriptive statistics for the data are given in Tables A.1 and A.2.

The data used to compute the trade balance are exports and imports from the U.N. Yearbook of International Trade Statistics and Statistics Canada CD-ROM. A more detailed classification in the Statistics Canada enables me to improve on the definitions provided by Tybout (1992) that are only at the three-digit ISIC level. The trade orientation of an industry is determined at a four-digit ISIC level, on the basis of Chilean trade balance in that particular industry. Plants that belong to a four-digit ISIC industry that exports more than 15% of its total output are characterized as export-oriented. Plants that belong to a four-digit ISIC industry whose ratio of imports to total domestic output exceeds 15% are characterized as import-competing. The rest of the plants belong to the nontraded-goods sector. Table A.3 summarizes import to output and export to output ratios for the three-digit ISIC sectors in my data. Table S.1 in the supplement to the paper on the Review's web page provides this information on a four-digit ISIC level.

Defining trade orientation in this manner raises two concerns: the presence of intraindustry trade and the endogeneity of the definition. Neither of these presents a problem in the Chilean data. Intraindustry trade was rarely an issue within three or four digit ISIC classifications. The Grubel–Lloyd index of intra industry trade averaged 0·30 from 1979 to 1986 on a four-digit ISIC level, and 0·35 on a three-digit ISIC level. The median import–output ratio was 0·257, the median export–output ratio was 0·017. As Table A.3 indicates and Figure A.1

TABLE A1

*Descriptive statistics*

| Variable | Mean | S.D. | Median |
|---|---|---|---|
| Output | 132,165 | 985,792 | 17,922 |
| Value added | 50,386 | 325,322 | 6,276 |
| Labour | 56 | 121 | 23 |
| Skilled labour | 15 | 41 | 5 |
| Unskilled labour | 41 | 87 | 18 |
| Capital | 53,066 | 360,274 | 3,682 |
| Investment | 3,861 | 41,624 | 0 |
| Materials | 73,337 | 700,712 | 9,643 |

*Note*: Quantities in thousands of 1980 pesos. Labour is measured by the number of employees.

TABLE A2

*Panel information*

| Year | Number of plants | Years in the panel | Number of plants |
|---|---|---|---|
| 1979 | 3,470 | 8 | 1,536 |
| 1980 | 3,704 | 7 | 716 |
| 1981 | 3,654 | 6 | 406 |
| 1982 | 3,396 | 5 | 400 |
| 1983 | 3,034 | 4 | 441 |
| 1984 | 2,928 | 3 | 385 |
| 1985 | 2,797 | 2 | 341 |
| 1986 | 2,508 | 1 | 154 |
| Total number of plant-years | 25,491 | Total number of plants | 4,379 |

*Note*: The left hand side of the table indicates the number of plants in a given year. The right hand side of the table indicates the number of plants that stay in the panel for a total of 8,7,... years.

TABLE A3

*3-digit ISIC industry trade orientation*

| Industry | Export–output ratio | Import–output ratio | Import Penetration |
|---|---|---|---|
| 312 | 0·174 | 0·078 | 0·072 |
| 313 | 0·046 | 0·045 | 0·043 |
| 321 | 0·006 | 0·271 | 0·211 |
| 322 | 0·004 | 0·174 | 0·145 |
| 323 | 0·008 | 0·135 | 0·117 |
| 324 | 0·004 | 0·097 | 0·085 |
| 331 | 0·254 | 0·019 | 0·019 |
| 332 | 0·016 | 0·089 | 0·081 |
| 341 | 0·418 | 0·096 | 0·087 |
| 342 | 0·023 | 0·062 | 0·059 |
| 351 | 0·824 | 1·326 | 0·567 |
| 352 | 0·002 | 0·113 | 0·101 |
| 353 | 0·029 | 0·114 | 0·099 |
| 354 | 0·019 | 0·262 | 0·170 |
| 355 | 0·040 | 0·296 | 0·227 |
| 356 | 0·002 | 0·102 | 0·092 |
| 361 | 0·092 | 0·716 | 0·320 |
| 362 | 0·017 | 0·318 | 0·240 |
| 369 | 0·003 | 0·078 | 0·072 |
| 371 | 0·063 | 0·112 | 0·100 |
| 372 | 0·733 | 0·012 | 0·011 |
| 381 | 0·097 | 0·255 | 0·203 |
| 382 | 0·053 | 2·141 | 0·676 |
| 383 | 0·036 | 1·649 | 0·621 |
| 384 | 0·210 | 2·010 | 0·666 |
| 385 | 0·089 | 7·381 | 0·876 |

*Note*: All reported figures are averages over 1980–1986.

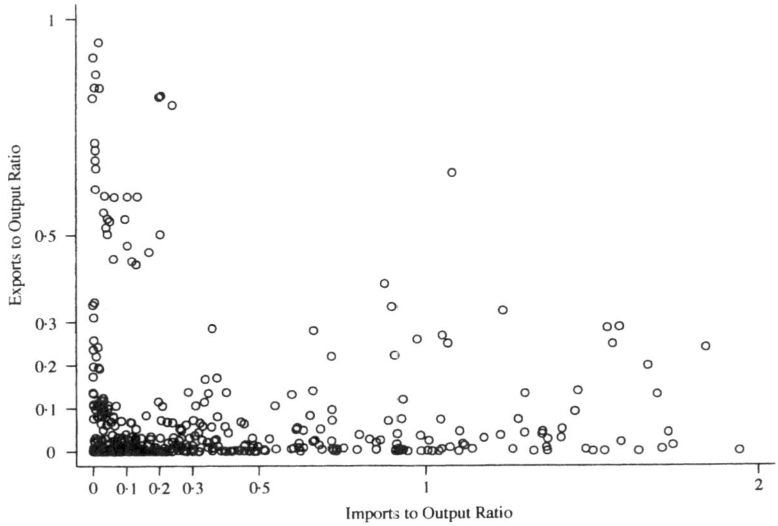


Source: Statistics Canada

FIGURE A.1
Export–output vs. import–output ratio (1980–1986, 4-digit ISIC industries)

illustrates, in the sectors that had both imports and exports, one of the categories significantly prevailed over the other so that the trade orientation was easily determined.

The endogeneity of trade orientation could arise from the traditional omitted variable problem: unobserved factors that affect a plant's productivity might also affect a plant's trade orientation during trade liberalization. One way of solving this problem is to define trade orientation of a sector using information on imports and exports preceding the sample period. Interestingly, trade orientation of the three- and four-digit ISIC industries does not change much over time. In my regression analysis I also account for plant specific effects, so that this specification eliminates the impact of any permanent unobserved plant characteristic that influence trade orientation and plant productivity.

Moreover, I could measure a plant's exposure to trade with tariff concessions or changes in protection. Yet, the change in tariffs does not completely depict the change in the trading environment. Some sectors might not experience an increase in imports regardless of the drop in tariffs because of transportation costs or other barriers to trade. Category 3117, manufacturing of bakery products is a good example. Despite low tariffs, it involves a good that is nontraded because it is perishable. Therefore, a definition of a trade orientation of a sector based on trade balance seems more appropriate. In addition, if one considers political economy issues, measures such as tariffs might be endogenous (Trefler (1993)), *i.e.* less productive industries might be more likely to lobby and receive higher tariffs. However, this is unlikely in Chile during the 1980s, since all tariffs and tariff changes were uniform across all manufacturing sectors.

*Acknowledgements.* I would like to thank Gene Grossman, Penny Goldberg and Bo Honore for guidance and time. Eric Edmonds, Hank Farber, Igal Hendel, Nancy Marion, John McLaren, and seminar participants at Cornell, Columbia, Dartmouth, Harvard, Michigan State, MIT Sloan School, NYU, Penn, Princeton, Stanford, the World Bank, Wisconsin, and Yale provided helpful comments and suggestions. The paper also benefited greatly from the comments of three anonymous referees and the editor. This research was supported by a Ford Foundation Fellowship.

REFERENCES

ANDREWS, D. (1991), "Asymptotic Normality of Series Estimators for Nonparametric and Semiparametric Regression Models", *Econometrica*, **59**, 307–345.

ARELLANO, M. and BOND, S. (1991), "Some Tests of Specification for Panel Data: Monte Carlo Evidence and an Application to Employment Equations", *Review of Economic Studies*, **58**, 277–297.

AW, B., CHEN, X. and ROBERTS, M. (1997), "Plant-level Evidence on Productivity Differentials, Turnover, and Exports in Taiwanese Manufacturing"(Mimeo, Pennsylvania State University).

BERNARD, A. and JONES, C. (1996), "Comparing Apples to Oranges: Productivity Convergence and Measurement Across Industries and Countries", *American Economic Review*, **86**, 1216–1238.

BERNARD, A., EATON, J., JENSEN, B. and KORTUM, S. (2000), "Plants and Productivity in International Trade: A Ricardian Reconciliation" (NBER Working Paper, No. 7688).

BLUNDELL, R. and BOND, S. (1998), "Initial Conditions and Moment Restrictions in Dynamic Panel Data Models", *Journal of Econometrics*, **87**, 115–143.

BLUNDELL, R., GRIFFITH, R. and VAN REENEN, J. (1999), "Market Share, Market Value, and Innovation in a Panel of British Manufacturing Firms", *Review of Economic Studies*, **66**, 529–554.

CAVES, D., CHRISTENSEN, L. and TRETHEWAY, M. (1981), "U.S. Trunk Air Carriers, 1972–1977: A Multilateral Comparison of Total Factor Productivity", in T. Cowing and R. Stevenson (eds.), *Productivity Measurement in Regulated Industries* (New York: Academic Press).

CORNWELL, C., SCHMIDT, P. and SICKLES. R. (1990), "Production Frontiers with Cross-Sectional and Time-Series Variation in Efficiency Levels", *Journal of Econometrics*, **46**, 185–200.

DORNBUSCH, R. and EDWARDS, S. (1994), "Exchange Rate Policy and Trade Strategy", in B. Bosworth, R. Dornbusch and R. Laban (eds.), *The Chilean Economy: Policy Lessons and Challenges* (Washington DC: The Brookings Institution).

EATON, J. and KORTUM, S. (1996), "Trade in Ideas: Productivity and Patenting in the OECD", *Journal of International Economics*, **40**, 251–278.

EATON, J. and KORTUM, S. (1997), "Technology and Bilateral Trade" (NBER Working Paper, No. 6253).

EDWARDS, S. and EDWARDS, A. (1987) *Monetarism and Liberalization. The Chilean Experiment* (Cambridge, MA: Ballinger).

ERICSON, R. and PAKES, A. (1995), "Markov-Perfect Industry Dynamics: A Framework for Empirical Work", *Review of Economic Studies*, **62**, 53–82.

GATT (1991) *Trade Policy Review: Chile* (Geneva: GATT).

GOOD, D., NADIRI, I. and SICKLES, R. (1996), "Index Number and Factor Demand Approaches to the Estimation of Productivity" (NBER Working Paper, No. 5790).

HARRISON, A. (1994), "Productivity, Imperfect Competition and Trade Reform", *Journal of International Economics*, **36**, 53–73.

KLETTE, T. (1996), "R&D, Scope Economies, and Plant Performance", *RAND Journal of Economics*, **27**, 502–522.

LEVINSOHN, J. (1996), "Plant Heterogeneity, Jobs, and International Trade: Evidence from Chile" (NBER Working Paper, No. 5808).

LEVINSOHN, J. and PETRIN, A. (1999), "When Industries Become More Productive, Do Plants? Productivity Dynamics in an Open Economy" (Mimeo, University of Michigan).

LIU, L. (1993), "Entry–Exit, Learning and Productivity Change: Evidence from Chile", *Journal of Development Economics*, **42**, 217–242.

LIU, L. and TYBOUT, J. (1996), "Productivity Growth in Chile and Colombia: The Role of Entry, Exit and Learning", in M. Roberts and J. Tybout (eds.), *Industrial Evolution in Developing Countries* (Oxford: Oxford University Press).

OLLEY, S. and PAKES, A. (1996), "The Dynamics of Productivity in the Telecommunications Equipment Industry", *Econometrica*, **64**, 1263–1297.

PAKES, A. (1994), "Dynamic Structural Models, Problems and Prospects: Mixed Continuous Discrete Controls and Market Interactions", in C. Sims (ed.), *Advances in Econometrics* (Cambridge: Cambridge University Press).

PAKES, A. and OLLEY, S. (1995), "A Limit Theorem for a Smooth Class of Semiparametric Estimators", *Journal of Econometrics*, **65**, 295–332.

ROBERTS, M. and TYBOUT, J. (1996) *Industrial Evolution in Developing Countries* (Oxford: Oxford University Press).

RODRIK, D. (1988), "Imperfect Competition, Scale Economies, and Trade Policy in Developing Countries", in

R. Baldwin (ed.), *Trade Policy Issues and Empirical Analysis* (Chicago: The University of Chicago Press).

RODRIK, D. (1991), "Closing the Technology Gap: Does Trade Liberalization Really Help?", in G. Helleiner (ed.), *Trade Policy, Industrialization and Development: A Reconsideration* (Oxford: Clarendon Press).

SCHMIDT, P. (1985), "Frontier Production Functions", *Econometric Reviews*, **4**, 289–328.

SCHMIDT, P. and SICKLES, R. (1984), "Production Frontiers and Panel Data", *Journal of Business and Economic Statistics*, **2**, 367–374.

TREFLER, D. (1993), "Trade Liberalization and the Theory of Endogenous Protection: An Econometric Study of U.S. Import Policy", *Journal of Political Economy*, **101**, 138–160.

TYBOUT, J. (1992), "Linking Trade and Productivity: New Research Directions", *World Bank Economics Review*, **6**, 189–211.

TYBOUT, J. (1996), "Chile, 1979–1986: Trade Liberalization and Its Aftermath", in M. Roberts and J. Tybout (eds.), *Industrial Evolution in Developing Countries* (Oxford: Oxford University Press).

TYBOUT, J., De MELO, J. and CORBO, V. (1991), "The Effects of Trade Reforms on Scale and Technical Efficiency: New Evidence from Chile", *Journal of International Economics*, **31**, 231–250.

TYBOUT, J. and WESTBROOK, M. (1995), "Trade Liberalization and the Dimensions of Efficiency Change in Mexican Manufacturing Industries", *Journal of International Economics*, **39**, 53–78.

UNCTAD (1992) *Trade Liberalization in Chile: Experiences and Prospects*, Trade Policy Series No. 1 (New York: United Nations).

# [17]

*Econometrica*, Vol. 71, No. 6 (November, 2003), 1695–1725

## THE IMPACT OF TRADE ON INTRA-INDUSTRY REALLOCATIONS AND AGGREGATE INDUSTRY PRODUCTIVITY

BY MARC J. MELITZ[1]

This paper develops a dynamic industry model with heterogeneous firms to analyze the intra-industry effects of international trade. The model shows how the exposure to trade will induce only the more productive firms to enter the export market (while some less productive firms continue to produce only for the domestic market) and will simultaneously force the least productive firms to exit. It then shows how further increases in the industry's exposure to trade lead to additional inter-firm reallocations towards more productive firms. The paper also shows how the aggregate industry productivity growth generated by the reallocations contributes to a welfare gain, thus highlighting a benefit from trade that has not been examined theoretically before. The paper adapts Hopenhayn's (1992a) dynamic industry model to monopolistic competition in a general equilibrium setting. In so doing, the paper provides an extension of Krugman's (1980) trade model that incorporates firm level productivity differences. Firms with different productivity levels coexist in an industry because each firm faces initial uncertainty concerning its productivity before making an irreversible investment to enter the industry. Entry into the export market is also costly, but the firm's decision to export occurs after it gains knowledge of its productivity.

KEYWORDS: Intra-industry trade, firm heterogeneity, firm dynamics, selection.

### 1. INTRODUCTION

RECENT EMPIRICAL RESEARCH using longitudinal plant or firm-level data from several countries has overwhelmingly substantiated the existence of large and persistent productivity differences among establishments in the same narrowly defined industries. Some of these studies have further shown that these productivity differences are strongly correlated with the establishment's export status: relatively more productive establishments are much more likely to export (even within so-called "export sectors," a substantial portion of establishments do not export). Other studies have highlighted the large levels of resource reallocations that occur across establishments in the same industry. Some of these studies have also correlated these reallocations with the establishments' export status.

This paper develops a dynamic industry model with heterogeneous firms to analyze the role of international trade as a catalyst for these inter-firm reallocations within an industry. The model is able to reproduce many of the most salient patterns emphasized by recent micro-level studies related to trade. The model shows how the exposure to trade induces only the more productive firms to export while simultaneously forcing the least productive firms to exit. Both the exit of the least productive firms and the additional export sales gained by

[1]Many thanks to Alan Deardorff, Jim Levinsohn, and Elhanan Helpman for helpful comments and discussions. This manuscript has also benefited from comments by the editor and two anonymous referees. Funding from the Alfred P. Sloan Foundation is gratefully acknowledged.

the more productive firms reallocate market shares towards the more productive firms and contribute to an aggregate productivity increase. Profits are also reallocated towards more productive firms. The model is also consistent with the widely reported stories in the business press describing how the exposure to trade enhances the growth opportunities of some firms while simultaneously contributing to the downfall or "downsizing" of other firms in the same industry; similarly, protection from trade is often reported to shelter inefficient firms. Rigorous empirical work has recently corroborated this anecdotal evidence. Bernard and Jensen (1999a) (for the U.S.), Aw, Chung, and Roberts (2000) (for Taiwan), and Clerides, Lack, and Tybout (1998) (for Colombia, Mexico, and Morocco) all find evidence that more productive firms self-select into export markets. Aw, Chung, and Roberts (2000) also find evidence suggesting that exposure to trade forces the least productive firms to exit. Pavcnik (2002) directly looks at the contribution of market share reallocations to sectoral productivity growth following trade liberalization in Chile. She finds that these reallocations significantly contribute to productivity growth in the tradable sectors. In a related study, Bernard and Jensen (1999b) find that within-sector market share reallocations towards more productive exporting plants accounts for 20% of U.S. manufacturing productivity growth.

Clearly, these empirical patterns cannot be motivated without appealing to a model of trade incorporating firm heterogeneity. Towards this goal, this paper embeds firm productivity heterogeneity within Krugman's model of trade under monopolistic competition and increasing returns. The current model draws heavily from Hopenhayn's (1992a, 1992b) work to explain the endogenous selection of heterogeneous firms in an industry. Hopenhayn derives the equilibrium distribution of firm productivity from the profit maximizing decisions of initially identical firms who are uncertain of their initial and future productivity.[2] This paper adapts his model to a monopolistically competitive industry (Hopenhayn only considers competitive firms) in a general equilibrium setting.[3] A contribution of this paper is to provide such a general equilibrium model incorporating firm heterogeneity that yet remains highly tractable. This is achieved by integrating firm heterogeneity in a way such that the relevance of the distribution of productivity levels for aggregate outcomes is completely summarized by a single "sufficient" statistic—an average firm productivity level. Once this productivity average is determined, the model with

[2]One of the most robust empirical patterns emerging from recent industry studies is that new entrants have lower average productivity and higher exit rates than older incumbents. This suggests that uncertainty concerning productivity is an important feature explaining the behavior of prospective and new entrants.

[3]Montagna (1995) also adapts Hopenhayn's model to a monopolistic competition environment (in a partial equilibrium setting), but confines the analysis to a static equilibrium with no entry or exit and further constrains the distribution of firm productivity levels to be uniform. Although it is assumed that only the more productive firms earning positive profits remain in the industry in future periods, the present value of these profit flows does not enter into the firms' entry decision.

productivity heterogeneity yields identical aggregate outcomes as one with representative firms that all share the same average productivity level.

This simplicity does not come without some concessions. The analysis relies on the Dixit and Stiglitz (1977) model of monopolistic competition. Although this modeling approach is quite common in the trade literature, it also exhibits some well-known limitations. In particular, the firms' markups are exogenously fixed by the symmetric elasticity of substitution between varieties. Another concession is the simplification of the firm productivity dynamics modeled by Hopenhayn (1992a). Nevertheless, the current model preserves the initial firm uncertainty over productivity and the forward looking entry decision of firms facing sunk entry costs and expected future probabilities of exit. As in Hopenhayn (1992a), the analysis is restricted to stationary equilibria. Firms correctly anticipate this stable aggregate environment when making all relevant decisions. The analysis then focuses on the long run effects of trade on the relative behavior and performance of firms with different productivity levels.

Another recent paper by Bernard, Eaton, Jenson, and Kortum (2000) (henceforth BEJK) also introduces firm-level heterogeneity into a model of trade by adapting a Ricardian model to firm-specific comparative advantage. Both papers predict the same basic kinds of trade-induced reallocations, although the channels and motivations behind these reallocations vary. In BEJK, firms compete to produce the same variety—including competition between domestic and foreign producers of the same variety. This delivers an endogenous distribution of markups, a feature that is missing in this paper. BEJK also show how their model can be calibrated to provide a good fit to a combination of micro and macro US data patterns. Comparative statics are then obtained by simulating this fitted model. The BEJK model assumes that the total number of world varieties produced and consumed remains exogenously fixed and relies on a specific parameterization of the distribution of productivity levels.

In contrast, the current paper allows the total range of varieties produced to vary with the exposure to trade, and endogenously determines the subset of those varieties that are consumed in a given country. Despite leaving the distribution of firm productivity levels unrestricted, the model remains tractable enough to perform analytical comparisons of steady states that reflect different levels of exposure to trade. Although the current model only considers symmetric countries, it can easily be extended to asymmetric countries by relying on an exogenously fixed relative wage between countries.[4] In this model, differences in country size—holding the relative wage fixed—only affect the relative number of firms, and not their productivity distribution. This straightforward extension is therefore omitted for expositional simplicity.

[4]This assumption is also made in BEJK. See Helpman, Melitz, and Yeaple (2002) for an extension of the current model that explicitly considers the asymmetric country case when the relative wage is determined via trade in a homogeneous good sector.

One last, but important, innovation in the current paper is to introduce the dynamic forward-looking entry decision of firms facing sunk market entry costs. Firms face such costs, not just for their domestic market, but also for any potential export market.[5] These costs are in addition to the per-unit trade costs that are typically modeled. Both survey and econometric works have documented the importance of such export market entry costs. Das, Roberts, and Tybout (2001) econometrically estimate these costs average over U.S. $1 Million for Colombian plants producing industrial chemicals. As will be detailed later, surveys reveal that managers making export related decisions are much more concerned with export costs that are fixed in nature rather than high per-unit costs. Furthermore, Roberts and Tybout (1977a) (for Colombia), Bernard and Jensen (2001) (for the U.S.), and Bernard and Wagner (2001) (for Germany) estimate that the magnitude of sunk export market entry costs is important enough to generate very large hysteresis effects associated with a plant's export market participation.[6]

## 2. SETUP OF THE MODEL

### 2.1. *Demand*

The preferences of a representative consumer are given by a C.E.S. utility function over a continuum of goods indexed by $\omega$:

$$U=\left[\int_{\omega\in\Omega} q(\omega)^{\rho}d\omega\right]^{1/\rho},$$

where the measure of the set $\Omega$ represents the mass of available goods. These goods are substitutes, implying $0<\rho<1$ and an elasticity of substitution between any two goods of $\sigma=1/(1-\rho)>1$. As was originally shown by Dixit and Stiglitz (1977), consumer behavior can be modeled by considering the set of varieties consumed as an aggregate good $Q\equiv U$ associated with an aggregate price

$$P=\left[\int_{\omega\in\Omega} p(\omega)^{1-\sigma}d\omega\right]^{\frac{1}{1-\sigma}}. \tag{1}$$

[5]Sunk market entry costs also explain the presence of simultaneous entry and exit in the steady state equilibrium.

[6]Sunk export market entry costs also explain the higher survival probabilities of exporting firms—even after controlling for their higher measured productivity. See Bernard and Jensen (1999a, 2002) for evidence on U.S. firms.

These aggregates can then be used to derive the optimal consumption and expenditure decisions for individual varieties using

$$(2)\qquad \begin{aligned} q(\omega) &= Q\left[\frac{p(\omega)}{P}\right]^{-\sigma}, \\ r(\omega) &= R\left[\frac{p(\omega)}{P}\right]^{1-\sigma}, \end{aligned}$$

where $R = PQ = \int_{\omega\in\Omega} r(\omega)d\omega$ denotes aggregate expenditure.

### 2.2. *Production*

There is a continuum of firms, each choosing to produce a different variety $\omega$. Production requires only one factor, labor, which is inelastically supplied at its aggregate level $L$, an index of the economy's size. Firm technology is represented by a cost function that exhibits constant marginal cost with a fixed overhead cost. Labor used is thus a linear function of output $q$: $l = f + q/\varphi$. All firms share the same fixed cost $f > 0$ but have different productivity levels indexed by $\varphi > 0$. For expositional simplicity, higher productivity is modeled as producing a symmetric variety at lower marginal cost. Higher productivity may also be thought of as producing a higher quality variety at equal cost.[7] Regardless of its productivity, each firm faces a residual demand curve with constant elasticity $\sigma$ and thus chooses the same profit maximizing markup equal to $\sigma/(\sigma-1) = 1/\rho$. This yields a pricing rule

$$(3)\qquad p(\varphi) = \frac{w}{\rho\varphi},$$

where $w$ is the common wage rate hereafter normalized to one. Firm profit is then

$$\pi(\varphi) = r(\varphi) - l(\varphi) = \frac{r(\varphi)}{\sigma} - f,$$

where $r(\varphi)$ is firm revenue and $r(\varphi)/\sigma$ is variable profit. $r(\varphi)$, and hence $\pi(\varphi)$, also depend on the aggregate price and revenue as shown in (2):

$$(4)\qquad r(\varphi) = R(P\rho\varphi)^{\sigma-1},$$

$$(5)\qquad \pi(\varphi) = \frac{R}{\sigma}(P\rho\varphi)^{\sigma-1} - f.$$

[7]Given the form of product differentiation, the modeling of either type of productivity difference is isomorphic.

On the other hand, the ratios of any two firms' outputs and revenues only depend on the ratio of their productivity levels:

$$(6) \qquad \frac{q(\varphi_1)}{q(\varphi_2)} = \left(\frac{\varphi_1}{\varphi_2}\right)^{\sigma}, \qquad \frac{r(\varphi_1)}{r(\varphi_2)} = \left(\frac{\varphi_1}{\varphi_2}\right)^{\sigma-1}.$$

In summary, a more productive firm (higher $\varphi$) will be bigger (larger output and revenues), charge a lower price, and earn higher profits than a less productive firm.

## 2.3. *Aggregation*

An equilibrium will be characterized by a mass $M$ of firms (and hence $M$ goods) and a distribution $\mu(\varphi)$ of productivity levels over a subset of $(0, \infty)$. In such an equilibrium, the aggregate price $P$ defined in (1) is then given by

$$P = \left[\int_0^\infty p(\varphi)^{1-\sigma} M\mu(\varphi)d\varphi\right]^{\frac{1}{1-\sigma}}.$$

Using the pricing rule (3), this can be written $P = M^{1/(1-\sigma)}p(\tilde{\varphi})$, where

$$(7) \qquad \tilde{\varphi} = \left[\int_0^\infty \varphi^{\sigma-1}\mu(\varphi)d\varphi\right]^{\frac{1}{\sigma-1}}.$$

$\tilde{\varphi}$ is a weighted average of the firm productivity levels $\varphi$ and is independent of the number of firms $M$.[8] These weights reflect the relative output shares of firms with different productivity levels.[9] $\tilde{\varphi}$ also represents aggregate productivity because it completely summarizes the information in the distribution of productivity levels $\mu(\varphi)$ relevant for all aggregate variables (see Appendix):

$$P = M^{\frac{1}{1-\sigma}}p(\tilde{\varphi}), \qquad R = PQ = Mr(\tilde{\varphi}),$$
$$Q = M^{1/\rho}q(\tilde{\varphi}), \qquad \Pi = M\pi(\tilde{\varphi}),$$

where $R = \int_0^\infty r(\varphi)M\mu(\varphi)\,d\varphi$ and $\Pi = \int_0^\infty \pi(\varphi)M\mu(\varphi)\,d\varphi$ represent aggregate revenue (or expenditure) and profit. Thus, an industry comprised of $M$ firms with any distribution of productivity levels $\mu(\varphi)$ that yields the same average productivity level $\tilde{\varphi}$ will also induce the same aggregate outcome as an industry with $M$ representative firms sharing the same productivity level $\varphi = \tilde{\varphi}$.

[8] Subsequent conditions on the equilibrium $\mu(\varphi)$ must of course ensure that $\tilde{\varphi}$ is finite.

[9] Using $q(\varphi)/q(\tilde{\varphi}) = (\varphi/\tilde{\varphi})^{\sigma}$ (see (6)), $\tilde{\varphi}$ can be written as $\tilde{\varphi}^{-1} = \int_0^\infty \varphi^{-1}[q(\varphi)/q(\tilde{\varphi})]\mu(\varphi)d\varphi$. $\tilde{\varphi}$ is therefore the weighted harmonic mean of the $\varphi$'s where the weights $q(\varphi)/q(\tilde{\varphi})$ index the firms' relative output shares.

This variable will be alternatively referred to as aggregate or average productivity. Further note that $\bar{r} = R/M$ and $\bar{\pi} = \Pi/M$ represent both the average revenue and profit per firm as well as the revenue and profit level of the firm with average productivity level $\varphi = \tilde{\varphi}$.

## 3. FIRM ENTRY AND EXIT

There is a large (unbounded) pool of prospective entrants into the industry. Prior to entry, firms are identical. To enter, firms must first make an initial investment, modeled as a fixed entry cost $f_e > 0$ (measured in units of labor), which is thereafter sunk. Firms then draw their initial productivity parameter $\varphi$ from a common distribution $g(\varphi)$.[10] $g(\varphi)$ has positive support over $(0, \infty)$ and has a continuous cumulative distribution $G(\varphi)$.

Upon entry with a low productivity draw, a firm may decide to immediately exit and not produce. If the firm does produce, it then faces a constant (across productivity levels) probability $\delta$ in every period of a bad shock that would force it to exit. Although there are some realistic examples of severe shocks that would constrain a firm to exit independently of productivity (such as natural disasters, new regulation, product liability, major changes in consumer tastes), it is also likely that exit may be caused by a series of bad shocks affecting the firm's productivity. This type of firm level process is explicitly modeled by Hopenhayn (1992a, 1992b). The simplification made in this model entails that the shape of the equilibrium distribution of productivity $\mu(\varphi)$ and the ex-ante survival probabilities are exogenously determined by $g(\varphi)$ and $\delta$. On the other hand, the range of productivity levels (for surviving firms), and hence the average productivity level, are endogenously determined.[11] Importantly, this simplified industry model will nevertheless generate one of the most robust empirical patterns highlighted by micro-level studies: new entrants (including the firms whose entry is unsuccessful) will have, on average, lower productivity and a higher probability of exit than incumbents.

This paper only considers steady state equilibria in which the aggregate variables remain constant over time. Since each firm's productivity level does not change over time, its optimal per period profit level (excluding $f_e$) will also remain constant. An entering firm with productivity $\varphi$ would then immediately exit if this profit level were negative (and hence never produce), or would produce and earn $\pi(\varphi) \geq 0$ in every period until it is hit with the bad shock and is

[10] This captures the fact that firms cannot know their own productivity with certainty until they start producing and selling their good. (Recall that productivity differences may reflect cost differences as well as differences in consumer valuations of the good.)

[11] The increased tractability afforded by this simplification permits the detailed analysis of the impact of trade on this endogenous range of productivity levels and on the distribution of market shares and profits across this range.

forced to exit. Assuming that there is no time discounting,[12] each firm's value function is given by

$$v(\varphi) = \max\left\{0, \sum_{t=0}^{\infty}(1-\delta)^t \pi(\varphi)\right\} = \max\left\{0, \frac{1}{\delta}\pi(\varphi)\right\},$$

where the dependence of $\pi(\varphi)$ on $R$ and $P$ from (5) is understood. Thus, $\varphi^* = \inf\{\varphi : v(\varphi) > 0\}$ identifies the lowest productivity level (hereafter referred to as the cutoff level) of producing firms. Since $\pi(0) = -f$ is negative, $\pi(\varphi^*)$ must be equal to zero. This will be referred to as the zero cutoff profit condition.

Any entering firm drawing a productivity level $\varphi < \varphi^*$ will immediately exit and never produce. Since subsequent firm exit is assumed to be uncorrelated with productivity, the exit process will not affect the equilibrium productivity distribution $\mu(\varphi)$. This distribution must then be determined by the initial productivity draw, conditional on successful entry. Hence, $\mu(\varphi)$ is the conditional distribution of $g(\varphi)$ on $[\varphi^*, \infty)$:

$$\text{(8)} \qquad \mu(\varphi) = \begin{cases} \dfrac{g(\varphi)}{1-G(\varphi^*)} & \text{if } \varphi \geq \varphi^*, \\ 0 & \text{otherwise,} \end{cases}$$

and $p_{in} \equiv 1 - G(\varphi^*)$ is the ex-ante probability of successful entry.[13] This defines the aggregate productivity level $\tilde{\varphi}$ as a function of the cutoff level $\varphi^*$:[14]

$$\text{(9)} \qquad \tilde{\varphi}(\varphi^*) = \left[\frac{1}{1-G(\varphi^*)}\int_{\varphi^*}^{\infty} \varphi^{\sigma-1} g(\varphi)\, d\varphi\right]^{\frac{1}{\sigma-1}}.$$

The assumption of a finite $\tilde{\varphi}$ imposes certain restrictions on the size of the upper tail of the distribution $g(\varphi)$: the $(\sigma-1)$th uncentered moment of $g(\varphi)$ must be finite. Equation (8) clearly shows how the shape of the equilibrium distribution of productivity levels is tied to the exogenous ex-ante distribution $g(\varphi)$ while allowing the range of productivity levels (indexed by the cutoff $\varphi^*$) to be endogenously determined. Equation (9) then shows how this endogenous range affects the aggregate productivity level.

[12]Again, this is assumed for simplicity. The probability of exit $\delta$ introduces an effect similar to time discounting. Modeling an additional time discount factor would not qualitatively change any of the results.

[13]The equilibrium distribution $\mu(\varphi)$ can be determined from the distribution of initial productivity with certainty by applying a law of large numbers to $g(\varphi)$. See Hopenhayn (1992a, note 5) for further details.

[14]This dependence of $\tilde{\varphi}$ on $\varphi^*$ is understood when it is subsequently written without its argument.

### 3.1. *Zero Cutoff Profit Condition*

Since the average productivity level $\tilde{\varphi}$ is completely determined by the cutoff productivity level $\varphi^*$, the average profit and revenue levels are also tied to the cutoff level $\varphi^*$ (see (6)):

$$\bar{r}=r(\tilde{\varphi})=\left[\frac{\tilde{\varphi}(\varphi^*)}{\varphi^*}\right]^{\sigma-1}r(\varphi^*), \qquad \bar{\pi}=\pi(\tilde{\varphi})=\left[\frac{\tilde{\varphi}(\varphi^*)}{\varphi^*}\right]^{\sigma-1}\frac{r(\varphi^*)}{\sigma}-f.$$

The zero cutoff profit condition, by pinning down the revenue of the cutoff firm, then implies a relationship between the average profit per firm and the cutoff productivity level:

$$\pi(\varphi^*)=0 \iff r(\varphi^*)=\sigma f \iff \bar{\pi}=fk(\varphi^*), \tag{10}$$

where $k(\varphi^*)=[\tilde{\varphi}(\varphi^*)/\varphi^*]^{\sigma-1}-1$.

### 3.2. *Free Entry and the Value of Firms*

Since all incumbent firms—other than the cutoff firm—earn positive profits, the average profit level $\bar{\pi}$ must be positive. In fact, the expectation of future positive profits is the only reason that firms consider sinking the investment cost $f_e$ required for entry. Let $\bar{v}$ represent the present value of the average profit flows: $\bar{v}=\sum_{t=0}^{\infty}(1-\delta)^t\bar{\pi}=(1/\delta)\bar{\pi}$. Also $\bar{v}$ is the average value of firms, conditional on successful entry: $\bar{v}=\int_{\varphi^*}^{\infty}v(\varphi)\mu(\varphi)d\varphi$. Further define $v_e$ to be the net value of entry:

$$v_e=p_{in}\bar{v}-f_e=\frac{1-G(\varphi^*)}{\delta}\bar{\pi}-f_e. \tag{11}$$

If this value were negative, no firm would want to enter. In any equilibrium where entry is unrestricted, this value could further not be positive since the mass of prospective entrants is unbounded.

## 4. EQUILIBRIUM IN A CLOSED ECONOMY

The free entry (FE) and zero cutoff profit (ZCP) conditions represent two different relationships linking the average profit level $\bar{\pi}$ with the cutoff productivity level $\varphi^*$ (see (10) and (11)):

$$\begin{aligned} &\bar{\pi}=fk(\varphi^*) && \text{(ZCP)},\\ &\bar{\pi}=\frac{\delta f_e}{1-G(\varphi^*)} && \text{(FE)}. \end{aligned} \tag{12}$$

In $(\varphi, \pi)$ space, the FE curve is increasing and is cut by the ZCP curve only once from above (see Appendix for proof). This ensures the existence and

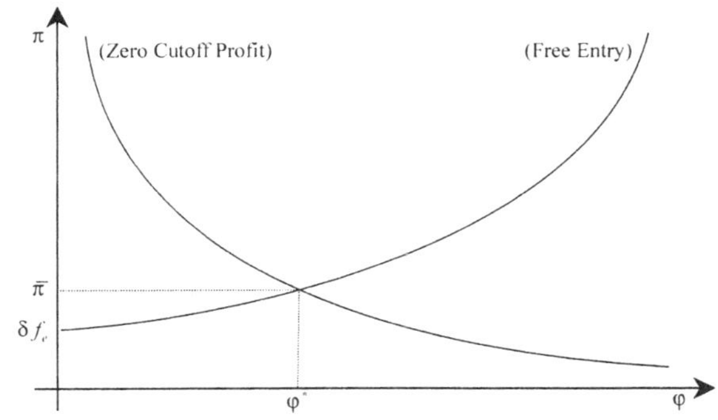


FIGURE 1.—Determination of the equilibrium cutoff $\varphi^*$ and average profit $\bar{\pi}$.

uniqueness of the equilibrium $\varphi^*$ and $\bar{\pi}$, which is graphically represented in Figure 1.[15]

In a stationary equilibrium, the aggregate variables must also remain constant over time. This requires a mass $M_e$ of new entrants in every period, such that the mass of successful entrants, $p_{in}M_e$, exactly replaces the mass $\delta M$ of incumbents who are hit with the bad shock and exit: $p_{in}M_e = \delta M$. The equilibrium distribution of productivity $\mu(\varphi)$ is not affected by this simultaneous entry and exit since the successful entrants and failing incumbents have the same distribution of productivity levels. The labor used by these new entrants for investment purposes must, of course, be reflected in the accounting for aggregate labor $L$, and affects the aggregate labor available for production: $L = L_p + L_e$ where $L_p$ and $L_e$ represent, respectively, the aggregate labor used for production and investment (by new entrants). Aggregate payments to production workers $L_p$ must match the difference between aggregate revenue and profit: $L_p = R - \Pi$ (this is also the labor market clearing condition for production workers). The market clearing condition for investment workers requires $L_e = M_e f_e$. Using the aggregate stability condition, $p_{in}M_e = \delta M$, and the free entry condition, $\bar{\pi} = \delta f_e/[1 - G(\varphi^*)]$, $L_e$ can be written:

$$L_e = M_e f_e = \frac{\delta M}{p_{in}} f_e = M\bar{\pi} = \Pi.$$

Thus, aggregate revenue $R = L_p + \Pi = L_p + L_e$ must also equal the total payments to labor $L$ and is therefore exogenously fixed by this index of country

[15]The ZCP curve need not be decreasing everywhere as represented in the graph. However, it will monotonically decrease from infinity to zero for $\varphi^* \in (0, +\infty)$ as shown in the graph if $g(\varphi)$ belongs to one of several common families of distributions: lognormal, exponential, gamma, Weibul, or truncations on $(0, +\infty)$ of the normal, logistic, extreme value, or Laplace distributions. (A sufficient condition is that $g(\varphi)\varphi/[1 - G(\varphi)]$ be increasing to infinity on $(0, +\infty)$.)

size.[16] The mass of producing firms in any period can then be determined from the average profit level using

$$(13) \qquad M = \frac{R}{\bar{r}} = \frac{L}{\sigma(\bar{\pi} + f)}.$$

This, in turn, determines the equilibrium price index $P = M^{1/(1-\sigma)} p(\tilde{\varphi}) = M^{1/(1-\sigma)} / \rho\tilde{\varphi}$, which completes the characterization of the unique stationary equilibrium in the closed economy.

### 4.1. *Analysis of the Equilibrium*

All the firm-level variables—the productivity cutoff $\varphi^*$ and average $\tilde{\varphi}$, and the average firm profit $\bar{\pi}$ and revenue $\bar{r}$—are independent of the country size $L$. As indicated by (13), the mass of firms increases proportionally with country size, although the distribution of firm productivity levels $\mu(\varphi)$ remains unchanged. Welfare per worker, given by

$$(14) \qquad W = P^{-1} = M^{\frac{1}{\sigma-1}} \rho\tilde{\varphi},$$

is higher in a larger country due only to increased product variety. This influence of country size on the determination of aggregate variables is identical to that derived by Krugman (1980) with representative firms. Once $\tilde{\varphi}$ and $\bar{\pi}$ are determined, the aggregate outcome predicted by this model is identical to one generated by an economy with representative firms who share the same productivity level $\tilde{\varphi}$ and profit level $\bar{\pi}$. On the other hand, this model with heterogeneous firms explains how the aggregate productivity level $\tilde{\varphi}$ and the average firm profit level $\bar{\pi}$ are endogenously determined and how both can change in response to various shocks. In particular, a country's production technology (referenced by the distribution $g(\varphi)$) need not change in order to induce changes in aggregate productivity. In the following sections, I argue that the exposure of a country to trade creates precisely the type of shock that induces reallocations between firms and generates increases in aggregate productivity. These results cannot be explained by representative firm models where the aggregate productivity level is exogenously given as the productivity level common to all firms. Changes in aggregate productivity can then only result from changes in firm level technology and not from reallocations.

[16]It is important to emphasize that this result is not a direct consequence of aggregation and market clearing conditions: it is a property of the model's stationary equilibrium. Aggregate income need not necessarily equal the payments to all workers, since there may be some investment income derived from the financing of new entrants. Each new entrant raises the capital $f_e$, which provides a random return of $\pi(\varphi)$ (if $\varphi \geq \varphi^*$) or zero (if $\varphi < \varphi^*$) in every period. In equilibrium, the aggregate return $\Pi$ equals the aggregate investment cost $L_e$ in every period—so there is no net investment income (this would not be the case with a positive time discount factor).

## 5. OVERVIEW AND ASSUMPTIONS OF THE OPEN ECONOMY MODEL

I now examine the impact of trade in a world (or trade bloc) that is composed of countries whose economies are of the type that was previously described. When there are no additional costs associated with trade, then trade allows the individual countries to replicate the outcome of the integrated world economy. Trade then provides the same opportunities to an open economy as would an increase in country size to a closed economy. As was previously discussed, an increase in country size has no effect on firm level outcomes. The transition to trade will thus not affect any of the firm level variables: The same number of firms in each country produce at the same output levels and earn the same profits as they did in the closed economy. All firms in a given country divide their sales between domestic and foreign consumers, based on the size of their country relative to the integrated world economy. Thus, in the absence of any costs to trade, the existence of firm heterogeneity does not affect the impact of trade. This impact is identical to the one described by Krugman (1980) with representative firms: Although firms are not affected by the transition to trade, consumers enjoy welfare gains driven by the increase in product variety.[17]

On the other hand, there is mounting evidence that firms wishing to export not only face per-unit costs (such as transport costs and tariffs), but also—critically—face some fixed costs that do not vary with export volume. Interviews with managers making export decisions confirm that firms in differentiated product industries face significant fixed costs associated with the entry into export markets (see Roberts and Tybout (1977b)): A firm must find and inform foreign buyers about its product and learn about the foreign market. It must then research the foreign regulatory environment and adapt its product to ensure that it conforms to foreign standards (which include testing, packaging, and labeling requirements). An exporting firm must also set up new distribution channels in the foreign country and conform to all the shipping rules specified by the foreign customs agency. Although some of these costs cannot be avoided, others are often manipulated by governments in order to erect

[17]The irrelevance of firm heterogeneity for the impact of trade is not just a consequence of negligible trade costs. The assumption of an exogenously fixed elasticity of substitution between varieties also plays a significant role in this result. The presence of heterogeneity (even in the absence of trade costs) plays a significant role in determining the impact of trade once this assumption is dropped. In a separate appendix (available upon request to the author), the current model is modified by allowing the elasticity of substitution to endogenously increase with product variety. This link between trade and the elasticity of substitution was studied by Krugman (1979) with representative firms. In the context of the current model, the appendix shows how the size of the economy then affects the aggregate productivity level and the skewness of market shares and profits across firms with different productivity levels. Larger economies have higher aggregate productivity levels—even though they have the same firm level technology index by $g(\varphi)$. Therefore, even in the absence of trade costs, trade increases the size of the "world" economy and induces reallocations of market shares and profits towards more productive firms and generates an aggregate productivity gain.

non-tariff barriers to trade. Regardless of their origin, these costs are most appropriately modeled as independent of the firm's export volume decision.[18]

When there is uncertainty concerning the export market, the timing and sunk nature of the costs become quite relevant for the export decision (most of the previously mentioned costs must be sunk prior to entry into the export market). The strong and robust empirical correlations at the firm level between export status and productivity suggest that the export market entry decision occurs after the firm gains knowledge of its productivity, and hence that uncertainty concerning the export markets is not predominantly about productivity (as is the uncertainty prior to entry into the industry). I therefore assume that a firm who wishes to export must make an initial fixed investment, but that this investment decision occurs after the firm's productivity is revealed. For simplicity, I do not model any additional uncertainty concerning the export markets. The per-unit trade costs are modeled in the standard iceberg formulation, whereby $\tau > 1$ units of a good must be shipped in order for 1 unit to arrive at destination.

Although the size of a country relative to the rest of the world (which constitutes its trading partners) is left unrestricted, I do assume that the world (or trading group) is comprised of some number of identical countries. This assumption is made in order to ensure factor price equalization across countries and hence focus the analysis on firm selection effects that are independent of wage differences.[19] In this model with trade costs, size differences across countries will induce differences in equilibrium wage levels. These wage differences then generate further firm selection effects and aggregate productivity differences across countries.[20] I therefore assume that the economy under study can trade with $n \geq 1$ other countries (the world is then comprised of $n + 1 \geq 2$ countries). Firms can export their products to any country, although entry into each of these export markets requires a fixed investment cost of $f_{ex} > 0$ (measured in units of labor). Regardless of export status, a firm still incurs the same overhead production cost $f$.

## 6. EQUILIBRIUM IN THE OPEN ECONOMY

The symmetry assumption ensures that all countries share the same wage, which is still normalized to one, and also share the same aggregate vari-

[18]The modeling of a fixed export cost is not new. Bernard and Jensen (1999a), Clerides, Lack, and Tybout (1998), Roberts and Tybout (1977a), and Roberts, Sullivan, and Tybout (1995) all introduce a fixed export cost into the theoretical sections of their work in order to explain the self-selection of firms into the export market. However, these analyses are restricted to a partial equilibrium setting in which the distribution of firm productivity levels is fixed.

[19]As was previously mentioned, another way to abstract from endogenous relative wage movements when countries are asymmetric is to introduce a freely traded homogeneous good sector. See Helpman, Melitz, and Yeaple (2002) for an example incorporating this extension.

[20]In these asymmetric equilibria with fixed export costs, large countries enjoy higher aggregate productivity, welfare, and wages relative to smaller countries.

ables. Each firm's pricing rule in its domestic market is given, as before, by $p_d(\varphi) = w/\rho\varphi = 1/\rho\varphi$. Firms who export will set higher prices in the foreign markets that reflect the increased marginal cost $\tau$ of serving these markets: $p_x(\varphi) = \tau/\rho\varphi = \tau p_d(\varphi)$. Thus, the revenues earned from domestic sales and export sales to any given country are, respectively, $r_d(\varphi) = R(P\rho\varphi)^{\sigma-1}$ and $r_x(\varphi) = \tau^{1-\sigma} r_d(\varphi)$, where $R$ and $P$ denote the aggregate expenditure and price index in every country. The balance of payments condition implies that $R$ also represents the aggregate revenue of firms in any country, and hence aggregate income. The combined revenue of a firm, $r(\varphi)$, thus depends on its export status:

$$(15) \qquad r(\varphi) = \begin{cases} r_d(\varphi) & \text{if the firm does not export,} \\ r_d(\varphi) + nr_x(\varphi) = (1 + n\tau^{1-\sigma}) r_d(\varphi) \\ & \text{if the firm exports to all countries.} \end{cases}$$

If some firms do not export, then there no longer exists an integrated world market for all goods. Even though the symmetry assumption ensures that all the characteristics of the goods available in every country are similar, the actual bundle of goods available will be different across countries: consumers in each country have access to goods (produced by the nonexporting firms) that are not available to consumers in any other country.

### 6.1. *Firm Entry, Exit, and Export Status*

All the exogenous factors affecting firm entry, exit, and productivity levels remain unchanged by trade. Prior to entry, firms face the same ex-ante distribution of productivity levels $g(\varphi)$ and probability $\delta$ of the bad shock. In a stationary equilibrium, any incumbent firm with productivity $\varphi$ earns variable profits $r_x(\varphi)/\sigma$ in every period from its export sales to any given country. Since the export cost is assumed equal across countries, a firm will either export to all countries in every period or never export.[21] Given that the export decision occurs after firms know their productivity $\varphi$, and since there is no additional export market uncertainty, firms are indifferent between paying the one time investment cost $f_{ex}$, or paying the amortized per-period portion of this cost $f_x = \delta f_{ex}$ in every period (as before, there is no additional time discounting other than the probability of the exit inducing shock $\delta$). This per-period representation of the export cost is henceforth adopted for notational simplicity. In the stationary equilibrium, the aggregate labor resources used in every period

[21] The restriction that export costs are equal across countries can be relaxed. Some firms then export to some countries but not others—depending on these cost differences. This extension would also generate an increasing relationship between a firm's productivity and the number of its export destinations.

to cover the export costs do not depend on this choice of representation.[22] The per-period profit flow of any exporting firm then reflects the per-period fixed cost $f_x$, which is incurred per export country.

Since no firm will ever export and not also produce for its domestic market,[23] each firm's profit can be separated into portions earned from domestic sales, $\pi_d(\varphi)$, and export sales per country, $\pi_x(\varphi)$, by accounting for the entire overhead production cost in domestic profit:

$$\pi_d(\varphi) = \frac{r_d(\varphi)}{\sigma} - f, \qquad \pi_x(\varphi) = \frac{r_x(\varphi)}{\sigma} - f_x. \tag{16}$$

A firm who produces for its domestic market exports to all $n$ countries if $\pi_x(\varphi) \geq 0$. Each firm's combined profit can then be written: $\pi(\varphi) = \pi_d(\varphi) + \max\{0, n\pi_x(\varphi)\}$. Similarly to the closed economy case, firm value is given by $v(\varphi) = \max\{0, \pi(\varphi)/\delta\}$, and $\varphi^* = \inf\{\varphi : v(\varphi) > 0\}$ identifies the cutoff productivity level for successful entry. Additionally, $\varphi_x^* = \inf\{\varphi : \varphi \geq \varphi^*$ and $\pi_x(\varphi) > 0\}$ now represents the cutoff productivity level for exporting firms. If $\varphi_x^* = \varphi^*$, then all firms in the industry export. In this case, the cutoff firm (with productivity level $\varphi^* = \varphi_x^*$) earns zero total profit ($\pi(\varphi^*) = \pi_d(\varphi^*) + n\pi_x(\varphi^*) = 0$) and nonnegative export profit ($\pi_x(\varphi^*) \geq 0$). If $\varphi_x^* > \varphi^*$, then some firms (with productivity levels between $\varphi^*$ and $\varphi_x^*$) produce exclusively for their domestic market. These firms do not export as their export profits would be negative. They earn nonnegative profits exclusively from their domestic sales. The firms with productivity levels above $\varphi_x^*$ earn positive profits from both their domestic and export sales. By their definition, the cutoff levels must then satisfy $\pi_d(\varphi^*) = 0$ and $\pi_x(\varphi_x^*) = 0$.

This partitioning of firms by export status will occur if and only if $\tau^{\sigma-1} f_x > f$: the trade costs relative to the overhead production cost must be above a threshold level. Note that, when there are no fixed export costs ($f_x = 0$), no level of variable cost $\tau > 1$ can induce this partitioning. However, a large enough fixed export cost $f_x > f$ will induce partitioning even when there are no variable trade costs. As the partitioning of firms by export status (within sectors) is empirically ubiquitous, I will henceforth assume that the combination of fixed and variable trade costs are high enough to generate partitioning, and therefore that $\tau^{\sigma-1} f_x > f$. Although the equilibrium where all firms export will not be

[22]In one case, only the new entrants who export expend resources to cover the full investment cost $f_{ex}$. In the other case, all exporting firms expend resources to cover the smaller amortized portion of the cost $f_x = \delta f_{ex}$. In equilibrium, the ratio of new exporters to all exporters is $\delta$ (see Appendix), so the same aggregate labor resources are expended in either case.

[23]A firm would earn strictly higher profits by also producing for its domestic market since the associated variable profit $r_d(\varphi)/\sigma$ is always positive and the overhead production cost $f$ is already incurred.

formally derived, it exhibits several similar properties to the equilibrium with partitioning that will be highlighted.[24]

Once again, the equilibrium distribution of productivity levels for incumbent firms, $\mu(\varphi)$, is determined by the ex-ante distribution of productivity levels, conditional on successful entry: $\mu(\varphi) = g(\varphi)/[1 - G(\varphi^*)]\ \forall\varphi \geq \varphi^*$. The ex-ante probability of successful entry is still identified by $p_{in} = 1 - G(\varphi^*)$. Furthermore, $p_x = [1 - G(\varphi_x^*)]/[1 - G(\varphi^*)]$ now represents the ex-ante probability that one of these successful firms will export. The ex-post fraction of firms that export must then also be represented by $p_x$. Let $M$ denote the equilibrium mass of incumbent firms in any country. $M_x = p_x M$ then represents the mass of exporting firms while $M_t = M + nM_x$ represents the total mass of varieties available to consumers in any country (or alternatively, the total mass of firms competing in any country).

### 6.2. *Aggregation*

Using the same weighted average function defined in (9), let $\tilde{\varphi} = \tilde{\varphi}(\varphi^*)$ and $\tilde{\varphi}_x = \tilde{\varphi}(\varphi_x^*)$ denote the average productivity levels of, respectively, all firms and exporting firms only. The average productivity across all firms, $\tilde{\varphi}$, is based only on domestic market share differences between firms (as reflected by differences in the firms' productivity levels). If some firms do not export, then this average will not reflect the additional export shares of the more productive firms. Furthermore, neither $\tilde{\varphi}$ nor $\tilde{\varphi}_x$ reflect the proportion $\tau$ of output units that are "lost" in export transit. Let $\tilde{\varphi}_t$ be the weighted productivity average that reflects the combined market share of all firms and the output shrinkage linked to exporting. Again, using the weighted average function (9), this combined average productivity can be written:

$$\tilde{\varphi}_t = \left\{\frac{1}{M_t}\left[M\tilde{\varphi}^{\sigma-1} + nM_x(\tau^{-1}\tilde{\varphi}_x)^{\sigma-1}\right]\right\}^{\frac{1}{\sigma-1}}.$$

By symmetry, $\tilde{\varphi}_t$ is also the weighted average productivity of all firms (domestic and foreign) competing in a single country (where the productivity of exporters is adjusted by the trade cost $\tau$). As was the case in the closed economy, this productivity average plays an important role as it once again completely summarizes the effects of the distribution of productivity levels $\mu(\varphi)$ on the aggregate outcome. Thus, the aggregate price index $P$, expenditure level $R$,

[24]Even when there is no partitioning of firms by export status, the opening of the economy to trade will still induce reallocations and distributional changes among the heterogeneous firms—so long as the fixed export costs are positive. In the absence of such costs (given any level of per-unit costs $\tau$), opening to trade will not induce any distributional changes among firms, and heterogeneity will not play an important role.

and welfare per worker $W$ in any country can then be written as functions of only the productivity average $\tilde{\varphi}_t$ and the number of varieties consumed $M_t$:[25]

$$(17)\quad \begin{aligned} P &= M_t^{\frac{1}{1-\sigma}} p(\tilde{\varphi}_t) = M_t^{\frac{1}{1-\sigma}} \frac{1}{\rho\tilde{\varphi}_t}, \qquad R = M_t r_d(\tilde{\varphi}_t), \\ W &= \frac{R}{L} M_t^{\frac{1}{\sigma-1}} \rho\tilde{\varphi}_t. \end{aligned}$$

By construction, the productivity averages $\tilde{\varphi}$ and $\tilde{\varphi}_x$ can also be used to express the average profit and revenue levels across different groups of firms: $r_d(\tilde{\varphi})$ and $\pi_d(\tilde{\varphi})$ represent the average revenue and profit earned by domestic firms from sales in their own country. Similarly, $r_x(\tilde{\varphi}_x)$ and $\pi_x(\tilde{\varphi}_x)$ represent the average export revenue and profit (to any given country) across all domestic firms who export. The overall average—across all domestic firms—of combined revenue, $\bar{r}$, and profit, $\bar{\pi}$ (earned from both domestic and export sales), are then given by

$$(18)\quad \bar{r} = r_d(\tilde{\varphi}) + p_x n r_x(\tilde{\varphi}_x), \qquad \bar{\pi} = \pi_d(\tilde{\varphi}) + p_x n \pi_x(\tilde{\varphi}_x).$$

### 6.3. *Equilibrium Conditions*

As in the closed economy equilibrium, the zero cutoff profit condition will imply a relationship between the average profit per firm $\bar{\pi}$ and the cutoff productivity level $\varphi^*$ (see (10)):

$$\begin{aligned} \pi_d(\varphi^*) = 0 \quad &\Longleftrightarrow \quad \pi_d(\tilde{\varphi}) = fk(\varphi^*), \\ \pi_x(\varphi_x^*) = 0 \quad &\Longleftrightarrow \quad \pi_x(\tilde{\varphi}_x) = f_x k(\varphi_x^*), \end{aligned}$$

where $k(\varphi) = [\tilde{\varphi}(\varphi)/\varphi]^{\sigma-1} - 1$ as was previously defined. The zero cutoff profit condition also implies that $\varphi_x^*$ can be written as a function of $\varphi^*$:

$$(19)\quad \frac{r_x(\varphi_x^*)}{r_d(\varphi^*)} = \tau^{1-\sigma}\left(\frac{\varphi_x^*}{\varphi^*}\right)^{\sigma-1} = \frac{f_x}{f} \quad \Longleftrightarrow \quad \varphi_x^* = \varphi^*\tau\left(\frac{f_x}{f}\right)^{\frac{1}{\sigma-1}}.$$

Using (18), $\bar{\pi}$ can therefore be expressed as a function of the cutoff level $\varphi^*$:

$$(20)\quad \begin{aligned} \bar{\pi} &= \pi_d(\tilde{\varphi}) + p_x n \pi_x(\tilde{\varphi}_x) \\ &= fk(\varphi^*) + p_x n f_x k(\varphi_x^*) \qquad \text{(ZCP)}, \end{aligned}$$

where $\varphi_x^*$, and hence $p_x$, are implicitly defined as functions of $\varphi^*$ using (19). Equation (20) thus identifies the new zero cutoff profit condition for the open economy.

[25]In other words, the aggregate equilibrium in any country is identical to one with $M_t$ representative firms that all share the same productivity level $\tilde{\varphi}_t$.

As before, $\bar{v} = \sum_{t=0}^{\infty}(1-\delta)^t \bar{\pi} = \bar{\pi}/\delta$ represents the present value of the average profit flows and $v_e = p_{in}\bar{v} - f_e$ yields the net value of entry. The free entry condition thus remains unchanged: $v_e = 0$ if and only if $\bar{\pi} = \delta f_e / p_{in}$. Regardless of profit differences across firms (based on export status), the expected value of future profits, in equilibrium, must equal the fixed investment cost.

### 6.4. *Determination of the Equilibrium*

As in the closed economy case, the free entry condition and the new zero cutoff profit condition identify a unique $\varphi^*$ and $\bar{\pi}$: the new ZCP curve still cuts the FE curve only once from above (see Appendix for proof). The equilibrium $\varphi^*$, in turn, determines the export productivity cutoff $\varphi_x^*$ as well as the average productivity levels $\tilde{\varphi}$, $\tilde{\varphi}_x$, $\tilde{\varphi}_t$, and the ex-ante successful entry and export probabilities $p_{in}$ and $p_x$. As was the case in the closed economy equilibrium, the free entry condition and the aggregate stability condition, $p_{in}M_e = \delta M$, ensure that the aggregate payment to the investment workers $L_e$ equals the aggregate profit level $\Pi$. Thus, aggregate revenue $R$ remains exogenously fixed by the size of the labor force: $R = L$. Once again, the average firm revenue is determined by the ZCP and FE conditions: $\bar{r} = r_d(\tilde{\varphi}) + p_x n r_x(\tilde{\varphi}_x) = \sigma(\bar{\pi} + f + p_x n f_x)$. This pins down the equilibrium mass of incumbent firms,

$$M = \frac{R}{\bar{r}} = \frac{L}{\sigma(\bar{\pi} + f + p_x n f_x)}. \tag{21}$$

In turn, this determines the mass of variety available in every country, $M_t = (1 + np_x)M$, and their price index $P = M_t^{1/(1-\sigma)}/\rho\tilde{\varphi}_t$ (see (17)). Almost all of these equilibrium conditions also apply to the case where all firms export. The only difference is that $\varphi_x^* = \varphi^*$ (and hence $p_x = 1$) and (19) no longer holds.

## 7. THE IMPACT OF TRADE

The result that the modeling of fixed export costs explains the partitioning of firms by export status and productivity level is not exactly earth-shattering. This can be explained quite easily within a simple partial equilibrium model with a fixed distribution of firm productivity levels. On the other hand, such a model would be ill-suited to address several important questions concerning the impact of trade in the presence of export market entry costs and firm heterogeneity: What happens to the range of firm productivity levels? Do all firms benefit from trade or does the impact depend on a firm's productivity? How is aggregate productivity and welfare affected? The current model is much better suited to address these questions, which are answered in the following sections. The current section analyzes the effects of trade by contrasting the closed and open economy equilibria. The following section then studies the impact of incremental trade liberalization, once the economy is open. All of the following analyses rely on comparisons of steady state equilibria and should therefore be interpreted as capturing the long run consequences of trade.

Let $\varphi_a^*$ and $\tilde{\varphi}_a$ denote the cutoff and average productivity levels in autarky. I use the notation of the previous section for all variables and functions pertaining to the new open economy equilibrium. As was previously mentioned, the FE condition is identical in both the closed and open economy. Inspection of the new ZCP condition in the open economy (20) relative to the one in the closed economy (12) immediately reveals that the ZCP curve shifts up: the exposure to trade induces an increase in the cutoff productivity level ($\varphi^* > \varphi_a^*$) and in the average profit per firm. The least productive firms with productivity levels between $\varphi_a^*$ and $\varphi^*$ can no longer earn positive profits in the new trade equilibrium and therefore exit. Another selection process also occurs since only the firms with productivity levels above $\varphi_x^*$ enter the export markets. This export market selection effect and the domestic market selection effect (of firms out of the industry) both reallocate market shares towards more efficient firms and contribute to an aggregate productivity gain.[26]

Inspection of the equations for the equilibrium number of firms ((13) and (21)) reveals that $M < M_a$ where $M_a$ represents the number of firms in autarky.[27] Although the number of firms in a country decreases after the transition to trade, consumers in the country still typically enjoy greater product variety ($M_t = (1+np_x)M > M_a$). That is, the decrease in the number of domestic firms following the transition to trade is typically dominated by the number of new foreign exporters. It is nevertheless possible, when the export costs are high, that these foreign firms replace a larger number of domestic firms (if the latter are sufficiently less productive). Although product variety then impacts negatively on welfare, this effect is dominated by the positive contribution of the aggregate productivity gain. Trade—even though it is costly—always generates a welfare gain (see Appendix for proof).

### 7.1. *The Reallocation of Market Shares and Profits Across Firms*

I now examine the effects of trade on firms with different productivity levels. To do this, I contrast the performance of a firm with productivity $\varphi \geq \varphi_a^*$ before and after the transition to trade. Let $r_a(\varphi) > 0$ and $\pi_a(\varphi) \geq 0$ denote the firm's revenue and profit in autarky. Recall that, in both the closed and open economy equilibria, the aggregate revenue of domestic firms is exogenously given by the country's size ($R = L$). Hence, $r_a(\varphi)/R$ and $r(\varphi)/R$ represent the firm's market share (within the domestic industry) in autarky and in the equilibrium with trade. Additionally, in this equilibrium with trade, $r_d(\varphi)/R$ represents the

[26] Because $\tilde{\varphi}_t$ factors in the output lost in export transit (from $\tau$), it is possible for $\tilde{\varphi}_t$ to be lower than $\tilde{\varphi}_a$ when $\tau$ is high and $f_x$ is low. It is shown in the Appendix that any productivity average that is based on a firm's output "at the factory gate" must be higher in the open economy.

[27] Recall that the average profit $\bar{\pi}$ must be higher in the open economy equilibrium.

firm's share of its domestic market (since $R$ also represents aggregate consumer expenditure in the country). The impact of trade on this firm's market share can be evaluated using the following inequalities (see Appendix):

$$r_d(\varphi) < r_a(\varphi) < r_d(\varphi) + nr_x(\varphi) \quad \forall \varphi \geq \varphi^*.$$

The first part of the inequality indicates that all firms incur a loss in domestic sales in the open economy. A firm who does not export then also incurs a total revenue loss. The second part of the inequality indicates that a firm who exports more than makes up for its loss of domestic sales with export sales and increases its total revenues. Thus, a firm who exports increases its share of industry revenues while a firm who does not export loses market share. (The market share of the least productive firms in the autarky equilibrium—with productivity between $\varphi_a^*$ and $\varphi^*$—drops to zero as these firms exit.)

Now consider the change in profit earned by a firm with productivity $\varphi$. If the firm does not export in the open economy, it must incur a profit loss, since its revenue, and hence variable profit, is now lower. The direction of the profit change for an exporting firm is not immediately clear since it involves a trade-off between the increase in total revenue (and hence variable profit) and the increase in fixed cost due to the additional export cost. For such a firm ($\varphi \geq \varphi_x^*$), this profit change can be written:[28]

$$\Delta\pi(\varphi) = \pi(\varphi) - \pi_a(\varphi) = \frac{1}{\sigma}([r_d(\varphi) + nr_x(\varphi)] - r_a(\varphi)) - nf_x$$
$$= \varphi^{\sigma-1} f\left[\frac{1 + n\tau^{1-\sigma}}{(\varphi^*)^{\sigma-1}} - \frac{1}{(\varphi_a^*)^{\sigma-1}}\right] - nf_x,$$

where the term in the bracket must be positive since $r_d(\varphi) + nr_x(\varphi) > r_a(\varphi)$ for all $\varphi > \varphi^*$. The profit change, $\Delta\pi(\varphi)$, is thus an increasing function of the firm's productivity level $\varphi$. In addition, this change must be negative for the exporting firm with the cutoff productivity level $\varphi_x^*$:[29] Therefore, firms are partitioned by productivity into groups that gain and lose profits. Only a subset of the more productive firms who export gain from trade. Among firms in this group, the profit gain increases with productivity. Figure 2 graphically represents the changes in revenue and profits driven by trade. The exposure to trade thus generates a type of Darwinian evolution within an industry that was described in the introduction: the most efficient firms thrive and grow—they export and increase both their market share and profits. Some less efficient firms still export and increase their market share but incur a profit loss. Some even less efficient firms remain in the industry but do not export and incur losses of both market share and profit. Finally, the least efficient firms are driven out of the industry.

[28] Using $r_d(\varphi) = (\varphi/\varphi^*)^{\sigma-1}\sigma f$ and $r_a(\varphi) = (\varphi/\varphi_a^*)^{\sigma-1}\sigma f$.

[29] Since $\pi_x(\varphi_x^*) = 0$ and $r_d(\varphi_x^*) < r_a(\varphi_x^*)$.

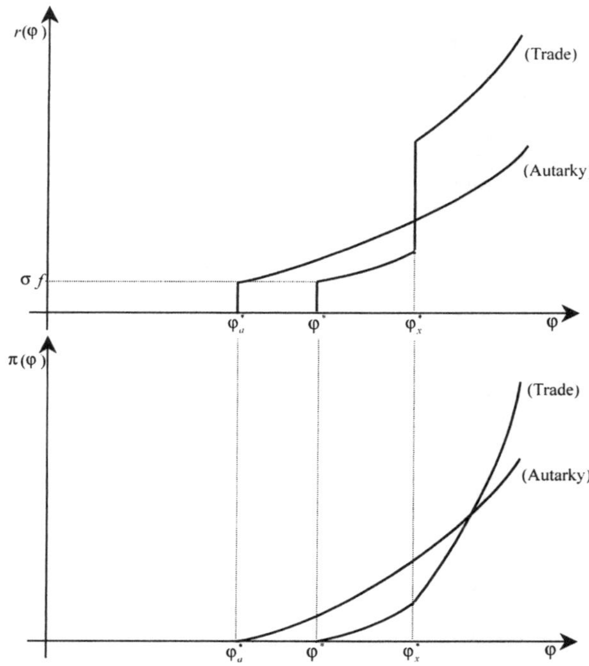


FIGURE 2.—The reallocation of market shares and profits.

### 7.2. *Why Does Trade Force the Least Productive Firms to Exit?*

There are two potential channels through which trade can affect the distribution of surviving firms. The first to come to mind is the increase in product market competition associated with trade: firms face an increasing number of competitors; furthermore the new foreign competitors, on average, are more productive than the domestic firms. However, this channel is not operative in the current model due to the peculiar and restrictive property of monopolistic competition under C.E.S. preferences: the price elasticity of demand for any variety does not respond to changes in the number or prices of competing varieties. Thus, in the current model, all the effects of trade on the distribution of firms are channeled through a second mechanism operating through the domestic factor market where firms compete for a common source of labor: when entry into new export markets is costly, exposure to trade offers new profit opportunities only to the more productive firms who can "afford" to cover the entry cost. This also induces more entry as prospective firms respond to the higher potential returns associated with a good productivity draw. The increased labor demand by the more productive firms and new entrants bids up the real wage and forces the least productive firms to exit.

The current model thus highlights a potentially important channel for the redistributive effects of trade within industries that operates through the exposure to export markets. Recent work by Bernard and Jensen (1999b) suggests that this channel substantially contributes to U.S. productivity increases within manufacturing industries. Nevertheless, the model should also be interpreted with caution as it precludes another potentially important channel for the effects of trade, which operates through increases in import competition.

## 8. THE IMPACT OF TRADE LIBERALIZATION

The preceding analysis compared the equilibrium outcomes of an economy undergoing a massive change in trade regime from autarky to trade. Very few, if any, of the world's current economies can be considered to operate in an autarky environment. It is therefore reasonable to ask whether an *increase* in the exposure of an economy to trade will induce the same effects as were previously described for the transition of an economy from autarky. The current model is well-suited to address several different mechanisms that would produce an increase in trade exposure and plausibly correspond to observed decreases in trade costs over time or some specific policies to liberalize trade. The effects of three such mechanisms are investigated: an increase in the number of available trading partners (resulting, for example, from the incorporation of additional countries into a trade bloc) and a decrease in either the fixed or variable trade costs (resulting either from decreases in real cost levels or from multilateral agreements to reduce tariffs or nontariff barriers to trade). These three scenarios involve comparative statics of the open economy equilibrium with respect to $n$, $\tau$, and $f_x$. The main impact of the transition from autarky to trade was an increase in aggregate productivity and welfare generated by a reallocation of market shares towards more productive firms (where the least productive firms are forced to exit). I will show that increases in the exposure to trade occurring through any of these mechanisms will generate very similar results: in all cases, the exposure to trade will force the least productive firms to exit and will reallocate market shares from less productive to more productive firms. The increased exposure to trade will also always deliver welfare gains.[30]

### 8.1. *Increase in the Number of Trading Partners*

I first investigate the effects of an increase in $n$. Throughout the comparative static analyses, I use the notation of the open economy equilibrium to describe

[30]Formal derivations of all the comparative statics are relegated to the Appendix.

the old equilibrium with $n$ countries. I then add primes ($'$) to all variables and functions when they pertain to the new equilibrium with $n' > n$ countries.

Inspection of equations (20) and (19) defining the new zero cutoff profit condition (as a function of the domestic cutoff $\varphi^*$) reveals that the ZCP curve will shift up and therefore that both cutoff productivity levels increase with $n$: $\varphi^{*\prime} > \varphi^*$ and $\varphi_x^{*\prime} > \varphi_x^*$. The increase in the number of trading partners thus forces the least productive firms to exit. As was the case with the transition from autarky, the increased exposure to trade forces all firms to relinquish a portion of their share of their domestic market: $r_d'(\varphi) < r_d(\varphi)$, $\forall \varphi \geq \varphi^*$. The less productive firms who do not export (with $\varphi < \varphi_x^{*\prime}$) thus incur a revenue and profit loss—and the least productive among them exit.[31] Again, as was the case with the transition from autarky, the firms who export (with $\varphi \geq \varphi_x^{*\prime}$) more than make up for their loss of domestic sales with their sales to the new export markets and increase their combined revenues: $r_d'(\varphi) + n'r_x'(\varphi) > r_d(\varphi) + nr_x(\varphi)$. Some of these firms nevertheless incur a decrease in profits due to the new fixed export costs, but the most productive firms among this group also enjoy an increase in profits (which is increasing with the firms' productivity level). Thus, both market shares and profits are reallocated towards the more efficient firms. As was the case for the transition from autarky, this reallocation of market shares generates an aggregate productivity gain and an increase in welfare.[32]

### 8.2. *Decrease in Trade Costs*

A decrease in the variable trade cost $\tau$ will induce almost identical effects to those just described for the increase in trading partners. The decrease from $\tau$ to $\tau' < \tau$ (again I use primes to reference all variables and functions in the new equilibrium) will shift up the ZCP curve and induce an increase in the cutoff productivity level $\varphi^{*\prime} > \varphi^*$. The only difference is that the new export cutoff productivity level $\varphi_x^{*\prime}$ will now be below $\varphi_x^*$. As before, the increased exposure to trade forces the least productive firms to exit, but now also generates entry of new firms into the export market (who did not export with the higher $\tau$). The direction of the reallocation of market shares and profits will be identical to those previously described: all firms lose a portion of their domestic sales,

[31]There is a transitional issue associated with the exporting status of firms with productivity levels between $\varphi_x^*$ and $\varphi_x^{*\prime}$. The loss of export sales to any given country—from $r_x(\varphi)$ down to $r_x'(\varphi)$—is such that firms entering with productivity levels between $\varphi_x^*$ and $\varphi_x^{*\prime}$ will not export as the lower variable profit $r_x'(\varphi)/\sigma$ no longer covers the amortized portion of the entry cost $f_x$. On the other hand, incumbent firms with productivity levels in this range have already incurred the sunk export entry cost and have no reason to exit the export markets until they are hit with the bad shock and exit the industry. Eventually, all these incumbent firms exit and no firm with a productivity level in that range will export once the new steady state equilibrium is attained.

[32]As pointed out in footnote 26, the productivity average must be based on a firm's output "at the factory gate."

so that the firms who do not export incur both a market share and profit loss. The more productive firms who export more than make up for their loss of domestic sales with increased export sales, and the most productive firms among this group also increase their profits. As before, the exit of the least productive firms and the market share increase of the most productive firms both contribute to an aggregate productivity gain and an increase in welfare.[33]

A decrease in the fixed export market entry cost $f_x$ induces similar changes in the cutoff levels as the decrease in $\tau$. The increased exposure to trade forces the least productive firms to exit ($\varphi^*$ rises) and generates entry of new firms into the export market ($\varphi_x^*$ decreases). These selection effects both contribute to an aggregate productivity increase if the new exporters are more productive than the average productivity level. Although the less productive firms who do not export incur both a market share and profit loss, the market share and profit reallocations towards the more productive firms, in this case, will not be similar to those for the previous two cases: the decrease in $f_x$ will not increase the combined market share or profit of any firm that already exported prior to the change in $f_x$—only new exporters increase their combined sales. However, as in the previous two cases, welfare is higher in the new steady state equilibrium. Both types of trade cost decreases described above also help to explain another empirical feature, reported by Roberts, Sullivan, and Tybout (1995), that some export booms are driven by the entry of new firms into the export markets.[34]

## 9. CONCLUSION

This paper has described and analyzed a new transmission channel for the impact of trade on industry structure and performance. Since this channel works through intra-industry reallocations across firms, it can only be studied within an industry model that incorporates firm level heterogeneity. Recent empirical work has highlighted the importance of this channel for understanding and explaining the effects of trade on firm and industry performance.

The paper shows how the existence of export market entry costs drastically affects how the impact of trade is distributed across different types of firms. The induced reallocations between these different firms generate changes in a country's aggregate environment that cannot be explained by a model based on representative firms. On one hand, the paper shows that the existence of such costs to trade does not affect the welfare-enhancing properties of trade: one of the most robust results of this paper is that increases in a country's exposure to trade lead to welfare gains. On the other hand, the paper shows how the export costs significantly alter the distribution of the gains from trade

[33]See footnote 32.

[34]Over half of the substantial export growth in Colombian and Mexican manufacturing sectors was generated by the entry of firms into the export markets.

across firms. In fact, only a portion of the firms—the more efficient ones—reap benefits from trade in the form of gains in market share and profit. Less efficient firms lose both. The exposure to trade, or increases in this exposure, force the least efficient firms out of the industry. These trade-induced reallocations towards more efficient firms explain why trade may generate aggregate productivity gains without necessarily improving the productive efficiency of individual firms.

Although this model mainly highlights the long-run benefits associated with the trade-induced reallocations within an industry, the reallocation of these resources also obviously entails some short-run costs. It is therefore important to have a model that can predict the impact of trade policy on inter-firm reallocations in order to design accompanying policies that would address issues related to the transition towards a new regime. These policies could help palliate the transitional costs while taking care not to hinder the reallocation process. Of course, the model also clearly indicates that policies that hinder the reallocation process or otherwise interfere with the flexibility of the factor markets may delay or even prevent a country from reaping the full benefits from trade.

*Department of Economics, Harvard University, Littauer Center, Cambridge, MA 02138, U.S.A.; CEPR; and NBER.*

*Manuscript received April, 2002; final revision received April, 2003.*

## APPENDIX A: AGGREGATION CONDITIONS IN THE CLOSED ECONOMY

Using the definition of $\tilde{\varphi}$ in (7), the aggregation conditions relating the aggregate variables to the number of firms $M$ and aggregate productivity level $\tilde{\varphi}$ are derived:

$$\begin{aligned} Q &= \left[\int_0^\infty q(\varphi)^\rho M\mu(\varphi)d\varphi\right]^{1/\rho} \qquad \text{(by definition of } Q \equiv U\text{)} \\ &= \left[\int_0^\infty q(\tilde{\varphi})^\rho \left(\frac{\varphi}{\tilde{\varphi}}\right)^{\sigma\rho} M\mu(\varphi)d\varphi\right]^{1/\rho} \\ &= M^{1/\rho}q(\tilde{\varphi}), \end{aligned}$$

and using the definition of $R$ and $\Pi$ as aggregate revenue and profit,

$$R = \int_0^\infty r(\varphi)M\mu(\varphi)\,d\varphi = \int_0^\infty r(\tilde{\varphi})\left(\frac{\varphi}{\tilde{\varphi}}\right)^{\sigma-1} M\mu(\varphi)\,d\varphi = Mr(\tilde{\varphi}),$$

$$\Pi = \int_0^\infty \pi(\varphi)M\mu(\varphi)\,d\varphi = \frac{1}{\sigma}\int_0^\infty r(\varphi)M\mu(\varphi)\,d\varphi - Mf = M\left[\frac{r(\tilde{\varphi})}{\sigma} - f\right] = M\pi(\tilde{\varphi}).$$

## APPENDIX B: CLOSED ECONOMY EQUILIBRIUM

### B.1. *Existence and Uniqueness of the Equilibrium Cutoff Level $\varphi^*$*

Following is a proof that the FE and ZCP conditions in (12) identify a unique cutoff level $\varphi^*$ and that the ZCP curve cuts the FE curve from above in $(\varphi, \pi)$ space. I do this by showing that

$[1-G(\varphi)]k(\varphi)$ is monotonically decreasing from infinity to zero on $(0,\infty)$. (This is a sufficient condition for both properties.) Recall that $k(\varphi)=[\tilde{\varphi}(\varphi)/\varphi]^{\sigma-1}-1$ where

$$\tilde{\varphi}(\varphi)^{\sigma-1}=\frac{1}{1-G(\varphi)}\int_{\varphi}^{\infty}\xi^{\sigma-1}g(\xi)\,d\xi \tag{B.1}$$

as defined in (9). Thus,

$$\begin{aligned} k'(\varphi) &= \frac{g(\varphi)}{1-G(\varphi)}\left[\left(\frac{\tilde{\varphi}(\varphi)}{\varphi}\right)^{\sigma-1}-1\right]-\left(\frac{\tilde{\varphi}(\varphi)}{\varphi}\right)^{\sigma-1}\frac{\sigma-1}{\varphi} \\ &= \frac{k(\varphi)g(\varphi)}{1-G(\varphi)}-\frac{(\sigma-1)[k(\varphi)+1]}{\varphi}. \end{aligned}$$

Define

$$j(\varphi)=[1-G(\varphi)]k(\varphi). \tag{B.2}$$

Its derivative and elasticity are given by

$$j'(\varphi)=-\frac{1}{\varphi}(\sigma-1)[1-G(\varphi)][k(\varphi)+1]<0, \tag{B.3}$$

$$\frac{j'(\varphi)\varphi}{j(\varphi)}=-(\sigma-1)\left(1+\frac{1}{k(\varphi)}\right)<-(\sigma-1). \tag{B.4}$$

Since $j(\varphi)$ is nonnegative and its elasticity with respect to $\varphi$ is negative and bounded away from zero, $j(\varphi)$ must be decreasing to zero as $\varphi$ goes to infinity. Furthermore, $\lim_{\varphi\to 0} j(\varphi)=\infty$ since $\lim_{\varphi\to 0} k(\varphi)=\infty$. Therefore, $j(\varphi)=[1-G(\varphi)]k(\varphi)$ decreases from infinity to zero on $(0,\infty)$.

## APPENDIX C: Open Economy Equilibrium

### C.1. *Aggregate Labor Resources Used to Cover the Export Costs*

It was asserted in footnote 22 that the ratio of new exporters to all exporters was $\delta$, and hence that the aggregate labor resources used to cover the export cost did not depend on its representation as either a one time sunk entry cost or a per-period fixed cost. As before, let $M_e$ denote the mass of all new entrants. The ratio of new exporters to all exporters is then $p_x p_{in} M_e / p_x M$. This ratio must be equal to $\delta$ as the aggregate stability condition for the equilibrium ensures that $p_{in}M_e=\delta M$.

### C.2. *Existence and Uniqueness of the Equilibrium Cutoff Level* $\varphi^*$

Following is a proof that the FE condition and the new ZCP condition in (20) identify a unique cutoff level $\varphi^*$ and that this new ZCP curve cuts the FE curve from above in $(\varphi,\pi)$ space. These conditions imply $\delta f_e/[1-G(\varphi^*)]=fk(\varphi^*)+p_x n f_x k(\varphi_x^*)$, or

$$fj(\varphi^*)+nf_x j(\varphi_x^*)=\delta f_e, \tag{C.1}$$

where $\varphi_x^*=\tau(f_x/f)^{1/(\sigma-1)}\varphi^*$ is implicitly defined as a function of $\varphi^*$ (see (19)). Since $j(\varphi)$ is decreasing from infinity to zero on $(0,\infty)$, the left-hand side in (C.1) must also monotonically decrease from infinity to zero on $(0,\infty)$. Therefore, (C.1) identifies a unique cutoff level $\varphi^*$ and the new ZCP curve must cut the FE curve from above.

## APPENDIX D: THE IMPACT OF TRADE

### D.1. *Welfare*

Using (14), welfare per worker in autarky can be written as a function of the cutoff productivity level:[35]

$$W_a = M_a^{\frac{1}{\sigma-1}} \rho \tilde{\varphi}_a = \rho \left( \frac{L}{\sigma f} \right)^{\frac{1}{\sigma-1}} \varphi_a^*.$$

Similarly, welfare in the open economy can also be written as a function of the new cutoff productivity level (see (17)):[36]

$$W = M_t^{\frac{1}{\sigma-1}} \rho \tilde{\varphi}_t = \rho \left( \frac{L}{\sigma f} \right)^{\frac{1}{\sigma-1}} \varphi^*. \quad \text{(D.1)}$$

Since $\varphi^* > \varphi_a^*$, welfare in the open economy must be higher than in autarky: $W > W_a$.

### D.2. *Reallocations*

PROOF THAT $r_d(\varphi) < r_a(\varphi) < r_d(\varphi) + nr_x(\varphi) = (1 + n\tau^{1-\sigma})r_d(\varphi)$: Recall that $r_a(\varphi) = (\varphi/\varphi_a^*)^{\sigma-1}\sigma f$ $(\forall \varphi \geq \varphi_a^*)$ in autarky and that $r_d(\varphi) = (\varphi/\varphi^*)^{\sigma-1}\sigma f$ $(\forall \varphi \geq \varphi^*)$ in the open economy equilibrium. This immediately yields $r_d(\varphi) < r_a(\varphi)$ since $\varphi^* > \varphi_a^*$. The second inequality is a direct consequence of another comparative static involving $\tau$. It is shown in a following section that $(1 + n\tau^{1-\sigma})r_d(\varphi)$ decreases as $\tau$ increases. Since the autarky equilibrium is obtained as the limiting equilibrium as $\tau$ increases to infinity, $r_a(\varphi) = \lim_{\tau \to +\infty} r_d(\varphi) = \lim_{\tau \to +\infty}[(1 + n\tau^{1-\sigma})r_d(\varphi)]$. Therefore, $r_a(\varphi) < (1 + n\tau^{1-\sigma})r_d(\varphi)$ for any finite $\tau$.

### D.3. *Aggregate Productivity*

It was pointed out in the paper that aggregate productivity $\tilde{\varphi}_t$ in the open economy may not be higher than $\tilde{\varphi}_a$ due to the effect of the output loss incurred in export transit. It was then claimed that a productivity average based on a measure of output "at the factory gate" would always be higher in the open economy. Define

$$\Phi = h^{-1}\left( \frac{1}{R} \int_0^\infty r(\varphi)h(\varphi)g(\varphi)d\varphi \right) \quad \text{(D.2)}$$

as such an average where $h(.)$ is any increasing function. The only condition imposed on this average involves the use of the firms' combined revenues as weights.[37] Let $\Phi_a = h^{-1}((1/R)\int_0^\infty r_a(\varphi) \times h(\varphi)g(\varphi)d\varphi)$ represent this productivity average in autarky. Then $\Phi$ must be greater than $\Phi_a$—for any increasing function $h(.)$—as the distribution $r(\varphi)g(\varphi)/R$ first order stochastically dominates the distribution $r_a(\varphi)g(\varphi)/R$: $\int_0^\varphi r(\xi)g(\xi)d\xi \leq \int_0^\varphi r_a(\xi)g(\xi)d\xi$ $\forall \varphi$ (and the inequality is strict $\forall \varphi > \varphi_a^*$).[38]

## APPENDIX E: THE IMPACT OF TRADE LIBERALIZATION

### E.1. *Changes in the Cutoff Levels*

These comparative statics are all derived from the equilibrium condition for the cutoff levels (C.1) and the implicit definition of $\varphi_x^*$ as a function of $\varphi^*$ in (19).

[35]Using the relationship $(\tilde{\varphi}_a/\varphi_a^*)^{\sigma-1} = r(\tilde{\varphi}_a)/r(\varphi_a^*) = (R/M_a)/\sigma f = (L/M_a)/\sigma f$.
[36]Using $(\tilde{\varphi}_t/\varphi^*)^{\sigma-1} = r_d(\tilde{\varphi}_t)/r_d(\varphi^*) = (R/M_t)/\sigma f = (L/M_t)/\sigma f$.
[37]This is the standard way of computing industry productivity averages in empirical work.
[38]This result is a direct consequence of the market share reallocation result.

*Increase in n*: Differentiating (C.1) with respect to $n$ and using $\partial\varphi_x^*/\partial n = (\varphi_x^*/\varphi^*)\partial\varphi^*/\partial n$ from (19) yields

$$\text{(E.1)}\qquad \frac{\partial\varphi^*}{\partial n} = \frac{-f_x\varphi^* j(\varphi_x^*)}{f\varphi^* j'(\varphi^*) + nf_x\varphi_x^* j'(\varphi_x^*)}.$$

Hence $\partial\varphi^*/\partial n > 0$ and $\partial\varphi_x^*/\partial n > 0$ since $j'(\varphi) < 0\ \forall\varphi$ (see (B.4)).

*Decrease in* $\tau$: Differentiating (C.1) with respect to $\tau$ and using $\partial\varphi_x^*/\partial\tau = \varphi_x^*/\tau + (\varphi_x^*/\varphi^*)\partial\varphi^*/\partial\tau$ from (19) yields

$$\text{(E.2)}\qquad \frac{\partial\varphi^*}{\partial\tau} = -\frac{\varphi^*}{\tau}\frac{nf_x j'(\varphi_x^*)\varphi_x^*}{f\varphi^* j'(\varphi^*) + nf_x\varphi_x^* j'(\varphi_x^*)} < 0$$

since $j'(\varphi) < 0\ \forall\varphi$, and

$$\frac{\partial\varphi_x^*}{\partial\tau} = -\frac{fj'(\varphi^*)}{nf_x j'(\varphi_x^*)}\frac{\partial\varphi^*}{\partial\tau} > 0.$$

*Decrease in* $f_x$: Differentiating (C.1) with respect to $f_x$ and using $\partial\varphi_x^*/\partial f_x = (\varphi_x^*/\varphi^*)\partial\varphi^*/\partial f_x + [1/(\sigma-1)]\varphi_x^*/f_x$ from (19) and $j'(\varphi_x^*)\varphi_x^* = -(\sigma-1)[j(\varphi_x^*) + 1 - G(\varphi_x^*)]$ from (B.2) and (B.4) yields

$$\frac{\partial\varphi^*}{\partial f_x} = \frac{n[1 - G(\varphi_x^*)]}{fj'(\varphi^*) + nf_x j'(\varphi_x^*)(\varphi_x^*/\varphi^*)} < 0$$

since $j'(\varphi) < 0\ \forall\varphi$, and

$$\frac{\partial\varphi_x^*}{\partial f_x} = \frac{-1}{nf_x j'(\varphi_x^*)}\left[nj(\varphi_x^*) + fj'(\varphi^*)\frac{\partial\varphi^*}{\partial f_x}\right] > 0.$$

*Welfare*: Recall from (D.1) that welfare per worker is given by $W = \rho(L/\sigma f)^{1/(\sigma-1)}\varphi^*$. Welfare must therefore rise with increases in $n$ and decreases in $f_x$ or $\tau$ since all of these changes induce an increase in the cutoff productivity level $\varphi^*$.

## E.2. *Reallocations of Market Shares*

Recall that $r_d(\varphi) = (\varphi/\varphi^*)^{\sigma-1}\sigma f$ ($\forall\varphi \geq \varphi^*$) in the new open economy equilibrium. $r_d(\varphi)$ therefore decreases with increases in $n$ and decreases in $f_x$ or $\tau$ since all of these changes induce an increase in the cutoff productivity level $\varphi^*$. Thus $r_d'(\varphi) < r_d(\varphi)\ \forall\varphi \geq \varphi^*$ whenever $n' > n$, $\tau' < \tau$, or $f_x' < f_x$ (since $\varphi^{*\prime} > \varphi^*$).

The direction of the change in combined domestic and export sales, $r_d(\varphi) + nr_x(\varphi) = (1 + n\tau^{1-\sigma})r_d(\varphi)$, will depend on the direction of the change in $(1 + n\tau^{1-\sigma})/(\varphi^*)^{\sigma-1}$. It is therefore clear that a firm's combined sales will decrease in the same proportion as its domestic sales when $f_x$ decreases since $1 + n\tau^{1-\sigma}$ will remain constant. On the other hand, it is now shown that these combined sales will *increase* when $n$ increases or $\tau$ decreases as $(1 + n\tau^{1-\sigma})/(\varphi^*)^{\sigma-1}$ will then increase.

*Increase in n*: From (E.1),

$$\frac{\partial\varphi^*}{\partial n}\frac{1}{\varphi^*} = -\left[\frac{f}{f_x}\frac{\varphi^* j'(\varphi^*)}{j(\varphi_x^*)} + n\frac{\varphi_x^* j'(\varphi_x^*)}{j(\varphi_x^*)}\right]^{-1}$$

$$= -\left[\tau^{\sigma-1}\frac{(\varphi^*)^{\sigma-1}j(\varphi^*)}{(\varphi_x^*)^{\sigma-1}j(\varphi_x^*)}\frac{\varphi^* j'(\varphi^*)}{j(\varphi^*)} + n\frac{\varphi_x^* j'(\varphi_x^*)}{j(\varphi_x^*)}\right]^{-1} \qquad \text{(using (19))}$$

$$< [(\sigma-1)(\tau^{\sigma-1} + n)]^{-1}$$

since $-\varphi j'(\varphi)/j(\varphi) > \sigma - 1\ \forall\varphi$ (see (B.4)) and $(\varphi^*)^{\sigma-1}j(\varphi^*)/[(\varphi_x^*)^{\sigma-1}j(\varphi_x^*)] > 1$.[39] Hence,

$$\frac{\partial\left[\frac{1+n\tau^{1-\sigma}}{(\varphi^*)^{\sigma-1}}\right]}{\partial n} = \frac{1+n\tau^{1-\sigma}}{(\varphi^*)^{\sigma-1}}\left[\frac{1}{\tau^{\sigma-1}+n} - (\sigma-1)\frac{\partial\varphi^*}{\partial n}\frac{1}{\varphi^*}\right] > 0.$$

*Decrease in $\tau$*: From (E.2),

$$\begin{aligned}
-\frac{\partial\varphi^*}{\partial\tau}\frac{\tau}{\varphi^*} &= \left[\frac{f}{nf_x}\frac{\varphi^* j'(\varphi^*)}{\varphi_x^* j'(\varphi_x^*)} + 1\right]^{-1} \\
&= \left[\frac{f}{nf_x}\frac{[1-G(\varphi^*)][k(\varphi^*)+1]}{[1-G(\varphi_x^*)][k(\varphi_x^*)+1]} + 1\right]^{-1} && \text{(using (B.3))} \\
&= \left[\frac{f}{nf_x}\left(\frac{\varphi_x^*}{\varphi^*}\right)^{\sigma-1}\frac{\int_{\varphi^*}^{\infty}\xi^{\sigma-1}g(\xi)\,d\xi}{\int_{\varphi_x^*}^{\infty}\xi^{\sigma-1}g(\xi)\,d\xi} + 1\right]^{-1} && \text{(using (B.1))} \\
&= \left[\frac{\tau^{\sigma-1}}{n}\frac{\int_{\varphi^*}^{\infty}\xi^{\sigma-1}g(\xi)\,d\xi}{\int_{\varphi_x^*}^{\infty}\xi^{\sigma-1}g(\xi)\,d\xi} + 1\right]^{-1} && \text{(using (19))} \\
&< \left[\frac{\tau^{\sigma-1}}{n} + 1\right]^{-1}
\end{aligned}$$

since $\int_{\varphi^*}^{\infty}\xi^{\sigma-1}g(\xi)d\xi/[\int_{\varphi_x^*}^{\infty}\xi^{\sigma-1}g(\xi)d\xi] > 1$ as $\varphi^* < \varphi_x^*$. Hence,

$$\begin{aligned}
\frac{\partial\left[\frac{1+n\tau^{1-\sigma}}{(\varphi^*)^{\sigma-1}}\right]}{\partial\tau} &= \frac{1+n\tau^{1-\sigma}}{(\varphi^*)^{\sigma-1}\tau}\left[\frac{(1-\sigma)n\tau^{1-\sigma}}{1+n\tau^{1-\sigma}} - (\sigma-1)\frac{\partial\varphi^*}{\partial\tau}\frac{\tau}{\varphi^*}\right] \\
&= \frac{1+n\tau^{1-\sigma}}{(\varphi^*)^{\sigma-1}\tau}(\sigma-1)\left[-\frac{\partial\varphi^*}{\partial\tau}\frac{\tau}{\varphi^*} - \left(\frac{\tau^{\sigma-1}}{n}+1\right)^{-1}\right] \\
&< 0.
\end{aligned}$$

### E.3. *Reallocations of Profits*

*Increase in $n$*: All surviving firms who do not export (with $\varphi < \varphi_x^{*\prime}$) must incur a profit loss since their profits from domestic sales decrease ($r_d'(\varphi) < r_d(\varphi)$) and those who would have exported previously (with the lower $n$) further lose any profits from exporting. Similarly, the firm with productivity level $\varphi = \varphi_x^{*\prime}$ also incurs a profit loss (although the firm exports, it gains zero additional profits from doing so and still incurs the loss in domestic profits). The profit change for all exporting firms (with $\varphi \geq \varphi_x^{*\prime}$) can be written:

$$\begin{aligned}
\text{(E.3)}\qquad \Delta\pi(\varphi) &= \pi'(\varphi) - \pi(\varphi) \\
&= \frac{1}{\sigma}[r'(\varphi) - r(\varphi)] - (n'-n)f_x \\
&= \varphi^{\sigma-1}f\left[\frac{1+n'\tau^{1-\sigma}}{(\varphi^{*\prime})^{\sigma-1}} - \frac{1+n\tau^{1-\sigma}}{(\varphi^*)^{\sigma-1}}\right] - (n'-n)f_x.
\end{aligned}$$

This profit change increases without bound with $\varphi$ and will be positive for all $\varphi$ above a cutoff level $\varphi^\dagger > \varphi_x^{*\prime}$.[40]

[39]Note that $\varphi^{\sigma-1}j(\varphi)$ must be a decreasing function of $\varphi$ since its elasticity with respect to $\varphi$ is $(\sigma-1) + \varphi j'(\varphi)/j(\varphi) < 0$.

[40]The term in the bracket in (E.3) must be positive as $1 + n\tau^{1-\sigma}/(\varphi^*)^{\sigma-1}$ increases with $n$.

*Decrease in $\tau$*: As was the case with the increase in $n$, the least productive firms who do not export (with $\varphi < \varphi_x^{*\prime}$) incur both a revenue and profit loss. There now exists a new category of firms with intermediate productivity levels ($\varphi_x^{*\prime} \leq \varphi < \varphi_x^*$) who enter the export markets as a consequence of the decrease in $\tau$. The new export sales generate an increase in revenue for all these firms, but only a portion of these firms (with productivity $\varphi > \varphi^\dagger$ where $\varphi_x^{*\prime} < \varphi^\dagger < \varphi_x^*$) also increase their profits. Firms with productivity levels $\varphi \geq \varphi_x^*$ who export both before and after the change in $\tau$ enjoy a profit increase that is proportional to their combined revenue increase (their fixed costs do not change) and is increasing in their productivity level $\varphi$:

$$\Delta\pi(\varphi) = \frac{1}{\sigma}[r'(\varphi) - r(\varphi)]$$
$$= \varphi^{\sigma-1} f\left[\frac{1 + n(\tau')^{1-\sigma}}{(\varphi^{*\prime})^{\sigma-1}} - \frac{1 + n\tau^{1-\sigma}}{(\varphi^*)^{\sigma-1}}\right],$$

where the term in the bracket must be positive.

### E.4. *Changes in Aggregate Productivity*

Any productivity average based on (D.2) must increase when $n$ increases or $\tau$ decreases as the new distribution of firm revenues $r'(\varphi)g(\varphi)/R$ first order stochastically dominates the old one $r(\varphi)g(\varphi)/R$: $\int_0^\varphi r'(\xi)g(\xi)\,d\xi \leq \int_0^\varphi r(\xi)g(\xi)\,d\xi \ \forall\varphi$.[41] Note that this property does not hold when $f_x$ decreases as the revenues of the most productive firms are not higher with the lower $f_x$. Nevertheless, the productivity average $\Phi$ will rise when $f_x$ decreases so long as the new exporters are more productive than the average ($\varphi_x^* > \Phi$).

## REFERENCES


AW, B. Y., S. CHUNG, AND M. J. ROBERTS (2000): "Productivity and Turnover in the Export Market: Micro-level Evidence from the Republic of Korea and Taiwan (China)," *World Bank Economic Review*, 14, 65–90.

BERNARD, A. B., J. EATON, J. B. JENSON, AND S. KORTUM (2000): "Plants and Productivity in International Trade," NBER Working Paper No. 7688, forthcoming in the *American Economic Review*.

BERNARD, A. B., AND J. B. JENSEN (1999a): "Exceptional Exporter Performance: Cause, Effect, or Both?" *Journal of International Economics*, 47, 1–25.

——— (1999b): "Exporting and Productivity," NBER Working Paper No. 7135.

——— (2001): "Why Some Firms Export," NBER Working Paper No. 8349.

——— (2002): "The Deaths of Manufacturing Plants," NBER Working Paper No. 9026.

BERNARD, A. B., AND J. WAGNER (2001): "Export Entry and Exit by German Firms," *Weltwirtschaftliches Archiv—Review of World Economics*, 137, 105–123.

CLERIDES, S. K., S. LACK, AND J. R. TYBOUT (1998): "Is Learning by Exporting Important? Micro-dynamic Evidence from Colombia, Mexico, and Morocco," *The Quarterly Journal of Economics*, 113, 903–947.

DAS, S., M. J. ROBERTS, AND J. R. TYBOUT (2001): "Market Entry Costs, Producer Heterogeneity and Export Dynamics," Mimeo, Pennsylvania State University.

DIXIT, A., AND J. STIGLITZ (1977): "Monopolistic Competition and Optimum Product Diversity," *American Economic Review*, 67, 297–308.

HELPMAN, E., M. J. MELITZ, AND S. R. YEAPLE (2002): "Export Versus FDI," NBER Working Paper No. 9439.


[41] Again, this is a direct consequence of the market share reallocation results.

HOPENHAYN, H. (1992a): "Entry, Exit, and Firm Dynamics in Long Run Equilibrium," *Econometrica*, 60, 1127–1150.

——— (1992b): "Exit, Selection, and the Value of Firms," *Journal of Economic Dynamics and Control*, 16, 621–653.

KRUGMAN, P. R. (1979): "Increasing Returns, Monopolistic Competition, and International Trade," *Journal of International Economics*, 9, 469–479.

——— (1980): "Scale Economies, Product Differentiation, and the Pattern of Trade," *American Economic Review*, 70, 950–959.

MONTAGNA, C. (1995): "Monopolistic Competition with Firm-Specific Costs," *Oxford Economic Papers*, 47, 318–328.

PAVCNIK, N. (2002): "Trade Liberalization, Exit, and Productivity Improvements: Evidence from Chilean Plants," *The Review of Economic Studies*, 69, 245–276.

ROBERTS, M. J., T. SULLIVAN, AND J. R. TYBOUT (1995): "Micro-Foundations of Export Booms," Mimeo, World Bank.

ROBERTS, M. J., AND J. R. TYBOUT (1997a): "The Decision to Export in Colombia: An Empirical Model of Entry with Sunk Costs," *American Economic Review*, 87, 545–564.

——— (1997b): *What Makes Exports Boom?* Washington, D.C.: The World Bank.

# [18]

# Plant- and Firm-Level Evidence on "New" Trade Theories

**James R. Tybout**

## Chapter Outline

By relaxing the assumption of perfect competition, the "new" trade theory has generated a rich body of predictions concerning the effects of commercial policy on price–cost mark-ups, firm sizes, exports, productivity and profitability among domestic producers. This chapter critically assesses the plant- and firm-level evidence on these linkages. Several robust findings are identified. First, mark-ups generally fall with import competition. Second, import-competing firms cut back their production levels when foreign competition intensifies. Third, trade rationalizes production in the sense that markets for the most efficient plants are expanded, but large import-competing firms tend to simultaneously contract. Fourth, exposure to foreign competition often improves intra-plant efficiency. Fifth, firms that engage in international activities tend to be larger, more productive, and supply higher quality products. Finally, the short-run and long-run effects of commercial policy on exports and market structure depend upon initial conditions, sunk entry costs, and the extent of firm heterogeneity.

## 1 Introduction

Two decades ago, in an effort to become more relevant, trade economists began developing models with imperfectly competitive product markets. The result was a richer body of theory that describes how commercial policy might affect price–cost mark-ups, firm sizes, productivity, exports, and profitability among domestic producers. The literature also yielded formal representations of the channels through which commercial policy might influence growth. This chapter selectively surveys and interprets the firm- and plant-level evidence that has emerged on these theories.

Section 2 focuses on three static predictions of the "new" trade theory that have attracted attention from empiricists. First, protection can change firms' pricing behavior, thereby affecting the allocative efficiency of the economy and the distribution of real income. Second, when trade policies affect prices, they generally also change the set of active producers and/or their output levels. These adjustments induce productivity changes through scale effects and market share reallocations. Finally, changes in the intensity of foreign competition and/or in firms' opportunities to export can affect their technical efficiency.[1]

Section 3 continues to discuss firm-level responses to policy reforms in terms of pricing decisions, output levels, exports and productivity. However, rather than focus on comparative statics, the models and evidence in this section are explicitly dynamic. They allow for sunk entry costs, firm heterogeneity, and uncertainty. Thus they highlight the relation between responses, expectations and initial conditions. Finally, Section 4 briefly recaps what is known and what we would like to know, then mentions some directions for future research.

## 2 STATIC RESULTS: MARK-UPS, SCALE, AND PRODUCTIVITY

### 2.1 Pricing

#### 2.1.1 THEORY

Except when collusive equilibria are considered, trade models with imperfect competition treat firms' pricing decisions as determined by static profit maximization. Accordingly, the ratio of output prices ($p$) to marginal costs ($c$) is typically a decreasing function of the elasticity of demand ($\eta$) that firms face:

$$\frac{p}{c}=\left(\frac{\eta}{\eta-1}\right). \tag{13.1}$$

It follows that when trade liberalization increases $\eta$, mark-ups should fall.

This kind of elasticity effect has been generated by a variety of modeling devices. For example, under the "Armington assumption" that foreign and domestic goods are imperfect substitutes, the demand elasticity for domestic goods rises as the relative price of foreign goods falls (e.g., Devarajan and Rodrik, 1991). Or, when protection takes the form of non-tariff barriers (NTBs), the removal of a quota can create heightened competitive pressures (Bhagwati, 1978). Finally, when liberalization makes more product varieties available (Krugman, 1979) and/or reduces the market share of domestic firms (Helpman and Krugman, 1985, pp. 85–112), these producers may perceive their demand elasticities to rise.

When collusive equilibria are modeled, trade liberalization can change the payoff to defecting, change firms' ability to punish defectors, or make it more difficult to detect them (Prusa, 1992; Staiger and Wolak, 1989).[2] It is possible that cooperative behavior will become unsustainable and mark-ups will fall. Or, some have argued that collusive firms are likely to use the (exogenous) tariff-distorted price of imports as a reference price.[3] By construction, models that begin from this latter pricing rule predict that trade liberalization will depress the price of import-competing goods.

### 2.1.2 EVIDENCE

Several simple methodologies have been used to link mark-ups to import competition. Prices and marginal costs are rarely observable, so each technique infers mark-ups indirectly. The most common approach is to use the price–cost margin (*PCM*) – that is, sales net of expenditures on labor and materials over sales. If one assumes that unit labor and material costs are flat with respect to output, and we interpret $c$ as short-run marginal costs, this statistic is a monotonic transformation of the mark-up in equation (13.1):

$$PCM_{it} = \frac{p_{it}q_{it} - c_{it}q_{it}}{p_{it}q_{it}} = \frac{p_{it} - c_{it}}{p_{it}},$$

where $q_{it}$ is the physical output of the $i$th firm in period $t$. The *PCM* is also current economic profits ($\pi_{it}$) over sales plus the competitive return on capital over revenues:

$$PCM_{it} = \frac{\pi_{it}}{p_{it}q_{it}} + \frac{(r_t + \delta)k_{it}}{p_{it}q_{it}},$$

where $k_{it}$ is the capital stock, $r$ is the market return on capital, and $\delta$ is the depreciation rate.[4] By this logic, after controlling for the ratio of capital stocks to sales, variables that measure the intensity of foreign competition should contribute nothing to the explanation of price cost margins in industries where free entry drives profits to zero. On the other hand, if economic profits are present ($\pi_{it} > 0$), these variables should correlate negatively with the *PCM* whenever trade liberalization increases demand elasticities or destroys collusive equilibria.

Most analyses of mark-ups based on the *PCM* begin from a simple regression like:

$$PCM_{it} = \beta_0 + \beta_1(k_{it}/p_{it}q_{it}) + \beta_2 I_{it} + \ldots + \varepsilon_{it} \qquad (13.2)$$

where $i$ may index either firms or industries, and $I_{it}$ is a proxy for the intensity of import competition – either the import penetration rate, the effective protection rate, or a license coverage ratio. (Import competition can only be observed at the industry level, so when firm-level data are used, $I_{it}$ takes the same value for all firms within each industry.) When industry-level, cross-sectional data are used, the typical finding is that "the ratio of imports to domestic consumption tends to be negatively correlated with the profitability of domestic sellers, especially when domestic concentration is high" (Schmalensee, 1989, p. 976).[5]

A handful of studies have implemented equation (13.2) with plant-level panel data, controlling for permanent cross-industry differences in technology with industry dummies, and controlling for efficiency-related variation in mark-ups by including plant-level market shares.[6] Results for Mexico (1985–90), Colombia (1977–85), Chile (1979–86), and Morocco (1984–9) all reveal the same basic pattern: "In *every* country studied, relatively high industry-wide exposure to foreign competition is associated with lower [price–cost] margins, and the effect is concentrated in larger plants" (Roberts and Tybout, 1996, p. 196, emphasis in original). This pattern seems robust with respect to measures of import competition. In the case of Mexico, where it was possible to explore alternative measures of protection, the pattern appears whether one uses import penetration rates, effective protection rates, or license coverage ratios (Grether, 1996).

The standard interpretation for these *PCM* findings is that large firms and/or concentrated industries enjoy the most market power, hence their prices are the most responsive to heightened foreign competition. But other explanations are also plausible. For example, it might be that "relatively efficient industries are more profitable, and thus better able to compete against potential imports (low import penetration)" (Roberts and Tybout, 1996, p. 195). Or, concentration might reflect large sunk entry costs instead of market power (e.g., Hopenhayn, 1992). Then, rather than squeezing monopoly profits, unanticipated foreign competition cuts into the revenues that firms had expected would cover their entry costs and makes them sorry, ex post, that they entered (e.g., Albuquerque and Rebelo, 2000). If this latter interpretation is correct, one should observe output contractions in high-sunk-cost industries and exit in the others when trade is liberalized. There is some evidence that this happens, as I shall argue shortly.

An alternative methodology for linking foreign competition and pricing begins from the standard Tornqvist growth decomposition. Suppose the *i*th firm produces output according to $q_{it} = A_{it}h(\mathbf{v}_{it})$, where $\mathbf{v}_{it} = (v_{it}^1, v_{it}^2 \ldots v_{it}^J)$ is the vector of $J$ factor inputs it uses and $A_{it}$ measures its productivity level at time $t$. Then, suppressing time subscripts, output growth can be decomposed into a weighted-average of growth rates in the factor inputs and a residual productivity growth term:

$$d\ln(q_i) = \sum_{j=1}^{J} \frac{\partial \ln(h)}{\partial \ln(v_i^j)} d\ln(v_i^j) + d\ln(A_i). \qquad (13.3)$$

Hall (1988) notes that when product markets are imperfect, this expression can be combined with equation (13.1) and the cost-minimization conditions $c_i = w_j/(\partial q_i/\partial v_i^j)$, $\forall_j$, to link output growth, input growth, productivity growth and mark-ups:

$$d\ln(q_i) = \left(\frac{\eta}{\eta - 1}\right) \sum_{j=1}^{J} \left(\frac{v_i^j w_j}{p_i q_i}\right) d\ln(v_{ij}) + d\ln(A_i). \qquad (13.4)$$

Further, he argues that a regression of output growth on the share-weighted rate of input growth, treating $d\ln(A_i)$ as the mean productivity growth rate plus noise, should reveal the price-cost mark-up as the slope coefficient.

By allowing $\eta$ to vary through time with trade reforms, one can test whether import competition affects mark-ups. Similarly, one can look for trade-related shifts in the mean rate of productivity growth. Several analysts have performed these exercises by fitting generalized versions of equation (13.4) to plant-level panel data.[7] Studying Turkey and Côte d'Ivoire, respectively, Levinsohn (1993) and Harrison (1994) conclude that certain protected sectors had significant mark-ups during the sample period, and that these mark-ups fell with trade liberalization or exchange rate appreciation. Krishna and Mitra (1998, p. 447) repeat the exercise using a panel of Indian firms and report "strong evidence of an increase in competition (as reflected in price-marginal cost mark-ups)" after the 1991 trade liberalization. Thus studies based on Hall's approach are consistent with studies based on the *PCM* – both methodologies suggest that heightened foreign competition forces down mark-ups among domestic firms.

However, Hall's approach is subject to several criticisms. First, profit-maximizing firms should adjust their factor demands in response to productivity shocks. Hence consistent estimators of the slope coefficient in (13.4) require instruments that are correlated with factor stock growth but not with transitory productivity growth. It is difficult to argue that any available instruments satisfy this criterion, so mark-up estimates are probably biased upward, and may exhibit spurious correlation with the trade regime (Abbott et al., 1989).

Second, the framework presumes that firms face no adjustment costs. If some or all of the factors are subject to such costs they will be paid less than their marginal revenue product during upswings (when factor inputs are growing rapidly) and more during downswings (when factor inputs are growing slowly or shrinking). This measurement error is counter-cyclic and productivity growth tends to be *pro*-cyclic, so the estimated mark-up may be understated. Further, if import competition depresses demand for domestic goods, it may appear to eliminate monopoly power when it merely creates under-utilization of capacity.

Third, inputs and outputs are typically poorly measured and year-to-year fluctuations in these variables are particularly noisy. For example, due to gestation lags and changes in capacity utilization, growth in capital stocks is quite different from growth in capital services.[8] Perhaps more importantly, growth rates in physical output are not really observed; what we observe is growth in nominal revenue deflated by a broad price index. If firms that expand rapidly also tend to drive their output prices down relatively rapidly, as one would expect in a differentiated product market, than true output growth is understated when input growth is rapid, and the mark-up estimate should be biased downward.[9] I will discuss these measurement problems further in section 2.3.

## 2.2 The Firm Size Distribution and Its Effects On Productivity

### 2.2.1 Theory

The output changes that accompany price adjustments depend upon whether markets are segmented and whether entry or exit barriers inhibit adjustments in the number of producers. Head and Ries (1999) provide a useful synopsis of some alternative theories. In the absence of collusive behavior, unilateral trade liberalization either reduces firm size (when there are entry/exit barriers or markets are segmented) or leaves it unchanged (when entry and exit are free).[10] Alternatively, when firms collude to slightly undercut the tariff-inclusive price of imports, trade liberalization *cum* free entry and scale economies forces import-competing firms that remain in the market to operate on a larger scale.

As Head and Ries (1999) acknowledge, the invariance of firm size under free entry and no collusion is an artifact of the Dixit–Stiglitz demand system that is used in the models they consider. More generally, free entry is consistent with firm size adjustments whenever trade liberalization induces changes in the demand elasticities ($\eta$) that domestic firms perceive. In particular, when demand elasticities rise with liberalization, price–cost mark-ups are squeezed according to equation (13.1), and this should induce exit until the remaining firms can make up on volume what they lost on margin.

Business and labor groups care about policy-induced output adjustments because they are generally accompanied by job creation or destruction and by capital gains or losses. But trade economists have focused mainly on the ways the changes in the size distribution affect productivity. To summarize these effects, I shall adopt Tybout and Westbrook's (1995) decomposition of industry-wide productivity growth. As before, let output at the $i$th firm in year $t$ be given by $q_{it} = A_{it}h(\mathbf{v}_{it})$, but now write $h(\mathbf{v}_{it}) = \gamma(g(\mathbf{v}_{it}))$ where $g(\mathbf{v}_{it})$ is a constant-returns homothetic function of the input vector, $\mathbf{v}_{it}$, and $\gamma(\cdot)$ captures any scale economies. Also, let $S_{it} = g(\mathbf{v}_{it})\Big/\sum_{k=1}^{n_t} g(\mathbf{v}_{kt})$ be this firm's market share in terms of its input use and let $B_{it} = q_{it}/g(\mathbf{v}_{it})$ be its productivity level. Then the rate of growth in industry-wide average productivity, $B_t = \sum_{i=1}^{n_t} B_{it}S_{it}$, can be decomposed as:

$$\frac{dB_t}{B_t} = \sum_{i=1}^{n_t}\left(\frac{dg_{it}}{g_{it}}\right)(\mu_{it}-1)\left(\frac{q_{it}}{q_t}\right) + \sum_{i=1}^{n_t} dS_{it}\left(\frac{B_{it}}{B_t}\right) + \sum_{i=1}^{n_t}\left(\frac{dA_{it}}{A_{it}}\right)\left(\frac{q_{it}}{q_t}\right) \qquad (13.5)$$

where $\mu_{it} = d\ln(q_{it})/d\ln(g_{it})$ measures returns to scale at the $i$th plant in year $t$. The first right-hand-side term above quantifies efficiency gains due to scale economies at the margin, the second term quantifies gains due to market share reallocations toward relatively efficient producers, and the last term picks up residual intra-firm average efficiency changes that are unrelated to internal scale economies. I shall hereafter refer to these three quantities as *scale effects*, *market share effects* and *technical efficiency effects*.

In most trade models, all firms within an industry are characterized by a common technology and face identical demand conditions, so they expand or contract together in response to liberalization. Productivity gains or losses, when they are present, thus come exclusively from scale effects.[11] However, several models deal explicitly with intra-industry heterogeneity and show how size adjustments (including entry or exit) might affect productivity through the market share effects. For example, Bond (1986) shows how heterogeneous workers might endogenously allocate themselves between entrepreneurial positions and salaried employment. In his "normal" case, protection of the industrial sector increases firm heterogeneity and lowers average productivity by drawing low quality entrepreneurs into managerial roles.

Melitz (2000a) obtains a related set of results in a forward-looking model of steady state trade with firm heterogeneity and imperfect competition. Movement toward freer trade increases a country's imports and erodes each domestic firm's domestic sales and profits.[12] Firms at the lowest end of the productivity distribution contract or exit, while firms at the high end of the productivity distribution expand their exports more than they contract their domestic sales. Accordingly, aggregate productivity improves.

Still another version of the same basic idea can be found in Bernard et al. (2000), who use a static model to study the effects of liberalization on the size and productivity mix of producers. They show that when firms use Bertrand pricing rules to compete, trade liberalization expands the market shares of the most efficient firms by providing them with larger export markets, and it forces firms at the low-end of the productive efficiency spectrum to shut down as they face competition from abroad.

### 2.2.2 The Evidence, Part 1: Size Distributions and Trade

What do we know empirically about size distributions and trade? Many analysts have fit cross-sectional regressions that relate firm size measures to the intensity of import competition, controlling for a few other factors like domestic market size.[13] Whether the competition proxy is the import penetration rate or a measure of the industry-wide rate of protection, this literature finds that import competition reduces the average plant size, if it has an effect at all. Further, studies that include export shares in the explanatory variable set find that average plant sizes are relatively large in the export-oriented industries.

One limitation of this literature is that domestic output appears in the denominator of import penetration rates, so there may be spurious negative correlation between output per firm and this foreign competition proxy. A second problem is that causality may run from size to protection. Concentrated industries that are dominated by a few large producers may have an easier time coordinating lobbying efforts because they face less of a free-rider problem. Finally, most of these studies presume that firms in all industries will adjust to foreign competition in the same way. This runs contrary to theory, which tells us that industries with low entry barriers, like apparel, are likely to show relatively less size adjustment and more adjustment in the number of active firms.

Several more recent studies handle the first two criticisms by measuring exposure to foreign competition with policy variables like tariff rates and license coverage ratios; and by focusing on intra-industry *changes* in average firm size rather than cross-industry differences. Comparing industrial census data before and after Chile's trade liberalization, Tybout et al. (1991, p. 236) find that plants in "sectors with relatively large declines in protection have shown a greater tendency toward employment reductions."[14] Similarly, Tybout and Westbrook (1995) find that during

Mexico's unilateral trade liberalization of 1984–9, firms in the sectors that underwent relatively large reductions in license coverage ratios tended to grow relatively slowly, while firms grew quickly in sectors with rapid export growth.[15]

A subset of studies that deal with the first two criticisms also deal with the third by allowing intra-industry changes in firm size to vary with entry costs (proxied by industry-specific plant turnover rates). Perhaps the best is Head and Ries's (1999), which uses the Canada–US Free Trade Agreement as a natural experiment. Their regressions suggest that "Canadian tariff reductions lowered scale [in Canada] while U.S. tariff reductions increased scale" (p. 309). Further, they confirm that entry barriers affect the way that firms respond: industries with high turnover (low entry costs) show relatively mild reductions in scale in the face of heightened import competition. Roberts and Tybout (1991) obtain similar findings by contrasting industry-specific size distributions in Chile and Colombia and relating them to cross-country industry-specific differences in effective protection.

### 2.2.3 THE EVIDENCE, PART 2: TRADE-INDUCED SIZE ADJUSTMENTS AND SCALE EFFICIENCY

In sum, the finding that foreign competition is associated with smaller firms in import-competing industries seems robust. There is also some evidence that foreign liberalization increases the size of exporting firms. We might reasonably ask, then, how dramatically these trade-induced adjustments have affected scale efficiency.

Most of the studies that address this question are based on computable general equilibrium (CGE) models, and they suggest that the scale-based efficiency gains when trade is liberalized can range from 1 to 5 percent of GDP.[16] However, these findings are suspect for two reasons. First, while CGE models often predict firm-size expansion in *all* traded goods industries, the econometric evidence clearly suggests that firms in import-competing sectors *contract* when import competition intensifies, at least in the short run. Second, even if exporter expansion were the dominant effect of liberalization, it is unlikely that the gains in scale efficiency would amount to much. Although CGE studies often presume returns to scale ranging from 1.10 to 1.25 at the margin, this is probably a gross overstatement of the extent of unexploited scale economies. Exporting plants tend already to be the largest in their industry (Aw et al., 1997; Bernard and Jensen, 1995, 1997; Bernard and Wagner, 1997; Das et al., 2001). Thus they are not likely to exhibit much potential for further scale economy exploitation. Similarly, since most of the production in *any* industry comes from large plants, scale efficiency losses due to contraction in import-competing sectors are also typically minor (Tybout and Westbrook, 1996).

As an alternative to CGE analysis, Tybout and Westbrook (1995) used panel data on Mexican firms to estimate returns to scale ($\mu_{it}$) as a function of size. Then they combine these estimates with the firm-specific growth rates observed during Mexico's unilateral trade liberalization of 1984–90 to implement equation (13.5). Although the cumulative weighted-average growth rate in output was 53 percent for the manufacturing sector, they find that the associated productivity growth rate due to scale efficiency effects was only one-half of one percentage point. This reflected the fact that large plants were operating in the flat portions of their average cost schedule, and these plants accounted for the bulk of the output adjustments.

## 2.2.4 THE EVIDENCE, PART 3: MARKET SHARES AND PRODUCTIVITY EFFECTS

Of course, scale effects are not necessary to link size adjustments and productivity growth. Trade-induced market share reallocations can affect industry-wide performance so long as firms are heterogeneous in terms of $A_{it}$ (see equation 13.5). What do we know empirically about these effects?

A simple way to address this question is to view firms' sizes as reflecting their productivity.[17] Then, if liberalization causes large firms to expand while small firms contract or exit, the associated market share reallocations should improve efficiency. From this perspective, the very robust finding that larger firms are more likely to export suggests that access to foreign markets allows the most efficient firms to become larger, thus pulling up industry-wide productivity levels.

However, studies that associate *changes* in trade protection with changes in the intra-industry size distribution deliver mixed evidence. Head and Ries (1999) find that large Canadian firms grew the most dramatically with US tariff reductions, and they shrank the most dramatically in response to Canadian tariff reductions. Similarly, Roberts and Tybout (1991) find that shrinkage in response to import competition – proxied by import penetration rates or effective protection rates – was relatively dramatic among the large firms in Chile (1979–85) and Colombia (1977–87). But Dutz (1996) finds that as Morocco dismantled NTBs during the 1980s, *small* plants shrank relatively dramatically and their exit probabilities increased relative to others'. Also, Tybout et al. (1991) find that in Chile, reductions in effective protection between 1967 and 1979 were associated with balanced percentage reductions in employment across the entire size distribution.

These mixed findings could mean that the selection effects emphasized by Melitz (2000a) are not robust, or they could mean that size is a poor proxy for productivity, or both. To get at the latter issue, several studies measure share effects directly by constructing firm- or plant-specific $B_{it}$ trajectories. Tybout (1991) simply uses revenue per worker as his productivity measure and measures share-based gains for Chile (1979–85), Colombia (1977–87) and Morocco (1984–7).[18] He finds that market share reallocations contribute to productivity growth among tradeable goods, but his data span periods of major macro shocks rather than major trade liberalization episodes so it is difficult to argue that the gains are trade-induced. Using the same Chilean data set Pavcnik (2000) measures total factor productivity much more carefully and also finds that the shifting of market shares toward more efficient plants was an important source of efficiency gain during the sample period. However, she does not investigate the link between market share reallocations and foreign competition. Similarly, Liu (1993), Liu and Tybout (1996), Tybout (1991), and Pavcnik (2000) all find that exiting plants were substantially less productive than surviving plants in Chile (and elsewhere), but none of these studies links this gap to import competition or exporting opportunities.[9]

Tybout and Westbrook (1995) have a better basis for inference in the unilateral Mexican liberalization of 1984–9. Using equation (13.5), as well as a similar decomposition based on cost functions, they find that this liberalization was associated with efficiency gains, and that some of these gains were due to market share reallocations. However, they do not find strong evidence that rationalization effects were concentrated in the tradeable goods industries. Similarly, studying the Canada–US FTA, Trefler (2001) finds little evidence that turnover-based productivity gains were concentrated in the industries subjected to the largest tariff reductions.[20]

In sum, market share reallocations (including entry and exit) do matter, but it is difficult to find empirical studies that convincingly link these processes to the trade regime.[21] This is not surprising, given that the effects of import competition on industrial evolution are inherently dynamic, and poorly captured by contemporaneous, reduced-form correlations. I will return briefly to this issue when I discuss transition dynamics in section 4.

## 2.3 Other Intra-firm Productivity Gains

Leaving aside productivity effects due to adjustments in the firm size distribution, there are many other linkages between commercial policy and efficiency gains. These are bundled together in the third right-hand-side (technical efficiency) term in equation (13.5). Some have to do with changes in the incentives to innovate or eliminate waste. For example, foreign competition or access to foreign markets may change the effort that a firm's managers put forth and/or the rate at which they improve their products and processes. However, a diverse body of theory suggests that the direction of change in efficiency hinges critically upon model specifics (Corden, 1974; Goh, 2000; Hart, 1983; Miyagawa and Ohno, 1995; Rodrik, 1992; Scharfstein, 1988; Voustden and Campbell, 1994).

Other effects on intra-firm productivity are more robust. As Ethier (1982) noted, intra-firm productivity gains may accompany trade liberalization if it expands the menu of intermediate inputs available to domestic firms. This allows each producer to match his or her input mix more precisely to the desired technology or product characteristics. Similar comments apply concerning access to capital goods, as de Long and Summers (1991) have stressed.

Trade may also act as a conduit for disembodied technology diffusion if firms learn about products by observing imported varieties, or by exporting to knowledgeable buyers who provide them with blueprints and give them technical assistance (e.g., Grossman and Helpman, 1991). Similar knowledge transfers may occur when domestic firms enter into joint ventures or sell equity to foreign multinationals, although these activities are less directly related to commercial policy.

Finally, domestic knowledge spillovers further confound the picture. If learning externalities are generated by experience producing a good, then changes in a country's product mix induced by commercial policy can change the rate at which domestic efficiency grows (e.g., Krugman, 1987; Young, 1991). Whether trade liberalization helps or hurts in this respect depends upon which productive processes generate the most positive externalities, and whether they expand or contract as protection is dismantled.

## 2.3.1 THE EVIDENCE, PART 1: PRODUCT VARIETY AND PRODUCTIVITY

Very little firm-level empirical work has been done on the popular notion that increases in the menu of available inputs improve productivity. This lack of micro evidence reflects practical difficulties with identifying a firm's desired input mix, observing the actual input mix, and relating discrepancies between the two to measures of firm performance. It may also reflect a presumption that diversification of input bundles makes input use more heterogeneous at the industry level but not at the firm level.

Feenstra et al. (1992) provide the only exception I am aware of.[22] They argue that Korean conglomerates (*chaebols*) are vertically integrated, and thus when new intermediate producers join a conglomerate they effectively diversify the input menu for its final goods producers. Regressions confirm that, over a four year period, total factor productivity growth among final goods producers in 45 *chaebols* was positively correlated with the fraction of input expenditure going to new intra-*chaebol* intermediate goods suppliers.

This innovative study provides tantalizing evidence that input diversification contributes to productivity gains. However, data limitations prevent the authors from observing the connection between input variety and productivity as directly as one would like. Simultaneity bias is also an issue, since *chaebol*s with high productivity growth are probably inclined to expand and incorporate new firms regardless of whether input diversification occurs.

## 2.3.2 THE EVIDENCE, PART 2: IMPORT DISCIPLINE EFFECTS

It is much more common to relate firm-level productivity measures to proxies for the vigor of import competition. Most micro empirical studies that do so are based on first- or second-order approximations to the production function $q_{it} = A_{it}h(\mathbf{v}_{it})$, expressing the log of productivity, $\ln(A_{it})$, as a function of import competition proxies, $I_{it}$, and noise. In the first-order (Cobb–Douglas) case, this amounts to estimating:

$$\ln(q_i) = \sum_{j=1}^{J} \beta_i \ln(v_{ij}) + \gamma I_{it} + \varepsilon_{it} \tag{13.6}$$

Alternatively, the log of productivity can be thought of as a draw from a one-sided productivity distribution (e.g., $\alpha_{it} < 0$) plus an orthogonal transitory shock beyond the control of managers: $\ln(A_{it}) = \alpha_{it} + \varepsilon_{it}$.[23]

$$\ln(q_i) = \sum_{j=1}^{J} \beta_i \ln(v_{ij}) + \alpha_{it} + \varepsilon_{it} \tag{13.7}$$

Then, treating the distribution of $\alpha_{it}$ as dependent upon import competition, one can investigate whether mean productivity levels and/or productivity dispersion respond to trade liberalization.

Regardless of whether one uses equation (13.6) or equation (13.7), one cannot measure import competition at the firm level. Thus its effect is identified by cross-industry or temporal variation in $I_{it}$. The former type of identification is problematic because cross-industry regressions describe long run equilibria, and all industry characteristics – including import penetration rates, protection rates, and concentration – are endogenous in the long run (Schmalensee, 1989). Nonetheless, Caves and Barton (1990) use equation (13.7) to characterize the $\alpha_{it}$ distribution for each US manufacturing industry, and they use cross-industry variation in $I_{it}$ to infer that "import competition (measured by imports' share of total supply) increases efficiency in industries whose domestic producers are concentrated" (p. 111).

Other studies use temporal variation in $I_{it}$ to link import competition and productivity via equation (13.6) or (13.7). As I mention in Tybout (2000, p. 34), these studies "tend to find that trade liberalization is associated with rising average efficiency levels" (Harrison, 1996; Nishimizu and Page, 1982; Pavcnik, 2000; Trefler, 2001; Tybout et al., 1991; Tybout and Westbrook, 1995). Similarly, liberalization drives down measured productivity dispersion relatively more in import-competing industries (Haddad and Harrison, 1993; Pavcnik, 2000; Tybout et al., 1991).[24] Both sets of findings are consistent with the import discipline hypothesis, but they also could reflect the kind of selection effects described by Bond (1986), Melitz (2000a), and Bernard et al. (2000).

The implications of these studies are further clouded by methodological problems. Excepting Pavcnik (2000), they do not deal with the simultaneity bias that results from the dependence of factor inputs on productivity levels. Also, all of the studies use industry-wide price deflators to convert plant-specific revenues to plant-specific measures of physical output. But since products within each industry are heterogeneous, this procedure attributes relative price fluctuation to physical output fluctuation, and it thus confounds efficiency with monopoly power. Trade-induced reductions in measured "productivity" dispersion may be no more than the reductions in mark-ups among firms with market power that I discussed in section 2.1.

Finally, a general problem with this literature is that it tends to equate measured efficiency gains with welfare improvements. Thus when these gains are associated with trade liberalization, they are touted as a beneficial effect of foreign competition. But the costs of productivity gains are often embodied in overheads, license fees, training and other items that do not get measured in the input vector. Further, the benefits these expenditures generate are not fully reaped in the same periods in which they are incurred. I know of no study that attempts to measure the present value of firms' productivity-enhancing expenditures and compare them to the present value of the resulting productivity gains.

### 2.3.3 THE EVIDENCE, PART 3: TRADE AND TECHNOLOGY DIFFUSION

Does trade serve as a conduit for technology diffusion? Many studies have established that exporters tend to be bigger, more skill-intensive, and more productive than their domestically oriented counterparts (Aw and Hwang, 1995; Aw et al., 1997;

Bernard and Jensen, 1995, 1997; Bernard and Wagner, 1997; Chen and Tang, 1987; Handoussa et al., 1986). Further, the case study literature on exporters documents instances in which technologically sophisticated buyers transmit blueprints and proprietary knowledge to the exporting firms.[25] However, there is some doubt as to whether the cross-sectional correlation between performance and exporting mainly reflects causality from the latter to the former. Firms may self-select into export markets and/or be sought out by foreign buyers *because* they are high quality.

Several authors have attempted to resolve this issue by studying temporal *changes* in firms' performance and their relation to export market participation. These studies amount to Granger causality tests based on variants of the autoregressive specification:

$$\ln(A_{it}) = \beta_0 + \sum_{j=1}^{J} \beta_j \ln(A_{it-j}) + \sum_{j=1}^{J} \gamma_j y_{it-j} + \ldots + \varepsilon_{it}, \qquad (13.8)$$

where $y_{it}$ is a dummy variable that indicates whether the $i$th firm exports in period $t$. Causality tests in this context establish whether exporting experience in the past helps explain productivity in the present, once other determinants of current productivity (including previous productivity) are controlled for. Given that $y_{it}$ responds to productivity shocks, the distributed lag $\sum_{j=1}^{J} \gamma_j y_{it-j}$ will be orthogonal to $\varepsilon_{it}$ only when $\varepsilon_{it}$ is serially uncorrelated, so it is key to use a generous lag length ($J$) for the term $\sum_{j=1}^{J} \beta_j \ln(A_{it-j})$.

Fitting a version of equation (13.8) to plant-level panel data from Colombia, Mexico and Morocco, Clerides et al. (1998) find very little evidence that past exporting experience improves performance. Bernard and Jensen (1999, p. 14) obtain similar results using US data: "Exporting does not Granger-cause productivity, but does Granger-cause employment, shipments and wages." On the other hand, Kraay (1997) finds that lagged $y_{it}$ values help explain current productivity among Chinese firms; Bigsten et al. (1999) find evidence that exporting Granger-causes productivity among African firms, and Aw et al. (1997) obtain similar findings using census data from Taiwan and Korea.[26]

There are at least four problems with this literature. First, the contact between an exporting firm and its foreign client may occur well before export flows are actually observed in the data.[27] Second, as with the import discipline literature, there is a strong tendency to interpret productivity gains as good, but no effort to quantify the *costs* of these gains. Third, the measures of performance are quite crude, as discussed in connection with the import discipline literature. Fourth, almost all of these studies focus on single conduits for technology transfer. But international activities like exporting, importing intermediates, importing capital goods, and selling equity abroad are often complementary, so firms pursue them in bundles (Kraay et al., 2001). Studies that focus on one at a time may generate misleading conclusions regarding channels of international technology diffusion.

Kraay et al. (2001) tackle the third and fourth methodological problems using the same data sets that Clerides et al. (1998) used to study learning by exporting.

First, they document that international activities indeed come in bundles – exporting, importing intermediate goods, importing capital goods, and sales of equity to multinationals are clearly not independent activities.[28] Next, by using a nested logit representation of demand for the differentiated products, and by exploiting information on the market share of each product, they are able to separately measure product and process innovations at each firm.[29] Finally, they relate quality trajectories and average cost trajectories to firms' international activities, using generalized versions of equation (13.8). They find that activity histories don't usually help to predict future product quality or reduce average production costs, once the histories of these performance variables are controlled for. Nonetheless, Colombian firms that engage in at least some international activities – especially those that import their intermediate goods – tend to have higher product quality.[30] This finding suggests the kind of static efficiency effect that Ethier (1982) envisioned.

### 2.4 Summary

Measurement and methodological problems plague the literature I have reviewed in this section, but some findings seem robust. First, the evidence suggests that mark-ups fall with import competition. The most likely interpretation is that foreign competition increases the elasticity of demand that domestic firms face. However, it is not clear whether these trade-induced reductions in mark-ups reflect the elimination of market power or the creation of negative economic profits.

Second, contrary to the predictions of many simulation models, import-competing firms cut back their production levels when foreign competition intensifies. This is not consistent with the Helpman and Krugman (1985) monopolistic competition model, under which some domestic plants would exit and the remaining plants would either remain the same size (if their demand elasticities do not change) or expand (if their demand elasticities rise). Instead, it suggests that sunk entry or exit costs are important in most sectors.

Third, trade does seem to rationalize production in the sense that markets for the most efficient plants are expanded. Further, if we discount the methodological problems with measuring productivity, most studies suggest that exposure to foreign competition improves intra-plant efficiency. (At what cost, we don't know.) Finally, while firms that engage in international activities tend to be larger and more productive, it is not obvious whether the activities caused these characteristics or vice versa.

## 3 Transition Dynamics

The theories I have mentioned thus far describe static or steady state equilibria, and the regressions that give them empirical content deal mostly with patterns of contemporaneous correlation. But some important issues are inherently dynamic. For example, when a developing country dismantles its trade barriers and devalues its currency, as the World Bank often recommends, the effect of the new regime on the

Central Bank's foreign currency reserves will depend upon the resulting changes in the export trajectory. Further, the political support for a given reform package will depend upon the associated changes in firms' market values and employment trajectories that business representatives and workers anticipate. All of the literature that I have reviewed thus far is silent on these high profile issues.

The dynamic effects of policy reforms are difficult to characterize because they reflect complex decisions on the part of firms. Faced with an uncertain future, some managers find themselves weighing the earnings effects of shutting down plants and/or firing workers against the associated severance costs and the option value of retaining plants or workers for possibly better days. Others must weigh the sunk costs of breaking into foreign markets, building new plants, and/or hiring workers against the net revenue streams that these activities might generate. Their decisions are further complicated by the need to anticipate the decisions of other managers producing competing products. Below I discuss a nascent literature that tackles the relation between commercial policy reforms and industrial responses in settings with these features.

## 3.1 Export Dynamics

### 3.1.1 Theory

In the past 15 years, several theoretical contributions to the trade literature have incorporated sunk costs and uncertainty in dynamic models. Among the first to do so were the papers by Dixit (1989), Baldwin (1988) and Baldwin and Krugman (1989) on the role of sunk costs and expectations in driving exporters' behavior. Generalizing their specification in anticipation of discussion to follow, let us specify an export profit function for the *i*th firm that depends on the exchange rate ($e_t$), marginal production costs ($c_{it}$), a foreign demand shifter ($x_{it}$), and serially uncorrelated noise ($\varepsilon_{it}$): $\pi^f(e_t, c_{it}, x_t) + \varepsilon_{it}$.[31] Further, let us assume that firms without prior exporting experience must establish distribution channels, repackage their products, and learn bureaucratic procedures. Call the sum of these entry costs for new exporters $\Gamma_S$. Then, defining the indicator variable $y_{it}$ to take a value of unity in periods when the *i*th firm exports and zero otherwise, the pay-off from being an exporter in year *t* may be written as:

$$u(e_t x_{it}, \varepsilon_{it}, y_{it}, y_{it-1}) = \begin{cases} \pi^f(e_t, x_t) + \varepsilon_{it} & if\ y_{it} = 1;\ y_{it-1} = 1 \\ \pi^f(e_t, x_t) - \Gamma_S + \varepsilon_{it} & if\ y_{it} = 1;\ y_{it-1} = 0 \\ 0 & if\ y_{it} = 0;\ y_{it-1} = 0 \end{cases}$$

Presuming that the vector $(e_t, c_{it}, x_t)$ follows a first-order Markov process, risk-neutral managers do best to choose a sequence of decision rules, $y_{it} = g_t(e_t, c_{it}, x_{it}, \varepsilon_{it}, y_{it-1})$, that maximizes their expected profit stream from export market participation: $E_t = \sum_{j=t}^{\infty} u(e_j, c_{it}, x_{ij}, \varepsilon_{ij}, y_{ij}, y_{ij-1})\delta^j$. Equivalently, their patterns of export market participation should satisfy the following Bellman equation:

$$V(e_t, x_{it}, c_{it}, \varepsilon_{it}, y_{it-1}) = \max_{y_{it}} \{\pi^f(e_t, c_{it}, x_{it}) - (1 - y_{it-1})\Gamma_S + \varepsilon_{it} + \delta E_t V(e_{t+1}, c_{it+1}, x_{it+1}, \varepsilon_{it+1}, y_{it})\} \quad (13.9)$$

Here expectations are taken conditioned on $(e_t, c_{it}, x_t)$ and the Markov process that governs this vector's evolution.

This framework implies that seemingly identical policies and macro conditions can lead to different levels of exports, depending upon how many firms have a history of export market participation: when firms have no exporting experience, they weigh the sunk costs of entry against the expected profit stream. But when most firms are already exporters, the aggregate response to export incentives reflects volume adjustments and has little to do with entry costs. Second, firms that begin exporting in response to a shock – say, a large devaluation – may not cease exporting when that shock is reversed. Third, expectations about future exchange rate trajectories and commercial policies may play a critical role in determining whether firms invest in becoming exporters today. Finally, export responsiveness to any shock or regime switch depends critically upon the amount of cross-firm heterogeneity in marginal costs and foreign demand, $x_{it}$. Many firms may be poised on the verge of exporting, or just a scattered few.

### 3.1.2 Evidence

Several studies have explored the empirical relevance of the sunk-cost export model sketched above. Roberts and Tybout (1997) begin from the implication of (13.9) that firms will find it optimal to export whenever:

$$\pi^f(e_t, c_{it}, x_{it}) - (1 - y_{it-1})\Gamma_S + \varepsilon_{it} + \delta[E_t V(e_{t+1}, c_{it}, x_{it+1}, \varepsilon_{it+1} | y_{it} = 1) - E_t V(e_{t+1}, c_{it}, x_{it+1}, \varepsilon_{it+1} | y_{it} = 0)] > 0$$

The second bracketed term describes the option value of being an exporter in period $t$, that is, the expected current value of being able to export in period $t + 1$ without having to pay sunk entry costs. Accordingly, its magnitude depends upon expectations about the future operating profits one might generate by exporting. Combining terms that depend upon current values of the state variables, the $i$th firm will do best to export whenever:

$$f(e_t, c_{it}, x_{it}) + y_{it-1}\Gamma_S + \varepsilon_{it} > 0,$$

where:

$$f(e_t, c_{it}, x_{it}) = \pi^f(e_t, c_{it}, x_{it}) + \delta[E_t V(e_{t+1}, c_{it+1}, x_{it+1}, \varepsilon_{it+1} | y_{it} = 1) - E_t V(e_{t+1}, c_{it+1}, x_{it+1}, \varepsilon_{it+1} | y_{it} = 0)]$$

Using a reduced form approximation to $f(\cdot)$, and assuming a particular distribution for the error term, $\varepsilon_{it}$, this equation implies a dynamic discrete choice model of export market participation. Bernard and Jensen (1999), Campas (1999), Roberts and Tybout (1997), and Sullivan (1997) have fit this model as a dynamic Probit or logit and tested whether sunk entry costs affect export market participation. This simply amounts to testing whether lagged exporting status affects current status, once the other sources of persistence in behavior have been controlled for: $(x_{it}, e_t, \varepsilon_{it})$. Critically, if other sources of persistence are *not* completely controlled for, this approach to inference mis-attributes serial correlation in exporting status to sunk costs. So it is important to treat $\varepsilon_{it}$ as a serially correlated disturbance when estimating the equation.

The universal finding of these studies is that sunk costs are important. Even after serial correlation in $\varepsilon_{it}$ is treated, the probability that a firm will export, given $(x_{it}, e_t, \varepsilon_{it})$, can be up to 0.70 higher if it exported last period. From this, researchers have typically concluded that export aggregates are subject to important hysteresis effects and that sunk costs matter.

More recently, Das et al. (2001) revisited the question of how sunk costs shape export responsiveness among Colombian chemical producers. Instead of using a reduced-form version of the decision rule, they fit a structural model that explicitly describes the profit function and the autoregressive processes that govern the vector $(x_{it}, c_{it}, e_t, \varepsilon_{it})$. Using their estimates, they then examine the option value of export market participation for each firm: $\delta[E_tV(e_{t+1}, x_{it+1}, \varepsilon_{it+1}|y_{it} = 1) - E_tV(e_{t+1}, x_{it+1}, \varepsilon_{it+1}|y_{it} = 0)$. This expression measures the importance of expectations about the future in shaping exporting decisions. They find that it is quantitatively important for small-scale exporters, whose foreign demand is relatively limited. However, the firms that supply the bulk of total exports earn operating profits that far exceed the option value term. Hence, hysteresis effects are important only for fringe players in the export markets, and *aggregate* exports are relatively insensitive to history or expectations. Put differently, if one is interested only in the aggregates, sunk entry costs and the subtleties they introduce may be ignorable for many industries.[32]

One robust finding concerning exporters is that they tend to sell very small fractions of their output abroad (Aw et al., 1997; Campas, 1999; Sullivan et al., 1995). In principle this could mean that foreign demand for each firm's product is very limited and inelastic, but this is not the way most people view foreign markets. A second explanation is that firms export just enough to exploit duty drawback schemes and purchase the imported intermediates or capital goods at duty-free prices. To my knowledge this hypothesis has not been pursued, although it would be easy to do so. A third hypothesis is that firms export partly to diversify their earnings stream, exploiting the imperfect correlation between foreign and domestic shocks. Small stable shares in foreign markets might be rational under these assumptions.

Maloney and Azevado (1995) develop a simple model of this diversification motive for exports and fit it to firm-level panel data from Mexico. They find, among other things, exchange rate volatility and the covariance between domestic and international demand shocks are significant determinants of export volumes. Hence, for example, when an over-valued exchange rate is allowed to float, the export response may be counter-intuitive.

In sum, the initiation of exports appears to invoke some sunk start-up costs. These costs matter a good deal for marginal exporters, but are unimportant relative to the operating profits that large exporters earn. Thus their effect on aggregate export responses to regime shifts or exchange rate shocks may not be large. Other determinants of export responsiveness that may be relevant include risk diversification considerations and domestic market demand shocks (when marginal costs aren't flat). There is some evidence that the former matters; the latter remains largely unexplored.

## 3.2 Industrial Evolution

### 3.2.1 Theory

Theoretical models of industrial evolution demonstrate how the combination of sunk entry costs with imperfect foresight and cross-firm heterogeneity can lead to continual flux in the population of active firms (Ericson and Pakes, 1995; Hopenhayn, 1992; Jovanovic, 1982). They also describe the implications of this flux in terms of job turnover patterns and productivity growth. However, very little theoretical work has been done on the effects of commercial policy in an economy with these features.

Two exceptions merit note. The first is Melitz (2000a), who focuses on the relation between openness and the steady state distribution of firm types (see section 2). The other is Albuquerque and Rebelo (2000), who abstract from intra-industry heterogeneity to derive some analytical results about dynamic responses to trade liberalization. Only the latter paper deals with transition issues, so I shall focus on it here.

Albuquerque and Rebelo consider an open economy with homogeneous firms in each of two sectors. New firms must pay a sunk fee to initiate production, so incumbents may earn positive profits in steady state without inducing entry and multiple equilibria are possible. Further, responses to policy shocks depend upon the pre-reform equilibrium. When profits net of entry costs are zero in the exportable goods, and when profits *before* entry costs are zero in the import-competing sector, small reductions in the rate of protection should generate entry in the former and exit in the latter. Unanticipated reforms also induce inter-sectoral reallocations of variable factors in the period before entry and exit occur. Pre-announcing eliminates this short-run adjustment period. On the other hand, if the economy begins from an interior steady state and reforms are too mild to trigger entry or exit, the effects of policy reforms are limited to variable factor movements and capital gains or losses for the owners of incumbent firms.

The dichotomy between responses beginning from zero-profit *versus* interior profits is an artifact of the assumption that firms within each sector are homogeneous. Intra-industry heterogeneity will generally mean that operating profits are close to zero for the marginal incumbent, and profits net of entry costs will be close to zero for the marginal entrant. Nonetheless, the results I mentioned above suggest how responses to reforms should depend on the *density* of incumbents and potential entrants near the zero-profit margin.

### 3.2.2 THE EVIDENCE, PART 1: DESCRIPTIVE STUDIES

It is well established that, even within narrowly defined industries, plants are quite heterogeneous in terms of their size and measured productivity (see, for example, the references in section 2.2.2). Also, simultaneous plant entry and exit are the norm, as are market share reallocations and job creation/destruction among incumbent firms (e.g., Baldwin et al., 1998; Davis et al., 1996; Dunne et al., 1989; Roberts and Tybout 1996). These are the stylized facts that inspired the modern theory of industrial evolution and they are commonly cited as evidence of its relevance.

We know much less about the effects of commercial policy shocks on industrial evolution patterns, or how these effects depend upon the initial population of firms. A number of studies document patterns of contemporaneous correlation between openness, firm size distributions, and entry/exit or market-share-based efficiency gains (see section 2). There is also a small amount of evidence relating openness to patterns of job turnover (Levinsohn, 1999).[33] However, these studies tell us little about the dynamic responses to reforms when threshold costs and uncertainty make firms' adjustments forward-looking, gradual, and/or dependent upon initial conditions.

### 3.2.3 THE EVIDENCE, PART 2: A STRUCTURAL MODEL

Lu and Tybout (2000) attempt to go beyond patterns of contemporaneous correlation and quantify these dynamic relationships. Drawing heavily on Ericson and Pakes (1995) and Pakes and McGuire (1994), they develop an empirical model with sunk costs, heterogeneity, and uncertainty. It portrays an import-competing industry populated by a finite number of potential entrepreneur/owners, including those already in the industry (*incumbents*) and those contemplating entry (*potential entrants*). Each incumbent is characterized by a unique product and a time-varying productivity index that summarizes both his product's appeal and his unit production costs. Imports are represented by a single foreign variety whose price responds to exchange rate shocks and commercial policy reforms, but not to domestic producers' behavior.

Entrepreneurs in this industry play a Markov-perfect dynamic game against one another. Each period, each entrepreneur attempts to maximize his discounted net profit stream, given the available information set. Potential entrants choose whether to enter the market, given their privately observed entry costs. Incumbents decide whether to remain in the market or exit, given the privately observed scrap value of their firms. The incumbents who remain active engage in Bertrand–Nash product market competition with one another, given the current price of the import-competing good and a simple logit demand system.

At the beginning of each period, all entrepreneurs learn the productivity level of each incumbent firm (*industry structure*), as well as the current realizations on the number of consumers and the real effective exchange rate (*market conditions*). If an incumbent firm remains in the industry, its productivity evolves from period to period according to a common knowledge exogenous Markov process, as do the exchange rate and the number of consumers. Firms solve for their optimal strategies and make their exit or entry decisions simultaneously. From period to period, the industry structure evolves with entry, exit, and random shocks to each firm's productivity.

Using Colombian panel data on the pulp and paper industry, Lu and Tybout (2000) estimate the demand parameters of their model. Combined with observed market shares these allow them to impute productivity trajectories for each producer, and to estimate the associated Markov processes. Finally, given these primitives, they calibrate the entry cost and exit cost distributions so that simulated plant turnover rates approximate the industry's actual figures.

Lu and Tybout's main computational experiment is to simulate responses to a change in the exchange rate process that gradually intensifies import competition. The impact effect of this regime switch is to squeeze price–cost mark-ups, just as the econometric evidence suggests. However, the new exchange rate regime also discourages entry (but not exit), so over time, the number of domestic producers gradually shrinks. With the menu of varieties falling, elasticities of demand for each variety fall too, allowing the remaining incumbents to restore their mark-ups and cover their operating costs. This transition path suggests that the robust margin squeeze effects and output contraction effects identified by contemporaneous correlation patterns may not be permanent (see sections 2.1 and 2.2 above).

Although consumers initially benefit from cheaper imported goods and cheaper domestic goods, they are ultimately left with fewer domestic varieties at prices close to pre-appreciation levels. Hence, in the scenario that Lu and Tybout analyze, the present value of consumer welfare actually falls with heightened import competition.[34] Producers suffer capital losses, of course, so they are worse off too.

Extra costs are also imposed on workers, who endure higher job destruction rates during the transition period. Indeed, the job turnover effects predicted by this model are implausibly high, suggesting that it should be generalized to include severance costs and/or screening costs, as in Hopenhayn and Rogerson's (1993) simulations. By the same token, the apparent importance of hiring and firing costs means that firms' expectations are critical and suggests that static calculations of the employment effects of trade policies can be very inaccurate.

Finally, this framework provides a conceptually rigorous way to address the question of how changes in the intensity of import competition affect the market-share-based efficiency changes that are described by the second term in equation (13.5). Lu and Tybout (2000) find that this type of efficiency gain is small for two reasons. First, most of the adjustment in varieties comes from less entry rather than more exit. Incumbent firms that are relatively inefficient don't increase the rate at which they jump out of the market because their entry costs are already sunk, their scrap values are small, and they perceive a possibility that conditions will improve in the future. Second, the firms that do enter or exit account for a relatively small fraction of total production. This is consistent with what we actually observe in the data, as discussed in section 2.2.

These simulations are subject to several criticisms. Most fundamentally, they are partial equilibrium and thus do not document the capital gains and growing number of product varieties in sectors that benefit from exchange rate appreciation. Second, they do not permit the number of imported varieties to adjust. If foreign firms face sunk entry costs when breaking into the domestic market, there will probably be some new ones that are induced to enter by the change in the exchange rate regime. Third, the model is highly stylized in many respects, including the demand system, the productivity growth process (which is presumed exogenous) and the distributions for entry costs and scrap values. Nonetheless, at a minimum the model demonstrates that conclusions based on contemporaneous patterns of correlation can be very misleading, and it brings together in a unified framework the phenomena that firms, workers, and consumers care about.

## 4 An Agenda

I shall close with a few observations on directions for future trade research using firm- or plant-level data. First, as the previous section suggests, I am personally enthusiastic about the new insights that we might gain from dynamic structural models that link trade regimes and industrial evolution. These models suffer from some serious limitations, but they integrate many pieces of the response story that were heretofore treated in disjoint literatures. They also provide a basis for counterfactual simulations in the presence of threshold costs, uncertainty and heterogeneous firms. As computers become more powerful and solution algorithms improve I am hopeful that econometrically estimated industrial evolution models can be made more realistic and used for applied policy work.

Second, despite the large volume of research on the link between trade and productivity, there are several senses in which this literature might be improved. One is to get away from pretending that firms in manufacturing industries produce homogeneous products, and to deal with pricing, output and productivity measurement in unified frameworks (e.g., Melitz, 2000b). Another is to tighten the link between theory and tests. Theory has emphasized the effects of enhanced input variety – including both capital and intermediate goods – and, more recently, efficiency gains due to geographic agglomeration. But we have very little direct micro evidence on the importance of either. These are relatively difficult topics to tackle, but creative empiricists should be able to make progress on both fronts.

Finally, although the relationship between trade and wages has attracted considerable attention, we have only limited evidence on the micro details of worker displacement, job-search processes and reemployment patterns that are triggered by changes in the trade regime. The census bureaus of several countries (including the US) have recently devoted some resources to matching household survey data with establishment survey data, so the characteristics of plants and workers can now be analyzed together and workers can be tracked as they change jobs. These matched data sets should provide a much better basis for inference on the employment effects of commercial policy reforms or changes in the exchange rate regime.

### *Acknowledgments*

I am grateful to James Harrigan and participants in workshops at the NBER, the University of Toronto and the University of Texas-Austin for many useful comments.

## Notes

1 I shall ignore the empirical literature on multinationals and foreign direct investment, which is treated in chapter 10.
2 In these models protection takes the form of institutional arrangements for anti-dumping measures.
3 See Head and Ries (1999) for discussion and references.
4 This measure presumes that intermediate input use and labor use are proportional to output, and the proportions are fixed across plants. See Schmalensee (1989) for further discussion of the limitations of *PCM* as a performance measure.
5 See also Lee (1991) and Roberts and Tybout (1996, pp. 188–99) for surveys of the literature on developing countries.
6 "Efficient plants should be larger and have higher profits, so a positive correlation is generally expected between market shares and price-cost margins, regardless of whether firms have market power . . ." (Roberts and Tybout, 1996, p. 196).
7 Generalizations have included allowing for non-constant returns to scale, and letting $\eta$ and the mean productivity growth rate vary across firms. For example, see Harrison (1994).
8 Pakes and Griliches (1984) estimate that it may take several years for newly installed capital to reach full productivity.
9 Klette and Griliches (1996) and Melitz (2000b) discuss the consequences of this measurement problem for estimates of production function parameters.
10 The most common form of entry/exit barrier is sunk start-up costs. Firms will continue to operate so long as their expected earnings stream covers their expected future expenditures, even if *ex post*, they discover they cannot also recoup the sunk costs that they paid to enter (e.g., Albuquerque and Rebelo, 2000). Uncertainty about future market conditions is likely to increase the option value of remaining in operation, effectively compounding persistence in status. Firms that enjoyed excess profits before import competition intensified will also fail to exit.
11 I will not treat external returns to scale because these are nearly impossible to measure.
12 The cases he analyzes are: autarky versus free trade, more versus fewer countries in a customs union, and high versus low non-tariff barriers (at home and abroad).
13 These studies span a wide range of countries. See Baldwin and Gorecki (1986, table 7.1), Caves (1984), Muller and Owen (1985), Scherer et al. (1975), and Schwalbach (1988). Tybout (1993a, table 2a) provides further details on these studies.
14 This pattern is less apparent when size is measured with output or value-added, suggesting that efficiency gains occurred in the import-competing industries.
15 On the other hand, they find no significant cross-industry correlations between firm size and effective protection rates or import penetration rates.
16 See, for example, Brown et al. (1991), Harris (1984), Norman (1990), and Smith and Venables (1988). Tybout and Westbrook (1996) provide a more detailed discussion.
17 The size-productivity linkage is common in models with heterogeneous firms. See, for example, Bernard et al. (2000), Hopenhayn (1992), and Melitz (2000a).
18 His decomposition does not distinguish intra-plant productivity gains due to scale efficiency from other sources of intra-plant gains. Bernard et al. (2000) show that revenue per unit output is a monotonic function of true total factor productivity if firms compete Bertrand.
19 In any case, as Liu and Tybout (1996) point out, the impact of this differential on productivity growth was minor, given that they typically account for a very small fraction of output.

20 Trefler's (2001) intra-industry data are grouped by plant size, so he cannot rule out the possibility that the FTA generated productivity gains through reallocations *within* size classes or through entry and exit.

21 Bernard and Jensen (2000) link entry and exit patterns to trade indirectly by arguing that, with output prices pinned down by international arbitrage, Rybczynski effects should induce net entry in the sectors intense in the factors that are growing relatively rapidly. They confirm this conjecture using data from the US, first with cross-industry regressions at the national level, then with similar regressions at the regional level. They find that where human capital and physical capital have grown relative to unskilled labor, exit rates have been low among skill-intensive goods and high among low-skill goods.

22 While not at the firm level, Feenstra et al. (1999) do use detailed data on trade flows to link sectoral productivity to the diversity of final good and upstream exports.

23 Detailed discussions of this approach to productivity analysis may be found in the "stochastic frontier" literature (e.g., Greene, 1993).

24 There is also evidence that innovative activities are stimulated by import competition. See Blundell et al. (1999).

25 Much of this literature focuses on East Asia. Pack (2000) and Westphal (2002) provides recent surveys.

26 Both Kraay (1997) and Bigsten et al. (1999) are based on annual data with short lag lengths, $J$, and do not provide tests for serial correlation. Hence they may be picking up spurious correlation. Aw et al. (1997) compare censuses at five year intervals, so their study is likely to suffer from this problem.

27 For interesting discussions of the case study literature on pre-exporting contacts with buyers, see Pack (2000) and Westphal (2002).

28 Aw et al. (2001) document similar dynamic complementaries between worker training, R&D, and exporting using multinomial probit models.

29 One unappealing feature of their approach is that one must assume that the ratio of physical output to intermediate input use is constant across all producers in a given four digit industry and geographic region.

30 Given the way that Kraay et al. (2001) impute quality, this is almost a corollary to the finding that firms engaging in international activities have large domestic market shares.

31 Domestic product market conditions are kept out of the analysis by assuming flat marginal cost schedules with respect to output.

32 Using a reduced-form econometric model and descriptive statistics, Campas (1999) draws similar conclusions from Spanish data.

33 Levinsohn finds that job turnover patterns in Chile during the 1980s were not closely linked to commercial policy or exchange rate shocks. He does argue, however, that turnover rates were higher among tradeable goods than among non-tradeables. Thus, liberalization in economies like Chile's should reduce job security, and may meet resistance for the political economy reasons detailed by Fernandez and Rodrik (1991).

34 This result is partly an artifact of the demand system they use, which probably overstates the value consumers place on goods with small market shares.

## References

Abbott, Thomas, Zvi Griliches, and Jerry Hausman 1989: Short-run movements in productivity: Market power versus capacity utilization. Harvard University, Department of Economics, working paper.

Albuquerque, Rui and Sergio Rebelo 2000: On the dynamics of trade reform. *Journal of International Economics*, 51, 21–48.

Aw, Bee-Yan and Amy Hwang 1995: Productivity and the export market: A firm-level analysis. *Journal of Development Economics*, 47, 313–32.

Aw, Bee-Yan, Xiaomin Chen, and Mark Roberts 1997: Firm-level evidence on productivity differentials and turnover in Taiwanese manufacturing. NBER working paper no. 6235.

Aw, Bee-Yan, Mark Roberts, and Tor Winston 2001: Investment in knowledge and the evolution of firm productivity in the Taiwanese electronics industry. Pennsylvania State University, Department of Economics, working paper.

Baldwin, John and Paul Gorecki 1986: *The Role of Scale in Canada–U.S. Productivity Differences in the Manufacturing Sector: 1970–79*. Toronto: University of Toronto Press.

Baldwin, John, Timothy Dunne, and John Haltiwanger 1988: A comparison of job creation and job destruction in Canada and the United States. *Review of Economics and Statistics*, 80, 347–56.

Baldwin, Richard 1988: Hysteresis and the beachhead effect. *American Economic Review*, 78, 773–85.

Baldwin, Richard and Paul Krugman 1989: Persistent trade effects of large exchange rate shocks. *Quarterly Journal of Economics*, 104, 635–54.

Bernard, Andrew and J. Bradford Jensen 1995: Exporters, Jobs and Wages in U.S. Manufacturing, 1976–87. *Brookings Papers on Economic Activity: Microeconomics*, Washington, DC: The Brookings Institution.

Bernard, Andrew and J. Bradford Jensen 1997: Why some firms export: Experience, entry costs, spillovers, and subsidies. Yale University.

Bernard, Andrew and J. Bradford Jensen 1999: Exceptional exporter performance: Cause, effect, or both? *Journal of International Economics*, 47, 1–26.

Bernard, Andrew and J. Bradford Jensen 2000: Who dies? International trade, market structure and plant closures. Dartmouth College, Tuck School of Business.

Bernard, Andrew and Joachim Wagner 1997: Exports and success in German manufacturing. *Weltwirtschaftliches Archiv*, 133, 134–57.

Bernard, Andrew, Jonathon Eaton, Samuel Kortum, and J. Bradford Jensen 2000: Plants and productivity in international trade. NBER working paper no. 7688.

Bhagwati, Jagdish 1978: *Foreign Trade Regimes and Economic Development: Anatomy and Consequences of Exchange Control Regimes*. Lexington: Ballinger for NBER.

Bigsten, Arne et al. 1999: Exports and firm-level efficiency in the African manufacturing sector. University of Montreal, School of Business.

Blundell, Richard, Rachel Griffith, and John van Reenen 1999: Market share, market value and innovation in a panel of British manufacturing firms. *Review of Economic Studies*, 66, 529–54.

Bond, Eric 1986: Entrepreneurial ability, income distribution and international trade. *Journal of International Economics*, 20, 343–56.

Brooks, Eileen L. 2001: Why don't firms export more? Manuscript, Harvard University.

Brown, Drucilla, Alan Deardorff, and Robert Stern 1991: A North American free trade agreement: Analytical issues and a computational assessment, University of Michigan: Department of Economics.

Campas, Jose 1991: Exchange rates and trade: How important is hysteresis in trade? New York University, Stern School of Business.

Caves, Richard 1984: Scale, openness and productivity in manufacturing. In Richard Caves and Lawrence Krause (eds.), *The Australian Economy: A View from the North*, Washington, DC: The Brookings Institution.

Caves, Richard and David Barton 1990: *Efficiency in U.S. Manufacturing Industries*. Cambridge, MA: MIT Press.

Chen, Tain-jy and De-piao Tang 1987: Comparing technical efficiency between import-substituting and export-oriented foreign firms in a developing country. *Journal of Development Economics*, 36, 277–89.

Clerides, Sofronis, Saul Lach, and James Tybout 1998: Is learning by exporting important? Micro dynamic evidence from Colombia, Mexico and Morocco. *Quarterly Journal of Economics*, 113, 903–47.

Corden, W. Max 1974: *Trade Policy and Economic Welfare*, Oxford: Clarendon Press.

Das, Sanghamitra, Mark Roberts, and James Tybout 2001: Micro-foundations of export dynamics. Pennsylvania State University, Department of Economics.

Davis, Steven, John Haltiwanger, and Scott Schuh 1996: *Job Creation and Destruction*, Cambridge, MA: MIT Press.

De Long, J. Bradford and Lawrence Summers 1991: Equipment investment and economic growth. *Quarterly Journal of Economics*, 56, 445–502.

Devarajan, Shanta and Dani Rodrik 1991: Pro-competitive effects of trade reforms: Results from a CGE model of Cameroon. *European Economic Review*, 35, 1157–84.

Dixit, Avinash 1989: Entry and exit decisions under uncertainty. *Journal of Political Economy*, 97, 620–38.

Dunne, Timothy, Mark Roberts, and Larry Samuelson 1989: Plant turnover and gross employment flows in the U.S. manufacturing sector. *Journal of Labor Economics*, 7, 48–71.

Dutz, Mark 1996: Oligopolistic firms' adjustment to quota liberalization: Theory and evidence. In Mark Roberts and James Tybout (eds.), *Industrial Evolution in Developing Countries*, New York: Oxford University Press.

Ericson, Richard and Ariel Pakes 1995: Markov-perfect industry dynamics: A framework for empirical work. *Review of Economic Studies*, 62, 53–82.

Ethier, Wilfred 1982: National and international returns to scale in the modern theory of international trade. *American Economic Review*, 72, 950–9.

Feenstra, Robert, Dorsati Madani, Tzu-Han Yang, and Chi-Yuan Liang 1999: Testing endogenous growth in South Korea and Taiwan. *Journal of Development Economics*, 60, 317–41.

Feenstra, Robert, James Markusen, and William Zeile 1992: Accounting for growth with new inputs: Theory and evidence. *American Economic Review: Papers and Proceedings*, 82, 415–21.

Fernandez, Raquel and Dani Rodrik 1991: Resistance to reform: Status quo bias in the presence of individual specific uncertainty. *American Economic Review*, 81, 1146–55.

Goh, Ai-Ting 2000: Opportunity cost, trade policies and the efficiency of firms. *Journal of Development Economics*, 62, 363–83.

Greene, William 1993: Frontier production functions. New York University, Stern School of Business, working paper no. EC-93-20.

Grether, Jean-Marie 1996: Mexico, 1985–90: Trade liberalization, market structure and manufacturing performance. In Mark Roberts and James Tybout (eds.), *Industrial Evolution in Developing Countries*, New York: Oxford University Press.

Grossman, Gene and Elhanan Helpman 1991: *Innovation and Growth in the Global Economy*. Cambridge, MA: MIT Press.

Haddad, Mona and Ann Harrison 1993: Are there positive spillovers from direct foreign investment? Evidence from panel data for Morocco. *Journal of Development Economics*, 42, 51–74.

Hall, Robert 1988: The relation between price and marginal cost in U.S. industry. *Journal of Political Economy*, 96, 921–47.

Handoussa, Heba, Mieko Nishimizu, and John Page 1986: Productivity change in Egyptian public sector industries after the "Opening," 1973–1979. *Journal of Development Economics*, 20, 53–73.

Harris, Richard 1984: Applied general equilibrium analysis of small open economies with scale economies and imperfect competition. *American Economic Review*, 74, 1016–32.

Harrison, Ann 1994: Productivity, imperfect competition and trade reform: Theory and evidence. *Journal of International Economics*, 36, 53–73.

Harrison, Ann 1996: Determinants and effects of foreign direct investment in Côte d'Ivoire, Morocco, and Venezuela. In Mark Roberts and James Tybout (eds.), *Industrial Evolution in Developing Countries*, New York: Oxford University Press.

Hart, Oliver 1983: The market mechanism as an incentive structure. *Bell Journal of Economics*, 14, 366–82.

Head, Keith and John Ries 1999: Rationalization effects of tariff reductions. *Journal of International Economics*, 47, 295–320.

Helpman, Elhanan and Paul Krugman 1985: *Market Structure and Foreign Trade: Increasing Returns, Imperfect Competition and the International Economy*. Cambridge, MA: MIT Press.

Hopenhayn, Hugo 1992: Entry, exit and firm dynamics in long run equilibrium. *Econometrica*, 60, 1127–50.

Hopenhayn, Hugo and Richard Rogerson 1993: Job turnover and policy evolution: A general equilbrium analysis, *Journal of Political Economy*, 101, 915–38.

Jovanovic, Boyan 1982: Selection and the evolution of industry. *Econometrica*, 50, 649–70.

Klette, Tor J. and Zvi Griliches 1996: The inconsistency of common scale estimators when output prices are unobserved and endogenous. *Journal of Applied Econometrics*, 11, 343–61.

Kraay, Aart 1997: Exports and economic performance: Evidence from a panel of Chinese enterprises. The World Bank, Development Economics Department.

Kraay, Aart, Isidro Soloaga, and James Tybout 2001: Product quality, productive efficiency, and international technology diffusion. Pennsylvania State University, Department of Economics.

Krishna, Pravin and Devashish Mitra 1998: Trade liberalization, market discipline, and productivity growth: New evidence from India. *Journal of Development Economics*, 46, 447–52.

Krugman, Paul 1979: Increasing returns, monopolistic competition and international trade. *Journal of International Economics*, 9, 469–79.

Krugman, Paul 1987: The narrow moving band, the Dutch disease, and the consequences of Mrs Thatcher: Notes on trade in the presence of scale economies. *Journal of Development Economics*, 27, 41–55.

Lee, Norman 1991: Market structure and trade in the developing countries. In Gerald K. Helleiner (ed.), *Trade Policy, Industrialization and Development: New Perspectives*, Oxford: Clarendon Press.

Levinsohn, James 1993: Testing the imports-as-market-discipline hypothesis. *Journal of International Economics*, 35, 1–12.

Levinsohn, James 1999: Employment responses to international liberalization in Chile. *Journal of International Economics*, 47, 321–44.

Liu, Lili 1993: Entry-exit, learning and productivity change: Evidence from Chile. *Journal of Development Economics*, 42, 217–42.

Liu, Lili and James Tybout 1996: Productivity growth in Colombia and Chile: Panel-based evidence on the role of entry, exit and learning. In Mark Roberts and James Tybout (eds.), *Industrial Evolution in Developing Countries*, New York: Oxford University Press.

Lu, Shihua and James Tybout 2000: Import competition and industrial evolution: A computational experiment. Pennsylvania State University, Department of Economics.

Maloney, William and Rodrigo Azevado 1995: Trade reform, uncertainty and export promotion: Mexico 1982–88. *Journal of Development Economics*, 48, 67–89.

Melitz, Marc 2000a: The impact of trade on intra-industry reallocations and aggregate productivity. Harvard University, Department of Economics.

Melitz, Marc 2000b: Estimating productivity in differentiated product industries. Harvard University, Department of Economics.

Miyagawa, Kaz and Yuko Ohno 1995: Closing the technology gap under protection. *American Economic Review*, 85, 755–70.

Muller, Jurgen and Nicholas Owen 1985: The effects of trade on plant size. In Joachim Schwalbach (ed.), *Industry, Structure and Performance*, Berlin: Edition Sigma.

Nishumizu, Mieko and John Page 1982: Total factor productivity growth, technological progress, and technical efficiency change: Dimensions of productivity change in Yugoslavia. *Economic Journal*, 92, 920–36.

Norman, Victor 1990: Assessing trade and welfare effects of trade liberalization. *European Economic Review*, 34, 725–51.

Pack, Howard 2000: Modes of technology transfer at the firm level. University of Pennsylvania, The Wharton School.

Pakes, Ariel and Zvi Griliches 1984: Estimated distributed lags in short panels with an application to the specification of depreciation patterns and capital stock constructs. *Review of Economic Studies*, 51, 243–62.

Pakes, Ariel and Paul McGuire 1994: Computing Markov-perfect Nash equilibria: Numerical implications of a dynamic differentiated product model. *RAND Journal of Economics*, 25, 555–89.

Pavcnik, Nina 2000: Trade liberalization, exit, and productivity improvements: Evidence from Chilean plants. Dartmouth College, Department of Economics.

Prusa, Thomas J. 1992: Why are so many antidumping petitions withdrawn? *Journal of International Economics*, 33, 1–20.

Roberts, Mark and James Tybout 1991: Size rationalization and trade exposure in developing countries. In Robert Baldwin (ed.), *Empirical Studies of Commercial Policy*, Chicago: University of Chicago Press for NBER.

Roberts, Mark and James Tybout (eds.) 1996: *Industrial Evolution in Developing Countries*, New York: Oxford University Press.

Roberts, Mark and James Tybout 1997: The decision to export in Colombia. *American Economic Review*, 87, 545–65.

Roberts, Mark, Theresa Sullivan, and James Tybout 2001: Micro-foundations of export booms. Manuscript, World Bank.

Rodrik, Dani 1992: Closing the technology gap: Does trade liberalization really help? In Gerald Helleiner (ed.), *Trade Policy, Industrialization and Development: New Perspectives*, Oxford: Clarendon Press.

Scharfstein, David 1988: Product market competition and managerial slack. *RAND Journal*, 19, 47–55.

Scherer, Frederic M. et al. 1975: *The Economics of Multi-Plant Operation: An International Comparison Study*, Cambridge, MA: Harvard University Press.

Schmalensee, Richard 1989: Inter-industry studies of structure and performance. In Richard Schmalensee and Robert Willig (eds.), *Handbook of Industrial Organization*, Amsterdam: North-Holland.

Schwalbach, Joachim 1988: Economies of scale and intra-community trade. In Commission of the European Communities, *Research on the "Cost" of Non-Europe: Basic Findings*, vol. 2, Brussels: Commission of the European Communities.

Smith, Alistair and Anthony Venables 1988: Completing the internal market in the European Community. *European Economic Review*, 32, 1501–25.

Staiger, Robert W. and Frank A. Wolak 1989: Strategic use of antidumping law to enforce tacit international collusion. NBER working paper no. 3016.

Sullivan, Theresa 1997: Estimating the manufactured export supply function for Morocco, PhD dissertation, Georgetown University.

Sullivan, Theresa, Mark Roberts, and James Tybout 1995: Micro foundations of export booms. Pennsylvania State University working paper.

Trefler, Daniel 2001: The long and short of the Canada–U.S. Free Trade Agreement. NBER working paper no. 8293.

Tybout, James 1991: Linking trade and productivity: New research directions. *World Bank Economic Review*, 6, 189–212.

Tybout, James 1993a: Internal returns to scale as a source of comparative advantage. Georgetown University working paper no. 93–101.

Tybout, James 1993b: Internal returns to scale as a source of comparative advantage: The evidence. *American Economic Review: Papers and Proceedings*, 83, 440–4.

Tybout, James 2000: Manufacturing firms in developing countries: How well do they do, and why? *Journal of Economic Literature*, 38, 11–44.

Tybout, James and M. Daniel Westbrook 1995: Trade liberalization and dimensions of efficiency change in Mexican manufacturing industries. *Journal of International Economics*, 39, 53–78.

Tybout, James and M. Daniel Westbrook 1996: Scale economies as a source of efficiency gains. In Mark Roberts and James Tybout (eds.), *Industrial Evolution in Developing Countries*, New York: Oxford University Press.

Tybout, James, Jaime de Melo, and Vittorio Corbo 1991: The effects of trade reforms on scale and technical efficiency: New evidence from Chile. *Journal of International Economics*, 31, 231–59.

Voustden, Neil and Neil Campbell 1994: The organizational cost of protection. *Journal of International Economics*, 37, 219–38.

Westphal, Larry 2002: Technology strategies for economic development in a fast-changing global economy. *Economics of Innovation and New Technology*, Aug–Oct, 11(4–5), 275–320.

Young, Alwyn 1991: Learning by doing and the dynamic effects of international trade. *Quarterly Journal of Economics*, 106, 369–405.

# Name Index


Abbot 385
Abbott, T. 461
Abramovitz, M. 241
Acemoglu, D. 235
Acheson, A.L.K. 120
Aghevli, B. 343
Aghion, P. 181, 235, 236, 237, 247
Agrawal, D. 193
Agrion 193
Aitken, B. 242, 253
Albuquerque, R. 460, 474, 478
Anand, S. 329
Anant, T.C.A. 236, 292
Andrews, D. 401, 404
Arellano, M. 360, 398
Arellano-Cadena, R. 45
Arrow, K. 239, 311
Aten, B. 259
Aw, B.-Y. 140, 395, 409, 414, 416, 420, 427, 464, 468, 469, 473, 479
Azevado, R. 473

Bacha, E. 54
Backus, D. 292
Balassa, B. 30, 31, 32, 39, 40, 41, 46, 48, 50, 52, 55, 88, 323, 356
Baldwin 475
Baldwin, J. 478
Baldwin, R. 246, 319, 327, 331, 471
Banerjee, A. 235
Bardhan, P. 329
Barro, R.J. 5, 6, 7, 8, 9, 11, 15, 20, 21, 23, 24, 85, 103, 104, 116, 120, 141, 142, 143, 302, 360
Bartel, A. 257
Bartelsman, E. 241
Barton, D. 468
Basu, S. 259
Becker, G. 8, 271
Ben-David, D. 87, 89, 90, 124, 125, 126, 129, 132, 143, 182
Bental, B. 201
Bernard, A.B. 140, 247, 248, 250, 251, 395, 405, 414, 427, 428, 429, 438, 447, 463, 464, 468, 469, 472, 478, 479
Bernstein, J.I. 228
Berthelemy, J.-C. 39
Bevan, D. 359
Bhagwati, J. 33, 35, 37, 46, 95, 322, 323, 324, 329, 330, 351, 374, 458
Bhalla, S. 96
Bigsten, A. 469, 479
Blalock, G. 244, 254
Bliss, C. 322
Blomström, M. 252
Blundell, R. 244, 398, 419, 420, 479
Bond, E. 462, 468
Bond, M. 39
Bond, S. 244, 360, 398
Boone, P. 360
Bosworth, B.P. 104, 340
Bottazzi, L. 255, 256
Bowden, R. 385
Bradford, C., Jr. 63
Bradford, C.I. 34
Brainard, L. 243
Branson, W.H. 34
Branstetter, L. 242, 252, 253, 255
Bresnahan 389
Brown, D. 478
Bruno, M. 31, 322, 323
Bruton, H. 28
Buffie, E. 91
Burnside, C. 104, 361

Caballero, R. 238
Campas, J. 472, 473, 479
Campbell, N. 466
Caselli, F. 257
Caves, D. 409
Caves, R. 241
Caves, R.E. 88, 468, 478
Celasun, M. 343
Chakwin, N. 63
Chang, S.J. 228
Chen, T.-j. 469
Chen, X. 395, 409, 414, 420
Chenery, H.B. 319, 322, 325
Chhibber, A. 40
Choksi, A.M. 35, 36, 45, 47
Christensen, L. 241, 409
Chung, S. 140, 427
Clague, C. 120

Clark, P. 322
Clerides, S. 140, 246, 250, 251, 252, 261, 427, 438, 469
Cline, W.R. 322
Cobban, A. 128
Coe, D.T. 152, 180, 181, 185, 195, 227, 228, 229, 234, 242, 243, 245, 248, 249, 250, 258
Cohen, W. 257
Coleman, W., II 257
Collier, P. 358, 359
Collins, S.M. 104, 340
Cooley, T.F. 5
Cooper, R. 34, 37
Corbo, V. 48, 396, 398, 399
Corden, W.M. 31, 32, 40, 271, 323, 324, 466
Cornwell, C. 398, 401
Cox-Edwards, A. 43, 48
Cuthbertson, K. 159

Dam, K. 320
Das, S. 429, 464, 473
David, P. 236, 239
Davis, S. 475
de la Caudra, S. 43
De Long, J.B. 9, 63, 466
de Melo, J. 30, 48, 374, 396, 398, 399
Dean, J. 359, 361, 365
Dervis, K. 30, 323
Desai, P. 322
Devarajan, S. 458
Díaz-Alejandro, C. 132, 322
Diewert, E. 241
Dinopoulos, E. 200, 236, 292
Dixit, A. 32, 246, 291, 428, 471
Dollar, D. 19, 23, 63, 85, 89, 90, 95–104, 115, 141, 361
Domowitz, I. 374, 375
Doms, M. 241
Dornbusch, R. 248, 395
Dosi, G. 236
Dunne, T. 475
Dunning, J.H. 227, 233
Dutz, M. 465

Easterley, W. 360
Easterly, W. 63, 235, 342, 363
Eaton, J. 195, 198, 201, 214, 219, 236, 237, 238, 247, 248, 255, 257, 259, 395, 405, 428
Edmonds, C. 243
Edwards, A. 416
Edwards, S. 5, 34, 37, 38, 43, 45, 48, 58, 59, 87, 88, 89, 90, 115, 116, 119, 122, 123, 142, 143, 355, 356, 395, 416
Emery, R. 50

Englander, A.S. 167
Engle, R.F. 159, 162
Ericson, R. 399, 400, 474, 475
Esfahani, H.S. 52, 54, 57, 88
Ethier, W. 241, 245, 272, 291, 304, 466, 470
Evenett, S. 182
Evenson, R. 236, 239

Fagerberg, J. 194, 236
Falvey, R. 97
Feder, G. 5, 6, 20, 49, 50, 58, 63, 88
Feenstra, R. 92, 292, 467, 479
Feldman, M. 239
Fernandez, R. 479
Findlay, R. 271
Fischer, S. 20, 63, 71, 85, 248, 360
Fishlow, A. 28
Fosfuri, A. 252
Frankel, J.A. 63, 67, 71, 72, 87, 88, 89, 90, 133, 134, 135, 136

Galor, O. 257
Gelb, A.H. 119
Gemell, N. 97
Gerschenkron, A. 128, 194, 257, 259
Gertler, P. 244, 254
Ginarte, J.C. 120
Girma, S. 244, 253
Globerman, S. 252, 253
Goh, A.-T. 466
Good, D. 409
Gordon, D.F. 39
Gorecki, P. 478
Görg, H. 252, 253
Granger, C.W.J. 159, 160, 162
Gray, P. 51, 53
Greenaway, D. 137, 252, 253, 355, 358, 359
Greene, W. 479
Grether, J.-M. 460
Grier, K. 5, 6, 20, 21
Griffith, R. 244, 253, 254, 257, 258, 419, 420
Griliches, Z. 152, 162, 175, 176, 177, 181, 194, 198, 240, 241, 242, 243, 244, 246, 251, 271, 478
Grossman, G.M. 16, 58, 91, 92, 152, 153, 154, 155, 167, 181, 182, 194, 200, 202, 207, 235, 236, 238, 245, 249, 272, 278, 292, 310, 311, 331, 374, 466
Grossman, H. 120
Gulde, A.M. 176
Gulhati, R. 109
Gutierrez, E. 219, 247

Haber, S. 132

Hachette, D. 43
Haddad, M. 468
Hagen, E.E. 322, 326, 331
Hall, A.R. 69
Hall, R.E. 73, 74, 75, 104, 135, 235, 374, 375, 461
Hallward-Driemeier, M. 250, 251
Hamilton 319
Handoussa, H. 469
Hanson, G. 108, 252
Harberger, A.C. 333
Harhoff, D. 195
Harrigan, J. 39, 358
Harris, R. 478
Harrison, A. 30, 63, 89, 90, 96, 108, 136, 137, 242, 253, 387, 396, 399, 404, 461, 468
Hart, O. 466
Haskel, J. 252, 253, 254, 258
Hausman, J.A. 72, 243
Head, K. 462, 464, 465, 478
Heitger, B. 56
Helfgott, S. 197, 199
Helleiner, G.K. 51, 52, 55
Helliwell, J.F. 167
Helpman, E. 16, 58, 63, 91, 92, 152, 153, 154, 155, 167, 180, 181, 182, 194, 195, 200, 202, 207, 227, 228, 229, 234, 235, 236, 238, 242, 243, 245, 248, 249, 250, 258, 272, 278, 292, 310, 311, 373, 374, 428, 438, 458, 466, 470
Henderson, R. 255, 256
Heston, A. 8, 13, 23, 24, 67, 96, 97, 103, 131, 132, 141, 143, 144, 196, 197, 198, 248, 249, 259
Hirschman, A. 28, 318
Hoffmaister, A. 249
Hopenhayn, H. 427, 428, 432, 433, 460, 474, 476, 478
Howitt, P. 181, 193, 235, 236, 237, 247
Hulten, C. 241
Husted, S. 89
Hutchinson, M. 57
Hwang, A. 468

Iarossi, G. 250, 251
Im 229
Irwin, D. 255
Iyer, L. 235

Jaffe, A. 155, 198, 238, 240, 255, 256
Javorcik, B.S. 254
Jay, K. 50
Jensen, J.B. 140, 250, 251, 405, 414, 427, 429, 438, 447, 464, 469, 472, 479
Jenson, J.B. 428
Johnson, B.T. 143
Johnson, H.G. 31, 323, 326, 328, 334
Johnson, S. 235
Jones, C.I. 73, 74, 75, 104, 135, 139, 194, 207, 235, 237, 395
Jones, R.W. 88, 326, 329
Joshi, V. 329
Jovanovic, B. 194, 213, 474
Judd, K. 273
Jung, W.S. 57

Katayama, H. 241
Kavoussi, R.M. 51
Keefer, P. 114, 142
Kehoe, P. 292
Kehoe, T. 292
Keller, W. 182, 190, 195, 229, 235, 242, 243, 244, 245, 248, 249, 250, 253, 254, 255, 256, 257, 258, 259
Kim, I.-M. 243
Kim, K.S. 44, 45
Kim, M. 120
Klenow, P. 74, 255
Klette, T. 241, 409, 478
Knack, S. 114, 142
Kogut, B. 228
Kohli, I. 51, 52, 54
Kokko, A. 252, 253
Kormendi, R. 5, 6, 7, 11, 12, 20, 21, 22, 63
Kornai, J. 104
Kortum, S. 194, 195, 198, 201, 214, 219, 236, 237, 238, 247, 248, 255, 257, 259, 395, 405, 428
Kraay, A. 469, 479
Kravis, I. 50, 51
Krishna, P. 461
Krueger, A.O. 33, 35, 36, 37, 38, 40, 41, 42, 42, 44, 46, 85, 95, 321, 323, 324, 326, 330, 355, 356
Krugman, P. 89, 246, 283, 289, 291, 373, 436, 437, 458, 466, 470, 471
Kugler, M. 254

Lach, S. 140, 213, 246, 250, 251, 252, 261
Lack, S. 427, 438
Lal, D. 34
Lancaster, C. 40
Lancaster, K. 291
Landau, D. 5, 14
Larrain, B.F. 242, 252, 254, 261
Lau, L.J. 96
Leamer, E.E. 5, 6, 7, 18, 23, 30, 116, 143, 238, 256
Lee, J.-W. 63, 64, 85, 89, 90, 103, 104, 116, 135, 136, 141, 142, 143

Lee, N. 478
Leonard, H. 6
Lerner, A.P. 98
LeRoy, S.F. 5
Levin, A. 160, 161, 162, 178, 229
Levin, R.C. 203
Levine, R. 5, 8, 15, 63, 138, 235, 359, 363
Levinsohn, J. 238, 256, 461, 475
Levinthal, D. 257
Lewis, W.A. 319
Lichtenberg, F. 228, 229, 239, 240, 246, 257
Lin, C.F. 160, 161, 162, 178, 229
Linneman, H. 63
List 319
Little, I. 30, 31, 32, 45, 88, 323, 330, 342, 343
Liu, L. 398, 399, 421, 465, 478
Lopez-Calva, L. 242, 252, 254, 261
Lorch, K. 382
Lu, S. 241, 475, 476
Lucas, R.E., Jr. 20, 40, 58, 255, 271, 292, 310
Lumenga-Neso, O. 249

Maddala, G.S. 243
Maddison, A. 125, 126, 127, 132, 143, 271
Mahalanobis, P.C. 322
Mairesse, J. 251
Maizels, A. 50
Maloney, W. 473
Mankiw, N.G. 8, 9, 71, 193
Mansfield, E. 203, 209, 213
Markusen, J. 252
Marquez-Ruarte, J. 343
Marshall, P.J. 57
Matsuyama, K. 92
McAleer, M. 6, 8
McFetridge, D. 120
McGuire, P. 475
McKinnon, R.I. 323
Meguire, P. 5, 6, 7, 11, 12, 20, 21, 22, 63
Melitz, M. 428, 438, 463, 465, 468, 474, 477, 478
Melvin, M. 89
Michaely, M. 35, 36, 37, 38, 42, 45, 47, 48, 51, 55, 56, 63, 330
Michalopoulos, C. 50
Milner, C.R. 355
Mirrlees, J.A. 323
Mitra, D. 461
Miyagawa, K. 466
Moghadam, R. 152
Mohnen, P. 227, 228, 232, 233
Mollett, J.A. 39
Montagna, C. 427
Morgan, W. 137
Morrison, C. 39
Mosley, P. 39, 358
Motta, M. 252
Muller, J. 478
Murphy, K.M. 271, 322

Nadiri, M.I. 181, 228, 409
Nallari, R. 109
Nelson, C.R. 69
Nelson, R.R. 194, 257
Neven, D. 228
Newbold, P. 160
Newey, W. 385
Nishimizu, M. 374, 388, 468
Norman, V. 291, 478
Nurske, R. 319, 322

O'Rourke, K.H. 128
Obstfeld, M. 89
Ocampo, J.A. 54
Oehmke, J. 292
Ohno, Y. 466
Okada, Y. 198
Olarreaga, M. 249
Olley, S. 244, 251, 395, 396, 397, 399, 404, 409, 420
Owen, N. 478

Pack, H. 479
Page, J.M., Jr. 374, 388, 468
Pakes, A. 203, 210, 244, 251, 253, 395, 396, 397, 399, 400, 404, 409, 420, 474, 475, 478
Papageorgiou, D. 35, 36, 45, 47, 356
Parente, S.L. 194
Park, W. 120, 195
Parker, J.C. 39
Pasinetti, L. 274
Patel, P. 228
Pavcnik, N. 427, 465, 468
Pavitt, K. 236
Pedroni, P. 229
Peled, D. 201
Penrose, E.T. 194
Pereira, S. 252, 253, 254, 258
Peri, G. 242, 247, 255, 256
Pesaran 229
Phelps, E.S. 194, 200, 257
Pinto, B. 40
Pitt, M. 324
Polanyi, M. 239
Pollard, S. 127
Prebisch, R. 27, 28, 321, 338
Prescott, E.C. 194, 235
Press, W.H. 223
Pritchett, L. 18, 19, 139

Prusa, T.J. 459
Pursell, G. 250
Putnam, J. 195, 198

Quah, D. 58, 59, 236

Radelet, S. 135, 141
Rajapatirana, S. 34
Ram, R. 5, 6, 15, 51, 52, 57
Ramaswami, V.K. 323
Ramos, J. 48
Rana, P.B. 52
Ranis, G. 332
Rapp, R. 209
Rauch, J.E. 58, 59
Rebelo, S. 309, 310, 460, 474, 478
Redding, S. 244, 253, 254, 257, 258
Renelt, D. 5, 8, 63, 138, 359
Rhee, Y.-W. 250
Richardson, P. 132
Ries, J. 462, 464, 465, 478
Rivera-Batiz, L. 16, 235, 238, 245, 305
Roberts, M. 140, 374, 395, 396, 409, 414, 420, 427, 429, 437, 438, 449, 460, 464, 465, 466, 472, 475, 478
Robinson, J. 235
Rodríguez, F. 103, 108, 114, 132, 139
Rodriguez-Clare, A. 74, 242, 252, 255, 261
Rodrik, D. 63, 103, 108, 114, 115, 132, 139, 252, 341, 342, 344, 345, 351, 355, 356, 359, 394, 458, 466, 479
Rodriquez 355, 359
Rogerson, R. 476
Rogoff, K. 99
Rogowski, R. 128
Romeo, A. 203, 209, 213
Romer, D. 71, 72, 87, 89, 90, 133, 134, 135, 136, 193, 359
Romer, P.M. 5, 6, 8, 9, 14, 15, 16, 17, 21, 40, 58, 59, 152, 191, 193, 207, 235, 236, 238, 245, 271, 272, 274, 280, 282, 286, 289, 292, 294, 296, 297, 305
Rønde, T. 252
Rosenberg, N. 194, 236, 291
Rosenstein-Rodan, P. 322
Ross-Larson, B. 250
Rozek, R. 209
Rushing, F. 120

Sachs, J.D. 29, 34, 63, 85, 89, 90, 103, 104, 105, 106, 108, 109, 110, 111, 112, 115, 135, 136, 137, 141, 142, 325, 359, 361, 363
Saggi, K. 252
Sala-i-Martin, X. 8, 63, 104, 105, 302, 361
Salvatore, D. 57
Samuelson, P. 248
Sapsford, D. 358
Sargan, J.D. 385
Schankerman, M. 203, 210
Scharfstein, D. 466
Scherer, F.M. 155, 195, 242, 478
Schiff, M. 249
Schmalensee, R. 374, 389, 460, 468
Schmidt, P. 386, 398, 401
Schultz, T.W. 317
Schulze-Ghattas, M. 176
Schwalbach, J. 478
Schwartz, M. 209
Scitovsky, T. 30, 31, 32, 45, 88
Scott, M. 30, 31, 32, 45, 88
Segerstrom, P. 236, 292
Sheehy, T.P. 143
Sheikh, M.A. 324
Shell, K. 194
Sherman, R. 30
Shin 229
Shiue, C.H. 235
Sickles, R. 398, 401, 409
Simonsen, M.H. 344
Simpson, H. 244, 253, 254, 258
Singer, H.W. 27, 51, 53
Singh, J. 252, 253
Singh, N. 51, 52, 54, 57
Siotis, G. 228
Sjöholm, F. 250, 252, 253
Slaughter, M. 132, 252, 253, 254, 258
Smith, A. 27, 271, 291, 478
Soete, L. 228, 236
Sokoloff, K. 250, 251
Solow, R.M. 271, 374
Spraos, J. 319
Srinivasan, T.N. 91, 324, 329
Staiger, D. 69
Staiger, R.W. 459
Startz, R. 69
Stiglitz, J.E. 85, 428
Stock, J.H. 69, 159, 160
Stockman, A.C. 20
Streeten, P. 32
Strout, A. 322, 325
Sullivan, T. 438, 449, 472, 473
Summers, L. 466
Summers, L.H. 63
Summers, R. 8, 13, 23, 24, 67, 96, 97, 103, 131, 132, 141, 143, 144, 196, 197, 198, 248, 249, 259

Tamura, A. 193

Tang, D.-p. 469
Taylor, L. 29, 39
Teece, D. 239
Temple, J. 359
Terleckyj, N.E. 152
Thompson, M. 120
Thompson, P. 200
Tornell, A. 120
Toye, J. 39
Trajtenberg, M. 198, 240, 255, 256
Trefler, D. 423, 468, 479
Tretheway, M. 409
Tsiang, S.C. 324, 332
Tsiddon, D. 257
Tullock, G. 5, 6, 20, 21
Turkington, D. 385
Twain, M. 84
Tybout, J. 30, 48, 140, 241, 246, 250, 251, 252, 261, 374, 395, 396, 398, 399, 421, 427, 429, 437, 438, 449, 460, 462, 463, 464, 465, 466, 468, 472, 475, 476, 478
Tyler, W. 50

Urata, S. 374

Vamvakidis, A. 132
van Ark, B. 197, 198
van der Willingen, T.A. 39
Van Pottelsberghe de la Potterie, B. 228, 229, 246
Van Reenen 419, 420
Van Reneen, J. 257
Venables, A. 478
von Hippel, E. 239
Vopel, K. 195
Voustden, N. 466

Wacziarg, R. 89, 90, 104, 136, 137, 138
Wagner, J. 429, 464, 469
Wagner, S. 209
Wakelin, K. 244, 253
Wang, J. 249
Warner, A. 63, 85, 89, 90, 103, 104, 105, 106, 108, 109, 110, 111, 112, 115, 136, 137, 141, 142, 359, 361
Weil, D. 193, 259
Weintraub, S. 322
Westbrook, M. 399, 462, 464, 468, 478
Westphal, L. 236, 239, 479
White, H.L. 119, 120
Williamson, J. 316
Willig, R. 389
Winter, S. 236
Wolak, F.A. 459
Wolf, H. 116, 143
Wright, P. 137

Xu, B. 249, 253, 257, 258

Yamawaki, H. 228
Yarbrough, B.M. 88
Yarbrough, R.M. 88
Yeaple, S. 244, 253, 254, 258, 428, 438
Young, A. 292, 466